EDWARD HYDE, IST EARL OF CLARENDON
*After* A. Hanneman

*Reproduced by permission of the*
*National Portrait Gallery, London*

# Clarendon and the English Revolution

## R. W. HARRIS

*It is such a lecture of Government for an
English Prince as I won't distrust but you may
yet live to be thanked and
to thank God for.*

Samuel Pepys on the publication
of Clarendon's *History*

STANFORD UNIVERSITY PRESS
STANFORD, CALIFORNIA
1983

STANFORD UNIVERSITY PRESS
Stanford, California

© 1983 R. W. Harris

Originating publisher:
Chatto & Windus, London

First published in the U.S.A. by Stanford University Press,
1983

Printed in Great Britain

ISBN 0-8047-1216-6
LC 83-40092

# Contents

*To my Former Students*

# Preface

The purpose of this book is to go rather beyond the limits of biography in order to relate the career of the Earl of Clarendon to the world of thought and action in which he lived. The Victorian 'Life-and-Times' approach is properly denigrated today, yet it seems to me that unless the subject of a biography is sufficiently related to the problems and ideas of his period, the book must be of limited use, either to the student or the general reader. In the case of the Earl of Clarendon, this has involved the survey of some forty of the most dramatic and important years in English history, during most of which Clarendon was a principal actor, and which he himself brilliantly recorded. The writer therefore has the double task of relating the developments of the age with special reference to Clarendon himself, and of assessing the value of Clarendon's own history of those events. He must also relate Clarendon's account, written in exile, to the letters he wrote at the time of the events. The portrait which emerges is of a warm and humorous character, with a profoundly serious and moral view of life and politics, with a caustic pen, yet essentially truthful in all that he wrote. His final disgrace at the hands of Charles II ('that paragon of ingratitude', as Trevor-Roper calls him) was undeserved, and takes on the aspect of tragedy. Yet without it Clarendon might never have completed his *History* or written his *Life*. Without them historians would be incomparably the poorer.

I am greatly indebted to the Leverhulme Trust for their research grant, and to the Dean and Governing Body of Christ Church, Oxford, for their Studentship, hospitality and the use of their magnificent library. My thanks are also due to St John's College, Oxford for their hospitality over the years, to the Bodleian Library, to the library of the University of Kent, to the Archivist of Canterbury Cathedral and to the St Augustine's Library, Canterbury. I owe personal debts of gratitude to Mr William Thomas, Dr Jonathan Wright, Dr John Mason and Professor J McManners, of Christ Church Oxford; also to Mr Robert Franklin of All Soul's, Dr Blair Worden of St Edmund Hall, Miss Flair Kennett, and Canon Peter Pilkington. Lord Rotherwick very kindly allowed me to visit Cornbury Park, and Earle W Reiley Esq to explore Clarendon's old home at Purton. I owe more than I can say to my wife for her constant help and encouragement.

# Early Life and Intellectual Influences

Edward Hyde, first earl of Clarendon, was the greatest royalist statesman of the seventeenth century, and the first of the great English historians. In a sense the study of history was the governing factor in his life. Trained as a lawyer, he nonetheless spent much of his youth and formative period among the most stimulating literary and intellectual men of his time. It would be wrong to see the second and third decades of the seventeenth century merely as years of growing political and religious conflict; they were also, as Clarendon remembered them, halcyon years of peace and plenty, in which many men of moderation attempted to resolve current conflicts by a new appeal to history and reason. For how could men decide between the rival claims to infallibility by Rome and Geneva but by an appeal to the Scriptures, to the early history of the church, and to the rights of reason and conscience? Similarly in political conflict, how could questions be resolved but by a study of history, tradition and constitutional law? At a time when the Catholic Church, following the path laid down by the Council of Trent, employed Baronius to produce the twenty volumes of erudition, the *Annales Ecclesiastici*, to buttress its claims by an appeal to history (a work to which Isaac Casaubon did not live long enough to complete his answer); when Paolo Sarpi wrote history to contradict those claims, and when Davila wrote his great narrative of the civil wars in France, history seemed the most natural way to approach the urgent problems of the time.

Under the influence of great antiquarians like Sir Henry Spelman, Sir Robert Cotton and John Selden, men turned to history with a new sense of purpose, as providing the answer to unsubstantiated claims of dogmatism, and it produced a new spirit of liberal tolerance which pervaded the lives and works of men as different as Peter Heylin, Robert Burton, John Earle, Charles Cotton, Sir Henry Wotton and Sir Kenelm Digby. As a member of the Great Tew circle, Edward Hyde imbibed the new humanist spirit which was fully in accord with the thought of Erasmus, Hooker and Grotius. He rejected the rival intolerances of Calvinism and Catholicism in favour of a reliance on the Scriptures, the Early Fathers, and sixteen hundred years of tradition. At the same time he was offended by the infringement of the common law by the executive power. In 1640 therefore he emerged as a reformer. But reform turned to revolution, threatening to destroy both the monarchy and the Anglican church, and the same ideas which had made him a reformer then led him to wish to restore continuity in both church and state. Whether seeking to limit Stuart executive power, or striving desperately to find a peaceful *modus vivendi* between king and parliament, his attitude was shaped by his interpretation of history, and when he had sufficient leisure, it was natural that he should turn to writing the history of the events through which he lived. He both made history and recorded it, and it is this double function which it is the purpose of this book to explore.

The Hydes were seated at Norbury in Cheshire from the time of Henry III when Sir Roger de la Hyde married his cousin, the heiress of Thomas de Norbury. Connection with Wiltshire began in the time of the Chancellor's great-grandfather, Robert Hyde of Norbury, whose first wife was Margaret Hollard of Dinton in Wiltshire. His son Laurence Hyde was auditor of the Exchequer in the reign of Queen Elizabeth,* and, marrying Anne the wealthy widow of Matthew Colthurst of Claverton, Somerset, he purchased an estate at West Hatch and other lands in Wiltshire. They had four sons and four daughters to provide for, and as the bulk of the estate went to the eldest son there was but a modest inheritance for the younger sons who necessarily chose the career most likely to offer security and fortune – the law. The second son became Sir Laurence Hyde and Attorney-General to Queen Anne of Denmark, wife of James I. The fourth son Nicholas rose to be Lord Chief Justice of the King's Bench. The third son, Henry, studied at Oxford and the Middle Temple, but never practised the law. Instead he spent a period travelling on the continent, even visiting Rome, a dangerous thing to do in the days of Queen Elizabeth, before returning to the impropriated rectory of Dinton in Wiltshire and a modest £40 a year. He married Mary, daughter of Edward Langford a merchant of Trowbridge, and she brought with her a substantial fortune. Henry, who was known for his meticulous honesty, sat in several of the Elizabethan parliaments, but otherwise lived a simple rustic life among his books. Clarendon said that his mother Mary, in all her forty years of married life never once visited London. The couple had four sons and five daughters. Laurence the eldest and Nicholas the fourth son died in infancy; the second son Henry died aged twenty-six or twenty-seven, and only Edward, the third son, and subject of this book, lived to be his father's heir.

Edward Hyde was born on 18 February 1609 in the village of Dinton, six

---

* Laurence Hyde made a name for himself in the parliament of 1601 for his opposition to monopolies, and in the parliament of 1604 for his attacks on purveyance, when he and John Hare were known as 'tribunes of the people'. His brother Nicholas was a member of the 1610 parliament, where he showed his hostility to recusants.[1] There was then some tradition of political independence in the Hyde family.

miles from Salisbury, and was baptised four days later. His first education was partly from the village schoolmaster, but more from his father, who was a good classical scholar. At the tender age of thirteen he was sent off to the University of Oxford. Clarendon tells us only the bare minimum about his days there. As the younger son of a younger son, it was clear to him that he had 'to make his own fortune by his own industry',[2] and he appeared to start with considerable advantages – his uncles were influential lawyers, and his brother Henry already an Oxford MA. Family influences obtained a letter from King James to the President of Magdalen recommending Edward for a demyship, but he did not get it, and he entered Magdalen Hall as a commoner. He later thought it unfortunate that a boy of thirteen should have been given so much freedom, and his brother Henry, who was a drunkard, led the boy into bad habits. However he always had respect for his tutor John Oliver, and later rewarded him with the deanery of Worcester. Edward's father at first thought of removing him from Oxford, without a degree, and of sending him to the Inns of Court, where, it was hoped, he would receive better training, and where he would be under the indulgent but careful eye of his uncle Nicholas. However, the plague was raging in London, so he remained at Oxford long enough to take his degree. His academic performance was modest. He wrote later that the discipline at Oxford had been too lax, and that, although he was 'a young man of parts and pregnancy of wit', yet he had done little to improve himself by his industry.

The Inns of Court had become an indispensable part of the education, not only of lawyers, but also of gentlemen before they retired to their estates (as Hyde's father had done) to take an active part in the affairs of their counties and to enter parliament. Since the Reformation there had been an enormous expansion in the study of the law, and the Inns of Court had grown up as London clubs where practising lawyers could stay, and where students received instruction in the law and a wide range of cultural subjects. W R Prest estimates that between 1590 and 1640 the total admissions were over 12,000. Clarendon wrote that the Inns of Court were most desirable places for young gentlemen to stay, 'where it is probable they will find their friends, and can never miss men of good manners and good conversation'. He loved the convivial life and the stimulus of good conversation, and he greatly enjoyed these years in London.[3]

Years later Clarendon vividly remembered the morning in 1625 when, at the age of sixteen, he left Marlborough with his uncle Nicholas to be entered at the Middle Temple where Nicholas, then a circuit judge, was treasurer. But almost at once he was struck down with a serious illness which entailed his return home, now at Pirton in north Wiltshire, where his father had purchased an estate. It was feared that the boy had developed consumption, and it was almost a year before he was strong enough to return to the Middle Temple. When he did so, at Michaelmas 1626, it was with no great enthusiasm for the study of the law. He wrote later that he spent much time with the soldiers who were gathered in London for Buckingham's expedition to France, and although they were rough company, they were exhilarating companions for a boy of seventeen. However he found some time for his law books, and almost every night his uncle would set him a case for exposition. Moreover the teaching at the Inns of Court was by no means confined to the law, but included history, literature, logic and rhetoric. Hyde himself especially enjoyed what he called 'polite learning and history, especially the Roman'. Roman history he had enjoyed since his early days in Wiltshire. In 1628 he rode the Norfolk circuit with his uncle, now Chief Justice, and at Cambridge he again fell ill with what this time was thought to be smallpox. This necessitated another period of recuperation at Pirton, and it was there that he well remembered reading Camden's *Annals* to his father when the news arrived in August 1628, of the assassination of the duke of Buckingham. This was a matter of some seriousness to the Hyde family, for Buckingham had been the patron of Sir Nicholas Hyde, who owed his promotion to Lord Chief Justice to his readiness to defend the claims of the royal prerogative. But Sir Nicholas died in 1631 of gaol fever, and it was now more than ever necessary for Edward Hyde to make his own way in the world.

His first step was to make a successful marriage. In 1629 he had married Anne the daughter of Sir George Ayliffe, a Wiltshire landowner, whose mother (a St John) was related to a number of noble families. But six months later Anne died of smallpox and a miscarriage; Hyde later wrote that 'he bore her loss with so great passion and confusion of spirit, that it shook all the frame of his resolutions', and he thought for a time of throwing up his studies and going overseas. If this unlikely possibility really presented itself to him, it was presumably the lingering influence of the London soldiery which had fired his imagination. But the thought of himself as a soldier must have seemed ludicrous, and instead he persevered with the law and was called to the bar. In whose chambers he began we do not know, but with his powerful family influences he had no difficulty in obtaining ready access to the Court, and the acquaintance of such nobles as Viscount Grandison and the marquis of Hamilton. He hints darkly at being involved in some Court scandals,[4] and it is clear that he was no stranger to the factions and rivalries which were destroying the nation's confidence in the king and his Court.

If Clarendon's account is to be accepted, the three years following the death of his first wife were years of indecision and uncertainty as to his future career. Two events of 1632, however, combined to stabilise him. The first was his marriage to Frances, daughter of Sir Thomas Aylesbury who had been Buckingham's secretary and was Master of Requests and Master of the Mint. This marriage greatly widened Hyde's social and political connections, and all the evidence suggests that it was happy, blessed with nine children and lasting for over thirty-five years, through times of prosperity and hardship. But Hyde always kept his family life private, and there is little in his correspondence or his writings to throw much light upon it, or upon the character of his seemingly placid and entirely domestic wife.

The second event was the death of his father, in his seventieth year. Hyde regarded this as a great loss; his father had been, he said, the best friend and the wisest man he had ever known. He had lived a life of rural happiness, enjoying 'a competent, and, to him a plentiful fortune', and he left his affairs in the scrupulous condition they had always enjoyed: 'Never man ordered his wardrobe more exactly for a journey than my father did his estate for death – no possible scruple to arise, no party not fully satisfied.'[5] Years later Burnet recounted a story which he had from Lady Ranelagh, who had it from Clarendon himself, that shortly before his father died, he had warned his son that lawyers were inclined to 'stretch law and prerogative to the prejudice of the liberty of the subject', and urged him never to 'sacrifice the laws and liberties of his country to his own interests, or the will of a prince'.[6] It is perhaps a strange fact that Clarendon tells us very little about either the political or the religious views of his family in his early days, so this anecdote is all the more valuable in suggesting the viewpoint of a country gentleman, suspicious of lawyers, suspicious of the prerogative, and deeply committed to traditional laws and liberties. No doubt his father was thinking of his brothers, Sir Laurence and Sir Nicholas, both good friends to the prerogative, and it was advice Edward Hyde took much to heart.

These are the bare biographical details of Hyde's early life, but they throw little light on the formation of his opinions. On this he was understandably reticent, first because it was irrelevant to the *History*, and second because the prime purpose of the *Life* was to reveal the mind of a mature statesman, not to trace a mental evolution through devious paths. We have therefore to depend a good deal upon inference.

We have seen that when in 1626 Hyde returned to the Middle Temple after his illness it was, on his own admission, with no great enthusiasm for intensive study of the law. For an intelligent youth of seventeen with good connections, London and Westminster were heady places and there was one centre above all others which attracted him: Ben Jonson's sick room in Westminster. In many ways these were sad years for Jonson as he struggled with disease, in urgent need of patronage, and bereft of so many of his old friends. But he was a greatly respected literary figure and sage, and surrounded himself with a group of young lights, 'the Tribe of Ben', as well as members of the aristocracy. Viscount Falkland later gave a genuine portrait of the time:

> To him how daily flockt, what reverence gave,
> All that had wit, or would be thought to have. . . .
> How the wise too, did with mere *wits* agree,
> As Pembroke, Portland and grave Aubigny,
> Nor thought the rigid'st senator a shame
> To contribute to so deserved a fame![7]

Of the earl of Pembroke we shall have more to say later. Sir Richard Weston, Viscount Portland, and his son were not close members of the group, but Jonson had great hopes of their patronage when Portland became Lord Treasurer. D'Aubigny, later duke of Lennox, was a willing patron, and Jonson's host for five years. Another friend and admirer was that complete Renaissance man, Sir Kenelm Digby, a man of action, dashing soldier, diplomat, man of affairs, man of fashion and scholar, who was said to have admired Jonson's verses as second only to Spenser's. Another occasional member of the group was William Cavendish, the romantic and exuberant earl of Newcastle. Another was the brilliant and accomplished poet Thomas Carew. He was too old and too critical of Jonson to be a disciple but he enjoyed his company. James Howell recounted Carew's criticism of Jonson at supper, when there was 'good company, excellent cheer, choice wines and jovial welcome', but Ben Jonson 'began to engross all the discourse, to vapour extremely of himself, and, by vilifying others, to magnify his own Muse'.[8] His 'Ode to Ben Jonson' was a reprimand that he should so resent contemporary criticism when his reputation with posterity was secure:

> Let others glut on the extorted praise
> Of vulgar breath, trust thou to after days.

Jonson's rough and turbulent ways might repel, but he was the most distinguished literary figure alive, and his circle of friends the most distinguished gathering of the time. How and when the young Edward Hyde gained an entry to it is not exactly known. It could not have been earlier than 1629. Clarendon wrote that Ben Jonson 'had for many years an extraordinary kindness for Mr. Hyde, till he found he betook himself to business, which he believed ought never to be preferred before his company'.[9] This has the ring of truth. Hyde re-married in 1632 and was determined to pay more attention to the law. Moreover, by now he was a more likely guest at Great Tew, than at Westminster, and the sick and failing Jonson no doubt showed his resentment. We may therefore safely date Hyde's membership of Ben's Tribe as between 1629 and 1632.

Clarendon later wrote inimitable pen portraits of some members of the tribe who most impressed him. There was Charles Cotton, who is now remembered only as being the father of the poet, but as a young man had 'all those qualities which in youth raise men to the reputation of being fine gentlemen', a learning derived from Cambridge and residence in France, less deep than it appeared, but combined with a charming civility. He later retired to his estate at Beresford Hall and built up a fine library. Another was the young law student John Vaughan, who was a friend of Hyde's, and a devoted disciple of John Selden. Clarendon, who had good reason not to like him when he wrote, described his supercilious and rough manner, and said that 'he looked most into those parts of the law which disposed him to least reverence to the crown, and most to popular authority, yet without inclination to any change in government'. This did not prevent him from building up a prosperous Star Chamber practice. He later sat in the Long Parliament, helped to defend Strafford, and adhered to the king in 1642, but soon retired to his country estate at Trawscoed, and was treated as a delinquent. At the Restoration Clarendon sought to renew the old friendship by offering him a seat on the Bench. He declined on the not unreasonable grounds that he had been out of touch with the law for twenty years. But he sat in the Cavalier Parliament and became a leader of the opposition to Clarendon, and one of the chief promoters of the impeachment of 1667.

A third member of the group was the poet Thomas May, a student of Gray's Inn, but who was prevented by a stammer from following the law. His father squandered most of his fortune, and the son was forced to live in modest circumstances. He turned to literature, wrote plays, and gained considerable reputation as a translator of the classics. For a time he had the favour of Charles I, but was said to have been embittered at being refused a royal pension. In any case he supported parliament during the Civil War. But the two men who made the most profound impression upon Edward Hyde and with whom he formed the firmest friendships were John Selden and Lucius Cary. John Selden was in his forties, at the time Hyde first knew him, with an enormous reputation as a scholar and lawyer. He had been called to the Bar in 1612, but by then had spent some seven years, in company with the antiquarians Camden and Sir Robert Cotton, in probing into Anglo-Saxon and Norman institutions. Selden was a great defender of the traditions of common law, and he shared in the widespread anti-clericalism which was a feature of the time. He declared that the clergy had always resisted the progress of true knowledge, and had opposed the 'noble studies' of Roger Bacon, Reuchlin, Budaeus and Erasmus. Later, in the Long Parliament, he was to express his hostility to episcopacy. As a member of the parliaments of 1623-29 he, together with Sir Edward Coke and Sir John Eliot, was increasingly concerned at the threat of the prerogative to the common law and the traditional liberties of England. When parliament was dissolved in March 1629, Selden was one of the nine members sent to the Tower, and he remained in prison until 1631. In describing his early encounters with Selden Clarendon makes no mention of his political opposition, but it is clear that as a young man he had boundless admiration for him: 'he was a person whom no character can flatter, or transmit in any expressions equal to his merit and virtue'. He was impressed by his 'stupendous learning', his courtly manners, and the clarity of his discourse. 'Mr. Hyde was wont to say that he valued himself upon nothing more than upon having had Mr. Selden's acquaintance from the time he was very young; and held it with great delight as long as they were suffered to continue together in London.'[10] In the Long Parliament they often agreed, and when Hyde withdrew to York and Selden remained with parliament, Hyde was indulgent in defence of Selden's decision. Clarendon made the significant remark that he had so much affection and reverence for Selden 'that he always thought himself best when he was with him'.[11] It seems probable therefore that Hyde had something approaching hero-worship for the elder man, and if so it is most likely that Hyde's constitutional ideas were moulded at least in part by Selden.

In no period of our history were the views of lawyers of greater importance to the outcome of political events. The central issue of the early Stuart period was the relationship of the prerogative to the rule of law. If there was one principle upon which all lawyers were agreed it was that in England the rule of law was paramount. As early as the fifteenth century Sir John Fortescue had declared that the famous maxim 'What pleased the Prince has the force of law' had no place in England (although it had in France):

The laws of England do not sanction any such maxim, since the king of that land rules his people not only regally but also politically, and so he is bound by oath at his coronation to the observance of his law.[12]

It is often forgotten that when James I declared in 1610 that

The state of monarchy is the supremest thing upon earth; for kings are not only God's lieutenants upon earth, and sit upon God's throne, but even by God himself they are called gods,

although he was using language common enough in the Tudor period, he went on to say that

every just king in a settled kingdom is bound to observe that paction made to his people by his laws, in framing the government agreeable thereto.

On this there was no difference of opinion among the lawyers. Sir Robert Berkeley, in giving judgment in the Ship Money Case in February 1638, declared:

I hope that none doth imagine that it either is, or can be drawn by consequence, to be any part of the question in this case, whether the King may at all times and upon all occasions impose charges upon his subjects in general, without common consent in Parliament. If that were made the question, it is questionless that he may not. The people of the kingdom are subjects, not slaves, freemen, not villeins to be taxed *de alto et basso*. Though the King of England hath a monarchical power, and hath *jura summae majestatis*, and hath an absolute trust settled in his crown and person for government of his subjects, yet his government is to be *secundum leges regni* . . .

The fundamental issue was to decide, in Fortescue's words, what was *regal* and what was *political*; or in Berkeley's words, what limits might be placed on *jura summae majestatis*. For the judges it posed questions of formidable difficulty. Neither James I nor Charles I attempted to overthrow the law, but there was genuine doubt as to what the law actually was. Thus in the Five

Knights' Case in the King's Bench in November 1627, John Selden cited Magna Carta that no free man should be imprisoned *nisi per legem terrae*, but he admitted that everything turned on the question what exactly was *lex terrae*. Clarendon's uncle, Lord Chief Justice Hyde, declared:

We are sworn to maintain all prerogatives of the King, that is one branch of our oath; and we are likewise sworn to administer justice equally to all people.

But he went on to declare that all the precedents were against the defence, and he found the imprisonment lawful.[13]

John Selden brought the cool judgment of history to bear upon the problems of his time. He would have nothing to do with mystical explanations of political power, such as the *Jure Divino* of kings.

A King is a thing men have made for their own sakes, for quietness' sake . . . To think all Kings alike is the same folly.

There were good kings and bad kings, tyrants and beneficent rulers, and they were to be judged, not by Divine Right, but by the happiness of their subjects. As for the bishops, they 'are now unfit to govern because of their very learning. They are bred up in another law; they run to the text for something done among the Jews that nothing concerned England.' That is to say, their study of the Old Testament, and their knowledge of canon and of civil law, rather than of common law, made them allies of the prerogative.

Some of the Bishops pretend to be *Jure divino*, yet the practice of the kingdom has been ever otherwise; for whatsoever Bishops do otherwise than what the law permits, Westminster Hall can control.

Yet this was not to say that bishops should be abolished:

Bishops have the same right to sit in Parliament as the best of the Earls and Barons, that is, those which were made by writ . . . Bishops were in the Parliament ever since there is any mention or sign of a parliament in England.

Selden asked neither that the bishops should be exalted into willing allies of the prerogative, nor as rulers *Jure Divino*, but simply that they should be regarded as part of the traditional English constitution.

The Bishops being put out of the house, whom will they lay the fault upon now: when the dog is beat out of the room, where will they lay the stink?

And again:

They are both equally mad who say Bishops are so *Jure Divino* that they must be continued, and they who say they are so anti-christian that they must be put away. All is as the State likes.

Selden was a complete Erastian who rejected equally the extreme views of Arminian episcopacy and those of Presbyterians and Independents. Those who advocated the abolition of bishops were making themselves greater than bishops.

Men cry out upon the High Commission as if only clergymen had to do in it; when I believe there are more laymen in Commission there than clergymen. . . . So of the Star Chamber, the people think the Bishops only censured Prynne, Burton and Bastwick, when they were but two there, and one spake not in his own cause.*

As to the growth of Independency:

Independency is in use at Amsterdam, where you have forty Churches of Congregations having nothing to do one with another, and 'tis no question, agreeable to the primitive times before the Emperor became Christian. . . . But when the civil state became Christian they appointed who should govern whom. . . . Both the Independent man and the Presbyterian man do equally exclude the civil power, though after a different manner.

No man took a more dispassionate view of the religious conflicts of his time than John Selden:

Disputes in religion will never be ended because there wants a measure by which the business should be decided, the puritan would be judged by the word of God (if he would speak clearly he means himself, but that he is ashamed to say so), and he would have me believe him before a whole Church that have read the word of God as well as he. One says one thing and another another, and there is, I say, no measure to end the controversy. . . . There's all the reason in the world Divines should not be suffered to go a hair's breadth beyond their bounds for fear of breeding confusion, since there be now so many religions afoot.

He was contemptuous also of the impassioned attacks upon the Roman Catholic Church by the Protestant clergy:

When our clergy preach against the pope and Church of Rome, they preach against themselves, and crying down their pride and their power and their riches has made themselves poor and contemptible enough. They did it at first to please their prince, not considering what would follow. . . . We charge the prelatical clergy with popery to make them odious, though we know they are guilty of no such thing.

As to the prickly doctrine of Predestination:

it is a point inaccessible out of our reach, we can make no notion of, 'tis so full of intricacy, so full of contradiction 'tis in good earnest as we state it half a dozen Bulls one upon another.

Selden's opinions, drawn from his *Table Talk*,[15] have been given at some length because they had profound influence upon Clarendon, helped to mould his views on constitutional and religious issues, and explain why he held Selden in such veneration. Rejecting both divine-right and puritan

---

* Laud at his trial showed that he had not voted in the sentences on Prynne, Burton and Bastwick because he was personally involved.[14]

mysticism, he sought a middle way which would appeal to a reasonable man. How far this was also Clarendon's view will appear in the course of this book. When the Civil War came, arguing that 'wise men say nothing in dangerous times', Selden withdrew from politics and absorbed himself with legal history until his death in 1654. Hyde however pursued the more dangerous path of practical politics. The second great influence upon Edward Hyde was that of Lord Falkland.

Lucius Cary was, by general agreement of contemporaries and later generations, one of the noblest men of his age. He was the son of the first Viscount Falkland, born in 1610, and at the age of nineteen he inherited from his maternal grandfather the estate of Great Tew in Oxfordshire, said by Clarendon to be worth about £2,000 a year. His father, the first viscount, was a client of Buckingham's, through whose influence he became Lord Deputy of Ireland in 1622, and it was in Ireland that Lucius was educated. It was an unhappy family. His mother was a Roman Catholic, and it was her fervent wish to effect the conversion of her eldest son; but Lucius resisted, and the disappointed lady had to be content with seeing all of her four daughters take the veil. Lucius offended his father by marrying a lady with no dowry, and in 1632 settled down to a life of study and literature at Great Tew. He inherited his father's title in 1633. His earliest interest in literature drew him irresistibly to Ben Jonson's circle. He was himself a poet, though of modest ability, and his admiration for Ben Jonson, whom he called his 'noble father', was unstinted. He submitted his 'Anniversaries' and his 'Pindaric Ode' to Jonson, and after the latter's death wrote 'Eglogue', already quoted, and edited the *Jonsonius Virbius* (1638).*

According to Clarendon, Falkland had been well educated at the University of Dublin, and when he came to England at the age of eighteen he was already a master of Latin and French, and widely read in the poets. He had however, Clarendon noted, a grave superficial disadvantage:

> His stature was low, and smaller than most men; his motion not graceful; and his aspect so far from inviting that it had somewhat in it of simplicity; and his voice the worst of the three, and so untuned, that instead of reconciling, it offended the ear, so that nobody would have expected music from that tongue; and sure no man was less beholden to nature for its recommendation into the world.[16]

But, he continued, beneath this unpromising exterior there was a great heart, a fearless disposition, an excellent mind, and 'a nature so gentle and obliging, so much delighted in courtesy, kindness and generosity, that all mankind could not but admire and love him'. If a man wanted a recommendation to posterity, he could not do better than choose Clarendon for its author.

Lucius Cary's marriage had led to an irreparable breach with his father, and after a short period in Holland, when he contemplated a military career, he

---

* Virbius was a figure in the Roman cult of Diana, brought back to life by the goddess.

retired to Great Tew to devote himself to a life of study. Clarendon dated his acquaintance with Cary from 1630; and when he turned to a closer study of the law, about 1632, and Lucius Cary was entering upon his patronage of learning at Great Tew, a close friendship developed. To his interest in literature Lucius Cary added an extended study of theology. Clarendon wrote that Cary 'read all the Greek and Latin fathers, all the most allowed and authentic ecclesiastical writers, and all the councils with wonderful care and observation'.[17] At Great Tew he established almost a second university from Oxford,[18] where he kept open house for men of scholarly interests; according to Archbishop Mathew 'the first conscious oasis of learning since the break-up of the circle of Sir Thomas More'.[19] Clarendon wrote that Falkland's 'whole conversation was one continued *convivium philosophicum* or *convivium theologicum*, enlivened and refreshed with all the facetiousness of wit and good humour and pleasantness of discourse, which made the gravity of the argument itself very delectable'.[20] There some of the leading men of religion of the time, Gilbert Sheldon, George Morley, John Earle, John Hales and William Chillingworth, met men of the world like Sidney Godolphin, Edmund Waller, Sir Francis Wenman, Sir John Suckling and Thomas Hobbes. Clarendon said that men came and went with the greatest freedom, and the master of the house never knew how many he had in the house until he came to sit down to dinner, and it appears that from the study and the discussions which took place at Great Tew, something like a common viewpoint on religious affairs emerged. To understand their position it is necessary to say something of the background. Both the Reformation and the Counter Reformation had thrown up their own brands of dogmatism and intolerance. The Reformation of Henry VIII had been anti-papal but essentially Catholic; Henry certainly did not think in terms of a complete break with the past, and had no intention of going along with the continental reformers. Under Edward VI there was a rapid advance towards a Protestant Reformation, and in 1553 the Forty-two Articles of Religion marked the extent of the advance. But within seven weeks the whole process appeared to be reversed with a return to Rome under Queen Mary. Yet within five years Mary was dead, and Queen Elizabeth was faced with the problem of what the religion of England should be. As the welcome alternative to Mary she had a strong vested interest in Protestantism. What she really believed no man could say; her instincts were entirely political and suggested a return to the doctrinal position of her father. The overwhelming need seemed to be to achieve a new stability in religious affairs. The Lord Keeper's opening speech to Elizabeth's first parliament emphasised the point:

that you will in this your assembly and conference clearly forbear and, as a great enemy to good council, flee from all manner of contentious reasonings and disputations and all sophistical, captious and frivolous arguments and quiddities, meeter for ostentation of wit than consultation in weighty matters, comlier for scholars than for counsellors, more beseeming for schools than for parliament houses ... And like as in council all contention would be eschewed, even so by council provision would be made that all contentious, contumelious or opprobrious words, as 'heretic', 'schismatic', 'papist' and such like names and nurses of seditious factions and sects may be banished out of men's mouths, as the causers, continuers and increasers of displeasure, hate and malice, and as utter enemies to all concord and unity, the very mark that you are now to shoot at. (25 January 1559.)[21]

This was undoubtedly in accord with the wishes of the queen, but she did not anticipate the strength of militant reform which came with the Marian exiles who returned from the continent. They differed among themselves in many things but were united in their hatred of all things Roman. They found a bewildered or indifferent laity, a widespread continuance of Roman practices and an unlearned and grossly inadequate clergy. Only a tiny minority of the queen's subjects could at that time be said to be Protestants. The 1559 church settlement was on the whole, in accordance with the queen's wishes, although in some respects it went further than she would have wished. For her, however, it was intended to be a final settlement. On the other hand for the Protestant reformers it was only the first step towards a truly Protestant church.

The Church of England was based on the Acts of Uniformity and Supremacy and on the Prayer Book of 1552. Its weakness lay in the uncertainties of its theology, faced as it was on the one side by the certainties of the Roman Catholic Counter Reformation, and on the other by the certainties of Calvinism. The Elizabethan bishops were often hard-working administrators, but they were faced with formidable difficulties, their revenues often plundered by the State, some ten per cent of livings vacant, and no suitably educated ministers to fill them at a time when ninety per cent of the livings were less than £26 a year, and nearly a half were worth less than £10.[22] One of the great changes which the reformers wished to bring about was from a sacramental priesthood to a pastoral ministry, and this was the main reason why the reformers were so anxious to eliminate all vestments or ceremonies which emphasised priestly status at the expense of a pastoral and caring ministry. With the spread of Renaissance humanism the laity were now better educated, and were not ready to tolerate an ignorant clergy who were 'dumb dogs' and quite incapable of preaching. Often the church seemed fair game for spoliation by the queen, the nobility, lay patrons and even by the bishops themselves. The queen herself kept the see of Oxford vacant for forty-one years, and bishop Edwin Sandys was a notorious spoliator of the see of Worcester. On the other hand many powerful patrons like the earls of Leicester, Warwick, Huntingdon and Pembroke were strongly Puritan. In theology most of the prelates were Calvinist according to the basic test of belief in Predestination.

'Puritanism' is an elastic word which might imply a serious desire to reform the church, combined with a devotion to the literal interpretation of the Scriptures, and a hatred of all things Roman. It might seek to reform the church from within, or it might seek separation, as with the Sectaries. The Anglican Church was prepared to tolerate some diversity of opinion, and many bishops certainly had Puritan and Calvinist sympathies. Archbishop Parker sympathised with the Puritan desire to improve the quality of the clergy. The queen, whose attitude was that of a *politique*, asked only that there should be outward conformity; and with the dangers from Spain, the Queen of Scots and the rebellion of the Northern Earls, Catholicism might seem a greater danger than Puritanism. But when in 1569 Cartwright, Lady Margaret Professor of Divinity at Cambridge, launched a frontal attack on church order, and when the Puritan campaign in parliament began in 1571–2, the Puritan threat clearly emerged. *The Admonition to the Parliament* of 1572 was a challenge the government could not ignore. When Archbishop Grindal attempted to defend Puritan practices, the queen sequestrated him, and when Whitgift became Archbishop in 1583 he initiated a policy of discipline which effectively muzzled militant Puritanism.

The Anglican Church lacked a clear-cut theological position, and Richard Hooker attempted to remedy this in his great work the *Laws of Ecclesiastical Polity*. It was aimed against the certainties of Calvinism, and the disruptive influences of the sectaries. Religion could not be based solely on the Scriptures, but must embrace the law of nature, which was the law of reason, and the lessons of history. He rejected Predestination and the doctrine of the Elect at a time when it was the prevailing theology of the Church of England. At this time, as Sir John Neale showed, 'Elizabethan England, as mirrored in the House of Commons, was overwhelmingly Puritan in its sympathies'.[23] When in 1595 William Barrett, a young chaplain of Gonville and Caius, preached a sermon against Predestination, the Heads of Houses at Cambridge forced him to recant and to assert that election was part of the doctrine of the Church of England. A long dispute followed in which there were appeals to the Archbishop and to Burghley. Whitgift somewhat wearily tried to restore peace by issuing the nine Lambeth Articles, which nonetheless remained Calvinist in thought, although he made it clear that they were only his personal opinions ('certain propositions which we are persuaded to be true'). The queen intervened to inform him that she misliked his support for Predestination, and the whole incident began to mark a turning of the tide. More and more members of the Church of England were beginning to react against rigid Calvinism. At the Hampton Court Conference the Calvinists failed to have the Lambeth Articles inserted into the Book of Common Prayer, and thereafter the Articles fell into disuse.

Predestination was under challenge from Jacobus Arminius, Professor of Theology at Leyden in 1602. He rejected the doctrine on the grounds that

God could not be so unjust as to decree the election or damnation of men, and he appealed for toleration and freedom of discussion in order to permit the search for truth, and to avoid schism and the growth of conflicting sects. After his death in 1609 the conflict continued under his successor Vorstius, and in 1610 Uyttenbogaert and Episcopius, leading Arminians, drew up a *Remonstrance to the States* which flatly rejected Predestination, and declared that Christ died for all, and that all men were capable of salvation. Vorstius' book *Tractatus Theologicus de Deo* enfuriated James I for reasons not easy to understand, and he declared to the States General that no heretic ever deserved the stake better than Vorstius. Arminius had sought to bring about peace by challenging the dogmatism of the Calvinist position, and no one sought peace more sincerely than Episcopius. But in the event the conflict was only enflamed. The Synod of Dort in 1618, to which King James sent representatives, condemned Arminianism. The Anglican position remained as uncertain as before, for whereas the Anglican representatives all signed the doctrinal decrees, according to the wishes of the King, they protested at the assertion that there was Scriptural basis for an equality of ministers, since this denied the validity of the status of bishops. John Hales left the conference rejecting Calvin. Some bishops in England found it politic not to define their doctrinal position too closely. Lancelot Andrewes, bishop of Winchester, for instance, probably held views nearer to those of the Arminians than of the Calvinists, but he never said so openly.

As the upper and nether millstones of doctrinal certainties, Catholic and Calvinist, ground hard, the idea of toleration slowly emerged, harking back to the spirit of Erasmus, seeking to reconcile the conflicting Christian sects. It spread among the Polish Socinians, and it imbued the work of Hugo Grotius. 'All my life', he wrote in 1641, 'I have burned with the desire to bring reconciliation to the Christian world', and he said that he wished to be in the pacific company of Erasmus, Melanchthon, Witzel and Cassander. Another great scholar seeking the same end was Isaac Casaubon, who had been professor of Greek at Geneva, but who rejected Calvinism without being able to accept Roman Catholicism, and who came to England in 1610 to see whether he could accept the Church of England as the true church. Archbishop Bancroft received him kindly, and gave him a prebend in Canterbury Cathedral. He accepted Anglicanism, and when he died four years later he was honoured by the bishops who welcomed their recognition by a scholar of such international eminence.

Casaubon corresponded with Dutch Arminians, Vorstius and the others, and with Grotius, and there was general agreement upon the need to bring about peace among the churches. He warned of the dangers of encouraging free preaching among the unlearned: theology, he argued, was a matter for the experts. Grotius himself was sent to England in 1613 as one of the Dutch commissioners to discuss commerce, and he seized the opportunity to try to further his cause in England. With many he made an unfavourable impression. James I found him 'a pedant, full of words and of no great judgment', and when he was invited to dinner by the bishop of Ely, he bored the company by tedious theological discussions. Archbishop Abbot came to the conclusion that the Arminians were as dangerous as the Puritans in their zest for controversy.[24] But this was to miss the central point of his thought. In 1632 his *True Religion Explained and Defended* was translated into English, and had great influence among the Great Tew Circle. His book sought to distinguish between the essentials and the inessentials in Christian belief. Christians could unite upon the fundamentals, that there is one eternal and omnipotent God, that Christ rose from the dead, that Christianity is superior to all other religions, that there is nothing in Christian belief contrary to right reason, that Christ's law is superior to that of Moses, and so on. But he argued that Christ's apostles were gentle and tolerant, and the early Christians meek and simple, that there was much agreement between the chief points of Christianity and the beliefs of the heathens, and Grotius's book entirely excludes controversial issues of theology, such as Predestination. The whole was a plea for toleration and agreement. Elsewhere he wrote:

Some dogmas are such that any educated adult should understand them and accept them with a sincere faith, under pain of imperilling his salvation. These dogmas constitute the foundation of faith. All Protestant Churches agree that there is only a small number of them, and that they are clearly expressed in one place or another in the Scripture, with a promise of salvation for those who believe in them and a threat of damnation for those who do not. The other points of doctrine are not the basis, but a superstructure. ... Men who build up a superstructure of hay and straw on the true foundation, do not endanger their salvation ... The weakness of such men must be tolerated, not judged, and we should accept them among us until the day when the whole truth will be revealed.[25]

Francis Bacon urged the same need to separate essentials from inessentials:

We contend about Ceremonies, and things indifferent, about the externe policy and government of the Church: in which kind, if we would but remember, that the ancient and true bonds of unity, are one Faith, one Baptism, and not one Ceremony, one Policy. If we would observe the league among Christians that is penned by our Saviour Christ (He that is not against us, is with us) . . . : if we would leave the overwhelming and turbulent humours of these times, and renew the blessed proceedings of the Apostles and Fathers of the Primitive Church, . . . not to enter into assertions and positions, but to deliver counsels and advices, we should need no other remedy at all . . .
Whilst the Bishops and governors of the Church continue full of knowledge and good works, whilst they feed their flocks indeed, . . . so long the Church is situate, as it were, upon an hill, no man maketh question of it, or seeks to depart from it. But when these virtues in the Fathers and Elders of the Church have lost their light, and that they wax worldly, lovers of themselves, and pleasers of men: then

men begin to grope for the Church as in the dark, they be in no doubt whether they be the successors of the Apostles, or of the Pharisees.
These things I in all sincerity and simplicity, set down touching the controversies which now trouble the Church of England, and that without all art or insinuation: and therefore not likely to be grateful to either part.[26]

These were exactly the views adopted by the Great Tew Circle, and which governed Clarendon's thinking throughout his life. One of those who found them congenial was John Hales, a Fellow of Merton who in 1612 was appointed Professor of Greek at Oxford. In 1618 Hales went to The Hague as chaplain to the ambassador Sir Dudley Carleton, and he attended the Synod of Dort as an interested observer. What he heard led him to 'bid John Calvin good night', but he left without being converted to Arminianism. Clarendon, who wrote a 'Character' of Hales[27] said that Hales's memorial of the Synod was the best record of the 'ignorance and passion and animosity and injustice of that convention; of which he often made very pleasant relations: though at that time it received too much countenance from England'. In 1619, on his return to England, he settled into an Eton Fellowship, to spend the rest of his life among his books, as Clarendon wrote, 'the most separated from the world of any man then living'. Yet he delighted in the company of friends, and once a year would travel to London to join the literary circle around Ben Jonson. He refused preferment in the church and was content to live on £50 a year; yet 'made a greater and better collection of books than were to be found in any other private library that I have seen; as he has sure read more, and carried more about him in his excellent memory, than any man I ever knew, my Lord Falkland only excepted, who I think sided him'.

John Hales' thought was entirely in the Erasmian and humanist tradition. Deeply devoted to scholarship, he was well aware of the limits to certainty in knowledge and belief, and he was convinced therefore of the need for tolerance. Clarendon wrote:

Nothing troubled him more than the brawls which were grown from religion; and he therefore exceedingly detested the tyranny of the Church of Rome; more for their imposing uncharitably upon the consciences of other men, than for the errors in their own opinions: and would often say that he would renounce the religion of the Church of England tomorrow, if it obliged him to believe that any other Christians should be damned; and that nobody would conclude another man to be damned who did not wish him so. . . . He thought that pride and passion, more than conscience, were the cause of all separation from each other's communion; and he frequently said that that only kept the world from agreeing upon such a liturgy as might bring them into one communion, all doctrinal points upon which men differed in their opinions, being to have no place in any liturgy.

In 1638 Hales wrote a little pamphlet on *Schism and Schismatics* in which he argued that words such as heresy and schism were used as 'theological scarecrows' to uphold a party in religion, and to frighten away those who wished to make an impartial enquiry into its truth. Heresy, he wrote, was an offence against truth, and schism an offence against charity, 'and both are deadly'. To quarrel over such matters as the date of Easter, or over Donatist doctrine, seemed to him to be absurd. The reference to the Donatists was aimed against the Presbyterians, but he was equally critical of Roman Catholicism, which 'pretend that we are bound to receive more doctrine as necessary than appears to us to be so'. Indeed Hales was equally reproving of any church which thought it had a monopoly of the truth:

To say 'That one tittle of God's word shall not pass away' is not to say that God will keep here always a known company of men to teach us all Divine Truths, which from them, because of their authority, we may without more ado accept.

For most people, he argued, religion was not a matter of conscious thought and acceptance, but of inheritance and custom, and the religion of the vulgar had little to do with reason:

It hath been the common disease of Christians from the beginning not to content themselves with that measure of faith which God and the Scripture have expressly afforded us; but, out of a vain desire to know more than is revealed, they have attempted to discuss things of which we can have no light, neither from reason nor revelation; neither have they rested herein, but upon pretence of Church authority, which is none, or tradition, which for the most part is but figment.

Thus arose heresies such as Arianism and Nestorianism, not because Arius or Nestorius 'did maliciously invent', but because they made mistakes. And thus there was a simple remedy for schism:

Consider of all the liturgies that are or ever have been, and remove from them whatsoever is scandalous to any party, and leave nothing but what all agree on, and the event shall be that the public service and honour of God shall no ways suffer; whereas to load our public forms with private fancies upon which we differ is the most sovereign way to perpetuate schism unto the world's end.[28]

The pamphlet attracted the attention of Archbishop Laud, who sent for Hales, and, according to Clarendon, 'chid him very kindly for having never come to him, having been his old acquaintance at Oxford'. The two fell to discussing the pamphlet and the interpretation of the Early Fathers, and the Archbishop 'concluded with saying that the time was very apt to set new doctrines on foot, of which the wits of the age were too susceptible; and that there could not be too much care taken to preserve the peace and unity of the Church'. Laud asked if Hales wanted anything; he replied 'Nothing'; however, later Laud persuaded him to accept a canonry at Windsor. But Hales always preferred the peace and security of his own library; he was, Clarendon concluded, 'one of the least men in the kingdom; and one of the greatest scholars in Europe'.[29]

Whether the Archbishop encouraged him to write further, or whether he felt it necessary to defend himself against such criticisms as Laud had made, is not clear, but in either case Hales wrote a further *Letter by the Rev. John Hales of Eton to Archbishop Laud upon Occasion of his Tract Concerning Schism*. In it he declared that his whole life had been devoted to the pursuit of truth: 'For this I have spent my moneys, my means, my youth, my age, and all I have . . . And truth itself shall give me this testimony at last, that if I have missed of her, it is not my fault but my misfortune'. His sole purpose, he wrote, was to obtain peace in religion, but this could not be done by submission to authority. He would not accept the authority of Antiquity untested by reason, nor would he accept the authority of the church without the test of reason. 'For Authority is not wont to dispute, and it goes but lazily on, when it must defend itself by argument in the Schools.' There was nothing subversive in his attitude; 'quiet and peaceable men will not fail of their obedience', so long as they are not driven to perjure their consciences. 'It is a fearful thing to trifle with conscience, for most assuredly, according unto it a man shall stand or fall at the last.'

W E Gladstone once declared to John Morley, with some surprise: 'Do you know whom I find the most tolerant Churchman of that time? Laud! Laud got Davenant made Bishop of Salisbury, and he zealously befriended Chillingworth and Hales.'[30] There was much truth in this. Laud was liberal in his theology; what angered him was what he felt was the rebellious cocksureness of the Puritan extremists, and, as Archbishop, unlike his predecessor George Abbot, he thought it his first duty to enforce conformity throughout the Church. The liberal nature of his theology is revealed in his *Conference between William Laud and Mr. Fisher the Jesuit, by the command of King James*, which took place in 1622, when Laud was bishop of St David's. It was then published in 1624 with Laud's name concealed under the letter 'B'; but in 1639 it was published under his own name, dedicated to Charles I, and it seems probable that John Hales helped him to prepare it for publication.

James I had adopted a policy of limited toleration towards those Roman Catholics who took the Oath of Allegiance, and in these conditions of comparative safety Fisher and other Jesuits carried on missionary work with some success. Thus the poet Crashaw, Sir Francis Cottington and William Chillingworth were converts to Catholicism. Chillingworth later explained that in his state of doubt, the Catholic Church seemed the only one to claim infallibility, while its historical claims seemed irresistible. Chillingworth was appalled at the way in which Protestantism had fragmented the Christian Church into warring sects. He argued that the Scripture was inadequate as the sole arbiter of religious faith, or how did it happen that there were so many conflicting interpretations? In his search for peace and Christian unity the Catholic Church seemed to offer the best chance of success. Clarendon says that Chillingworth went to St Omer to complete his conversion, though it was more probably Douai.[31] He soon found however that Catholic theology no more settled his doubts than the Anglican had done, and he returned to England after only a few months, in a state of considerable depression. His godfather Archbishop Laud treated him kindly, and wrote him letters to remove his doubts. Those letters which have been unfortunately lost would undoubtedly throw considerable light on the tolerance and liberalism of Laud. At one point Chillingworth seems to have returned to the continent to consult with Grotius, who was still much concerned with the need to re-unite Christendom. When he returned he was taken in by Lucius Cary's mother, Lady Falkland, in the belief that he was still a Catholic, but when she found him telling one of her daughters that Roman Catholicism was 'founded on lies and maintained on them', she quickly sent him packing. To her annoyance her son Lucius gave Chillingworth a home at Great Tew, and made him a tutor to his young brothers. The state of Chillingworth's religious beliefs was a matter of considerable concern, for at the news of his conversion to Rome, a number of young men at Oxford had considered following his example. The re-conversion was a slow business, and Laud and Sheldon must have shown unwonted patience in their task. They offered him an Anglican living, since he had no visible source of income except the generosity of his father and friends. But Chillingworth refused because he could not bring himself to subscribe to the Thirty-Nine Articles:

I am firmly and unmoveably resolved, that if I can have no preferment without subscription, neither I can nor will have any ... I will not juggle with my conscience, and play with God Almighty ... If I subscribe, I subscribe to my own damnation.[32]

Not until 1635 was he willing to subscribe, and it was not until 1638 that he became Chancellor of Sarum.

Chillingworth's *The Religion of Protestants*, composed at Tew, revealed his reluctance to admit the justice of any church to exercise dogmatic authority over its members, partly because he thought that the clergy were as open to corruption as other men, partly because he hated persecution, and partly because he believed that dogmatism led to schism. He rejected the claim to infallibility for the Roman as for any other church, because all human institutions were liable to error. He likewise rejected the Calvinist God because it was an unjust God. To Chillingworth, as to Falkland, 'Our God is a gracious God, and requires of no more than we are able to do.'[33] His was no recipe for scepticism:

By the 'religion of Protestants', I do not understand the doctrine of Luther, of Calvin or Melanchthon; nor the confession of Augusta, or Geneva, nor the Catechism of Heidelberg, nor the Articles of the Church of England, no nor the harmony of Protestant confessions; but that wherein they all agree, and which they all subscribe with a greater harmony, as a perfect rule of their faith and actions, that is, the BIBLE. The BIBLE, I say, the BIBLE only, is the religion of Protestants.[34]

All other beliefs were matters of opinion. Thus he rejected Calvinist Predestination, not only because it seemed to reflect upon God's justice, but because it could be no more than an opinion. When the Jesuits challenged Chillingworth to show the grounds for certainty for the Protestant faith, he replied that Protestants did not presume to certainty, but that the truth could be *sought* in the Scripture and in history. He rejected the claims to certainty made by any church; the Divine Right of Presbyterianism was as obnoxious to him as the Divine Right of Catholicism. All his life he yearned after Grotius's ideal of a union of all Protestant churches on the simple fundamentals of Biblical Christianity.

The Great Tew circle were conscious of the importance of history in a way that many earlier thinkers were not. They thought less of the Reformation as a complete break with the past, and more in terms of the importance of continuity in the search for the truth. Hales and Falkland were deeply read in the works of the Early Fathers. Falkland's most important written work was *A Discourse of Infallibility, and a Reply* in which he displayed the new reliance on man's reason, and the need for tolerance. He denied that any church could claim infallibility because no church could prove it. If the Church of Rome appealed to the Scriptures, why may not the Protestant interpretation be also acceptable? If men follow their reason in the interpretation of the Scriptures, 'God will either give his Grace for assistance to find the Truth, or his pardon if they miss it'. There is no such thing as an infallible guide, no better test of man's belief than his reason. What particularly angered him was the persecution of those who would not accept the Catholic position. 'When there is fire for them that disagree, they need not brag of their Uniformity who consent!' He could not accept that God's Grace was not freely available to all men: 'I should rather be a Pelagian than a Calvinist, since the first doth not wholly overthrow God's grace'. Theological conclusions derived from tradition can be only matters of belief, since they derive from the philosophy of ages which may have been faulty, and may still be shown to be so. Yet men have been accounted heretics merely for doubting them. Suppose a church to claim the truth of tradition, and another to deny it, how could one choose between them but by the application of one's reason? Falkland frequently quoted Erasmus as a model, one who 'having suffered and long by the bigots of both parties', remained 'a dear friend both to Fisher and his colleague in martyrdom, Sir Thomas More'. The whole work is indeed in the Erasmian tradition, a plea for tolerance and an appeal to reason.

These new ideas of reason and tolerance were not without their influence within the Anglican Church. Indeed the earlier Stuart bishops have as yet had scant justice at the hands of historians. Mention here should be made of the career of John Dury (1596–1680), a Protestant minister who, while minister to the English Company of merchants at Elbing in Prussia conceived the idea of reconciliation between the Protestant churches, and won the encouragement of Gustavus Adolphus and Chancellor Oxenstierna. Dury spent most of his life travelling about northern Europe, including England, in the attempt to bring about Protestant unity. In England he was well received by Archbishop Laud, but his especial friends and supporters were bishops Morton of Durham, Hall of Exeter, and Davenant of Salisbury. In his *Good Counsells for the Peace of Reformed Churches*, published in 1641, he revealed their answers to his questions. Bishop Davenant denied that such matters as Predestination and Freewill could be sufficient ground for schism and separation, and he quoted St Paul: 'if it be possible and as much as in you lies, live peaceably with all men':

Now I leave it to every man's conscience to judge, what manner of Charity that is, which sees and suffers Christian Churches (without all just cause and necessity) to stand still at distance and defiance one with another, and perpetually to shun a Reconciliation and Union. Is it not enough for us to separate from the hay and stubble, I mean, from the errors of other Churches, but must we by a voluntary separation forsake the Churches themselves, which as yet have not forsaken Christ or his Truth?

Thomas Morton declared 'that 'tis easy for peaceable and moderate men to be reconciled'. The real rock of division seemed to him to be Predestination, but he urged that on this even Luther, Calvin and the Pope were not irreconcilable. Bishop Hall of Exeter saw three points of difference, namely the omnipotence of Christ, the manner of receiving the Eucharist and Predestination, and he thought there could be reconciliation on all three:

The foundation of the Christian Faith is, amongst us all, one and the same, entire and unshaken; there's not so much as one stone in it, or the least piece of cement, about which any question either is or can be made. Upon this Foundation there are built certain points of School divinity about which alone we so hotly contend, but what are these to a Christian? What are these to Salvation? In what a safe and quiet state might the affairs of Christendom have been, if such nice disputes of curious and over-busy heads had never been heard of.[35]

There was therefore the beginnings of a real Oecumenical movement before 1640. It is true that John Dury in fact achieved little. He put his faith in the triumph of parliament, and was sorely disappointed at the result. He was not in touch with the Great Tew circle, except through John Hales, but the response of Morton, Davenant and Hall shows that the new spirit was abroad in the Church of England, and might have borne fruit if it had not been swallowed up in civil war. Civil war was indeed a catastrophe for the Great Tew circle, as for other men of moderation. Falkland, more than any of the others, was plunged into despair by the conflict. Their ideas however were not destroyed, but lived on in the thought of the Cambridge Platonists, while Hyde, Sheldon and Morley played their parts in the Restoration Church. Young Ned Hyde had had a stimulating education as a member of the group. From his father, from Oxford and private reading, he had acquired a great love of history and literature. At the Inns of Court, and above all under the influence of John Selden, he developed a profound belief in the common law as the foundation of stability in church and state. From his friends at Great Tew he was initiated into a humanist and tolerant theology which owed much to the study of history, and which rejected the bigoted certainties which were the cause of so much religious conflict. Moreover, by the 1630s he was a prosperous and highly successful London lawyer, practising in the courts, and not unknown at Court, and soon to be caught up in the developing political situation. It is to this we must now turn.

2

# The Seeds of Conflict

In November 1646, when the Civil Wars were all but over, and Edward Hyde was in virtual exile on the isle of Jersey, he wrote to his friend Secretary Nicholas:

As soon as I found myself alone, I thought the best way to provide myself for new business against the time I should be called to it (for, Mr. Secretary, you and I must once again to business) was to look over the faults of the old; and so I resolved (which you know I threatened you with long ago) to write the history of these evil times, and of this most lovely Rebellion . . . I write with all fidelity and freedom of all I know, of persons and things, and the oversights and omissions on both sides, in order to what they desired; so that you will believe it will make mad work among friends and foes, if it were published.

Hyde tackled the task with relish: in some ways it was more congenial to him than the rigours of politics. He intended, he said, to write for three hours a day, and for the rest of the time to give himself to study, 'so I doubt not after seven years' time in this retirement, you will find me a pretty fellow'. He wrote with the knowledge and approval of the king, but his work was in no sense intended to be an apology for the monarchy. The king, he said, 'will not find himself flattered in it, nor irreverently handled: though the truth will better become a dead than a living man'. He did not intend that it should be published in his own lifetime.[1]

Hyde wrote with a deep sense of the continuity of history, and the conviction that historical laws were discernible in events; or as he put it, that 'the immediate finger and wrath of God must be acknowledged in these perplexities and distractions'. Great events could not arise without cause, and once God's purpose was seen, once the causes of strife were understood, 'we may not yet find the cure so desperate, but, by God's mercy, the wounds may be again bound up'. He did not doubt that after an interval the continuity of history would be resumed. For there was a grand paradox, in that whereas the conflict had arisen from a zeal to protect religion, the laws, liberties and the rights of parliament, all noble ideals, yet it had led to the destruction of both law and liberty, and a very threat to the constitution it sought to preserve.[2] Nor did he believe that the conflict could have arisen without grave errors in Stuart government.

It was not his intention to seek the causes earlier than the death of James I. He was not so sharp-sighted, he wrote, as those who found causes as early as the reign of Queen Elizabeth, and in this modern historians have tended to agree with him.[3] He began therefore with the mistakes of the early years of Charles I, in particular the disastrous wars with Spain and France. James I may have learned the lesson of history, but his son did not, that foreign wars always brought grave dangers to the monarchy. The war with Spain was at first popular, and the Commons had voted supplies, three subsidies and two fifteenths in 1624, and further subsidies in 1625 and 1628; but the yield of such taxes was inadequate to meet the needs of a war which cost a million pounds a year, and there was the additional burden of £600,000 debt left by James I. When the people saw the miserable results of the war, they soon got tired of paying for it, and had good reason to complain.

The second mistake Hyde discerned was in the king's handling of the parliaments of the years 1625–9. Genuine grievances had needed remedies, and members were in constructive mood: 'the habit and temper of men's minds were, no question, very applicable to the public ends'. He did not defend the turbulent events of 1628–9; they were, he wrote, 'not fit for the dignity and honour of those places, and unsuitable to the reverence due to his majesty and his councils'. But they were the consequence of Buckingham's policies, and above all of repeated dissolutions of parliament, which were no answer to the problems, and merely encouraged the suspicions which were growing up between the Court and the nation. The blame he placed on Buckingham for the first two dissolutions, and on Weston for the third.

Whereas, if they had been frequently summoned, and seasonably dissolved, after their wisdom in applying medicines and cures, as well as their industry in discovering diseases had been discerned, they would easily have been applied to the uses for which they were first instituted.[4]

But Buckingham was 'utterly ignorant of the ebbs and floods of popular councils', and could think of no better way of dealing with parliament than by encouraging factions, or by speedy dissolutions. Clarendon was especially critical of Buckingham's attempts to build up a faction in the Commons, and his impeachment of the earl of Middlesex on trumped-up charges, in both of which he had the aid of the feckless Charles. Clarendon saw the full significance of James I's warning to Buckingham: 'By God, Stenny, you are a fool, and will shortly repent this folly, and will find that, in this fit of popularity, you are making a rod with which you will be scourged yourself', words borne out when the Commons attempted to impeach Buckingham in 1626. Still more ominous was his warning to Charles, 'that he would live to have his bellyful of parliaments; and that when James should be dead, he would have too much cause to remember how much he had contributed to the weakening of the Crown, by this precedent he was now so fond of'. Clarendon saw the forging of the weapon of impeachment against Middlesex as carrying deadly implications for Strafford and the monarchy in 1641, and modern historians have again agreed with him.[5]

Clarendon wrote that once Charles I was on the throne the truth of his father's words became apparent. An attack was launched against Buckingham in parliament:

all the actions of his life ripped up and surveyed, and all malicious glosses made upon all he had said and all he had done: votes and remonstrances passed against him as an enemy to the public; and his ill management made the ground of their refusal to give the king that supply he had reason to expect, and was absolutely necessary to the state he was in.[6]

The attacks of parliament were met by dissolutions, which Clarendon regarded as highly ill-conceived. The disastrous expedition to the Isle of Rhé, and John Felton's assassination of Buckingham were events which Clarendon could well remember among his early experiences. Moreover his first wife had been distantly related to the duke, and his father-in-law had been Buckingham's secretary, and through him had become Master of Requests and Master of the Mint.[7] When Clarendon wrote that the duke did 'many things which only grieved his friends and incensed his enemies'[8] one may catch an echo of the discussions which must have gone on in the Hyde family circle. He described the private grief the king experienced at the loss of his friend, and how, as he had good reason to know, 'from that time almost to the time of his own death, the king admitted very few into any degree of trust who had ever discovered themselves to be enemies to the duke'.[9] Thus a further barrier was erected between the king and his subjects.

It is a mark of Clarendon's quality as a historian that having criticised the disastrous consequences of Buckingham's policy, he redressed the balance by emphasising the personal qualities of charm and generosity which made Buckingham a great courtier, prodigal to his friends, formidable to his enemies, and a valiant soldier in the field. But so over-mighty a subject could not but belittle the monarch and make rival factions. His greatest misfortune was to have risen too quickly, and never to have made a single friend who could have influenced him in statesmanship.[10] His possessiveness over the Prince of Wales when in Spain had amounted to an obsession, and was a grave reflection on the prince's maturity. At the time of Buckingham's death the Hyde family could be regarded as clients, and Edward Hyde was persuaded to write a pamphlet in defence of the duke. This he openly admitted in his *History*. He wrote

so far from any acrimony to the memory of that great favourite, whose death he had lamented at that time, and endeavoured to vindicate him from some libels and reproaches, which vented after his death, that he took delight in remembering his many virtues, and to magnify his affability and most obliging nature.[11]

But this personal view did not influence Clarendon's strictures on the duke's statesmanship.

Buckingham's disastrous policies resulted in the growth of a formidable political opposition both at Court and in parliament, headed by the earl of Arundel, Earl Marshal of England, the ablest of the Howards, and his brother-in-law the earl of Pembroke, and including a formidable array of political talent with the earls of Bristol and Clare, John Williams bishop of Lincoln, Sir John Eliot, Sir Thomas Wentworth, Sir Dudley Digges, Sir Robert Cotton and John Selden. Clarendon wrote vivid pen-portraits of some of these men including a eulogy of the third earl of Pembroke as 'the most universally loved and esteemed of any man of that age'. Pembroke had been highly critical of Buckingham's Spanish policy, but the two were reconciled in 1626, when it was agreed that the eldest son of Pembroke's brother Philip (who became the fourth earl) should marry Buckingham's daughter. On the death of Buckingham the Hydes, with their west country interests, naturally looked towards the earl of Pembroke as patron, and Clarendon described him as 'a great lover of his country and of religion and justice'. He was a man of great fortune, especially after his marriage with the daughter and heir of the earl of Shrewsbury, but it was an unhappy marriage, and 'he was immoderately given up to women'. He was also (although Clarendon did not mention it) a considerable patron of literature, and Shakespeare himself. He died in 1630, and it is unlikely that the young Edward Hyde knew him personally.

Of Pembroke's brother and successor, the fourth earl, Clarendon wrote contemptuously, as one who rose to power at Court under James I simply because of the latter's partiality for handsome young men, yet 'he pretended to no other qualifications than to understand horses and dogs very well'.[12] Clarendon thought he drifted into the parliamentary camp during the Civil War without ever intending to, but with the single intention of preserving Wilton House, which he rebuilt in the 1630s, and where he gathered a fine collection of Van Dycks, all of which constituted his great monument in history. Hyde's later relations with him when the two were on opposite sides in the Civil War did not improve his low opinions of the earl's abilities.

Against Arundel Clarendon had a strong prejudice. He was Earl Marshal of England, and it was the Earl Marshal's court which in 1624 inflicted what was thought to be an injustice on Hyde's uncle. This was never forgotten by the family, and Edward Hyde had his revenge in the Long Parliament, when he led the attack on the court and secured its abolition. Clarendon described Arundel as 'a man supercilious and proud', 'always in disgrace, and once or twice in the Tower'; with 'no other affection for the nation of the kingdom than as he had a great share in it, in which, like a great leviathan, he might sport himself'. Modern historians have not been able to endorse this estimate, and it is now clear that Arundel was a great exponent of the traditional forms of government, as well as being a great patron of the arts, and singularly uncorrupted by the politics of the time.[13]

Clarendon's portrait of Sir Richard Weston, earl of Portland, the Lord Treasurer, is equally unflattering, 'a mean and abject spirit', avid for patronage for his family and friends. Hyde as a young lawyer had crossed swords with the Lord Treasurer with a petition from London merchants which Portland had rejected, and this may have influenced his judgment. He did however praise his handling of the royal finances at a time when economy was the great need of the monarchy.[14]

Clarendon was a vivid portraitist, although it is clear that his judgments were often somewhat influenced by personal considerations. From the 1630s he was a prosperous barrister, often appearing in the courts, and meeting the leading men of his day, and no doubt the way in which great men received him had much to do with his estimates of them. Thus he wrote that Lord Keeper Coventry 'manifested kindness for him as often as he came before him'; and that he was 'looked upon as a favourite' in the Court of Requests, which the Lord Privy Seal, the earl of Manchester, 'had raised to do as much business as the chancery itself was possessed of'; of that Lord Chamberlain, the earl of Pembroke, received him with 'familiarity', and so on. Clarendon was very interested in people, was very sensitive to stature, to the sound of a voice, or the clothes people wore, and he loved nothing better than to reveal the quirks and paradoxes in human behaviour. There was always the artistic urge to compose a complete character-study, warts and all, in a paragraph or two. His assessments of men before his time are always significant. He greatly admired Archbishop Bancroft as one who had 'almost rescued the Church out of the hands of the Calvinian party', but he was contemptuous of his successor in 1610, George Abbot, whose ability, Clarendon wrote with caustic humour, was such as to fit him to be head of a poor Oxford college. He believed that the church would have been different if Lancelot Andrewes or bishop Overall had succeeded Bancroft. But Clarendon's observation and knowledge of human nature make his historical judgments of men he knew personally of special value. In the 1630s Hyde could fairly claim to have many friends at Court and 'among great persons in the country'; and the greatest of these was Archbishop Laud.[15]

William Laud, born in 1573, and twenty years later a fellow of St John's, Oxford, became chaplain to bishop Neile of Rochester in 1608, who remained his patron for many years. In 1611 he became President of St John's. Archbishop Abbot roundly condemned him as 'at least a Papist at heart',[16] but he had the favour of James I who made him, first dean of Gloucester (1616) and then bishop of St David's (1621). In 1622 he was sent by the king to converse with the countess of Buckingham who at the time was considering becoming a Roman Catholic. Henceforth he had the patronage of the all-powerful duke, and in due course the favour of Charles I who insisted on having him (as prebend of Westminster) at his coronation in place of the dean and bishop of Lincoln, John Williams. Henceforth the Arminian party in the church rose rapidly to influence in the favour of the king, and in 1627 Laud became bishop of London, and on the death of Abbot in 1633, archbishop of Canterbury. Clarendon really began his account in 1635 when, on the death of Lord Treasurer Portland, the king decided to put the treasury into commission, and appointed Archbishop Laud, Lord Keeper Coventry and Lord Cottington to the commission. Clarendon saw this as an ominous event for previously Laud had been concerned only with the good government of the church, in which he was a formidable disciplinarian, convinced that 'if the schismatics were not with rigour suppressed, they would put the whole kingdom into a flame'.[17] In this capacity alone he was in a position of great power, but now in addition both as treasury commissioner and Privy Councillor he was at the heart of public affairs, and more than anyone else in the position of chief minister to the king; and being a man of great energy he would make it his business to be concerned in every aspect of government. Clarendon put his finger on the real character of Laud when he wrote of him that

too secure in a good conscience, and most sincere worthy intentions, with which no man was ever more plentifully replenished, he thought he could manage and discharge the place and office of the greatest minister in the court without the least condescension to the arts and stratagems of the court, and without any other friendship or support than what the splendour of a pious life, and his unpolished integrity, would reconcile to him; which was an unskilful measure in a licentious age, and may deceive a good man in the best that shall succeed.[18]

Hyde's first contact with the archbishop well illustrated the officious industry that Laud always displayed. On his weekly visits to his home town of Reading Laud met a merchant, Daniel Harvey, who complained that a petition of London merchants to the Lord Treasurer Portland had been ignored. Laud detested Portland, and was eager to unearth any matter which might put him in a bad light. He asked who had drawn up the petition, and was told a young lawyer named Hyde, who was the son-in-law of Sir Thomas Aylesbury. Aylesbury told the archbishop that his son-in-law lived with him, and had chambers in the Middle Temple. Laud sent for the young lawyer and received him kindly, saying that he had recently, against his will, become a commissioner of the treasury, that he knew little of commercial matters, but was anxious to serve the king, and therefore to know more. He made it clear to Hyde that what he desired was to find as much evidence as possible against Portland and Hyde returned later with enough evidence to 'please him abundantly'. Henceforth Hyde was a protégé of the archbishop. He said he frequently appeared as counsel in cases before the Privy Council, and that he 'well knew how to cultivate those advantages' which accrued from so powerful a patron, with the result that he was 'used with more countenance by all the judges in Westminster Hall and the eminent practisers, than was usually given to men of his years, so that he grew every day in practice, of which he had as much as he desired; and having a competent estate of his own, he enjoyed a very pleasant and a plentiful life, living very generously, and much above the rank of those lawyers whose business was only to be rich'.[19]

Clarendon described his daily routine as a young lawyer. He made a point of meeting his friends about court and the town at dinner, where they enjoyed lively conversation; he worked at his law in the mornings and afternoons, but found time for the reading of literature which he loved, and always avoided eating supper, which prevented him from working into the night.[20] Apart from two months in the country during the summer, he spent his whole time in London. He afterwards regretted never having ridden a country circuit, which would have given him a clearer view of the opinions of the counties.

One of his closest friends during these years was a fellow-lawyer Bulstrode Whitelocke, who was four years his senior. Bulstrode was the son of Sir James Whitelocke who in 1624 was appointed a judge in the King's Bench. The two became friends while students at the Middle Temple, and Hyde greatly admired Whitelocke for his 'stupendous learning' and his 'faculty of making hard things easy'. Like Hyde, Whitelocke was a great admirer of Selden, of whose library he made full use, and from whom he learnt a love of history. His inheritance of Fawley Court and a comfortable fortune, had much to do in Clarendon's opinion, with Whitelocke's decision to continue to support parliament.

William Prynne had published *Histriomastix*, a humourless attack upon play-acting which was interpreted as an insult to the Queen, was sentenced by the Star Chamber to be expelled from Lincoln's Inn, fined £5000, to lose his ears and to be imprisoned for life. Prynne later became a popular hero, but he was not so regarded in 1634. The Inns of Court decided to repudiate their connection with him by presenting a masque before the king and queen, and they chose *The Triumph of Peace* by James Shirley. An organising committee of two representatives from each of the Inns of Court included Edward Hyde and Bulstrode Whitelocke for the Middle Temple, and John Selden and William Noy the Attorney-General were among the others. The whole production was on the most lavish scale with Inigo Jones designing the scenery and costumes, and Whitelocke responsible for the music. The masque was performed on 3 February 1634, preceded by a vast procession through the city to Whitehall, with trumpeters, musicians, dancers, torch-bearers, mounted gentlemen of the Inns of Court, footmen in scarlet and silver, with anti-masquers representing beggars and cripples, miming a satire on the monopolists. The masque itself was performed in the Banqueting Hall. The king and queen were delighted with the performance, and the queen danced until morning, when there was a banquet. Ten days later, by royal request, the masque was repeated in Merchant Taylors' Hall. The whole cost over

£21,000, and Whitelocke proudly claimed that it was the finest ever performed in England.[21]

Charles I and his queen loved masques and plays, and basked in the lavish and exotic atmosphere of baroque glorification of monarchy. Historians have of course been struck by the contrast between this world of make-believe and a gathering storm of political conflict in the nation. But again it is important not to ante-date the storm. John Selden had suffered imprisonment after the last parliament, but was ready to help organise a great display in honour of the monarchy. Whitelocke and Hyde were young lawyers with an eye to the main chance, and were undoubtedly hoping to further their advancement at Court and in their profession. They were much interested in the great test cases of their time, Bate's Case, the Five Knights' Case, ship money and so forth, but they regarded them as legal cases to be settled in the courts by common law rather than issues to be settled by political means.

Edward Hyde's surviving correspondence for these years is scanty, but we have occasional glimpses of his way of life. A letter of 5 August 1635 shows him to be working in the Middle Temple on the extension of ship money from the maritime parts to the whole country: it was a direction he apparently accepted without comment. About the same time there was an undated letter to Whitelocke which revealed something of his life-style, fears and aspirations:

Our best news is, that we have good wine abundantly come over; and the worst that the plague is in town and no judges die. For your bishops, I know no new additions . . .[22]

Hyde early acquired the reputation of a *bon viveur*; plague was almost an annual cause for alarm; and it is clear that both young men intended to follow their family traditions, and had their eye on the judicial bench. The reference to 'your bishops' is a reminder of the interest attached to the episcopal bench at the time. The bishops were attracting to themselves a great amount of public interest, and if Hyde was persona grata to the archbishop, Whitelocke was not. His first wife had died in May 1634, and in November Whitelocke eloped with Frances Willoughby, niece and ward of the earl of Rutland, who had forbidden the marriage. It was the talk of the town, and Hyde heartily congratulated his friend on his romantic adventure. But the officious Laud took a different view. He already disapproved of Whitelocke for his leniency towards the Puritans, both in the courts and out of them, and now he summoned him and roughly reprimanded him for daring as a commoner to marry the daughter of a nobleman without permission, treating Whitelocke 'more like a porter than a gentleman'. Afterwards he seems to have regretted his remarks, for he summoned Whitelocke to dinner and apologised. Apparently Whitelocke did not bear a grudge, but the incident illustrates one reason for the growing unpopularity of the archbishop. At first the Willoughby family would not recognise the marriage, but there were some powerful mediators, including Bishop Williams of Lincoln; Edward Hyde won over the bride's brother, Lord Francis Willoughby, and the wounds were eventually healed.[23]

Another of Hyde's letters to Whitelocke, in his characteristically bantering and buoyant style, announced his intention of visiting Fawley Court (undated):

I will not so far lessen my devotion to Fawley, to tell you it is fit I breathe the country air; indeed this beloved town [London] is to me all health; yet I intend nothing more than to visit you this Lent, and be merry with you, that you shall perceive you have much of my heart in your keeping. The time exactly I dare not promise; however it shall not be before the twenty-ninth; for I am in doctor Moor's disposal for one week's physic.[24]

In another letter he congratulated Whitelocke on the birth of a son (which dates the letter to 1635), and promised to send him a doe, which however seems never to have arrived. He concluded: 'My pen is deep in a star-chamber bill, and therefore I have only the leisure and the manners to tell you, I am very proud that you are a friend to Your most affectionate servant Edward Hyde.'

Even the scanty correspondence which has survived has shown both Whitelocke and Hyde much concerned as lawyers with ship money. Whitelocke had expressed some opposition to the extended tax and it is possible that Hyde agreed with him. He certainly understood the implications for Charles I's government. He wrote on 18 February 1638:

The King is now thoroughly possessed of his ship money, which all the judges of England have assured him may be levied by law, which is a notable revenue annexed to the Crown since you went, and amounts to a greater proportion than was ever given by Parliament. This and a spiritual Treasurer may in time make the King very rich.[25]

On 10 February Lord Chief Justice Finch and Sir Robert Berkeley had given judgment in favour of the crown in the Hampden case, and the legality of ship money was clearly asserted. Bishop Juxon was Lord Treasurer, and Hyde feared that now that the king had an assured revenue independent of parliament there might never again be another parliament.

When he came to write his *History* he made the mature judgment that the judges' confirmation of the legality of ship money made it less, and not more likely that the people would accept the tax. When it was regarded as an extraordinary imposition to meet a real national defence emergency, people were prepared to pay it with no more than a grumble. But when they saw it erected into a legal and permanent tax,

when they heard this demanded in a court of law, as a right, and found it, by sworn judges of the law, adjudged so, upon grounds and reasons *as every stander-by was able to swear was not law*, they regarded the rights of property at risk, and 'they had no reason to hope that that doctrine, or the preachers of it, would be contained within any bounds'.[26] Clarendon regarded the judgment of the judges as mistaken, and believed that thereby they had brought the law into contempt, 'there being no possibility to preserve the dignity, reverence and estimation of the laws themselves, but by the integrity and innocency of the judges'. If later in the 1640s the House of Commons rode roughshod over the law, if the prestige of the House of Lords was shaken, it 'could be imputed to no one thing more than to the irreverence and scorn the judges were justly held in'.

If these men had preserved the simplicity of their ancestors, in severely and strictly defending the laws, other men had observed the modesty of theirs, in humbly and dutifully obeying them.[27]

Clarendon argued that in earlier times the prerogative had been exerted more forcefully, but without bringing the law into contempt. As it was, 'my lord Finch's speech in the exchequer-chamber made ship money much more abhorred and formidable than all the commitments by the council-table, and all the distresses taken by the sheriffs in England'. For in exalting the power of the King, in declaring that 'no Act of Parliament can bar a King of his regality', Finch belittled parliament.[28] Some things were better left undefined. The other lawyer, particularly blamed by Clarendon, was the Attorney-General, William Noy, for his ingenuity in framing such devices as monopolies and ship money.

Clarendon thus identified the main causes of the coming conflict as, first, the disastrous policies of the duke of Buckingham, and the mishandling of the parliaments of 1625–9; and second, the imposition of ship money, together with the other impositions of tonnage and poundage, the forest laws and fines for knighthoods, all with the aid of the Prerogative Courts and the Courts of Common Law, by which the law and the judges were brought into disrepute. The third and crowning blunder was the intervention in Scotland.

Charles's purpose, Clarendon wrote, was nothing less than 'to unite his three kingdoms in one form of God's worship, and in a uniformity in their public devotions',[29] and in this he had the ever-active assistance of Archbishop Laud. Clarendon was very critical of the lack of consultation even with the friends to episcopacy in Scotland, and of the king's obliviousness to the Scots' attachment to the old liturgy, and their fears of becoming a mere province of England. Charles failed to remember his father's experiences at the hands of 'the most turbulent and seditious ministers of confusion that could be found in the kingdom'; or to recognise how little authority Scottish bishops possessed in Scotland.[30]

To the great conflict between the so called Arminians ('though' wrote Clarendon 'many of them had never read a word written by Arminius') and the Puritans, Clarendon adopted the attitude of the Great Tew Circle, blaming each for enflaming a controversy which need not have occurred. For the Puritans declared that the Arminians sought to introduce Popery, while the latter regarded all Puritans as seeking to overthrow the government of the church and establish the Genevan system,

whereas in truth, none of the one side were at all inclined to popery, and very many of the other were most affectionate to the peace and prosperity of the church, and very pious and learned men.[31]

Laud, a man of courage, convinced of his own piety and the justice of his cause, pursued a single-minded course regardless of the storm he aroused. Not only did he have the king's full support, but he secured the appointment of Juxon, bishop of London as Lord Treasurer, 'a man so unknown that his name was scarce heard of in the kingdom, who had been within two years before but a private chaplain to the king, and the president of a poor college in Oxford'.[32] Laud believed he was strengthening the church when in fact he was merely promoting a nonentity. Clarendon described how Laud's enemies deliberately provoked him into a rage which he would afterwards greatly regret and make amends for by inviting them to dinner.

To Clarendon it seemed that the handling of Scotland was a litany of errors. In January 1636 new canons were published on the authority of the king, and without consultation with the Scots. It enjoined the observance of a new Prayer Book which did not appear until 1637. When it was published it had made a few concessions to Scottish opinion, but did nothing to remove the unfounded fear that Charles and Laud intended a return to Roman Catholicism. Neither the Canons nor the Prayer Book had been submitted to the clergy of Scottish Council, but had been issued on the sole authority of the king, and the Prayer Book contained 'too much nourishment to be administered at once to weak and queasy stomachs'.[33] The result was the carefully timed explosion of resistance in the cathedral of St Giles, Edinburgh on 23 July 1637. Clarendon had no special information as to its organisers, but he noted that no member of the rabble was brought to justice. He noted also that people in England were so ignorant of Scottish affairs that they knew more of events in Germany or Poland. Thus for a long time the seriousness of the challenge from Scotland was not realised. The National Covenant was drawn up in February 1638, but it was not until late in the year that the king began to raise an army. In September the king revoked the Prayer Book and Canons, but with no intention of surrendering. Clarendon probably did not know that the king's instructions to the marquis of Hamilton, his commissioner in Scotland, had been: 'Flatter them with what hopes you please . . . until I be ready to suppress them.'[34] Clarendon thought that speedy military action at the outset might have succeeded. When the king did resort to military action it was to summon the nobility to his aid in the mistaken belief that the people would rally behind their king to fight their old enemies the

Scots.[35] The general in command, the earl of Arundel, was no soldier; the earl of Holland, commander of the horse, was duped by the supposed strength of the forces at Leslie's command. The earl of Pembroke was opposed to the war, and Lords Saye and Sele and Brooke were in opposition to the king. The royalist forces were demoralised and mutinous. The king therefore was forced to accept the Pacification of Berwick (18 June 1639) by which both sides agreed to disband, and the king agreed to come to Scotland in the autumn for the meeting of a parliament and assembly. Clarendon knew that the Scots found good friends among the English, and had convinced them that their main aim was the removal of the unpopular marquis of Hamilton. He said he never discovered what prevailed on the king to make so disadvantageous an agreement. Clarendon did not suspect disloyalty, but he did accuse the king's advisers of gross incompetence. The only man to emerge with increased reputation, he said, was the earl of Essex. The king's prestige had suffered a severe blow, and Scottish resistance was enormously encouraged. The general assembly which opened at Edinburgh in August condemned episcopacy as contrary to the law of God; and the Scottish Parliament, when it met, was dominated by the Covenanters. A letter from the latter to the King of France fell into Charles's hands, and he hoped it would rally English opinion against the Scots. He determined on a further military venture, but for this a parliament in England was necessary, and it was summoned to meet on 13 April 1640. It was an event which was to transform Hyde's whole life.

Looking back on the years 1629–40 Clarendon's view was ambivalent, personal nostalgia and historical judgment vying with each other. On the one hand

England enjoyed the greatest measure of felicity that it had ever known; the two crowns of France and Spain worrying each other, by their mutual incursions and invasions of each other. ... All Germany weltering in its own blood, and contributing to each other's destruction. ... Of all the princes of Europe, the king of England alone seemed to be seated upon that pleasant promontory, that might safely view the tragic suffering of all his neighbours about him, without any other concernment than what arose from his own princely heart and Christian compassion. ... His three kingdoms flourishing in entire peace and universal plenty, in danger of nothing but their own surfeits . . .[36]

While on the other

the court full of excess, idleness and luxury, and the country full of pride, mutiny and discontent; every man more troubled and perplexed at that they called the violation of one law, than delighted or pleased with the observation of all the rest of the charter: never imputing the increase of their receipts, revenue and plenty, to the wisdom, virtue and merit of the crown, but objecting every little trivial imposition to the exorbitancy and tyranny of the government.[37]

He himself more than once hinted at the temptations which had beset him as a

young man in the bad company he sometimes kept, and said that he felt like
the horseman who having passed over Rochester bridge, found that it had
collapsed behind him. He admitted particularly enjoying eating and drinking,
and the epicurean conversation of men such as the earl of Dorset, Lord
Conway and Lord Lumley, 'men who excelled in gratifying their appetites'.[38]

Looking back on these years from the discomforts and poverty of exile in
Jersey or Rouen, Clarendon set out to understand how such a revolution could
have come about.

## 3

# Edward Hyde the Reformer

With the Scottish revolt upon his hands Charles I was beset with conflicting advice. Sir Thomas Wentworth urged strong military action such 'insolency as is not to be borne by any rule of Monarchy', and he urged the king not to distrust 'the loyalty and cheerfulness of your English subjects . . . for, upon my faith to God, I believe they will be found very ready and trusty in pursuance of your commands'.[1] There were few however who shared his optimistic outlook. Lord Lorne (soon to become Argyll) wrote to Wentworth from Inverary that the Scots 'could hardly be brought back one step to Rome, which on so good grounds they have cast off and settled their own laws' and Sir Edward Stanhope wrote that if only the Scots could secure their 'laws, privileges and immunities', they would be loyal subjects. By January 1639 Northumberland, the Lord High Admiral, was writing:

I assure your Lordship, to my understanding (with sorrow I speak it) we are altogether in as ill a posture to invade others, or to defend ourselves, as we were a twelvemonth since, which is more than any man can imagine that is not an eye-witness of it. The discontents here at home do rather increase than lessen, there being no course taken to give any kind of satisfaction. The King's coffers were never emptier than at this time.[1]

With an empty treasury the king had no choice but to summon parliament.

Clarendon was very reticent about the circumstances which led to his becoming a member of parliament. In November 1639 he wrote with some excitement to Whitelocke announcing that after eleven years the king had summoned a parliament, and it seems probable that he at once determined to seek a seat, as his father had done long before. In the *Life* he says merely that he was elected for two boroughs, Wootton Bassett in Wiltshire and Shaftesbury in Dorset, and chose to sit for the former. The earl of Pembroke had extensive electoral influence in numerous boroughs, and Shaftesbury was one of them. The franchise however lay with the mayor and burgesses, and there was always a contest between the earl and the civic authorities. It seems probable that Hyde was the earl's nominee, and that this secured his election. But Hyde perhaps preferred not to sit as the earl's nominee, for we have seen that he rarely had a good word to say about the great man. This may explain his preference for Wootton Bassett, which was in any case much nearer the family property. At first Whitelocke decided not to stand 'because of the danger of the time and of the employment', but he was finally persuaded to stand for Abingdon, and was defeated.[2]

Clarendon tells us something of the proceedings of the Short Parliament, but he was writing without the necessary documents, and consequently misdates events. He said that it was unusual for a parliament to do much during the first fortnight, as late members drifted in, but this parliament plunged into business at once. Parliament met on 13 April, and was addressed by the king and Lord Keeper Finch. The latter declared that the Scots had taken up arms against 'the Lord's anointed, their rightful Prince'. There was an urgent need for supplies, and if the Commons would grant them, the king would allow them time afterwards to consider grievances. As a sop to expected critics he declared that the king collected tonnage and poundage only *de facto*, until parliament should legalise it. But the Commons preferred to deal with grievances first. On 16 April Harbottle Grimston made a bitter speech, declaring that there was as great a danger at home as there was from Scotland; that

The Commonwealth hath been miserably torn and massacred, and all property and liberty shaken, the Church distracted, the Gospel and the professors of it persecuted, and the whole nation is overrun with multitudes and swarms of projecting cankerworms and caterpillars, the worst of all the Egyptian plagues.[3]

Grimston turned out to be a moderate who throughout the period 1640–60 pursued a middle course, and was devoted to the old constitution which he believed to have been violated, but at this point his speech seemed too provocative, and he was followed by Sir Benjamin Rudyerd who tried to strike a more conciliatory note. Aged sixty-eight, he had been a Surveyor of the Court of Wards and Liveries, and had sat in the parliament of 1620 for Portsmouth, and since 1623 for Wilton, as a client of the earl of Pembroke. He was above all anxious that an unconciliatory Commons should not force the king to an early dissolution. 'A great door', he said, 'is opened unto us of doing a great deal of good, if we do not shut it against ourselves.'

That we are here together in this house is an evident demonstration that the king's heart stands right towards us, for which we do owe him a thankful and bountiful retribution.

They must, he urged, avoid the mistakes of previous parliaments, for 'the main causes of the infelicity and distractions of these times have been the frequent breaking of parliaments'. Kings were naturally concerned with power, and subjects with liberty, and the two must be reconciled. The crux of the situation lay in the royal need for revenues, and 'I do hope before this parliament be finally concluded, we shall establish such a constant revenue to his majesty as shall enable him to live plentifully . . .' He urged that 'we may all of us strive to make this a breeding, teeming parliament, that it may be the mother of many more . . .'[4]

Sir Francis Seymour followed, warning of the dangers of voting subsidies before grievances were debated, and reciting a long list of grievances, against the judges, the seminary priests of the Queen's chapel at Somerset House, pluralism in the church, 'dumb dogs that cannot speak a word for God', preachers who do nothing but exalt the king's prerogative, and finally the threat to property implicit in ship money. John Pym then proposed a Committee of Grievances, and it was carried.[5]

Next day, 17 April, Pym launched into a major speech outlining the grievances of the Commonwealth. It was this speech which Clarendon remembered as opening the proceedings of this parliament. He made clear that the House should not vote supplies until grievances had been redressed, and that in discussing the latter 'I shall take care to maintain that great prerogative of the King that he can do no wrong'. The grievance he put first was the threat to 'the privilege of parliament' (for him a key phrase during the coming years) which had been violated by the dissolution of the 1629 parliament. The second was religious, the encouragement given to Papists, the setting up of altars, the encroachments of the Court of High Commission, and the bishops' claim to *jure divino*. The third was the taking of tonnage and poundage without consent of parliament, knighthood fines, monopolies, ship money and the forest laws.

On 18 April Edward Hyde rose to point out that Pym had omitted one grievance as important as any other, namely the activities of the Court of Honour, of the Earl Marshal, a court erected, he said, without a shadow of legality, which fined and imprisoned at will. He recited the case of a citizen imprisoned for insulting an earl's crest by mistaking a swan for a goose; and another in which a tailor was fined for saying that he was as good as a gentleman. He had heard it said that a knight could not live as cheaply as a gentleman; now he could not die as cheaply, for he must pay £5 (or £10) to the heralds of the Earl Marshal. When a lawyer said that such a fee was not legal, he had been imprisoned. Perhaps this was too specialised an issue to capture the interest of the House, which preferred to pass on to the consideration of the legality of ship money, but at any rate Hyde had shown himself at the outset as a reformer.

The king was becoming impatient, and on 21 April the Lord Keeper addressed both Houses in the Banqueting House to urge them to grant speedy supplies, after which the king would listen to just grievances. As for ship money, he declared, the king had never intended it as an annual levy, nor was it for his own advantage, and parliament was welcome to see how the money had been spent. The Commons were staggered at the extent of the king's requirements of £100,000 a month, and next day they preferred to discuss the acts of Convocation. But on the 23rd they came to the king's business. Sir

Benjamin Rudyerd urged the House to trust the king as the best means to 'bring all things to a happy conclusion', but Sir Ralph Hopton said that there were many thorns to be pulled out before they could serve the king. The Comptroller of the Household, Sir Thomas Jermyn, made it clear that the king would gladly exchange ship money for an alternative source of revenue. As the debate continued it was clear that speakers preferred the settling of grievances before supply, and so it was decided.

Next day, the 24th, the king sought the aid of the Lords. He told them of the Commons' decision, and declared that they had 'put the cart before the horse'; but his necessities were so urgent that there could be no delay. He would allow no innovation in religion; he intended no threat to property, and the money would be used, not for his own profit, but to preserve sea power. The kingdom was in danger, and 'this time I must be trusted'.[6] The Lords were impressed, and by about three to one voted that supply should precede examination of grievances, although the earl of Manchester and Viscount Saye opposed. All the bishops voted for the motion.

Pym at once saw the danger, and requested a conference between the two Houses. Lord Keeper Finch recounted the king's plea that his affairs would suffer no delay, and that he must be trusted. Pym took his stand on the privilege of parliament, which to him transcended all other matters, and argued that the lords had violated the privilege of the Commons by interfering in a matter of supply. On the 29th the Lords took their stand on their own privileges. Strafford (ironically in view of his own fate) urged the Lords to retain their jurisdiction intact, saying that the Commons could do nothing effectively without the Lords. Arundel, the Earl Marshal, smarting under Hyde's attack, declared that the Lords, and not the Commons, were a court of jurisdiction. By 60 votes to 25 the Lords agreed 'that the matter of his Majesty's supply should have precedence . . . was no breach of the privileges of the House of Commons'.[7] Pym, who by now was effectively directing the course of the Commons, at a further conference with the Lords on the 30th declared that by their vote

You have not only meddled with the matter of supplies, but have concluded both the matter and order of proceedings which the House of Commons takes to be a breach of their privileges, for which I am commanded to desire reparation from your Lordships.[8]

In the Commons Pym kept up the impetus of the attack. On the 29th he urged the House not to be afraid to call crimes crimes if they were so, and to bring criminal charges against guilty parties, adding that 'if we were faint in this place we should discourage all others', meaning his friends in the Lords. But this was too strong for the House, which decided to treat their complaints 'not as crimes but as grievances only'. Next day he switched his attack to a sermon preached by Dr Beales, Vice-Chancellor of Cambridge in 1635, which seemed to reflect on the privilege of parliament, and the House voted that Beales be required to purge himself before the House.

In the conference between the two Houses, the Lords refused to give way. Lord Keeper Finch declared that 'their Lordships as persons moving in an orb nearer the King's person than the House of Commons, and as persons at least equally interested with the House of Commons in the good of the Kingdom, could not but more timely discern and give their advice', and the Lords reiterated that supply should have priority. Pym had thus managed to produce a deadlock between the two Houses, not on the issue of supply, but on the privileges of the House of Commons. This to him, for the rest of his life, was the most important issue, transcending all others.

When on 2 May the king sent a further anguished message requesting supplies, some members were anxious to find a compromise formula. Charles Price, for instance, suggested that a petition of grievances and a supply bill might proceed together. Pym however preferred a committee to examine precedents for the relations between the two Houses. When Sir Francis Seymour said that if the king would give satisfaction on ship money, he was ready to trust the king, Strode and Hampden opposed, and Pym declared that the question went far beyond ship money, and that he wanted enactment that *no* charges should be laid on the people without consent in parliament. He recognised the prerogative of the king to make war, but the Commons, he said, were not bound to pay for it. After a hot debate the House agreed with Pym that grievances must precede supply.[9]

On 4 May Sir Henry Vane brought a further offer from the king: he would part with ship money in return for twelve subsidies spread over three years. Sir Benjamin Rudyerd advised acceptance. However the speech which most impressed Clarendon was that of Serjeant Glanville, who said that five subsidies would cost him a mere £10, whereas ship money cost him £20:

As for twelve subsidies, to give so gracious a King in three years, this was nothing: five in the first year, four the second, three the third, was nothing to stagger our gratuity to so good a king.[10]

Clarendon wrote that the speech was so persuasive that an immediate vote might have carried the House with him. But others spoke against, and Sir Roger Cooke, member for Gloucester declared that the king was fighting a *bellum Episcopale*, and that the bishops themselves might be left to fight it. Clarendon spoke urging the House to take a clear vote whether they proposed to vote a supply or not, but no record of the speech has survived. (His account of the debate of 2–4 May, written from memory is muddled as to the sequence of speeches.) In the end the House decided to take no vote. Next day the king summoned both Houses. He thanked the Lords for their help, and said he would not be so uncharitable as to blame the whole House of Commons, but 'it hath been in some cunning and ill-affected men that hath been the cause of this misunderstanding'. He then dissolved parliament.[11]

Hyde had spoken at most twice during this parliament, but it is clear that he was accounted one of the reformers. A study of the composition of committees in both the Short and the Long Parliaments shows the skill with which Pym and his friends arranged the membership to further their policies. Hyde was a member of a committee to consider the commission granted to Convocation and another to consider ship money (21 April). He was a member of the committee to consult with the Lords on religion and supply (23–4 April).[12] When it was feared that the delays in the Commons in granting supply might lead to an early dissolution, Hyde hurried to Lambeth to see Archbishop Laud, and found him walking in the garden 'sad and full of thoughts'. Hyde begged him

to use all his credit to prevent such a desperate counsel (as that the king should dissolve parliament), which would produce great mischief to the king and to the church: that he was confident the House was well constituted and disposed as ever house of commons was or would be: that the number of the disaffected to church and state was very small; and though they might obstruct for some time the quick resolving upon what was fit, they would never be able to pervert their good inclinations and desires to serve the king.[13]

Laud replied that he believed the king was angry, and if he had decided to dissolve parliament, he would not try to dissuade him. Clarendon blamed Secretary of State Sir Henry Vane, and Solicitor-General Herbert for advising the king to dissolve parliament, presumably to prevent a vote in the House condemning ship money.

Clarendon always regarded the speedy dissolution of the Short Parliament as a major blunder on the king's part, for never again would he have so good a chance of winning national conciliation.

It could never be hoped that more sober and dispassionate men would ever meet together in that place, or fewer who brought ill purposes with them; nor could any man imagine what offence they had given, which put the king to that resolution.

There is some truth in this in that it is clear that Pym and his friends had not yet a sure command of the House. He had not always had his way, as when he wished the grievances to be declared crimes, but he had achieved his main objectives: he had opened up the major grievances of the previous eleven years; he had succeeded in defeating the voting of supplies; he had almost gratuitously picked a quarrel with the House of Lords with the object of asserting the ascendancy of the Commons, and he had shown his intention of bringing offending ministers and judges to 'justice'. In both this parliament and the next Pym's prime objective was to secure the ascendancy of the Commons, and it is probable that the longer the Short Parliament had continued, the clearer his leadership would have come. It is true that it contained many moderates such as Sir Benjamin Rudyerd, Sir Harbottle Grimston, Sir John Strangeways, Sir Francis Seymour and Serjeant Glanville, but they were no match for the political acumen of John Pym and Oliver St John. Within an hour of the dissolution of parliament Hyde, in considerable gloom, met St John who asked what troubled him. Hyde replied that he regretted the loss of so good a parliament. St John declared 'that all was well: and that it must be worse before it could be better: and that this parliament would never have done what was necessary to be done'.[14] Which, said Clarendon, was true enough.

Secretary Windebank wrote on 11 May that the dissolution was 'a very great disaster', but that there was no other way, since the king had 'offered redress of all the grievances, particularly the ship money'.[15] Sir Thomas Wentworth, now earl of Strafford, had returned from Ireland to advise the king, and was urging strong measures. When he heard that the deputy Lieutenants of Yorkshire had refused to raise 200 men, he declared that 'this insolence ought in my opinion to have been suffocated at birth . . . The Council-Board of late years have gone with so tender a foot in those businesses of Lieutenancy that it hath almost lost that power to the Crown'.[16] Strafford was clearly still for a policy of Thorough, and the king seemed to follow his advice when after the dissolution of parliament he arrested those he thought to be the ringleaders of the opposition, the earl of Warwick and Lords Brooke and Saye and Sele, John Pym, John Hampden and Sir Walter Earle. But it was clear that he had learnt nothing from the experience of the previous year. The country was hostile or indifferent to a Scottish expedition. When the king attempted to raise a loan of £200,000 in the City, he was refused. There were May-Day riots among the London apprentices, and an angry crowd forced Archbishop Laud to flee from Lambeth. In August the Lords of the treasury committee, reviewing the financial situation, found it so grave that they had to order disbandment of Hamilton's troops, and to recommend further loans from private persons. The king replied, 'I approve this, and for God's sake haste monies all you can by all ways'. Indeed three successive letters from the king within a week begged the immediate despatch of money.[17] His position was becoming desperate. Short as the king was of money and troops, the council advised against summoning a general muster of the City of London, 'unless the city were in a better temper, and your Majesty's affairs in the north in a more prosperous condition'.[18] It was becoming dangerous to trust the populace with arms.

The king's ministers were clearly appalled and alarmed at the situation, and on 3 September they sent the king advice, timidly worded, urging that 'if your Majesty dislike it . . . they will in all humility . . . lay this aside'. The advice was that the king should summon the Lords in a Great Council. They recognised that the demand of the Lords would probably be the summoning of a parliament, and the question was 'whether your Majesty will not rather give the glory of redress of grievances, and of a Parliament, to your own Lords, or rather to yourself by their advice, than to the Rebels, if your power and force be inferior to theirs'.[19] They argued that without some such sweetener, 'monies and forces will be raised very coldly and slowly, and without a voluntary assistance of both these, the Kingdom must be in danger'. The Scots under Leslie had already crossed the Tweed, and routed Conway at Newburn. By-passing Berwick, they found to their amazement that the English had abandoned Newcastle, which they occupied in triumph. There was thus no doubt about the reality of the danger. Charles's crass policy in Scotland had put him at the mercy of his enemies in both Scotland and England.

The only justification for a Great Council, rather than a parliament, would be that it played for time, and might persuade the peers to part with their money.* But this was no long-term solution, for the organisers of resistance in England, the earls of Bedford, Hertford, Warwick and Essex, the Lords Saye, Brooke, Mandeville and Howard of Escrick, John Pym and Oliver St John, drafted a remonstrance which was a full resumé of all the grievances of the time, together with a warning to the king not to use the hated Irish troops Strafford had at his disposal. The Great Council at York was therefore a futile exercise, and when it broke up, a parliament was inevitable.

By now the only man who still believed in the king's success was the king himself: even Strafford, in command of the ragged royalist army,† had lost hope, although he pretended otherwise to the king. The Privy Council was so divided that Charles wrote in the margin of one of their letters, 'I see ye are all so frighted, ye can resolve on nothing'.[20] His army was costing him £40,000 a month, and he wrote in September that he could not pay them beyond October unless the Council could come up with something. In October he had no choice but to sign a truce with the Scots, by which the Covenanters were to occupy the six northern counties, and to receive £860 a day until peace was concluded. Worse still negotiations were to be transferred to London, so that parliament could be a party to the negotiations. Clarendon called this 'the last and most confounding error', for it enabled the Scots to enter into a secret alliance with the parliamentary opposition, while Scots presbyterian clergy preached inflammatory sermons all over London, and 'had liberty to erect a tribunal the most tyrannical over all sorts of men, and in all the families of the kingdom: so that the preacher reprehended the husband, governed the wife, chastised the children, and insulted over the servants in the houses of the greatest men'. When parliament met, the king must have known that he would be severely on the defensive.

---

* In this during the year the king had considerable success. Clarendon said that within a few weeks of the dissolution of the Short Parliament, some £300,000 had been collected from private subscribers.

† He acted as lieutenant-general under Northumberland, who was, perhaps conveniently, sick. Strafford himself was ill with dysentery, but took the command out of a sense of loyalty.

Meanwhile the religious situation was exacerbated by two developments which, Clarendon wrote, could not have been more convenient to the Scots and the parliamentary opposition if they had themselves planned them. The first was the ostentation with which the Roman Catholics enjoyed the new era of toleration which existed under Charles I and his queen, with Mass being celebrated in the presence of great numbers of the public in the Queen's chapel at Somerset House, and the Roman envoys Con and Rozetti being welcome visitors to the Court, to the scandal of good Protestants, and seeming to confirm the suspicion that the king intended to encourage Popish practices. The second was the activity of Convocation, which had voted the king six subsidies, and then had drawn up seventeen new canons of the church. They were in fact moderate in tone, but upheld the divine right of kings and condemned any resistance to royal authority, and also Popery, Socinianism and the sectaries, and, above all imposed the 'Etcetera Oath' on all clergy, teachers and graduates, who were required to swear to do nothing to alter the established government of the Church by 'archbishops, bishops, deans and archdeacons etc.' Parliament could claim that the Convocation had no constitutional validity, because it had continued to sit after the dissolution of the Short Parliament, and that in any case Convocation had no power to impose such an oath upon the people. Clarendon commented that as the canons had been approved by the Privy Council, they were certainly as guilty as the clergy, in that they had issued them. As for the prolonged sitting of Convocation, this was not the work of Laud, but of the king himself.[21]

Clarendon gave a vivid picture of Charles I's chief ministers on the eve of the Long Parliament: Bishop Juxon, the ineffectual Lord Treasurer; Archbishop Laud, indefatigable in pursuit of church discipline; and Strafford who, a sick and weary man, had by the sharpness of his tongue, made enemies on all sides. 'The weight and the envy of all great matters rested upon these three.' Cottington, Chancellor of the Exchequer and Master of the Wards, was better at foreign than at domestic affairs, but his zeal in extending wardship had 'alienated all the rich families of England'. The earl of Northumberland Clarendon regarded as 'mere ornament'. Sir Henry Vane and Windebank were the Secretaries of State: Vane was a sworn enemy of Strafford because the latter had appropriated the barony of Raby, which Vane thought to be rightly his; Clarendon called Strafford's 'an act of the most unnecessary provocation'. Finally the marquis of Hamilton, the Scotsman who possessed the king's complete confidence: Clarendon believed that Hamilton had the king's permission to consort with the opposition in order to find out their secrets. It was indeed a sadly divided group which made up 'the committee of state', the 'Junto' or 'cabinet council'. But in all things the final word always lay with the king, and during his negotiations with the Scots Strafford was almost his sole adviser. But in always urging the king to strong action Strafford had become the most hated man in the country. When

Charles left the north for London to continue the negotiations with the Scots, Strafford would have preferred to remain with his troops in Yorkshire, but the king insisted on his coming to London to continue to act as his adviser. Perhaps they both realised the likelihood that he would be impeached, but Strafford was convinced that he could defend himself, or that he might strike first, by accusing the opposition of treasonable correspondence with the Scots. In any case he had the king's word that he need not fear for his life or fortune. But perhaps he knew how little that was worth, for he said to his friend George Radcliffe, 'I am tomorrow to London with more danger beset, I believe, then ever man went with out of Yorkshire'.[22] As to the remainder of the King's Council, Clarendon judged them to be broken reeds

everyone thought it enough to preserve his own innocence, and to leave the rest to those who should have authority to direct.[23]

The elections to the Long Parliament engendered great popular interest, and were often hard fought. The Court exerted every influence to secure the election of favourable candidates, especially in the duchies of Cornwall and Lancaster, in the principality of Wales, in the Cinque Ports and Admiralty towns, while Strafford exerted a baleful influence in Yorkshire. But some elected as Court candidates later went over to the reformers, just as some elected as reformers later joined the royalists. On the whole the Court did badly, for they were fighting a determined and well organised opposition. There is evidence that the reformers had had some organisation since 1629. It was certainly active in the elections to the Short Parliament[24] and still more so during the elections later in 1640. Lords Lieutenant like the earls of Essex, Warwick, Bedford and Lords Saye and Brooke were able to return their own candidates in counties and boroughs under their influence. In London John Pym and an organising committee sat in London, and succeeded in defeating Sir Thomas Gardiner the king's nominee for the City (and the Speaker's chair), and securing the election of Sir John Clotworthy, one of Strafford's chief enemies. All four of the City members were supporters of the reformers. In many counties, like Middlesex, Essex, Norfolk and Kent, there were substantial parliamentary victories; in others like Lancashire, Yorkshire and Cornwall, representation was more evenly divided. But it must be remembered that in so far as elections were fought on national issues, such as opposition to ship money, fines for knighthood, the forest laws, opposition to Arminianism and the Scottish war, public opinion was clearly against the king. Nearly sixty of those elected had resisted the king's demand for loans or taxation, and perhaps one-fifth of the House had at some time or other been in trouble with the authorities. Strode and Valentine had been in prison for eleven years, but both were elected in 1640. But many of these later became royalists, when the full implications of the opposition were revealed.[25]

Edward Hyde, after the dissolution of the Short Parliament, had returned to his lucrative legal practice,[26] and was in touch with public opinion in Wiltshire, where he was a justice of the peace. He was completely silent in his writings on the reasons behind his exchange of Wootton Bassett for Saltash in Cornwall in these elections. Keeler suggests that he may have been invited to stand for Saltash by the Buller family, who favoured the reformers.* If so, this might explain his silence on the subject. Indeed, in one of the most doubtful paragraphs in the *Life*, he wrote that 'the temper and constitution of both houses of parliament (in November 1640) . . . was very different from the last [which indeed was true enough], and they discovered not more prejudice against any man than against Mr. Hyde . . . . whom they were sorry to find amongst them', because of his well known friendship with Archbishop Laud, and his devotion to the Anglican church, and that they first tried to unseat him in a disputed election. This may mean no more than that, even years afterwards, the indignity of a disputed election still smarted, and Clarendon goes on to say that when the attempt failed, the attitude of the House towards him improved. It is easy to understand why he should have emphasised his devotion to the church in his *Life*. But there is no evidence whatever of an early prejudice against him by the reformers, and much evidence on the other side. There were in fact a large number of disputed elections in November 1640, and it is true that the House more often than not decided them to the disadvantage of the royalists; by this test Hyde was not accounted a royalist, for his petition succeeded.† Clarendon noted that the Long Parliament, which met on 3 November 1640, was in a very different mood from the previous one, that members had 'a marvellous elated countenance', and whereas the same men six months before had wished to 'apply gentle remedies without opening the wound too wide', now they were anxious 'to make inquisition into the causes and original of the malady'. From the first Pym appeared the organiser and manager of the reformers. He was now aged 56, and having sat in the parliaments of the 1620s was one of the most experienced parliamentarians then alive. He had sprung from a family of small landowners well below the gentry class, and had been a Receiver of Crown Lands in the west country. His patrons were the earls of Bedford and Warwick. During the 1630s he lived mainly in London, or at Fawsley, Northants, the home of Richard Knightley, where he became friends with the future parliamentarians, Lord Saye and Sele, Sir Nathaniel Rich, John Hampden and Sir Arthur Hesilrige. He became a bitter opponent of the duke of Buckingham, whose policies appeared likely to wreck the monarchy, and he was imprisoned for his

* Saltash was a burgage borough, and the mayor and burgesses returned George Buller, of the Middle Temple, and son of one of the chief landlords, Sir Richard Buller of Shillingham. As Hyde was also of the Middle Temple, two years George Buller's junior, it is probable that they were old friends. The connection however did not last.[27]

† It is just possible that some of the unpopularity of his cousin Robert Hyde, Recorder of Salisbury and its member of parliament, who was unpopular for his support for ship money and his hostility to the Puritans, had rubbed off on him.

speeches after the parliament of 1621. In religion his guiding principle was hatred of Popery, and this explains his growing hostility to Charles I. After 1625 his ideas expanded with his parliamentary experience. He learnt for instance the power of impeachment. Arminianism and unparliamentary taxation had by the 1630s come to be prime issues, and he began to see the Protestant and parliamentary liberties of Englishmen threatened. He had powerful friends among the members of the Massachusetts and Providence Island Companies, and his conduct of affairs in both the Short and the Long Parliament leaves no room for doubt that he had a clear-cut plan to unfold. He could indeed speak with veneration of the monarchy, but he saw the fundamental issue of the time to be a struggle for political power in which the triumph of the king would mean the extinction of Protestant and parliamentary liberties. In one sense he was not by nature a reformer, still less a revolutionary; but was moved by a deeply conservative instinct that the traditional rights of personal liberty and private property were at stake, and no man was more skilled in manipulating the House of Commons to his purpose.[28]

From the outset Clarendon regarded Pym as the brains and organising genius behind the parliamentary opposition. A few days before parliament opened, Pym had said to him 'that they must now be of another temper than they were in the last parliament; that they must not only sweep the house clean below, but must pull down all the cobwebs which hung in the top and corners . . .; that they had now an opportunity to make their country happy, by removing all grievances, and pulling up the causes of them by the roots, if all men would do their duties'.[29] Phrases like 'pulling down' and 'pulling up by the roots' clearly indicated Pym's intention to pursue a ruthless policy.

Strafford arrived in London on 10 November. His advice to the king was that he should have the parliamentary leaders arrested on a charge of treason for complicity with the Scots. Pym saw that he must destroy Strafford, or Strafford might destroy him. Strafford was the only strong minister Charles had, and without him his position was greatly weakened. To ensure success, Pym must first whip up highly charged emotions. Thus on the 11th he rose to announce a conspiracy 'to change the whole frame, and to deprive the nation of all the liberty and property which was their birthright by the laws of the land, which were now no more considered, but subjected to the arbitrary power of the privy council, which governed the kingdom according to their will and pleasure'.[30] He was careful to avoid placing blame on the king; the fault lay with one man, and that was Strafford. Sir John Clotworthy then denounced Strafford's tyranny in Ireland. Strafford had many enemies, and in this hysterical atmosphere it was easy to carry a vote for impeachment. A committee was appointed to draw up the charges, and Pym hurried off to the Lords to ask for Strafford's sequestration, which was granted. Strafford left the House in the custody of Black Rod. If Strafford had any friends in the Commons they did not speak on his behalf, and Pym had made men believe that the arrest had forestalled a dissolution of parliament, or a military coup. The king made no move to save his minister.*

There is no reason to suppose that Edward Hyde was not among the majority who voted for Strafford's impeachment. Having surmounted the difficulty of a disputed election return, Clarendon said that his credit rose rapidly in the House. His chief interest was still his vendetta against the Earl of Marshal's Court, and on 23 November, two days before Pym delivered to the Lords the charges against Strafford, Hyde was appointed to a committee to enquire into the working of that Court. He was now clearly regarded as one of the reformers, and within a fortnight he had been appointed a member of four other committees, two concerning Strafford, two concerning religion, and one on the judges and ship money.[32]

The impetus to reform was powerfully aided by ecclesiastical grievances. Indeed much of the power of the reformers sprang from their ability to weave constitutional and religious issues into a single campaign, so that each seemed to reinforce and justify the other. Pym had struck the keynote when in his first speech, having recounted the other grievances he came to the religious:

the last and greatest grievance leads us a step higher, even as high as Heaven, as the throne of God, his word and truth. The ambitious and corrupt clergy, preaching down the laws of God, and the liberties of the kingdom; pretending divine authority and absolute power in the king to do what he will with us; and this preaching is the highway to preferment, as one Mainwaring, sentenced in the former Parliament for this doctrine, then a doctor, is now become a bishop.[33]

Sir Benjamin Rudyerd followed with the complaint that many honest men were being branded with the name Puritan:

Whoever squares his actions by any rule either divine or human, he is a *Puritan*; whosoever would be governed by the King's laws, he is a *Puritan*; he that will not do whatsoever other men would have him do, *he is a Puritan*: the great work (of the Arminians), their masterpiece, now is to make all those of the religion to be *the suspected party* of the kingdom.[34]

It was the religious issue which drew many moderate constitutionalists like Rudyerd into the reformers' camp. When two days later Sir John Culpepper, later to be a royalist and an associate of Hyde's in the service of Charles I, presented a petition of grievances from the county of Kent, the main complaints were of 'the great increase of Papists', the new ceremonies of religion 'as placing the Communion Table Altar-wise, and bowing and cringing towards it', and the new Canons and the Etcetera oath, which formed the bulk of the complaints.[35] On 21 November Sir Edward Dering, also from

---

* Clarendon says that only Lord Falkland wished to stay proceedings, saying that he did not doubt Strafford's guilt, but he thought the charges should be formulated first. Pym said that delay would mean ruin, for if Strafford should hear of it he would advise a dissolution of parliament 'or some other desperate course to preserve himself'.[31]

Kent, in the Grand Committee for Religion declared that 'God's true religion is violently invaded by two seeming enemies ... I mean the Papists for one party, and our prelating faction for the other', and he declared that many ministers had been deprived without any breach of the law.[36] In December a Root-and-Branch petition from the City of London asked for the abolition of government by Archbishops, bishops and deans. In a debate on 14 December Sir Edward Dering and Nathaniel Fiennes launched bitter attacks on the Canons of 1640. Next day the House resolved without a division that the clergy in Convocation had no power to make Canons or Acts binding on the clergy or laity, and on the 16th a committee headed by Pym was set up to consider 'how far the Lord Archbishop of Canterbury had been an actor in the great design of the subversion of the laws of the realm and of religion, and to draw up a charge against him'.[37] On the 18th the Commons sent a message to the Lords accusing the Archbishop of high treason. Next day it was the turn of Matthew Wren, bishop of Ely, who was accused of 'the setting up of idolatry and superstition in divers places'. During the debate Harbottle Grimston attacked Laud in the most vicious terms as 'the sty of all pestilential filth that hath infested the state and government of this Commonwealth ... the only man that hath raised and advanced all those that together with himself have been the authors and causers of all our ruins, miseries and calamities we now groan under'. And this vituperation seems to have met with general approval. Indeed only one voice of moderation and sanity seems to have been raised, that of Sir Benjamin Rudyerd, who declared that it was not his intention to overthrow episcopacy, but to reform it; that while he would not tolerate 'any proud Becket or Wolsey prelates', yet he wished 'their reformation rather than their ruin, and that if there was a Cranmer, a Latimer or Ridley, "I would esteem and prize them (as rich jewels) fit to be set in the King's own Cabinet".' If Falkland or Hyde agreed with Rudyerd on this occasion, they did not say so.

In fact Falkland and Hyde seem to have been chiefly concerned at this time with the issues of ship money and the responsibility of the judges for the constitutional crisis.

Under Pym's direction the business of the House proceeded with great speed, and according to a clear plan. Pym presented the charges against Strafford to the Lords on 25 November. On 7 December ship money was declared 'against the Law of the realm, the subjects' right of property, and contrary to the Petition of Right', and a committee was set up to enquire how the judges had come to support its levy.[38] During the debate Lord Falkland launched a bitter attack upon the judges in general, and Lord Keeper Finch in particular:

The cause of all the miseries we have suffered, and the cause of all our jealousies we have had, that we should yet suffer, is, that a most excellent Prince hath been most infinitely abused by his judges telling him that the policy he might do what he pleased . . . We must now be forced to think of abolishing our grievances, and of taking away this judgment, and these judges together, and of regulating their successors by exemplary punishment . . . . there being no law more fundamental than that they have already subverted, and no government more absolute than they have really introduced. Mr. Speaker, not only the severe punishment, but the sudden removal of these men, will have a sudden effect in one very considerable consideration. (One judge in particular was responsible) He it is who not only gave away with his breath what our ancestors had purchased for us . . . He declared that power to be so inherent to the Crown as that it was not in the power even of Parliaments to divide them . . . Nor do I look to tell you news when I tell you it is my lord Keeper.[39]

Accordingly a committee was appointed headed by Falkland, and including Edward Hyde, to consider how it was that the judges were coerced into giving their judgment upon ship money. Hyde undoubtedly agreed with Falkland's remarks, and hinted in his *History* that he had been impatient with the attacks on Laud, which delayed the assault on ship money and the judges, which he regarded as more important.[40] Lord Keeper Finch was allowed to speak in his own defence, and according to Rushworth made an excellent defence – 'Many were exceedingly taken with his eloquence and carriage.'[41] – but to no avail. His impeachment was voted, but by that time he had fled to Holland. Hyde wrote that this was with the connivance of the parliamentary leaders, but afterwards suppressed the passage, Warburton said out of deference to the Finch family. Finch remained in exile for eight years, but was eventually allowed to return after making an abject submission. Falkland and Hyde were relentless in their pursuit of the subject of the judiciary, and the king was forced to announce his decision that henceforth judges should hold office *quamdiu se bene gesserint*, and no longer *durante bene placito*. On 14 January 1641 Falkland delivered another savage attack on the Lord Keeper, and the House voted thanks to St John, Whitelocke, Falkland and Hyde 'for the great service they have performed to the honour of this House and the good of the Commonwealth'. Falkland throughout had been indignant that the law, which he conceived to be for the protection of the subject and private property, was being perverted into an instrument of oppression, and Hyde was particularly concerned that the law, which to him was the foundation of all stability, was being brought into disrepute.

Hyde's part in the parliamentary business of the time, although shrouded in some mystery in his own account, becomes clear in the Journals of the Commons, and it was certainly an active one. On 23 December he was a member of a committee to consider the jurisdiction of the prerogative courts of York and the Marches. On the 30th he was a member of a committee to consider the annual meeting of parliaments, and on 6 January he was a member of the committee to draw up charges against the earl of Strafford. On 8 January he was a member of the committee to decide upon the future order of business in the House, when Strafford, Laud and Lord Keeper Finch were given priority. On 13 January Falkland and he were engaged in reading the articles of impeachment against the latter. On 26 January he was a member of a committee to implement the execution of the laws against priests and Jesuits, and he reported a conference with the Lords on the priest Goodman, who was subsequently expelled from the country. On 6 February he reported from a committee for the judges on the case of Justice Bartlett. On the 10th he was chairman of the Grand Committee to decide the disposal of the £60,000 borrowed from the City, £50,000 of which was assigned to the army. On the 12th he reported the case of Judge Berkeley, recommending his impeachment, and on the same day he was appointed to a committee to consider the new Canons in relation to Archbishop Laud. On the 13th he was a member of the committee to consider 'an Act for the abolishing of Superstition and Idolatry', and on the 15th a member of a committee for the reform of the Court of Chancery. And so the list could be continued.

It is clear that when Hyde wrote that as he was never absent from the House in the mornings, so he was seldom free in the afternoons from committee work, he told no more than the truth.[42] Since the composition of committees was carefully vetted by John Pym, it is also clear that at this time Hyde was regarded as a reformer, and an adherent of Pym's. Hyde said as much when he described how, after the afternoon committee work, he was often invited to dine at Pym's lodging in Sir Richard Manly's house behind Westminster Hall, where Pym, Hampden, Sir Arthur Hesilrige and two or three others, 'transacted much business, and invited thither those of whose conversion they had any hope'. [43] Here much of the planning of the parliamentary campaign was conducted.

Within three months of the meeting of the Long Parliament the king had been deprived of his chief ministers; Strafford, Laud and Finch were impeached of high treason; the judges and prerogative courts were under attack; a Root-and-Branch petition had demanded the abolition of episcopacy; and a bill was set in motion which began with the assertion: 'Whereas by the laws and statutes of this realm the Parliament ought to be holden at least once every year for the redress of grievances,' and which on 16 February became the Triennial Act. The king was being fast driven into a corner. His most immediate concerns were to save Strafford and episcopacy. His only hope lay in moderating the severity of his opponents, and this suggested the course of action he pursued. He would draw a line between the removal of specific grievances and fundamental constitutional change. Thus on 25 January he addressed both Houses in the Banqueting Hall. His object, he said, was to hasten their procedure, not to interrupt it; but there were two expensive armies to be maintained on English soil, and distractions in the nation were encouraged by malicious people. He was ready to accept reforms in the Church and the Law, 'for my intention is clearly to reduce all things to the best and purest time, as they were in the time of Queen Elizabeth'. He would give up illegal revenues. But

I must tell you that I make a great difference between Reformation and Alteration of Government; though I am for the first, I cannot give way to the latter. [He would limit episcopal jurisdiction] But this must not be understood that I shall any way consent that their voices in Parliament should be taken away . . . . I am bound to maintain them in it as *one of the Fundamental Constitutions of this Kingdom.*[44]

Eleven days before, Lord Falkland had attacked Lord Keeper Finch on the grounds that 'his life appeared a perpetual warfare against our fundamental laws'.[45] Now it would appear that both the king and the moderate reformers were fighting to maintain the same fundamental laws.

It was upon the issue of church government that the rift first appeared among the reformers. On 19 January 1641, for instance, Lord Digby had made a notable speech in favour of frequent parliaments:

I take this to be the Unum Necessarium: Let us procure this, and all our desires will effect themselves; if this Bill miscarry, I shall have left me no public hopes. . . . Wicked Ministers have been the proximate causes of our miseries; but the want of Parliaments the primary, the efficient Cause.[46]

But on 8 February Lord Digby rose to defend episcopacy. There was, he said, no one more anxious than he to 'clip the wings of the Prelates, whereby they have mounted to such insolencies'. But 'a total extirpation of Bishops . . . is against my heart'. The government of the Church of England had been established by Act of Parliament, but episcopacy derived from Apostolic times:

I am confident that instead of every Bishop we put down in a diocese, we shall set up a Pope in every parish . . . I do not think a King can put down Bishops totally with safety to Monarchy.[47]

In the same debate Lord Falkland launched a formidable attack on the bishops for their divisive policies, especially for their persecution of puritan ideals and practices. The bishops might well be deprived of their *offending* powers, but they should not be abolished:

I do not believe them to be *Jure divino*, nay I believe them not to be *Jure divino*; but neither do I believe them to be *Iniuria humana*; I neither consider them as necessary, nor as unlawful, but as convenient or inconvenient: But since all great mutations in government are dangerous . . . my opinion is that we should not root up this ancient tree, as dead as it appears, till we have tried whether by this or the like lopping of the branches, the sap which was unable to feed the whole, may not serve to make what is left both grow and flourish.[48]

It was a spirited debate, spread over two days in which the great issue was whether episcopacy should be reformed or abolished. The king's warning of 25 January was disregarded. Those who, like Nathaniel Fiennes were for total abolition argued that bishops were the supporters of divine right of kings and tyranny. Of those merely for reform, Sir Harbottle Grimston, so recently the abusive enemy of Archbishop Laud, now argued that the ill-doing of bishops was no reason for abolishing episcopacy, any more than the failures of judges would be a cause for abolishing the common law! Fiennes wanted the bishops deprived of all temporal jurisdiction, excluded from the Star Chamber and High Commission, and perhaps from parliament, except as advisers. But he made it plain that he was chiefly opposed to the jurisdiction of the Prerogative Courts as a threat to the Courts of Common Law.

A week later, on 15 February, the king was presented with the Triennial Bill which provided for the automatic assembly of parliament within three years of the dissolution or prorogation of the last. He must have recognised the serious invasion of his prerogative that was implied in the Bill. But it was essential that he should have the four subsidies promised by the Commons, and he must do all he could to save Strafford. He declared with truth to the two Houses:

I think never Bill passed here in this House of more favour to the subjects than this is. . . . I do not know what you can ask, for ought I can see at this time, that I can make any question to yield unto: therefore I mention this, to shew unto you the sense that I have of this Bill, and the obligation, as I may say, that you have to me for it. For hitherto, to speak freely, I have had no great encouragement to do it. . . . You have taken the government all in pieces, and I may say it is almost off the hinges.[49]

The king was making a desperate bid to win the sympathy and co-operation of the Houses, but so open an admission of his weakness could only convince Pym and his friends that they were near victory.

Two days later Edward Hyde's committee reported the Earl Marshal's Court as a grievance. On 26 February Pym presented to the Lords the Articles of Impeachment against Laud, 'that he hath traiterously endeavoured to subvert the Fundamental Laws and Government of this Kingdom; and instead thereof, to introduce an arbitrary and tyrannical Government against Law'.[50] The charges were wild and had little relation to the facts but Pym was little concerned with judicial accuracy. The object was to destroy the structure of Charles's government, and in this he carried the House with him. Laud was sent to the Tower. Pym's purpose was relentlessly pursued. On 6 March the king agreed to abrogate the Forest Laws. On the 11th the Commons resolved that the legislative and judicial powers of bishops in the House of Lords should be abolished. On the 22nd the trial of Strafford opened in Westminster Hall.

Hyde was a member of most of the committees concerned with drawing up the charges against Strafford, but he was not a member of the committee (dominated by Pym, Hampden and St John) set up to manage the trial. The bishops were excluded on the grounds that *clericus non debet interesse sanguini*. The earl of Arundel, a known enemy of Strafford, presided at the trial as Lord

High Steward of England, and the king attended in a private box (which, Clarendon said, he later regretted). Clarendon greatly admired the skill with which Strafford defended himself, 'with great show of humility and submission; but yet with such a kind of courage as would lose not advantage; and, in truth, made his defence with all imaginable dexterity'.[51] After six days of trial the Lords had reached only the fifth article, and charge after charge appeared merely malicious, trivial or false. One charge was that Strafford had said 'that the king's little finger should be heavier on the loins of the law', but Strafford was able to show that what he had said was 'that the little finger of the law was heavier than the King's loins'. The most damaging charge was made on 5 April. The younger Vane had rifled his father's cabinet, and had produced notes of a council meeting where Strafford was alleged to have said to the king: 'you have an army in Ireland which you may employ here to reduce this kingdom'. Strafford said that if the words were spoken they referred to Scotland, not England, and the earl of Northumberland, the marquis Hamilton and bishop Juxon being Privy Councillors, said that they could not remember the words being spoken at all. Clarendon thought the accusations of oppression in Ireland were more nearly proved.

By 10 April Pym knew that the impeachment would fail, and in the Commons he set in motion a Bill of Attainder. The technique used was one he employed on several occasions. He was a master of the dramatic, and in a tense and excited House he said he would reveal the true evidence against Strafford. He then produced a copy of the paper the younger Vane had procured, and interpreted it line by line as treasonable.[52] The younger Vane followed 'in some seeming disorder', confessed that the discovery would reflect heavily on his father, but said that his patriotism required him to reveal the document. It was a highly theatrical but very effective performance, which the House eventually approved by 204 to 59.[53] Strafford's trial had in fact ceased to be a judicial matter, and had become purely political: Strafford must be destroyed, not for what he had done, but because he was dangerous. It was said however that many members voted for attainder for fear of Pym, and others took comfort in the hope that the Lords would reject the Bill, or that the king would veto it.[54] But some dared to resist Pym. On 21 April Lord Digby declared that, although he regarded Strafford as 'the most dangerous Minister', and a 'grand Apostate to the Commonwealth', yet judicial and political decisions must not be confused, and he therefore voted against the attainder. Those who were brave enough to vote with him found their names posted in Old Palace Yard as 'Enemies of Justice'. The list included Hyde's cousin, Serjeant Hyde. How little the attainder had to do with justice was revealed by the assertion of St John, the king's Solicitor-General but a follower of Pym, that such a man might be condemned without any evidence at all, and that it was sufficient 'to knock foxes and wolves on the head as they can be found, because they be beasts of prey'.[55]

Edward Hyde almost certainly voted for Strafford's attainder. A week later he was chosen to bear a message to the Lords that the House feared that there was a plan to effect Strafford's escape, and he returned with the message that the Lords had ordered the prisoner to be kept in close confinement.[56] His closest friend Lord Falkland was certainly an enemy of the earl, and declared in the House that 'in equity Strafford deserved to die'. Indeed, Falkland's reputation as an honest man may well have influenced many doubters to condemn Strafford. In the *History* Clarendon made no mention of his own part in the trial and attainder. There was indeed no reason why he should, for he was attempting to write with the mature perspective of a historian recollecting in tranquillity the events of the past, not tracing his own early life. For instance it seemed to him on reflection that one of the most regrettable aspects of the case was that the oath of secrecy of Privy Councillors had been violated; the business of the council chamber had been divulged, and henceforth Privy Councillors would be chary of giving the king honest advice for which they might later be accountable to parliament.[57] But the fact remains that Hyde almost certainly voted for the attainder of Strafford, and we must ask why. The reason is not hard to find. We have seen that Hyde had been especially concerned with what he regarded as the abuses of the Prerogative Courts, and that from the outset he had attacked the Court of the Earl Marshal. He regarded the Court of the President of the Council of the North as equally culpable. The day after Lord Digby had refused to vote for the attainder Hyde, at a conference of both Houses, delivered an attack upon the Council of the North, his first major speech and thought by Rushworth worthy of being reported at length.[58] He called the Court 'a great and crying grievance', 'the grievance of the whole Kingdom', which 'hath almost overwhelmed that country under the sea of arbitrary power, and involved the people in a labyrinth of distemper, oppression and poverty'. He had gone into the subject thoroughly, and traced the history of the Court from the reign of Henry VIII and the Northern Rebellion. Its powers then were only those of a commission of Oyer and Terminer, and had subsequently been extended, especially under Strafford's presidency. But the Courts of Law were settled at Westminster, not at York, and 'his Majesty cannot by commission erect a new Court of Chancery, or a proceeding according to the rules of the Star Chamber', this was 'most clear to all who have read Magna Carta'. In short, the Court at York had superseded the Courts of Westminster, and 'disfranchised the good northern people of all their privileges by Magna Carta and the Petition of Right'. He called not for its reform but for its abolition. These then were the grounds of Hyde's hostility to Strafford. Hyde was displaying the principles he had learnt at the feet of John Selden, who might indeed have been uttering the indictment. How he reconciled the use of attainder with his principles of justice it is impossible to say.

The king worked desperately to save Strafford. It must be remembered that in the Long Parliament from the beginning there was virtually no Court party. Only twenty-seven officials and twenty-two courtiers had been elected to the Commons, and they for the most part had proved broken reeds. Charles had been deprived of his chief ministers. Unless he could find councillors who would do his business he would become the mere recipient of the will of the Commons. From the beginning of the Short Parliament, the chief of the leaders of the reformers in the Lords, whom Clarendon called 'the great contrivers and designers'[59] was the fourth earl of Bedford, who for years had been the patron of John Pym. He was a man of great wealth; he had been an active supporter of the Petition of Right in 1628, and had appeared before Star Chamber in 1629, although no charges were brought against him. In the Short Parliament he was one of the minority of twenty-five peers who voted that redress of grievances should precede supply. He was in close touch with the Scots during the summer of 1640, and was one of the twelve peers who signed a petition to the king to summon parliament, to dismiss his ministers and to make peace with the Scots. He used his great electoral influence in the elections to the Long Parliament, and in November 1640 appeared clearly the leader of the opposition. His views were moderate; he was no enemy to monarchy, but was exasperated by Charles's mismanagement of affairs. Clarendon wrote of him with great respect as 'a wise man, and of too great and plentiful a fortune to wish a subversion of government; and it quickly appeared that he only intended to make himself and his friends great at court, not at all to lessen the court itself'.[60] In short, he was no enemy to monarchy, but thought he could manage the king's affairs a good deal better than the king himself. Clayton Roberts[61] has unravelled the sequence of this complicated period, and believes that Bedford was ambitious for high office at least as early as November 1640. Lady Carlisle was reporting his plan to fill the great office of state as early as 3 December, but she added that 'the King makes himself merry at it'.[62] Similar rumours continued to circulate during January and February 1641, but when Charles made his first appointments, on 20 January they were of Sir Edward Littleton as Lord Keeper, and Sir John Bankes, Chief Justice of Common Pleas, both nominees of Strafford. On 29 January however he appointed Bedford's nominee Oliver St John as Solicitor-General. No doubt he hoped that St John's high standing in the Commons would be beneficial to the monarch's cause, but if so he was disappointed, for the appointment in no way weakened St John's links with the reformers, and he continued his attacks upon ship money. This may well have discouraged the king from making further precipitate appointments.

However, negotiations to bring Bedford and his friends into office seem to have continued. The proposal had the strong support of the king's favourite the marquis of Hamilton, whom Clayton Roberts rightly describes as 'a born schemer, a man of little intellect and no fixed principles', who was rumoured to wish to marry Bedford's daughter. The queen and her favourite Henry

Jermyn also joined in the pressure upon Charles, and she gave Bedford, Saye and Pym a private audience, which was thought to be a prelude to office. Clarendon said that Bedford was to be Treasurer, Pym Chancellor of the Exchequer, Kimbolton Lord Privy Seal, with places to be found for others. This was to be in return for a financial settlement which Clarendon thought would include an excise (Pym's special idea) and tonnage and poundage for life to the king. Clayton Roberts thinks this financial settlement improbable since it would have made the king independent of parliament, but that it probably included an improved collection of subsidies, increased fines on recusants, seizure of the lands of the deans and chapters, and tonnage and poundage perhaps for three years. This might have had some attraction for the king, although the seizure of church lands would certainly have been refused by him. But to Charles there was one matter which transcended all others, the need to save Strafford. If Bedford could ensure that, he might have been persuaded to agree to the appointment. So on 19–21 February he made a move by appointing Bedford, Hertford, Essex, Warwick, Saye, Savile and Kimbolton to the Privy Council.

But the difficulties were immense. There was a great wall of suspicion to be overcome before the king could accept the reformers as ministers. Clarendon makes it clear that Bedford, for his part, was not anxious to take office unless he could carry the House of Commons with him: for instance, before taking office he wanted a financial settlement to be enacted. He had been the patron of Pym and St John, but they had ideas of their own which went far beyond Bedford's wishes, and it was by no means clear that he could control them. Above all, there was the question of the fate of Strafford. Whether Bedford had given the king some kind of promise on this is not known, although Clarendon thought he had. For the king, his sole end in the negotiations had been to save Strafford. Bedford was probably in favour of a reprieve for Strafford, but he was not likely to carry his followers in the Commons with him, for, as Clarendon said, there were few of them who thought 'their preferment to office would do them much good, if the earl were suffered to live'.[63]

Hyde, as we have seen, had played an active part in bringing about the trial of Strafford, and on 22 April he had made his great attack on the judicial powers of the Council of the North, which, he wrote, 'had a wonderful approbation in both houses'. The same afternoon he said that he was walking in Piccadilly, 'which was a fair house for entertainment and gaming, and handsome gravel walks with shade, and where were an upper and lower bowling-green, whither very many of the nobility and gentry of the best quality resorted, both for exercise and conversation'; there he met the earl of Bedford.[64] Bedford 'lamented the misery the kingdom was like to fall into, by their own violence and want of temper', that 'the earl of Strafford was a rock upon which we should all split, and that the passion of the parliament would destroy the kingdom'; that the king was ready to make any concession if the life of the earl might be spared, that he would agree to his banishment or imprisonment, but that he could never consent to his execution. Bedford hoped to persuade his friends to accept this compromise, and asked Hyde's help in talking to Essex. Hyde then went to Essex, who congratulated him on having that day stoked the fires against Strafford. Hyde replied that that had not been his purpose, and that it was sufficient that Strafford should be rendered harmless for the future. Essex shook his head, and answered: 'Stone-dead hath no fellow'. He feared that if Strafford were spared, the king would pardon him as soon as the parliament was ended. From this position Hyde could not move him. When he argued that the king's conscience should not be strained so far, Essex replied that the king's conscience must be governed by his parliament.[65]

How far this conversation, remembered long afterwards, reflected Hyde's true feelings in April 1641 we cannot be certain, for on the 27th he was sent to the Lords with a message that the House believed that there was a design to effect Strafford's escape, and he returned with the answer that the Lords had ordered the earl's close confinement. On 1 May the king addressed both Houses in a last desperate attempt to modify their attitude. He told them that he could not in conscience condemn Strafford of high treason, and that there had never been any proposal that he should rule contrary to law. It was reported that the Commons 'seemed to be much troubled and discontented with what the King had spoken, and immediately adjourned'.[66] If there were doubts in the minds of many moderate members, Pym had a sovereign remedy which he always used in moments of crisis when his control was threatened. He alarmed the House with news of 'desperate designs, both at home and abroad, against the Parliament and the peace of the nation'.

The so called Army Plot had originated during March among discontented officers, who were also members of parliament; Henry Percy, brother of the earl of Northumberland, William Ashburnham and Hugh Pollard. They proposed to persuade officers to sign a declaration that they would stand by the king if he were forced to exclude bishops from the Lords, disband the Irish army, and accept other indignities at the hands of parliament. Henry Jermyn and Sir John Suckling wanted to go further and overawe parliament by bringing in the troops. They had the misfortune to bring in George Goring, a man guaranteed to wreck any cause with which he was concerned. The king rejected the offers from both groups, until the attainder of Strafford made his case desperate. He then contemplated an occupation of the Tower with loyal troops, and Strafford's escape. On 2 May a Captain Billingsley presented the Lieutenant of the Tower with an order from the king to admit a hundred men. Sir William Balfour refused to admit them and informed parliament. Sir John Suckling also had sixty men assembled at the White Horse tavern, who he said were destined for Portugal, but who may have been for the king's protection.

The plan failed, and on 5 May Jermyn and Suckling fled to France, and Henry Percy followed shortly afterwards. They were found guilty of high treason in their absence. Pym made full use of the incident, not only in parliament, but also in the City, and enquiries went on until late in the summer.

Thus on 3 May the Commons were stampeded into agreeing to a Protestation complaining of 'the designs of priests and Jesuits to undermine and ruin the reformed religion, to subvert the fundamental laws of England, and to introduce arbitrary and tyrannical government', and all members of Parliament were required to sign the protestation; 429 of them hastened to sign. Falkland and Hyde were presumably taken in by Pym's exaggerations, for they both signed. Two Lords were brave enough to refuse. Meanwhile the London crowds were demonstrating about Westminster to add momentum to Pym's purpose, and in Palace Yard a list of fifty-six supposed supporters of Strafford was posted under the heading 'Betrayers of their Country'. The list included Lord Digby, Sidney Godolphin and John Selden. Most significantly of all for the future, in the prevailing excitement, a bill was hurried through prohibiting the dissolution of the Long Parliament without its own consent. It was cleverly worded, claiming that it was necessary in order to secure credit without which the army could not be paid. Thus the most fundamental of all the constitutional changes introduced before the Civil War, passed almost unnoticed, and Pym had scored the greatest triumph of his parliamentary career.*[67]

On 4 May Strafford wrote a noble letter to the king urging him to accept the attainder, which finally passed the Lords on 8 May. Twenty thousand people in London petitioned for Strafford's death. Still the king delayed, consulted the judges, consulted the bishops, but was persuaded by the fear that his wife and children might be attacked by the mob. Finally at 9.00 pm. on 9 May with an anguished spirit he signed the attainder; he also accepted the bill perpetuating the Long Parliament, almost without noticing it. Three days later Strafford was executed.

On the day that Charles signed the attainder, the earl of Bedford died of smallpox, thus finally ending the possibility of political compromise between the king and the reformers; and the question must be asked whether a great opportunity had been lost in not making the ministerial appointments Bedford had suggested. Clarendon spoke with two voices on the subject at different times. On the appointment of Bedford and his friends to the Privy Council in February he commented that it was dangerous for the king to appoint men who were not loyal to the monarchy, and that they had refused to give him any

---

* The king admitted his fundamental error in a letter to the queen 21 Nov. 1646: he said he had allowed himself to sin against his conscience: 'For the truth is, I was surprised with it instantly after I made that base unworthy concession concerning Strafford; for which, and likewise for that great wrong and injustice to the Church, of taking away the Bishops' votes in Parliament, I have been most justly punished.'[68]

advice which was not in accord with the will of the Commons.[69] Later however he said that it was a pity that the ministerial appointments had not been made, 'that the king might have had some able men to have advised him or assisted; which probably these very men would have done, after they had been so thoroughly engaged'.[70] Clarendon's dilemma is understandable. If Bedford and his friends were so ineffectual as Privy Councillors, was there any reason for supposing that they would serve the king better as ministers? On the other hand the king had virtually no ministers of consequence, and any experiment in his desperate situation might have been worth trying. Yet the chance of success was small. Bedford's conversation with Hyde revealed his dilemma. He feared the growth of extremism, but was unable to check it. He could no longer control Pym, and it was becoming apparent that Pym could not guarantee to control his own extremists or the London mob. Bedford had genuinely wished to save Strafford but had failed, and without Strafford's life the bargain had little attraction for the king. Bedford himself was doubtful about office; hence his wish to secure a financial settlement before taking office. But it is unlikely that the Commons would have agreed to his terms. They were chary of voting money at the best of times; there was an enormous debt of £800,000, and they would not willingly have made the crown independent. What is most likely to have happened is that if Bedford had taken office and attempted to stem the extremist tide, he would have found his parliamentary influence melt away. In June 1641 the extremists attempted to pass a bill that no member of the House should accept office without the approval of the House. The intention clearly was, not to find agreement with the king, but to strip him of all means to effective power. Bedford's views were moderate and statesmanlike, but they would not have stemmed the tide of revolution.

So far Edward Hyde had been carried along by the impetus of reform, but the speed and nature of change was rapidly outrunning his limited vision, and would soon require reassessement of his position. The issue was to be that of the church.

# The Assault on the Monarchy

The political developments of the first months of the Long Parliament, which had become so disadvantageous to the king, were immensely exacerbated by ecclesiastical issues, and as it was these which in the end proved the final impasse, we must be sure exactly what those issues were.

The earliest attacks on the church in the Long Parliament were motivated by political considerations and were aimed particularly at offending clergy. In his opening speech John Pym made it clear that the fault lay with 'the ambitious and corrupt clergy, preaching down the laws of God, and liberties of the kingdom; pretending divine authority and absolute power in the king, to do what he will with us; and this preaching is the highway to preferment, and one Mainwaring . . . is now become a bishop'.[1] What was resented was the part played by the bishops in affairs of state, the influence of Arminians at Court, and the fear of a Popish conspiracy against the reformed church. Rudyerd complained of the use of 'Puritan' as a term of abuse against every serious-minded man. Sir Edward Dering made the same point, and identified those he thought the enemies of 'God's true religion' as 'the Papists for one party and our prelating faction for the other'.[2]

The London Petition of 11 December 1640 went much further. It demanded that 'the government of archbishops, lord bishops, deans, archdeacons, and their courts and administrations in them, with all its dependencies, roots and branches may be abolished, as dangerous to the Church and Commonwealth'.[3] As it purported to be signed by 15,000 persons, and as similar petitions came in from twelve counties in January, the organisation was clearly considerable. Clarendon explained the 'mountebankery' behind the mass petitions which reached parliament. He thought that some moderate petition would be drawn up, for instance protesting against the new Etcetera oath which had been imposed by the Canons of 1640, which would readily be signed by great numbers. Then a new and more extreme petition would be substituted, which the signatories had never seen.[4] Another way for reformers to increase the virulence of the attack on the church was to attack a few bishops, such as William Piers of Bath and Wells or Matthew Wren of Ely, and then to imply that they were typical of the whole church, and a threat to the laws and liberties of the people. Clarendon realised the extent to which events had played into the hands of the enemies of the church. The Canons of 1640 had been issued regardless of the tensions of the time, but Clarendon blamed the judges, who had pronounced on their legality, and the Privy Council, who had authorised their publication, as much as the bishops who had formulated them. Yet the whole clergy were made to bear the burden of guilt.

It was one thing to demand the removal of particular abuses, but quite another thing to sweep away the whole ecclesiastical system. George Digby had bitterly attacked the Canons of 1640, and Sir John Culpepper had denounced the new Arminian ceremonies, but both were later stout defenders of episcopacy as an institution.[5] On 15 December Sir Benjamin Rudyerd declared that he wanted the reformation, not the ruin of the bishops, that although he detested 'any proud Becket or Wolsey prelates', he loved the memory of a Latimer or Ridley. The Canons of 1640 were duly voted to be illegal (14 December), and Archbishop Laud was impeached (18 December). On 25 January 1641, as we have seen, the king told both Houses that he was ready to consider reforms, but not an alteration in the government of the church.[6]

In the major debate of 8–9 February 1641 on the Root and Branch petition against episcopacy a division of opinion slowly crystallised. On one side George Digby was in favour of 'clipping the wings of the prelates', but was against a total extirpation, and he warned against the danger of pulling down the bishops only to set up a pope in every parish. Lord Falkland delivered an impassioned speech in which he declared:

this kingdom hath long laboured under many and great oppressions both in religion and liberty . . . [and] a great, if not a principal cause of both these have been some bishops and their adherents . . . the destruction of unity; under pretence of uniformity to have brought in superstition and scandal, under the titles of reverence and decency to have defiled our Church . . . Nay, it hath been more dangerous for men to go to some neighbour's parish, when they had no sermon in their own, than to be obstinate and perpetual recusants; while Masses have been said in security, a conventicle hath been a crime, and, which is yet more, the conforming to ceremonies hath been more exacted than the conforming to Christianity; and whilst men for scruples have been undone, for attempts upon sodomy they have only been admonished.

Here we have a complete statement from the leader of the Great Tew Circle on the subject of episcopacy, and it is probable that Edward Hyde shared that opinion in February 1641. There is no word of support here for the Laudian bishops, and much sympathy for those who walked from village to village in search of a sermon. But Falkland went on to say that he wanted the bishops strictly regulated, not abolished. He did not believe them to be *Jure divino*, but neither did he believe them to be *iniuria humana*.

I neither consider them as necessary nor as unlawful, but as convenient or inconvenient: but since all great mutations in government are dangerous . . . my opinion is that we should not root up this ancient tree, as dead as it appears, till we have tried whether by this or the like lopping of the branches, the sap which was unable to feed the whole, may not serve to make what is left both grow and flourish.[7]

Harbottle Grimston came to the same conclusion. He argued that because there were bad judges one did not abolish judges, but he saw no purpose in ecclesiastics being included in the commissions of the peace, or sitting in Star Chamber, or in the Privy Council, and least of all should they sit in Parliament. On the other hand Nathaniel Fiennes and Holles were for total abolition. Pym spoke for a reformed episcopacy, but not its abolition. Thus by the spring of 1641 a divergence of opinion was emerging.

Few appeared willing to speak in defence of the Laudian bishops,* still less for their participation in government, but there was a division of opinion between reform and abolition. In any case Pym had tasks which he regarded as more immediate, namely to dismantle the structure of the king's government; and the first requirement was the impeachment of Strafford. For this purpose he wanted the exclusion of the bishops from taking part in the trial, and there the bishops came to his aid. John Williams, bishop of Lincoln, who had been imprisoned by Laud, and who saw an advantage in ingratiating himself with the reformers, proposed that the bishops should not take part in a trial involving blood. But this did not prevent the Commons from resolving on 11 March 'that the legislative and judicial power of bishops in the House of Peers is a great hindrance to the discharge of their spiritual function, prejudicial to the Commonwealth, and fit to be taken away'.[8] The bishops may have opted out of Strafford's trial, but they remained a solid bench of support for the king in the Lords. The emotional atmosphere aroused by Strafford's trial made the moment ripe for a strike at the bishops' legislative functions. On 30 March a bill was introduced into the Commons to exclude the bishops from the Lords, and from government. The bill was passed on 1 May and sent to the Lords.

However the bill raised an issue of great constitutional significance. A bill to remove the bishops from the Lords was a serious infringement of the Lords' privileges, and it was argued that if the Commons could remove the episcopal bench, they could remove the barons, or indeed the whole House. On 24 May the Lords informed the Commons that they could not accept the bill. There must have been some speedy consultation among the leaders of the reformers, and on the 27th, according to his own account, Sir Edward Dering had a bill thrust into his hands by Sir Arthur Hesilrige† with the urgent request that he should present it. Dering did so, although he said he had hardly time to read it;

* We cannot be sure of that, for it was said speeches for the bishops were suppressed.
† Dering misdated the incident to 21 May, and said it had been drawn up by Sir Henry Vane and Oliver Cromwell, but it is more likely to have been the work of Oliver St John.

it was a bill for the root and branch abolition of episcopacy. Dering called it 'a purging bill: I give it you, as I take physic, not for delight, but for a cure', and he urged that unless primitive episcopacy could be restored, he was for abolition.[9] Dering later spent much time explaining away his action on that occasion or wishing the words unsaid. He claimed that he had desired not to abolish episcopacy but to reform it, but it is clear that his thinking at the time was close to Presbyterianism, which he took to be the equivalent of primitive episcopacy. On the second reading the voting was 139 to 100. On the commital stage of the bill, Hyde spoke against it on the grounds that 'it was changing the whole frame and constitution of the kingdom, and of parliament itself'; that the bishops had always been part of the House of Lords, and as the clergy were the third estate of the realm, they deserved representation.[10] To his surprise, he wrote later, Lord Falkland, who always sat next to him in complete agreement, jumped up to say that he disagreed, that the bishops did *not* represent the clergy, and that he supported the bill. Clarendon wrote that the House was amused to see the two friends in disagreement, but Hyde had the satisfaction of seeing the bill put aside. The incident did nothing to diminish their friendship, and within six months Falkland had changed his mind.

It is not difficult to see the guiding hand of Pym through this period. He had the clear objective of dismantling the king's government, and this he had achieved to a remarkable degree. The complete abolition of episcopacy was not part of his plan. It was a contentious issue, and there was no general agreement on what was to be put in its place. The House continued to discuss the subject. On 11 June Hyde was chairman of a committee of the whole House which resolved that archbishops, bishops, deans etc. 'hath been found by long experience to be a great impediment to the perfect reformation and growth of religion, and very prejudicial to the civil state'; and on the 15th it was resolved that deans and chapters should be abolished, and their lands 'be employed to the advancement of learning and piety'.[11] But these were only resolutions, not legislative enactments. If it should seem strange that Hyde should have chaired such a debate, it must be remembered that it was often the practice to put in the chair one whose business it was to maintain judicial impartiality, and who was thus precluded from an active part in the discussion.* The degree of support for bishops and deans cannot be accurately assessed, for Nalson said that speeches in favour of episcopacy were deliberately suppressed, and some members were certainly afraid to speak for fear of the reformers. In any case, with a deadlock between the two Houses, the Root and Branch Bill made no further progress during the session.[13]

That Hyde was still regarded as a reformer, and an adherent of Pym, is

* cf. 'They who wished well to the bill having resolved "to put Mr. Hyde into the chair, that he might not give them trouble by frequent speaking, and so too much obstruct the expediting the bill"'. As it was, he did all he could to obstruct the Bill, so that Sir Arthur Hesilrige declared "that he would never hereafter put an enemy into the chair".[12]

illustrated by an incident he later described in the *Life*.[14] After a busy afternoon at committee work he was often invited to dine at Pym's lodging in Sir Richard Manly's house behind Westminster Hall, where Pym, Hampden, Sir Arthur Hesilrige and two or three more 'transacted much business, and invited thither those of whose conversion they had any hope'. On one such occasion Nathaniel Fiennes, son of Lord Saye, dined there and afterwards invited Hyde to ride in the fields between Westminster and Chelsea. Fiennes asked him why he was so attached to episcopacy. Hyde replied 'that he could not conceive how religion could be preserved without bishops, nor how the government of the state could well subsist if the government of the church were altered; and asked him what government they meant to introduce in its place'. Fiennes replied that there would be time enough to think of that, but 'if the king resolved to defend the bishops, it could cost the kingdom much blood, and would be the occasion of as sharp a war as had ever been in England'. This, Clarendon wrote, was the first indication he had ever had of what was in the mind of the reforming party. The vividness with which he remembered the incident suggests that it played a significant part in forming the doubts which were gathering in his mind.

Two days later Hyde met Henry Marten, another reformer, 'with whom he lived very familiarly'. Marten warned Hyde that 'he would undo himself by his adhering to the court; to which he replied that he had no relation to the court, and was only concerned to maintain the government and preserve the law'. Hyde asked him what he thought of the leading reformers, 'and he very frankly answered that he thought them knaves'. Hyde then asked him what his political objective was. Marten replied; 'I do not think one man wise enough to govern us all'.[15] This was a shock to Hyde, the first time he had heard of the anti-monarchist intentions of the extreme reformers. During the summer and autumn of 1641 it is clear that he and Falkland rethought their whole political position, and such conversations as those with Fiennes and Marten left a deep impression upon them.

The Root and Branch Bill had created a deadlock between the two Houses, but there was much other pressing work for the Commons. The first need was that the English and Scots armies be paid off and disbanded. The financial problem was desperate, for a Commons committee reported that nearly £650,000 was needed to pay off the armies and to settle immediate debts.[16] On 18 June Hyde was specially commissioned to consider a poll tax, and on the 22nd the Tonnage and Poundage Act received the royal assent. The latter made clear that collection without consent of parliament was illegal. At the same time bills to abolish the Courts of Star Chamber, High Commission and Requests, passed without difficulty.

Much of Hyde's time was spent with matters which had previously concerned him most. On 29 June he reported the articles of impeachment against Bramston LCJ, and on 1 July, against the Barons of the Exchequer for their part in the ship money cases. For once the case was fully reported, and it provides us with a rare opportunity to see Hyde in operation as prosecuting counsel before the Lords. The case for the impeachment of the three Barons of the Exchequer, Davenport, Weston and Trevor, opened on 6 July 1641, and shows how seriously Hyde regarded the alleged abuse of the law:

There cannot be a greater instance of a sick and languishing Commonwealth than the business of this day: Good God! how have the guilty these late years been punished, when the judges themselves have been such delinquents! 'Tis no marvel than an irregular, extravagant, arbitrary power, like a torrent, hath broke in upon us, when our banks and bulwarks, the Laws, were in the custody of such persons. ... 'Twas once said by one who always spoke excellently, *that the Twelve Judges were like Twelve Lions under the Throne of Solomon*; under the throne! in obedience! but yet lions. Your Lordships shall this day hear of six who ... were no lions.

The great fault of the judges had been to bring the law into disrepute, and Hyde looked to their lordships to 'restore the dejected, broken people of this island to their former joy and security'. The judges' decision in favour of ship money 'was a crime of so prodigious a nature, that it could not be easily swallowed and digested by the consciences even of these men', but they had been hardened to it by impositions on trade. They had aided in 'that universal destruction of the kingdom by ship money . . . by *doing the work of a Parliament to his Majesty in supplies*'. Their decision 'was the boldest piece of sophistry we have met with in a court of law'.

My lords, if the excellent, envied constitution of this kingdom hath been of late distempered . . [and] the king and people have been robbed of the delight and comfort of each other, and the blessed peace of this island been shaken and frightened into tumults and commotion . . these are the men that actively or passively, by doing or not doing, have brought this upon us.[17]

This was, of course, the speech of a professional lawyer acting as counsel for the prosecution, but it is clear from the *History* that Hyde sincerely believed that the law had been brought into contempt, and that the judges bore a heavy responsibility for dividing the king and the people.*

On 5 July the king addressed the two Houses, and reminded them of how much he had conceded:

I hope you remember that I have granted that judges hereafter shall hold their places *quamdiu bene se gesserint*. I have bounded the forests, not according to my

---

* cf. Lord Falkland's speech against ship money 5 Dec 1640: 'The constitution of this Commonwealth hath established, or rather endeavoured to establish to us the security of our goods, by appointing for us judges so settled, so sworn, that there can be no oppression . . . [and] the greatest person in this kingdom cannot continue the least violence upon the meanest. But this security has been almost our ruin, for it hath been turned, or rather turned itself into a battery against us: And those persons who should have been dogs to defend the sheep, have been as wolves to worry them. Mr. Speaker, the cause of all the miseries we have suffered, and the cause of all our jealousies we have had . . . is that a most excellent Prince hath been most infinitely abused by his judges, telling him that by policy he might do what he pleased.'[18]

right, but according to late customs. I have established the property of the subjects, as witness the free giving, not taking away of ship money. I have established by Act of Parliament, the property of the subject in tonnage and poundage* which never was done in any of my predecessors' times; I have granted a law for a triennial Parliament; and given way to an Act for the securing of moneys advanced for the disbanding of the Armies [this was how Charles preferred to view the Act for the prevention of the dissolution of the Long Parliament]; I have given free course of justice against delinquents; I have put the laws in execution against Papists. Nay, I have given way to everything that you have asked of me; and therefore methinks, you should not wonder if in some things I begin to refuse.[19]

The king spoke no more than the truth. Pym and his friends had dismantled Charles's government, destroyed his ministers, established parliamentary control of taxation, and perpetuated the life of the Long Parliament. By building up supposed Catholic and army plots to hysterical proportions in May and by attempting to impose a Protestation on all members of parliament on 3 May, which already appeared to envisage conditions of civil war, the reformers had driven Charles to the limits of endurance. What was desperately needed was a period of calm in which moderate counsels could prevail, but the conditions for confidence simply did not exist. The king could hardly be expected to accept the complete destruction of the prerogative. He announced his intention to go to Scotland in August, and this could only be with the intention of winning over the Scottish nobility against the Covenanters and perhaps the English parliament. Pym on his side kept up the temperature of alarm by continuing to probe the Army Plot, and by proposing the Ten Propositions of 24 June 1641, a document which, like the Protestation of 3 May, seemed to envisage the approach of civil war. It required that the armies be disbanded, that the king should delay his journey to Scotland, that he should take into his council only those acceptable to parliament; that no Catholic should serve the queen, that the trained bands be armed, and the Cinque Ports be placed under the command of those acceptable to parliament.† The myth of a Catholic menace was kept alive by such demands as that the king should have no Papists about the Court. These were presumably the terms upon which Pym was prepared to make a constitutional settlement. But a vicious circle had been created. The king could not accept as ministers or Privy Councillors men he could not trust, and the reformers could not feel safe until they could trust the king's councillors. Pym saw it in terms of just such a dilemma:

There is but one end and foundation of all these affections and counsels. . . . We cannot duly and truly serve God, but thereby we serve our King, nor serve God and our King as we ought without our service to the Commonwealth.[21]

* Granted to the king, almost insolently, for only two months at a time.
† This was aimed against the duke of Richmond. The reformers wanted to replace him by the earl of Warwick. Clarendon said that Richmond was almost the only man about the king who did not kowtow to the reformers in the Commons.[20]

Moreover, as the gap widened between the king and the reformers, no reformer would risk his reputation in the Commons by trying to build a bridge to the king, while the king, on his side, regarded all the concessions he had made as merely temporary.

The Commons viewed the king's intention to go to Scotland with grave apprehension, fearing that his intention was to win the support of the Scottish nobility not only against the Covenanters, but perhaps against the English parliament. They first tried to delay his journey, and when this failed, discussed whether some regency (*Custos regni*) might be appointed to operate in his absence, but this was abandoned as being without precedent.[22] They feared that the king might make use of the English army in the north, and Rushworth was sent post-haste to York to urge the earl of Holland, the commander, to complete the disbandment. Finally, when the king set out for Scotland on 11 August they appointed the earl of Bedford, Lord Howard of Escrick, Nathaniel Fiennes, Sir William Armyne, Stapleton and Hampden to accompany him, nominally as witnesses of the peace with Scotland, but actually, Clarendon affirmed, to spy upon him and keep the reformers fully informed.[23] In the absence of the king parliament could make no enactments, but this did not prevent them from issuing orders on their own authority to the country forbidding the use of crucifixes and ornaments, or the use of altars, or bowing at the name of Jesus; and all sports and dancing were forbidden on the Lord's Day.[24] The constitutional significance of this did not escape members,* and on 21 October Sir Edward Dering raised the question in the House, and questioned whether the orders of the Commons were binding:

Your Orders (I am out of doubt) are powerful, if they be grounded upon the laws of the land; upon that warranty we may by an Order, enforce anything that is undoubtedly so grounded; and by the same rule we may abrogate whatsoever is introduced contrary to the undoubted foundation of our laws. But, Sir, this Order is of another nature, another temper. . . . [Men of birth and fortune] sent us hither as their trustees, to make and unmake laws: they know they did not send us hither to rule and govern them by arbitrary, revocable and disputable orders, especially in religion.[26]

Dering was voicing the fears of moderate opinion at the course of events, and the triumph of radical reform. When on 9 September the most hectic session in parliamentary history came to an end, and members adjourned to the country until 20 October, they left a committee of 47, headed by Pym, to manage business during the recess. For the next few weeks he managed the affairs of government efficiently but at the expense of earning the nickname of 'King Pym'; Sir Peter Wroth said that the committee's orders lacked only the letter 'R' after Pym's name.[27]

* Clarendon said that the order had only been carried because attendance was thin that day. The Lords refused to join in the order and issued a contradictory order that services should be conducted as appointed by Act of Parliament.[25]

There were signs that Pym's domination was not accepted without protest. In some places the order of 9 September was resisted, it was reported that those called 'sectaries and orthodox' in St Giles's, Cripplegate 'were almost got to daggers drawing, the one about executing the order of the House of Commons, the other for preserving their church in its ancient condition, with the rails about the Communion-table', and the churchwardens and parishioners petitioned the Commons that the rails about the Communion table should remain as they had been for the past eighty years.[28] And it was clear that in some parishes the Puritans were regarded as the innovators, and Anglican practices as traditional. On 16 October Sir Simonds D'Ewes protested to the Commons' committee that the tearing up of brass inscriptions and the defacing of statues on tombs at the Wool Church in London 'had brought a great scandal upon the House of Commons as if we meant to deface all Antiquities'.[29] On 25 October Pym declared 'that he had received a letter from a porter of the House, and upon opening of it, a plaster which came from a wound, full of corrupt matter dropped out of it, and that the letter contained many menaces and much railing against him'. It was brought by a gentleman who gave the porter a shilling, but his identity was never discovered.[30]

Pym's cause was in some danger of losing impetus, and when Parliament reassembled on 20 October the clearest course was to renew the attacks on the bishops. The whole political conflict was immensely exacerbated by the way in which ecclesiastical and constitutional issues were intertwined. There was, as we have seen, little sympathy for the Laudian bishops, and there was general opposition to the active part they played in the king's Councils and in jurisdiction. There was general resentment against the Canons of 1640, and the bishops who had promulgated them. So long as the Commons concentrated on such supposed practical evils, there would be a consensus of opinion in the Commons. Similarly so long as the attacks were on supposed constitutional abuses such as ship money or the operation of the Prerogative Courts. If however it became clear that the intention of the reformers was to go far beyond practical abuses, and to dismember the constitution of Church and State, that consensus might disappear. Pym well understood this. His constitutional objectives were becoming clearly defined, but it was necessary to carry the House with him. The safest line to pursue was that from the last session, the exclusion of the bishops from the House of Lords. At this point Scottish affairs played into his hands.

In Scotland there had been an almost complete collapse of episcopacy and royal power, and in August Charles's main hope was that moderate Covenanters, who would readily condemn episcopacy, might not so readily see the collapse of royal power, especially if that meant the domination of the earl of Argyll. His favourite, the commissioner for Scotland, the marquis of Hamilton, despairing of the royal cause, had gone over to Argyll, but Charles found a new ally in the earl of Montrose. Henceforth Montrose and Argyll were great antagonists, 'like Caesar and Pompey', said Clarendon, 'the one would endure no superior, and the other would have no equal'. Clarendon wrote a vivid account of the so called Incident, in which Montrose laid before the king evidence of the treason of both Argyll and Hamilton, and offered either to present the evidence to the Scottish parliament, or 'to kill them both'. The king would not agree to the latter, but was prepared for a treason trial before parliament. On 12 October, however, Argyll, Hamilton and his brother the earl of Lanark, fled from Edinburgh to their estates, declaring that there was a plot to assassinate them. A lurid account of the incident was despatched to Westminster, with dark hints that the plot, involving the king, had wider implications which threatened England as well as Scotland. Pym made full use of the story when parliament reassembled on 20 October, and was able to magnify it into a great plot involving, as always, papists, bishops, the army and foreign conspirators, and to suggest that the king could not be trusted.[31] After the recess Pym's domination of the Commons was more pronounced than ever before.

Thus alarmed, the Commons on 20 October turned again to the subject of the Canons of 1640 and the position of the bishops in the House of Lords. The litany against the clergy was rehearsed by Sir Simonds D'Ewes, but his sweeping but vague accusations went beyond the limits of credulity for some members, and Falkland and Hyde intervened to move 'that we should leave the business of Scotland to the Parliament there, and not to take up fears and suspicions without very certain and undoubted grounds'.[32] We do not know whether Hyde spent the weeks of the recess with Falkland at Great Tew, but a new note of caution entered their interventions in debates from October onwards, as parliamentary affairs moved from concern with practical abuses to a more fundamental constitutional attack.

Sir Edward Dering was also having second thoughts. He argued that just as it was expedient that bishops should cease to exercise secular jurisdiction, it was equally dangerous for laymen to pronounce on points of theology and that though the complaint had been that laymen were excluded from making the Canons of 1640, the Commons were now committing the reverse error in attempting to exclude bishops. Dering suggested a national synod, but next day he revealed his fears of a rampant Puritanism:

If we let forth the Government into a loose liberty for all religions, we shall have none. Libertinism will beget Atheism. And truly, Sir, at present between Papism on the one hand and Brownism on the other, narrow is the way, and few there be that do find it, to right good Protestantism.[33]

Pym however steered the House to aim at the thirteen bishops who had voted for the Canons of 1640. He declared that they should be excluded from the Lords, since the Canons were 'against the Prerogative of the King, against the privilege of Parliament, against the Property of the subject, and against the peace of the kingdom'. His defence of the prerogative of the king made little sense since the king had issued the Canons, and Pym's claim that 'Parliament was the fountain of justice' was a significant reversal of the mediaeval tag which James I had so often affirmed.[34] The bill for their exclusion of the bishops from the Lords was rushed through in a thin House of 81, in spite of attempts by Hyde to delay it until the House was fuller. The Erastianism of many members was sufficient to give any anti-clerical measure an impetus. When for instance D'Ewes proposed that clergy should be excluded from all state affairs, he quoted the historian de Thou 'that in whatsoever kingdom the clergyman had intermeddled with state affairs, it had brought calamity and mischief into that Kingdom'. When Hyde asked whether he intended to exclude the clergy from being Masters of colleges or schoolmasters, D'Ewes said that he did not intend to go so far.[35] Hyde also opposed the bill on the grounds that it was an infringement of the privileges of the Lords to attempt to exclude the bishops, and contrary to constitutional precedent. Here he was on weak ground, for D'Ewes pointed out that Parliament had made greater changes in Henry VIII's time with the exclusion of abbots and priors, and that the bishops sat, not as ecclesiastics, but as barons created by William I.[36]

The dangers Pym had suggested seemed confirmed when on 1 November news arrived of a catastrophic rising in Ireland. Strafford's hold on Ireland had seemed secure, and he had built up an army there which he had offered to Charles for use in Scotland. But Pym and his friends had regarded it as a menace, and in May 1641 Charles ordered disbandment, while at the same time instructing Ormond, Strafford's successor, to keep together as many of the men as possible. He hoped by making ample concessions in Ireland to build up substantial support there. But concessions to the Protestants meant antagonising the Catholic Irish landowners, who saw their tenures threatened if the plantation system continued. The signal for revolt was an attack on Dublin castle on 23 October, which failed. On the 24th Sir Phelim O'Neill in Ulster issued a proclamation; the rebels, he said, were not in arms against the king, but only in defence of their rights. But the rising then got out of hand, and there were savage attacks on Protestants. England was horrified at stories of murders, and of Protestant families being stripped naked and left to die of privation. Lecky estimated that there were 4000 murders, and 8000 who died of cold and starvation, but these figures were magnified many times in accounts in England. The Long Parliament debated the Irish rebellion on 1 November, and in the heat of the moment the two Houses issued a declaration; 'That they do intend to serve his Majesty with their lives and fortunes for the suppressing of this wicked rebellion . . . And thereupon have ordered and provided for a present supply of moneys, and raising the number of 6000 Foot and 2000 Horse to be sent from England.'[37] The king appointed Ormond to command the forces in Ireland. But herein lay the rub for the reformers. The king had had nothing to do with the outbreak of the revolt, but there was the suspicion that in some undefined way he could turn it to his own advantage.[38] On 4 November for instance Sir Phelim O'Neill in Ireland had issued a proclamation in the king's name calling on the Catholics to take arms in his defence. It was a forgery, but it was taken as genuine, and increased the suspicion that there was a conspiracy between the king, the Catholics, Jesuit conspirators and foreign powers. The Irish rebellion, so far from aiding the king, was disastrous to his cause, as it increased fears and tensions just at the time when there might have been a prospect of their relaxation.

The news of the Irish rising and stories of plots spread panic throughout the country, so that any rumour might be believed. Irishmen were said to be in London waiting for the signal to rise. Houses were searched to find hidden Papists. There were stories of plots to kill members of parliament, and of a French army waiting to invade England. Richard Baxter wrote later:

There was nothing that with the people wrought so much, as the Irish massacre and rebellion . . . This filled all England with a fear both of the Irish, and of papists at home . . In so much that when the rumour of a plot was occasioned at London, the poor people, all the countries over, were ready either to run to arms, or hide themselves, thinking that the papists were ready to rise and cut their throats.[39]

Moderate men like Sir Simonds D'Ewes or John Selden saw the folly of such hysteria, but were quite unable to stem the tide.

John Pym's constitutional objectives were being pursued with great skill and care to carry the Commons and public opinion with him. In his Ten Propositions of 24 June his central demand was that the king's councillors should be only those who had the confidence of Parliament. In September 1641 the king had acquiesced in just such a demand in Scotland, namely that all officers of state, Privy Councillors and lords of sessions should be chosen 'with the advice and approbation' of the Scottish parliament. This re-enforced Pym's objective in England. On 28 October, in what D'Ewes thought to have been a carefully planned move, Robert Goodwin raised in the Commons the question of the king's councillors, and Strode followed with a violent speech, declaring that 'all we had done this Parliament was nothing unless we had a negative voice in the placing of the great officers of the King and of his councillors, by whom his Majesty was led captive'. Edward Hyde at once opposed this on the grounds that the appointment of councillors was undoubtedly part of the royal prerogative; that by abolishing the Prerogative Courts and ship money they had done much good, but he wished the structure of church and state to remain unchanged. D'Ewes followed, and in his speech revealed the difficulty which arose from the mingling of constitutional and ecclesiastical issues. He said that the appointment of councillors was an integral part of the royal prerogative, and he would always defend it; but he could not agree with Hyde that all was well with the church:

truly I rather think the Church is yet full of wrinkles amongst us and needs a great deal of reformation which I hope we shall shortly see effected . . . The way to make the King and kingdom happy is that godly and wise men may be placed about the King's person and in office in Court.[40]

In short, D'Ewes defended the royal prerogative, but wanted a Puritan church.

Previously attacks had been made, not on episcopacy itself, but on the quality of existing bishops. Charles attempted to forestall this criticism by appointing five new bishops to the vacant sees of Worcester, Lincoln, Exeter, Chichester and Bristol, all men of learning without special Laudian associations.* On 29 October these appointments were at once attacked in the Commons by Sir Walter Earle and Sir Simonds D'Ewes, who thought their appointment derogatory to the Commons while the fate of bishops was still under discussion. Sir John Hotham thought that by opposing the appointments the House laid themselves open to the charge of *praemunire*, and so no doubt they would have been in Tudor times, but the situation was very different in October 1641. Three days later the news of the Irish rebellion powerfully strengthened the hands of the extremists.[41] Thus on 5 November the House discussed whether they should seek the aid of the Scots to suppress the Irish rebellion, an idea which would appeal to the Puritan members who saw the Scottish Covenanters as natural allies against episcopacy. Lord Falkland opposed, urging that they should wait to see the extent of the problem in Ireland, but the majority voted for seeking Scottish help. Pym then returned to the matter nearest his heart, the appointment of the king's councillors, which had failed to secure acceptance on the 28th. Now in the new atmosphere of tension he was much more likely to succeed. D'Ewes said that there would have been a speedy acceptance had not Edward Hyde opposed it, and so did Edmund Waller, who argued that the House was implying that if the king did not dismiss his councillors the House was absolved from aiding him in Ireland. This was in fact exactly what Pym had in mind, but Waller was rash enough to liken the attitude of the House to that of the earl of Strafford, and that gave Pym the chance to call for Waller's censure. Waller was forced to ask the pardon of the House and Pym. With this victory, Pym was able to carry, on 8 November, the vote that 'if his Majesty should not be graciously pleased to grant [the appointment of councillors approved by Parliament] . . . we should take such a course for the securing of Ireland as might likewise secure ourselves'.[42] The motion was carried by 151 to 110, but, according to Clarendon, late at night when all the radicals were present but many moderates had gone home. Hyde feared that it was an act of provocation to the king, which would only widen the breach he was so anxious now to close. S R Gardiner regarded the vote of 8 November as the turning-point in the

---

* Dr Prideaux, regius professor at Oxford, Dr Winiff, dean of St Paul's, Dr Henry King, dean of Lichfield, Dr Brownrigg, master of Catherine Hall, Cambridge, and Dr Holdsworth, master of Emmanuel College.

division of the Commons into two irreconcilable parties. Mr Wormald thought the process more gradual than that, but the essential facts are not in dispute. Pym's victory was but a preliminary to his great stroke of policy which was to follow.

On the same day (8 November) Pym introduced the Grand Remonstrance. It was a massive document of 204 clauses and sought to encompass in one document all the grievances of the reign. It declared the root cause of the troubles of the kingdom lay in 'a malignant and pernicious design of subverting the fundamental laws and principles of government, upon which the religion and justice of this kingdom are firmly established'; that the conspirators were Papists, bishops and evil councillors; that the object was the exaltation of the prerogative, the advancement of Arminianism, and to divide the king from his parliament. The document was careful to say that 'we have ever been careful not to desire anything that should weaken the Crown either in just profit or useful power', and that the whole Remonstrance contained 'not so much as a shadow of prejudice to the Crown', but it announced parliament's intention of curbing 'the exorbitant power which the prelates have', and of setting up 'a general synod' for the reform of the church; and it demanded parliamentary control over the king's advisers. It was a cleverly worded document, re-opening old wounds which might have been regarded as having been healed, yet claiming complete loyalty to the monarchy, appealing to Puritan sentiment by attacks on the bishops and Papists and equating the two, and then coming to the clause which Pym regarded as the most crucial and important of all, namely the control of the king's councillors.

It took the Commons a fortnight to digest its contents, and there was some hard debating in which Edward Hyde emerged as a leader of the opposition to the Remonstrance. November 16 for instance was an uncomfortable day for the reformers, for Hyde attacked the clause which seemed to imply that the Book of Common Prayer was to be set aside, and D'Ewes reported, 'We saw that the party for episcopacy was so strong as we were willing to lay the clause aside without further trouble.' The clause to dispose of episcopal and dean-and-chapter lands was also resisted until it was laid aside. Then the clause alleging that the bishops had brought in idolatry and popery was opposed by Sir Edward Dering, only to have his earlier speeches thrown at him, and on a vote Dering was defeated by 124 to 99.

The final debate took place on 22 November. Clarendon more than once commented on the difficulty of persuading many members to attend debates regularly; that whereas the radicals attended in full force, the moderates and doubtfuls often preferred to stay away. So at the beginning of this debate at 9.00 am Hyde proposed that the Sergeant should go with his mace to call up members who were walking in Westminster Hall. D'Ewes said that this was reluctantly agreed to. When this had been done Hyde, Falkland, Sir John Culpepper and others attacked the Remonstrance. They argued that the document was unnecessary, that many of the grievances had already been satisfied, that the king had granted everything they had reasonably asked, that the Commons had no power to make such an appeal to the people without the concurrence of the Lords, that it would be deeply disturbing to the country when unity was needed in face of the Irish rebellion, that it was deeply offensive to the king, and so forth. Lord Falkland said that much that was written into the document was fit only for an Act of Oblivion, and phrases such as 'that the king had not bread to put in his head, or was able to subsist but by the bounty of his people' were gratuitously offensive. Dering and Culpepper argued that the blanket attack on all the bishops was grossly inaccurate. Culpepper said that this was a deliberate attempt to stir up the people, and was altogether without precedent. Pym replied roundly 'that the king's honour was the objection. The honour of the king is the safety of his people. That he had thrust home all the plots and designs to the Court, and it is time to speak plain English, lest posterity shall say that England was lost and no man durst speak the truth.' Or, in another version:

It was time to deal plainly with the king and posterity: and come nearer home yet; since all the projects have been rooted in Popery. Shall we forget that a Lord Treasurer died a Papist? that a Secretary was a Papist? If this king will join with us we shall set him upon as great grounds of honour and greatness in that all the world shall not be able to move him.[44]

The opposition were able to win some victories, some of the phrases offensive to the king being omitted, such as that Sir John Eliot had been committed to prison 'by the king's own hand'. The debate raged all day and far into the evening. The final vote was taken about 1.00 am, when the Remonstrance was carried by 159 to 148; a very narrow majority which would probably have disappeared had the vote been taken next day, but many of the older and more moderate members had left the House exhausted, and others such as D'Ewes had left because they disagreed with the Remonstrance, but thought further resistance useless. Even after the vote the debate continued, for the reformers proposed that the Remonstrance be published. This revealed their true purpose, which was to stir up public opinion. In vain did Sir John Culpepper protest that a Remonstrance was always addressed to the king, and for the redress of grievances, not an exercise in propaganda and in order to enflame public feeling. The temperature of the debate was reaching boiling point, and one member recorded that 'we had catched at each other's locks, and sheathed our swords in each other's bowels, had not the sagacity and great calmness of Mr. Hampden by a short speech prevented it'.[45] Sir Edward Dering declared:

When I first heard of a Remonstrance. . . . I did not dream that we should remonstrate downward, tell stories to the people, and talk of the king as of a third person.

The motion for publication was carried by 124 to 101. When Geoffrey Palmer, a lawyer of the Middle Temple, and a close friend of Hyde's, wished to enter a protest, he was prevented. Pandemonium followed, and two days later Palmer was called to account for his words, and sent to the Tower for a few days, in spite of Hyde's protest that the attack on Palmer 'took away the great privilege of freedom of speech'.[46]

According to his later account of the great debate on the Remonstrance, Hyde took a leading part in resisting it. Only fragments of his speeches have survived, but one remark stands out as specially significant:

We stand upon our liberties for the King's sake, lest he should be King of mean subjects and we subjects of a mean King.[47]

Hyde's theme throughout was that if the Remonstrance were intended as a means to a speedy constitutional settlement it could be defended, that the work of the Long Parliament had been to remove specific abuses, and that that had been largely achieved. But if it were intended to be an incitement to public agitation, and to prepare the ground for fundamental changes in church and state, it must be resisted. All his life Hyde sought, not a royal triumph, still less a parliamentary triumph, but a constitutional balance. When he came to write his *History* he commented that the authors of the Remonstrance had

left not any error or misfortune in government, nor any passionate exercise of power, then unmentioned and unpressed; with the sharpest and most pathetical expressions to affect the people, that the general observation of the wisest, or the particular animosity of the most disobliged or ill-affected person could suggest, to the disadvantage of the king, from the death of his father, to the unhappy beginning of the present parliament . . . They magnified their own services . . .[48]

As a move in the war against royal power the Remonstrance was an effective instrument, but it made an early constitutional settlement much less likely. It provided Pym with the impetus to continue the drive which had seemed to be losing momentum. In later years the problem which interested Clarendon was how

a handful of men, much inferior in the beginning, in number and interest, came to give laws to the major part; and to show that three diligent persons are a greater number in arithmetic, as well as a more significant number in logic, than ten unconcerned, they by a plurality of voices in the end, converted or reduced the whole body to their opinions.[49]

He saw the great disadvantage the king was under in having no one of stature in the Commons to defend his cause, and he returned to the question of whether Charles might not have been wise to have brought Pym, Hampden and Hollis into his government at the same time as St John, before Pym's hostility to the crown had hardened.[50]

Charles returned from Scotland on 25 November 1641, and was received with popular acclamation, and a magnificent entertainment provided by the Lord Mayor, Sir Richard Gurney. If this gave the king a false sense of his power, it certainly alarmed the reformers. On Sunday 28 November demonstrating crowds flocked to Westminster, and next day members, including Sir John Strangways, were jostled by the mob demanding their votes against bishops. During the king's absence in Scotland, Parliament had provided themselves with an armed guard drawn from the London trained bands, commanded by the earl of Essex. The king regarded this as a dangerous precedent, and on his return dismissed the guard, and when the Commons protested, he appointed his own guard drawn from the Westminster trained bands, and commanded by the earl of Dorset, Lord Lieutenant of Middlesex. When this force was hard pressed on the 29th Dorset ordered his men to fire blanks if necessary.

The debate on the Grand Remonstrance, and especially the order to publish the document, the rough usage by the House of Geoffrey Palmer, the growth of mob violence, and the increasing suspicion of the real intentions of the reformers, strengthened the need for a party of moderation and order. It included Lord Falkland, Edward Hyde, Edmund Waller, Sir John Culpepper, Sir John Strangways and George Digby. On 30 November they raised the question of mob violence in the Commons, Edward Hyde and others pointing out the pressure which had been brought to bear on Strangways. Strangways went further and produced evidence that an apprentice named Cole had been summoned to Palace Yard Westminster, with a thousand others, armed with swords, and sent by their masters at the behest of 'some Parliament men', who had thought their help necessary to secure a vote in the Commons. Edward Kirton, a Somerset gentleman and agent for the marquis of Hertford, produced evidence from a citizen that Captain Venn, a member of the House, had sent word to a Mr Farlow in Wood Street 'to desire him to come away speedily armed to the house of Commons, for swords were there drawn and the well affected party was like to be overborne'. Unfortunately for the moderates, William Chillingworth, a protégé of Great Tew, who had been gathering information, had said to a lawyer of Clement's Inn that he thought some of the members of the Commons as guilty of treason as the earl of Strafford. Pym was able to divert attention to Chillingworth, who was sent for, proved to be a lamentable witness, and was sent to the Tower.[51]

Many members of the Commons must have been bewildered by the speed of events and the confusion of arguments. Two parties were emerging, one emphasised the dangers from royal power and the untrustworthiness of the king; the other believed that the reforms had gone far enough, and was suspicious of the intentions of the reformers and of the dangers which would follow from social revolution. For the time being the majority of the Commons thought the king the greater danger, and this was why the impetus of the Grand Remonstrance had been so important for Pym. That impetus Pym had no difficulty in maintaining. On 1 December twelve members were appointed to present the Remonstrance to the king at Hampton Court. They were carefully chosen to include Sir Simonds D'Ewes, Sir Ralph Hopton and Sir Edward Dering, moderate men who were thus committed to a document on which they had doubts.* The king made a measured reply. He reproached them for the disrespect shown in the Remonstrance. He asked who were the 'wicked and malignant' councillors of whom they complained. As for religion, he was willing to call a national synod. To the imputation that there was a Catholic conspiracy, he replied with the double-edged outburst: 'The devil take him, whomsoever he be, that had a design to change religion'. To the clause referring to the disposal of rebel lands in Ireland he replied that 'we must not dispose of the bear's skin till he be dead'. He sought to question the commission further, but they replied that they had no authority to enter into discussions. The king then promised to send a reasoned reply, and instructed them not to publish the Remonstrance until his reply had been received. The commissioners were then entertained 'with great respect'.[53] If Pym's intention had been to goad the king into an ill-considered or hasty reply, he was disappointed.

For the next two days the Commons discussed the recent tumults. Some attacked the actions of the earl of Dorset for showing force against the loyal Londoners; others, like Sir John Culpepper, defended him. On 3 December the king addressed both Houses in an attempt to calm the fears of those 'disturbed with jealousies, frights and alarms of dangerous designs and plots, in consequence of which Guards have been set to defend both Houses'.[54] But his words had little effect, for Pym had two objectives he was determined to pursue.

The first was to end the procrastination of the Lords about the impeachment of the bishops. On 3 December a committee was appointed, headed by Pym to present the Lords with what amounted to an ultimatum. One of the most remarkable features of the period after November 1640 was the way in which the House of Lords had lost the status and power which had formerly been theirs. Now the Commons came near to claiming full sovereignty, 'this House being the Representative Body of the whole Kingdom, and their Lordships being but as particular Persons, and coming to Parliament in a particular capacity'. If then the Lords were unwilling to accept the decisions of the Commons, the latter would legislate 'together with such Lords that are more sensible of the safety of the kingdom'. The Commons' ultimatum amounted to an offer of acquiescence or extinction to the Lords.[55]

The second of Pym's objectives was to secure control of the armed forces. One purpose of the king's address to the two Houses had been to urge them to

* Nicholas Ms: Sir Ralph Hopton was named to present the Remonstrance, which he endeavoured to avoid, having declared against it, but the House required him to obey. The king treated him with special respect.[52]

raise forces for Ireland, but this was just what Pym had no intention of doing so long as those forces remained under the king's command. The fear was that any such force might be turned against parliament. On 7 December Sir Arthur Hesilrige brought in a bill to place the militia and trained bands under the command of a Lord General of their own appointment, and the navy under a parliamentary admiral. It was bitterly opposed by Edmund Waller and Sir John Culpepper, the latter arguing that the bill would but replace one arbitrary power for another. It was a difficult decision for members to make. D'Ewes said he would support it if it had the king's agreement since 'we know that what we do here is but *lumen opacum*, a body only capable of light which his Majesty only must give'.[56] In the end the bill was carried by 158 to 125.

With London in turmoil, and the Irish atrocities continuing, the question of the armed forces was urgent, and on 7 December the king thought to hasten events by reminding the Lords that he would accept no diminution of the royal prerogative in the control of the militia, and demanding that a *salvo jure* clause be included in Hesilrige's proposed bill. Pym saw his position threatened, for the moderates would certainly have regard to the king's wishes. He must make it a great issue. He rushed to the Commons with a Protestation at the intervention of the king, and late at night, on 15 December hurried through by 135 to 83 a vote that it should be printed. Next day he inaugurated a full-dress debate urging that the privilege of parliament had been violated by the king's attempt to influence the debate. After a heated debate the Protestation was approved. Pym carried it to the Lords, and on the 17th a deputation headed by John Williams, archbishop of York, presented it to the king. Charles replied 'in a low voice' that he would return a considered answer.[57]

Meanwhile the situation in the City of London was becoming more acute. Brian Manning has distinguished two levels of agitation,[58] first the middle class of merchants and shopkeepers who had supported the moderate reformers, and below them the apprentices, craftsmen and journeymen, whipped up into a fury of hostility to bishops, papists and the Prayer Book by preachers and agitators. It was the latter who increased the nervousness of moderates. Yet when they presented a petition said to be signed by 30,000, on 23 December, for the abolition of episcopacy, the House agreed to receive it since it had been presented peacefully, although some members were for 'casting it out of the House'.[59] On the 21st the elections to the Common Council of London were a victory for Pym and his friends, and the risk of armed conflict was brought perceptibly nearer. The king felt it necessary at least to control the Tower of London. Sir William Balfour, thought to be too favourable to the reformers, was on the 23rd replaced by Sir Thomas Lunsford. Not much was really known about Lunsford, but he was at once denounced as a drunken and desperate character, and in face of renewed demonstrations the king again gave way and dismissed him.*

* He was replaced by Sir John Byron.

Again it had been shown that a display of force or determination could drive the king into retreat. Since his return from Scotland he had been required to accept a deliberately provocative and insulting Remonstrance; he had seen the continued campaign against the bishops, and the campaign to deprive him of all control over the armed forces. His attempt to influence the terms of the Militia Bill had been denounced as a breach of the privilege of parliament, with the implication that in future the Crown was expected to rubber-stamp any matter the Commons chose to enact; and if the Crown was to be reduced to a cipher, so also was the House of Lords, who had been told by the Commons that they represented no one but themselves. Mob violence had introduced a new and sinister element into the situation. During the twelve days of Christmas, when apprentices were on holiday, there was continued brawling in the streets. Finally, Pym maintained his assault by a campaign of vilification and exaggeration:

> that there had long been a design of the papists to ruin the true religion, that the placing of Colonel Lunsford to be Lieutenant of the Tower did shew that the same design was now growing to a maturity. . . . ; that we had done our utmost for the saving of this Church and Kingdom from ruin and from the plots of the cruel and bloody Papists . . . [and so on].[60]

When on 28 December the dangers arising from the street violence were discussed in the Commons, and some proposed that the king be asked that a guard be set for the protection of members, Pym replied that the people were 'our surest friends', and 'God forbid that the house of Commons should proceed in any way to dishearten people to obtain their just desires in such a way'.[61] Clarendon said that when writs were issued under the great seal to the justices to appoint constables to preserve the peace, the Commons countermanded the orders and declared them to be 'a breach of privilege'. Henceforth this became a phrase elastic enough to cover any action, however legal, of which the Commons disapproved.[62]

So the turmoil continued in the streets. In the days after Christmas the archbishop of York John Williams had to be rescued from a hostile crowd. Next day a mob tried to storm Westminster Abbey and were repelled with difficulty. The bishops indeed dared not risk leaving their homes in order to attend the Lords. Clarendon wrote that in the prevailing spirit of hostility towards them they would have done well to have lain low, but instead, putting justice before expediency, they were unwise enough to petition the Lords, protesting that they were being prevented from taking their places. Further, they asked that all business conducted in their absence should be null and void. The purpose of the latter demand was to reverse a vote in the Lords on 28 December and to ensure that the bill for the exclusion of bishops would not be voted on in their absence. It was undoubtedly the work of Archbishop Williams, who headed the petition, and Clarendon commented that the bishops were unwise to have submitted to the leadership of such a 'proud, restless and overweening spirit'. The Lords might have claimed jurisdiction over their own members; instead they at once informed the Commons. Pym seized the chance offered him and proposed the impeachment of the twelve bishops. During the year the campaign against the bishops had made slow progress, but now their precipitate action sealed their fate. The Lords at once committed the twelve bishops to confinement, ten to the Tower, and two, in view of age and respect, to the custody of Black Rod.

The repeated humiliation of the king, and the growth of popular violence, had led to some reaction in favour of the monarchy, and on 30 December a few hundred gentlemen of the Inns of Court marched to the Court to demonstrate their loyalty and to offer protection against the mob. Again Pym turned the occasion to his advantage. D'Ewes vividly described how Pym dramatically rose to demand that the doors of the Commons be shut, and then to announce 'that there being a design to be executed upon the House of Commons this day, we might send instantly to the City of London that there was a plot for the destroying of the House of Commons this day'.[63] This was too much for the moderates. D'Ewes doubted whether there was really a plot, and regarded it as a dangerous move 'since the citizens are not all the sons of one mother nor of one mind', and there was no knowing what violence might ensue. Pym's proposal of course had been to ignore the king, and to call on the City, but in the end the House decided that a committee should wait upon the king to ask for a guard drawn from the trained bands. Next day the king gave his answer that

We are wholly ignorant of the grounds of your apprehensions, but this we do protest before Almighty God . . that had we any knowledge or belief of the least design in any of violence . . against you, we would pursue them to condign punishment.[64]

In his *History* Clarendon several times commented on the disadvantage a member of the Commons was at, once he was labelled a friend of the Court, and that the only hope lay with independent members who might by reason and moderation stem the tide of extremism. For him, as for Lord Falkland, the turning point had been the Grand Remonstrance when it became clear to them that Pym's intentions went far beyond the removal of specific grievances, which had already been largely achieved, and that the radicalism and even insolence of the Grand Remonstrance would make accommodation with the king increasingly unlikely. In his *Life* he was at pains to emphasise his entire independence of the Court, until an incident occurred, which unfortunately cannot be precisely dated, and which in his telling seems to contain some inaccuracies. One day Henry Percy came to tell Hyde that the king wished to speak with him. Hyde replied that there must be some mistake, since he had never spoken with the king, and that the other Hyde in the House must be intended. However Percy led him to the king, who received him graciously and thanked him for the concern he had shown for the Anglican Church. The king asked him for his help in staving off an attack on episcopacy until the disbandment of the armies and the king's journey to Scotland:

If you will look to it that they do not carry it before I go to Scotland . . when the armies shall be disbanded, I will undertake for the church after that time.[65]

The timing would appear therefore to be about August 1641, but if Henry Percy was the intermediary, the date is wrong, since he had been on the run since May from the so called army plot, and was in Paris by July. Clarendon therefore was mistaken either in the date or in the intermediary. The question is not important, for the king was merely expressing thanks and attempting to win a likely ally. While in Scotland the king wrote to Nicholas, who was already acting as Secretary of State, again to express thanks for Hyde's services, and to ask him for his views on current events.[66]

It is clear that by November 1641 Hyde was no longer dining familiarly with Pym and his friends, but moving in a different circle. Clarendon described how he had drafted a private answer to the Grand Remonstrance, purely for his own interest, and how his new friend Lord Digby, coming upon it, asked to show it to the king. Hyde refused, since it 'might prove ruinous to him if the house should have the least imagination that he exercised himself in such offices', and since no one except Lord Falkland had seen it. The reply well illustrates the fear which existed in the minds of those who might be regarded as at all accommodating to the Court. Pym's majorities were obtained more by frightening away the timid from voting than by a free vote. No wonder that the king 'seemed to wonder very much that a person who had appeared so publicly in defence of his service, should be wary of assisting him in private'. Hyde's reluctance however sprang not from timidity but from the fear that if he were thought to be an adherent of the Court, his influence on the side of moderation in the House would disappear. He also knew how impulsive and rash Digby could be; but he gave way and sent the paper to the king on condition that it was submitted to the full Privy Council. The king's answer which was given to the Commons on 23 December, and which was eventually published, was therefore written by Hyde. It complained of the disrespect shown in publishing the Remonstrance against his expressed wishes, affirmed that all things should be done 'in a parliamentary way'; that the right of bishops to sit in the Lords was 'grounded upon the fundamental law of the kingdom'; that the inordinate power of the clergy had been sufficiently curbed by the abolition of the Court of High Commission; that he was prepared to summon a synod to achieve a religious settlement, although he affirmed his belief in the purity of the Anglican Church; he would shield no councillor found guilty in a court of law, but he must have the right of all free men to choose his own advisers; finally he took note of the Commons' concern at the alienation of rebel lands in Ireland.[67] However moderate the wording of the king's reply, in the pandemonium of late December in the Commons it fell upon deaf ears.

It must have been following Hyde's authorship of the reply, in November or December, that the king sent Lord Digby to bring Hyde at night by the queen's back stairs, into his presence, and offered him the post of Solicitor-General in place of Oliver St John, 'who had served him so ill'. Hyde's reply was a startled 'God forbid!'. The reasons he gave were his youth and inexperience, and his belief that St John would do the king far more harm out of office than in it. But his motives for refusal may well have been different. He knew the wretched figure which Court appointments cut in the Commons unless like St John they in fact worked with the reformers, and he genuinely believed that the only hope of bridging the gulf between crown and parliament lay with the independent moderates who might, if the king made no false or rash move, gather strength once the fever of hysteria then raging had subsided.[68] His friends thought otherwise and on 2 January 1642 Lord Falkland became the king's Secretary of State, and Sir John Culpepper Chancellor of the Exchequer.

'That the king should make no false or rash move' was the operative clause in Hyde's thinking. The king must show himself the guardian of the traditional values in the law and constitution until political opinion was soothed and turned away from the radicalism of the reformers and the violence of the mob. For the forces of stability were still there if they could be mobilised. Men such as Sir Edward Dering who had shown bitter enmity to the Laudian bishops and to the earl of Strafford, had modified their position, and recently Dering had made a speech in which he found much that was good in many of the bishops.* But there were others, especially Lord Digby, who saw things differently. They saw the royal power in tatters as the king made concession after concession. Many unemployed soldiers had drifted to London and to the Court, in readiness perhaps for an Irish expedition, or indeed for any enterprise which promised action. Ministers had been driven out and impeached for high treason; the bishops were in the Tower on the same fatuous charge. Surely two could play at that game. Were not the reformers guilty of treason in inviting in the Scots? Above all, were they not guilty of treason in stirring up the London mob to intimidate parliament? It was a measure of the king's desperation that he accepted Digby's reckless plan. What neither of them saw was that in doing so they were playing directly into John Pym's hand.

On 3 January the Attorney General Sir Edward Herbert submitted articles of high treason against Lord Mandeville, John Pym, John Hampden, Sir Arthur Hesilrige, Denzil Holles and William Strode, and their trunks and rooms were sealed. The charge was that 'they have traiterously endeavoured

* When he attempted to publish his speeches the Commons ordered the stationery company to seize the copies C J 5 Feb 1642.[69] He was expelled from the House and sent to the Tower.

to subvert the fundamental laws and government of England, to deprive the King of his royal power'. The Serjeant at Arms demanded the surrender of the five members. The Commons replied that they would return an answer, but ordered that the seals be broken on the doors and trunks. After a hasty conference with the Lords, a committee was appointed to inform the king that the sealing of the possessions of the five members was a breach of privilege. Sir William Fleming and another who had performed the sealing were taken into custody on Mr. Speaker's warrant. The king's reply to the deputation was that all that had been done had been by his orders. That some sort of military action was to be expected was common knowledge, and the House sent a warning to the Inns of Court and denounced the demonstrators of 30 December as delinquents.

Next day, 4 January, the Commons assembled with the five members in their places. Pym knew that he was in great danger. The arrest of the five might lead to the collapse of the opposition. On the other hand, if the king could be driven into committing a public act of violence, Pym could turn it to decisive advantage. In a sense both the king and Pym were banking on winning the support of the City of London. Charles had substantial military aid at hand, and if the London trained bands could be relied upon to control the mob, he might be able to restore royal authority. But Pym had a more accurate assessment of the situation in the City. He had firm allies in Alderman Pennington, Venn, Foulke and Mainwaring. He could rely on the activity of the apprentices led by Samuel Barnardiston, son of Nathanial Barnardiston, a wealthy Suffolk landowner and member of the House, Sir Richard Wiseman, a half-crazed victim of the Star Chamber, and the redoubtable John Lilburne.[70] There were also the Puritan preachers, Cornelius Burgess, Calamy, Marshall and others who could be relied upon to whip up their congregations. Thus on 3 January Pym had seen to it that an order was sent from the Commons to the Lord Mayor, Aldermen and Common Council to call out the trained bands of the City 'for the safety of the King's person, the City and the Commonwealth'.[71]

So on 4 January the five members sat in their places in the Commons to await events. Pym had early warning that the king was approaching, sent to him by the countess of Carlisle, one of the queen's ladies, and sister to the earl of Northumberland.* Henrietta Maria in her anxiety for her husband had revealed his departure, an act for which she ever afterwards reproached herself, but which in fact could have made little difference. About 3.00 pm the House heard that the king was approaching with an armed guard, and they at once ordered the five to depart by barge. When the king entered the House accompanied by the Elector Palatine, he glanced to the right to the seat normally occupied by Pym. He approached the Speaker's chair with the words

* But Clarendon thought the secret was betrayed by William Murray, a Gentleman of the Bedchamber, a great friend of Lord Digby.[72]

'By your leave, Mr. Speaker, I must borrow your chair a little.' The Speaker stood down, the king sat, while members stood uncovered:

Gentlemen, I am sorry for this occasion of coming among you. Yesterday I sent a serjeant-at-arms to apprehend some that, by my command, were accused of high treason; whereupon I did expect obedience, and not a message. And I must declare unto you here that albeit no king that ever was in England shall be more careful of your privileges, to maintain them to the uttermost of his power, than I shall be, yet you must know that in cases of treason no person hath a privilege . . . Well, since I see all the birds are flown, I do expect from you that you shall send them unto me as soon as they return hither. But I assure you, in the word of a king, I never did intend any force, but shall proceed in a legal and fair way, for I never meant any other.

He asked the Speaker whether any were present, and received the famous reply: 'I have neither eyes to see, nor tongue to speak, in this place, but as the house is pleased to direct me.' Charles then strode out in anger to cries of 'Privilege! Privilege!'[73]

The only possible jusification for such an act would have been that it had succeeded; instead the whole attempt had been grossly bungled. It revealed indeed how primitive were the resources open to the king to achieve secrecy or effective action on such an occasion. It was a blunder that the king should have gone himself, but any deputy would have been open to the charge of treason. As it was, Charles had suffered a grave reverse, which he did his best to repair next day. Clarendon was presumably in the House on 4 January, and described the events in detail. He was in no doubt that the whole affair had been planned by Digby alone, and it was Digby who advised the next move. It was, in effect, to appeal to the authorities of the City of London over the heads of the Commons. The five had taken refuge in the City, and according to Clarendon, Digby offered to seek them out and capture them by force or kill them,[74] 'but the king liked not such enterprises'. Instead the king rode by coach to the City next morning, accompanied by only a few lords, and dined at the house of Alderman Garret. He then went on to Guildhall, where he asked for the surrender of the members accused of treason. He was civilly received by the authorities, but in the streets he was met with cries of 'Privilege of parliament!', and one stalwart cried 'To your tents, O Israel'.* The Lord Mayor, Sir Richard Gurney, who courteously escorted the king out of the City, was on his return attacked by a crowd, who broke his chain and tore his gown. The king had learnt to his surprise and bitter disappointment that he had lost London. It was a situation he had never contemplated. The weakness of his position was plainly revealed, and he had no plans as to what to do next. One thing was certain, that he should remain in Whitehall in order to rally moderate support, but instead he withdrew to Hampton Court, his immediate

* I Kings 12:16: 'So when all Israel saw that the king hearkened not unto them, the people answered the king, saying . . . to your tents, O Israel!'

concern being the safe departure of the queen with her daughter to Holland. In fact the next time Charles would see Whitehall it would be as a prisoner.

On 5 January the Commons had adjourned until the 11th, but, as if to emphasise their alliance with the City, a committee was appointed (including Lord Falkland) to sit at Grocers' Hall. On the 11th the five members returned in triumph; the House ignored the charge of treason, and condemned the breach of privilege. Thousands of people milled around Whitehall, 'asking with much contempt what was to become of the king and his cavaliers? and whither was he gone?'[75] Three thousand Buckinghamshire men had ridden in to defend their hero Hampden and their Parliament. Clarendon regarded 11 January as a turning-point:

From this day we may reasonably date the levying of war in England; whatsoever hath been since done being but the superstructures upon those foundations which were then laid.[76]

During the next few weeks columns of men from the home counties flocked to Westminster, many with petitions against economic hardship, for trade had been badly hit, and many of the poor faced destitution. Pym and his friends had to tread a difficult path between the need for popular support and the dangers of social revolt. Pym admitted as much in a speech on 24 January, when he spoke of the danger of tumults and insurrection:

of the meaner sort of people, by reason of their ill vent of cloth and other manufactures, whereby great multitudes are set on work, who live for the most part by their daily gettings, and will in a very short time be brought to great extremity if not employed. Nothing is more sharp and pressing than want; what they cannot buy they will take, and from them the like necessity will quickly be derived to the farmers and husbandmen, and so grow higher, and involve all men in an equality of misery and distress, if it be not prevented.[77]

It was the popular movement which had given the reformers impetus in their assault on royal power, but Pym saw that it could also bring about a royalist reaction.

Meanwhile the Commons proceeded to impeach the Attorney General for his accusations against the Five, and he was expelled the House. They impeached Lord Digby and Colonel Lunsford for a supposed military plot, although all that had happened had been that a few officers had met together at Kingston-upon-Thames, and then dispersed quietly. Digby had found it prudent to fly to Holland, but Lunsford was sent to the Tower.[78] The extent of the damage done by the attempt on the five members was now apparent. Pym's position was immensely stronger, resting as it did largely on the fears of the king's intentions, and belief in some kind of Catholic plot. His influence in the Commons had never been stronger. As Clarendon wrote: 'All men were now in union in both houses: the lords had not yet recovered the courage to dissent in any one proposition made to them from the commons.'[79] Here Clarendon was not quite fair to the Lords. The Commons in January turned to the problem of defence, and in doing so began acting almost as a soverign body. On 13 January they approved a declaration to the counties to put themselves in a state of defence.[80] Next day they appointed a committee to consider the fleet. They also resolved to enjoin the Lords that the Prince of Wales should be placed under the care of the marquis of Hertford. Next day they demanded that Sir John Byron should be dismissed as Lieutenant of the Tower. On the 25th they demanded that not only the Tower, but the principal forts of the kingdom (they had Hull and Portsmouth chiefly in mind), and the whole militia, should be placed under the command of those who had the confidence of parliament. This last demand was too much for the Lords, who refused to agree; but the Commons petitioned the king in their own name.

Since 4 January the king had been strictly on the defensive. He was anxious that the queen and princess should safely leave the country, and he was relieved when they sailed in February. Also, with the departure of Lord Digby, Charles came increasingly to rely on the advice of Falkland, Culpepper and Hyde. It is significant that after early December 1641 Hyde seems to have fallen silent in the House, and ceased to be appointed to committees. Clarendon made no secret of the fact that the three friends were deeply discouraged by the attempt to arrest the five members, but he said that they met together, usually at Hyde's house, every night to discuss the intelligence of the day, and then Hyde sent their advice to the king. They were convinced that the moderates in the Commons would respond to leadership. Clarendon said that from the debate on the Grand Remonstrance he was as unpopular as any man in the House, and although no one believed that he had anything to do with the events of 4 January, yet his friendship with Digby, and his nightly meetings with Falkland and Culpepper left the radicals in little doubt where Hyde stood. Hampden once snapped that he well knew that Hyde would like them all to be in prison.[81] For the next few months the king relied on Hyde's skilful pen to draft his replies to the Commons' demands, but the final decision always lay with the king, and we cannot be sure that the final document always reflected Hyde's views. Thus on 7 February the king gave a soft answer to the demand that those who commanded the militia and the forts should have the approval of parliament. He asked what powers these commanders should have, for how long, and what were the names proposed. The House proceeded to make their nominations, and meanwhile Charles escorted his wife out of England. When he returned and the Commons pressed for an answer, they were met with a firm refusal. He said that their proposal amounted to a complete alteration of government, deprived the king of all power, and gave the Commons a power greater than the law had given to the Crown. In anger the House resolved 'that those that advised the king to give this answer are enemies to the state, and mischievous projectors against the safety of the king and the peace of the kingdom'.[82] Hyde's advice henceforth was always that the king should take his stand firmly on constitutional precedent, admitting frankly that the incident of 4 January was a grievous error, but that the king must defend his just prerogative. Clarendon later stated his own position clearly:

He [Hyde] had a most zealous esteem and reverence for the construction of the government; and believed it so equally poised, that if the least branch of the prerogative was torn off, or parted with, the subject suffered by it, and that his right was impaired: and he was as much troubled when the crown exceeded its just limits, and thought its prerogative hurt by it.[83]

This was the view, he thought, most likely to attract moderate support. There were many who shrank from depriving the king of all military power. As Bulstrode Whitelocke argued in a speech on 2 March, the only happy situation was when king and parliament agreed, and since parliament had control of the purse-strings the independent powers of the king were limited:

I shall conclude then in my humble opinion, the power of the Militia is neither in the King alone nor in the Parliament, but if anywhere in the eye of our law, it is in the King and Parliament both consenting together. And I think it best that it should be there still. I cannot join in that advice to you, to settle the Militia of ourselves without the King, but rather with those worthy gentlemen who have moved that we yet again should petition his Majesty that the Militia may be settled in such hands as both he and you shall agree upon.[84]

Some such compromise would certainly have been welcomed by Falkland and Hyde. Four days before, the king was informed at Theobalds that unless he agreed to the Commons' terms, they would dispose of the militia by their own authority, and on 2 March they resolved 'that the kingdom be forthwith put into a posture of defence by authority of both houses'. On the 4th Pym made an inflammatory speech repeating the old exaggerations, that there was a design to alter the religion of the country, that the papal nuncio and the queen were in collusion, that the rebellion in Ireland was part of the plot, that the queen was preparing an army abroad, that Spain and France were preparing to send 4000 men apiece to alter religion and destroy parliament, and so on.[85] In this atmosphere of panic the Militia Ordinance was approved on 5 March. The Commons thus assumed sole legislative authority, nominated the Lords Lieutenant of the counties and authorised them to recruit and train the militia.[86]

Since 4 January the king had adopted a conciliatory role. He had withdrawn the charges against the five members, and on 13 February, on the advice of Sir John Culpepper had accepted the Clerical Disabilities Act excluding the bishops from the Lords, and all clergy from any executive authority in central or local government; and on the same day he accepted an Impressment Act.[87] The Militia Ordinance was however virtually an act of war against him. All commissions of lieutenancy granted under the great seal were declared illegal.

It was not sufficient that the king had withdrawn the charges against the Five, but on 8 March the impeachment of the Attorney General was instituted for bringing the charges in the first place.* On 15 March one Thomas Shawbridge was brought to the Bar of the House for calling Pym 'King Pym' and 'Rascal', and was sentenced to a fine of £100 and imprisonment, and the University of Cambridge was required to cancel his doctor's degree.†[88] The Star Chamber may have been abolished, but the House of Commons was proving to be an effective substitute. All this provided the moderate members with food for thought. Pym might have an assured majority in the Commons, but how far would this be accepted in the constituencies? Henry Killigrew, a stout Cornishman raised the question on 1 April. They stood, he said

here upon slippery places, and before we imposed the militia upon the people, or laid a tax on them, a knight and a burgess should do well to go into the country to see if they would consent and obey, lest we feel the weight of the major part of the people.[90]

Cornwall would certainly not stand for it, but Killigrew was censured by the House for saying so. He was the member who later, when members were invited to subscribe to Essex's army, made the famous reply that 'he would provide a good horse, a good sword and a buff coat, and then would find a good cause'.

Freedom of speech was becoming increasingly difficult in parliament. When the duke of Richmond made the sensible suggestion that parliament should adjourn for six months to allow a cooling-off period, he was denounced by the Commons as a malignant.[91] When Sir Ralph Hopton strongly defended the king's prerogative at the time of the Militia dispute, declaring that the House was condemning the king 'upon less evidence than would serve to hang a fellow for stealing a horse', he was sent to the Tower.[92] Clarendon wrote that spies were everywhere, and when the member for Plymouth, Thomas Trelawnay, said in private conversation 'that the house could not appoint a guard for themselves without the king's consent, under pain of high treason', he was sent to the Tower. A similar fate was dealt out to Sir Edward Dering who attempted to publish his speeches. Thus, commented Clarendon 'in this sad condition was the king fallen .. from a height and greatness that his enemies feared, to such lowness that his servants durst hardly avow the waiting on him'.[93]

Many members were intimidated, and after 4 January the prestige of John Pym was assured. But this cannot be the only explanation for his extraordinary success. The fear of royal power was widely felt, and was enhanced by the skilful way in which the reformers associated it with supposed dangers from

---

* On 29 April he was sentenced by the Lords to imprisonment in the Fleet.
† On 3 April for the same offence Edward Sanderford, a tailor was sentenced to be fined, pilloried, publicly whipped and imprisoned for the rest of his life.[89]

some papist conspiracy and plots to bring in troops from France or Spain. Every move of the king was regarded with suspicion, every rumour was credited, and it was very difficult for a moderate member to assess the situation dispassionately. Thus in Februrary Lord Falkland reported to the House on the aid France was reputed to be sending to Ireland. Presumably his report was negative, for the House decided not to protest to the French ambassador. On the same day he was teller against the motion that the Attorney General should be impeached, but it was carried by 65 to 48.[94] In February the House feared that the king might be intending to send the Prince of Wales abroad, and on the 24th ordered that the prince should remain at Hampton Court. Hyde was a member of a deputation of three sent to the king at Canterbury to express their fears concerning the prince. Charles gave a sharp reply, but Hyde begged a private audience and persuaded him to delay his answer until they reached Greenwich. At Greenwich Hyde had a long private audience at which the King bade Falkland, Culpepper and Hyde to draft what answer they would, 'for now I have gotten Charles [with him], I care not what answer I send them'. He said he now regretted having accepted the Bishops' Bill, which he did only for the safety of the queen. He told Hyde that he intended to go north, and would probably not see him again, but he required the three to keep him fully informed of parliamentary business. He promised absolute secrecy, 'that he would himself transcribe every paper in his own hand before he should shew it to any man', and before his secretary should write it out. Hyde replied that 'he writ a very ill hand' (which was true enough!), and that he would trust Secretary Nicholas. The king however insisted on carrying out the laborious task of copying his letters himself, and Clarendon said he adhered to this even when the communications were long and took him several days and far into the night.[95] It was such insights as this into his character that rapidly dispelled Hyde's earlier suspicions of the king, and convinced him that the loyalty of the nation could be recovered by gentle handling.

The king's answer was simply that he had sent for the prince to join him in Greenwich, and 'as to the fears and jealousies [expressed by the House], His Majesty knows not what answer to give, not being able to imagine from what grounds they proceed'.[96] On 2 March he referred again to these 'fears and jealousies':

You speak of jealousies and fears: Lay your hands to your hearts and ask yourselves whether I may not likewise be disturbed with fears and jealousies and, if so, I assure you this message [on the Militia] hath nothing lessened them . . . I assure you upon my honour, that I have no thought but of peace and justice to my people.[97]

The Militia Bill was a challenge to royal power which he could not tolerate, and it was in these circumstances that he took the fateful decision to move northwards to York.

# The Search for Peace

Hyde received the news of the king's intention to go northwards with considerable disquiet. He had hoped that now that the queen, who was the centre of so much suspicion, had gone to Holland Charles might return to Whitehall and pursue a policy of conciliation. For the moderates were alarmed at Pym's intentions, and especially with the Militia Bill, while others feared the rise of mob rule with the prospect of social upheaval. But Charles felt that with hostile crowds in Whitehall, and the threat of impeachment hanging over the heads of his servants, he would be deprived of freedom of action and might soon find himself a prisoner of Pym and his friends.[1]

At Newmarket, on his way north, the king received another list of grievances presented by a deputation headed by the earl of Pembroke, to which he gave a sharp reply:

I must tell you that I rather expected a vindication for the imputation laid on me in Master Pym's speech, than that any more general rumours and discourses should get credit with you . . . What would you have? Have I violated your laws? Have I denied to pass any one Bill for the ease and security of my subjects? I do not ask what you have done for me . . . All this considered, there is a judgment from heaven upon the nation, if these distractions continue.[2]

When Pembroke urged that the militia might be granted as parliament desired for a time, his Majesty swore by God: 'Not for an hour. You have asked that of me in this was never asked of any King, and with which I will not trust my wife and children.' Hyde was alarmed at the sharpness of the king's reply, and wrote off at once to beg him to send a more conciliatory answer from Huntingdon, pointing out that he had made no mention of Ireland, although that was an urgent problem; and warning him:

Men's discourses here are full of your Majesty's designs of immediate force, of a retreat into Scotland, of the divisions there, to none of which your servants give the least credit; assuring themselves that, however your affairs and conveniences have invited you to York, [that] you intend to sit as quietly there as if you were at Whitehall. For your Majesty well knows that your greatest strength is in the hearts and affections of those persons who have been the severest asserters of the public liberties, and so besides their duty and loyalty to your person, are in love with your inclinations to peace and justice, and value their own interests upon the preservation of your rights.[3]

This was a bold intimation to the king of the policy Hyde wished him to pursue, that he should avoid any act of violence, and rely upon rallying the support of moderate opinion, even of those who like Hyde had so far opposed him, once it was seen that he stood for the rule of law; that the king must not 'give the least hint to your people that he relied upon anything but the strength of his laws, and their obedience'.

The king complied so far as to send Hyde's message from Huntingdon, announcing his intention to take up residence in York (15 March). But there were few signs of conciliation from the Commons. They replied by insisting on the Militia Ordinance, and resolving that,

When the Lords and Commons in Parliament, which is the supreme Court of Judicature in the Kingdom, shall declare what the law of the land is, to have this not only questioned and controverted, but contradicted, and a command that it should not be obeyed, is a High Breach of Privilege of Parliament.

This referred to the king's rejection of the Militia Ordinance and amounted to a claim to complete legislative sovereignty for parliament, and the virtual elimination of the Crown from effective politics. When the king sent a long defence of his policy, parliament replied on 26 March by again raking over the past:

We beseech your Majesty to remember that the Government of this Kingdom, as it was in a great part managed by your Ministers before the beginning of this Parliament, consisted of many continued and multiplied acts of violation of laws; the wounds whereof were scarcely healed when the extremity of all those violations was far exceeded by the late strange and unheard of breach of our laws in the accusation of the Lord Kimbolton and Five Members of the Commons House and in the proceedings thereupon, for which we have received no full satisfaction.[4]

In one sense Pym's harping on this single incident was a sign of the weakness of his position, and it must have occurred to many that the attempt on the Five was certainly no worse than the imprisonment of the bishops on the flimsiest of pretexts. But as propaganda it seems to have been effective.

Hyde regarded it as essential that the dialogue should continue, for the alternative must be armed conflict, and that the king's constitutional position should be carefully defined. That definition during the ensuing months was largely the work of Falkland, Culpepper and Hyde, rather than of the king himself. It is merely confusing the issue to talk of Hyde having become a royalist, or of changing sides. He had occupied the middle ground throughout, discountenancing acts which he regarded as unconstitutional, such as the levy of ship money, but never endorsing Pym's emerging intention of destroying royal power. When he came to write his *History* he thought he might be accused of advising the king to make too many concessions, and himself of being too subservient to parliament. But, he wrote, 'it was necessary to remember the incredible disadvantage his majesty suffered by the misunderstanding of his going to the house of commons, and by the popular mistake of the privilege of parliament . . and, on the contrary, the great height and reputation the factious party had arrived at'. Hyde had a clearer view of the weakness of the king's position than many of his more flamboyant followers.

In these circumstances the position of the three friends in the Commons was becoming increasingly difficult, for since February, when Hyde had been seen twice in private conversation with the king at Canterbury and Greenwich, he was a marked man. The three expected to be sent to the Tower, and therefore decided never to attend the Commons at the same time.[5] Their official duties required the attendance of Falkland and Culpepper, but Hyde attended rarely, and this aroused suspicion. On 23 March the Commons ordered that Hyde should attend the House next day, and Falkland sent him a hurried note, beginning 'Dear Sweetheart', saying that he had made the excuse that Hyde was suffering from the stone, and was in the country for his health, but he urged him to attend next day.[6] The House was far from satisfied, and on 29 March ordered 'that Mr. Hyde be summoned forthwith to attend the service of the House, all excuses laid aside'.[7] It was clear that he could not remain much longer at Westminster, but his departure would mark the failure of his policy of conciliation.

Hyde's insistence that the dialogue must continue rested on the conviction that once the fear of the royal use of force was overcome moderate opinion would grow for a constitutional settlement. The main constitutional reforms had already been carried; the Prerogative Courts and ship money had been abolished, triennial parliaments secured, and church reform for the time being was shelved. But the Militia Ordinance had raised a fundamentally new issue which had alarmed moderate opinion not only in the Commons, but in the counties, where there was genuine uncertainty whether men were to obey parliament or the king. During his leisurely progress northwards Charles had been well received at many points, and this had given him somewhat premature confidence in the strength of his support in the counties. At York, Clarendon wrote: 'the king found himself at ease; the country had received him with great expressions of joy and duty, and all persons of quality of that great county, and of the counties adjacent, resorted to him, and many persons of condition from London who had not the courage to attend upon him at Whitehall; so that the court appeared with some lustre'.[8] But this display of loyalty was in some respects illusory. In 1640 the Yorkshire gentry had been practically united against Wentworth, and some of them like Thomas, Lord Savile had certainly been in correspondence with the Scots. The opposition then was led by Sir Hugh Cholmley and Sir John Hotham. It is true that by the beginning of the Civil War royalist gentry in Yorkshire outnumbered the parliamentary gentry by two to one, but there were as many neutral families as royalist ones.[9] What the great majority of the gentry wanted in the spring of 1642 was a peaceful settlement of the constitutional issue.

The same was true of Kent, which had petitioned against the bishops in January 1641, and which had then had Sir Edward Dering as its mouthpiece. During the course of the year Dering changed his mind: the debate on the Grand Remonstrance was a parting of the ways. He denied that the bishops stood for idolatry, and above all he objected to the use of the Remonstrace as a propagandist appeal to the people. So far his political stance had been shaped by ecclesiastical issues, but by 1642 he was forced to question the basic tenets of Pym's policy. So were many of his Kentish constituents.[10]

This is nowhere better illustrated than in the Journal of Dering's friend and neighbour Sir Roger Twysden. He wrote that no man had welcomed the summoning of the Long Parliament more than he did, but his doubts began with the destruction of the earl of Strafford, for how would it benefit the people if the domination of Strafford was replaced by the domination of Pym? What Twysden wanted was the passing of good laws by which the king must govern, not a struggle for power. His doubts increased when in January 1641 the justices of the peace for Aylesford received an order of the Commons to imprison recusants who refused to give their names, and again in August when the Commons required JPs to disarm all Popish recusants. He said he knew no law justifying these orders.

That which troubled me in my Lord's (Strafford's) execution was, that if penal Statutes, even those concerning treason, might be expounded, not according to the letter, but by equity, I did not see any man could be certain not to be impeached of treason.

Still more was he alarmed by the Act perpetuating the life of Parliament:

The perpetuating of the houses I did ever look at as the second part of the XXX tyrants of Athens [of whom Xenophon] that would never end unless forced. Men in authority do not easily quit that they have possessed themselves of . . . I dare boldly say there is no example in history of any temporary Court having a perpetuity annexed to it, that did cver end but necessitated.

That Act of March 1641, he declared, was 'initium malorum nostrorum'. Moreover the Commons inflicted punishments on those who offended them, without any shadow of legality, in the name of 'breach of privilege'. After the attempt to arrest the five members in January 1642, Twysden noted that the Commons stirred up the counties to petition against the act, and that the petitions were drawn up in London, not the counties:

I never doubted the true and real intent of the Parliament in encouraging men to this [petition] was to see the strength of their party, and intimidate the King.

One remark of the king particularly impressed him:

That which wrought most on me was one clause in his Majesty's speech at Newmarket, 9 March 1642, wherein he urged them to say whether he had refused to pass any one bill for the ease and security of the subject, adding: 'I do not ask what you have done for me', intimating they had done nothing.[11]

It is probably true that there were few who saw the issues quite so clearly as Sir Roger Twysden, but doubts were growing, and the Militia Ordinance forced men to take sides. In February 1642 a small group of Kentish Puritans led by Sir Michael Livesey and Sir Anthony Weldon sent a petition to parliament which was based on a model sent down from London, and was held to represent the views of only a minority of the Kentish gentry. On 21 March, before the Assizes at Maidstone, a number of gentlemen, including Sir Roger Twysden, Sir Edward Dering, Sir George Strode, met together at the Star Inn and discussed the political situation, and decided upon a petition to parliament. Twysden wrote that there were many things they wanted to include in the petition which discretion dictated should be omitted. The first draft was several times amended, but finally accepted in open court. It was a moderate document requesting the observance of the liturgy of the Church of England; that changes should be only by a national synod; and that 'the precious liberty of the subject, the common birth-right of every Englishman, may be preserved entire; that no order of either or both Houses, not grounded on the laws of the land, may be enforced on the subject, until it be fully enacted by Parliament'. It was this clause, aimed as it was against the Militia Ordinance and the exercise of jurisdiction by the Commons, which enraged the reformers. Finally the petition asked for a speedy understanding between king and parliament. Twysden wrote:

I saw nothing of ill in this petition. Neither had I other intent in the assenting to it than that there might be a fair intelligence between the King and the two Houses by their complying with his Majesty, without ever trying who was the strongest, and the subject governed by laws, not by arbitrary revocable votes.

The right of citizens to petition was traditional, but when the petition was to be presented to the Commons on 29 March, Pym forestalled it. After a conference with the Lords a committee of twelve peers (ten of whom were close adherents of Pym's) and twenty-four of the Commons (almost every one was a follower of Pym) was appointed to hear the evidence. Witnesses were examined: the earl of Bristol, Twysden, Dering and Strode were ordered to be detained. Dering had disappeared, but his impeachment was begun. Mr. Justice Malet, who had presided over the Maidstone Assizes, was imprisoned. Pym sought thus to make a simple petition into a conspiracy against parliament, and to discourage similar petitions. The petition was nonetheless presented on the 30th, not by the authors, but by two Cavaliers, the poet Richard Lovelace and Sir William Boteler, both of whom were committed to prison.[12]

S. R. Gardiner underlined the significance of The Kentish petition: 'if any one moment can be selected as that in which the Civil War became inevitable, it was that of the vote of March 28 by which the Kentish petitioners were treated as criminals'.[13] It has been recounted at some length here because it provides a fitting background to Hyde's thinking at this time, and it illustrates the way in which Pym was driving the king into a position from which force would appear the only escape. Hyde's assessment of the situation was almost exactly that of Sir Roger Twysden and his friends who met at the Star Inn at Maidstone and drew up the petition; who wanted the maintenance of episcopacy, were concerned at the growing pretensions of the Commons, and earnestly longed for an agreement between parliament and the king. It is not of course suggested that this was the opinion of all the Kentish gentry. The Oxinden family, for instance, were split down the middle in their support for the king and for parliament, but in their case the side chosen was determined almost entirely on religious grounds, with little apparent understanding of wider constitutional issues. Even so, one of their correspondents wrote in August 1642 that in his area (Leeds Abbey), he thought that five gentlemen would obey the king's commission of array for every one who adhered to parliament.[14] Pym however would use all the power of the Commons to suppress moderate, as well as royalist opinion, and thus make armed conflict inevitable.

The war of words continued between York and Westminster during the Spring and Summer of 1642, but both sides thought increasingly of armed conflict. If there was to be war Hull and Portsmouth were of first importance. Hull was not only a gateway to the continent, but had a large magazine which both sides were determined to possess, and parliament was preparing to ship the arms to the Tower of London. It was necessary therefore for the king to act quickly. On 22 April the young duke of York and the Elector Palatine visited the city, and were entertained to a banquet by the Governor, Sir John Hotham, when the news arrived that the king himself intended to dine with them, and that he was accompanied by three hundred horse. Hotham sent a message begging the king not to come since he could not admit him without a breach of trust. The drawbridge was then raised and the gates closed. When the king appeared before the Beverley gate, Hotham professed his loyalty, offered to admit the king and twelve followers, but no more. After some hours the king retired to Beverley and pronounced Hotham a traitor. On 28 April the Commons resolved that declaring Hotham a traitor, being a member of the Commons, was 'a high breach of the privilege of Parliament'.[15]

The incident was a grave shock to royal prestige, and what most concerned Hyde and his friends was that it increased the conviction in the Commons that the king intended to make war. Most men, both in parliament and in the country required only a peaceful settlement of an issue which was confusing, and in which faults were not all on one side. Whichever side was made to appear the aggressor would be at a disadvantage. Clarendon wrote:

if the king should commit such an outrage as to levy war against his parliament, to destroy the religion, laws and liberty of the kingdom, good men were persuaded that such a resistance might be made as might preserve the whole.[16]

Once the king had been declared the aggressor, it would be easy to persuade many men to defend parliament, and thus men who wanted only peace would be led into war. This was why Hyde and his friends strove desperately to keep the dialogue going, and hence the formidable number of lengthy documents which passed between Westminster and York.

Clarendon said that about the end of April the king had required him to go to York, but that the friends agreed that he could still be more useful at Westminster. Despatches were sent to the king almost daily, and so efficient was the courier system that he said that a letter sent at midnight on Saturday would bring the king's answer by 10 am on Monday.[17] But by the middle of May Hyde concluded that it was too dangerous to remain any longer. He had, as we have seen, been in the country in March ostensibly for his health, only to be peremptorily ordered to return to the House. Now he slipped away to the house of Lady Lee, at Ditchley, near Oxford, and lay in hiding until he learned that Lord Keeper Littleton had also gone to York, sending the Great Seal by a groom of the privy chamber and another route. Henceforth, with the Great Seal, royal documents would regain their legal validity. Hyde then left Ditchley with William Chillingworth as guide, and by a circuitous route through Leicestershire and Derbyshire, reached Nostell Priory, some twenty miles from York, the home of Sir John Worstenholme, where he was expected. Next day the king sent John Ashburnham to him, and he set about preparing yet another reply to parliament. A few days later he was summoned to the king at York, and his first task was to beg him not to dismiss Littleton, who had alienated the king by his timidity. He reminded Charles that Littleton 'had newly escaped out of that region where the thunder and lightning is made; and that he could hardly yet recover the fright he had been often in, and seen so many others in'. Such was the fear inspired by the power of the Commons in 1642.[18] Nor did Hyde find welcome at the lodgings provided for him in York, for it transpired that his landlord held a grudge against him for the part he had played in abolishing the Council of the North, in which he had had good employment, and Hyde hastily moved to accommodation provided by a prebendary of York Minster.[19] By now there was a considerable exodus of members and peers from Westminster to York, including Lord Falkland and Sir John Culpepper.

On 1 June the truncated houses of parliament agreed to the Nineteen Propositions to be sent to the king. They were intended to be their final ultimatum before open conflict. After a statement of their duty to the king the demands were that all members of the Privy Council and all officers of state should require the consent of parliament; that all business of state should be debated in parliament, and not elsewhere; that the education of the king's children, and any royal marriages, should be approved by parliament; that the reform of the church and liturgy should be as parliament should advise; that parliament should have control of the militia; that judges should be appointed with the approval of parliament; that all forts should be under the command of those approved by parliament; that Lord Kimbolton and the five members be cleared of all charges by Act of Parliament; and that all future peers would require the approval of parliament. If all this was accepted the parliament would regulate the royal revenues to his advantage.[20]

Clarendon summed it up accurately when he wrote that the Nineteen Propositions 'contained the disinherison of the crown of all its choice regalities, and left only the shadow and empty name of the king'.[21] Falkland and Culpepper prepared the king's answer before they reached York, dividing the paragraphs between them, Culpepper dealing with the constitutional paragraphs. They sent the draft to the king with the request that it be published after Hyde had approved it. When they reached York they were surprised to find it still in Hyde's possession. Clarendon wrote that he was dissatisfied with what he thought to be a constitutional gaffe in Culpepper's version. Culpepper had accepted that the king, the house of peers and the house of commons were the three estates of the realm. If this were true, then the king could always be outvoted by the other two. But the traditional theory was that the three estates of the realm were the lords spiritual, the lords temporal and the commons, the king being above the three estates. However Clarendon wrote that when Falkland arrived and found the answer still unpublished, he quarrelled with Hyde, saying that 'he disliked it because he had not writ it himself'. Hyde was so hurt that he at once accepted the answer, which went that night to the printers. Later, Clarendon said, both the king and Falkland recognised the error, and regretted it.

This interpretation has recently been questioned by Weston and Greenberg, who thought that Hyde himself was more concerned with the omission of the bishops as an estate of the realm than with the reflection on the status of the king, and that at the time Hyde was content that the king should be regarded merely as one of the estates in the legislative process. However that may be, the reference to the three estates was omitted in the 1643 edition of the king's answer. By then however the damage, if any, had been done.[22]

The king's answer to the Nineteen Propositions was of profound importance in establishing the principles upon which under Hyde's guidance the monarchy henceforth based its constitutional position. The king professed his willingness to leave any of his councillors or ministers to the justice of the law where they could be shown to have offended, but this would not apply to those whose only fault was that they follow their conscience, and preserve the established laws, and agree not in such votes, or assent not unto such Bills, as some persons who have now too great an influence even upon both Houses, judge or seem to judge to be for the public good, and as are agreeable to that new Utopia of Religion and Government into which they endeavour to transform this kingdom.

Nor would the king agree to dismiss ministers who had served him well. Since parliament required the judges to hold their places *quamdiu se bene gesserint* 'we are resolved to be as careful of those we have chosen as you are of those you would choose'.

But this demand, as unreasonable as it is, is but one link of a great chain, and but the first round of that ladder, by which Our Just, Ancient, Royal Power is endeavoured to be fetched down to the ground. For it appears plainly, that it is not with the persons now chosen, but with Our choosing that you are displeased.

In practice all the king's nominations would be rejected by virtue of the fact that he had made them. If all ministers and councillors were to be, in effect, appointed by parliament, and all business to be discussed only in parliament, this would be tantamount 'to depose both Ourself and Our Posterity'.

These being passed, We may be waited on bare-headed, We may have Our hand kissed, the style of Majesty continued to Us, and the King's authority declared by both Houses of Parliament may be still the style of your commands; We may have swords and maces carried before Us, and please Ourself with the sight of a crown and sceptre (and yet even these twigs would not long flourish, when the stock upon which they grew were dead), but as to true and real power, We should remain but the outside, but the picture, but the sign of a King.

It was true that laws could be made only in the High Court of Parliament, but the king was part of that parliament, and had as much right to reject a bill as the Commons had, and he had as much right to take advice from whom he pleased as the Commons had. The constitution of England was a mixed government.

The experience and wisdom of your ancestors hath so moulded this out of a mixture [of monarchy, aristocracy and democracy] as to give this Kingdom the conveniences of all three, without the inconveniences of any one, as long as the balance hangs even between the three Estates, and they run jointly on in their proper channel . . . The ill of absolute monarchy is tyranny; the ill of aristocracy is faction and division; the ills of democracy are tumults, violence and licentiousness. The good of monarchy is the uniting a nation under one head, to resist invasion from abroad, and insurrection at home; the good of aristocracy is the conjunction of council in the ablest persons of a state for the public benefit; the good of democracy is liberty, and the courage and industry which liberty begets.

In England there was a 'regulated Monarchy' based on law and the rights of property. The House of Commons was 'an excellent conserver of liberty, but never intended for any share in government, or the choosing of them that should govern'. Their power lay in control of taxation and the powers of impeachment. The House of Lords were entrusted with the judicatory power, and were 'an excellent screen and bank between the Prince and the People'. To secure the rights of parliament the king had agreed to Triennial Parliaments, and had surrendered the right to dissolve the present parliament, in return for which he expected a similar moderation from parliament. The powers of parliament were sufficient to prevent tyranny, but what was demanded by them was 'a total subversion of the Fundamental Laws, and that excellent Constitution of this Kingdom', and 'there would be nothing left for Us but to look on'. Nor would this be the end, for the decline of royal power would soon be followed by the destruction of the House of Lords, and this would be followed by the destruction of

all Rights and Properties, all distinctions of family and merit; and by this means this splendid and excellently distinguished form of government end in a dark equal chaos of confusion, and the long line of our many noble ancestors in a Jack Cade or a Wat Tyler. For all these reasons to all these demands Our answer is, *Nolumus Leges Angliae mutari*: but this we promise, that we will be as careful of preserving the laws in what is supposed to concern wholly our subjects, as in what most concerns Our Self.

As to the Church of England, the king declared that there was no church on earth with more purity of doctrine, but in matters indifferent, on which there were differences of opinion, he was prepared to agree to liberty for tender consciences, provided that could be done peacefully and decently. He was ready to listen to further proposals from parliament on church reform.

It was a masterly document, and represented genuine concessions on the part of the king, setting forth as it did the theory of a 'regulated monarchy' to which Edward Hyde adhered for the rest of his life, and almost exactly mirroring the Restoration settlement of 1660. The historian is tempted to conclude that if it had been accepted in 1642 England would have been saved much misery and two civil wars. But on neither side was there a delay in military preparations. On 5 May 1642 parliament issued the Militia Ordinance which the king at once forbade his subjects to obey.

Honest citizens were placed in an uncomfortable dilemma. Thomas Knyvett, living in the strongly Puritan area of East Anglia, received an order from the earl of Warwick to take up his militia commission for parliament:

I was surprised what to do, whether to take or refuse. 'Twas no place to dispute, so I took it.[23]

But a few hours later he heard of the command of the king:

This distraction made me to advise with some understanding men what condition I stand in, which is no other than a great many men of quality do.

He concluded that in such an unpleasant circumstance he must listen to the dictates of his conscience. Surrounded by a rampant Puritanism, Knyvett commented, 'Poor King, he grows still in more contempt and slight here every day'. He still had great confidence that parliament would be able to achieve a legal settlement, but on 24 May he saw the faults on both sides:

They are extreme bad councillors that shall excite the King to begin a war against his people. The first blows will wound deep. There is another remonstrance coming out from the Parliament that runs higher yet. . . . I think we have no peace makers left.

A week later he despaired of a peaceful settlement, while putting his finger on the essential irony of the situation:

Both strive for the maintenance of the laws, and the question is not so much how to be governed by them, as who shall be master and judge of them; a lamentable condition to consume the wealth and treasure of such a kingdom, perhaps the blood too, upon a few nice wilful quibbles.

Thirteen months later, when he was in prison as a royalist, Knyvett concluded that what God really wanted was that

he will have neither side be absolutely prevalent in this quarrel, but that a middle way of accommodation that might settle a peaceable government in the Church and Commonwealth would best please him.

There were still men of moderation on both sides, but as usual they seemed powerless to stem the tide of war. Hyde's old friend Bulstrode Whitelocke, who had remained at Westminster, and supported both the Militia Ordinance and the Nineteen Propositions, was nonetheless full of foreboding, as any man might be with an estate worth £3800 a year:

It seems to me to set us at the pit's brink, ready to plunge ourselves into an ocean of troubles and miseries . . . It is strange to note how we have insensibly slid into this beginning of a civil war by one unexpected accident after another, as waves of the sea which have brought us this far and we scarce know how . . . What the issue of it will be no man alive can tell. Probably few of us here may live to see the end of it.[24]

But, he concluded,

When I have said this, I am not for a lame resignation of our Religion, lives and liberties into the hands of our adversaries, who seek to devour us; nor do I think it inconsistent with your great wisdom to prepare for a just and necessary defence of them.[25]

Men of moderation found it difficult to gain a hearing, for Pym refused to suspend war preparations, and frequently stifled discussions of peace terms. It was easy for 'fiery spirits' like Holles and Strode, bent as they were on war, to silence men of peace like Edmund Waller and Sir John Potts. But the most impressive of all the speeches for peace came from old Sir Benjamin Rudyerd on 9 July 1642: they were, he said on the brink of war:

I am touched, I am pierced, with an apprehension of the honour of the House and success of this Parliament. The best way to give a stop to these desperate imminent mischiefs, is to make a fair way for the King's return hither; it will likewise give the best satisfaction to the people and will be our best justification.

The times were full of danger, but how much they had already achieved!

We have a Parliament, ship money is abolished, monopolies, High-Commission Court, Star Chamber, the votes of bishops all taken away, the Council regulated, forests limited, triennial parliaments, and a perpetual parliament.

Had they been told all this three years before they would have thought it 'a dream of happiness',

yet now we are in the real possession of it, we do not enjoy it, although his Majesty hath promised and published he will make all this good to us. . . . Let us beware we do not contend for such a hazardous unsafe security as may endanger the loss of what we have already. Let us not think we have nothing because we have not all we desire; and though we had, yet we cannot make a mathematical security, all humane caution is susceptible of corruption and failing . . . Mr Speaker, It now behoves us to call up all the wisdom we have about us, for we are at the very brink of combustion and confusion. If blood begins once to touch blood, we shall presently fall into a certain misery . . .*26

Such warnings were ignored, and three days later the Commons resolved that an army should be raised 'for the safety of the King's person, defence of both Houses of Parliament . . . and the true religion, laws, liberty and peace of the Kingdom'.27

For many men there was now a second parting of the ways. Lord Paget, as he journeyed northwards to join the king, wrote to Hyde that he had so far supported reform, but now he must

desert the cause. Most true it is, that my ends were the common good, and that as long as it was prosecuted, I was ready to lay down my life and fortune. But when I found a preparation of arms against the King under the shadow of loyalty, I rather resolved to obey a good conscience than particular end; and now am on my way to his Majesty, where I will throw myself at his feet, and will die a loving subject.28

In contrast the earl of Pembroke was in an agony of indecision, and tried to keep a foot in both camps, thus earning Clarendon's contempt when he came to write his *History*. Hyde in July tried to win him over to the king's side. Pembroke's son, Lord Herbert, professed loyalty to the king, but said it was necessary for his health to take the waters at Tunbridge Wells. His father had retired to Wilton, but Herbert said he could be won over if the king would assure him of 'the preservation of parliaments, laws, liberties and religion'. What however was no doubt the principal consideration to Pembroke was that

* The king was so pleased with the speech that he ordered its immediate publication.

the earls of Warwick and Bedford were within striking distance of Wilton. In the end Pembroke threw in his lot with parliament.[29]

Clarendon wrote that by July 1642 the House of Lords had been reduced to about one-fifth, and the Commons by one-half, and an impressive number of peers and gentry had gathered around the king at York, but that few preparations had been made for war, partly because most of the king's Council doubted whether parliament would actually make war, but still more because 'the king had no possibility to procure either arms or munitions but from Holland'.[30] Also, many feared the thunders of parliament, and no doubt remembered the fate of Strafford, who had been accused of levying war on parliament. The most that many would do would be to defend the king against attack, but, in Clarendon's phrase, they 'lacked the mettle' for offensive war. It was indeed essential that the king should not appear the aggressor. Thus on 13 June was published a statement that the king had no intention of making war, and desired only a settlement respecting the privileges of parliament, and the liberty of the subject, signed by the duke of Richmond, the marquis of Hertford, eighteen earls and fifteen peers.[31] Clarendon asked wryly why such an impressive collection of peers had not made greater use of their numbers in the House of Lords at Westminster! His answer was that they had been driven out by intimidation, and that the same was true of the Commons where moderate men were declared to be enemies of their country, and where free speech had become impossible. Thus when moderate men were driven out, it was easy for Pym and his friends to carry their policies:

What had been, upon full and solemn debates in a full house, rejected, was many times, in a thin house, and at unsual and unparliamentary hours, resumed, and determined contrary to the former conclusions.[32]

In answer to parliament's Militia Ordinance the king issued Commissions of Array. The great lawyer John Selden condemned both as being equally illegal. When the royalist Lord Mayor of London, Sir Richard Gurney, and the Recorder Sir Thomas Gardiner, attempted to implement the king's commission, they were impeached by parliament and imprisoned. (18 August 1642).[33] Clarendon wrote that at this time, while the earl of Essex was gathering a sizeable force,

the king had not one barrel of powder nor one musket, nor any other provision necessary for an army; and, which was worse, was not sure of any port to which they might be securely assigned; nor had he money for the support of his own table for the term of one month.[34]

The king's commander of the fleet, Sir John Pennington, was replaced by the parliamentary earl of Warwick, and the only port the king could safely use was Newcastle. In Holland the queen was selling the royal jewels and attempting to raise money from the Dutch; in the end she had considerable success, raising a total of two million pounds. But progress was slow, and when she managed to send one small ship through the blockade, the king had greatly to exaggerate the supplies of 200 barrels of gunpowder, the two or three thousand arms and the few field pieces he actually received.[35] Beyond this he was dependent on the subscriptions of the nobility, who, Clarendon said, thought the conflict would be over in three months.

On 15 July a final effort at peace was made when the earl of Holland brought a petition from the two Houses, offering to cancel military preparations if the king did the same. The earl reminded the king that his father had been famed as a peacemaker, and he hoped that his majesty would be one also. The king, who had just returned from Lincoln, was angry at the news of parliament's military preparations; and the petition seemed to make few concessions. His reply therefore was sharp. It must have been written by Hyde, and Sir Philip Warwick[36] later complained that Hyde had been carried away by the fluency of his pen, and was too niggling in his objections to the petition, especially as the earl of Holland had given a private guarantee that the king would be given satisfaction. The king demanded that the town of Hull be handed over to him, that the command of the navy be restored to his nominee, and that all armies be disbanded. Without these conditions there could be no peace.

Hyde therefore must bear some responsibility for the king's rejection of parliament's offer, however unpromising the terms might have appeared and he admitted as much in his *History*.[37] As it was the earl of Holland, who might have been won over, was alienated and threw in his lot with the parliamentarians. On 12 July the Commons resolved 'that an army be forthwith raised for the safety of the king's person, defence of both houses of parliament ... and preserving of the true religion, the laws, liberty and peace of the kingdom'; and the earl of Essex was appointed General.[38] However, it is more likely that Holland's mission had been a mere exercise in public relations, for on 4 July Pym had established a Committee of Safety for the conduct of the war, and was already seizing the property of many who had joined the king. The duke of Richmond, Lord Dorset, Sir Thomas Fanshawe, Sir Arthur Capel, and others suffered in this way. No wonder that the earl of Pembroke chose to remain at Wilton to see which way the wind blew.

In contrast the king's preparations for war were faltering. Clarendon wrote that Charles was so short of money that he could not maintain tables at Court for his officers of state. There were few arms and munitions, and recruitment was slow, for landowners were more concerned to harvest their crops than to prepare for war.[39] When the king raised his standard at Nottingham on 22 August the response was poor. It was clear to him that he was in no condition to advance on London. He appeared to be strong in the north, although Hull in parliamentary hands deprived him of a convenient port. Parliament was strong in the east of England. It was important then that Charles should secure the west country which with Wales would be a valuable recruiting ground, and enable him to maintain contact with Ireland. An early success came when Colonel Goring seized Portsmouth for the king. There was a hopeful sign from Somerset in June, when the knights, gentry, clergy and freeholders of the county petitioned parliament for the maintenance of the established church and the restoration of peace. But in fact in most of the western counties except Cornwall (which was strongly royalist) public opinion was fairly evenly divided between the two sides; Wiltshire and Gloucestershire were predominantly for parliament, and the parliamentarians were more successful at recruitment than the royalists. In fact the country gentry were sorely divided by the development of an unexpected and unwanted civil war. Many of them had opposed the forced loans and ship money levies of Charles I; some had embraced Puritanism. In 1640 they had presented a fairly united front in favour of moderate reform, such as Hyde had supported. The first doubts had been raised in some minds at the political murder of the earl of Strafford, and some were opposed to the attacks on the Prayer Book and episcopacy. But the real test had come with the Militia Ordinance which traditionalists saw as an infringement of the royal prerogative. The historically and traditionally minded could not admit the transference of sovereignty from the king to parliament. They shrank from revolution, but they shrank also from civil war. They opposed arbitrary government whether of the king or of parliament, and this sentiment was reinforced if they also opposed alteration in religion. A natural conservatism, family traditions and religious sentiment drew many to the king's side. But in most counties they were opposed by a well-organised and determined parliamentary party, who were equally convinced that they were defending the law and the rights of Englishmen. It was not always a division based on class;* many families were internally split. It was often more a matter of temperament and reaction to circumstances.

Clarendon had a vivid memory of a conversation with Sir Edmund Verney, shortly before the battle of Edgehill. Verney said that Hyde was lucky in that he was sure that the king's cause was right,

but for my part, I do not like the quarrel, and do heartily wish that the king would yield and consent to what they desire; so that my conscience is only concerned in honour and in gratitude to follow my master. I have eaten his bread, and served him near thirty years, and will not do so base a thing as to forsake him; and choose rather to lose my life (which I am sure I shall do) to preserve and defend those

---

* Clarendon however saw a class basis to the division:

For though the gentlemen of ancient families and estates in that county (Somerset) were for the most part well affected to the king, and easily discerned by what faction the parliament was governed; yet there were a people of an inferior degree, who, by good husbandry, clothing, and other thriving arts, had gotten very great fortunes; and, by degrees, getting themselves into the gentlemen's estates, were angry that they found not themselves in the same esteem and reputation with those whose estates they had; and therefore, with more industry than the other, studied all ways to make themselves considerable. These, from the beginning, were fast friends to the parliament.[40]

things which are against my conscience to preserve and defend: for I . . . have no reverence for the bishops, for whom this quarrel (exists).

So Verney fought out of traditional loyalty, was the king's standard-bearer, and was killed, as he had foretold.[42]

The king's General-in-Chief was the earl of Lindsey, an elderly and ineffectual man of little military experience. Command in the west was given to the marquis of Hertford, with commissions issued to Sir Ralph Hopton and Lord Berkeley to raise armies in the six western counties, while a Cornish army was raised by Lord Mohun and Sir Bevil Grenville, mainly from the tenantry of the gentry and at their expense. The war began badly for the royalists. The marquis of Hertford surrendered Sherborne Castle in September; most of his troops retired to Wales, while Hopton retreated into Cornwall. Hopton was a Puritan in religion and a constitutionalist in politics. He had supported the Grand Remonstrance, but refused to accept the Militia Ordinance, and went over to the king's cause. In Cornwall, with the powerful aid of Sir Bevil Grenville, he recruited a substantial army, supplied with arms by the queen from France, and paid for by Cornish tin. The queen's aid at this time was invaluable, and by November she had sent into Newcastle, Weymouth and Falmouth arms sufficient for 10,000 foot and 2000 horse.[42] Plymouth and Exeter were formidable obstacles in Hopton's way, but in January 1643 he defeated Colonel Ruthven and parliamentarians at the battle of Braddock Down, near Liskeard, and thus secured Cornwall for the king. He went on to capture Saltash, although Plymouth was too strong for him. In February little Sidney Godolphin, one of the Great Tew circle, was killed in the engagement. Clarendon was by no means the only one who paid tribute to his nobility of character. Hobbes wrote of him as 'my most noble and honoured friend . . . who hating no man, nor hated of any, was unfortunately slain . . . in a public quarrel, by an undiscerned and an undiscerning hand'.[43] He was a minor poet of great charm:

> 'Tis true, the object sanctifies
> All passions which within us rise,
> But since no creature comprehends
> The cause of causes, end of ends,
> He who himself vouchsafes to know
> Best pleases his creator so.

Meanwhile the king, advancing westwards towards Worcester, in September 1642, encountered part of Essex's army at Powick Bridge. Prince Rupert's cavalry attacked and dispersed them in the first major battle of the war. Clarendon wrote that the victory was 'of unspeakable advantage and benefit to the king, rendering the name of prince Rupert very terrible', and giving his cavalry the reputation of invincibility. Charles then collected reinforcements from Shrewsbury and advanced towards London. Essex who was at

Worcester, moved in pursuit, and the two armies, roughly equal in size, met at Edgehill, in Northamptonshire (23 October). At Rupert's first cavalry charge one wing of the enemy fled, but he threw away the chance of complete victory by a reckless pursuit, and the royalist centre were badly mauled. Clarendon thought that if either side had had the vigour for a final charge they must have won a complete victory.[45] However next morning both armies remained in the field, but with no desire to renew the battle, and next day the earl of Essex withdrew to Warwick, pursued by Rupert's cavalry. The advantage therefore lay with the king, for the way lay open to London, and this was perhaps his greatest chance of victory. But he was badly shaken by the carnage of the battle, full of uncertainty, and having taken Banbury castle, he retired instead to Oxford, which, Clarendon commented, 'was the only city of England that he could say was entirely at his devotion'.[46]

While military operations continued, so did the war of words. On 16 September Parliament declared that there could be no peace until 'the authors and instruments of these mishiefs' were handed over to the justice of parliament; and the king was accused of 'leading in your Person an Army against [Parliament] as if you intended by conquest to establish an absolute and illimited power over them'. The king, on his side, repeated that his sole intention was 'to defend the true reformed Protestant religion, the known laws and the liberty and property of the subject'.[47] On 22 October the king's 'Declaration to his loving subjects' urged:

Let all honest men remember the many gracious acts we have passed this Parliament for the ease and benefit of our people, that when there was nothing left undone, or unoffered by us, which might make this nation happy, these mischievous contrivers of ruin, instead of acknowledging our grace and justice, upbraided us with all the reproaches malice and cunning could invent, in a Remonstrance to the people.[48]

The king could live in considerable comfort at Christ Church; the great shortage was of money and munitions. One course of action was to spend the winter at Oxford, relying on the prestige the royalists had gained at Edgehill, and await overtures of peace, for there was a growing peace party at Westminster. The alternative was an early attack on London with a view to a speedy end to the war. Success would have great advantages, especially in view of the king's limited resources, but failure would alarm and embitter London and defeat the chances of a negotiated peace. The king chose action, and in November advanced to Reading. At Colnbrook on 11 November he received a parliamentary deputation headed by the earls of Northumberland and Pembroke, asking him to receive peace commissioners. He agreed, and Clarendon discussed whether it might have been better to await the commissioners rather than press on. But Rupert swept on, sacked Brentford, and advanced to Turnham Green, where he found the earl of Essex and the trained bands blocking his way. The royalists had to retire, leaving Londoners with renewed fears of the king's intentions, and allowing parliament to accuse him of bad faith in attacking during peace negotiations. They were able to turn the king's failure to considerable advantage. They published the king's letters to the queen, which had been intercepted, announcing his intention to attack London. They were also able to use the alarm to justify an ordinance for a forced loan from the City, which soon developed into a monthly tax of £6000, a far heavier burden than Charles I had ever imposed. When the king received parliament's terms at Reading, they proved to be merely insulting, requiring him to return to Westminster without his army or councillors. Charles gave an immediate reply in 'indignation and scorn', that those who had failed to snatch the crown from his head, now asked him to surrender it voluntarily.[49] He then went into winter quarters at Oxford.

To those about the Court there was a strong feeling that although the military advantage lay with the king, yet parliament was far more successful in raising money, and had the advantage in the propaganda war. In December therefore Hyde wrote and the king published a Declaration intended to reverse the situation and encourage the moderates at Westminster. They were no mere propaganda points, but contained some of Hyde's fundamental beliefs. The conflict, he declared, was about 'the interest, property and liberty of the subject', yet these were the very things threatened by the raising of a parliamentary army, and the levy of heavy parliamentary taxation. Was property safer from arbitrary taxation than before? Were men freer from arbitrary arrest since the Commons, with no constitutional powers of judicature, had taken to itself the power to impose oaths and imprison subjects by their own authority? By what right did the Commons exclude half the members legally elected by their constituents? The authority of king, lords and commons was the highest in the land, but that of the Commons alone had no legislative or judicial validity. What had happened to the fundamental laws Pym had once appealed to, when he had said 'if you take away the law, all things will be in confusion'? It was now sufficient for a man to be called 'malignant' for him to be imprisoned without trial. Nor were the decisions of the Commons taken by its 500 members, but by less than eighty, and those of the Lords by one-fifth of their number. The implication of the whole Declaration was that without the king there could be no guarantee of law and liberty.[50]

Hyde's appeal to political opinion seemed a necessary exercise in view of its volatile nature. It is worth investigating this more fully. According to Keeler the maximum number of seats in the Commons of the Long Parliament was 493, but in fact the largest attendance at any one division was 379, and even the vote on the Grand Remonstrance in November 1641 numbered only 307. Some members had such shadowy existence that Keeler could not always be sure of their existence, and the total membership of those of whose political views we can be certain was 429. Of these 236 can be labelled parliamentarians in the period 1640–48, that is up to the time of Pride's Purge, and in the same period 193 were royalists. There was indeed overwhelming support for the early reforms carried by the Long Parliament; the impeachment of Strafford was carried by 204 to 59. Pym was able to steer through a great programme of reform including the outlawing of unparliamentary taxation, the abolition of the Prerogative Courts, the abrogation of the forest laws, the enactment of Triennial Parliaments and the perpetuation of the Long Parliament. The great dividing line came with the Grand Remonstrance and the Militia Ordinance. Few if any of those voting against the Grand Remonstrance were 'royalists' in the sense of wanting royalist absolutism. What the great majority wanted was the achievement of a constitutional balance such as Hyde suggested in his Declaration; some were more influenced by the threat to the Anglican (although not the Laudian) church than by the threat to the king. Some like Sir Thomas Danby, Robert Hyde, Richard Edgcombe, John Russell (third son of the earl of Bedford) and Thomas, Lord Wentworth, always tended to support the king. Others, like Lord Falkland, Edward Hyde, Sir Thomas Ingram, George Fane and Henry Coke, although they had often voted with the reformers, had to make a choice when the king withdrew to York, and when the war began.

Hyde greatly regretted the king's withdrawal to the north, partly because it presaged a war which he abhorred, and partly because it placed the moderates in such an invidious position. If they remained at Westminster they were in increasing danger from their opponents, but if they left they lost their voice in bringing about a compromise. If the 193 royalists could have remained at Westminster without intimidation, they might well have gained a moderate majority capable of a settlement. But some had been expelled as monopolists as early as 1641, and others as royalists by 1642, and many more by 1644, leaving parliamentary decisions to be taken by less than half the original Commons, and often by a much smaller minority. But without the king, the royalists were demoralised and intimidated, and they withdrew, some of them to their country estates and into oblivion, some to fight for the king. Historians have studied very carefully the parliamentarians who remained, but until recently have paid much less attention to the royalists, who were almost as numerous, and had as much right to sit at Westminster as their opponents.[51] The prestige of the name of parliament gave the latter a great advantage. The king's attempt to establish an Oxford Parliament was a failure, for it seemed clear to most people that parliament must be at Westminster or nowhere.

Edward Hyde was right to appeal to moderate opinion, for at Westminster in the early months of 1643 there was almost certainly a majority in favour of peace. The peace initiative at Colnbrook in November had been stunted by the king's attack on Brentford, and on 12 November parliament protested, 'we thought it a strange introduction to peace that your Majesty should send your army to beat us out of our quarters at Brentford'; to which the king made the entirely unconvincing answer that 'his Majesty had no intention to master the city by so advancing'.[52] But the correspondence continued. On the 24th they invited the king to 'return to your Parliament with your royal, not your martial attendance, to the end that religion, laws and liberties may be settled'; to which Charles replied that he would be pleased to do so whenever it was safe. The City of London took the hint, and in a petition expressed the City's loyalty, and begged him to return. Charles asked 'what hope his Majesty can have of safety there whilst Alderman Pennington, their pretended Lord Mayor (the principal author of those calamities, which so nearly threaten the ruin of that famous city), Venn, Foulke and Mainwaring (all persons guilty of schism and high treason . . .' together with preachers, Brownists, Anabaptists and Sectaries held sway there?[53]

However, with a moderate majority in the Commons the peace initiative was resumed in January 1643, and in preparation for this Charles proposed to make Secretary Nicholas Master of the Wards to make room for Hyde as Secretary of State. 'I must make Ned Hyde secretary of state, for the truth is, I can trust nobody else', he wrote to the queen in fulfilment of a fatal promise to consult her before making changes. It was highly embarrassing to both Nicholas and Hyde when the letter fell into enemy hands and was published, and when the king told Hyde of his intentions the latter begged him to think again, since it would cause grave offence to a servant as honest as Nicholas. Lord Falkland however provided the solution. The Master of the Rolls had just died, and Sir John Culpepper had long coveted the office. Culpepper was appointed Master, and Hyde succeeded him as Chancellor of the Exchequer. He was thus sworn of the Privy Council and knighted. Falkland was relieved to have his old friend a member of the Council, and the only disappointed man was Culpepper, who had hoped to continue to hold the office together with the Mastership.

In February a peace deputation arrived at Oxford headed by the earls of Northumberland, Pembroke, Salisbury and Holland, and including eight members of the Commons, all moderates, sincerely desiring peace, 'none of them', wrote Clarendon, 'having ever had inclination to alter the government'.[54] It is not easy to see why Professor Hexter found the terms so satisfactory,[55] for they seemed to require full concessions from the king, while parliament made very few. The king and his evil councillors were blamed for the conflict; the old story of a papist conspiracy was repeated; the king must disband his army, and leave delinquents and papists to the law; he must agree to the abolition of bishops and deans; he must settle the militia in accordance with the will of parliament; he must accept the appointment of such judges as parliament chose; he must dismiss the earl of Bristol, Lord Herbert, Lord Digby and the earl of Newcastle, and leave them to the rigours of the law. If the king granted all this, parliament would disband its forces.[56]

Bulstrode Whitelocke, one of the commissioners, said that they were received 'with great favour and civility' by the king at Christ Church. The king's advisers often dined with the commissioners, and the king accepted gifts of wine and provisions from Northumberland's ample supplies. The king, who was accompanied usually by Prince Rupert, Lord Keeper Littleton, the earl of Southampton, Lord Chief Justice Bankes, and other members of the Council, allowed free debate. However he alone spoke to the commissioners, his advisers merely occasionally reminding him of particular points. Whitelocke was impressed by the abilities Charles showed:

In this treaty the King manifested his great parts and abilities, strength of reason and quickness of apprehension, with much patience in hearing what was objected against him; wherein he allowed all freedom, and would himself sum up the arguments, and give a most clear judgment upon them.

However Whitelocke discerned one weakness which Charles certainly possessed:

His unhappiness was that he had a better opinion of others' judgments than of his own, though they were weaker than his own; and of this the Parliament's commissioners had experience to their great trouble.

Charles had from his early days lacked a self-confidence which perhaps resulted from a contrast with his more brilliant brother Henry, and which led him into disastrous dependence on the duke of Buckingham. By the 1640s he showed an unfortunate desire always to seek the advice and approval of the queen, and thus to discuss with her dangerous questions of policy in letters which too often fell into enemy hands. Whitelocke described how they would often debate an issue until midnight, and the king would agree with the commissioners, but next morning he had changed his mind.[57] Edward Hyde was an old friend of Whitelocke's, and the two got along well together; but while Hyde and Falkland worked for peace, the earl of Bristol and others were known to be opposed to it, believing in the need for military victory. However, this was not the only difficulty. Pym had bound the commissioners by the strictest instructions, so as to leave them almost no freedom to negotiate. The commissioners themselves disliked the terms; had pointed out before they left Westminster that similar terms had already been rejected, only to be told that the purpose was to see what concessions the king would make. When the king heard that the commissioners had no powers to negotiate, he replied tartly that the terms might as well have been sent by common courier. Every point raised in discussion had to be referred to Westminster, and when the king made a proposal, the parliamentary committee in Westminster would require further clarification. Moreover the commissioners were given only twenty days in which to reach a treaty. The question arises whether either side was sincere in its efforts for peace. It is always extremely difficult to have fruitful discussions about peace while a war continues, and both sides were continuing their military operations. The terms Pym was offering were hardly such as to suggest genuine conciliation. It was hardly tactful to begin by placing all blame for the past on the king and his ministers, while making no reference to the substantial concessions the king had already made. Nor could the king be expected to agree to hand over his advisers to receive the same fate as Strafford at the hands of a vengeful parliament. Most suspicious of all was the clause suppressing episcopacy. Although Pym had been determined to exclude bishops from voting in the Lords, he had shown much less enthusiasm for disbanding the entire Anglican church. Why then was such a bill rushed through the Commons at this time, when he must have known that the king would on no account accept it, if it were not to make certain that the peace offer would fail? Why were the moderate commissioners deprived of all powers of negotiation, even though the constant reference back to Westminster was intolerably cumbrous? There was indeed a majority at Westminster sincerely anxious for peace, but there was also a war party, and Pym had to steer events between the two if he was to retain the support of both. The same was true in the king's counsels. Men like the earl of Dorset, Falkland, Culpepper and Hyde certainly wanted peace, while the earl of Bristol and his friends wanted war. The only hope of peace lay in giving the moderate men on both sides a chance freely to negotiate a compromise. Clarendon wrote:

The commissioners, who had all good fortunes and estates, had all a great desire of peace, but knew well that there must be a receding mutually on both sides from what they demanded; for if the king insisted on justice, and on the satisfaction and reparation the law would give him, the lives and fortunes of all who had opposed him would be at his mercy . . . On the other side, if the parliament insisted on all that they had demanded, all the power of the crown and monarchy itself would be thrown off the hinges, which as they could never imagine the king would ever consent to, so they saw well enough their own concernment in it, and that themselves should be as much involved in the confusion as those they called their enemies.[58]

According to Clarendon, William Pierrepoint suggested a solution. It was clear that the king would never accept the abolition of episcopacy, while the parliamentarians would not agree to restoring the armed forces to the king. Pierrepoint suggested to Secretary Nicholas that if the latter obstacle could be removed, the former might be left in abeyance, and that a solution might be found if the king appointed the earl of Northumberland Lord High Admiral. Nicholas failed to convince Charles, and asked Hyde to try personal persuasion. During Charles's morning walk, Hyde raised the whole question. He recognised the objections to Northumberland,

yet he desired him [the king] to consider his own ill condition; and how unlike it was that it should be improved by the continuance of war; and whether he could ever imagine a possibility of getting out of it upon more easy conditions than what was now proposed; the offer of which to the parliament could do him no signal prejudice, and could not but bring him very notable advantages.[59]

Charles however rejected the proposal, and Clarendon regarded this as a disastrous decision. The blame Clarendon placed squarely upon the queen, who he said delighted in the power she had established over the king, and who had extracted from Charles the promise that he would make no important appointment without her approval. She detested Northumberland, and moreover had set sail from The Hague on 13 February, and landed in Yorkshire on the 22nd with substantial arms and forces. The suspicion was therefore that the king was merely drawing out the negotiations until his reinforcements arrived. Clarendon lamented that 'it was her majesty's and the kingdom's misfortune, that she had not any person about her, who had either ability or affection, to inform and advise her of the temper of the kingdom or humour of the people, or who thought either worth the caring for'.[60]

The one concession obtained was an extension of treaty time from March into April. Everything turned now on whether the two sides could agree to conditions for the cessation of hostilities; but, as Hyde had foreseen, there was deadlock over the control of the armed forces. The king refused to surrender so integral a part of the prerogative. As Lord Falkland put it on 15 April, the king's claims were founded on law, and if parliament wished to change it, they must show that they had a fundamental right superior to that of the king, and he added, somewhat naively, that if the powers of the crown were really as dangerous as they feared, they would have been restricted long ago. The king wanted only the law of the land and the traditional rights of the crown.[61] Charles summed up his position: he asked only for his legal rights, and that as soon as his revenues, magazines, ships and forts were restored to him, and all members of both Houses could return to their seats, and as soon as king and parliament were free from tumultuous assemblies, he would agree to the disbandment of both armies. All other matters could then be left to the free discussion of parliament.

At least the discussions had made it clear that without a cessation of the conflict, peace terms were impossible, and that the greatest need was for a free return of king and members to Westminster.* In fact neither side had called a halt to the war. There was always a peace party in the king's council,† but the

---

* 'Concerning the king's return to the parliament, they said "they had no instructions to treat upon it", which the king much wondered at.'[62]
† The king's council consisted of:
Lord Keeper Littleton, the duke of Richmond, the marquis of Hertford (brother-in-law to Essex), the earl of Southampton, the earl of Leicester ('rather a speculative than a practical man'), the earl of Bristol, the earl of Newcastle, the earl of Berkshire (a man of 'little understanding'), Lord Dunsmore ('rough and tempestuous nature, violent in pursuing what he wished without judgment or temper to know the way of bringing it to pass'), Lord Seymour (brother to Hertford),

war party argued that his military position was good, with the earl of Newcastle controlling the north, Wales loyal, and Hopton ready for an advance in the west. What however impressed Hyde more was the fact that parliament was now levying monthly assessments which amounted to £1,742,936 a year, a huge sum compared with the subsidies amounting to £150,000 which the king had occasionally received before the war.[64] How could the king succeed against such a concentration of power?

---

Lord Savile ('false ... ambitious and restless nature') Lord Falkland, Sir John Culpepper, Secretary Nicholas, Sir Edward Hyde, Sir John Bankes, Sir Peter Wych (comptroller of the household, who on his death was succeeded by Sir Christopher Hatton).[63]

# 'Two Sovereign Contending Powers'

Clarendon was clearly of the opinion 'that the king was too severe in the Oxford treaty, and insisted too much upon what was his own by right and law'. The appointment of the earl of Northumberland to high office would have been a useful gesture, but it would not have brought about a peace, for the abolition of bishops and deans and the sequestration of their lands, and the calling of the Westminster Assembly, gave no grounds for supposing a peace to be possible.[1] Almost before the negotiations were ended the war was resumed, and the superiority of parliament's resources in supplies and arms was soon apparent. On 25 April Sir William Waller took Hereford; on the 27th the earl of Essex took Reading and Clarendon thought that if he had proceeded to attack Oxford, the king would have had to withdraw northwards, and would have been cut off from the west country. On 20 May the king made a further appeal to the Lords 'to send such an answer as may open a door to let in a firm peace and security to the whole kingdom'. Pym's reply three days later was to institute the impeachment of the queen, who was now at York with a considerable army, and with plans for a strong royalist campaign in the west. None the less her impeachment was an act of provocation bitterly resented by the king.[2]

The failure of the peace negotiations gravely disappointed many moderates, not least the earl of Northumberland, and the royalist Edmund Waller, who had remained a member of the Commons. S. R. Gardiner estimated that at least one-third of Londoners were royalists[3] and many of them were anxious to bring pressure to bear on an obstinate parliament. Waller discussed the possibilities of resistance with his brother-in-law Tompkins. At the same time a wealthy citizen, Sir Nicholas Crisp, who had been prosecuted by the Commons, and had fled to Oxford, persuaded the king that London was ready to rise in revolt, and Lady Daubigny, whose husband had been killed at Edgehill, agreed to carry to London the king's commission of array, safely in her bosom. A servant of Tompkins overheard a conversation with Waller and reported it to Pym. Pym well knew how to make the most of such opportunities. The whole city was placed on the alert, and Waller was interrogated. He was so shattered by his arrest that he recounted everything he had heard from the many, including the earls of Northumberland and

Portland and Lord Conway, who, like himself, had probably expressed little more than discontent at the course of events. It took Pym but a few days to get to the bottom of the plot, or, perhaps more accurately, to build it into a mighty edifice, and to startle parliament with its details on 6 June. Under the impact of the news he persuaded both Houses to take a vow and covenant that they would not lay down their arms 'so long as the papists, now in open war against the parliament, shall by force of arms be protected from the justice thereof'.[4] Tompkins and one Challoner were executed on 5 July, and Waller, whose abject submission had provided most of the evidence, was expelled the House and condemned to death by the Council of War. He was reprieved by the earl of Essex but imprisoned and fined £10,000, and after a year was able to escape to the continent. The whole incident had weakened the king's position, discouraged the royalists and moderates in the City, and greatly strengthened Pym's hold over parliament. Clarendon made it clear that there was no single conspiracy, that Waller's discussions had nothing to do with the king's commission for array; and he wrote that he had good reason for asserting that no such plot was seriously considered by either Lord Falkland or by the king.[5]

War was resumed in the west country in May, when the earl of Stamford, the parliamentary general, marched into Cornwall with a strong army of 5000 foot and 1400 horse, well equipped with canon and supplies. Lord Mohun, Sir Ralph Hopton and Sir Bevil Grenville had inferior numbers, but gave battle at Stratton and won a great victory, capturing 1700 of the enemy, together with all their equipment of cannon, food and £5000 in cash. Hopton and Grenville were two of the finest soldiers the royalists produced, and Clarendon gave a graphic and accurate description of the battle, although, according to Miss Coate, he was less than fair to the defeated general.[6] Now Hopton could advance to join Prince Maurice in Somerset. General Chudleigh had fought gallantly on the parliamentary side in the battle, but afterwards was persuaded to join the royalists: a great blow to parliamentary morale, for he was their ablest general in the west.[7] Hopton had built up a high morale among his royalist forces, instilled discipline, and punished vice and plunder.[8] It was Miss Coate's judgment that 'had he been able to impose on the Royalist forces as a whole his own standard of loyalty, discipline and piety, the fate of the monarchy might have been different.'[9] But once he joined up with the forces of the marquis of Hertford and Prince Maurice at Chard, discipline fell apart, plundering was permitted, and the royalist cause had to pay a heavy price for alienating the yeoman and clothiers of Somerset. Still the royalist position looked strong, with the bulk of the army of 4000 foot and 2300 horse being provided by Hopton's Cornishmen. They advanced to take Taunton, Bridgwater and Glastonbury. At Wells, Hopton wrote to his old friend William Waller, the parliamentary general, asking for an interview. Waller refused, but wrote a touching reply:

Certainly my affections to you are so unchangeable, that hostility itself cannot vitiate my friendship to your person, but I must be true to the cause wherein I serve.[10]

The two men met in battle on 5 July at Lansdowne, near Bath. It was bitterly fought, and although the royalists were victorious, they suffered irreparable casualties. Hopton was terribly burnt, and blinded by an explosion, and Sir Bevill Grenville was killed. In him, Miss Coate wrote, 'were finely blended the humanism of the Renaissance, the strength of Puritanism, and the ardour and loyalty of his Cornish ancestry'.[11] The royalist cause could ill afford the loss of such commanders. It was the first time that the royalist cavalry had been heavily mauled. With severe shortage of supplies the royalists fell back to Devizes. Waller attacked at Roundway Down and found himself between Hopton's forces and newly arrived reinforcements from Oxford. His army was shattered with heavy losses; the severest defeat the parliament-men were to sustain during the war. In July Prince Rupert laid siege to Bristol and carried the city by assault, but with heavy losses. Colonel Nathaniel Fiennes, the parliamentary governor, was heavily outnumbered, but could have held out somewhat longer. Among the royalist dead were Sir Nicholas Slanning and Colonel John Trevannion, whom Clarendon called 'the life and soul of the Cornish regiments', and Colonel Harry Lunsford and Nathaniel Moyle, all young men inspired by the most romantic royalism. Royalist victories were being won but at the price of the loss of such men who could not be replaced.[12] Equally ominous was the disintegration of the Cornish army, whose losses at Lansdowne and Bristol, coupled with the loss of their great leaders, broke their spirit.

The king's grand strategy had so far aimed at a three-pronged attack on London, with the earl of Newcastle advancing from Yorkshire, the king from Oxford, and Hopton's army from the west. But at this point a fateful decision was made. Three parliamentary fortresses still held out, namely Hull, Gloucester and Plymouth, and the king decided they should first be reduced. The earl of Newcastle was besieging Hull, the king laid siege to Gloucester, and Prince Maurice marched into the west country, took Exeter and advanced on Plymouth. The morale of the parliamentary garrison in Plymouth was so low that a sudden attack might have succeeded. Alexander Carew, hitherto a strong parliament-man, member of one of the most honoured of west country families, intrigued to betray the city, but was discovered, and was sent to London for trial and execution. Still Maurice delayed, in spite of the fact that he controlled all Devonshire, and in Dorset only Poole and Lyme remained in parliamentary hands. Both Gloucester and Hull continued to hold out, and on 5 September Charles abandoned the siege of Gloucester and marched off towards London, in order to place himself between the earl of Essex and London. At Newbury on the 20th a hard-fought but indecisive battle allowed

Essex to march towards London. Charles had ordered the earl of Newcastle to abandon the siege of Hull and to march towards London, but Newcastle replied that his men absolutely refused to leave a strong garrison in their rear. Nonetheless in October he was forced to abandon the siege of Hull. For the king the battle of Newbury proved to be the turning of the tide: after his failure to win an outright victory, he was never in so favourable a position again. His difficulties now increased rapidly.

For Edward Hyde, the battle of Newbury had cost him the life of his closest friend, Lord Falkland, 'which he lamented so passionately that he could not in many days compose himself to any thoughts of business'. Falkland died, Clarendon wrote, 'as much of the time as of the bullet: for, from the very beginning of the war, he contracted so deep a sadness and melancholy, that his life was not pleasant to him, and sure he was too weary of it'.[13] Hyde's last letter to Falkland had been to beg him to take fewer risks on the battlefield, saying that it was not necessary for a Privy Councillor and Secretary of State thus to expose himself; but Falkland replied that since he was known to be so passionately anxious for peace, he must show that he was not personally a coward. At Newbury he seemed to sense that he would die, and he threw himself into the hottest part of the conflict.[14] He had never been a party man, but was equally opposed to both extremes, as much to Strafford as to Pym, or to Laud as to the Puritans. He was primarily a philosopher, ill-suited to politics, and still less to warfare. S. R. Gardiner wrote truly: 'The desire to secure intellectual liberty from spiritual tyranny was the ruling principle of his mind. His claim to our reverence lies in the fact that his mind was as thoroughly saturated as Milton's was with the love of freedon'.[15] To Matthew Arnold, he was the greatest martyr of the civil war.

Clarendon makes it clear that the king's Court was torn by dissensions, ready to embrace wildcat schemes, and with the courtier's usual hunger for office and influence. The queen was jealous of Prince Rupert's influence with the king, and the two virtually headed opposing factions. Every victory was taken to indicate the approaching end of the war, and every set-back was followed by mutual recrimination.[16] Yet there continued during the year to be a steady stream of desertions from both houses of parliament to Oxford, and often there was little tact shown in receiving them. The most important were the earls of Bedford, Holland and Clare, all monarchists at heart, who had been disappointed at the failure of the Oxford negotiations. More cautious was the earl of Northampton, whose sentiments were the same, but who preferred to withdraw from Westminster to Petworth, to see how the earls were received. The latter encountered much hostility at Court, although Hyde did everything possible to welcome them. They persevered, and joined the king at the siege of Gloucester, and fought afterwards at Newbury. But the king treated Holland with especial coldness, because he made no submission for his past faults. Holland, on his side, was certainly greedy for a return of his old office of Groom of the Stole, which however the king preferred to confer on the marquis of Hertford. After waiting some time in vain for evidence of the king's good will, Holland slipped away one night and made his peace with parliament. The king was said to owe him £30,000, so he had some reason for feeling Charles's ingratitude. Hyde was under no illusions as to Holland's motives of self-interest, but he was nonetheless exasperated at the stupidity of the Court:

this unhappy ill carriage of the earl doth not absolve the king's council from oversight in treating him no better; which was a great error; and made the king, and all those about him, looked upon as implacable, and so diverted all men from farther thoughts of returning to their duty by such application, and made those who abhorred the war, and the violent counsels in carrying it on, choose rather to acquiesce, and expect a conjuncture when a universal peace might be made, than to expose themselves by unseasonable and unwelcome addresses.[17]

Holland's loyalty was certainly understimated, for he was to join the king again in the second Civil War, and was eventually executed by parliament.

The worst news Charles received during 1643 was of the threatened intervention of the Scots, and it may be convenient at this point to summarise his relations with his troubled northern kingdom.

The ineptitude of Charles's policy in the 1630s had united the Scottish nobles and kirk against king and episcopacy, and brought about a humiliating defeat of the king in the first Bishop's War of June 1639. But thereafter the solidarity of Scottish resistance diminished. Some Scottish nobles led by the earl of Montrose had no desire to see the Estates destroy royal authority, or to accept the domination of Archibald Campbell, marquis of Argyll and in August 1640 they drew up the Cumbernauld Bond expressing their loyalty both to the crown and the Covenant against the ambitions of certain men. When war began in England in 1642 the kirk wished to aid the English parliament with a view not only to limiting royal power, but also to extending Presbyterianism in England, and it suited Argyll to put himself at the head of the kirk party. The king's party was headed by James, duke of Hamilton, with his brother the earl of Lanark, Secretary of State for Scotland, and the earl of Traquair, the king's treasurer. The king's visit to Scotland in August 1641 failed to break the alliance between the English and the Scots, but the Scots were finally paid off and returned home, to the great relief of the English, and church bells were rung to celebrate the event (September 1641). Scotland returned to conditions of peace under the domination of the Covenanters. As the English Civil War approached, the English parliament again sought Scottish help, but the Scots would agree only if episcopacy was abolished and Presbyterianism established in its place. But this was too much to ask of a country where Presbyterianism was never popular, and Pym was not likely to bring in the Scots again except as a last resort. By 1643 however stalemate seemed to have been reached in the war, and in these circumstances Pym again turned to the Covenanters. The king played into his hands by the use of Papist troops from Ireland (the so-called Antrim Plot of 1643) which enabled the kirk to disseminate wild rumours of the king's intentions.[18]

The moderates in the Westminster parliament disliked a further approach to the Scots, and Pym had to use all his political skill to convince them otherwise. The resounding defeat of Sir William Waller at Roundway Down, the so-called plot of Edmund Waller and the impeachment of the queen were all played up to the full by Pym to create the necessary atmosphere of crisis, and in August he had his way. A delegation of six were sent to Edinburgh to request an alliance. Its leader was Sir Henry Vane the younger, one of the most enigmatic of the parliamentarians. He was the son of Charles I's Secretary of State and a wealthy landowner in Durham. At the age of twenty-three he was elected governor of Massachusetts, but the colony was soon torn by religious dissensions, and in 1637 he returned to England in disgust. With the influence of the earl of Northumberland, he became Joint Treasurer of the Navy in 1639. When Strafford took the barony of Raby, which the Vanes coveted, he became an inveterate enemy of the earl, and in September 1640 disclosed to Pym a transcript of his father's notes of a Privy Council meeting which formed the basis of the principal charge against Strafford. He was a bitter enemy of episcopacy, and always opposed negotiations for peace with the king. However in most matters he followed Pym, and it was not until late in 1643 that he emerged as one of the leaders of the war party. Clarendon described him as 'of very profound dissimulation', and said that few could 'make a guess of what he intended', for 'he was inferior to no other man in all mysterious artifices'.[19]

At the time of the Oxford negotiations the Scots sent Lord Loudoun and Alexander Henderson (author of the National Covenant) to Charles to warn him that he could prevent Scottish intervention only by agreeing to Presbyterianism in the English church. On Hyde's advice the king gave a frosty response, on the grounds that he would no more permit the Scots to dictate to the English church than he would the King of France. Scotland was operating now virtually as a republic, and in June a Convention was called without royal warrant. In August, when the English commissioners arrived, the General Assembly was also sitting. Vane's diplomatic skill proved superior to the Scots', and on 17 August the Solemn League and Covenant was drafted providing for the preservation of the reformed faith in Scotland, and the reformation of religion in England and Ireland 'according to the word of God and the example of the best reformed churches'. The churches of the three kingdoms were to be assimilated, and peace and union between England and Scotland established. Vane was no Presbyterian, but an Independent, and the phrase 'according to the word of God' provided him with an escape clause. The Westminster parliament accepted the Solemn League and Covenant on

25 September, and in November a military agreement provided for 18,000 foot and 2000 horse from Scotland to aid the English. To the English the Solemn League and Covenant was no more than a disagreeable necessity upon which Scots' military aid depended. To the Scots it was a sacred mission for the conversion of England.* In December Robert Baillie and his colleagues arrived from Scotland to take part in the Westminster Assembly of divines with the object of effecting this. But they were to be gravely disappointed. The so-called Presbyterian party in England, headed by Denzil Holles, were not really Presbyterians at all, and only the need for Scots' military help kept the charade going.

The Scots' alliance was the last achievement of John Pym, who died on 8 December 1643. C V Wedgwood rightly described him as a man of 'phenomenal energy, persistence and political perspicacity', yet one who 'remains personally unknown to us'.[21] From the first meeting of the Long Parliament he had taken extraordinary control of its affairs, and was the man chiefly responsible for dismantling the royal government and stripping the royal prerogative of all but a ficition of power. Since Professor Hexter's *The Reign of King Pym*, historians have often accepted the idea of a 'middle group', led by Pym, somewhere between the peace and war parties in the Commons, but no man in the Commons did more to bring about war than Pym, and no one more effectively prevented peace talks from succeeding. What, then, were Pym's real objectives? In his *Declaration and Vindication* he claimed

I am, and ever was, and so will die, a faithful son of the Protestant Religion, without having the least relation in my belief to those gross errors of Anabaptism, Brownism and the like.

What he sought to destroy, he said, was the political power of the bishops 'to foment the civil differences between His Majesty and his Parliament'. As to royal power:

I neither directly nor indirectly, ever had a thought tending to the least disobedience or disloyalty to His Majesty, whom I acknowledge my lawful King and Sovereign, and would expend my blood as soon in his service as any subject he hath.[22]

If this is not to be regarded as a downright untruth, the explanation may lie in a remark of his that his position was very like that of Cicero's in the Catiline conspiracy of 63 AD. Cicero forestalled the plot and executed the conspirators. It was a far-fetched comparison, but Pym clearly regarded himself as defending the consitution against a Stuart conspiracy. However in doing so he would have reduced the monarch to the position of a Doge of Venice.

---

* There was also the motive of self-preservation: cf. 'Declaration of Reasons for assisting the Parliament of England: If the Parliament of England that now is, be destroyed, who shall undertake for our safety?'[20]

Clarendon wrote that Pym had greater knowledge of the business of parliaments than any man living, and, becoming the dominating influence in the Commons, 'no man had more to answer for the miseries of the kingdom, or had his hand or head deeper in their contrivance'. Yet he believed that Pym had become more deeply involved than he had intended, that he was by nature 'a man of a private quality and condition of life'; and that he had at first taken seriously the prospect of taking office with the earl of Bedford. But then he discovered that office under the crown would destroy his influence in the Commons. He was an inveterate enemy of Strafford, and Clarendon believed he used bribery to obtain evidence against him.

From the time of his being accused of high treason by the king . . . he never entertained thoughts of moderation, but always opposed all overtures of peace and accommodation.[23]

His last achievement was to bring in the Scots, with all the disastrous consequences that entailed.

After the death of Falkland, the king wished Hyde to become Secretary of State, but for the second time he refused it. The reason was the queen's known preference for her favourite Lord Digby, a much more dashing and reckless character. There was an urgent need for reorganisation of the government, if only to limit the confusion and dissensions which too often prevailed. The Privy Council was clearly too large a body for daily business, especially as members were often away on military affairs. Charles therefore established a junto, consisting of the duke of Richmond, Lord Cottington, the two Secretaries of State (Nicholas and Digby), Sir John Culpepper and Sir Edward Hyde. Exasperated by the Scottish alliance, Charles cast about for means to limit the stranglehold the Westminster parliament had achieved, and in September he consulted Hyde about the possibility of declaring it dissolved, on the grounds that the Act perpetuating the existence of the Long Parliament was unconstitutional. Hyde did not think this could be upheld in law, and he doubted whether anyone would listen to it. But he did think that the Westminster parliament might no longer be regarded as a true parliament, since about half the members of the Commons were excluded from it, and since the House of Lords had shrunk to about twenty-two peers.[24] He argued that

since the whole kingdom was misled by the reverence they had to parliaments, and believed that the laws and liberties of the people could not be otherwise preserved than by their authority, and that it appeared to be to no purpose to persuade them that what they did was against the law when they were persuaded that their very doing it made it lawful, it would therefore be necessary . . . to convince them, that they who did those monstrous things were not the parliament, but a handful of desperate persons, who, by the help of the tumults raised in the city of London, had driven away the major part of the parliament, and called themselves the parliament, who were, in truth, much the less, and the least considerable part of it.[25]

This passage contains the essence of Hyde's constitutional thought, that the government of England was a balance of king, Privy Council, Lords and Commons, each held in check by law. In 1640 Hyde had regarded the balance as tilted dangerously in favour of the king; now the balance had been completely overthrown, and the Westminster parliament had assumed virtual sovereignty. Both the king and Hyde thought that the greatest blunder was the acceptance of the bill perpetuating the Long Parliament. The second greatest blunder was to have drawn off the royalist and moderate members of both Houses, leaving Pym in undisputed control. A total of 256 Lords and Commons had withdrawn from Westminster, and if they had still been there, a peace surely might have been arranged. The next best thing was to summon a rival parliament of the king's supporters to Oxford. The king accepted Hyde's proposal. A proclamation to this effect was issued on 22 October 1643, requiring the parliament to assemble on 21 January 1644. Charles did regard it with some trepidation, concerned that an Oxford parliament might be as troublesome as the Westminster parliament had been, and fearing that it might enter into fruitless peace negotiations with Westminster.[26] He need not have worried on these scores, but it was a forlorn hope that the Oxford parliament would steal any thunder from Westminster. Its first act was to condemn the Westminster parliament's alliance with the Scots.

The Solemn League and Covenant was sworn by a total of 229 members at Westminster on 22 September. On 9 October the king issued a Proclamation, a little late in the day, forbidding his loyal subjects to take the Covenant, and in December he declared that the two Houses at Westminster could no longer be regarded as a free parliament, and that he could not treat with them. There was indeed considerable misgiving in London at the news of a new Scottish invasion, and there were many exasperated at the failure of the Oxford treaty. A hare-brained scheme was suggested to Charles that since direct negotiations with parliament seemed useless, the City of London might act as go-between to bring about a peace. Sir Basil Brooke agreed to act for the king in the City, but long before developments were possible, captured letters were passed to the Committee of Safety, and Brooke and others were arrested. It was a desperate and ill-considered idea, springing mainly from the frustrated desire for peace, and hostility to further intervention by the Scots. As so often happened the failure merely strengthened the hand of the war party.

The king, desperately short of money, men and supplies, asked his Oxford parliament freely to give advice. Clarendon wrote that members recognised that the greatest difficulty was not in making peace, but in persuading the Westminster parliament to negotiate;[27] and that the great obstacle was fear of the fate of the leaders once the king regained power. They advised therefore an approach to the earl of Essex, well known for his moderation. The king left the management of the Oxford parliament largely to Hyde, and the latter almost certainly had a hand in composing a letter sent from the parliament to the earl of Essex on 29 January 1644, begging him to intercede for peace, and promising an absolute pardon for all past offences.

This letter was subscribed by his highness the prince (of Wales), the duke of York, and three and forty dukes, marquises, earls, viscounts, and barons of the house of peers, and one hundred and eighteen members of the house of commons; there being such expedition used in the despatch that it was not thought fit to be deferred for a greater subscription: albeit it was known that many lords and commoners were upon the way, who came within a few days; and there were at that time near twenty peers absent with his majesty's leave and employed in his affairs and armies.[28]

Only twenty-two peers still remained at Westminster. The earl of Essex however returned a chilling reply, pointing out that as no reference had been made to the Westminster parliament, he could not communicate the letter to them, 'The maintenance of the parliament of England, and of the privileges thereof, is that for which we are all resolved to spend our blood; as being the foundation whereupon all our laws and liberties are built'; and for good measure he included a copy of the National Covenant. Clarendon commented wryly on the fanaticism of the Covenant:

They . . . talked how clearly the light of the gospel shined amongst them; that they placed not their confidence in their own counsels and strength; but their confidence was in God Almighty, the Lord of Hosts, who would not leave nor forsake his people. It was his own truth and cause, which they maintained against the heresy, superstition and tyranny of Antichrist.[29]

In exile later Clarendon pondered the meaning of it all, and drew a conclusion to which he adhered for the rest of his life,

that posterity may observe the divine hand of Almighty God upon the people of these miserable kingdoms; that after they had broken loose from that excellent form and practice of religion, which their ancestors and themselves had observed and enjoyed, with a greater measure of happiness than almost any nation lived under so long a time; and after they had cancelled and thrown off those admirable and incomparable laws of government, which was compounded of so much exact reason, that all possible mischiefs were foreseen and provided against, they should now be captivated by a profane and presumptuous entitling themselves to God's favour, and using his holy name in that manner, that all sober Christians stand scandalised and amazed at; and be deluded by such a kind of reasoning and debate, as can only impose upon men unnurtured and unacquainted with any knowledge or science.[30]

Clarendon defended neither the mistakes of the Stuarts, nor the excesses of the high church. What he defended was the broad continuity of English history since the Reformation, and he saw that continuity being broken by what he called 'new and strange' doctrines in church and state.

The king was persuaded, with some difficulty, to send another appeal to Westminster for a free conference between the two parliaments, but this was at once rejected since Westminster did not recognise the Oxford parliament. Thus ended yet another attempt at peace negotiations. Meanwhile the Oxford parliament turned to the urgent problems of finances. Clarendon said that, in spite of the fact that they called themselves a parliament, they dared not impose taxation which would alienate the countryside. They therefore appealed to rich royalists to contribute, and by this means raised £100,000. But this was a source which would soon dry up, and could not compare with the sum of over a million pounds a year which the Westminster parliament could levy. Plate was brought in for coining, and crown lands were sold. The Westminster parliament borrowed from the continent the idea of the new excise, which proved an efficient source of revenue, while monthly assessments on the counties provided money which made ship money appear a very modest tax.

While Hyde and the Oxford parliament were seeking peace, the king, who had little faith in these attempts, was preparing for war. The invasion of the Scots greatly increased the military dangers, and led Charles to review his position in all three kingdoms. The Irish rebellion of 1641 had been inspired by the Scottish rebellion against Charles I, but whereas the Long Parliament sought the alliance of the Scots, they had nothing but hostility for the Irish Catholic rebels, and king and parliament were supposed to be jointly engaged in suppressing them. The earl of Leicester was Lord Lieutenant of Ireland, but as he preferred to stay in England the brunt of the war fell on the commander, James Butler, earl of Ormond, who was in the difficult position of a man who had to serve two masters. Ormond was of an old Anglo-Irish family, a Protestant, chiefly concerned to defend the English settlements around the Pale. Strafford had built up a useful army in Ireland, but the king could not afford to strengthen it, and Pym's chief concern was that it should not be used to reinforce royal power in England. In January 1643 the king ordered Ormond to make peace with the rebels, with the view ultimately to transferring the troops to England. Ormond was in no hurry to comply, but finally signed an armistice in August, known as the 'cessation'. In Ulster there was a separate force, sent by parliament and the Scots, under the command of Colonel Robert Monro. Parliament roundly condemned the armistice, and Monro did not observe it. So far Ormond had tried to obey both king and parliament, but it was clear that that could not continue when the king ordered the transport of his five regiments to England, and when Ormond imposed on them an oath of loyalty to the king. Colonel Monck, who refused to take the oath, was sent to England under arrest. Those troops were English and Protestant, only too glad to have escaped from Ireland; but they were treated by parliament and the Scots as if they were Papist and Irish. Charles gave Monck a personal interview, and persuaded him to throw in his lot with the royalists. The five regiments landed at Chester, to reinforce the royalists under Lord Byron. All Cheshire and Lancashire were royalist except for

Manchester and Nantwich, and Byron laid siege to the latter in December. Sir Thomas Fairfax, the parliamentary general, marched to its relief, and on 24 January defeated Byron and relieved the town. Monck was taken prisoner. He had warned Charles that the royalist forces lacked professionalism, and included too many amateur generals, and Clarendon agreed with him. He wrote that 1500 prisoners and all the cannon had been lost, and that the main cause was 'the extreme contempt and disdain this body had of the enemy; and the presumption in their own strength, courage and conduct'.[31] Prince Rupert was sent to restore royalist fortunes in the area.

Charles's handling of Scottish affairs was as infelicitous as before. He continued to rely on the marquis of Hamilton for advice on Scottish affairs, but Argyll was clearly the greatest man in the country, and Hamilton decided that his best course was to come to a secret understanding with him while still advising the king. He gave Charles his word that Scotland would not interfere in English affairs during 1643. Argyll's greatest enemy was the earl of Montrose, who had once been a Covenanter and opponent of the king, but who had come to see the kirk subject to Argyll's domination, and Argyll likely to be dictator of Scotland. In March 1643 he slipped into England, and warned the queen of Argyll's alliance with the English parliament, and the threat of Scottish invasion. She passed the information to the king, who however mistrusted Montrose for his former attitude, and preferred to rely on Hamilton's advice. He was therefore one of the last to believe the alliance which Sir Henry Vane had achieved. He even made Hamilton a duke, while Montrose kicked his heels at Oxford during the autumn. At last however the truth dawned on the king, and when Hamilton arrived in October, he found himself under arrest. Charles was now ready to listen to Montrose, who proposed a desperate adventure, nothing less than an invasion of Scotland. As Montrose wrote,

> He either fears his fate too much,
> Or his deserts are small,
> That dares not put it to the touch,
> To gain or lose it all.

Charles could spare him only a hundred horse, but in February 1644 he appointed him his Captain General in Scotland, and Montrose, by his genius, recruited some two thousand more. The plan was for a double invasion of Scotland, Montrose from England, and Lord Antrim, the chief of the Irish McDonnells, who offered ten thousand of his clan from Ulster.[32] But Antrim's forces failed to appear, and Montrose had to be content with holding Westmorland and Cumberland for the king, and contacting the royalists in Scotland, especially the Gordons.[33]

The Scots by March 1644 had advanced to Newark in Nottinghamshire, a key royalist fortress which, if lost, would sever connections between Oxford and York. Meldrum, the Scottish commander besieged the garrison, who were hard pressed. Prince Rupert marched from Chester to its relief, took the Scots by surprise, put them to flight with a greatly inferior force, and captured 'four thousand arms, eleven pieces of brass cannon, two mortar pieces, and above fifty barrels of powder'.[34] It was to be Prince Rupert's greatest victory.

In the west country the king's cause appeared to prosper. Plymouth, Poole and Lyme Regis continued to hold out for parliament, but otherwise Devonshire, Somerset and most of Dorset seemed securely for the king. Bristol was in the king's hands, although Gloucester still held out. Sir Ralph Hopton, now raised to a peerage, manoeuvred eastwards as far as Farnham, which was strongly garrisoned by Sir William Waller (November 1644). He therefore turned into Sussex, surprised the parliamentary garrison in Arundel Castle, and captured it. Thereafter however he was completely out-manoeuvred by Waller, who had received ample reinforcements. Waller retook Arundel, where Hopton had left a very inadequate garrison, and on 29 March inflicted a complete defeat on the earl of Forth and Hopton at Cheriton, near Petersfield. Clarendon was severely critical of the way the royalists so frequently over-estimated their own strength and what they could achieve with their limited resources. It seemed to him that Hopton's ranging over Hampshire and Sussex with such a small force of about five thousand men was to court defeat.[35] As it was the west now lay open to Waller and the parliamentary forces.

Clarendon could judge of military affairs, of which he had no special knowledge, with a certain detachment, for he took no part in the king's military decisions. Charles tried to keep military and civil affairs separate, and his chief military advisers were General Ruthen, created the earl of Brentford, Prince Rupert, Lord Wilmot, Sir Jacob Astley, Lord Digby and Sir John Culpepper, only the last two of whom were members of the Privy Council. Clarendon described Brentford as a drunkard and an illiterate. Wilmot was a man 'of a haughty and ambitious nature, of a pleasant wit, and an ill understanding', usually at enmity with Prince Rupert. Lord Hopton was a great soldier, but his star sank rapidly after the defeat at Cheriton. Sir Jacob Astley was 'an honest, brave, plain man', one of the noblest of the old Cavaliers. Lord Digby was a spirited but unpredictable man whose superior qualities usually gained him his way in the military council, and he could usually count on the support of Sir John Culpepper.

The king's difficulties sprang from the need to control such large areas with so few troops, and he sorely needed at least three Prince Ruperts. In the spring of 1644 Waller took Reading and Abingdon and thus moved dangerously near to Oxford. In June the king was in Worcester, pursued by Waller, and there in a brilliant manoeuvre, of which he was afterwards very proud, Charles trapped Waller at Cropredy Bridge, and inflicted on him a sharp defeat. Meanwhile the earl of Essex marched into the west country and in July forced Sir Richard

Grenville to raise the siege of Plymouth. He then took the ill-conceived decision to march into Cornwall, to deprive the king of a source of manpower. It was a dangerous move, for Cornwall was a royalist county, and by August he found three armies advancing towards him, the king, Prince Maurice and Lord Hopton. The presence of the king was an inspiration to royalist troops, and the west was of special importance to the king, for the queen had lately been delivered of a daughter at Exeter. She had then withdrawn to France, but the young princess was left in the care of Lady Dalkeith.

Clarendon gives an inimitable picture of the confusion in the king's council at this time, with the earl of Brentford too deaf to know much of what was being said, and Lord Wilmot convinced that this was the time to try to win over the earl of Essex so that their combined forces could coerce Parliament into making peace. Wilmot made no secret of his discontents to his drinking companions, of whom, Clarendon wryly remarked, there were many; and said disrespectful things about the king, which were duly reported to him by Lord Digby. On 8 August Wilmot was suddenly arrested on a charge of treachery, and sent as prisoner to Exeter. The act caused discontent among the troops, for Wilmot was a popular general; and Clarendon was shocked that all this should have taken place almost within sight of the enemy lines. Wilmot in disgust threw up his command, and received leave to retire to France. Worse still, the king appointed the egregious Goring to succeed him as General of Horse.[36] Charles did make a personal appeal to the earl of Essex, using the latter's nephew, Lord Beauchamp, eldest son of the marquis of Hertford, as go-between. Essex however replied, expressing his loyalty to the king, but declaring that he had no orders from parliament to negotiate.[37]

However, Essex, with singular lack of generalship, had allowed himself to be penned in at Lostwithiel and Fowey. He decided therefore to send his horse at night through the enemy lines, while his infantry attempted an escape by sea. The first part of the plan succeeded, and Clarendon blamed Goring for his careless vigilance, saying that 'he was in one of his jovial exercises'.[38] Essex himself escaped by fishing-boat to Plymouth, leaving Major-General Skippon to capitulate. The infantry were given honourable terms, and some 6000 men marched out from Fowey. They were however dreadfully plundered on the way, and many died from starvation and exposure; only about a thousand reaching Poole. Skippon's leadership and courage won the admiration of the royalists. Charles should probably have followed this victory by a determined assault on Plymouth, but after a half-hearted attempt to secure a capitulation, he left Sir Richard Grenville to continue the blockade, and marched off to meet the challenge of Waller in the east.

Meanwhile, royalist successes in the west country had been overshadowed by utter disaster in the north. The key to the north lay in York, where the earl of Newcastle was besieged by the Scots under Lord Leven, Sir Thomas Fairfax, and the earl of Manchester's Eastern Association. In June Prince

Rupert restored royalist control of Lancashire, and then marched off to save York. Although heavily outnumbered, he relieved the beleaguered garrison by brilliant tactics. The parliamentarians then decided to fall back towards Tadcaster, and since he was outnumbered by three to two, Rupert might have been wise to allow them to do so; but he was determined to challenge them on the field. The two sides met on 2 July 1644 on Marston Moor. For once Rupert allowed the enemy to attack first. Cromwell's charge broke Rupert's cavalry on the right wing, but the royalist left wing put the parliamentarians to flight, so that Fairfax fled towards Hull, convinced that the battle was lost. The Scottish infantry however stood firm, and Cromwell's cavalry turned the tide. The royalist army was destroyed. Cromwell wrote triumphantly: 'God made them as stubble to our swords . . . I believe of twenty thousand the Prince hath not four thousand left. Give glory to God!' Rupert with the remains of his shattered army retreated towards Wales. The marquis of Newcastle fled to Scarborough, and took ship to Hamburg. York surrendered, and the whole of the north was virtually lost to the king. Montrose brought his little army to repair some of Rupert's losses of manpower, but at the expense of his own invasion of Scotland. The one crumb of comfort the royalists could extract from the disaster was that Marston Moor increased the divisions between the Scots and parliament. The Scots had hoped for their own military victory, but it was Cromwell who emerged as the hero of the battle, and the greater his strength the less he would need Scottish help.

It may be useful at this point to attempt a review of the situation in the Westminster parliament. It has become customary to speak of a war party, a peace party and a 'middle group' between the two, and some such grouping, if established, would ease the historian's task of making sense of so difficult and confused a period. The difficulty lies in establishing criteria for the groups, and the use of the word 'party' can be misleading in implying consistency in voting patterns. In fact most members found the situation intensely confusing, and might well be found supporting one group at one time, and another later. What we might term the 'old peace party', men like the Hothams, Edmund Waller, Sir Geoffrey Palmer, Sir Norton Knatchbull and Sir Harbottle Grimstone had for the most part absented themselves from the Commons, and therefore had ceased to influence events there. Others, like John Maynard, Sir Benjamin Rudyerd, John Selden, Sir Simonds D'Ewes and Sir John Coke remained in the House, and found their undisputed leader in Denzil Holles. Holles, a younger son of the earl of Clare, had been a strong supporter of Pym in the first years of the Long Parliament. He was a proud, bad tempered man, but he was devoted to parliament as the protector of law, religion and liberty. Parliament was for him 'the foundation and basis of government, and consequently of the peace and happiness of the kingdom'.[39] For him parliament was the central organ of the State, and there was no real place for the king in his idea of government. But a short period of military service cured him of the idea of settling issues by war, and by 1643 he stood forth as the leader of a peace party. Like Bulstrode Whitelocke and John Glyn, he came to hate war against the king, not because he had abandoned his belief in parliament, but because he now thought that a constitutional balance could be negotiated between them. He voted for the abolition of episcopacy in January 1643, but his biographer thinks that this was designed (as Clarendon thought it was) mainly as a bargaining counter with the king, to induce him to surrender control of the militia. In the Commons in February 1643 there was a clear majority for peace, and Holles warned the House that those who prolonged the struggle would be responsible for the blood shed.[40] When the negotiations failed however, as Pym saw to it that they did, the latter was able to regain control and press on with the war. Holles wrote in his *Memoirs* that the treaty failed solely because of parliament's unreasonable demands, 'as the Devil did to our Saviour, to have him fall down and worship them, lay his honour at their feet, his life at their mercy'. This was precisely the view of Sir Edward Hyde. It is usual to say that Charles was more concerned to win the war than to accept the terms, but it is not easy to see how he could have been expected to accept them in the form they were offered to him.

The war party was led by Sir Henry Vane and Henry Marten, and included William Strode, Zouch Tate, Francis Rous, Edmund Prideaux, and Lord Saye. They were opposed to any negotiations with the king, believing that victory must first be won. The last named was mainly activated by an insatiable hostility to the Anglican church.

Professor Pearl thinks that after Pym's death in December 1643 the true leader of the 'middle group' was Oliver St John, a lawyer by training and temperament, once defender of John Hampden in the ship money case, business manager to the earl of Bedford, and Solicitor-General to Charles I. From the beginning of the Long Parliament he was a close colleague of Pym's, and always exercised immense influence in the Commons. Much of his thinking was coloured by his Puritanism. Other members of the 'middle group' included Samuel Browne, St John's business manager in the Commons, whom Professor Pearl regards as 'one of the great organisers and manipulators in the Long Parliament'; Nathaniel Fiennes, William Pierrepoint and Sir John Evelyn.[41]

The difficulty with this three-fold division of opinion in the Commons lies in attaching any real meaning to the 'middle group', and Professor John MacCormack[42] denies that any such group existed after the death of Pym. Pym himself had exercised a dominating influence until his death, but the practical difference between him and the war party lay rather in his greater political skill and sagacity than in fundamental objectives. It would be anachronistic to think of the Commons as dividing between moderate constitutionalists and social revolutionaries; the House contained few, if any, of the latter. The most radical members of the House wanted to defeat the king, not to negotiate with him, and when negotiations took place the terms were usually such that the king could not possibly accept. The great majority of members would have claimed to be constitutional monarchists, but they found it impossible to trust Charles, or to accord him any more than the trappings of monarchy.

Even less successful has been the attempt to divide members into Presbyterians and Independents except as convenient political labels. Very few members were Presbyterians in the ecclesiastical and Scottish sense of the term. It is true that some of the more radical members were Independents, but many members of the House were Erastian rather than Presbyterian or Independent. The attack on the bishops' lands was dictated more by financial exigencies, and the need to pay the Scots than by ecclesiastical considerations.

The alliance with the Scots and the Solemn League and Covenant were a traumatic experience for England, and caused much bitter heart-searching. It was humiliating to have to admit that the king could not be beaten without Scottish help. The Scots would be an expensive ally, and the price would include a Presbyterianism which few people in England wanted. Even the bishops might seem preferable to the tyranny of the Presbyter.

The Westminster Assembly was summoned to meet on 1 July 1643. It consisted of thirty-one English lay assessors, headed by the earls of Northumberland, Bedford, Pembroke, Viscount Saye and Sele, John Selden, Sir Henry Vane, Oliver St John and John Pym, and about two ministers from each county. The king forbade their meeting, so some twenty-seven clerics did not attend at all, and some seventeen others soon ceased to attend, but there were ninety-six regular attenders.[43] To the king's prohibition the assembly returned the answer 'that the constitution at present was dissolved; that there were two sovereign contending powers in the nation; and if the war in which the parliament was engaged was just and necessary, they might assume this branch of the prerogative, till the nation was settled, as well as any other'. The Scottish general assembly sent a strong team of elders, the earl of Cassilis, Lord Maitland and Sir Archibald Johnston, together with the ministers Alexander Henderson, Robert Douglas, Samuel Rutherford, Robert Baillie and George Gillespie. The Scots came with a naive missionary enthusiasm to convert England to Presbyterianism, which, Robert Baillie was soon reporting, 'to this people is conceived to be a strange monster'.[44] They were soon engaged in a running battle with the Independents, through long debates, in which theological intepretations were interminably discussed. Thus after twenty sessions on the meaning of 'presbyter' in the Scripture, Baillie reported wearily, 'Truly, if the cause were good, the [Independents] have plenty of learning, wit, eloquence, and, above all, boldness and stiffness to make it out; but when they had wearied themselves and over-wearied us all, we found the most they had to say against the Presbytery was but curious, idle niceties.'[45] Clearly progress towards a Directory of Worship to replace the Book of Common Prayer would be slow.

More germane to the needs of the war party was the Committee of Both Kingdoms, established in February 1644 to co-ordinate the war effort of the two kingdoms. S. R. Gardiner saw the committee as the forerunner of the modern cabinet, but the immediate significance was the great powers granted to it by Parliament.[46] Sir Henry Vane and St John were members, and indeed the committee was packed with their friends, Lord Saye, Sir Arthur Hesilrige, John Crewe, Oliver Cromwell, Lord Wharton, Samuel Browne and John Glyn. The Committee became the scene of a bitter rivalry between the earl of Manchester and the earl of Essex. Hostility to Essex sprang primarily from the belief that his sympathies were too readily with the king, and that therefore he was reluctant to win outright victories. Charles had suspected this when he made overtures to him, and although Essex's replies were impeccable, they did nothing to remove suspicions. Some suspected that he might use the army to force a peace. Sir Henry Vane's mind worked in a different direction, and in June 1644 he was in York discussing with the Scots the possibility of establishing a republic. Another idea floated at the period was that Charles I might be replaced by Charles Lewis, the Elector Palatine (Charles I's nephew), and it brought the Elector hurrying to London in the summer of 1644. But most of the committee were shocked at the suggestion, and both ideas were shelved.

Cromwell's victory at Marston Moor greatly increased the prestige of the army of the Eastern Association, and the Scots were vexed to see him receive most of the credit when they had played so important a part in bringing it about. Henceforth there would be less dependence on the Scots. Sir Henry Vane was said to have inserted the word 'league' in 'Solemn League and Covenant' thinking that a league could be broken, and that 'covenant' would be limited by the phrase 'according to the word of God'. In the Westminster Assembly the Scots were horrified at the strength of Independency. Robert Baillie wrote in April 1644,

we are vexed and over-wearied with their ways . . . We are almost desperate to see anything concluded for a long time: their way is woefully tedious. Nothing in any Assembly that ever was in the world except Trent, like to them in prolixity.[47]

They had come to root out episcopacy, but now they found that the real enemy was 'anarchical schemes, and the heresies of Antinomians and Anabaptists';[48] and when they were not resisting Independents, with their hated defence of toleration, they were contesting with the Erastians. On 12 July Baillie reported, 'In our last debate with the committee of Commons . . . we were in the midst, over head and ears, of that greatest of our questions, the power of Parliament in ecclesiastical affairs. It's like this question shall be hotter here than anywhere else.'[49] A few days later he was horrified to hear a minister, Roger

Williams, say that 'there is no church, no sacraments, no pastors, no church-officers, no ordinance in the world, nor has been since a few years after the Apostles'.[50] In September Cromwell obtained an order from the Commons that the Assembly should accept toleration, and Baillie commented, 'we had need of your prayers in this hour of darkness'.[51]

The Scots had their own problems at home. In August 1644 Montrose slipped into Scotland with a single companion. At long last Antrim sent a force, not ten thousand, as he had promised, but eleven hundred ill-equipped McDonnells. Montrose raised the royal standard, and was joined by a few hundred clansmen. He swooped on Perth and Aberdeen, and led the pursuing Argyll a dance through desolate highland regions. In December he drove him from his own castle of Inverary, and in February 1645 routed the Campbells (Argyll having as usual fled) at Inverlochy. The Scottish commissioners in London were deeply depressed. The spectacular military successes they had expected in England had not materialised, and it was not until October 1644 that they managed to take Newcastle, after a long siege.

The year 1644 was therefore one of considerable confusion for both sides. The invasion of the Scots, and Cromwell's great victory at Marston Moor, had deprived the king of control of the north, but he had triumphed in the west. In October he marched back from the siege of Plymouth to fight the second battle of Newbury (27 October), an indecisive battle which enabled him to relieve Donnington Castle, and retire in good order to Oxford (23 November). But what most concerned Clarendon was that 'his necessities were still the same, and the fountains dried up from whence he might expect relief'.[52] On the other hand the intervention of the Scots, the conflicts between Presbyterians, Independents and Erastians in the Westminster Assembly, and the growing divisions in the Westminster parliament, and perhaps above all, the urgent longing for peace in the country, created confusion and uncertainty. Robert Baillie recognised this when he wrote in August 1644:

Since Pym died, no state head amongst them; many very good and able spirits, but not any of so great and comprehensive a brain as to manage the multitude of so weighty affairs as lies on them. If God did not sit at their helm, for any good of theirs, long ere this they had been gone.[53]

The earl of Essex had ruined his reputation at Lostwithiel, but his great rival the earl of Manchester, was wearying of the struggle, and becoming convinced that it was necessary to make peace:

If we fight a hundred times and beat him ninety-nine times, he will be King still. But if he beats us but once, of the last time, we shall be hanged, we shall lose our estates, and our properties be undone.

But Manchester had now a new rival in Oliver Cromwell, who replied:

My Lord, if this be so, why did we take up arms at first? This is against fighting ever hereafter; if so let us make peace, be it never so base.[54]

This quarrel developed at the second battle of Newbury, when Cromwell accused Manchester of deliberately avoiding a complete defeat of the king. According to Clarendon, Cromwell declared

My lord, if you will stick firm to honest men, you shall find yourself at the head of an army that shall give the law to king and parliament.[55]

These were prophetic words, but they alarmed more moderate men. The Scots were particularly concerned at the growing power of Independency and the army. The earl of Manchester, Baillie wrote, was 'a sweet, meek man', but Cromwell he regarded as a radical in a 'high and mighty plot of the Independent party'.[56]

In December the Westminster Assembly completed the new Directory of Worship. It laid aside the Book of Common Prayer, and proclaimed the *jus divinum* of presbyterian government, but by now Baillie despaired of ever making England Presbyterian:

the learnedst and most considerable part of (the clergy) were fully Episcopal; the Independents had brought the people to such a confusion that was insuperable by all the wit and strength which was here.[57]

The *jus divinum* of Presbyterianism was certainly too much for Bulstrode Whitelocke and John Glyn. They attacked it in the Commons, and succeeded in carrying a vote laying it aside.[58]

Since there was so much questioning and uncertainty, and since there was in the country such a genuine desire for peace, the question must be asked: why was the peace party at Westminster so ineffective? Clarendon thought that the main reason was intimidation, and this seems to have been the case.[59] The Waller and Brooke Plots had in essence been no more than attempts to get negotiations started, but they had led to accusations of treason and denunciations of 'malignancy'. Henceforth anyone who urged peace might be denounced as a malignant. When the earls of Bedford, Holland, Clare and Northumberland sought peace in the summer of 1643, the first three had to leave Westminster and join the king at Oxford, and Northumberland tried to act through the French ambassador. When that failed, Holland and Northumberland returned to make their peace with parliament. When the peace party asserted themselves, as they did in August 1643, Pym turned to the City, and pulpits rang with denunciations of talk of peace.

Pym and his friends had early learnt the value of demonstrations by the City apprentices, and the preachers who could stir up their congregations. Clarendon noted that 'It was an observation of that time that the first publishing of extraordinary news was from the pulpit; and by the preacher's text, and his manner of discourse upon it, the auditors might judge, and commonly foresaw, what was like to be next done in Parliament or Council of State.' Professor Trevor-Roper has shown how true this was for the whole period.[60] At the time of the attempt on the Five Members, Clarendon noted how 'their seditious ministers were despatched to inflame the neighbouring counties, and all possible art was used to inflame the city of London'.[61] It was true that there could be counter-demonstrations, as when crowds of women on 8 August 1643 denounced Lord Saye and Pym, and demanded peace[62] but these were exceptional. The radicals made use of the Brooke Plot in December 1643 to disenfranchise those electors to the Common Council of London who had been accused of 'malignancy', or who refused to take the Covenant. The Common Council was dominated by the radical John Foulke throughout 1644, and the Lord Mayor and aldermen found themselves neutralised in the face of such pressures.* Oliver St John was skilled also in winning the support of the Merchant Adventurers and the Levant Company, whose loans were invaluable to parliamentary finances.

Sir Henry Vane and his friends were in no mood for peace talks, and were more concerned with securing a Self-Denying Ordinance which would enable Essex to be ousted from the command of the army. But the pressure of Holles and the peace party, and the desire for peace in the counties could not be ignored. In November 1644 Holles and Whitelocke were among the commissioners sent to Oxford to discuss terms. They had some rough handling from royalists on the way, but were warmly received by Sir Edward Hyde, who expressed 'his earnest desire and endeavour' for peace.[64] The king received them civilly, and listened to the terms offered, saying that he would consider his answer. Holles and Whitelocke decided to make a courtesy call on the earl of Lindsey, who was recovering from his wounds, and while there, to their surprise, the king appeared, and drew them into conversation. He said he was disappointed with the terms offered. Holles admitted that they were less good than he would have liked. The king asked them what answer he should make. Embarrassed, they replied that they could not advise him. However, he pressed them as private individuals. Holles said that the best thing would be for the king to return to London, where he could rally moderate opinion. The king then pressed them to go into another room to write their thoughts on his reply. They did so, Whitelocke writing in a disguised hand. They left the paper on the table, and the king later took it. Holles, through the French agent Sabran, pressed the king not to reject the terms, lest he should wreck the efforts of the peace party, but to send his own terms to parliament. The commissioners returned with the king's answer, and a request for a safe conduct for the duke of Lennox and the earl of Southampton to bring the king's proposals. Eventually a treaty (i.e. a 'treating') was agreed upon at Uxbridge. The parliamentary commissioners included Northumberland, Pembroke, Salisbury, Denzil Holles, Sir Henry

---

* cf. Clarendon: 'Sir Henry Vane having diligently provided that men of his own principles and inclinations should be brought into the government of the city; of which he saw they should always have great need, even in order to keep the parliament well disposed'.[63]

Vane, Oliver St John and Bulstrode Whitelocke. The king's commissioners included Richmond, Hertford, Southampton, Culpepper, Nicholas and Hyde. The Scots also sent commissioners. The parliamentarians occupied the north side of the town, the royalists the south side. Meetings were held at the house of Sir John Bennet, where the commissioners sat each side of a table, with the Scots sitting by themselves at the end.

The king was offered in November terms which the war party, and the moderates, knew that he could not possibly accept. He was required to accept the Solemn League and Covenant; episcopacy was to be abolished and the work of the Westminster Assembly affirmed; all reformation of religion was to be by Act of Parliament. 'Malignants' were to be excepted from a general pardon, and the list included Prince Rupert, the earls of Bristol and Newcastle, Lord Digby, Edward Hyde, and many more. The armed forces were to be under commissioners nominated by parliament, and there were further clauses on Ireland. The king's own terms had been that his revenue, towns, forts and ships should be restored to him, that all laws should be by Act of Parliament, that there should be guarantees for the Protestant religion, and that if these were accepted, there should be a cessation of arms.[65] It was decided at the outset that three days (Clarendon says four days) should be devoted to each of the three subjects of religion, the militia and Ireland, after which the order would be repeated, the whole discussion to be limited to twenty days.

In the discussions on religion the Scots minister Alexander Henderson led the attack on the bishops, as the source of all misery in England and Scotland, and urging the need to bring England into line with continental Protestantism. Dr Steward saw an opening here, and asked *which* brand of continental protestantism, since the Directory seemed to conform to none? He defended episcopacy as an original institution of Christianity. Long discussions on the meaning of the Scripture brought them no nearer to a conclusion, although it became clear to the king's men that the English parliamentarians were less enthusiastic for the Directory than the Scots. When Hyde spoke he argued that whatever faults Archbishop Laud had committed, they were not sufficient to require an end to episcopacy which was as old as Christianity. In private conversation the earl of Pembroke admitted that he regretted that the Directory omitted the Lord's Prayer, the Creed and the Ten Commandments.[66]

When the commissioners passed to the subject of the armed forces, the demand of parliament was much more understandable, namely that control should be entirely in their hands. Clarendon summarised the problem succinctly,

they of that side (even they who most desired peace) both publicly and privately insisting upon having the whole command of the militia by sea and land, and all the forts and ships of the kingdom at their disposal; without which they looked upon themselves as lost and at the king's mercy; without considering that he must be at theirs, if such a jurisdiction was committed to them.[67]

Clarendon said they were convinced that the king would use force to liquidate his opponents.

On the subject of Ireland the parliamentary commissioners were convinced that the king favoured the rebellion there; they demanded that the cessation be revoked, and that the war against the rebels be renewed. Hyde was entrusted with the reply. He reminded them that parliament had paid too little attention to Ireland, that troops raised for service in Ireland had fought against the king at Edgehill; that the cessation had been inevitable in view of the king's limited resources; that money raised from the Adventurers in Ireland had been used to buy the aid of the Scots, not to suppress the Irish rebels. Since it was clear that any action in Ireland must depend on the settlement of the militia question, it was unlikely that any agreement was possible on the third proposition.

As the treaty continued, Hyde learned that there were three points of view on the parliamentary side; there were those who 'desired to have peace without any alteration in the government, so they might be sure of indemnity and security for what passed; there were the Scots who, so long as they had Presbyterianism would defer in other matters to the king; and there was a party who wanted no peace, but outright victory over the king. Clarendon said the last group were led by Sir Henry Vane, St John and Prideaux, who acted as commissioners, not for peace, but to act as spies on the others.[68] They knew that the three heads of the treaty were such that the king must reject them, and thus that the peace effort would fail. The doubts and uncertainties which existed among them were illustrated when, late one night, the earl of Pembroke came to Hyde's lodging. Hyde had once looked to the Herberts as patrons, and no doubt Pembroke felt safe in confiding to him. He begged that the king might be persuaded to accept the terms; 'that there never was such a pack of knaves and villains as they that now governed in the parliament'; that if the war party triumphed, Essex would be removed, the army would dominate parliament and defeat the king, and that the result would be a commonwealth. He admitted that they had been wrong, but it was too late for regrets. If the king accepted, the moderates would rally around him, and after a short time it would be possible for the king to overthrow the terms he had conceded.[69] Nor was this the view only of the earl of Pembroke, for the earls of Northumberland and Salisbury now saw the threat to the social position of the nobility, but Clarendon saw that they were men of straw, who had little credit in parliament or out of it. Clarendon had much greater respect for the earl of Denbigh, who also described the wretchedness of his position, and his willingness to do anything for the king which might bear fruit:

He informed more fully of the wicked purposes of those who then governed the parliament than others apprehended or imagined.[70]

As to the other members of the Commons, apart from Vane, St John and Prideaux, Clarendon believed they were all men of peace, but intimidated by the strength of the war party. They would speak freely of their opposition in private, but not in public. Holles doubted the strength of his following. Whitelocke had self-interest to consider:

All his estate was in their [parliamentary] quarters, and he had a nature that could not bear or submit to be undone: yet to his friends, who were commissioners for the king, he used his old openness, and professed his detestation of all their proceedings, yet could not leave them.

Pierrepoint and Crew showed more reserve, but were still men of moderation.

Rather than see the treaty fail completely, the moderates proposed that the king should concede control of the militia for seven years to a committee agreed by both sides, but it then proved impossible to agree upon the composition of such a committee. Thus after twenty days the negotiations were at an end without result. They had been exhausting days. Clarendon wrote

they who had been most inured to business had not in their lives ever undergone so great fatigue for twenty days together as at that treaty, the commissioners seldom parting, during that whole time, till one or two of the clock in the morning, and they being obliged to sit up long after, who were to prepare such papers as were directed for the next day.

The question remains whether the king at this time sincerely sought peace. Clarendon was certain that he did. He wrote that Charles was much depressed at the military situation, especially the loss of Shrewsbury during the negotiations, and he recognised the urgent desire for peace in the country. In October 1644 the gentry and freeholders of Somerset had petitioned the king for leave to appeal to parliament to seek peace. The king granted permission, and accordingly their petition to parliament requested

that as we now come to hazard our lives with his Majesty upon a well-grounded belief of his promises; so we will be no less ready to engage them in being sureties for his real performance, and therefore *desire you to lay by the too tender sense of those imaginary evils, which you only fear*, and to join hands with us in an happy treaty, for the removal of those real evils which we so sensibly suffer.[71]

This petition had considerable influence on the king. It is true that he was bombarded with letters from the queen in France begging him not to sign away his safety and honour. But Charles replied that the desire for peace was so great among his own followers, that he must pursue it. Yet there were two principles he could not concede. (1) 'I cannot yield to the change of the government by Bishops'; (2) the militia, 'this is certainly the fittest subject for a

King's quarrel, for without it the Kingly power is but a shadow'.[72] On these two principles the treaty broke down, as Vane and St John had intended that it should.

A clear indication of the king's real assessment of his prospects was his decision to send the Prince of Wales to the west country. When Lord Digby raised the topic with Sir Edward Hyde he painted a gloomy picture:

of the low condition of the king; of the discontent and murmur of the court and of the camp; how difficult a thing it was like to be to raise such an army as would be fit to take the field; and how much more unfit it would be for the king to suffer himself to be enclosed in any garrison; which he must be, if there were no army for him to be in. If the first difficulty should be mastered, and an army made ready to march, there could be little doubt, how great soever their distractions were at London, but that the parliament would be able to send another more numerous, and much better supplied than the king's could be; and then, if the king's army was beaten, he could have no hope ever to raise another, his quarters already being very strait; . . . London would pour out more forces; that all the west would be swallowed up in an instant . . .[73]

Digby had lost all the buoyant optimism in the early days of the conflict, and perhaps already sensed the military disasters which the year was to bring him. The chief hopes now lay in divisions in the Westminster parliament, and in Montrose's exploits in Scotland.* Hyde agreed that the prince must not be allowed to fall into the hands of parliament. He was less happy at the news that the king wished him to accompany the prince, and still more at the plan that, if the occasion demanded it, the prince should go to France to his mother. Not only would this have a depressing effect on the royalists in England, but also, Hyde feared the unpopularity of the queen, and the influence she might exercise over a fifteen-year old boy. Digby argued that if both king and prince were captured, parliament or army might murder the king with a view to placing the boy on the throne, whereas if the prince were out of the country there would be less purpose in the king's death. Charles on the other hand argued, somewhat naively, that parliament would never kill the king because at his death they themselves would be automatically dissolved.[74] Clarendon thought that Digby had spoken less with the voice of the king than of the queen, whose creature he was.[76]

In March 1645 Hyde was appointed to the Council of the Prince of Wales, and the king told him that he placed his trust particularly in Sir John Culpepper and himself. It was the last occasion Hyde ever saw Charles, for on 5 March the prince and his entourage set out for the west. The emotional strain was too much for Hyde, who, on the journey had his first attack of gout which was to plague him for the rest of his life. When he reached Bath he was unable to stand.

* Montrose wrote to the king during the Uxbridge Treaty urging him not to make concessions: 'The more your Majesty grants, the more will be asked; and I have too much reason to know that they will not rest satisfied with less than making your Majesty a king of straw.'[74]

# From Uxbridge to the Engagement

The failure of the Treaty of Uxbridge coincided with the opening of a darker and more embittered phase in the conflict. Hitherto there had been belief in a negotiated peace and a mutal tolerance, but now there was a new ruthlessness in which the influence of men of moderation was steadily eliminated. Even before the Uxbridge meeting there had been an act of provocation when Archbishop Laud had been attainted of treason, without a shadow of legality, and executed (10 January 1645). In his final sermon he declared:

I was born and baptised in the bosom of the Church of England established by law; in that profession I have ever since lived, and in that I come now to die. This is no time to dissemble with God, least of all in matters of religion: and therefore I desire it may be remembered, I have always lived in the Protestant religion established in England, and in that I come now to die.[1]

The Hothams, father and son, were executed for their attempt to surrender Hull to the earl of Newcastle. The Lords attempted a stay of mercy both with Laud and the Hothams, but were overruled by the Commons. In December a Self-Denying Ordinance, designed to eliminate the earl of Essex from the command of the army, passed the Commons; the Lords held it up until April, when it was allowed to pass. The Upper House had almost lost the will to independent action. Essex, Warwick and Manchester resigned their commands, and were replaced by Sir Thomas Fairfax and Cromwell. In April the New Model Army came into being. The areas of England under the king's control were now virtually restricted to parts of the Midlands and the west country. There was no longer the possibility of a royalist victory; the most which could be hoped for was a negotiated peace. The king had few cards left to play, and must rely upon divisions at Westminster, or the Scots, or the victories of Montrose.

When the prince and his council reached Bristol in March 1645 they found the royalist situation in the utmost confusion. The guard for the prince's protection had not materialised, nor had the hundred pounds a week for his maintenance; and Clarendon said that the prince had to borrow from Lord Hopton in order to buy bread. Instead of a willingness to work together among the royalists there were mutual recriminations. The prince was appointed

Generalissimo of the forces in the west, but in view of his age he was to act through his council, consisting of the earl of Berkshire, the duke of Richmond, the earl of Southampton, Lords Capel, Hopton and Culpepper and Sir Edward Hyde. The king had expressed his especial confidence in the last two to direct affairs in his interest. There was also a council to administer the lands and revenues of the duchy of Cornwall. There was inevitably friction between the two councils, and between the prince's council and the military men in the field. When failure engulfed the whole western venture, the Generals Grenville and Goring placed the blame on the interference of the council, and Hyde's account was written in 1646 to put the record straight. The events were fresh in his mind, and his account reasonably accurate.

The parliamentary forces were still holding out in Plymouth and Taunton, and had retaken Weymouth. Lord Goring, who was Lieutenant-General of the counties from Hampshire to Kent, and therefore had no authority in the west country, nonetheless proposed a joint attack on Taunton. It made good sense, and the prince's council approved. But Sir William Waller was marching westwards, and Goring revised his plans and asked for reinforcements to meet the threat. The prince's council accordingly ordered Sir Richard Grenville, who was besieging Plymouth, to march to Goring's assistance. Grenville replied that he would not stir a foot nor advance beyond Taunton until the town had been taken. It was true that his men objected to serving far from home, but in addition Grenville had no desire to serve Goring. The latter was able to inflict two sharp defeats on Waller in Wiltshire, but without reinforcements could not follow them up as Waller retired to Salisbury. Grenville was left grumbling that with six hundred men he could have taken Taunton. It was indeed imperative that Taunton should be taken if the west country was to be safe, and in April the prince's council gave Goring the choice of either pursuing Waller, or detailing his foot to join with Grenville in the siege of Taunton. Goring returned a 'sullen' reply, but complied with the latter alternative, and then retired to Bath on a plea of ill health. He had indeed a wound, but Clarendon said that he sported himself for several days in Bath, until he reprimanded him: 'For God's sake let us not fall into ill-humour which may cost us dear. Get good thoughts about you and let us hear speedily from you to a better tune'.[2] After which Goring returned to his command.

Meanwhile Grenville had been severely wounded before Taunton, and when Sir John Berkeley was appointed to the command of the siege of Taunton, Grenville's men refused to serve under him. Hyde, Capel and Culpepper were sent down to Exeter to settle disputes of jurisdiction and command. They found a bitter quarrel raging between Grenville and Berkeley which on investigation proved to arise from the fact that they both held commissions giving them command of the forces of Devon and Cornwall. Grenville complained that it troubled him to be confined to besieging Plymouth, when there was likelihood of much greater action. The commissioners agreed with Grenville, who, with all his faults, was the most influential leader in Devon and Cornwall; and they decided that Berkeley should take charge of the siege of Plymouth. Hyde also was busy apportioning the two thousand pounds weekly which were the revenues from Devon and the seven hundred pounds from Cornwall. The great need was for an overall commander in the west. The best man might well have been thought to be Lord Hopton, but in the interests of harmony Grenville was favoured by the council. The whole difficulty in the west illustrated the weakness of royalist organisation in controlling county committees. Grenville exercised a unique authority in Devon and Cornwall by scrupulously paying his troops regularly, and hanging those who plundered, or who failed to pay taxes.[3] The council therefore made the best arrangement in the circumstances.

In May 1645 however it was overthrown by the intervention of the king. In April he summoned Goring to Oxford. Goring developed a close friendship with Lord Digby, and gave his own version of these events, criticising the interventions of the council without which, he said, quite untruthfully, he would have defeated Waller. The king believed him, and on 10 May appointed him Generalissimo of the Western Army. It was a disastrous decision which upset the settlement the prince's council had made. Grenville was now required to serve under Goring, to his great discontent. Prince Rupert was anxious to march northwards to have his revenge for Marston Moor on the Scots who were embarrassed by Montrose's victories in the Highlands, and Goring's troops would have been a useful assistance. But he disliked Goring, and was not anxious to have him under his command. Thus Goring returned with 5000 foot and 4000 horse to the siege of Taunton, a force which would have been invaluable at Naseby. Goring was a soldier of dash and vigour, but also a debauchee, and he allowed his troops to terrorise the countryside of Somerset and Dorset, so that the population was alienated from the royalists. Most country people were in fact neutral in the conflict between king and parliament, and wanted only to be left alone. When they were harassed by the royalists they organised their own defence, calling themselves Clubmen. It is true that the prince's council wrote to the king on 24 May saying that the West would be lost if Goring's force was withdrawn, but in fact Goring did nothing to take Taunton.

On 31 May Prince Rupert captured Leicester and sacked it, thus revealing one of the worst aspects of royalist excesses. The New Model Army was as yet untried, but on 14 June Fairfax and Cromwell forced the king and Prince Rupert to fight at Naseby, near Market Harborough, although they were heavily outnumbered, and Rupert was in favour of avoiding battle. Clarendon was not impressed by the generalship shown by the royalists, and wrote that the troops had little to rely on except their courage.[4] Rupert's cavalry as usual attacked with vigour, but as at Edgehill, failed to regroup, and in the end the royalist army was shattered with the loss of nearly 4000 men. The king's treasure and, worse, his private papers, were captured. The battle, Clarendon wrote, lost the king his kingdom.

Charles fell back to Hereford, with the idea of raising a new army from Wales, a strange idea, Clarendon wrote, considering the exhausted state of that country, and considering that he had a ready-made army awaiting him in the west country. But that army was in considerable disarray. Grenville governed Devon and Cornwall with a brutal efficiency, collecting revenues which he retained entirely for the use of his own army, regardless of the needs of other royalists, and plundering and hanging countrymen at will. Goring did little to attempt to take Taunton, and was so debauched 'that he many times was not seen abroad in three or four days', while his men plundered the countryside. Finally his feebleness as a general was revealed on 9 July, when he allowed himself to be surprised by Fairfax at Langport, a few miles from Bridgwater, and utterly routed. Some two thousand royalists were taken prisoner, and many of those who escaped were killed by Clubmen. Bridgwater was taken, with great stocks of royalist supplies, which Hyde and the council had built up so laboriously. Meanwhile Grenville was summoned before the prince at Liskeard and asked by what authority he had acted so oppressively. Clarendon wrote that 'he answered little, but sullenly extolled his services and enlarged his sufferings'. When he spoke of spending his own estate he was reminded 'that he had no estate by any other title than the mere bounty of the king'.[5] Under the pressure of events royalist morale was breaking down. For a short time Hyde passed through a period of despondency:

I am weary of my life. . . . The burden is too great for us, and truly grief, anger and indignation have so broken my mind that I am not able to continue this life.[6]

Fortunately the mood soon passed, although he never forgave Goring nor Grenville for their exasperating and childish behaviour. Mary Coate writes that he

acted with energy; he was the brains of the Prince's Council, and his efforts to collect the royal revenue in Cornwall to support the failing cause are worthy of an attention which neither their author in his writings, nor his successive biographers have bestowed on them. Fortunately the Clarendon Mss. and the official documents of the duchy of Cornwall witness to his unceasing efforts and his marked ability as a financier.

She shows that he was able to raise £1175 from the revenues of the duchy of Cornwall. He raised the production of tin, which was shipped to the queen in France in payment for supplies and loans, and Jermyn had the difficult task of disposing of the exports. Hyde also had the problem of extracting the weekly rate of £750 from a county which was exhausted, and which had grown used to avoiding payment.[7]

Charles was in south Wales when he heard of the defeat at Langport and the surrender of Bridgwater, which he had supposed to be impregnable. He suspected treachery, and for a time he too was despondent. So was Prince Rupert, who wrote to the duke of Richmond that the only course the king could take was to make peace. Charles answered the letter himself:

As for your opinion of my business, and your counsel thereupon, if I had any other quarrel but the defence of my religion, crown and friends, you had full reason for your advice. For I confess, that speaking as a mere soldier or statesman, I must say, there is no probability but of my ruin; yet as a Christian, I must tell you that God will not suffer rebels and traitors to prosper, nor this cause to be overthrown: and whatever personal punishment it shall please him to inflict upon me, must not make me repine, much less give over this quarrel; and there is as little question that a composition with them at this time is nothing else but a submission, which, by the grace of God, I am resolved against, whatever it cost me, for I know my obligation to be, both in conscience and honour, neither to abandon God's cause, injure my successors, nor forsake my friends.

He begged Rupert not to press for peace terms, since he could not accept less than he had offered at Uxbridge, and if parliament would not accept them then, they certainly would not accept them after Naseby.[8] The letter is the clearest statement of the principles which guided Charles for the rest of his life. Whatever mistakes he had made in the past, he was now determined, come what may, not to give way on the church, the traditional powers of the crown, or betray his friends. He had indeed betrayed Strafford, and it was a matter of bitter regret to him always; indeed he believed that his subsequent misfortunes had been divine punishment for his betrayal. Hyde also believed absolutely in the need to observe these three principles; his only fear was that under superhuman stress, Charles might give way on them. But Charles did not, and it was this which finally converted Hyde from his earlier suspicions of monarchy to a veneration for Charles I.

The king summoned Hyde and Culpepper from Cornwall to attend him in south Wales. Hyde was again incapacitated by gout, but Culpepper hastened to Cardiff, and there received Charles' letter of instructions to the Prince of Wales (5 August, 1645):

It is very fit for me now to prepare for the worst. . . . Wherefore know that my pleasure is, whensoever you find yourself in apparent danger of falling into the rebels' hands, that you convey yourself into France, and there be under your mother's care; who is to have the absolute full power of your education in all things, except religion; and in that not to meddle at all, but leave it entirely to the care of your tutor, the bishop of Salisbury . . . And for the performance of this, I command you to require the assistance and obedience of all your council . . .

Your loving father, Charles R.[9]

(The bishop of Salisbury was Brian Duppa.) Hyde and the council were alarmed at the king's letter, not at the need to prevent the prince from falling into parliament's hands, with which they of course agreed, and indeed had a ship waiting at Falmouth for just such an extreme occasion; but at the king's instructions that he should go to France. The earl of Norwich, ambassador to France, wrote that such a move would be disastrous to the prince's cause, and the council prepared a letter to the king setting out the arguments against it, and asking that they be left freedom of action, since Ireland, or Scotland (if Montrose continued to be successful) would be possible alternatives. The influence of the queen, and of Catholic associations, would be a mortal blow to royalism in England. Meanwhile Hyde personally supervised the provisioning of a ship ready for the prince at Pendennis Castle.[10]

After his defeat at Langport, Goring had thrown himself with renewed energy into raising a new army in Cornwall, and talked of ten or twelve thousand men. But morale was low, money desperately short, and Clarendon wrote that although there was plenty of food in the west country, people were refusing to supply the royalists. Goring continued his feud against the prince's council, and made impossible demands for recognition as supreme commander. Worst of all, Fairfax took Sherborne Castle in August, and moved up to the siege of Bristol. As Bristol was the only remaining link between the west and the king in Wales, its defence was essential. By 4 September Prince Rupert found the city surrounded, although by a rather thin line. He might have achieved more by well planned sallies, but it is probable that royalist morale was low. A general assault on the city was begun on 9 September in the middle of the night, and by morning parts of the city were on fire, either deliberately or by accident. In the morning Prince Rupert asked for terms, and was allowed to march out of the Royal Fort in good order, he himself 'clad in scarlet, very richly laid in silver lace, mounted upon a very gallant black Barbary horse'.[11] The king was furious at the news of the disaster. Rupert had promised to hold out at least four months, and it was hoped that Goring might march his new army to the relief of the city. But there was a strong parliamentary force in the neighbourhood of Taunton under the command of Colonel Massey, and even if the royalist morale had been high enough to make the attempt, it is doubtful whether Goring could have got through. Rupert might have been expected to make a dash out of the city with his cavalry, but may have felt that further fighting would have brought needless slaughter. The king wrote him a savage letter:

the greatest trial of my constancy that hath yet befallen me; for what is to be done, after one that is so near me as you are, both in blood and friendship, submit himself to so mean an action? . . . My conclusion is, to desire you to seek your subsistence . . . somewhere beyond the seas.[12]

Rupert published a 'Declaration' defending his conduct, and demanded a court martial, which at least exonerated him from treachery. Clarendon hints that Charles's sharp reaction may have been the result of a suspicion that Rupert, like his brother the Elector Palatine, had some idea of replacing Charles as king, but if so the king was mistaken, for Rupert's loyalty was never in doubt.* Charles must however have felt a great sense of isolation at this time. Only in Scotland had he cause for satisfaction, for on 18 August 1645 Montrose completely defeated Argyll at the battle of Kilsyth; no other army opposed him, and he was master of Scotland. Glasgow and Edinburgh submitted, and for a short time Montrose was to enjoy the fruits of victory.

The loss of Bristol plunged the prince's council into 'such a desperate gulf of despair, that all the good news in the world beyond our horizon cannot change our complexion', Lord Culpepper wrote to Lord Digby. The only solution seemed to him to be the royalist garrisons in the west to remain on the defensive, while Goring led his horse to join the king in an attempt to reach Scotland and Montrose, after which, perhaps with Irish or French help, an attack might be staged on England. But, he wrote, nothing would be achieved without a reform of discipline in the royalist army:

Our energy is enerved by a lazy licentiousness; and good men are so scandalised at the horrid impiety of our armies, that they will not believe that God can bless any cause in such hands.[14]

After the battle of Edgehill Cromwell had told Hampden that their own troops were 'old serving-men and tapsters', who could never hope to defeat 'the sons of gentlemen that have honour and courage and resolution in them'.[15] In 1645 the situation was different. Three years of war had brutalised and demoralised many royalists, and the countryside was alienated by their depradations for which lack of food and pay were the only excuse.

Culpepper's strategic plan was quickly overtaken by events, for the fall of Bristol left the way open for Fairfax to advance into Devon. There was a move in the county to persuade the prince to make a separate offer of peace to parliament, but this the council managed to stave off. Goring was ordered to gather his forces and make a main stand at Tiverton, but he remained disgracefully inactive, and Fairfax was able to occupy the town almost without firing a shot. The royalists had now to fall back to Exeter, where they had some respite while Fairfax rested his troops at Ottery St Mary.

Meanwhile Hyde and Hopton were inspecting Pendennis, Bodmin and Truro to decide where the prince might make his last stand. The king wrote to the prince's council a letter which arrived only in the middle of October, virtually accepting Goring's proposal that Lord Goring's horse might be sent to Oxford, although he recognised that that might be impossible; but above all commanding that the prince be sent safely to France, and expressly forbidding Scotland or Denmark.[16] Hyde knew however that the departure of the prince would be a signal for the utter collapse of the royalists in the west, and the council wrote to the king begging that it be delayed as long as possible.

On 20 November Goring laid down his command and escaped to France, on the plea of ill health. Clarendon later wrote a damning indictment of

* He wrote a full submission to the king, 8 Dec. 1645.[13]

Goring's generalship, which modern historians have on the whole endorsed.[17] Clarendon concluded that 'if he had been confederate with the enemy, and been corrupted to betray the west, he could not have taken a more effectual way to do it'.[18] Goring had an army not much inferior in numbers to Fairfax's, but the latter never needed to worry that Goring would make much use of it. Goring was not treacherous, but he was an inferior general. It may well be argued that the king's defeat was inevitable after Naseby, but Goring hastened the end. Perhaps the real mistake was to have sent him into the west in May 1645. His horse would have been invaluable at Naseby, and Grenville would have been the better general in the west.

The prince's council regarded Goring's flight as a blessing rather than a loss. They reckoned that they still had some six thousand foot and five thousand horse, and if these could be assembled, and Exeter defended, they could still give a good account of themselves. The king wrote on 7 November urging the prince's withdrawal, this time to Denmark, and again on 7 December, even more imperatively, saying that he was about to propose a personal treaty with parliament, and that it was necessary that the prince should be safely in Denmark, France or Holland. John Ashburnham wrote to Culpepper on the 13th revealing the desperate state of Charles's affairs at Oxford. The king proposed, he wrote, to ask the Upper House, the Scots and the City of London (thus carefully avoiding asking the Commons) for a safe conduct to come to London for forty days to arrange a peace. Ashburnham continued:

The reasons that invited his Majesty to make a choice of this advice, I suppose, were these. First, his low condition in point of force, the strange necessity he is brought into not being longer able to supply his table, the like wants being fallen on all his party; the little hope he hath of being timely succoured by the earl of Montrose, or any other; the certainty of being blocked up here or in any other place his Majesty can now hie unto.[19]

Ashburnham's letter showed that the king placed his hopes now with the Scots. Lord Digby had written a persuasive letter to the Scottish earls of Leven and Callander, offering the king's guarantee of security for the Presbyterian Church in Scotland, and the settlement of the English Church by a national synod. The letter was found among Digby's papers when Sherborne Castle was taken. There was a piquancy in that Digby had complained bitterly of the king's carelessness in allowing his own papers to be captured after Naseby.[20]

Charles in fact was desperately seeking for a basis for a negotiated peace. The French ambassador Montreuil warned him that no settlement was possible without the acceptance of Presbyterianism in England. Charles replied that even if he wished it, he could not impose Presbyterianism in England, since Independency was so strong, and in any case English Presbyterians differed greatly from the Scots. He offered however firm guarantees for Presbyterianism in Scotland, and the settlement of religion in England to be left to a national synod. Montreuil replied that parliament would accept nothing less than the three conditions laid down at Uxbridge; that the war in the west was nearly over, and that time was running out, 'de sorte que j'ose encore repeter a V.M. qu'elle n'a plus de temps á perdre'.[21] On 25 December parliament rejected the king's request for a personal treaty or a safe conduct for his envoys to come to London, and letters went to and fro during January without result.[22] But, Charles wrote to the queen, he meant to persist in his attempts. The queen pressed him to abandon episcopacy, but this he would not do:

The difference between me and the rebels concerning the church is not bare matter of form or ceremony, which are alterable according to occasion, but so real that if I should give way as is desired, there would be no church, and by no human probability ever to be recovered; so that, besides the obligation of mine oath, I know nothing to be an higher point of conscience. . . . This I am sure of, which none can deny, that my yielding this is a sin of the highest nature.[23]

He was convinced that parliament meant to have his life, and hence the importance he attached to ensuring the prince's safety. With so many doubting counsellors about him ('there is none doth assist me heartily in my steady resolutions but Sir Edward Nicholas and Ashburnham') Charles held firm to the determination that, at whatever cost, he would not surrender on the Anglican Church, nor surrender the royal prerogative, nor betray his friends. As to the possibility of a treaty with the Scots, Charles revealed his real belief when he wrote to the queen on 1 February:

Now, for the Scotch treaty, it is not so much worth as to spend words about it; in short it is all fourbery [i.e. knavery].[24]

Culpepper and Hyde, on the other hand, in their desperation, seized on the idea of a Scots treaty as the best, indeed the only way out of the king's predicament. They wrote an urgent letter to Ashburnham:

This is again most earnestly to intreat you to bend all your wits to advance the Scotch treaty. It is the only way left to save the Crown and three Kingdoms; all other tricks will deceive you. This is no age of miracles; and certainly the King's condition is such that less than a miracle cannot save him without a treaty, nor any treaty probably but that. . . . If you can make the Scots your friends upon any honest terms, do it. Remember, that Kingdom united, and the North, and the King's friends at London, will quickly master any opposition which the independents can make. The question ought not to be, Whether, but how, you should do it.[25]

They continued that the west could not hold out beyond mid-summer, that Ireland would be a broken reed, and foreign aid 'but a vain dream'. Once Fairfax advanced again in the west the horse would be lost, and once lost, could never be recovered. They advised that the best course would be an open offer to Leslie (Leven) and Callander, and they hinted that the duke of Hamilton might be useful as in intermediary. Hamilton was still a prisoner in Pendennis Castle; Hyde had had interviews with him, and the Scot had offered his services to the king.* It was Hamilton's servant who was the bearer of this letter.

It crossed with one from the king of 2 February 1646 which revealed that his mind was now concerned with a different plan. He announced that he hoped to raise one thousand five hundred horse and a thousand dragoons as an 'army volant' for a sudden descent on Kent, to raise Sussex and seize Rochester, and he hoped that the queen would be able to send five thousand men from France to be landed near Hastings.† If this should fail, he would join the Prince of Wales, or require the prince to join him, and he asked the council to be prepared for either eventuality. He made it plain that his object was only to persuade parliament to negotiate.

It was a desperate scheme, and showed how far Charles was out of touch with the situation in the west. For in January Lord Wentworth was defeated by Fairfax near Bovey Tracy, and the prince was forced to fall back from Tavistock to Launceston, and from there to Pendennis Castle.[27] Grenville found it impossible to control his men, and threw up his command. Only the greatest sense of loyalty persuaded Lord Hopton to replace him. Perhaps if he had been given the command in May 1645 the situation would have been happier. As it was, he was now required to take charge of 'a dissolute, undisciplined, wicked, beaten army', in which 'both officer and soldier was desirous to take any occasion and to find any excuse to lay down his arms'.[28] It was now an army 'only terrible in plunder, and resolute in running away'. When Grenville refused to serve under him, the prince had him imprisoned. In spite of Grenville's harsh government, this was not a popular move, and many of the gentlemen of Cornwall thought he had been unfairly treated. Grenville's advice had been to abandon Devon, and hold a strong line at the river Tamar, since Cornwall was the only completely royalist county. This would have been militarily feasible, but would have made sense only if the prince had contemplated a separate peace with parliament which neither prince nor council would entertain for a moment.

On 14 February 1646 Fairfax defeated Hopton at Torrington, and this was virtually the end of the resistance. As Fairfax advanced to Launceston and Bodmin, the prince retired to Pendennis Castle. There were rumours of a plan to seize him and hand him over to parliament.‡ Hyde and Culpepper felt themselves very vulnerable, not knowing even whether they could trust the prince's own servants or the governor of the castle. The council therefore agreed that the prince should sail to the Scilly Isles, which were part of

---

* When the fall of the castle was imminent, Hamilton was set free.
† His letter asking the queen for this is dated 19 Feb.[26]
‡ Secretary Nicholas warned Culpepper and Hyde of this on 4 Feb. from Oxford.[29]

Cornwall, where, it was given out, French help could be gathered for the relief of Cornwall. On the night of 2 March the prince went on board, and two days later landed at St Mary's in the Scillies. Hopton and Capel followed on 11 March. On 12 March the army accepted honourable terms: it was disbanded, and the officers might go overseas or compound for their estates. Pendennis Castle and St Michael's Mount were the only two places which continued to hold out, as Fairfax marched off to join the siege of Oxford. Exeter surrenderd on 18 April.

The prince and his following remained in the Scilly Isles from 4 March to 16 April. They found little in the way of supplies, food or money on the island. Moreover on 12 April a strong fleet of twenty enemy ships appeared. It was dispersed by a storm, but it was certain that it would return, and that the prince had no means of defence. Still the council hesitated: suppose the king's treaty with parliament should succeed? What if the prince's ship was driven on to the French coast? The prince settled the matter by producing a letter from his father dated 23 June 1645, commanding him to do nothing dishonourable even as a means of saving the king's life. This was interpreted to mean that he must not at any cost fall into rebel hands. The council at once agreed, and on 16 April the prince and his entourage set sail in the *Proud Black Eagle*, a frigate of 160 tons and 24 guns, and next day they landed before Elizabeth Castle, Jersey. Two other vessels followed, bringing servants, wives and tradesmen, some three hundred people in all.

The prince and his council took up residence in Elizabeth Castle, while his lesser followers found places in Saint Helier.[30] He was accompanied by the earl of Berkshire, Lords Capel, Wentworth and Hopton and Sir Edward Hyde. Lord Culpepper, who had been windbound in France, arrived a few days later, bearing a letter from the queen, full of anxiety for the prince's safety, and making it clear that her real objective was to have him in France.[31] This presented a problem the council had expected, and were prepared to resist. They argued that France had shown no real friendship for Charles I, that the prince would become a tool in French diplomacy, and they mistrusted the queen's influence. Meantime the prince lived in considerable state, receiving the gentry of the island, winning praises for his affability, and dining in public. Jean Chevalier, who saw him, was immensely impressed at the quantity of silver plate, the kneeling pages who served him, and the delicacy of the food. Such was the outward show, but in fact the prince had landed with less than twenty pounds, and from the beginning had to borrow 1500 pistoles from the governor, Sir George Carteret.[32]

In May Culpepper and Capel were sent to the queen to explain why the council advised the prince to remain in Jersey, but two days later, on 11 May, Sir Dudley Wyatt arrived with an importunate letter from Henrietta Maria, and enclosing a letter from the king dated 15 April. He hinted his intention of going to the Scots, and commanded the prince to join the queen in France.

Hyde undertook to write the reply. In a flowery and ironic letter to Lord Jermyn, the queen's favourite (20 May), he declared that nothing would please him better than to be at the most civilised Court in the world, and to have the protection of the queen. But there would be more point in the prince going to Paris if France were ready actively to send help to the king. He said he was far from believing that any good would come from the men at Westminster, but the rebels were divided; there were royalists in England who might reassert themselves, and they would be discouraged if they saw their prince in France when French intentions were so uncertain, and not least from the associations with Popery, however ungrounded the suspicions. The king's, and therefore the prince's hope of returning to power depended on their remaining loyal to the Anglican church:

so that the question is not, whether the Prince be like to be corrupted in his religion by going into France, but whether generally the people of England will be persuaded to believe that he is so . . . And truly, in this conjuncture of time, it may be the reputation of a pious and religious Prince, may do more towards the composing of the distractions of the three Kingdoms, than any other attribute that can be wished in him.[33]

In making such a decision the thoughts of the Scots, Irish, the Prince of Orange, the King of Denmark must also be taken into account, and finally the queen should consider what use the English parliament would make of the prince's obeying his mother's instructions. It was a stout letter, and one which carried with it Hyde's complete conviction.

His opinion was formed in the light of the dire circumstances of the king in England. Since December his repeated attempts to negotiate a personal treaty had been rejected by parliament. When he proposed to come to London, the two Houses voted (31 March) that if he should appear he should be placed under arrest.[34] He even wrote to Sir Henry Vane offering the Independents royal aid in overthrowing Presbyterian domination.[35] In letter after letter from the queen he was bombarded with reproaches, for she saw no reason why the Crown should be sacrificed for the sake of the Anglican church. In March he replied wearily:

really I should sink under my present miseries, if I did not know myself innocent of those faults which thy misinformed judgment condemns me of . . . I am blamed both for granting too much, and yet not yielding enough.[36]

She had won over Culpepper to her point of view, and both urged Charles to seek agreement with the Scots. She had also identified Hyde as the centre of resistance to her influence, and did her best to poison the king's mind against him. On 30 March he replied:

As for Culpepper I confess never to have much esteemed him in religion, though in other things I reverenced his judgment. But I believe thou mistaketh Ned Hyde, for I am assured he was, and am still confident that he is, fully of my mind; and thou much mistaketh me if anything hath all this while hindered my conjunction with the Scots, but their seeking to force my conscience.

The king's instinct was right, but Montreuil, the French ambassador, was also pressing for an agreement with the Scots, and by 6 April he seems to have convinced him, for he wrote to the queen that he would be received by them 'as their natural sovereign, with freedom of my conscience and honour'. A fortnight later Montreuil had to admit that he was wrong, that the Scots made no promises, and that the king's knowledge of that nation was much better than his.* But by now Charles was at the end of his resources. Oxford could not hold out much longer, and he thought of flight to Lynn where he might find a ship to take him to Montrose, or Ireland, France or Denmark. On 27 April, accompanied only by John Ashburnham and his chaplain Dr Hudson, he disappeared from Oxford. It is probable that he had still not made up his mind where to go, but after some days wandering in disguise, he appeared on 5 May at the Scots' camp before Newark. The Scots treated him as their prisoner, as they marched away to Newcastle.

Charles now learnt the bitter truth which he had apprehended before. The Scots would do nothing to risk their alliance with the English parliament.

It is daily more and more evident to me that the Scots resolve to clip the king's power in England just answerable to what it is in Scotland.

His servants were sent away ('None are suffered to come about me but fools and knaves') and he was bombarded with attempts to convert him to Presbyterianism. The only effect was to convince him more than ever that the crown and the Anglican church were inseparable. On 10 June he wrote

Indeed I have need of some comfort, for I never knew what it was to be barbarously baited before. . . . Nothing must serve but my signing the covenant . . . I answered them that what they demanded was absolutely against my conscience . . . I cannot but again remember thee that there was never man so alone as I . . .[38]

He felt he could not trust any advice, and could hardly any longer trust his own judgment. In this turmoil his mind repeatedly reverted to the idea that he was being punished for his betrayal of Strafford.

Charles was right in his assessment of Hyde, who regarded it as essential that the king should not weaken in his defence of the Anglican Church. On 1 June he wrote to Secretary Nicholas, who was still at Oxford, that all of them must be prepared to die rather than to give way more than the king had offered at Uxbridge. On the subject of the prince he wrote:

* Clarendon absolved Montreuil from any accusation of duplicity. On 1 April the Scots had promised him that the king would be received 'as their natural sovereign; and that he shall be with them in all freedom of his conscience and honour', but during the month they changed their minds. Montreuil kept the king fully informed of the change. The king therefore went to the Scots under no illusion, simply because 'he was clearly destitute of any other refuge'.[37]

I will not be hurried by any command whatsoever into an action that I think will prove so pernicious to the King, Queen, Prince and realm, as this unnecessary going of the Prince into France.[39]

This was his most immediate task. John Ashburnham, who had been forced to leave the king, arrived in France with a first-hand account of Charles's sad condition. He reported that the king was anxious that the prince should leave Jersey, but only because he feared for his safety. Henrietta Maria used this to re-enforce her demand that the prince should join her, and she now had powerful allies. When Lords Capel and Culpepper arrived at Saint Germain they were splendidly entertained, and when Lord Digby arrived a few days later he too received the same flattering treatment, not only by the queen, but also by Mazarin. Capel and Culpepper were not deceived by this, but Digby was. The queen then sent an impressive embassy to the prince, with an imperative letter that he should obey his father's wishes.[40] On 20 June 1646 Lords Capel, Culpepper, Digby, Witherington, Jermyn and Wentworth, together with an entourage of seventy or eighty, arrived in Jersey bearing the letter.

They met the council on Sunday, the 21st. The queen's friends assumed that there could be no question of the prince not agreeing, but the council put up a stout resistance and the debate became so hot that the prince suspended the meeting until the next day. The council argued that the island was stoutly defended by 500 or 600 men, and that the prince was in no danger. Lord Capel doubted whether the French had any intention of aiding the king. Digby and Jermyn however talked airily of French intentions of placing the prince at the head of 30,000 men for the invasion of England. Hyde led the resistance. Walking on the ramparts of the castle, Digby and Jermyn asked him whether his resistance was worth while. Jermyn argued that the king's cause was wholly dependent upon the French and the Scots, and that the French would do nothing without the presence of the prince in France. He agreed that the French would act only in their own interests, but thought that those interests required a restored monarchy in England. Digby also expressed complete confidence in the French. Hyde was quite unmoved. He had a clearer view of French motives, was certain that Mazarin would do nothing effective, and knew the damage which would be done to the royalist cause in England if the prince was in French hands. At the renewed meeting, five of the six councillors (Berkshire, Brentford, Capel, Hopton and Hyde) were opposed to the prince's going, while the sixth, Culpepper, although more doubtful, inclined to their view. But the prince was dazzled by the attractions of the French Court and by the prospects of 30,000 men under his command, and he opted for France. Further argument therefore, Clarendon wrote, was 'not only useless but indecent'. The council however (excepting Culpepper) made it clear that they would not accompany him to France.[41] The five councillors therefore took their leave of the prince, who announced his intention of going at once to France. Relations between the council and the queen's friends were so strained that they were no longer on speaking terms, and thus a breach was made which was never healed, and for which Hyde had to pay dearly in later years. He however regarded the whole affair as having been cleverly stage-managed by Mazarin, and he was proved to be right.

Clarendon wrote that there was another factor which the council feared, but could not openly express, namely that the queen and the French ambassador would continue to press the king to accept Presbyterianism as the price of retaining his crown. In this they underestimated the king, who in the end was prepared to be a martyr for his church. But Hyde's thoughts went further,

for I do more fear a French army, than the Presbyterians and Independents. It must be the resurrection of the English courage and loyalty must recover England to the King, and ... sure a foreign aid (except of arms and money) will never reconcile those hearts and affections to the King and his Posterity, without which he hath no hope of reigning.[42]

He adhered to this principle for the next thirteen years.

Meanwhile the king's position steadily deteriorated. His flight to the Scots was an act of desperation, but rested on the assumption that the Scots were more favourable to monarchy than the Westminster parliament, and that it would be possible to drive a wedge between Presbyterians and Independents. But the Scots merely used the king to their own advantage. They first demanded that Montrose should lay down his arms and disband his forces. Montrose was still virtually master of the military situation in Scotland, and his was the only royalist force left to Charles. But the king ordered him to disband, a gross error on his part. Montrose complied, and went into exile in Germany.

Charles also relied on the promises of Henrietta Maria that the French would assist him, but Clarendon complained that the new French ambassador, Bellievre, was obsequious to parliament, applied himself exclusively to the Presbyterian party, and merely advised the king to accede to the Scots' demands that he should accept the Covenant.[43] This was also the advice of Jermyn, Culpepper and John Ashburnham writing to the king from Saint Germain. They argued that agreements entered into now need not be observed later. Charles replied at length from Newcastle on 12 August:

if you think that I understand anything in religion, then believe me that the Presbyterian tenets and government are more erronious than those of the Church of Rome, and absolutely inconsistent with monarchy; which I irrevocably destroy, according to own rules, if legally I introduce that which is so destructive to it. But for all this endeavours must never be given over for gaining of the Scots to my side.

The interests of the church and the crown were inseparable,

for people are governed by pulpits more than the sword.

Where was there ever obedience where religion did not teach it? . . . I am most confident that Religion will much sooner regain the Militia, than the Militia will Religion.

To the Prince of Wales the king wrote:

Take it as an infallible maxim from me, that as the Church can never flourish without the protection of the Crown, so the dependency of the Church upon the Crown is the chiefest support of Regal Authority. . . . Next to Religion, the power of the sword is the truest badge and greatest support of sovereignty.

In July 1646 parliament presented Propositions to the king at Newcastle:* he must accept the Solemn League and Covenant and the abolition of episcopacy, and agree to a long list of his servants, including Edward Hyde, being excepted from a general pardon. The armed forces were to be under the control of parliament for twenty years. Charles was lectured by Lord Loudoun, Chancellor of Scotland: that parliament was now so strong that they could dictate terms; that many people no longer felt the need for a monarchy, although the common people did, and that if the terms were rejected he would be deposed.[44] Charles asked the envoys what powers remained to him and his heirs, and his reply to parliament was a proposal that he should come to London to negotiate a settlement. He knew this would not be accepted, but he played for time. He knew the tensions which existed between the English and the Scots, and between the so-called Presbyterians, like Denzil Holles, and the Independents like Sir Henry Vane and Cromwell. The absurdity of parliament's position was shown by their insistence on the Covenant and the Presbyterian settlement, which the Independents did not themselves want, simply in order to please the Scots. Now that the fighting was over, parliament wanted to get rid of the Scots, who were expensive allies. Even Holles and his friends wanted them to leave as a preliminary to disbandment of the New Model Army. There was therefore some hope of a concession by one side or the other.

Meanwhile Jermyn, Culpepper and Ashburnham were unrelenting in their pressure on the king to give way to Presbyterianism. In letter after letter Charles explained at length that Presbyterianism and monarchy were incompatible, that he knew the Scots better than they did, and that he and his successors would be left no power at all.[45] But he did go so far as to enquire of bishop Juxon of London, Brian Duppa of Salisbury, and Gilbert Sheldon, 'as they would answer it at the day of judgment', whether he might agree to accept Presbyterianism for three years (30 September 1646). Their reply of 14 October was that as he no longer had force at his disposal, it would not be contrary to his oath to accept a settlement for three years. Three days later the king received another broadside from Jermyn and Culpepper that unless he

---

* The terms were worked out between parliament and Argyll, who was in London.

accepted Presbyterianism he would bring ruin upon himself, his posterity and his party, and that Scottish terms would be preferable to the English. The queen had also sent Sir William Davenant, who (Charles wrote) 'threatened him' with the prospect of the queen's going into a nunnery if he refused. For Charles this was the last straw: his grief, he wrote, was near to bursting. He continued however to draft proposals for a settlement. On 15 October he proposed that if Presbyterianism was accepted for five years on condition that episcopacy was restored at the end of it, he would agree to hand over the militia to parliament for his lifetime, on condition that it was restored to his successor. But all such offers came to nothing. Without a full acceptance of Presbyterianism the Scots would do nothing for him, while the Westminster parliament were anxious to get rid of such expensive allies, and to secure the person of the king. In January 1647 Charles wrote to Lord Jermyn at Saint Germain that he was now a prisoner of the Scots, that escape, which might have been easy earlier, was now impossible, that the only question was whether he would be a prisoner in Scotland or in England, that he thought he might have better treatment in England, and that in any case he would play for time, hoping for some assistance from France. But his fate was already decided, for the Scots agreed to hand him over to the English in return for an immediate payment of £200,000, with a similar payment a year later. Parliamentary commissioners took possession of the king, and installed him at Holmby House in Northamptonshire.[46]

The question now was what were the real intentions of the Westminster parliament? We have already seen that the labels 'Presbyterians' and 'Independents' are misleading when applied to members of parliament. 'Moderates' and 'radicals' are more satisfactory labels, although the problem of definition still remains. Since August 1645 elections had begun to fill the vacancies left by expelled royalist members, and they continued for three years. Some 275 members were thus admitted. Some turned out to be extremists, like Thomas Scott of Aylesbury, but the majority of the 'recruiters' were moderates, offering Denzil Holles the prospect of a possible majority in the Commons. The radicals certainly wanted to dethrone Charles I, and in September 1645 there was talk of replacing him by either the Elector Palatine (who was given a pension of £8000 by parliament), or by the Prince of Wales. This was one reason why Charles was so anxious that the prince should not fall into enemy hands. It was a proposal which might have united radicals, moderates and royalists, each seeing in it satisfaction for their own interests; but it was one which alarmed Hyde more even than the deposition of the king. He wrote to Nicholas:

I pray God they have not such a nose of wax ready for their impression: this it is makes me tremble more than all their discourse of destroying Monarchy (12 December 1646).[47]

What he meant was that to set up a puppet king as a powerless figurehead would be worse than proclaiming a republic: the latter in due course would revert to monarchy, but a puppet king would remain always a puppet king. Another proposal was that the little duke of Gloucester might be a suitable candidate for a puppet throne.

On the other hand radicals like Ludlow were exasperated that there were any negotiations at all with the king, 'though he had not a sword left wherewith to oppose them'. The army too were becoming restive. One day, which may have been about March 1647, Cromwell was walking with Ludlow in Sir Robert Cotton's garden, and spoke so bitterly against parliament that Ludlow later concluded that 'he had already conceived the design of destroying the civil authority, and setting up of himself; and that he took that opportunity to feel my pulse whether I were a fit instrument to be employed by him to those ends'.[48]

It is misleading to suppose that the so-called moderates who followed Holles were much more favourable to monarchy than the radicals. They did not advocate the king's deposition, but they were no more ready to offer him terms he could reasonably be expected to accept. They were 'Presbyterian' only in the sense that they relied more on the Scots to aid them against the radicals, and therefore were prepared to pay the price of insistence on the king's acceptance of the Covenant. When in December 1646 the City of London petitioned for the Covenant, Presbyterianism and the disbandment of the New Model Army, it was a programme for the moderates against the sectaries and Levellers. The disbandment of the army was for the moderates their first priority.

So long as the Scots remained in England, it was necessary to maintain the New Model Army, but once the Scots had withdrawn, the moderates were anxious to disband the army, or to send them for the reconquest of Ireland. But the New Model Army had developed a strong political complexion, and demanded a say in the political consequences of their work in defeating the king. Moreover there were heavy arrears of pay, and unless these were honoured, disbandment was impossible. Indeed the grave financial problems influenced both political and religious developments. To pay off the Scots cost parliament £400,000, half of which had to be paid immediately, and was raised by Holles as a loan in the City. Neither the heavy monthly assessments nor the excise were sufficient to pay off the arrears of army pay and also send regiments to Ireland. Thus two new sources of revenue became attractive, namely the sale of bishops' lands and payments for compositions of the estates of delinquents.* Thus political, military, financial and ecclesiastical questions became closely linked, and men who might not otherwise have been hostile to episcopacy, were now committed to its abolition. Moreover financial

* The sale of bishops' lands raised £200,000.[49]

exigencies required parliament to retain the good will of the City of London. But during 1646 the City became increasingly concerned at the growing activities of turbulent sectaries, and on two occasions petitioned parliament for their suppression, and the enforcement of Presbyterian organisation. But the City had a strong Independent section among the lower classes, and also a significant royalist minority.

All these factors blur the distinctions between 'Presbyterians' and 'Independents', or 'moderates' and 'radicals' in the Commons, and perhaps historians have sought to impose labels where they did not in reality exist. For the truth seems to be that although there were a dozen or so members who were clearly adherents of Holles, and a dozen or so who were radical enough to be classed with Ludlow and Henry Marten, yet most members seem to have been carried along by the leaders from one decision to another with little to guide them but their fears. However, what is quite clear is the division between parliament and the army.

The army had established a general council of officers and representatives of each regiment, known as 'agitators', to act, as Clarendon says, as 'a kind of parliament'.[50] In March 1647 they drew up a petition complaining of the plan to disband the army, and declaring that they would not serve in Ireland until they were satisfied as to the rights and liberties of subjects in England. The Commons at once condemned the petition, and a quarrel developed between Holles and Ireton, in which Holles challenged Ireton to a duel. Ireton replied that honour did not permit him to fight a duel, at which Holles tweaked his nose, saying that 'if his conscience would keep him from giving men satisfaction, it should keep him from provoking them.'[51] Holles' lieutenant Sir Philip Stapleton assessed the situation accurately when he declared of the army, that 'we must sink them . . . or they sink us'.[52] The Commons made an attempt to do just that in April by raising another loan from the City for £200,000, and ordering the disbandment of the army, beginning with Fairfax's regiment. There was immediate resistance in the army, and Fairfax informed parliament that disbandment was impossible.

Meanwhile on 12 May Charles returned his third answer to the Newcastle Propositions, and it was notably conciliatory. He accepted a number of the proposals, and offered that on coming to London for further negotiations, he would confirm Presbyterian government for three years, and agree to parliament's control of the armed forces for ten years, and he declared that 'a general act of oblivion is the best bond of peace'.[53] Here was a basis for an agreement between Holles and his friends and the king, which might enable them to secure the disbandment of the army and at the same time placate the Scots. The army knew this well enough, and a meeting of army officers at Bury St Edmunds on 29 May decided that action was necessary. What action was not specified, but a meeting at Cromwell's house in Drury Lane two days later decided that the king must be seized. Cornet Joyce arrived at

Holmby House on 2 June at the head of five hundred troopers. He told the parliamentary commissioners he had come to forestall a plot to convey the king to London. When the king asked by what authority he came, he pointed to his troopers. He gave the king a promise that he would be well treated, and Charles agreed to go with him. Joyce wrote presumably to Cromwell, 'We have secured the King . . . I humbly entreat you to consider what is done and act accordingly'. It appears probable therefore that Joyce was acting on Cromwell's orders. Cromwell was playing a game of such duplicity at this time that he gave rise to charges of hypocrisy in which men as different as Clarendon, Ludlow and Lilburne joined.[54] Clarendon wrote that Cromwell 'carried himself with that rare dissimulation in which sure he was a very great master',[55] denouncing the army to parliament, and parliament to the army. When the news of Cornet Joyce's exploits reached the Commons they were ready to arrest Cromwell, but he had ridden away to join the army, one of his party declaring that 'they should bring the king to justice, try him for his life, and cut off his head'.[56]

Charles had no choice but to ride with Cornet Joyce; it must have been a nerve-wracking journey to Newmarket, for Clarendon said that the king suspected that he would be murdered by the troopers. Fairfax, the general, however was genuinely shocked at the seizure, and sent Colonel Whaley's regiment to protect the king. When Fairfax offered to return him to Holmby House, Charles refused. At Newmarket he found his position considerably improved. He was allowed to have Sheldon, Morley, Sanderson and Hammond as his chaplains, and to receive his friends, so that, Clarendon wrote, he 'began to believe that the army was not so much his enemy as it was reported to be'.

The best gentlemen of the several counties through which he passed daily resorted to him without distinction; he was attended by some of his old trusty servants in the places nearest his person; and that which gave him most encouragement to believe that they meant well, was, that in the army's address to the parliament, they desired that care might be taken for the settling the king's rights.[57]

At Holmby House Charles had evidence of the loyalty of the country folk in the way they sought to be touched for the king's evil,* and he knew that some of the officers in the army were royalists who had joined for want of a better occupation. Sir John Berkeley, who had defended Exeter, and John Ashburnham, who had accompanied the king on his ill-fated journey to the Scots at Newark, returned from France to join him. But what gave the king the greatest pleasure was that he was permitted to see his children, who were under the care of the earl of Northumberland at Syon.[59]

The great question however which faced the king was whether he should

---

* Henry Marten commented cynically that 'he knew not but the Parliament's Great Seal might do as well, if there were an ordinance for it'.[58]

look to agreement with the army or with parliament to give him a satisfactory settlement of his difficulties, or whether he should wait to see which of the two would seek his aid. Some historians have argued that Holles and his friends were the more favourable to an agreement with Charles, and that the king's third answer to the Newcastle Propositions provided a basis for such an agreement. But there is little evidence for this, and Holles's latest biographer thinks otherwise, for Holles, although not a republican, was a Presbyterian, and always took his stand on the Newcastle Propositions, even as late as 1660.[60] He certainly thought that sooner or later the king would have to accept his terms if he was to save his throne.

In any case the initiative lay not with parliament but with the army. In June there was alarm that the army would march on London, and in spite of parliament's order that the army should not approach within forty miles of the city, they reached St Albans by 12 June. On the 14th they declared that parliament was attempting to usurp power and establish a tyranny, and next day they demanded the impeachment of eleven members of the Commons, including Denzil Holles and Philip Stapleton, for 'attempting to overthrow the rights and liberties of the subjects of this nation'.[61] The Commons tried to ignore this while making desperate efforts to pay off some of the arrears of the troops, but when the army again started to move forward, the Eleven withdrew from the Commons. William Prynne emerged as the stout defender of the rights and liberties of parliament against the threat of the army, but the army replied that 'Princes have no prerogatives nor Parliaments any privileges but such as are consistent with and in no way prejudicial to the common good of man'. This was to speak with a new voice, and Kishlansky is right to argue that the whole incident underlined 'the fragility of Parliament's authority'. For parliament seemed likely to perpetuate its existence; it had used 'Privilege' to destroy its enemies and it showed every reluctance to come to agreement with the king. The question was being raised: which spoke for the nation, parliament or the army? The whole situation reinforced the view which the king and Hyde had held ever since their answer to the Nineteen Propositions, that no settlement was possible without a return to constitutional monarchy. Such was the gist of a petition claimed to be from ten thousand young men of the City calling for 'the preservation of the king, the vindication of the privileges of parliament, the settlement of the church, the suppression of conventicles and the disbandment of the Army'.[62]

The army certainly seemed at the time to offer a better chance of agreement with the king than parliament did. On 1 August 1647 their Heads of Proposals included the ending of the Long Parliament within a year, future biennial parliaments, more equal representation of constituencies, the militia to be under the control of parliament for ten years, a Council of State to exercise the functions of the Privy Council, the great officers of State to be appointed by parliament; bishops to be deprived of jurisdiction; and an Act of Oblivion. Of particular importance to the king was the clause that the Covenant was not to be enforced, and there was no prohibition of the use of the Prayer Book.[63] If the religious question could be disposed of (and on this the Heads of Proposals were far more conciliatory than the Newcastle Propositions) a settlement seemed possible, for even the militia was not an unsuperable obstacle. As early as November 1646 Charles had written to the queen from Newcastle

I am still of opinion that, except Religion can be preserved, the Militia will not be much useful to the Crown: Nay, without that, this will be but a shadow. For though it be most true that the transferring of the right of the Militia unto the two Houses dethrones the King, yet the retaining of it is not so much consequence as is thought, without the concurrence of other things ... If the pulpits teach not obedience, which will never be if Presbyterian government be absolutely settled, the Crown will have little comfort of the Militia.[64]

The Head of Proposals were in many ways a far-seeing political document, which might be thought to have offered the best prospects of peace so far. Parliament was disintegrating, and the army marched into Southwark on 6 August without resistance. Speaker Lenthall and the earl of Manchester fled from parliament to join them. In spite of all this the king rejected the Heads of Proposals. He was convinced that he was indispensable to a settlement, and he held firm to his principles that he must defend his church, his crown and his friends. Clarendon also gave the terms short shrift; he regarded them 'as ruinous to the church and destructive to the regal power as had been yet made by the parliament; and, in some respects, much worse, and more dishonourable'.[65] Perhaps he did not study the terms in great detail, for his chief concern at the time was that Charles would give away too many of the 'foundations' of the constitution. In any case the lack of trust between king and army made any settlement highly unlikely. Cromwell told Ashburnham

that the king could not be trusted; and that he had no affection or confidence in the army; ... that he had intrigues in the parliament, and treaties with the presbyterians of the city to raise new troubles; that he had a treaty concluded with the Scotch commissioners to engage the nation again in blood, [and so on].

Although there was exaggeration in all this there was also much truth, and it must have been an accurate summary of the thoughts Cromwell entertained at this time. The king was equally mistrustful of Cromwell, for one of his own officers, Major Huntingdon, had told him 'that Cromwell was a villain, and would destroy him if he were not prevented'.[66]

In fairness to Cromwell it must be said that, much as he mistrusted parliament and the Scots, he faced great difficulties within the army with the rise of the Levellers, a movement which reached a climax during the next two years. Discontent in the army had sprung from long arrears of pay* but was

*Amounting to £2½ millions by March 1647.[67]

whipped up by preachers and 'agitators' and by the democratic writings of John Lilburne, Richard Overton and William Walwyn. The establishment of the General Council of the Army, on which agitators sat alongside generals and field officers, gave the extremists a platform for their programme, which included a purge of the House of Commons, abolition of the Lords and monarchy, a democratic electoral system, legal equality, religious toleration and a complete separation of Church and State. All this went much further than officers like Cromwell, Ireton and Lambert wanted.[68] But for the moment unity was preserved when on 6 August the army marched into the City and was welcomed by the Lord Mayor. Speaker Lenthall and Manchester resumed their seats, Holles and his friends fled abroad, or were placed under arrest. Presbyterianism melted away, and the supremacy of parliament gave way to the supremacy of the army. As Clarendon said, the new parliament was the General Council of the Army.[69]

In August the king was moved to Hampton Court where he lived in considerable freedom and dignity, and was able to receive letters and advice from all sides. There were rumours that the army would restore him to his throne, that Cromwell would be made earl of Essex and captain of the King's Guard, rumours which did him much harm among the Levellers, who suspected the motives of any negotiations with the king. Historians can never be sure exactly what was in Cromwell's mind. Perhaps his complaints to Ashburnham were really a plea for the king to put all his trust in Ireton and him. But the very fact of his negotiating at all brought attacks from Colonel Rainborough and trooper Edward Sexby, whom Professor Aylmer describes as 'the stuff of which actual revolutionaries are made', whose career 'it can safely be said is one which only the most reckless historical novelist would dare to invent'.[70] Thus while Cromwell was pressing Charles to accept the Heads of Proposals, some of the Levellers were talking of getting rid of the king, even by murder.

The king had been much encouraged by the actions of counter-revolutionary mobs in London, who in July produced the so-called Solemn Engagement calling for the return of the king to London to treat with Parliament. On 20 July they invaded the Houses of Parliament demanding the restoration of the eleven members.[71] Pym had taught the London mob how to influence events; the difference now was that it was counter-revolutionary. From the king's point of view its great defect was that it also demanded the Covenant and the establishment of Presbyterianism as well as suppression of the sectaries.[72] The choice before the king was therefore one of extreme difficulty, lying as it did between the Newcastle Propositions and the acceptance of Presbyterianism, and the Heads of Proposals. But Presbyterianism and the parliamentary followers of Holles, and the counter-revolutionary movement in London, had all been silenced with the army's entry into London, and, when forced to make a choice in September, he replied that he preferred the Heads of Proposals. The Commons voted by 84 to 34 to set up a committee to continue the negotiations, Cromwell voting with the majority.

The dilemma which faced Cromwell was that failure to reach a moderate settlement would alienate the nation which desperately wanted peace, but a moderate settlement would infuriate the Levellers. How wide the division was in the army was revealed when in October the Levellers produced the Agreement of the People, and when the whole subject was debated in the famous Putney Debates of 28 October–11 November 1647. There has been some disagreement among historians as to exactly how democratic the intentions of the Agreement of the People really were, but it was rejected by the Grandees, and also by the Commons. A mutiny in the army was crushed by Cromwell at Corkbush field on 14 November at the cost of one execution, and this marked the end of the Leveller danger.

Whether this might have paved the way for a settlement on the lines of the Heads of Proposals will never be known, for three days before on 11 November the king, accompanied only by Ashburnham, Berkeley and Legge, slipped away from Hampton Court, and rode into Hampshire. Clarendon thought that Charles genuinely believed that there was an army plot to murder him and that this actuated the flight, but he could never discover what plans had been laid. Certainly no ship could be found, and the king rested at Titchfield, the seat of the earl of Southampton, while Ashburnham went to the Isle of Wight in the belief that Colonel Hammond the Governor might be royalist-inclined. But Hammond was a close friend of Cromwell's and had married John Hampden's daughter, and when Ashburnham approached him he gave no promises but insisted on returning with him to Titchfield. When the king heard of this 'he brake out in a passionate exclamation, "O Jack, thou hast undone me"!',[73] but there was nothing for it but to proceed to Carisbrooke Castle. Clarendon wrote that the whole enterprise was 'so far from a rational design and conduct' as almost to pass belief. If the purpose was to escape abroad it was incredible that no ship had been provided. In fact Hyde later discussed the whole affair with both Ashburnham and Berkeley without coming much nearer to certainty. He was inclined to believe that they left Hampton Court on the orders of the king, without any idea what was in his mind, and that both the ship and Carisbrooke Castle were afterthoughts. If Charles had a plan, he did not tell his attendants what it was.[74]

He left behind him a letter at Hampton Court saying that he was justified in escaping from captivity since all men, even kings, had a right to liberty; that there could be no peace until all interests were given a hearing, not only himself, but the Presbyterians, Independents, the army and the Scots; and he called for an Act of Oblivion, arrears of pay for the army, and toleration:

Let me be heard with Freedom, Honour and Safety, and I shall instantly break through this cloud of retirement and show myself ready to be Pater Patriae. Charles Rex.[75]

From Carisbrooke he wrote to parliament proposing a personal treaty. He could not, he declared, agree to the abolition of episcopacy nor to the alienation of church lands, but he would consent to the present church government for three years, with toleration for all except Catholics, and to the militia and the appointment to the great offices of State being under the control of parliament for the rest of the reign.

It was an offer redolent of moderation and statesmanship. Why then did not Cromwell and parliament respond to it? There is a story that Cromwell had intercepted a letter from Charles to the queen, hidden in a riding saddle which revealed the king's intrigues abroad, but the story is suspect, for if true, Cromwell would surely have published the letter.[76] However this might be, parliament's reply was to demand the king's immediate acceptance of four bills, (1) confessing his blood guilt, (2) abolishing bishops and alienating church lands, (3) placing the Militia in the hands of parliament, (4) sacrificing his followers to the mercy of parliament. Whatever Cromwell's motives at this time, these were terms Charles could not accept.

The king was encouraged by evidence of a royalist reaction in the country. On Christmas Day 1647 there were riots in Canterbury, with cries of 'For God, King Charles and Kent'.[77] On 30 December an attempt was made by a captain Burley to rescue the king from Carisbrooke Castle, and at Newport a drum was beaten and the cry raised 'For God and King Charles'. From other parts of the country there were disturbances which were to increase throughout 1648. There was no doubt of an overwhelming general desire for a peaceful settlement with the king. Moreover the Scottish Commissioners who attended Charles at Carisbrooke expressed their disapproval of parliament's terms, and signed an alliance with him (The Engagement) by which the king accepted the Covenant, provided that none should be forced to take it, agreed to Presbyterianism for three years, provided that he and his family were not required to conform to it, after which a religious settlement would be determined by an Assembly of Divines. The Sectaries were to be suppressed, and the Scots would provide the king with an army.[78]

If there was justification for the king's alliance with the Scots, it was to be found in the decision taken by Cromwell, Ireton and their officers at a prayer meeting two days before, that the king should be brought to trial for his life, a fact of which Charles was at once informed by Watson, the Q M G of the army. Clarendon said that the king found this difficult to believe, but he did think that he might be murdered.[79]

The king's reply to the four bills was that he could not make a piecemeal agreement, and he renewed his request for a personal treaty. The House treated this as a rejection and passed a resolution that there be no more addresses to the king. In future all government business was to be carried on without reference to him.[80] These were highly unpopular measures in the country, and discontent was increased by the heavy taxation of £150,000 a month, together with increased customs and excise. Clarendon also noted a change in the centre of gravity of political power in the countryside, where gentlemen tended to retire from offices of trust, and be replaced by men of more humble origin:

And they who were not above the condition of ordinary inferior constables six or seven years before, were now the justices of peace and sequestrators and commissioners, who executed the commands of the parliament in all the counties of the kingdom with rigour and tyranny.[81]

The Engagement was primarily the work of the duke of Hamilton who, on his release from Pendennis castle had made his way, first to London, and then to Scotland to head a royalist revival against the influence of Argyll. Among the Scottish nobility was the growing sense that in letting loose religious fanaticism they had released a force they could no longer control.* They were beginning to realise also the futility of attempting to force Presbyterianism on an unwilling England. The Engagers therefore had strong support in the Estates.

Clarendon severely condemned the Engagement. He was too loyal to criticise the king, but he did point out the futility of the Scots' attempting to defeat Cromwell's army, and their reliance on the aid of Presbyterians in England, when not one would rise to help them.[83] He wrote ironically that the king by the Engagement gave away too much 'for the wonderful service they were like to perform'. Why then did the king agree to it? Clarendon thought that it was because he knew that once victory was won, he could ignore most of his concessions. But the chance of its succeeding was slight. Clarendon, who greatly admired the statecraft of Cromwell, wrote that one of his clear-sighted achievements was to cease to think of the Scots as allies, and to think of them as mercenaries, to be paid off and despatched as quickly as possible. This was a highly popular attitude in England, and the king would do his cause no good by encouraging a further war with the Scots as his allies. The Engagement was equally mistaken from the point of view of the Scots. Clarendon argued that if they had wished to aid the king, the time to have done it was when he surrendered to them at Newark, when they could have taken him to Scotland instead of handing him over to the English.

* Hyde wrote that the Kirk was destroying the Scottish State, 'and if the nobility there do not find some way to restore Bishops, they shall become in seven years after their little army is disbanded, of as little power as they have made the King'. To Hopton. 2 May, 1648.[82]

# The Beginning of the *History* and the Fall of the Monarchy

When the prince sailed for France on 26 June 1646, Brentford, Witherington, Culpepper, Jermyn and others went with him; the earl of Berkshire left for Holland, but Capel, Hopton and Hyde remained in Jersey. They were well aware that their decision might lose them royal favour. Their financial position might have been serious but for the fact that a merchant prize brought into Jersey was sold on the prince's orders for 8000 livres for the benefit of Hyde and Culpepper. But Hyde was determined not to go to France for reasons he set out at length in his letters of the next few months. First, he mistrusted the influence of the queen, both in the advice she was giving the king, and in the influence she might have on the prince. The Stuart cause was already tainted with suspicions of Catholicism, and although Hyde was certain that they were unfounded, yet the presence of the prince in France would only increase them. His reasons however went deeper than this. He did not believe that the French would ever actively help in the restoration of the Stuarts. He believed that Mazarin was merely manipulating the situation to his own advantage. Nor did Hyde want the French to help. He argued that the king must be restored by the will of his own people, or he would not be restored at all. He did not want the introduction of French armies or French ideas because he believed passionately in England's ability to solve its own problems.

All Hyde's letters of the next few months reflect the pleasure he found in his new life in Jersey. After years of feverish change he could relax and take stock of his own thoughts and the political situation.

'Truly, Jack', he wrote to his friend Sir John Berkeley, 'it will not be unseasonable or unuseful to a mind and spirit so wasted and weakened as mine, to refresh and strengthen itself with sitting still, and revolving past omissions or mistakes, and forming and making up a resolution and constancy . . . to bear cheerfully the worst that can happen'.[1] From his early days he had loved to read history, and Great Tew had encouraged his appetite for intellectual activity, now he had the leisure to pursue it. And so, he wrote, 'he presently betook himself to his study; and enjoyed, as he was wont to say, the greatest tranquillity of mind imaginable'.[2] Hyde had begun to write while still in the Scillies, but now devoted himself to it in earnest. He described how he would write in the mornings, but two or three times a week met Capel and Hopton for morning prayers at 11.00 am. They dined at Lord Hopton's at their joint expense, went without supper, but rode or walked on the sands during the evening, or were entertained by Sir George Carteret, the Governor, who was a model host. Hyde found the life entirely congenial, and at once opened an extensive correspondence with old friends, both for companionship and in order to collect material for his book.[3] His chief correspondents were Secretary Nicholas, Lord Cottington, Sir John Berkeley, the earl of Bristol, and Dr John Earle; these were his especial friends. To Nicholas he explained his purpose:

As soon as I found myself alone, I thought the best way to provide myself for new business against the time I should be called to it (for, Mr. Secretary, you and I must once again to business) was to look over the faults of the old; and so I resolved (which you know I threatened you with long ago) to write the history of these evil times, and of this most lovely Rebellion. Well; without any other help than a few diurnals I have wrote of longer paper than this, and in the same fine small hand, above three score sheets of paper. I begin from the death of King James with those accidents and errors which contributed and indeed were the grounds of all the ill that hath followed. I write with all fidelity and freedom of all I know . . . so that you will believe it will make mad work among friends and foes, if it were published.[4]

But he did not intend that it should be published, at least for some time. The question arises why he should have begun to write at all if he was not writing to influence immediate events. Some writers have thought he began with the idea of writing something which would be for the guidance of the king, but he nowhere indicated that that was his purpose. Certainly the king knew of his intention of writing, and greatly encouraged him in the belief that he would write a royalist apologetic, but this was never Hyde's intention. Professor Trevor-Roper has suggested that he wrote in answer to Tom May's parliamentary apologetic, but Hyde did not mention the work, and had begun writing before it had appeared. The truest explanation is surely the one he himself gave, that he wanted to *understand* the events through which he had lived, and to indicate a philosophy for the future. He said he modelled his work on the Venetian historian D'Avila's *History of the Civil Wars in France*,

who hath written as ours should be written, and from whence no question our Gamesters learnt much of their play.[5]

He intended to

insert the declarations of both sides in the main body of the story, as the foundations upon which all that was afterwards done was built.

It was also to be a work of historical and legal philosophy and would include a discourse of the just regal power of the kings of England, and of his negative voice, of the militia, and of the great seal, by the laws of the kingdom, of the original, at least of the antiquity and constitution of parliaments, of their jurisdiction and privileges, of the power of the house of peers, by the law, and of the natural limits and extent of the Commons.[6]

This was not actually included in the *History*, but there are twelve sheets in his secretary Edgman's handwriting in the Bodleian MSS where some of these ideas are expanded. However the whole work is permeated with the idea of constitutional law here suggested.

Hyde said that he wrote for three hours a day, and spent the rest of his time with his books, 'so I doubt not after seven years time in this retirement, you will find me a pretty fellow'.[7] He worked with great enthusiasm. By February 1647, he told the earl of Bristol, he had written 'near four score sheets', and had reached the setting up of the king's standard at Nottingham. He had also planned the work as far as the treaty of Oxford. In almost every letter he begged his friends to send him special information which was in their possession.

One purpose of writing was certainly to assess the place of individuals in history, since 'the preservation of the fame and merits of persons, and deriving the same to posterity, is no less the business of history, than the truth of things'.[8] Thus he wrote to Dr Steward for special information on Archbishop Laud:

I take it to be no less the true end of history, to derive the eminency and virtue of those persons who lived and acted in those times of which he writes, faithfully to posterity, than the counsels which were taken, or the actions which were done. And truly I do not more promise myself to see some visible marks of the judgment of God for that execrable murder [of Laud] than for the rebellion and sacrifice which they have acted and intended.[9]

Certainly one of the greatest achievements of Clarendon's *History* lies in the vividness and truth of his character-drawings, although it may be thought that he did less than justice to Laud himself.

At the same time he tried to look beyond personality to deeper reasons for the conflicts of his time, which might explain God's retribution on his age. One was the way in which religion had been subordinated to politics:

I assure you, I have not been without many melancholy thoughts, that this justice of God which of late years hath seemed to be directed against Empire itself, hath proceeded from the divine indignation against those principles of Empire, which have looked upon conscience and religion itself, as more private, subordinate, and subservient faculties, to conveniency and the interest of kingdoms, than duties requisite to the purchase of the Kingdom of Heaven. And therefore God hath stirred up, and applied the people in whom Princes thought it only necessary to plant religion, to the destruction of Principalities, in the institution whereof religion hath been thought unnecessary.[10]

So in this sense the rebels were instruments of God against the Erastianism of the State.

Hyde also concerned himself with theological studies. In February 1647 he was writing to Dr Robert Creighton, Dean of St Buryan's, Cornwall, about the Apocryphal parts of the Bible, and the reasons why they were retained at the Reformation.[11] On another occasion it was to Dr Steward, asking him to verify a quotation from Grotius's *De Jure Belli ac Pacis* about kings who lost their kingdoms as a result of war. But current affairs interested him most. He was angry at the activities of the queen's party in France:

Oh my Lord, [he wrote to Cottington] it breaks my heart to see that the hopes of the king and the recovery of the kingdom, must be carried on, and depend upon the counsels and principles of a nation which hath brought all these miseries upon us, and I fear hath not a less fatal projection at this time upon the honour and interest of the king, than they have hitherto had.[12]

He resented the pressure brought to bear on the king by the queen and Jermyn to accept the Covenant as the price of an agreement with the Scots, because he believed, as Charles did, that this would deprive the Crown of all real power. His greatest fear was that in a moment of weakness the king might be prevailed upon to accept.

He rejected the arguments of royalists such as Jermyn and the earl of Berkshire that the best course for the king must be to work for an agreement with the Scots against the English. The Scots might be more favourable to monarchy than were the Independents, but it would still be a monarchy with no power. He foretold a coming struggle between the Scots and English, 'a brisk war you shall have, and a bloody, I warrant you',[13] and it would be a great error for the king to be on the wrong side. He feared that the mistaken belief that the Presbyterians were more favourable to monarchy would strengthen their position, while anti-Scottish feelings in England would strengthen the Independents. He saw no future for the monarchy in an accommodation with either; the only hope for the king lay in a resurgence of 'English courage and loyalty', which would one day 'repair the breaches they have made', but this would occur only when the fever which possessed the nation had burnt itself out. One of Hyde's strongest convictions was his faith in the English people and their traditions. It was this faith which had made him a reformer in 1640, and it was this which made him a constitutional monarchist for the rest of his life. He wrote that if he must make a choice between Presbyterians or Independents, he would choose the latter:

I have not the same opinion and contempt of the Independents that other men have, from the opinion of their abhorring Rules of Government. I find they admit as strict Government as is necessary for their purposes. Is not their army (upon which they depend) regularly and strictly governed? No Independency admitted there. Are not the heads of the party the best heads in the pack? Do you think that any philosopher sees more confusion than they do, or that they are not sufficiently informed of the inconstancy and fury of the rabble, that they would never trust their lives and fortunes to such a vain foundation? Believe it, they do as well know what they would have, as what they would not have; only they find it easier to pull down than to build up . . . Neither do I believe with other men, that they intend to change the form of government from Monarchy to Aristocracy or Democracy . . . the alteration whereof would bring many unprofitable changes to any private man's condition that is worth anything . . . they will keep Monarchy to the height, and probably improve it; but . . . change the Monarch and his line, and make choice of such a one as may owe his Crown to them . . . and then he shall not want Ministers for as full a tyranny as hath been exercised in any Kingdom.[14]

As an assessment of the Independents, and a forecast of the rise of Cromwell, this showed remarkable insight. At the moment it appeared to be a choice between a Presbyterian king devoid of power, and an Independent ruler who would not be a Stuart. Presbyterianism was a foreign import and did not spring from English soil. The monarchists must wait patiently for a turning of the tide in England, and that was why it was important that the king should keep himself immaculate, and not make concessions which could not later be reversed. Hyde believed as firmly as Charles himself in the principle of 'No bishop, no king':

I have heard him often say, if he could not live a King, he would die a Gentleman. And I am confident that resolution will sooner restore him to what he hath lost, than the signing the Propositions [of Newcastle] will do.[15]

Hyde was no bigot in religion. When Nicholas consulted him as to whether the prince of Wales should attend a Huguenot church in France, he replied that he should certainly do so, since nothing would increase the suspicion in England that the Stuarts were inclined to Catholicism, so much as the avoidance of contacts with continental Protestantism. It was a mistake, he wrote, for Anglicanism to be too exclusive. When Nicholas pressed him about the *ius divinum* of bishops, he replied that he did not believe that the bishops had *ius divinum*, but he did not believe that the king had it either; to emphasise this theological abstraction was to miss the point. Both monarch and bishops were established by the ancient laws of England, and it was this which made the two inseparable.

He wrote to Hopton, who was less sure about the need for bishops:

Before I consent to the taking away of bishops, I must be persuaded that the exercise of the Ministry is of no moment, and that christening and marrying and preaching and praying and receiving the Sacrament, are needless things, or may be done without having Ministers. For upon my word, I know not which way to have Ministers without Bishops.[16]

Hyde never lost faith in the ultimate restoration of both church and monarchy, because he believed that they alone offered conditions for stability.

That was why he was so concerned that Charles should not be forced to make concessions which could not subsequently be reversed:

To my understanding, it is much more natural to expect a restoration to his rights, from the faction, animosity and disunion between the Rebels upon their managery and disposition of the spoil, and a resurrection of the English affection and loyalty, from the awe and reverence to his unshaken mind and magnanimity, than from his yielding to them, whose appetite of asking will never be satisfied but by his quitting all power to give.[17]

The same letter contained a sentence which gives the key to Hyde's political and legalistic thought, 'In God's name, let them have all circumstantial temporary concessions; but *let not the landmarks be removed, no pillars upon which the fabric relies, be taken away.*' Hyde had not the least doubt that the king *would* give way, but he still wrote to Dr Steward, who had recently been with the king at Newcastle, to reassure himself of the king's determination. He frequently referred to *foundations* which might be destroyed by concessions from the king to Parliament:

Oh, Mr. Secretary, those stratagems have given me more sad hours, than all the misfortunes in war which have befallen the King.

And again:

What will he [the king] do if foundations be destroyed? for the King and Parliament may destroy foundations . . . I would rather he should have stayed in Oxford, and after defending it to the last biscuit, been taken prisoner with his honest retinue about him, and then relied upon his own virtue in imprisonment, than to have thrown himself into the arms of the Scots, who held them not fairly open.

Thus he hoped that the king would not attempt to escape:

I could wish the King should sadly apply himself to the part he is to act, that is to suffer resolutely, and to have no tricks.[18]

These were Hyde's thoughts in seclusion at Jersey, but he was also active on behalf of the king. He says little on the subject in the *History* and *Life*, and his letters for the period are few. But it is clear that the Governor, Sir George Carteret, and Hyde had established some line of communication with the king in Carisbrooke Castle. Hyde first wrote that his letters to Charles would be sent by passing ships, and he added rather insensitively that he would now be deprived of the documents the king had promised to send him! In January 1648 a French vessel left Jersey carrying linen and bacon, and reached the Isle of Wight without exciting suspicion, but it was a fortnight before a royalist could be found to deliver the letter. When they heard of the Parliamentary Vote of No Addresses, Nicholas and Hyde composed a major defence of the king's position, which was presumably intended for the king.[19]

In April 1648 Hyde reopened correspondence with the prince, telling him that his *History* had reached the year 1644, and that without the leisure afforded him by the island, he would not have achieved so much. He also tried to repair relations with the queen, and in June was rewarded with a message from Jermyn inviting him to Saint Germain. This, however, he was reluctant to accept, and at once excused himself 'for you will easily believe that a man who hath not had a boot on these two years, nor in truth hath a boot to put on, cannot in a moment put himself into an equipage for such a journey'. He complained of his gout and his penury, and said that he must borrow money from a merchant in order to make the journey. But a more congenial invitation arrived from Lord Digby on 23 June, telling him that the prince was on his way to Calais bound for Holland: at Calais would be a meeting of the prince's council, 'the importantest occasion that ever was of using the advices of the faithful and able persons concerning the whole frame and order for the future'.[20] Hyde's gout was miraculously cured, boots were found, and on 26 June he left Jersey for Caen to meet Secretary Nicholas, but learnt there that Nicholas had gone to Rouen. At Rouen he found Lord Treasurer Cottington, the earl of Bristol and Nicholas, and learnt that the prince had gone on to Calais, and that they were to await further orders. As the road between Rouen and Calais was so infested with robbers, they were not sorry to remain there for the time being. They then heard that the prince had sailed for Holland, so they decided to proceed to Dieppe and take a ship for Holland, although Nicholas, whose wife was dying, remained behind.[21] At Dieppe they found a small ship which seemed so dangerous to the earl of Bristol that he stayed behind, but the other two decided to take the risk. Clarendon wrote that he knew nothing of the sea, nor of the risks they ran. In the event they were robbed at sea by pirates, Cottington losing a thousand pounds, and Hyde two hundred pounds, all his clothes, and, what worried him more, his papers, and were landed as prisoners at Ostend. The Governor was profuse in his apologies and promises of recompense, but after several days it dawned upon them that the Governor was a party to the piracy, and the only compensation they received was 100 pistoles between them. This depredation at the hands of pirates made such an impression upon Hyde that, he said, he discouraged privateering in the war of 1665–7.*[22] Hyde and Cottington eventually reached The Hague in August 1648.

The prince must have left France with a considerable sense of relief. When he first arrived there from Jersey he found that few preparations had been made to receive him. Young Louis XIV, his cousin, received him civilly enough in August, but no separate provision was made for his maintenance. The French Court added a sum to the 12,000 crowns already paid to Henrietta

---

* Clarendon however did not mention that while at Jersey he had been able to live mainly by the proceeds of privateering. In March 1647 for instance a ship with a cargo worth £15,000 was brought to St Elizabeth, of which the Governor Carteret received the lion's share.

Maria, but she gave the prince no separate allowance, so that he was entirely dependent upon her. Hyde's suspicions increased with every rumour which came from France. The first was that the queen was trying to arrange a marriage between the prince and the fabulously rich Mlle de Montpensier. This failed because the match was not attractive enough to the young lady. Then in September Hyde heard from Lady Elizabeth Thynne that Jermyn planned to sell Jersey and Guernsey to the French, in return for a French dukedom for Jermyn. Nothing came of this, but it persuaded Hyde, Capel and Hopton to prepare the defence of the island with the Governor, in expectation of an attack. In October Hyde learnt from Dr Henry Jansen that the French intended to use the prince for their own ends, and that the queen and Jermyn were entirely devoted to an acceptance of Scottish terms for a settlement.[23] The letters with which they plied the unfortunate king on the subject showed how true this was. Many of the rumours were exaggerated, and Jermyn was not the traitor he was feared to be, but he did tend to see English affairs through the queen's eyes, and he was notoriously her favourite.

The prince's departure from France was in anticipation of the renewal of the Civil War. The queen hoped to see the prince at the head of a Scots' army invading England, and this was the prince's intention when he reached Calais. The royalist momentum was gathering strength in England, and part of the fleet had declared for the king. The prince's intention had been to sail for Scotland, but his fleet mutinied and demanded action against the parliamentary fleet under Warwick. There was certainly much which could be done; Warwick might be defeated, the Kentish rebels aided, the king might be rescued from Carisbrooke, and there were rich merchant prizes to be won at sea. The prince enjoyed the prospect of action, and agreed to put to sea although his ships were ill supplied with provisions. At sea they met Warwick's fleet, which avoided battle and beat a hasty retreat to the Isle of Sheppey. The prince could not bring Warwick to a battle, nor could he do much to aid the Kentish rebels, but he captured enough merchant ships as prizes to enable him to pay his men. It is not clear why a more determined attempt was not made to rescue the king from Carisbrooke, but at least the prince had been spared a disastrous expedition to Scotland, for meanwhile the Scots under Hamilton had invaded England in July, and been annihilated by Cromwell near Preston (17–19 August). Clarendon wrote with some complacency, 'And all this great victory was got by Cromwell with an army not amounting to a third part of the Scots number.'[24] He had neither favoured the intervention of the Scots nor expected their success, and when he came to describe Cromwell's peaceful occupation of Edinburgh, there was more than a hint of admiration and patriotic relish about his words.

From the first Clarendon took a jaundiced view of the Scottish invasion. For him a restoration of the king at the hands of the Scots would be no restoration at all.

It can hardly be believed that, after so long knowledge of England ... they [the Scots] should still adhere to that fatal combination against the Church, which they could never hope to bring to pass, except they intended only to change the hand, and to keep the king under as strict a restraint ... as he was under the domination of the parliament and army.[25]

In August 1648 he wrote a long letter to Culpepper, one of the chief exponents of the Scottish alliance, pointing out the disastrous consequences of the prince's intention to go to Scotland, and arguing that the maintenance intact of the powers of the monarchy was more important even than the life of the king himself:

If whilst the King gloriously suffers, to preserve this vital part of monarchy, his negative power ... we shall under the notion of expedients barter away the essential props and supports of the old Government, we shall hugely discredit the cause, and insensibly run ourselves into inconveniences we shall not be able to repair.[26]

The royalist reaction in England was widespread, but unable to stand against Fairfax's army. The most sustained protest was in Kent. The riots in Canterbury on Christmas Day 1647 were not specifically royalist in origin, but were a protest against the oppressive Puritanism of the Mayor. However they soon developed a Church-and-King aspect. The Mayor was man-handled, the notorious Richard Culmer, desecrator of Canterbury Cathedral, was pelted with mud, and arms seized from the castle. But the revolt was severely crushed, and the walls and gates of the city breached. There was widespread discontent in the county against oppressive parliamentary rule, and at the Maidstone Assizes in May a petition to parliament demanded a personal treaty with the king, disbandment of the army, the return to the rule of law, and lower taxes. Professor Everitt writes, 'It was not the rising of a single clique or class of the community. It was the revolt of a whole countryside. . . . It was the last, in fact, of the great local insurrections of English history'.[27] 27,000 people signed a declaration of intent to arm in defence of the Petition. But Fairfax marched into Kent with his army, the moderates deserted, the rebels were defeated at Maidstone, and 1300 more surrendered at Canterbury (June 1648). A revolt in Sussex also collapsed.

There were risings in Wales and the north of England. In Norwich in April angry crowds with the cry 'For God and King Charles', called for the restoration of the church and the ousting of the Roundheads. The arsenal was stormed, but a chance spark ignited the gunpowder, and the whole building blew up, with heavy casualties. In May 2000 men from Essex marched to Westminster to petition for the return of the king and the disbandment of the army. At Bury St Edmunds the rioters set up a maypole with the same royalist catchphrase. There were royalist demonstrations at Chelmsford, and at Colchester, which was besieged for two months by Fairfax and starved into surrender. The prince's fleet appeared off Yarmouth in July, but the town refused to surrender, and it sailed away. Everywhere the royalist reaction collapsed in face of the strength of Fairfax's army, and the defeat of the Scots gave the death-blow. The main result was to consolidate the power of the army, and to hasten the fate of the king.[28]

Hyde was concerned at the factious state of the prince's Court when at last he reached The Hague in September. Culpepper and Sir Robert Long, the prince's secretary, headed the queen's faction, and were the chief exponents of the plan for a Scottish venture on the part of the prince. They were opposed by Prince Rupert and his friends, who advocated the maximum use of the fleet to harass the enemy. When Hyde and Cottington arrived, they found the two factions at each other's throat.[29] The States General had received the prince amicably, and given him a thousand guilders a day for ten days, after which he was expected to fend for himself. His seamen were often riotous and unpaid, and were unwelcome guests to the Dutch. Some rich prizes had been captured at sea, but there were fierce disputes about the disposal of the cargoes, and accusations of corruption against both officers and councillors.

In August 1648 the earl of Lauderdale, on behalf of the Committee of Estates of the Parliament of Scotland, presented a letter to the prince inviting him to Scotland, but laying down the strict conditions that he must accept Presbyterianism and the Covenant, and must not bring his English councillors with him. His first instinct was to follow his mother's advice and accept, but circumstances had led him instead to sea, and it was not until the third week of September that the matter came before the prince's council in Holland, Hyde and Cottington being present for the first time. The news of the Scottish defeat made it easier for Hyde to have the decision deferred, but he thought it wise to make another attempt to explain his position to the queen. On 22 September he wrote:

that I am in conscience so entirely devoted to the Government of the Church of England, and to all the rights of it, that I cannot only not contribute, but not consent or submit to, anything that may reasonably hazard the destruction or real alteration of it.

Indeed, he wrote ominously, if the king or queen were to propose the destruction of the government of the church, he would be compelled to resist them.[30] These were strong words, and on second thoughts he decided not to send them to the queen, but to send a similar version to Lord Jermyn; but there is no doubt that the letter expressed his deep feelings on the subject of the prince's journey to Scotland. However, that issue was resolved for the moment by a letter to the prince from Chancellor Loudoun in Edinburgh, repudiating the Engagers and advising the king to make peace with his parliament on the basis of the Covenant, and including for good measure a message from the General Assembly urging the prince to be 'diligent in reading the Holy Scriptures', and to avoiding 'the counsel and company of wicked men'.[31] Hyde's advice was thus thoroughly vindicated. His arguments however had no effect upon Jermyn, who replied that he was not convinced, and that 'the Queen makes you no answer by this occasion'.[*32]

We must return now to the position of the king, whose offer of a personal treaty in December 1647 had been rejected, and who in turn had refused to accept Parliament's Four Bills. Parliament had then passed a Vote of No Addresses. Cromwell and Ireton held a solemn prayer meeting with their officers to seek divine guidance as to the reasons for their failure to achieve a settlement, and the Lord had vouchsafed them the answer that it was because they had sought agreement with the king, and

> that it was our duty, if ever the Lord brought us back again to peace, to call Charles Stuart, that man of blood, to an account for that blood he had shed, and mischief he had done to his utmost, against the Lord's cause and people in these poor nations.[34]

Their victories during the year 1648 seemed to persuade many of the army that this was indeed the Lord's will. On the other hand, parliament could not fail to recognise the widespread royalist reaction in the counties, and in London. In some counties like Dorset, Somerset, Kent and Nottinghamshire most of the leading gentry were royalists; in others they were more evenly divided, while in East Anglia they were strongly Puritan. In many instances the gentry above all wanted peace, and an end to heavy taxation and the oppressions of the county associations; few if any wanted a social upheaval, such as was already beginning to emerge. As in 1640 they had resisted Stuart power, so now they resented parliamentary domination. Too often the new masters of the counties were a strongly Puritan activist minority, associated with high taxation, quartering and heavy composition fines on royalists. In the west country parliamentary troops were guilty of the same brigandage and depredations which royalist troops had perpetrated before. In most parts Puritans were in a small minority, but they were activists who often controlled

---

* A further cause of conflict between the prince's council and St Germain's arose over the use of some nine hundred troops which the duke of Lorraine had gathered on the small Dutch island of Borkum, and which he offered for the king's use. If the Scots' invasion had prospered, it was thought that the Lorrainers might attempt to rescue Charles from Carisbrooke. When the Scots failed, the queen and Jermyn were keen to employ the Lorrainers in an attack on the island of Guernsey. This the Council unanimously opposed as having little prospect of success, and being of little use to the king. The queen and Jermyn as usual placed the blame for the refusal upon Hyde. Hyde wrote to Lord Digby on 30 November.

> I am not so weak a man as not to discern and conclude that the Queen ... believes my attendance on the Prince may be well dispensed with,

that the royalist cause was beset with 'a torrent of prejudice', but that:

> I will censure nor rebel against no conclusion the King shall make; but by the grace of God I will not contribute towards, nor have any hand in any, which in my judgment promises nothing but vexation and misery to himself, and all honest men.[33]

local affairs. Many moderates who had supported parliament had done so in the belief that they were defending the traditional law; they were not prepared to defend a new order; or, as John Maynard put it in the debate on the Vote of No Addresses, 'I will fight to maintain a law, but never to get a [new] law'.[35] It was this which Clarendon understood so clearly, and it was upon these moderates that he always pinned his faith in the ultimate restoration of the monarchy.

There were many who desired to have peace . . . but there was another party that would have no peace upon what conditions soever, who did resolve to change the whole frame of the government in State as well as Church, which made a great party in the army.[36]

It must be remembered that at the time he was no more in favour of a royal triumph by military means than of a parliamentary victory over the king. He wrote to Nicholas from Jersey in May 1647:

If it shall please God to restore his Majesty by his own admirable courage and virtue, how much happier will he and the kingdom be, than if he had recovered his rights by a victory! Seriously I have often thought how miserable his condition would have been, if he had prevailed that way, when every man who had not been a traitor would have thought his loyalty of so much merit that no preferment could have been a recompense, and every Colonel believe the King owed his crown to his sword.[37]

In short, a royalist military triumph and a cavalier domination of the country and government, was as much a nightmare to him as the triumph of the parliamentary Puritans.

But for the moment the voice of moderation from the counties was evident. In May 1648 the knights, gentlemen and freeholders of Essex petitioned

that a timely and ready concession to His Majesty, for a personal treaty with his high court of Parliament, may prove the most effectual and speedy means for the removal of all such misapprehensions and fears, which are yet the unhappy obstacles of the peace and quiet of our Kingdom.[38]

At the same time the gentlemen of Kent declared: 'The Laws of Nature are universal and perpetual, among which that of self-preservation is one . . . We invade not your right, but stand firm to secure our own, and so to do is neither tumult nor rebellion.' The Commons had already responded in April with a declaration, carried by 165 to 99, that they would not alter 'the fundamental Government of the Kingdom, by King, Lords and Commons'. In July London petitioned that the king be brought to Westminster 'in honour, freedom and safety' for negotiations. The Commons feared the support which the king would mobilise in London, and insisted that peace negotiations be held in the Isle of Wight, and in September they appointed commissioners to treat with the king. The Commissioners nominated were, from the Lords, Northumberland, Pembroke, Salisbury, Middlesex and Saye and Sele, together with ten from the Commons, among whom the moderates were well represented. They met knowing that the alternative to success would be the triumph of the army.

The king left a full and detailed account of the negotiations for the guidance of the prince, which is likely therefore to be entirely trustworthy. It is clear that Charles was in effect being asked to accept four principles, without which there could be no agreement. The first was that parliament had undertaken a just war in defence of their rights; without this, the Commissioners argued, members might afterwards be held guilty of treason. The king said that he 'had resolved not to bring the merits of the cause to question', and the best way would be to make it 'penal for either side to reproach the other'; whereas to try to decide where right lay 'was but to revive those differences we thought to bury'. But when he found that the proposed preamble was *sine qua non* of the treaty, he gave way and accepted it, with the thought that he was acting under duress, and that the law of treason was in no way changed by it. Next he was required to agree to the abolition of episcopacy, the alienation of church lands, and the disuse of the Prayer Book. The usual long discussion followed with the divines on the status of Timothy and Titus, the interpretation of such texts as xiv Acts 23, and the teachings and practice of the early church. Charles was hard pressed with arguments such as that as episcopacy was established by law, it could be removed by law, and that Charles had already agreed to the abolition of episcopacy in Scotland. He finally agreed to the abolition of archbishops, deans and chapters, but not the bishops, but their suspension for three years, after which a religious settlement would be made by an assembly of divines. But he made clear his opinion that 'Episcopacy was so interwoven in the laws of this land, that we apprehended the pulling out this thread was like to make the whole garment ravel.' The Prayer Book would continue to be used in the royal chapel. Next the militia: the king agreed to its control by parliament for twenty years, although he argued that if it was unsafe to be in the king's control, it was equally unsafe to be in that of parliament. The king told the prince that the main reason for his agreeing was to hasten the disbandment of the army. Parliamentary agreement to appointments to the great offices of state was to be required for ten years, and the king agreed to annul all grants made by him since 1642. He consented to the abolition of the Court of Wards in return for £100,000 p.a. All this was agreed by 21 October.[39]

Charles had thus given way on much, but he had not agreed to the abolition of bishops, though he agreed to their suspension for three years, and he had not agreed to the total alienation of church lands. These to him were the most vital of all the issues at stake. When parliament's reply arrived, episcopacy was still the main sticking-point, and the king concluded that there was a party in parliament which did not really want peace, that he had made great concessions, and parliament had made none. He was indeed the conquered party, but further concessions would have left the Crown with no powers at all.

Even at this late stage historians have sometimes assumed that Charles was not sincere, and was only playing for time (e.g. Underdown: *Pride's Purge*) but there is no evidence for this. Charles knew that his enemies were ready to bring him to trial and execution, and that there was no room left for manoeuvre, and his letter of 25 November to the prince included a solemn admonition:

You see how long we have laboured in the search of peace. Do not be disheartened to tread in the same steps; use all worthy ways to restore yourself to your right, but prefer the way of peace. Shew the greatness of your mind, if God bless you . . . rather to conquer your enemies by pardoning than punishing . . . Give belief to our experience, never to affect more greatness or prerogative than that which is really and intrinsically for the good of subjects, not satisfaction of favourites. And if you thus use it, you will never want means to be a Father to all. . . . The English Nation are a sober people, however at present infatuated . . . We know not but this may be the last time we may speak to you, or the world publicly. We are sensible into what hands we are fallen . . . If God give you success, use it humbly and far from revenge.[40]

One slim hope remained, for the moderate majority of the Commons were determined to reach agreement with the king, in spite of the deadlock on episcopacy, in order to forestall the army and the radicals. On 15 November they voted to accept the king's request to come to London in 'honour, freedom and safety' to complete a settlement. Cromwell was besieging Pontefract, the last royalist stronghold in England, and army affairs were controlled by Ireton, who was determined to prevent a restoration of the king. He decided to act quickly, and on the 16th at a council of army officers produced a Remonstrance which was presented to the Commons on the 20th. It proclaimed the sovereignty of the people, and demanded the trial of the king as a traitor to his people. The Commons knew that the acceptance of the Remonstrance would signal the triumph of the army, and their own annihilation. William Prynne fearlessly denounced it as 'Subversive of the law of the land', and it was agreed to put off the decision for a week. How genuine was the desire for peace was shown when, on the false rumour that agreement had been reached with the king, bonfires were lit in the streets of London. But on the 29th Carisbrooke Castle was surrounded by troops, and it was clear that the seizure of the king was intended. The earl of Lindsey and the duke of Richmond advised the king to attempt an escape, Richmond saying that Colonel Cook knew the password, and that they had just walked past the guard without difficulty. But the king decided against it, and, with a deep sense of danger, he went to bed, but did not undress. Just at daybreak officers rushed into his chamber and took him away to Hurst Castle.[41]

Some of the tensions of the time are revealed by a discussion which took place at the end of November between Lilburne, the Levellers and Ireton. Colonel Harrison, one of the Levellers made clear 'their absolute determination to destroy the king', and 'to root up the Parliament', to replace it by the Agreement of the People. He argued that the army must move quickly, since they feared a treaty between the king and parliament, after which there would be a move to disband the army. Lilburne on the other hand showed that he distrusted the army as much as he distrusted parliament, for the army 'might rule over us arbitrarily, without declared laws, as a conquered people, and so deal with us as the poor slavish peasants in France are dealt with, who enjoy nothing they can call their own'. Lilburne objected to the army's decision to end the parliament, and their intention to try the king before 'a new and unquestionable Representative was sitting'. He argued that if parliament was ended there would be an end to legality:

then there is neither legal Judges nor Justices of Peace in England, and if so, then all those that are executed at Tyburn . . . are merely murdered, and the Judges or Justices that condemned them are liable in time to be hanged.

Lilburne also objected to 'Parliament's punishing where no law provides', and he differed from Ireton in the limits the latter would place on religious toleration. He left the meeting in defeat and disgust:

I took my leave of them for a pack of dissembling, juggling knaves, amongst whom in consultation ever thereafter I should scorn to come.[42]

In the Whitehall Debates in the General Council on 14 December similar divisions were revealed. The Leveller Wildman argued that the real question at issue was how much power the people would agree to give the rulers, and he denied that it extended to control of religion and matters of conscience. Ireton on the other hand denied this: the real issue, he declared, had been the distribution of powers between the king and parliament, 'so that the ground of the war was not difference in what the supreme Magistracy was, but whether it was in the King alone'. For the time being Ireton needed the support of the Levellers, and therefore was prepared to some extent to dissemble, but the final decision lay not with the Levellers but with Cromwell and himself. Lilburne called Ireton 'the Army's Alpha and Omega', and 'the cunningest of Machiavellians'. He was beginning to realise that the execution of the king would settle nothing. For the moment however the conflict was resolved by the decision of the General Council that 'the supreme trust' should be placed in 'the Representatives', except in matters of private conscience.[43]

On 4 December the Commons disowned the capture of the king, debated the question of peace, and in the early morning of the 5th voted that His Majesty's concessions were sufficient for a treaty settling the peace of the kingdom. As Professor Underdown writes, it was a vote for 'a restoration eleven years too early'.[44] But the army was now in control, and a committee headed by Ireton, Harrison and Ludlow directed affairs. On the 6th Colonel Pride and his men surrounded the Commons, and arrested a total of forty-five members, while 231 were excluded from the House.[45] There was no possibility of resistance. Ireton would have been better advised to dissolve the Long Parliament and institute new elections; as it was, in the eyes of the public he had merely subordinated the Rump to the will of the army, and his massive violation of parliament made the king's attempt on the Five Members in 1642 appear puny. As for the Puritan extremists, sectaries and millenarians, as Underdown writes, 'it was the dawn of a new day'.

Ireton and the radicals were bent on the trial of the king. Cromwell is said to have offered Charles his life in return for the surrender of the prerogative, but when this was inevitably rejected he took it as a sign from Providence and threw himself into preparations for the trial.* On 1 January 1649 the Rump proposed a High Court of Justice for trying Charles Stuart. The Lords, who had shrunk into insignificance, and at best numbered sixteen, rejected the Commons' resolution, the earl of Northumberland declaring that 'Not one in twenty of the people of England are yet satisfied whether the King did levy war against the Houses first, or the Houses first against him.'[47] But on the 4th the Commons resolved, 'That the People under God are the Original of all just Powers . . . [and] have the supreme Authority of this Nation. They do likewise declare, That whatsoever is enacted and declared Law by the Commons of England assembled in Parliament, hath the force of Law.'[48] Prynne who stoutly denied the supremacy of the Commons was imprisoned. A letter from the Estates of Scotland condemning the trial of the king was ignored. Thus at the moment when the Commons had ceased to have any reasonable claim to represent the nation, or to be a free body, they chose to depart from any pretence to constitutional legality, to ignore the Lords, and to put the king on trial. The most responsible lawyers in the country like Selden, Whitelocke and Oliver St John would have nothing to do with the trial. Of the 135 judges nominated, less than half ever attended, and many who did were, in C V Wedgwood's phrase 'rogues and knaves'[49] although she thinks that of the 59 who signed the death warrant, 30 or 40 acted from genuine conviction.

A lawyer named Bradshaw was made President of the Court, but the whole proceedings were dominated by Cromwell. The most distinguished member was Sir Thomas Fairfax, who however cut a poor figure, and is generally supposed to have been hoodwinked or overawed by Cromwell. But his wife was made of sterner stuff, and when at the end of the trial Bradshaw referred to crimes against the good people of England, she cried from the gallery, 'Not half, not a quarter of the people of England. Oliver Cromwell is a traitor.'[50]

Charles played his part magnificently. At the time of the Treaty of Newport he had appeared unkempt, with grey, undressed hair,[51] but now he appeared trim in sober black, and repeatedly he scored legal points:

Sir, by your favour, I do not know the Forms of Law. I do know Law and Reason,

---

* This story may or may not be true. It is accepted by Abbott, but rejected by C V Wedgwood.[46]

though I am no Lawyer professed. But I know as much law as any Gentleman in England; and therefore I do plead for the Liberties of the People of England more than you do.

He refused to plead until he knew by what authority he was being tried:

The Commons of England was never a Court of Judicature; I would know how they came to be so.

He did however submit his argument in writing. He rejected the President's claim that he was being tried by the will of the people:

for certainly you never asked the question of the tenth man in the Kingdom, and in this way you manifestly wrong even the poorest ploughman, if you demand not his free consent: nor can you pretend any colour for this your pretended commission, without the consent at least of the major part of every man in England of whatsoever quality or condition, which I'm sure you never went about to seek, so far are you from having it. Thus you see that I speak not for my own right alone, as I am your King, but also for the true liberty of all my subjects . . .

If power without law may make laws, may alter the fundamental laws of the Kingdom, I do not know what subject he is in England that can be sure of his life, or anything that he calls his own.[52]

However the conclusion was foregone, and the death sentence was pronounced on 27 January. Charles then asked to be allowed to address the two Houses of Parliament saying that he had a new proposal to make, but the Court would not allow it. Ludlow thought that Charles intended to abdicate in favour of his son. Bradshaw declared that the king

had endeavoured throughout the whole course of his reign to subvert those good laws, and to introduce an arbitrary and tyrannical government in the room of them: that . . . he had attempted from the beginning of his reign, either wholly to destroy Parliaments, or to render them only subservient to his own corrupt designs,

and that he had levied war against his people.[53] Fifty-nine commissioners signed the death warrant, some of them because they feared Cromwell more than the king.

On the scaffold before the Banqueting Hall in Whitehall on 30 January, Charles declared that he had not begun the war, but that his death was God's judgment for deserting Strafford. He continued:

Truly I desire their [the people's] liberty and freedom as much as anybody whomsoever; but I must tell you their liberty and freedom consists in having of government, those laws by which their life and their goods may be most their own. It is not for having a share in government, Sir, that is nothing pertaining to them. A subject and a sovereign are clear different things . . . Sirs, it was for this that now I am come here. If I would have given way to an arbitrary way, for to have all laws changed according to the power of the sword, I needed not to have come here, and therefore I tell you . . . that I am the Martyr of the people.

Charles died therefore rejecting the democratic principle, as his opponents were doing, but as a martyr for the traditional law and constitution of England as the best guarantee for the liberty and property of subjects, as well as for the Anglican Church. The manner of his death did much to efface the memory of earlier mistakes, and to royalists he could now shine forth as the noble figure of 'Eikon Basilike'. In this sense his death was, as Clarendon always recognised, a necessary preliminary to the restoration of the monarchy.

Clarendon commented that it was a paradox that at the moment of Charles' death, 'he had as great a share in the hearts and affections of his subjects in general, was as much beloved, esteemed and longed for by the people in general of the three nations, as any of his predecessors had ever been'.[54] Charles's fight to the death to defend the church and royal prerogative according to law, won Clarendon's veneration. His conclusion on the king's character is well known:

he was the worthiest gentleman, the best master, the best friend, the best husband, the best father, and the best Christian, that the age in which he lived had produced. And if he were not the best king, if he were without some parts and qualities which have made some kings great and happy, no other prince was ever unhappy who was possessed of half his virtues and endowments, and so much without any kind of vice.[55]

The news of the king's death was received with shock and horror by most of the nation, but there were no disturbances; the army was too strong for that. In Europe too there were expressions of horror, but no inclination to interfere. Mazarin expressed deep concern for the king's fate, but had too many problems of his own to act, and was torn between fear of the English parliament and the possibility of an alliance between the regicides and the Fronde. The Dutch had some sympathy for the English republic, although the House of Orange did all it could for the Stuarts. The States General sent two envoys to intercede for the king's life, but they were brushed aside. Portugal was an English ally, but could do nothing, and Spain had little incentive to aid the Stuarts. The Pope would do nothing without a clear promise of toleration for Catholics. The only powers ready to offer any practical help were the rulers of Denmark and Russia.[56] None of this surprised or disappointed Hyde, who from the first had been suspicious of French intentions, and who always believed that a solution would be found by the English people themselves, or it would not be found at all.

# Ireland, Scotland and Spain

Until the end of Charles I's life, Sir Edward Hyde's view of royal policy entailed an adamantine opposition to compromise on fundamental issues. He was convinced that with military defeat the position of the king was so weak that concessions would lead only to demands for more concessions, until the reality of monarchy and church was destroyed. The crown had one inestimable attribute; it was the keystone of a constitutional structure without which there could be no fundamental legality. In the course of time there must be a return to legality, and it was essential that meanwhile the foundations should not have been eroded. Thus Hyde rejected out of hand the terms offered, whether at Newcastle, Newport, or in the Heads of Proposals because they destroyed the fundamentals of Church and State. He even rejected the plan for a 'moderate episcopacy' which Archbishop Ussher had formulated, and which seemed to many royalists so attractive a compromise. 'Moderate episcopacy', he wrote,

is a new word to cozen men into a consent for extirpation. They would moderate their number by new nonsense, double or treble them; and they would moderate their revenue, that is, take three parts from them; and they would moderate their jurisdiction, that is, leave them no more authority or power than the parson of the parish: besides, I must tell you, these prudent men, who desire to moderate episcopacy, will nullify deans and chapters; and, on those righteous terms, they will be content that some men shall be called bishops.[1]

But would not this rejection of compromise lead to the overthrow of the monarchy and the death of the king? Hyde recognised this, but he took the hard view that it were better the king should die than that the king's successors should be for ever shorn of power.

Looking back on the course of events since 1640 Hyde concluded that the reason for the king's failure had been his tendency to give away too much in the belief that it would buy a settlement:

If I were now to die, I can impute the ill success of the King's affairs in these contentions to no one thing more than that supine temper in many honest men, of endeavouring expedients to satisfy those who were confessedly, wickedly in the wrong, and breaking the quarrel into pieces. This particular was not worth a war, and should the Kingdom be destroyed for this thing, or that word, by which the enemy gathered both courage and strength, whilst they found any one unreasonable or unlawful act countenanced? Whereas there ought to have been no more matter in issue on the King's part, than that they would compel his Majesty by arms to consent to laws and acts, which it was in his power to refuse; this was, and is in truth, the quarrel; and when you change it you will have a worse; yield to one thing, you justify the demand of another; and it is an even lay there will be more reason to demand the second than the first, you having by that yielded and receded from the best argument you had to deny. I do confess it is the office of wise men to find expedients to reform and reconcile the affections of distempered men, but it must be still to reduce them to just and true principles, not to quit the proper ends, for preservation only whereof an union and reconciliation is to be desired. I pray God the King's party do dispassionately weigh this, and not suffer themselves to be made a property to either party, out of animosity to the other.[2]

Thus it seemed to Hyde in 1648 that the reason for the king's failure lay in the concessions he had made in such instances as sanctioning the death of Strafford, or accepting the perpetuation of the life of parliament, each of which served to undermine his position and increase the demands of his opponents, until the foundations were worn away. It followed that attempts to seek agreements with Presbyterians, Independents, the army or the Scots must fail. He prayed that the king would stand firm, and when he did so he venerated his memory for doing so. Even the death of a king was not too high a price to pay for the defence of the fundamentals of the constitution:

I would not, to preserve myself, wife and children from the lingering pain of want and famine (for a sudden death would require no courage) consent to the lessening any part which I take to be in the function of a bishop, or the taking away the smallest prebendary in the church, or be bound not to endeavour to alter any such alteration.

The execution of his father left the eighteen-year-old Charles II, in Hyde's words, in 'deep amazement and confusion'.[3] Surrounded on all sides with conflicting advice, with few resources, and the prospects of poverty before him, it was difficult to know what course to pursue. His mother pressed him to return to France, and to make no appointments to his council until he had consulted her. But Charles had had enough of the humiliating tutelage at Saint Germain, and decided that any other course was preferable to that. On what that should be there was conflicting advice: the choice seemed to lie between an Irish or a Scottish venture.

The Irish rising of 1641, which had so embarrassed Charles I, had developed into a nation-wide Catholic revolt, with religion as the central issue. The Catholic Confederacy proclaimed their loyalty to the king, but demanded complete religious freedom for Catholics. Much as Charles I needed Irish support once the Civil War began, he could not offer complete religious toleration to the Irish Catholics, as this would gravely offend the English parliament, where Pym was already accusing the king of collusion with the

Papists. Moreover the loyalty of Irish Catholics was said to be in doubt; that their true allegiance was to the Pope and not the king, and, as James I had said, that they were 'only half-subjects'. Charles I therefore could neither win Irish support nor suppress the rebellion. All he could do was to leave it to his faithful Lord Lieutenant, the marquis of Ormond, to make the best settlement he could. Any agreement with the Catholic Confederacy would alienate the Ulster Protestants. In 1644 for example Lord Inchiquin informed Ormond that he could not serve in any combination with the Papists, and Sir Thomas Wharton urged Ormond to advise the king 'rather to think of an accommodation with his Parliament in England to subdue these rebels, than, by giving them any countenance or assistance, to bring ruin upon himself, religion and kingdoms'.[4]

However, Charles's need for Irish troops was desperate by 1645, and the earl of Glamorgan, according to his own account[5] had authority under the king's signet to barter Catholic privileges in return for military aid. Pope Innocent X sent Rinuccini to Ireland as Papal Nuncio, and in December 1645 reached agreement with Glamorgan. Meanwhile in November an agreement was reached in Rome by the Pope and Sir Kenelm Digby acting on behalf of Queen Henrietta Maria, offering the Catholics even more favourable terms. But no Irish troops materialised to help the king, and moreover Glamorgan's agreement was leaked both to parliament and to Ormond. There was an outcry, and the king had to repudiate Glamorgan.

After the battle of Naseby the king's military position rapidly collapsed, and Ormond had no alternative but to seek an agreement with the Confederates on the best terms he could get (March 1646). But Rinuccini and the clergy, with an utter lack of realism, rejected the peace terms, and pronounced an interdict on all who accepted them. A period of complete confusion followed, ending in June 1647 with the arrival in Dublin of a small parliamentary force under Colonel Michael Jones. The Confederacy was hopelessly divided, but Rinuccini was supporting a move to repudiate Charles I and to choose an independent king for Ireland. Faced with a choice between this and the English parliament, Ormond chose the latter, handed over to Jones, and sailed for England. Charles I confirmed Ormond in his appointment as Lord Lieutenant, and in February 1648 he was sent to France, with the king's instructions to act in future according to the orders of the queen and the Prince of Wales, since Charles was no longer a free agent. Ormond returned to Ireland in September, when he found the situation much the same. His great need was for Irish Catholic military aid, but for this he could give no firm religious guarantees, and Rinuccini rejected a peace without them. However, the trial and execution of the king were a shock to Irish Catholics and Ulster Scots alike. Charles II was proclaimed king in Ireland; the queen was now anxious that her son should go there, confirm Catholic privileges, and thus gather a military force.

Scotland seemed to offer an alternative. The Scots' interventions in English affairs had disappointing results for them in that they had gained neither quick military success nor imposed Presbyterianism on England. Historians have tended to assume that although the Scots were fanatical about Presbyterianism, they were less concerned with constitutional issues, and more favourable to monarchy than the English war party. There is little evidence for this, and Clarendon certainly thought otherwise. The Scots, it is true, did not propose to dethrone the king, but Argyll and the kirk party clearly intended to reduce him to a figurehead, and after the failure of the Newcastle Treaty, were ready to sell him to the English. Only gradually did the magnitude of the blunder of that act dawn upon the Covenanters, for if the king was eliminated as a factor, there would remain Independency and the army triumphant in England. Moreover the domination of Argyll and the kirk in Scotland was alienating the Scottish nobility, and the duke of Hamilton emerged to challenge that supremacy. At Hampton Court in October 1647 the earls of Lauderdale, Lanark (Hamilton's brother) and Loudoun told the king of their desire to restore him to his 'throne, dignity and royal government', but the price was the acceptance of the Covenant. The king enquired why then they had chosen to sell him to the English nine months before? When he fled from Hampton Court in November, it was not to the Scots, but to Carisbrooke Castle. There his position so worsened that in December he accepted the Engagement, including the Covenant and agreeing to Presbyterianism for three years. Hyde at once disapproved of the Engagement, as likely to be disastrous to the royal cause, and it proved equally disastrous to the Scots. However it won for Hamilton a majority in the Scots' parliament, and for the moment Argyll had to acquiesce. Hamilton, opposed by the kirk, got together a scratch army, which was destroyed by Cromwell at Preston in August 1648.

Hamilton's attempt to reconcile the monarchy and the Covenant had failed, and with his defeat the Engagers were driven from office. Argyll and the kirk reasserted their control, and it would take another three years of the domination of the kirk before the Scots finally tired of it. Cromwell in October worked out a settlement in Edinburgh acceptable both to him and to Argyll. But the Scots had no part in the trial and execution of the king in January 1649, and the Scottish parliament at once proclaimed Charles II king of Great Britain.

Lauderdale had been sent to the Prince of Wales in August to persuade him to put himself at the head of the Scottish army, but before any decision was made, the news of Hamilton's defeat had settled the matter. Lauderdale returned to Scotland, but finding a persecution of the Engagers in full swing, Lanerick and he escaped to Holland and rejoined the Prince.[6]

The problem which faced the young king in 1649 was therefore very similar to that which had faced his father, and the question was what conclusions might be drawn from his father's handling of it. In Scotland there was a triumphant kirk, upon which Argyll depended for much of his power; there were the Engagers, now in disgrace and driven from office, and there were the royalist nobility, strong in the north, yet powerless to achieve much. A royalist rising led by Sir Thomas Mackenzie seized Inverness in February, but was soon suppressed. The marquis of Huntly was executed, although he had nothing to do with the rising. Montrose however on the continent was in close touch with the prince and with Hyde, and was as eager as ever for another chance to raise Scotland for the king. Any offers of restoration from the triumphant Argyll and the kirk would have the same strings of submission to the Covenant as had been attached to offers to Charles I. Hyde wrote that he had not logic enough to understand those Scots who proclaimed the king, and yet wished to strip him of all regal powers.[7] But he thought they spoke for only a minority of Scots:

it is evident the poison and rancour there lies within a little compass, and is contracted within the breasts of few men, who, no question, were as consenting to the parricide as Cromwell or Ireton. If a full and clear encouragement were given to all the loyal party there, instead of application to the other [i.e. to Argyll and the kirk], I am persuaded Scotland would in a short time be in good posture of obedience.

In the choice between Ireland and Scotland as the king's destination, Hyde preferred Ireland, but in March Scots commissioners arrived in Holland to press him to come to Scotland. Their initial demand, that Montrose should be excluded from his counsels, was not encouraging. If Charles chose Scotland there were two rival policies advocated. The Engagers, Lauderdale, Lanark and Callander advised him to accept the Covenant and go to Scotland with the intention of overthrowing Argyll and the kirk once he was installed. But this was the disastrous policy which had led Hamilton to execution at the hands of the English in March 1649. The alternative was the policy of Montrose, that the only solution lay in a royalist invasion and military victory. Charles relied heavily on Montrose for advice, and that advice was that acceptance of the Covenant could mean ruin for the king, as for his father. Clarendon commented that since both the Engagers and Montrose were equally enemies to Argyll and the kirk, one would have expected them to combine against them, but instead the Engagers would not even meet Montrose.[8] Instead they pressed the king to accept their terms. Hyde wrote with exasperation of

those who, as if they had rescued his Majesty from destruction, not sold his Father to those who murdered him, press him wholly to be advised by them; and, at the same time they have cut off the Marquis of Huntly's head, insolently require the King to abandon my lord Montrose . . . I assure you an honest English heart is shrewdly put to it to continue wise and honest together.[9]

He believed that Argyll had deliberately made the terms harsh in the hope that Charles would reject them.

Finally the king listened to the advice of Montrose and Hyde, and the Scots returned empty-handed to Scotland, while he renewed plans for an Irish expedition. It was in any case necessary that he should leave Holland, for on 2 May 1649 a Dr Dorislaus, a doctor of civil law at Leyden, who had taught at Cambridge, and helped to draw up the indictment against Charles I, was murdered at The Hague by some followers of Montrose. Although the king was entirely ignorant of the plot, and although the assassins fled to Brussels, the Dutch authorities let it be known that the continued presence of the refugees would not be welcome. Charles consulted the Dutch about the course he should pursue, in the hope that they would offer him aid. They preferred the Scottish venture, and so did the Prince of Orange who lent him £20,000 to speed his departure. The queen offered to pawn her jewels to finance an expedition to Ireland.

Although Hyde favoured the Irish venture he saw that it had the great disadvantage of lack of resources, and also that it threw the king back into dependence upon his mother, for the expedition could be launched only from France. Lord Hatton wrote to Hyde in March:

I hold Lord Jermyn's counsels and designs as pernicious and destructive as ever, and his power as vast and exorbitant. His present endeavour is to procure a speedy meeting between the King and Queen here in France, to engage and tie up the King as much as ever his father was to the counsels of the Queen . . . To show you the rottenness and corruption of his heart, Lord Hatton heard him say in the Queen's bedchamber upon Sunday last that if the King did restore Lord Cottington, Sir Edward Hyde or any such person to be officers under his Majesty, the King would ruin himself. Sir, I beseech you, use all to prevent the King's journey to any such meeting.[10]

Hyde wrote soothing letters to Saint Germain:

My duty to the Queen is a part of my Religion; and I shall as soon take the Covenant as commit any fault willingly against her,[11]

but the hostility of the queen and Jermyn towards him remained inveterate. Hyde wrote to Nicholas, 'you cannot imagine the care hath been taken to infuse prejudice into the King of all his Father's council'.[12]

In April 1649 Lord Cottington, the Lord Treasurer placed before the king a proposal to send an embassy to Spain to enlist the aid of Madrid for the royalist cause. Spain seemed almost the last hope of acquiring money and aid without which even an expedition to Ireland seemed doomed to failure. It was true that Spain had done nothing to aid Charles I, but the Spanish had always shown a special interest in the fate of Ireland, where the Catholic cause was strongest, and where the Pope's aid might be enlisted. But Cottington had a personal interest in the plan. He had for years been ambassador to Spain, was passionately pro-Spanish, and now at the age of seventy-five longed for Spain's more congenial climate. But at his age he felt the need for Hyde's assistance, he being his closest friend, and the two sharing a house in the Hague. When Charles told Hyde of the proposal his first reaction was to suspect that it was a plot from Saint Germain to get him away from the king's council, but on further thought he warmed to the idea, for he was tired of the constant feuds which surrounded the unfortunate king. Both Jermyn and the Scots were pleased that Hyde's influence would be removed, although the queen was convinced that the Spanish venture was doomed to failure. Only Montrose took the news bitterly, regarding Hyde's departure as a desertion of his cause. Avid for action as usual, but now convinced that nothing further could be obtained in Holland, Montrose went off to Hamburg to enlist help from Denmark, Sweden and the Scottish exiles who roamed Europe.[13] Hyde drew up the ambassadors' instructions which were to seek aid and a loan from his Catholic Majesty in return for an alliance, and a promise of a repeal of the penal laws against the Catholics when the king was restored to his throne.[14]

How deeply Charles's advisers were divided was shown when it was decided that since the king had made no declaration to England since the death of his father, he should do so before leaving Holland, and Hyde was entrusted with its composition. However this proved an impossible task. The Prince of Orange and the Scots wanted an appeal to the Presbyterians, which Hyde who wanted a royalist manifesto resolutely opposed. On the question of amnesty, should it except the regicides? or more? or merely Cromwell and Bradshaw? In the end the whole idea was abandoned. However, Hyde drew up a memorandum for the guidance of the king during his absence, concerning the search for allies in England. It is an important document for understanding the working of Hyde's mind. Hyde argued, as he had done once before, that if there was to be a choice of Presbyterians or Independents as allies he would prefer the latter:

They are not so full of animosity and uncharitableness to the King's party as the Presbyterians are . . . and, being men of meaner condition and less pride, will find themselves to stand in need of the assistance and countenance of better men, which the other will despise. Lastly, they are possessed of power and interest in the Army and in Towns and Garrisons, and probably have a good influence in the Navy; whereas the Presbyterians (I mean those Presbyterians who pretend any inclination to the King) are as void of power and strength as the Cavaliers are, and without any credit or reputation with the People.

He thought that the Independents might be wooed with offers of a general amnesty, 'ease of tender consciences', legal reforms, poor relief and a promise of frequent Parliaments, 'these and the like specious concessions will comprehend all which they can insist on without evident invalidating the Regal power'. On the other hand agreement with the Presbyterians would present much greater difficulties, involving the abrogation of the Solemn League and Covenant, a church settlement by national synod, and the rejection of the Newport Treaty.[15] The whole document revealed a shrewd assessment of the Presbyterians, who, in his opinion, had done more than any other group to defeat the prospect of peace with the king. The Covenant had been a powerful political weapon in both Scotland and England for resisting the monarchy, but it failed lamentably to provide either a social, religious or political alternative for England. It remained in the last instance a foreign importation from Scotland.

Hyde and Cottington left The Hague in May and Hyde settled his wife and children in a house in Antwerp before proceeding to Brussels to deliver credentials to the archduke and to the duke of Lorraine. The latter, having been driven from his dominions by the French, still retained his army, and cherished an ambition to carve out for himself a new territory in Ireland. Cottington was able to persuade him to lend them two thousand pistoles to cover the expenses of the embassy.[16] Charles meanwhile passed through Antwerp and Brussels, where he was royally entertained by the Spanish authorities, before proceeding to Saint Germain. When the two ambassadors arrived there they found the court 'full of jealousy and disorder'. Henrietta Maria still had hopes of directing her son but Charles made it plain that he intended to conduct his own affairs, and 'seemed not to desire to be so much in her company as she expected'. To add to the confusion, Charles had again met a young man named Thomas Elliott, who had been a gentleman of the bedchamber to the prince at Oxford, and whose influence on the prince was so bad that the king had forbidden him to attend the Court. The two met again at The Hague, and Elliott quickly established an influence over Charles, encouraging his resistance to his mother's influence, and doing his best to blacken the reputations of old royalists such as the earl of Bristol and Lord Digby. The latter poured out their troubles to Hyde in Paris, and he learnt with alarm that Elliott was pressing the king to appoint his father-in-law, Colonel Wyndham, as his Secretary of State. In this situation of crisis, the queen turned to Hyde for help. Hyde readily agreed, and taxed Charles with the absurdity of appointing Wyndham as Secretary, when Nicholas was the obvious candidate for the post. But Charles remained obdurate, and it was Cottington who finally settled the matter, by asking the king to appoint one of his falconers as his chaplain, since, being an honest man, he was as fit to be a chaplain as Wyndham was to be Secretary. Courtiers laughed, and no more was heard of Wyndham's appointment.[17]

Meanwhile the plan for an Irish expedition failed, not only because of the King's deplorable lack of resources, but also because the royalist cause in Ireland was facing collapse. Ormond's only hope had been to unite the Catholic Confederacy, Inchquin's Ulstermen and his own force under a single command. But the Confederacy refused to accept his leadership, and in August 1649 his attempt to take Dublin failed when he was defeated by Jones at Rathmines. Thirteen days later Cromwell landed with 12,000 men, for the end of the Civil War had released ample manpower for an Irish campaign.

Thereafter the royalist cause rapidly collapsed. Cromwell stormed Drogheda in September and massacred its inhabitants, and Wexford suffered the same fate in October. Ormond hung on in Ireland until December 1650, but long before that, all hope of a royalist success had disappeared.

Charles's plight was now wretched. The French were anxious that he should be gone from France, and the queen could only acquiesce. On 12 September he left Saint Germain, almost penniless but with all the dignity he could muster, with six coaches each with six horses, and a retinue of some 300 noblemen, gentlemen and others. They were bound for Jersey, the only bit of his kingdom which remained to him. So large an invasion of a small island placed a severe strain upon the Governor, Carteret, and the squabbles of the impoverished courtiers increased the difficulty. With the failure of the Irish expedition, the queen and Jermyn renewed their pressure for an agreement with the Scots. Nicholas, who had been promised the Secretaryship of State, did his best to resist. Jermyn, he wrote to Ormond, was 'esteemed the head of the Scots' Presbyterian party', and he bitterly regretted the absence of Hyde. 'The truth is, Sir Edward Hyde being so unnecessarily and unskilfully employed in Spain, hath given an infinite advantage to the Scots presbyterians; for he was expert in all their jigs and artifices, and, only [he], understood their canting.'[18]

When therefore the Scots made further representations to the king in January 1650, his council agreed to discussions to take place at Breda. Most of the Scottish nobles were in favour of the king's return, the kirk was losing ground, and Argyll saw the monarchy as the best means of satisfying public opinion and achieving social stability; and if this was the case, who better to be king-maker than Argyll? Yet Charles and his council completely failed to understand the complexity of the situation. Montrose had been extraordinarily successful in gathering assistance in north Germany, particularly from Denmark and Sweden, and in September 1649 he sent a small advance party to Orkney under the command of the earl of Kinnoull, he himself following in March 1650. By then however the news of Charles's negotiations with Argyll had persuaded Denmark and Sweden to draw back. Charles informed Montrose of his intention to negotiate, but nonetheless ordered him to attempt a speedy victory. This was nothing less than a stab in the back,[19] for how could Scottish royalists be expected to join Montrose against Argyll when the king was in alliance with Argyll? Charles at the head of Montrose's army would have been a more honourable, and perhaps a more successful undertaking, than as a puppet to Argyll. As it was Montrose, smarting under the rebuff, passed to the mainland in April with a mere 1200 men and was at once attacked and routed by the Covenanters. He fled and went into hiding, but was betrayed by the MacLeods, captured, carried to Edinburgh and executed with the usual barbarities. If Charles I felt remorse for the death of Strafford, his son certainly should have felt it for the death of Montrose.

The terms which Cassilis, Lothian and George Wynrame presented to the king at Breda, required him to accept the Solemn League and Covenant and the Presbyterian government of the church. He must also repudiate Montrose, and all concessions made to the Irish Catholics.[20] He was reminded that these were the terms offered to his father at Newcastle, and the condition of the monarchy had worsened since then. If he accepted, he would be invited to Scotland. Charles in return asked for a guarantee of the safety of his person, the full exercise of his regal authority, and the reinstatement of the Engagers. He asked also for assistance in recovering his other kingdoms. Some of the Commissioners were anxious to gain his acceptance and returned favourable answers; others were less inclined to trust him. On 2 May he gave a general acceptance, but the Scottish parliament was not satisfied, and demanded further commitments, insisting on the exclusion from the kingdom of Engagers such as Hamilton, Seaforth, Calander, Traquair and Lauderdale, and making it clear that the Scots were not committed to a war with England. The kirk required further assurance that concessions to Irish Catholics were cancelled, and protested that the king continued to take communion on his knees according to Anglican practice. Above all he must sign the Covenant before landing in Scotland. Charles finally agreed to all the demands except that concerning communion, and on 24 June he was permitted to land at Garmouth.*

From the first Hyde was opposed to the Scottish venture, and at first did not believe that Charles would be misled into making it. On one occasion he wrote that it would be as great a miracle that the king should trust Argyll as that the men of Westminster would invite him to be king.[22] He placed his trust entirely upon Montrose at the head of a substantial royalist army:

We hope the Marquis of Montrose will advance this treaty better than all the devotion of the Presbyterians, and that the King will never do anything to lessen the power and trust he hath committed to him, who sure must be thought worthier of it than any person of that other party.

To the queen he wrote:

I pray . . . that the king may not throw off servants of unquestionable faith and integrity, of whom he is possessed, in expectation of great services from those who have done all the mischief to his Majesty and his father, and to your Majesty, and do not appear to repent anything they have done, and so are the more like to act over the same part again.[23]

The Scots, he wrote, dealt with the king like honest men,

---

* The queen, who approved of the Scottish negotiations, did not approve of Charles taking the Covenant. Cottington and Hyde wrote to her in July 1650: 'Few will believe that your Majesty ever advised or concurred in the point of the Covenant; nor in truth can the Scots have any other ground for pressing the King in it, than to expose him to dishonour'.[21]

and tell him plainly that they will never do him good; and yet we are so mad as to believe that they will do better than they promise.[24]

In March 1650 Hyde wrote to Dr Morley that if the Scots had come to the king renouncing the revolution, the Covenant and Presbyterianism, and ready to unite under Montrose, there would be good grounds for accepting:

but when they deal so frankly and honestly with him, and tell him that he is to expect the same usage from them his Father had, that they will swear over again to be as bad as ever, and that everybody else that will keep them company shall swear the same; and that they will destroy every honest man of his three kingdoms, and that he shall join with them to destroy them; that he shall renounce his Kingdom of Ireland and extirpate all the Catholics in all his Dominions: These conditions are so plain, that he hath nothing to do but to consider whether all they can do for him be worth this price.[25]

To Sir John Berkeley, whom he deemed a close friend, and who was in favour of a Presbyterian alliance, he wrote in some anguish:

Hath there been any avowed proposition made by that party [the Presbyterian] which doth not directly imply the destruction both of Catholic and King's party? Must he not, to gain the men of Edinburgh, plainly renounce the peace of Ireland, and consequently all his reasonable hope of that Kingdom? For God's sake, speak clearly to me, that I may know what hath transported so good an understanding as thou hast, and even corrupted so excellent a nature.[26]

But, he wrote, the king knew all the facts, and the final decision must be his alone. Berkeley did not share Hyde's exclusive royalist and Anglican views, and was in favour of an agreement with the Presbyterians on principles of the merest opportunism:

we must not pretend conscience where there is none, as Papists do infallibility, and Puritans the spirit; and as they do, when they are by rational arguments beaten out of all their strengths, retire to fastnesses, where no man can come at them; but rather make a conscience not to suffer a glorious and flourishing church and state for ever to perish, rather than it should be recovered by those against whom we have passionately engaged ourselves.[27]

Berkeley expressed a cynicism which shocked Hyde, and which he resisted for the rest of his life. Berkeley wrote that he had universality on his side, very few now agreeing with Hyde in opposing the Scottish venture. He asked why Charles I had failed, why he had not conceded at Oxford, or at Uxbridge the principles he was ready to concede at Newport; and answered that he was bound, 'tied by imaginary bonds that he could never unloose until it was too late'. Would not earlier concessions have saved him?

I, and many thousands more are persuaded it would; and yet the most powerful reason I ever heard was, that such concessions were absolutely unlawful in themselves, and afterwards were not thought so, nor indeed were not so in their nature.[28]

All this was implied criticism of the stand Hyde had always made, and it hurt him deeply. Secretary Nicholas on the other hand reproached him on quite different grounds, for deserting the King just when he needed his advice most. Hyde replied:

you do not know, Mr. Secretary, the difficulties I had to contend with, and such as were more incumbent to me than to any other person, and such as will make an honest man willing to shift the scene of his action.

The only criticism he cared about, he wrote, was that which came from royalists,

and when I found myself struck at by some letters from [the King's own party in England] . . . as an enemy to moderate counsels, and a breaker of treaties . . . I began to think myself of less use to the King's service than I had done before; for I have been always of opinion that the King's restoration depends exceedingly upon the reputation of his Ministers.[29]

Charles soon found his position humiliating and powerless. Clarendon brilliantly describes his predicament:

the king's table was well served; and there he sat in majesty, waited upon with decency: he had good horses to ride abroad to take the air, and was then well attended; and in all public appearances seemed to want nothing that was due to a great king. In all other respects, with reference to power to oblige or gratify any man, to dispose or order anything, or himself to go to any place than was assigned to him, he had nothing of a prince, but might very well be looked upon as a prisoner.[30]

All his attendants, including his secretary Robert Long, and Sir Edward Walker, clerk of the Council, and his Engager friends, Hamilton and Lauderdale, were sent away. Only the duke of Buckingham managed to insinuate himself into Argyll's favour, and was allowed to remain, to exercise his usual baleful influence.

There never was a better courtier than Argyll, who made all the possible address to make himself gracious to the king, entertained him with very pleasant discourses, with such insinuations, that the king did not only very well like his conversation, but often believed that he had a mind to please and gratify him; but then, when his majesty made any attempt to get some of his servants about him, or to reconcile the two factions, that the kingdom might be united, he gathered up his countenance, and retired from his address, without ever yielding to any one proposition that was made to him by his majesty.[31]

Cromwell from the first had seen the great propaganda value which lay in the challenge of both Scotland and Ireland. In March 1649 he reported to the General Council:

I had rather be overrun with a Cavalierish interest than of a Scotch interest; I had rather be overrun with a Scotch interest than an Irish interest; and I think of all this is most dangerous. If they shall be able to carry on their work they will make this the most miserable people in the earth, for all the world knows their barbarism. Now it should awaken all Englishmen who perhaps are willing enough he [the king] should have come in upon an accommodation but see now that he must come from Ireland or Scotland.[32]

In short, even royalists, as good Englishmen, would hesitate to accept a king brought in by Scots and Irish forces. Hyde saw this also, but Charles II listened to other advice.

Cromwell did not wait for the Scots to attack him, if that were their intention, but crossed the Tweed on 22 July. He did his best to avoid battle, urging the General Assembly to study Isaiah 28, 5–15, and asking,

is it infallibly agreeable to the Word of God all that you say? I beseech you, in the bowels of Christ, think it possible you may be mistaken.[33]

Leslie had an army considerably larger than Cromwell's, but ill-armed, untrained, and demoralised by repeated purgings of royalists and Engagers by the indefatigable kirk. Cromwell's chief problem was one of supply, and if Leslie had delayed action, the English might have been in difficulties. But, outnumbering Cromwell's army by two to one, he gave battle before Dunbar, and his army was shattered (3 September). Cromwell reported triumphantly to the Speaker of the Commons 'one of the most signal mercies God hath done for England', in which 'I do not believe we have lost twenty men'.

If the victory was a triumph for Cromwell, it was, Clarendon perceptively remarked, 'the greatest happiness that could befall' the king, for it broke the domination of the kirk, and released him from its tutelage. In August he had been forced to submit to the ultimate humiliation of having to 'humble himself before God for his father's opposition to the covenant, for the idolatry of his mother, the toleration of which in his house was a great provocation to God'.[34] Now he might become an important factor in rallying royalists and Engagers to resist the English. He used his physician Dr Fraser, and Henry Seymour, as agents to arouse support in the highlands among the marquis of Huntly and the earls of Airlie and Atholl, and a rising was planned for early October. But Charles revealed the plan to Buckingham, who was a friend of Argyll's. Perhaps he revealed it to Argyll; at any rate the latter heard of it and took speedy action. Charles was frightened and fled to the highlands ('The Start'), but a day or two later was persuaded to return to Perth and apologise for his conduct. Leslie was sent to deal with the royalists, who however were leniently treated by an Act of Indemnity. Charles was crowned at Scone on 1 January 1650, the crown being placed on his head by Argyll, a formidable sermon being preached by Robert Douglas on the theme that 'A king abusing his power to the overthrow of religion, laws and liberties … may be controlled and opposed'.[35]

Charles's plan now was to attempt to win the support of Argyll, royalists and

Engagers in a united movement against England. For this he must flatter Argyll, even to agreeing to marry his daughter Anne Campbell. Thus in February 1651 Captain Titus, of the king's Bedchamber, was sent to France to obtain the queen's permission for the marriage.[36] Charles must have known that permission would be refused, but meanwhile Argyll's good will might be obtained. Hamilton, Lauderdale and Atholl returned to the king, and he was able to build up a substantial army. The royalist recruiting ground was in the highlands, and it was in order to cut off this supply that Cromwell in July crossed the Forth and occupied Perth. Charles must either wait until Cromwell chose to attack him, or make a desperate attempt upon England. The latter was exactly what Cromwell hoped that he would do. Argyll at once broke with the king, and many Scots refused to join the English venture. Plans for royalist risings in England were discovered and the commonwealth government swooped on some two thousand royalists. Hyde's cousin, Henry Hyde, was executed. Many royalists just had time to escape to the continent. This was disastrous to Charles's cause, for he was relying on a rising in the west country to be led by Lord Beauchamp (one of those arrested), and to be aided by a force landed at Torbay from Holland and sent by the Prince of Orange. Charles wrote to the latter that this aid from Holland was crucial, and that he could not trust the Scots, 'the truth is, they seek themselves and their own interests too much to be a solid aid, or to be totally relied upon'.[37]

Charles advanced into England with a force of between ten and eleven thousand men, dispersed a small force blocking his way to Appleby, and was joined by the earl of Derby and some 300 men at Stoke-on-Trent. Beyond these, attempts to raise recruits in Lancashire failed, for the Presbyterians mistrusted Derby and refused to help unless he took the Covenant. After a march of twenty-three days, during which there were no further recruits, Charles was forced to rest his exhausted men at Worcester. Worcester was a loyal city, and in a strong defensive position, but Leslie and the Scots were demoralised, and Cromwell, who had three times the number of troops, could place himself between Worcester and London and surround the city at his leisure. When the final attack came on 3 September Charles commanded and fought with great courage. A contemporary who was there wrote afterwards:

Certainly a braver Prince never lived, having in the day of the fight hazarded his person much more than any officer of his army, riding from regiment to regiment, and leading them on upon service with all the encouragement (calling every officer by his name) which the example and exhortation of a magnanimous General could afford.[38]

Leslie in contrast was dazed and dispirited. When Cromwell forced his entry into the city, a terrible slaughter followed: he himself said that it was 'as stiff a contest as ever I have seen'. Some 2000 Scots were killed, and nearly 10,000 taken prisoner. Only when the battle was clearly lost did Charles decide to make good his escape. Some other gentlemen who escaped were sheltered by countrymen, but many were robbed and murdered. The duke of Hamilton was killed early in the battle, the earl of Derby was captured and executed, Lauderdale and Leslie were taken and imprisoned until the Restoration. Charles himself had an amazing escape, and with a reward of £1000 on his head, remained in hiding for six weeks, until he was able to take ship at Shoreham on 15 October. The families who helped him, the Lanes, the Penderels, the Wyndhams and others, were rewarded at the Restoration. By 20 October he was safely in the Louvre.[39]

Lord Cottington, Sir Edward Hyde and an entourage of twenty people, left Paris on their Spanish mission on 29 September 1649, and travelled via Bordeaux to the Spanish frontier. At the time they assumed that the king intended to go to Ireland, and their mission to Philip IV of Spain was to obtain Spanish money to finance the expedition. The incentive to help on the part of Spain, it was hoped, would be a sense of the brotherhood of monarchs, and the prospect of easing the lot of the Catholics of Ireland. There was also another possibility. Mazarin had always expressed sympathy for the Stuarts, but had said that his aid must be limited so long as he was at war with Spain. He now asked the ambassadors to convey to Spain his desire for a Franco-Spanish peace.[40] This opened to Cottington and Hyde the prospect of being mediators in bringing about peace talks, the successful conclusion of which might pave the way for Spanish as well as French aid for Charles. But these were flimsy prospects in view of the realities of the situation. The Spanish government was beset with formidable problems of its own. The war with France continued, Portugal had won its independence from Spain, Catalonia and Naples were in revolt, Roussillon and Cerdagne in French hands. Spanish military power had received a shattering blow on the field of Rocroi in 1643, and the French were pushing into Flanders. Spain had neither money nor resources to aid the Stuarts, nor much incentive to do so, when it was more important to establish good relations with the English Commonwealth. All this Henrietta Maria had realised when she warned Hyde that no good would come of the Spanish embassy.

Thus the ambassadors were met with an exasperating combination of Spanish courtesy and dilatoriness which made it plain to Hyde that the Spanish government 'heartily wished they had not come'.[41] When they reached Madrid no accommodation had been provided for them, and they had to stay incognito at the house of an English royalist merchant, Sir Benjamin Wright. The Spanish Minister Don Luis de Haro was all politeness, and entertained them at a bull-fight which Hyde watched with a fascinated horror, but when it came to business it was a different matter. Hyde formed a poor opinion of Don Luis's political ability, believing that 'the affairs of Spain declined more in the time they were under his government than at any time before'.[42] But in his concern for Charles' affairs, Hyde paid too little attention to the difficulties of European statesmen.

They were not received by King Philip IV until 22 December, when they asked for his help in obtaining the Pope's assistance in Ireland, in persuading Owen O'Neil to accept Ormond's leadership, and persuading other Catholic princes in Italy and Germany to lend Charles money. The king regretted the great disorder into which his own affairs had fallen; he could not do as he would have wished, but if Charles could assist in mediating a peace between France and Spain, he would be able to do more.[43] There was little further that Cottington and Hyde could do. At this time they still expected Charles to go to Ireland, and they argued that the best thing would be to wait until he was actually there. They agreed to this all the more readily because they found a life of leisure in Spain very agreeable, and Hyde was able to learn the language, study Spanish government and theology, and also to begin a study of the Psalms of David, which he was to complete during his second exile.

The envoys realised that the Spanish government was far more concerned to establish good relations with the Commonwealth than to aid Charles. It was particularly embarrassing for them when in May 1650 the English Parliament sent Anthony Ascham as envoy to Madrid. Cottington and Hyde protested that Spain should be the first monarchy to recognise the Commonwealth, but Don Luis declared that Ascham did not have ambassadorial status. There were in Madrid many exiled English royalists, some of whom had served in the Spanish army, and on 27 May six of them headed by a Captain John Williams, walked into Ascham's lodging and killed him. Clarendon said that they had plenty of time to disappear in the crowd, but they were amateurs, without plans or forethought. Five of them took sanctuary in a neighbouring church, and the sixth escaped to the Venetian embassy. Unfortunately for Cottington and Hyde, the last was one of their servants, Harry Progers. The five were taken out of sanctuary by the authorities, to the scandal of the Church, and imprisoned. Progers hid for a few days in the Venetian embassy, and then escaped to France. Four of the five, after a long imprisonment, made their escape, and in the end only one was hanged, his fate being sealed by the fact that he was a Protestant. The whole affair was an embarrassment to the ambassadors, although Don Luis told them privately that he wished his master had such loyal subjects as the assassins, ready to die for his service.[44]

News that Charles had gone as king of Scotland did something to raise his status, but the fact that he had signed the Covenant more than counter-balanced it in Catholic Spain. When in October 1650 Prince Rupert appeared off the Spanish coast with a royalist fleet anxious for ports where he might victual and dispose of captured prizes, Hyde wrote to him that 'the disposition of the Spaniards is friendly, but they are so absolutely afraid of the rebels that they dare not publicly avow any kindness for the King',[45] and when Blake and a parliamentary fleet appeared, the Spaniards were anxious only that Prince Rupert should be gone. In December Spain formally recognised the Commonwealth, and in January 1651 Cottington and Hyde were invited to leave, in return for a promise to pay Charles 50,000 pieces of eight in Flanders.[46] News of Cromwell's victory at Dunbar in September had convinced Spain that Charles's cause was now hopeless, and Don Luis's mask of courtesy fell away as he made it clear that he wished them to be gone. Hyde thought that one reason was his intention to bring to Madrid art treasures purchased by the Spanish ambassador from the effects of Charles I. Lord Cottington was aged seventy-six, unwilling to face a journey to the north, and moreover had secretly become a Catholic. He therefore obtained Spanish permission to reside privately in Valladolid, where he remained until his death a year later.

However slight Charles's expectations of obtaining foreign aid, it was not for want of trying. Robert Meynell was sent to Rome to engage the assistance of Pope Innocent X, and he kept in close touch with Cottington and with Hyde in Madrid. He found the Curia as reluctant to help as Spain was, without explicit guarantees of religious freedom for Catholics which Charles could not give. When Charles negotiated the agreement at Breda, Meynell wrote to Cottington, 'Now you see my Lord where the shoe pinches', for Rome would do nothing for a monarch who had signed the Covenant. Other ambassadors were sent further afield, Lord Culpepper to Moscow, William Crofts to Poland, and Viscount Bellamont even to Persia. Culpepper had the greatest success, with a loan of 20,000 roubles in corn and furs from the Tsar Alexis.[47] Crofts obtained a small sum of money from the king of Poland, but Bellamont never reached Persia at all, having perished in a sandstorm. Almost everywhere in Europe Charles's cause was thought to be hopeless; when he went to Scotland his acceptance of the Covenant alienated Catholic rulers, and Cromwell's victory at Dunbar was taken as placing a seal upon Charles's failure. In November 1650 the death of his brother-in-law, the Prince of Orange, was a serious further blow, for he had provided him with a refuge, and with money to the limit of his resources.

During his absence Hyde had been kept well informed by his correspondents of the dissensions in the royalist camp, which had become deeper and more bitter. What was now called by their enemies, 'the Louvre party' was headed by the queen and her favourite Lord Jermyn. Her attachment to him was so strong as to cause resentment even within the royal family. When the duke of York declared that 'the Queen loved and valued Lord Jermyn more than she did all her children', she admitted that it was true.[48] Adherents to the Louvre party included Lord Culpepper, Lord Percy, Lord Digby, Sir John Berkeley, and Robert Long. They were strong in their persuasions to the king to ally himself with Argyll, Hamilton and the Covenanters in the belief that once he was king he could overthrow the domination of the kirk. The queen however very much regretted that Charles signed the Covenant, knowing the effect the news would have on the Catholics. Lord Hatton said that she was in tears when she heard the news, and exclaimed, 'God forbid that I should ever have had a hand in persuading him to sacrifice his honour or conscience'.[49]

Opposed to the Louvre party stood Sir Edward Hyde, Secretary Nicholas, Lord Hopton and Lord Hatton. They were strong Anglicans; they feared the Presbyterian connection, and knew how reluctant the English royalists would be to combine with Argyll, Hamilton and the Scots. When the news of Cromwell's victory at Dunbar arrived, Lord Hatton commented, 'we see as yet but ill symptoms that a kingdom can be securely bought at the rate of conscience and honour'.[50] Nicholas wrote that he could not forget that Argyll was almost as guilty of the late king's death as Cromwell, and he grieved that the king should be combining with him; and to Hatton he declared 'that those kingdoms are rarely happy or long-lived whose kings govern by favourites more than by well-composed councils' (clearly a reference to Lord Jermyn).[51] What made things worse was the penury to which many of the royalists were reduced unless they had the queen's favour. Nicholas wrote to Hyde:

I do not conceive I am obliged to suffer my wife and children to starve in the streets, when I may, without oaths or engagements, purchase a poor subsistence out of my own even from the worst of thieves, which I conceive to be no submission but a patient bearing of the punishment God lays on me.

Lord Hopton was even more explicit, and wrote to Nicholas that he was thinking of returning to England and compounding for his estates.[52] There were many royalists who were loyal to the king but who disliked the Louvre party and were sick of poverty and who did indeed return to England to compound for their estates.* To many, like the marquis of Ormond at Caen, the news of the king's defeat at Worcester came as a shattering blow. The only hope to Ormond seemed to be either that the rebels would fall out among themselves, or that Europe would combine against them, and 'both these to us seem like drowsy speculations'.[54]

When Hyde left Madrid in March 1651 he owed Sir Benjamin Wright a total of 25,656 reals for their joint expenses, and he gave a promise that the king would one day repay it.[55] A personal gift promised by Don Luis was never forthcoming. When later he reached Antwerp, to cover his travelling expenses, he had to draw on the 50,000 pieces of eight granted by Spain to the king. Expenses were heavy, for at Bayonne and then again at Bordeaux he had prolonged bouts of gout, and had had to travel part of the way in a litter 'more like a dead than a living man'. If these attacks were in any way psychosomatic (for they often came at times of crisis) they perhaps indicated the reluctance

---

* 'There are abundance of Royalists gone for England from these parts (The Hague), and many more are going, as having little hopes left them, seeing they hear his Majesty intends to make use of the Louvre counsels.'[53]

with which Hyde returned to the gloomy prospects of poverty which awaited him. To Nicholas he wrote that they must find some cheap place to live together, not at the Hague, for that was as expensive as Spain. He was grieved at the news that his nephew Harry Hyde was on trial for his life in England. He was well received by the queen in Paris in April, and was entrusted by her with a ruby of 333 carats to be sold in Amsterdam. When he reached Antwerp he was at least able to send Nicholas a thousand guilders which he owed him, and which would relieve his poverty, and help to dissuade him from returning to England. Hyde was reconciled, he wrote, to losing his own estates in England. The greatest concern however was for the safety of the king and Hyde even despatched his secretary Edgeman to Scotland to learn of his circumstances.* Early in November there were rumours that the king had been seen in Holland, but a few days later news arrived that Charles was in Paris, and on the 15th Hyde and Nicholas received a royal summons to attend him in Paris. Hyde's first letter to Charles had the chilly note of an 'I told you so' reprimand. He wrote that God, in subjecting the king to these dangers, had instructed him in much knowledge which could not have been purchased but at that price, and now his own fate, and that of his three kingdoms depended on his own virtue. At the time, the king was inclined to agree with him, for he was determined never to repeat his Scottish mistakes. Hyde wrote grimly to Nicholas, 'If the King be improved as much as is reported, all will have comfort in following him, if not, he is not yet ripe for deliverance'.

Hyde's immediate problem was to persuade Nicholas to accompany him to Paris as the king had ordered. Nicholas's first thought was that he could not afford the journey, and the second was that he was too ill to travel. The real reason however was his extreme reluctance to be again in conflict with the Louvre party. Hyde tried to make it easy for him by suggesting that they travelled together in a coach, with Hyde's two sons on horseback, at a total cost of only 200 guilders. Eventually Hyde was forced to travel alone, and reached Paris in December. When Hyde saw the king, he told him that Nicholas feared the displeasure of the queen; Charles replied that the queen was in the wrong, and that he would compose all differences when Nicholas reached Paris.[56]

Strained as were the relations between the Louvre party and its opponents, Hyde was able to earn the queen's gratitude in at least one respect. The duke of York, aged seventeen in 1650, revolted against the tutelage of his mother and the egregious Lord Jermyn. He greatly admired Prince Rupert as a man of action, who never lost an opportunity to oppose the queen. He was surrounded by a little group of advisers, including Sir Edward Herbert, who had been Attorney General to Charles I, and Sir George Ratcliffe, who urged him to get away from his mother and go to Brussels to meet the duke of Lorraine, whom James admired for his reputation as a soldier. The difficulty

---

* He did not get beyond Amsterdam, for news of the king's return arrived.

was that James had no money of his own, and was entirely dependent upon his mother, but in spite of this, and against her wishes, he and his little entourage travelled to Brussels in October 1650. The duke of Lorraine was an adventurer who hoped to carve out for himself a principality in Ireland. He received the boy and presented him with a thousand pistoles for his subsistence, in the hope that he was bringing with him some concrete plan. But there was no plan, and James's council talked fatuously of his marriage to Lorraine's natural daughter. Lorraine's interest rapidly cooled, and Clarendon commented, 'so apt are inexperienced men, when they are once out of the way, to wander into bogs and precipices, before they will be sensible of their false conduct'.[57] When they found that there was nothing for them in Brussels, they advised the duke to go to his sister, the recently widowed Princess of Orange, but the queen forbade her to receive him, and the princess had too many problems of her own to welcome further responsibility. Instead he found a refuge for a time with his aunt the exiled queen of Bohemia, in Holland. When Hyde returned to Paris the queen begged him to advise the duke to return. Hyde saw the duke at Breda, found the councillors quarrelling bitterly among themselves, and had no great difficulty in persuading James to return to Paris.* Henceforth the danger was that there would be not two, but three, royalist parties opposing each other, with a third headed by the young duke.

A matter which concerned Hyde still more deeply on his return from Spain was the fate of the Anglican church. Many of the royalists who had gone to France after the Civil Wars were Anglicans, and their care was specially entrusted by Charles I to John Cosin, who had been a prebendary of Durham, dean of Peterborough and Master of Peterhouse, Cambridge, until his ejection in 1644. He was a great ritualist, and his *Book of Devotions*, which was admired by Charles I, especially enraged the Puritans. Charles I appointed him royal chaplain to the queen's household in Paris, and during the king's lifetime he was well provided for, and had a chapel in the royal household where he conducted Anglican services. But Anglicans came under heavy pressure from French Catholics, with arguments which Cosin summarised in a letter to Dr Morley in 1650:

You have lived a long while in heresy, which hath brought God's anger and indignation upon you: your kingdom of England is ruined; your Church is lost: your bishops and priests are put out of their places, and are never likely to be restored: your nine-and-thirty Articles are at an end, nobody regards them: your Service-book and your Sacraments are come into the contempt and scorn of the world.[59]

Cosin debated the question of the validity of the Anglican orders with the Prior of the English Benedictines in France, in a conference lasting several

* Clarendon had no high opinion of the duke's intelligence at this time. He mistook him for fourteen, when he was in fact seventeen, and wrote that he was 'backward enough for that age'.[58]

hours, in which he thought the Prior showed 'no great skill', and Cosin was all the more convinced that Anglicans must maintain their separate identity from both Roman Catholicism and continental Protestantism. The queen had no loyalty to the Anglican church, and the Louvre party had the idea that the king could be restored only by an alliance of Presbyterians and Catholics.* She was under pressure from the French court to close the Anglican chapel. Although she had a pension of 1200 livres a day from the French court, the queen said she could no longer afford to pay Cosin a stipend. Lord Hatton wrote to Nicholas in December 1649 that Cosin had been given a derisory four pistoles, and that the intention was to drive him from Court. Hyde reproached the queen with the neglect when he returned from Spain, but she declared that it was by the wishes of the queen-mother of France. Cosin continued to hold services in the house of the English Resident, Sir Richard Browne, but henceforth he lived in poverty, dependent on the gifts of the faithful. With the king in Scotland, Hatton suspected that the queen looked forward to the early extinction of Anglicanism.[61] Pressure on Anglicans to embrace Catholicism was certainly great, and Cosin himself was offered rewards if he was converted. Perhaps for this reason he established close relations with the Huguenots at Charenton, near Paris. Hyde had himself advised the Prince of Wales to attend their services in order to emphasise his Protestantism, and to offset rumours in England that he had become a Catholic. Cosin also held discussions with the Archbishop of Trebizond, and discovered a close agreement between the Greek Orthodox and Anglican churches. He encouraged the duke of York to attend Greek mass.[62] The position of the Anglican Church was a problem never far from Hyde's mind during these years of exile. At Antwerp, where he retained the status of ambassador, he was proud to have his own chapel which was attended by exiled Protestants like the marquis of Newcastle and the earl of Norwich.[63]

---

* Berkeley wrote to Hyde 'we ought to give one hand to the Catholic Roman, and the other to the Presbyterians, and join with them both to the destruction of our common enemy'.[60] Such advice was anathema to Hyde.

# Royalists and the Commonwealth

The English monarchy was declared abolished on 17 March 1649, and the House of Lords was abolished two days later, but the Commonwealth was not proclaimed until 19 May, when supreme authority was vested in the representatives of the people in parliament.[1] Europe expressed horror at the execution of the king, and the new government seemed to face ostracism in Europe. In August 1649 the queen regent of France issued an edict prohibiting trade with England, and condemning those who had 'bathed their hands in the blood of their king'. Philip IV of Spain expressed similar sentiments, sufficient to persuade Charles II to send his embassy to Madrid. The Prince of Orange, who had married Charles's sister, negotiated an alliance between the Dutch and France, aimed against Spain, but including a provision for joint action to restore the king of England.

These threats were to prove illusory. The death of the Prince of Orange in November 1650 was a disaster for the Stuarts, for not only did the French alliance collapse, but the Republican party re-asserted itself in the United Provinces; and France and Spain soon showed that they did not intend to follow up words with action. But for a time the Commonwealth appeared to be in danger, and royalist hopes rose. From the summer of 1650 the government became aware of royalist plans for insurrection. In July a Captain Levinz was hanged for bringing in a commission from Charles Stuart, and two other conspirators were executed in August, the victims of agents provocateurs. These were small fry, but more extensive plans were afoot. In January 1651 a Commonwealth agent, George Bishop had some leading royalists in his pay, and discovered most of their plans, which involved risings in the counties while a force was landed in Kent. A premature rising in Norfolk in December 1650 was easily suppressed, and the leaders hanged. Parliament was sufficiently alarmed to prohibit horse races, hunting and sporting matches which might serve as a cloak for military gatherings. As a Scottish invasion was expected, the government took the crisis seriously. On 4 March Sir Henry Hyde, Sir Edward's cousin, was executed for having accepted an embassy to Constantinople from the king in an attempt to persuade the Sultan to seize merchants' goods for the use of the king. Little is known of the trial or the details of the charges,* but his death was a serious blow to Sir Edward, since Sir Henry had been his chief agent in England. In March a group of royalists were seized as they were embarking for the Isle of Man in order to concert a rising with the earl of Derby in Lancashire. One Birkenhead, a captain in Charles's service, was captured with all the correspondence, and the Council of State was put in full possession of the facts. Tom Coke, Massey and the duke of Buckingham were implicated. Coke was finally captured in the Strand (31 March) and promptly revealed all he knew, including a list of the royalist leaders in each county. He also revealed a projected rising in London, and implicated some of the leading Presbyterians, like Calamy, Vines, Jenkins and Love.[3]

The Presbyterian party seems to have been divided. Some were certainly in favour of a restoration of the monarchy on some such terms as the Newport Treaty, and they were increasingly alarmed at the growing power of the army and Independency. One group plotted to rise in support of the invading army of Scots and Charles II. The eleven Presbyterian leaders, expelled from the Long Parliament, had retired to the country or gone abroad. Denzil Holles retired to France, where he composed his *Memoirs* and reconsidered the situation. He had been a persistent opponent of Charles I, but had come to detest the consequences. He venerated the idea of parliament, but feared the social upheaval which the Levellers, Independents and army brought with them. As early as 1647–8 he wrote, 'The wisest men saw it to be a great evil, that servants should ride on horses, and princes walk as servants on the earth: an evil now both seen and felt in our unhappy kingdom'. He now thought that the offences of Charles I were as nothing to the crimes committed by his opponents, that 'we were chastised with whips, but now with scorpions'.[4] The royalist Presbyterians hoped that Holles would enter the service of Charles II; and Secretary Nicholas, who conducted relations with the Presbyterians in England, seems to have made some attempt to win him over. But Holles preferred to remain an observer. He expected a Presbyterian rising in England, and thought that Charles would soon be restored, yet when in March 1651 the king offered him office as Secretary of State, he refused. Charles sent him fifty blank king's commissions which he filled up and sent to England so carelessly that they were captured (March 1651) thus incriminating the conspirators, and going far to ruin the earl of Derby's projected rising. The Council of State decided to put one of the Presbyterians, Christopher Love, on trial in June 1651. The evidence was not conclusive, but he was condemned to death. Parliament granted a month's reprieve while the case was considered, but Milton joined in a cry for his execution, and this took place in August. The defeat of Charles II at Worcester in the following month

---

* Hyde wrote that the evidence which cost Sir Henry his life was supplied by the son of Sir Francis Doddington, who had received great favours from Sir Henry.[2]

put an end to the crisis. The Presbyterians had had a serious setback, and the royalists a humiliating defeat.[5]

Cromwell's victories in Ireland and Scotland, and the collapse of the royalist cause, enabled the Commonwealth to speak with a new authority, and with an army of 70,000 men and a rapidly expanding fleet it could exercise an influence in Europe which the Stuarts never had. Thus in November 1650 Admiral Blake and his fleet put into Cartagena, and forced the Spanish government to refuse shelter to Prince Rupert's ships. Spain saw the prospect of winning an English alliance against the French, and hastened to recognise the Commonwealth, while in January 1651 Servien, special adviser to Mazarin, urged that since 'England was now the master of the seas', France could not afford to antagonise the new republic. In March 1651 an English delegation, led by Chief Justice St John and Walter Strickland, arrived at The Hague to negotiate a confederation of Protestant maritime powers. But commercial rivalry stood in the way of improved relations between England and both France and the Dutch. The Commonwealth had imposed a ban on French wines and silks, and in October 1651 it passed the Navigation Act which dealt a blow at the Dutch carrying trade. English privateers were inflicting heavy losses on French shipping, and negotiations were refused so long as France failed to recognise the Commonwealth. In the summer of 1652 England and the Dutch went to war over their commercial rivalry, this relegating religious considerations to the background. When earlier in the year Admiral Blake defeated the French fleet and helped the Spaniards to take Dunkirk, the Venetian envoy commented that Dunkirk showed how much good England could do to its friends, and how much harm to its enemies. Hyde and Nicholas concluded that it would not be long before Charles II was asked to leave France.[6] Hyde had never placed the least confidence in the hope that European rulers would aid the Stuarts; he wrote that they were 'so infatuated as to think the madness and fury of that people will be terminated within these dominions for which they now contend – whereas they may see that they are rebels of a more large-hearted extent, and contend not for the liberty of England, but for the liberty of mankind'.[7] He meant that the revolution which had begun in England might one day engulf western Europe.

Cromwell himself had probably been opposed to war with the Dutch because he dreamed of a great Protestant anti-Catholic alliance, but he was overborne by a popular enthusiasm for commercial expansion and an assertion of English naval power. The Dutch faced great difficulties in the war. Their fleet was larger and more experienced than the English, but they were torn between protecting their trade by massive convoys, or abandoning the protection of commerce and seeking out the English fleet to inflict decisive defeat. In the event the Dutch fell between two stools, and both Tromp and De Ruyter suffered heavy defeats in battle, while the Dutch fishing fleet was driven from the North Sea. By October 1652 some 400 Dutch merchantmen were bottled up in Dutch harbours. In June 1653 Tromp was defeated off Harwich, and henceforth the English were able virtually to blockade Holland. A Dutch mission sought peace, which was finally signed by the Treaty of Westminster in April 1654. The Commonwealth agreed not to help the House of Orange, and the Dutch promised not to help the Stuarts. During the war Charles II's offer to help the Dutch with his ships in the hope of persuading some English to desert, had been firmly rejected by De Witt, who made it plain that the king would be far more of an embarrassment than a help to the Dutch.[8]

The growth of military and naval power, the conquest of Scotland and Ireland, and victory over the Dutch, greatly increased the prestige of the Commonwealth abroad. This fact however made the political uncertainty at home all the more paradoxical. The motive force which had brought about the trial and execution of the king had come mainly from the radical element in the army, the Levellers. But a Leveller mutiny in the army was crushed in May 1649, Cromwell declaring 'you have no other way to deal with these men but to break them ... (or) they will break you'. Thereafter Leveller enthusiasm rapidly died away as the nation found a measure of unity in witnessing the victories in Ireland and Scotland. But the constitutional question remained. The Commonwealth proclaimed the sovereignty of the people in parliament, but neither the army nor the Rump dared propose that the people should be consulted. Blair Worden has shown that the Rump could in no sense be said to represent the nation,* and Ivan Roots has summed up its defect as 'a government regarded from the start as a stop-gap, a mere expedient, never an experiment'.[10]

Pride's Purge has been rightly seen by modern historians as a decisive turning-point in the history of the English revolution.[11] Superficially it represented the triumph of the army, the first consequence of which was the trial and execution of the king. More significantly it represented less a revolutionary move than a moderate alternative to a complete dissolution of the Long Parliament and the triumph of Leveller radicalism. To many Levellers the death of the king was to herald the dawn of a new age of democracy, legal reforms, agrarian changes and religious toleration. Ireton, who, as we have seen, had found it necessary to carry the Levellers with him so far, succeeded also in neutralising their radicalism, and so there followed, not a radical triumph, but a return to a conservative solution to constitutional problems. Clarendon recognised this, and thus thought that time, rather than the efforts of the royalists, would bring about a Restoration; or, as he put it, God had 'reserved the deliverance and restoration of the king to himself, and resolved to accomplish it when there appeared least hope of it'.[12]

* 'Bedford was not represented by a single Rumper, and many counties were represented by only one. Oxfordshire, Devon, Chester, Lancashire, all centres of opposition to the Commonwealth, were among the counties seriously under-represented after the purge.'[9]

Many essentially moderate men who had voted for the death of the king, had done so in the belief that there would be no peaceful settlement so long as he lived, or out of a simple fear of the army, but with no clear idea of what they would substitute for monarchy. They knew what they opposed, but not what to put in its place. If the threat of royal vengeance was removed, the threat of social upheaval and military despotism remained. For the next two years the army would be fully engaged in Scotland and Ireland, but at heavy cost, which by the autumn of 1650 had reached the enormous sum of £120,000 in monthly assessment. By 1652 the army would have reached the unprecedented total of 70,000 men. The execution of the king had never been endorsed by the nation; free elections were therefore out of the question, and politicians moved under the shadow of growing unpopularity. The early months of the Commonwealth were therefore marked by uncertainty and alarms, fears of royalist conspiracies and French hostility, of isolation in Europe, with threats from Ireland and Scotland.

Pride's Purge had removed about 270 members, leaving a total of about 213.[13] Blair Worden has shown that the composition of the Rump was by no means simple, that it still contained probably a majority of moderates, but also a strong radical and republican nucleus, so that since attendance was irregular, the latter could often carry the day. The radicals included men such as Henry Marten, Thomas Scot, Sir Arthur Hesilrige, Sir Henry Vane, Thomas Chaloner, Thomas Harrison, Sir James Harrington and Lord Grey of Groby, while the moderates included Speaker Lenthall, Bulstrode Whitelocke and Sir Thomas Widdrington. But Blair Worden warns against attempts to categorise rumpers into 'revolutionaries' and 'conformists', since men took highly individual views upon particular issues, and he points out how impossible it would be to place Cromwell in either category.[14] Executive power was vested in a Council of State, with the army represented by Fairfax, Skippon and Cromwell, and the remainder attempting some balance between moderates and radicals. The greatest weakness was the lack of a broadly-based support in the country, and thus for a time politicians reflected an air of gloom. Bulstrode Whitelocke reported the arrest of one Henderson who proclaimed at Newark, 'I pronounce Charles II . . . as king of England, although his father suffered wrongfully; yet you cannot be governed without a head, but now you are governed by a stinking lousy committee'. In April 1650 he noted apprehensively the petition of the diggers

for universal freedom, to make the earth a common treasury, that every one may enjoy food and raiment freely by his labour upon the earth without paying rents or homage to any fellow-creature of his own kind, that every one may be delivered from the tyranny of the conquering power, and so rise up out of that bondage to enjoy the benefit of his creation.[15]

Sir Henry Vane reflected the same pessimism when he declared 'that the whole kingdom would rise and cut their throats upon the first good occasion; and that they knew not any place to go unto to be safe'.[16] Hence the attempt of the new Commonwealth to impose an oath of loyalty known as the Engagement – a foolish move, since many secret royalists were ready to take it, while conscientious Presbyterians who regarded it as contrary to the Covenant, refused.

Clarendon noted the dilemma Cromwell found himself in; that in order to avoid dependence on the Presbyterians, he was tolerant of Independency, Anabaptists and Quakers, yet these were the last people to accept a military dictatorship.[17] However the fundamental issue had ceased to be religious, and was now constitutional. Cromwell returned from the victories over the Scots and Charles II with immensely enhanced prestige, and with a real determination to find a constitutional settlement which would be acceptable to the nation, and would offer stability for the future. Some time during the autumn of 1651 he called together a select number of army officers and members of parliament to discuss such a settlement. Bulstrode Whitelocke put his finger on the fundamental issue, which he defined as whether there should be 'an absolute republic, or with any mixture of monarchy'. Sir Thomas Widdrington said that a mixed monarchy would be most acceptable to the nation. Oliver St John and Speaker Lenthall agreed with him. Whitelocke argued that

the laws of England are so interwoven with the power and practice of monarchy, that to settle a government without something of monarchy in it, would make so great an alteration in the proceedings of our law, that you have scarce time to rectify, nor can we well foresee, the inconveniences which will arise thereby.

Widdrington suggested that the young duke of Gloucester, third son of Charles I might be a suitable choice for king. Colonel Desborough and the soldiers on the other hand were for a republic. Cromwell had leaned towards the idea of a monarchy, but, if Whitelocke's account is to be believed, shied away from the idea of choosing a Stuart, and the meeting broke up without a decision. Whitelocke was annoyed to find that, although the lawyers present were in favour of a monarchy, the soldiers were opposed to it. However, the discussion is significant as indicating the direction of the thoughts of men of moderation. They had seen Charles II accept the Scottish throne on the most humiliating terms, and after his defeat at Worcester it seemed clear that parliament could dictate almost any terms of royal restoration in England, if not of Charles himself, at least his young brother. But the most significant fact was the recognition by the lawyers that constitutional law required a monarch as guarantee of stability and continuity.

The question of supreme importance to both king and Commonwealth was the state of public opinion in the country. This was difficult to gauge, for whereas Commonwealth politicians believed in the existence of widespread royalist conspiracies, royalists were intimidated by the overwhelming military strength and vigilance of their opponents. It must be remembered that in most counties neutralism had been prevalent during the civil war. Many gentry took the view of the Birmingham gentleman who declared:

I never had an intention, nor yet have, of taking up arms of either side, my reasons this, my protestation already taken binds me both to king and parliament. I am not so senseless (though it were almost to be wished I were) that there are two armies, the one the king's, the other parliament's, each seeking to destroy the other, and I by oath bound to preserve both, each challenging the Protestant religion for their standard, yet the one takes the papists, the other the schismatics for their adherents, and (for my part) my conscience tells me they both intend the Protestant religion. What reason have I therefore to fall out with either?[18]

This was much the view of the tenants of William Davenport of Bramhall when he attempted to recruit them to fight for the king. They replied:

Howsoever we would not for the world harbour a disloyal thought against his Majesty, yet we dare not lift up our hands against that honourable assembly of Parliament, whom we are confidently assured doth labour for the happiness of his Majesty and all his kingdom.[19]

However, when it came to conflict, neutralism was not recognised by either side, and neutrals were likely to be plundered by both sides. Parliament, with its greater financial resources, was always more successful at recruitment than the royalists, and once parliamentarians gained authority in a county, they exercised an efficient control through county committees such as the counties had never before experienced. Thus in Kent Professor Everitt estimated that under the ruthless control of Sir Anthony Weldon, the annual assessment in the 1640s amounted to £570,000, possibly one-eighth of the total county income. Sales of episcopal lands of Canterbury and Rochester yielded some £82,990, and Chapter lands yielded a similar amount. Sequestrations of the estates of malignants following the Kentish rebellion of 1648 yielded total receipts of £105,597, with 595 compounders, the duke of Richmond paying £9856 and the earl of Thanet £9000, with a total yield from ecclesiastical and composition sources amounting to about £350,000 by 1652.[20]

Clarendon wrote that by 1650

the spirits of all the loyal party were so broken and subdued, that they could scarce breathe under the insupportable burdens which were laid upon them by imprisonments, compositions and sequestrations . . . They [the Commonwealth] sequestered all their estates, and left them nothing to live upon till they should compound; which they were forced to do at so unreasonable rates, that many were compelled to sell half, that they might enjoy the other towards the support of their families; which remainder was still liable to whatever impositions they at any time thought fit to inflict upon them, as their persons were to imprisonment, when any unreasonable and groundless report was raised of some plot and conspiracy against the state.[21]

This sweeping statement certainly reflected the opinions of royalists both at the time and after the Restoration, but researches of Mrs Thirsk, Professor Habakkuk and others in recent years have enabled historians to make a more accurate appraisal of the condition of the royalists during the Interregnum.[22] Between 1646 and 1654 the state confiscated and sold property belonging to the bishops to the total value of £676,387; of the deans and chapters to the value of £1,170,000; of the crown and fee-farm rents of well over £2,000,000, and of royalists of £1,224,916 (Professor Habakkuk's figures). At the Restoration the property of the crown and the church was recovered, although some purchasers remained after 1660 as leaseholders, but the situation of the royalists was more complicated. Those who were willing to compound were fined according to the degree of their delinquency, at a rate varying from one-tenth to one-third of the capital value of their estates. Such fines, Professor Habakkuk shows, could be burdensome, but were not often back-breaking, and most families paid less than two years' family income, often no more than a man might pay as dowry on the marriage of his daughter. When their estates were sequestrated many gentry were able to buy them back again within a short time. Some however were forced to make heavy sales of lands: the earl of Northampton sold land worth nearly £40,000, and the earl of Westmorland sold estates in Wiltshire and Leicestershire worth £17,000 but the families who suffered most were those already heavily indebted before 1642. Habakkuk writes that 'Delinquents who were not already heavily indebted before the imposition of the fine found it easy to pay the fine without selling any land; they rode out the difficulties of the Interregnum with no obvious long-term effects'. Mrs Thirsk agrees: 'Some of the lesser Royalist gentry disappeared into social oblivion as a result of the sale, but a larger number, including most of the nobility, managed to reassemble all or part of their estates before Restoration'. Most of the delinquents had regained their estates before 1660, or at least within a year or two of the Restoration. Moreover it must be remembered that by Professor Habakkuk's calculation, only about 3225 persons compounded for their delinquency, and 780 had their properties confiscated, and this represents about one-quarter of the gentry class. Even fewer could be counted as parliamentarians, and thus at least one-half of the gentry class were neutral.

However, having said this, the fact remains that the royalists suffered heavily. Many fathers or sons died on the battle-field. The marquis of Worcester was said to have given over £700,000 to the royal cause, and the duke of Newcastle £930,000. Many estates were already encumbered with debts before 1642, and these remained to hamper the families long after 1660. P G Holiday shows that in Yorkshire the heaviest burdens fell on Roman Catholic delinquents, most of them of no political significance. Even when properties were offered for sale it was not easy to find buyers in a glutted market. Often they were bought back by friends or agents of the owners, and sometimes by London speculators. Many individuals suffered great hardship, and were left with a permanent sense of grievance, but the whole process did not amount to a social revolution. Nor did the fines and confiscations solve the financial problems of the Commonwealth and Protectorate. Professor Habakkuk shows that the actual cash receipts were disappointing, and that it is quite wrong to suppose that by these means the Protectorate was able to balance its accounts. The State found it difficult to borrow money, a clear indication of the lack of confidence in the regime, and without credit it could not finance the enormous expenditure on the army and navy. Cromwell's wars pushed the regime further into debt, and thus prepared the way for the fall of the Protectorate and the return of the monarchy.

Reconciliation was a fundamental principle of Cromwell's policy during the 1650s, and in this respect the royalists who remained in England presented him with an awkward dilemma. Many royalists received Charles II's permission to compound for their estates, and even to take the Engagement expressing a loyalty to the Commonwealth they did not intend to honour. It was a moot point whether sequestrations and compositions would cow the royalists into quiescence, or would be a spur to rebellion. Certainly many royalists accepted the situation, and wished only to be forgotten, burying themselves in the country with their books and their families. As one of them wrote 'Wisdom and necessity, rather than good will, inclines them to be quiet'.[23] Cromwell himself protested against unnecessary harassment, when 'poor men, under this arbitrary power, were driven like flocks of sheep, by forty in a morning, to the confiscation of goods and estates, without any man being able to give a reason why two of them had deserved to forfeit a shilling!'[24] When he appointed Matthew Hale a justice of Common Pleas, the seizure of royalist estates ceased, and there was a greater return to legality. Ludlow, who detested Cromwell, complained that while he dealt harshly with his old radical supporters like Harrison, Rich and Carew, he did all he could to placate the royalists: 'This usurper endeavouring to fix himself in his throne by all ways imaginable, gave direction to the judges, who were ready to go their several circuits, to take especial care to extend all favour and kindness to the cavalier party.'[25] Many royalists therefore came to accept, or at least to acquiesce in Oliver's government. But the conspiracies went on, and Hyde and Nicholas found themselves at the centre of them.

The drive to abolish episcopacy was partly motivated by the urgent need for money to pay off the Scots in 1646. When the City of London was approached for a loan of £200,000, they required the excise and the bishops' lands as security. Ian Gentles calculates that a total of £884,000 was raised on the security of episcopal lands, a good deal more than their actual sale value.[26] He shows that most of the purchasers were speculators in episcopal lands, were from London and the south of England, mainly gentry, merchants and tradesmen, and that only a small proportion of the land was bought by tenants.

Members of Parliament and army officers did well out of the sales, Arthur Hesilrige was nicknamed the bishop of Durham by virtue of his huge acquisitions of episcopal lands valued at over £20,000. Speaker Lenthall, John Lambert, Edmund Ludlow and Thomas Scot were all large purchasers. Dean and Chapter lands were also dispersed in the same way.

The position of the Anglican clergy during the civil war was first investigated by John Walker in 1714, chiefly in order to show that the Anglican clergy suffered much worse under the Puritans than the Puritans suffered at the Restoration. His figures were revised by A G Matthews in 1947, with much greater accuracy.[27] They have recently been further examined by Dr I M Green, and a definitive picture now emerges.[28] Dr Green calculates that there were about 8600 English rectories and vicarages, and that if incumbents, curates, chaplains and lecturers are included, some 2780 men would have been dispossessed. He shows that dispossession might be for a number of reasons, that 'scandalous' might mean evil living, such as drunkenness, or false doctrine. But the Committee for Plundered Ministers set up in 1642 was bent on replacing 'delinquent' clergy by Puritans. Commissions issued to local militants in 1644 enabled them to listen to local complaints and to enforce wholesale ejections. High church and royalist clergy had short shrift, but on the other hand there were many clergy who were neither Laudians nor Puritans, and these were often left undisturbed, and, as Dr Green shows, 'there is some evidence of continued use of the Prayer Book in the late 1640s and the 1650s'. Militant Puritans, Presbyterians, Independents and Baptists were always in a minority, and many moderate clergy continued undisturbed through the Interregnum and into the Restoration period. Moreover sequestrations were most frequent in Puritan areas such as East Anglia and Wiltshire, or in Kent, where men like Sir Anthony Weldon became 'the scourges of the parish clergy', whereas in the north of England they were far fewer.[29]

Extensive research in local history in recent years, following the pioneer work of Professor Everitt in Kent, has shown that each area had its own special reaction to the civil war and its aftermath, and that simple generalisations are not likely to be wholly accurate. However it does appear that with the collapse of the royalist cause after 1646 there were, as J S Morrill writes, 'persistent demands from the moderate gentry throughout the country for a return to "normality"', and the end to the power of the county committees which had so frequently abused them.[30] The struggle between radicals and moderates at Westminster was mirrored in the counties as moderates were replaced by radicals on the county committees. Clarendon saw the conflict in class terms, as men of the lower classes ousted gentlemen from positions of authority. Often the radicals were an activist minority, strongly Puritan in outlook, who tended to seize power, and soon became associated with all the concomitants of military government, namely high taxes, quartering, plundering and oppression. Indeed one of the perennial problems facing parliament was how to restrain the local excesses of the county committees. Professor Underdown writes: 'By the end of the war the old leadership is being pushed aside by energetic new men lower down the social scale, lesser gentry and townsmen, often of radical Puritan inclinations, aiming at power as well as Reformation'.[31]

However this view has been modified by the researches of J S Morrill in Cheshire. He writes that it is quite wrong to stress 'the repressive and harsh Puritan mind leading to unsympathetic and unimaginative local government'.[32] In many ways local administration was more efficient in the 1650s than in the 1630s, but local government had become much more complicated, and the problems much greater, as administrators struggled with the burdens of heavy taxation, some of the worst harvests of the century, and the problems of unemployment. Charles I had been resisted in 1640 because it was felt that the central government was steadily encroaching upon local independence, but during the civil war and its aftermath that encroachment went on apace, with unprecedented taxation, and, worst of all, the threat of military government.

The complexity of the situation is well illustrated by the case of the city of Newcastle upon Tyne. A royalist city, at the outset of the civil war, it had to sustain a royalist garrison which must needs live off the town, and thus became a grievous burden. It also suffered heavily when parliament blockaded it, and cut off the coal trade with London. When therefore it was captured by the Scots in 1644 it accepted parliamentary control without too much complaint, and Roger Howell has shown that most citizens were neither markedly for parliament nor the King, neither Puritan nor Laudian, 'at best *politiques*, at worst Vicars of Bray'.[33] Newcastle was a parliamentary town, 'a parliamentary pocket in a Cavalier county', yet by November 1647 the Northern Association petitioned parliament:

We daily groan under the insupportable weight of oppression, taxes, free-quarter (besides murders, rapine, robberies, not mentioning the deep exhaustings during the late time of war, and since, both by the English and Scottish forces, no part of the Kingdom being so infested. We humbly desire a speedy alleavement and retardation thereof, that yet (if it be possible we may have bread to sustain the lives of our poor wives and children; many thousands being ready to perish through want . . .).

The citizens of Newcastle were for the most part asking only to live their lives free from parliamentary or royalist partisanship. Royalist delinquents were made to suffer severely: Sir Thomas Liddell was fined £4000, and Sir Arthur Hesilrige, the Governor of the town, although an efficient administrator, spent much of his energies in building up a fortune for himself in the area. But in the 1650s Newcastle 'settled into an easy acceptance of existing conditions', and at the Restoration was equally ready to accept the monarchy.[34]

The city of Norwich illustrates another aspect of the situation. John Evans[35] has shown that in 1640 the grievances of Norwich had little to do with ship money, but much to do with Puritan complaints against bishop Wren. Norwich had a strong Puritan party who by 1641 controlled the Court of Aldermen, and petitioned parliament against their bishop. Yet of the two members returned to parliament for Norwich, one was a royalist, and the other made little mark. When civil war became inevitable in 1642, Norwich was divided into two clear-cut camps, royalist and parliamentary, but the royalists were ousted from office during the next two years. John Evans thinks there may have been a royalist conspiracy in March 1643 which was suppressed, and which 'confirmed the supremacy of the parliamentary Puritans'. In November the cathedral was desecrated, stained glass windows and monuments smashed and the altar demolished. But if parliamentary-puritanism triumphed in Norwich, there always remained a strong minority of moderates or royalists. By 1646 however the conflict in Norwich was not between these two parties, but between the Presbyterians who wanted classical presbyteries, and the Independents who wanted individual congregations and religious toleration, while many people wanted neither. A royalist rising in March 1648, John Evans thinks, was primarily a conservative protest against the Independents and the dominance of the army, but it ended disastrously when an ammunition dump blew up, killing two hundred people, and thereafter Norwich conformed to parliamentary government.[36]

The City of London was naturally much more closely concerned with national politics than were the provincial towns. The Common Hall of the City's liverymen returned four anti-Court members to both the Short and the Long Parliament, and London radicalism became a powerful ally of Pym's in his struggle against the king in the period 1641–3. Professor Pearl and R Brenner[37] have shown that the rise of London radicalism was closely associated with the declining influence of the old monopoly companies, the Merchant Adventurers, and the Levant and East India Company traders, and the rise of the 'new' merchants particularly associated with colonial trade. But the radicalism which provided Pym with such convenient mobs at times of crisis, alarmed the moderates who, without wishing to return to the old order, nonetheless saw the king as a symbol of stability, and who turned to Presbyterianism as offering social discipline. By 1646 the Common Council placed all the blame for the confusion on the sectaries, and, as R Brenner writes; 'When on 1 June 1646 the Common Council resolved that the circulation in London of mass radical petitions for presentation to Parliament "tended to sedition", the City had come full circle from the insurrectionary days of 1641–2', and when in July they drafted a letter to the king to request his return, they were prevented from sending it only by the intervention of the army. The establishment of army control in the City during 1647–8 ensured the political victory of the Independents, who previously had been very weak in the City. The Independents were mainly tradesmen, well below the merchant-class, and the 'old' merchant-class were reduced to political impotence. In October 1647 some of the leading Presbyterians were impeached, and in December 1648 a parliamentary ordinance excluded all malignants (i.e. royalists) from office. The way was thus open for the 'new' merchants and tradesmen to rise to political power in support of the republic. The 'old' merchants could survive if they eschewed politics and concentrated upon their business. As Cromwell steadily abandoned his radical allies in the 1650s, he could hope to win the support of the merchants by a policy of religious toleration and commercial imperialism. Merchants and politicians could combine in support of the mercantilist policy embodied in the Navigation Act, and this policy had the active support of men like Arthur Hesilrige, Thomas Scot, Oliver St John, Thomas Chaloner and Sir Henry Vane.

After Worcester Charles returned to France to face the most wretched conditions of poverty and uncertainty. He was again thrown into a humiliating dependence upon his mother and the Louvre party, and on a frail hope that France might be induced to aid his cause. How remote that possibility was, a glance at the political situation in France will show.

Since 1643 Anne of Austria had been queen regent of France, governing in the name of her young son Louis XIV, with the aid of her favourite, Cardinal Mazarin. From the outset she had met with serious opposition which superficially resembled the opposition Charles I encountered in England. The heavy financial burdens of the wars against the Empire and Spain, the inequitable tax system, the opposition of the nobility to the growth of royal power, the unpopularity of the Italian Mazarin, and the inevitable difficulties attendant on a minority, all contributed to the unrest. In 1643 she had crushed an incipient revolt, known as the Cabale des Importants. In 1648 the Parlement of Paris asserted the right of veto over legislation, and proposed a series of reforms. The queen attempted to crush the revolt by the arrest of some of the ringleaders, but there were riots in Paris, and they were released. In January 1649 she was forced to leave Paris, and the first stage of the Fronde had begun. No wonder the queen said that the execution of Charles I was 'a blow to make all kings tremble'. Edward Hyde wrote that the violence shown in Paris was much worse than anything that London had experienced. A peace was patched up at Rueil in April, but it was only a temporary halt. In January 1650 the queen had the leaders of the nobility arrested, the Prince of Condé, his brother the Prince of Conti, and their brother-in-law the duc de Longueville. This however was the signal for a revolt in the provinces where the strength of the prince lay, especially in the Bordeaux area. The queen gave way, the princes were released early in 1651, and Mazarin, the object of general hatred, went into exile. Hitherto the queen had refused to part with him, remembering the consequences of Charles I's desertion of Strafford. But when in the autumn the princes staged another revolt, she recalled him. A second exile followed from August 1652 until February 1653, and it was not until August 1653 that the revolt in Bordeaux collapsed, and the Fronde could be said to be over.

These bald facts will give little idea of the complexity of French politics during these years, but they will help to explain some of the difficulties which faced the queen regent and Mazarin, and why the presence of the exiled Stuarts could be regarded only as an encumbrance and a nuisance. Queen Henrietta Maria, as the daughter of Henri IV, and aunt of Louis XIV, had to be given an honourable refuge in France, but the presence of her son presented more complicated problems. Mazarin had followed Charles I's problems with close interest. He had no sympathy with the pretensions of the English parliament, but he had no objection to Charles being kept weak, so long as there was no civil war. When war began, he wanted Charles to win, but he could not spare resources from his own wars to help him. Moreover he was careful not to alienate the English parliament when the chance of the king's victory faded. He also found much that was exasperating in the conflict. He could not understand why Charles was so concerned to risk everything in defence of the bishops, an attitude very different from that of Henri IV when 'Paris was worth a Mass'. Nor could he understand why the Presbyterians pressed Charles so far, nor why the Irish Catholics seemed to do everything possible to embarrass their king. He thought that Charles's desertion of Strafford was the beginning of all his troubles: he wrote that it was 'the beginning of the abolition of the monarchy; for the Parliament considered itself strong enough afterwards to obtain everything'.[38] He thought that Charles should have abandoned the Anglican Church and sought an alliance with the Irish Catholics and Presbyterians of Scotland and England, or failing that, with the Independents. All this showed how little Mazarin really understood the complexities of the situation in the three kingdoms, or the mind of Charles I. He was baffled that the men of property were prepared to bring down the monarchy, and that parliament should seem to hate monarchy so much.[39] He seriously doubted Charles I's political judgment, not only in deserting Strafford, but also in fleeing to the Scots when he had already been stripped of all bargaining power.

All this helps to explain why Mazarin had not been disposed to do more for Charles I. His policy was one of outward neutrality with some secret help for the Stuarts. He did not recall his ambassador until May 1649, but he recognised Charles II as king of England. The Commonwealth therefore viewed French policy with deep suspicion. There was a rumour that Condé would be employed to lead an army into England. A commercial war followed, with France placing an embargo on English textiles, and the Commonwealth retaliating with an embargo on French wines. This was a futile conflict in which both sides suffered equally. There was also conflict at sea, with each side employing privateers to prey on enemy shipping. Prince Rupert and his squadron were able to join in, and by the end of 1650 had captured booty worth £550,000 to aid Stuart funds. As the Franco-Spanish war continued, Mazarin feared that the English might seek a Spanish alliance against France. There was also the possibility that Cromwell might send help to the rebel Frondeurs of Bordeaux. But for the time being Cromwell was busy in Scotland, and in February 1651 Mazarin was forced into exile. However the Commonwealth sent Colonel Sexby and Thomas Scot on secret missions to negotiate some kind of deal with the rebel Bordelais, while Henry Vane visited Paris to explore the possibility of a renewal of the Fronde there.

Spain was the first of the European monarchies to recognise the Commonwealth in January 1651, and Mazarin saw the need for similar recognition on the part of France. He wished however to make it conditional on a commercial agreement and compensation for losses at sea, but the Commonwealth would not negotiate, and required immediate recognition. Meanwhile hostilities continued, and in September Admiral Blake and his fleet combined with the Spanish to inflict a sharp defeat on the French in their attempt to relieve Dunkirk. Two days later, on 16 September, Dunkirk fell to the Spaniards. Mazarin realised that he must repair relations with England, and sent Antoine de Bordeaux to London to offer immediate and unconditional recognition. But it suited Cromwell to drag out the negotiations, and meanwhile the depredations at sea continued, in which France suffered heavily. Not until November 1655 was Bordeaux able to sign the Treaty of Westminster which made peace and ended the trade war and the activities of the privateers. Charles II's fleet could no longer use French ports, and each country promised not to harbour the enemies of the other which was bad news for the Stuart cause in France. To Mazarin the good will of Cromwell was more important than that of Charles Stuart, and thus, as Hyde wrote, Mazarin's policy was 'of unspeakable disadvantage to our poor master'.[40]

Henrietta Maria had a pension of 8000 pistoles a year from the French Crown, and Charles II had an allowance of 6000 livres a month from the same source, although the French were not always in a position to pay it. Clarendon said that the queen took most of Charles's allowance for his board, and that great care was taken to see that nothing was left over to maintain his councillors, so that Ormond and Hyde had to find lodgings 'with a poor English woman, the wife of one of the king's servants, at a pistole a week for their diet', and Ormond had to walk the streets, being unable to afford a carriage, 'whilst Lord Jermyn kept an excellent table for those who courted him, and had a coach of his own, and all other accommodations incident to the most full fortune'.[41] Jermyn also obtained warrants from the king to draw on the loans which Culpepper and Crofts had obtained from Russia and Poland, so that the king 'never received five hundred pistoles from the proceeds of both of those embassies'. Nicholas complained that, while the queen gave rich presents at the marriage of two of her servants, the king's servants went unpaid. Thus the bitter rivalry between the Louvre party and their opponents was exacerbated by the poverty which faced many who did not seek Jermyn's favours. The queen seems to have been comfortably provided for, having substantial gifts from the Condé family, while Mazarin loaned her 300,000 livres. But some of the king's servants certainly lived in penury. Hyde complained to Nicholas in December 1652 that it cost him seven or eight livres a week for postage on the king's letters, which he could afford only by borrowing from friends, since he received nothing from the king,

yet it is to no purpose to complain, though I have not been master of a crown these many months, am cold for want of clothes and fire, and owe for all the meat which I have eaten these three months.[42]

Charles II formed a small privy council to advise him, consisting of the marquis of Ormond, Lord Jermyn, Lord Wilmot (who had served the king so loyally on the Scottish venture) and Sir Edward Hyde (the only member of Charles I's council who remained about the king). Hyde, who now met Ormond for the first time, found him a tower of strength in the difficult years ahead. In contrast, Sir John Berkeley, whom Hyde had always regarded as a close friend, now showed himself a bitter enemy. Hyde had remonstrated with him in letters from Spain for his strong support for the Scottish venture, and for his new attachment to Jermyn and the Louvre party. Since then Berkeley had attached himself to the duke of York, and was one of those urging him to break away from his mother's apron-strings. Berkeley was annoyed at being excluded from the king's council, and he pressed his claim to the office of Master of the Wards on the basis of a dubious promise of the late king. When he failed to obtain it, he blamed Hyde, and told him that their friendship was at an end. The royalists were rapidly sinking into quarrelsome factions which too often vented their spleen on Hyde for his influence with the king.* Nicholas was so hostile to the Louvre party that he long resisted Hyde's pressure to come to Paris. Like many royalists, he yearned to escape poverty by salvaging something of his estates in England, by returning to compound with the Commonwealth. However in October 1652 he wrote to Hyde that his estates, worth £1050 a year, had been sold off by the rebels, and he had little choice but to remain.[44]

The queen sought for a way out of financial difficulties by successful

---

*'The vexations he [the king] underwent cannot be expressed; and whoever succeeded not in his unreasonable desires imputed it only to the ill nature of the chancellor of the exchequer, and concluded that he alone obstructed it.'[43]

marriages for the king and duke of York. She first suggested in 1645 the marriage of Charles to Grande Mademoiselle Anne-Marie de Montpensier, daughter of the Duc d'Orléans, and she returned to the idea in 1649. But Charles had proved a reluctant lover, apparently unable to speak French, and making a poor impression upon his cousin. Henrietta Maria returned to the subject yet again in 1651, when it was proposed that the duke of York might also marry the daughter of the duc de Longueville. Charles now became an ardent lover, much interested in the Montpensier fortune, but the difficulties proved insuperable. Mademoiselle was implicated in the Paris Fronde, and thus earned Louis' ill will. Mazarin was determined to prevent a marriage which would fritter away the lady's fortune on English enterprises, and he whispered that there was a prospect of her marrying Louis XIV himself. It was assumed that the marriage could not take place unless Charles became a Catholic, but this was obviously impossible if he were ever to regain his throne. Moreover the hope of achieving that throne seemed remote, and without it Charles was a penniless exile. The lady therefore rapidly lost interest in the match. The Longueville marriage with the duke of York was soon abandoned when the queen decided it was not a good enough match for her son. Ormond and Hyde had advised against both marriages, a fact which did nothing to endear them to the Louvre party. 'They besought him [the king] to set his heart entirely upon the recovery of England, and to indulge in nothing that might reasonably obstruct that.' Charles replied ungallantly that he had favoured the marriage only as a means to acquiring the lady's fortune![45] But he was young, with an appetite for enjoyment which gave Hyde some concern. The Commonwealth 'Mercurius Politicus' reported (5 Nov. 1651): 'The King of Scots, the Duke of York, the Duke of Beaufort and Mademoiselle d'Orléans are much given to hunting, dancing, balls and masking.' Mademoiselle in fact held assemblies every evening and Charles was often there; when she tired of Charles he turned his attention to Isabelle-Angélique de Montmorency, duchesse de Châtillon, widow of Admiral Coligny. She was young, a great beauty, and surrounded by passionate admirers, including the Prince of Condé, the duc de Nemours and Lord Digby. Charles was infatuated with her, but there was always the restraining hand of Sir Edward Hyde who wrote to Nicholas in May 1652:

there are, and always will be, some actions of appetite and affection committed which cannot be separated nor banished from the age of twenty-one, and which we must all labour by good counsel to prevent and divert ... and must always remember that Kings are of the same mould and composition as other men, and must have the same time to be made perfect.[46]

What was much more serious at the time was that the queen and Charles were involved in the cross-fire between the French Court and the Fronde, and in July they had to escape from Paris to Saint Germain. They were able to return to the Louvre in September, and when the Fronde collapsed in 1653, Louis thanked Charles and his mother for their support. But their position was in no way improved, and Hyde longed for the time when the king could leave Paris for good. He wrote to Nicholas:

If I sought my own quiet and contentment, I would sure starve with my wife and children rather than expect the same fate to us both severed, with so many vexations as this place administers; but I conceive I am undergoing what I cannot with a good conscience decline.[47]

Hyde's depression was greatly increased by the ceaseless bickering and rivalry which tore the king's little Court apart. The Louvre party kept up a steady hostility to Hyde and Nicholas, and the latter was so resentful of their influence that he still resisted attempts to persuade him to join the king in Paris. In the king's Council Jermyn, Norwich and Wilmot usually opposed Ormond and Hyde, and the latter had to sustain constant effort to retain his influence over the king. He wrote that the queen and Jermyn were 'mad with the thought' that they could not control Charles.[48] The more hopeless the royalist cause appeared, and the greater the poverty, the more disillusioned members seemed disposed to quarrel. The worst incident concerned Robert Long, who had been Secretary to the Prince of Wales's Council in the west in 1645, and had continued as Charles II's secretary until the latter went to Scotland. He was reappointed when the king returned to France, but then a Colonel Wogan accused him of treachery and responsibility for the collapse of the military resistance at Torrington in that he had supplied Ireton with military facts concerning the royalist position. Since Long had offended the Louvre party by opposing the queen and Jermyn, Hyde was disposed to regard the affair as a Louvre conspiracy, although he seems to have believed the charges himself. However he wrote to Nicholas in February 1652, 'Mr Long behaves himself as ill as in the defence [i.e. of Torrington], but really appears as much fool as knave; no doubt the King will have no more to do with him.'[49] Accordingly Long was dismissed from the king's service, and henceforth blamed Hyde for his dismissal. In May 1652 Long received a letter from one Massonet, who had been employed by Hyde as a letter-writer, declaring that a maid who had once been in his wife's service, and had since served Cromwell, was ready to swear that she had once brought Hyde secretly to Cromwell's bedchamber. The implication was that Hyde had secretly visited England on his return from Spain, and was now in the pay of Cromwell, and Massonet added that if the maid was brought over, Long could do 'good service to his Majesty and take vengeance of an adversary'.[50] Long sat on the information until July 1653, when he informed Sir Richard Grenville of the strong accusation, but asked that his name should not be mentioned. Grenville told the king the story in September. Charles demanded the full details and all the correspondence, including the names of those who accused Hyde of being in receipt of a pension. Long was required to draw up a full indictment of Hyde, which ran into seven pages, and for good measure he wrote to Charles to recount a conversation he had once had with Hyde, in which the latter had said

that the King was given to pleasure, like other young men of 23 or 24 years old, and that I knew how indisposed and unactive he was; which I thought to be words of great malice and iniquity from a councillor.

This was no doubt true, for Hyde had written as much* to Nicholas,[51] but it had no influence on the king, whose investigations during December 1653 led to Hyde's exoneration. Hyde wrote to Nicholas in January 1654:

Of the conspiracy against me I shall say . . . only this, there hath no-one professed that he does believe it himself, though there are too many who are willing others should. His Majesty hath been more angry than I, and declared it to be false and malicious scandal.

To Hyde the significance of the incident was that it revealed how many enemies he had. Long, for instance, who had earned the hostility of the Louvre party, now found them his champions. Hyde wrote to Nicholas: 'you cannot imagine with what importunity the Queen, Lord Keeper [Sir Ed. Herbert], Jermyn and the duke of Buckingham are concerned for him [Long], and what foul malice the Lord Keeper and Jermyn have expressed against Sir Edward Hyde'.[53] Hyde realised the frustrations and strain under which the exiles lived, but such incidents made him wish 'I were quiet at my book in any part of the world, for I am not for these conflicts.'

Hyde's months in Paris were the most miserable of his entire exile. Surrounded by the malice of his enemies, and miserably poor ('though I am so cold, that I am scarce able to hold my pen, and have not three sous in the world to buy a faggot')† he had difficulty in keeping the king's mind on business, although the case of Robert Long showed that Charles could act effectively when he chose. Hyde wrote on one occasion:

When anything is to be done by the King's own hand we must sometimes be content to wait, he being brought very unwillingly to the work, which vexes me exceedingly . . . The truth is, if I did not serve the King for God's sake, I would not stay here a day longer, and seriously, if he do not speedily remove from this place, I shall not be able to continue with him for many reasons.[55]

---

*cf. March 1653, 'All the king's fault is loving pleasure and being with great difficulty gotten to write himself three or four hours together.'[52]

† Hyde's financial position is difficult to determine, for although such statements as these to Nicholas must have been the truth, yet Sir Richard Grenville's reason for believing the story that Hyde was in Cromwell's pay was that 'it is a known truth that his estate known cannot defray the tenth part of the monies which now, and for divers late years, have maintained his wife and children, at a higher rate of expense than any else can live at which are out of England'. Yet in August 1652 Hyde wrote that he had 'not received one penny from the King since I came hither which is eight months, so that you will easily conclude my condition is bad enough'.[54]

In his next weekly letter to Nicholas he declared:

I . . . have the good fortune to be equally disliked by those who agree in nothing else, my unpardonable crime being that I would have the King do his business himself and be governed by nobody; and my reason is, that by truth itself he hath more judgment and understanding by many degrees than many who pretend it, and that is the only thing that breaks my heart, that he makes no more use of it. But all is at worst . . .

It is clear that Hyde had the greatest difficulty in persuading Charles to pay attention to the seemingly fruitless task of following the political events of the time. On 20 June he wrote:

it cannot be denied the King is exceedingly fallen in reputation . . . besides I must tell you he is so much given to pleasure that if he stay here he will be undone.

A week later he wrote:

I am sure the penury [of the Court] is not to be imagined by you. It is very true I do not know that any man is yet dead for want of bread, which really I wonder at; I am sure the King himself owes for all he hath eaten since April, and I am not acquainted with one servant of his who hath a pistole in his pocket; five or six of us eat together one meal a day for a pistole a week, but all of us owe for God knows how many weeks to the poor woman that feeds us. I believe my Lord of Ormond hath not had five livres in his purse this month, and hath fewer clothes of all sorts than you have, and yet I take you to be no gallant.[56]

This was indeed in answer to Nicholas's complaint that royalists in England were refusing to send money for the support of the king, since the English press was making much of the social pleasures he was enjoying in Paris.

Hyde and Nicholas both followed events in England closely, and kept up a correspondence with friends whenever that was possible. Hyde's chief correspondent, and the one who looked after his affairs, was his cousin Sir Harry Hyde, and it was an irreparable loss to him when the latter was executed as a royalist adherent to Charles II in 1651. Nicholas kept up a correspondence especially with London, and Hyde frequently referred humorously to Nicholas's 'Presbyterian' friends. Travellers to and from France or Holland might be persuaded to carry letters, but many of them fell into the hands of vigilant Commonwealth agents. The information to be gleaned from such letters was small, but Hyde realised the importance of maintaining contacts. He knew the extent of a latent royalism in England, but he knew also the formidable strength of Cromwell's government and army. He put no faith at all in the possibility of foreign aid, at a time when, as he wrote, 'scarce a Prince is not infected and almost worn out with domestic troubles or foreign wars, and therefore very capable of receiving great damage by provoking a barbarous enemy [Cromwell] which hath so much power to do hurt'. If the monarchy were to be restored it would be because of the failure of the republican experiments, and this would take time. So he wrote to Nicholas that 'the consideration of doing his duty and depending upon God, keeps him from being over-concerned or afflicted with what he hears'. And always there was the longing to return to his books. In November 1651 he was trying to obtain the twelve volumes of Baronius's *Annales ecclesiastici.*\* Later he was enquiring eagerly as to Grotius's recent books, especially his history of the Low Countries, adding:

thus you see I please myself with the talk of books, and indeed desire nothing so much as to have leisure and leave in any corner to read them, for I find I grow old and infirm.[57]

By that time however England was on the verge of momentous changes which were to give the royalists a new ray of hope.

---

\* Baronius (1538–1607) wrote his history of the church 1588–1607 in refutation of Protestantism. They later formed part of Clarendon's library.

# Royalists and the Protectorate

The execution of Charles I, the conquest of Ireland and Scotland, and Cromwell's victory over Charles II at Worcester were formidable expressions of the power of the Commonwealth, and of the prestige of Cromwell himself, but there were widely divergent views as to what should follow those victories. Most people received the news of the execution of the king with horror, but to the Fifth Monarchy men it was the dawn of a new era characterised by the rule of the saints, and to the Levellers it was the dawn of freedom. Both hoped for the destruction of a national church, a purification of the clergy, the abolition of tithes, reform of the law and an end to the privileges of the rich. The Presbyterians looked with alarm at both these extremes, and hoped for a national church on the lines of the decisions of the Westminster Assembly. Unless some kind of constitutional stability could be achieved there would be a danger of a drift towards anarchy, or a return to monarchy. The chief barrier to either was the power of the army, but no one favoured a permanent military despotism.

The Rump Parliament showed itself on the whole a responsible and conservative-minded body. It spent much time discussing reforms, but it carried none.[1] There was a general desire that the life of this parliament should be ended, but how could this be done until parliamentary reform had been carried; if reform was attempted, how could a Leveller democracy be avoided, and what reform would prevent the return of a royalist House? Finally Cromwell lost patience and in April 1653 turned the Rump out of doors. The news was received with jubilation by the army, but with alarm by moderate opinion. Whitelocke wrote:

Now [the army] rose against [Parliament], and most ingratefully and disingenuously, as well as rashly and imprudently, they dissolved that power by which they themselves were created officers and soldiers; and now they took what they designed, all power into their own hands. All honest and prudent indifferent men were highly distasted at this unworthy action.[2]

Whitelocke venerated the legality of parliament, and saw that the last constitutional link with the past had been broken. Henceforth Cromwell stood forth as a usurper entirely dependent upon the support of the army. When on the afternoon of the 20th Cromwell informed the Council of State that they too were dissolved, Serjeant Bradshaw replied, 'Sir, you are mistaken to think that the Parliament is dissolved; for no power under heaven can dissolve them but themselves; therefore take you notice of that'.[3]

The royalists, glad in one sense that the Long Parliament was at last at an end, nonetheless commented that Charles I's attempt to arrest the Five Members had once been regarded as an unheard-of breach of the privilege of parliament, but was now insignificant compared with Cromwell's expulsion of a whole parliament.[4] There were rumours that Cromwell would himself restore the king, that Charles II might marry his daughter, that Cromwell would become a duke and be made Lord Deputy of Ireland.[5] We have seen that Cromwell in his search for constitutional stability had had the monarchical idea in mind in the autumn of 1651, and he returned to it in a discussion with Whitelocke in November 1652:

Cromwell: What if a man should take upon him to be king?
Whitelocke: I think that remedy would be worse than the disease.
Cromwell: Why do you think so?
Whitelocke: As to your own person the title of king would be of no advantage, because you have the full kingly power in you already, concerning the militia, as you are general.

This did not satisfy Cromwell. What he was seeking was not so much the Crown for himself but a permanent form of legality. He continued:

I have heard some of your profession observe, that he who is actually king, whether by election or by descent, yet being once king, all acts done by him as king are lawful and justifiable, as by any king who hath the crown by inheritance from his forefathers ... And surely the power of a king is so great and high, and so universally understood and reverenced by the people of this nation, that the title of it might not only indemnify in a great measure those that act under it, but likewise be of great use and advantage in such times as these, to curb the insolences and extravagances of those whom the present powers cannot control.

Clarendon himself could not have made a better justification for the restoration of the monarchy, and Cromwell's words underlined the ultimate inevitability of the restoration of 1660. Whitelocke argued truly that the real issue of the time was between monarchy and democracy, and that if the latter was rejected, then Charles Stuart rather then Cromwell, would be the choice of the nation.[6]

Sir Edward Hyde's first reaction to the news of the dissolution of the Rump was delight that it was the end of 'this accursed assembly of rogues', but this was overtaken by the sombre thought that Cromwell was now 'possessed of so absolute a power that nothing can stand in his way'. He wrote in December 1653 that he 'dreaded more than anything that can happen', Cromwell's taking the title of Protector or King,[7] since any step towards constitutional stability would be detrimental to Stuart hopes of a restoration of the monarchy. In his *History*, on more mature consideration he regarded Cromwell's seizure of power as the only alternative to a growing political confusion. Cromwell had dispersed a parliament, but, Clarendon added sarcastically, 'he was not so well satisfied in the general temper [of the nation], as to trust the election of [another parliament] to the humour and inclination of the people'.[8] Instead he discussed the matter with a new council of ten, seven of them from among his own generals. Lambert wished such a council to undertake the business of government without the aid of a new representative, but Harrison wanted a 'Sanhedrin' of seventy men on the Old Testament model.

Cromwell knew that he must clothe his military despotism with some constitutional form as quickly as possible, and he favoured an assembly of godly men who might lead the nation to accept the new order, bring wars to an end, enable the army to be reduced and taxation to be cut, and thus make the regime acceptable to the nation. He thus endorsed the idea of a Nominated Parliament, supposedly selected by the godly congregations, but in fact severely 'edited' by the army officers, so as to ensure their own representation. The Barebones Parliament included a fair number of able men, but also a sufficient number of Harrison's extremist followers to give the whole the ineffectual reputation which it has acquired in history. Clarendon's assessment was not unfair:

There were among them some few of the quality and degree of gentlemen, and who had estates, and such a proportion of credit and reputation as could consist with the guilt they had contracted. But much of the major part of them consisted of inferior persons, of no quality or name, artificers of the meanest trades, known only by their gifts in praying and preaching; which was now practised by all degrees of men, but scholars, throughout the kingdom . . . In a word, they were a pack of weak senseless fellows, fit only to bring the name and reputation of parliament lower than it was yet.[9]

A news-letter from London reported, 'I have seen a private list of them, and find that many of them are no better than attorneys, tanners, wheelwrights and of the meanest sort of mechanics'.[10] Praise-God Barebone (or Barbon), a leather-seller of Fleet Street, an otherwise undistinguished member, gave the assembly its derisory name, and Cromwell endowed them with the supreme authority of the nation until November 1654, by which time they were to make the choice of their successors.

To endow them with supreme authority, and to leave them to do as they wished, without executive guidance, was an elementary blunder on Cromwell's part. They took him at his word, and plunged into many of the issues which the Levellers and Fifth Monarchists had raised. Thus they attacked the lawyers, called for legal reforms, assailed the quality of ministers and opposed the continuance of tithes. The moderates fought a rearguard action, but the prospect of anarchy raised its head. Cromwell found himself under attack from John Lilburne and the Levellers, and Harrison and the Fifth Monarchists. As disillusionment with the Nominated Parliament spread, some eighty moderate members, taking advantage of the fact that the extremists were at prayers, on 12 December voted their own dissolution, and handed back power to the Lord General. The Instrument of Government had already been prepared, and four days later Cromwell was solemnly installed as Lord Protector.

By the Instrument of Government, supreme authority was vested in the Protector, his Council and a Parliament, which should meet in September 1654, and there was provision for an army of 30,000 men. Clarendon could not conceal a touch of admiration for Cromwell's achievement, when he wrote that thus

this extraordinary man . . . mounted himself into the throne of three kingdoms, without the name of king, but with a greater power and authority than had ever been exercised or claimed by any king; and received greater evidence and manifestation or respect and esteem from all the kings and princes in Christendom than had ever been shewed to any monarch of those nations: and which was so much the more notorious, in that they all abhorred him, when they trembled at his power and courted his friendship.[11]

Elections to the new parliament took place in July 1654. For the first time parliament represented all three kingdoms, and a new franchise gave better representation to the counties at the expense of 'rotten' or 'pocket' boroughs. Clarendon wrote with approval of the new franchise, and seems to regret not to have been able to retain it after 1660.[12] But known royalists were excluded from the franchise, and a vetting committee excluded elected Levellers from the House. Some 120 members seem never to have attended at all, yet some noted republicans hostile to the Protectorate were present, and, led by Haselrig, were bent on restoring the sovereignty of parliament. They found themselves in a vicious circle, for they existed as a parliament only by virtue of the Instrument of Government, the only authority for which lay in the predominance of the army. Could parliament question the constitution by which it existed? When they met on 3 September 1654 they showed themselves no more ready to accept the authority of the Protector than the Long Parliament had been to accept that of Charles I. Hesilrige's motion to discuss the whole issue, at first defeated by 187 to 130, was carried a few days later by 141 to 136, thus revealing how narrow a margin divided the two parties in the House.[13] For once Cromwell acted swiftly. On 12 September he addressed the House in the Painted Chamber in a long meandering speech, which ended with the requirement that members should accept the 'Recognition', a simple acceptance of the principle of government by one man and parliament. It was a statement a monarchist could accept, but not a republican. Some 240 members agreed, but 100 members preferred to withdraw from the House. However, those who remained continued to discuss the rest of the

Instrument, and in ensuing debates they edited the document. They showed a singular lack of grasp of political realities, and Cromwell, who could not again dismiss a parliament so quickly, had to endure the five months of their existence before he was permitted to end the session.

All this provided some crumbs of comfort for the royalists. Their main hope was that the Levellers and republicans in the army would try to unseat Cromwell. John Lilburne, Cromwell's staunchest Leveller opponent, was brought to trial in August 1653. With 6,000 citizens demonstrating on his behalf outside the court-room, he made a strong defence in the name of liberty, and the jury returned a verdict of not guilty. Public opinion had saved his life:

> And what, shall then honest John Lilburne die?
> Three score thousand will know the reason why.[14]

Nonetheless he was returned to prison, and remained there until his death four years later. But Lilburne had raised the hopes of the royalists. Secretary Nicholas had been in touch with him, and a news-letter from London in June reported that Lilburne 'proposed to the duke of Buckingham to bring in the king if he had but £10,000'.[15] Hyde was always sceptical of Nicholas's correspondents, but he wrote on one occasion that if Cromwell did not hang Lilburne, Lilburne would certainly hang Cromwell.[16] Hyde always placed more faith in the confusion in England than in anything the royalists themselves could do, and declared that 'if the nation were united, he should despair of prevailing against them'.[17] There was plenty of evidence of discontent. In 1653 *A Charge of High Treason exhibited against Oliver Cromwell* appeared as a pamphlet, probably written by the Leveller John Wildman, declaring that 'not having the fear of God before his eyes, but being instigated by the devil, [he] did traiterously and villainously, by force of arms, dissolve the late parliament'.[18] In October a clash between troops and civilians at St Paul's led to a riot, while London seamen demonstrated over arrears of pay. In 1654 the Fifth Monarchists became virulent critics of the Protectorate. They had opposed the Rump, and welcomed the rule of the saints, embodied in the Barebones Parliament. Its dissolution was accordingly a great shock to them, and regarded as a betrayal of the saints by Cromwell and his friends. There were important Fifth Monarchists in the army command, Major-General Harrison, Overton and Rich among them. Three colonels, Matthew Alured, John Okey and Thomas Saunders were found guilty of distributing subversive literature, and were cashiered. The government clamped down upon the others. Harrison, Courtney, Carew and Rich were all imprisoned. From their London pulpits Fifth Monarchist ministers such as Christopher Feake, John Simpson and George Cockayne thundered forth their attacks, but by Cromwell's government were treated with a good deal of tolerance.

The first parliament of the Protectorate considerably modified the

Instrument of Government. They gained the right to approve the members of the Council; they shared with the Protector the power of making peace and war. They called for a reduction in the size of the army, which was imposing a crippling burden on the cost of government, and creating a heavy annual deficit which the Protectorate never succeeded in solving. Parliament thus went a long way towards asserting its claim to be the ultimate constitutional authority. Yet the fundamental fact remained that they, like Cromwell's Protectorate, rested on the authority of the army, and unless some basis for stability and permanence could be achieved, and the size of the army reduced, the chance of survival was limited. Cromwell's health was failing, and royalists liked to say that he went in fear of assassination, so that he would not sleep in the same bed two nights running. There were indeed assassination plots, and the problem of the succession became increasingly urgent. Cromwell was annoyed when Lambert's motion in the first parliament that the Protectorate should be made hereditary was heavily defeated. But that the subject of monarchy was increasingly in men's minds is shown by a conversation between Cromwell and the future earl of Orrery late in 1654. Lord Broghill told Cromwell that the rumour in the City was that he intended 'to marry his daughter Frances to Charles Stuart, and that most people 'thought it the wisest thing he could do, if he could accomplish it'. Cromwell listened attentively to Broghill's arguments, but finally dismissed the idea, with the remark, 'The king cannot and will not forgive the death of his father.'[19] Thus the prime consideration which seemed to stand in the way of the restoration of the Stuarts was the fate which would befall those who had effected the death of the late king. It was a tenuous thread upon which to hang the continued existence of the Protectorate, which was a monarchy in all but name.

It was one thing to see the need for stability, and even to recognise the logic of monarchy if government was to be in accordance with legal precedence, but it was quite another thing to bring it about. In the early 1650s the royalist outlook seemed bleak indeed.

The correspondence of Sir Edward Hyde in the months after Charles II returned to France after the defeat at Worcester, makes depressing reading. He was intensely unhappy in Paris, where the factions were ever more embittered. For months Hyde was under the shadow of Long's accusations of treachery, and although the king in the end exonerated him, it was a trying time for him. He had become the chief target of the frustrations and hatred of the Louvre party. He longed to hear that the king intended to leave Paris, but there seemed nowhere to go, and no money to transport them anywhere. They were so poor, he wrote, that some of the king's Court could afford only one meal a day, and the king himself owed tradesman's bills for months at a time.[20] He complained frequently of the king's love of pleasure, and his unwillingness to attend to business.[21] The London press made the most of such stories, and a news-letter of 24 June 1653 reported that 'the King is so whelmed in pleasures, especially women, so that the whole town rings of him, that the Queen and Council have urged him to leave'.[22] This was an exaggeration, but, reported in England, it gave the royalists the impression that the king lived in luxury and idleness, and that therefore financial help from them was unnecessary.

Hyde, himself often wracked with gout 'so tortured that he cannot sit',[23] and Nicholas were kept busy with a voluminous correspondence, with the royalists in England, not only in order to keep their fingers on the pulse of events, but also in the hope that they could solicit money for the king's use. There was also correspondence with Denmark (where Lord Wentworth was, the king's envoy), Sweden, the Dutch and the German princes, from whom Charles hoped to gain help. Hyde complained to Nicholas 'of the multitude of despatches he has to write every week, so that really he has not Sundays to himself'.[24] Sometimes these efforts paid off, as in November 1653, when the Elector of Brandenburg wrote that the Imperial Diet had granted Charles 200,000 rix-dollars. But the sum was not paid for months, and it is a little disconcerting to find that a month before Hyde had written to Lord Rochester, Charles's envoy to the Empire, that the king wished him to purchase 'a good set of seven coach-horses, as he is told that in those parts [Cologne] they are the best in the world, and I am sure he hath the worst'.[25] However even in poverty and exile it was necessary for a king to keep up appearances. Hyde also kept up a correspondence with Rome, in the forlorn attempt to win for the king the good will of the Catholics in the three kingdoms.

Scotland continued to be a centre of interest. In April 1652 the Union of England and Scotland was proclaimed, and for the moment Scotland submitted, as the English army attempted a systematic occupation. Only Dunnottar Castle still held out for the king. It was of special importance to Charles because it contained not only rich plate and furniture worth £20,000, but also the regalia of Scotland. Charles did all he could to raise an expedition to take possession of them, but failed, and the castle surrendered in May. However George Ogilvy managed to smuggle out the regalia and conceal them beneath the floor of Kinneff church, where they remained until after the Restoration. For the moment Scotland was quiet, but in March 1652 Lieutenant-General Middleton, who had been taken prisoner at Worcester, and imprisoned in the Tower, but had escaped, arrived in Paris, bringing with him a Scottish minister, Henry Knox. Knox was the agent of Lord Balcarres, from whom he brought a proposition to the king. He said that the Highlanders resented the domination of the English and the oppressions of Argyll, and were ready to rise, if Middleton or Ormond were sent to take command. They stipulated that the Louvre party should not be informed of the plan, since the queen and they 'had too good an opinion of the marquis of Argyll, who would infallibly come to know whatever was known to either of the other'.[26]

In view of past experience, Hyde was instinctively mistrustful of Scottish projects. Clarendon wrote that Charles, Ormond and Hyde all 'believed that the king had nothing at this time to do but to be quiet, and that all his activity was to consist in carefully avoiding to do anything that might do him hurt'.[27] But this was clearly written in the light of what happened, and did not reflect Charles's opinion at the time. Hyde always mistrusted the Scots, and pointed out how impossible it would be to keep any activity secret from the queen, but he reluctantly agreed to conduct the affair. The king was much more ready for action, and sent Macdonald of Glengarry a commission for him and his friends to elect a leader pending Middleton's arrival, and the latter was appointed commander-in-chief for Scotland. Thus in June 1653 the earl of Glencairn was elected general, but with only 7000 men he was confined to raiding expeditions. However, royalist hopes rose, and in July 1653 Nicholas reported optimistically,

The King's party in Scotland increases daily. There are thirteen Earls and Barons there declared for the King, whereof the Marquis of Huntly, the young Earl of Seaforth, Lord Lorne, son of the Marquis of Argyll, the old Chancellor Loudoun, the Lord Balcarres, and the Earl of Athol are some.[28]

But Charles was penniless, and unable to mount even a modest expedition unless he could gain help from the Dutch, who, being at war with Cromwell, might be interested in a diversion. In December the Dutch did agree to send arms and gunpowder in return for a promise of fishing rights off the Scottish coast. In February 1654 the Princess Royal managed to raise 5000 guilders, and, thus equipped, Middleton sailed for Scotland with 100 men. His presence in Scotland was badly needed, for the Scottish chiefs were already quarrelling among themselves, and their main activity so far had been sneak raids and horse stealing.

In November 1653 an adventurous young royalist, Colonel Edward Wogan, who had come from Ireland with Ormond, produced a daring but foolhardy plan of going to England, raising a force of royalists, and marching to Scotland to join Middleton. Hyde warned him of the incredible risks he would run, but he was so eager that the king gave him leave to go. He managed to reach London, gathered a force of about eighty men, and together they rode out of the city as if they were Cromwell's men, and proceeded unmolested to Scotland, where they joined up with Glencairn in December. However, a few weeks later Wogan died of a simple wound, through lack of a competent surgeon, and when Middleton arrived in February, he found the Scots in 'rude chaos'. In April Cromwell detached General Monck from the Dutch war and sent him to take command in Scotland. In May he launched his offensive, and by August it was all over. Most of the clan chiefs submitted.

Middleton fled to the Isle of Skye, and eventually made his way back to Europe.[29]

Hyde still looked desperately for an opportunity for the king to escape from France, and the Anglo-Dutch war seemed to offer one. In November 1653 Alderman Charles Bunce and a group of Presbyterian exiles in Holland suggested that the Dutch would welcome the king's presence as an inducement to Cromwell to make peace, but that peace was ratified in February 1654, and it was made clear that the king would no longer be made welcome there.[30] For a time it seemed that Scotland might offer another opportunity, but by the summer of 1654 that too was a lost cause. The French made it plain that they wished Charles to leave France as a condition of peace with England. Charles was very ready to go, although he tried to sell his departure as dearly as possible by a financial agreement with Mazarin. At this point his financial position improved. Mazarin agreed to purchase brass cannon, the proceeds of Prince Rupert's prizes at sea, although at knock-down prices, and also to continue to pay Charles his pension. He received 3000 pistoles for the cannon, and with the promise of 100,000 thalers from the Imperial Diet, and the receipt of £3000 from England, his finances looked respectable. Germany remained the only resort open to him.

Hyde set about seeing that the money was not squandered. He budgeted for a monthly expenditure of 6000 guilders, and a royal Household of thirty-eight, headed by Ormond, Rochester, Wentworth, Norwich, Culpepper and Hyde, with 2000 guilders a month for the royal table and stable, and 1000 guilders for the robes and privy purse. It was clear that the king could not afford a large establishment, and Hyde had an invaluable opportunity to shed a considerable number of hangers-on, and in particular to sever connection with the Louvre party, and those who had been Hyde's most persistent enemies and whom he referred to significantly as 'the Presbyterian gang'. Thus Lord Keeper Herbert was left behind in Paris on the grounds that the king no longer had need for the Great Seal, and Hyde took over his duties. Prince Rupert went off to seek his fortune in Germany. Sir Richard Grenville's hostility towards Hyde had dated from the western campaign. He had published a pamphlet vilifying Hyde's part in it, and was so eaten up with enmity and passion that the king did well to dispense with his services. Robert Long, who had accused Hyde of treachery, was dismissed, and went off to England to sell his services to Cromwell. In January 1654 the stigma was finally lifted from Hyde's shoulders, when the King declared, under the sign manual that

He has examined the charges against Hyde ... which the King looks upon as a libel derogatory from his own honour and justice as also full of malice against Hyde; and that, upon the whole matter, he consequently pronounces that the accusation is a groundless and malicious calumny, that he is very well satisfied of Hyde's constant integrity and fidelity in the service of his father and himself, that he will hereafter further enquire into the conspiracy when he shall be better able to punish those who may be found guilty of it, and in the meantime he renews his former judgment that Sir Richard Grenville shall not presume to come into his presence.[31]

Henceforth correspondence between the king and the Louvre party became scanty indeed, and the hostility of the latter towards Hyde became more intense than ever. Richard Watson, formerly Lord Hopton's chaplain, a strong Anglican and firm friend of Hyde's, wrote to Hyde's secretary Edgeman in February 1654 that he found people far too ready to credit any charge against the Chancellor of the Exchequer, but he admitted that Hyde was in some degree to blame:

he fears that some little height of spirit, some passionate expressions dropped from it, and some unsatisfactory answers given to the importunities of necessitous persons, have laid the foundation for all this malice. Nothing is left (besides innocency) for Hyde to do himself right but the publication of his *History*.[32]

In short, some of Hyde's unpopularity arose from the influence he had over the king, combined with too rough a tongue, an inability to suffer fools gladly, and a sheer inability to satisfy the crowd of beggars who habitually besieged the impecunious king.

Before leaving France in July 1654 Charles paid a final romantic visit to the lovely duchesse de Châtillon. Hyde was less fortunate in being granted a final audience with the queen, which entirely failed to thaw any of her coldness towards him. The breach was complete. Policy forced Charles to travel incognito, and poverty required him to ride on horseback, without a carriage. He met his sister, the Princess of Orange, at Spa, where she was taking the waters; and when an outbreak of smallpox drove them away, they moved to Aix, 'famous for its hot baths, whither many come after they have drunk the cold waters of the Spa'. Here at last Secretary Nicholas joined them, having always refused to go to France because of the queen's hostility towards him. Henceforth Charles would rely on the triumvirate of Ormond, Nicholas and Hyde for the conduct of policy, and this made for much greater smoothness and efficiency than had been possible in the turbid atmosphere of Paris. Charles disliked Aix, so they moved on to Cologne, where he was relieved to find that he was well received, and where he had the friendship of the duke of Neuburg at Dusseldorf. There Charles spent the winter, much of the time, according to Clarendon, studying Italian and French, 'and in the whole spent his time very well'.[33]

However from May 1654 onwards a more immediate task awaited the king. During the winter of 1653–4 a kind of high command of royalists in England was formed under the name of the Sealed Knot, of about six members. It was so secret that we do not know for certain who they were, for their identities were carefully concealed under fictitious names. Three of its members were probably Lord Willoughby of Parham, Lord Belasyse and Sir William Compton. The king was in correspondence with them from March onwards, and in May he sent commissions for the appointment of leaders in every county. By July a general rising was planned, to include Surrey, Sussex and Kent. Strongholds such as Warwick, Denbigh, Tynemouth and Ludlow were to be seized; Sir Philip Musgrave was to occupy Carlisle, Sir John Grenville to seize Plymouth, Sir Humphrey Bennett Portsmouth, Lord Byron Nottingham, Sir Thomas Peyton Sandwich, Colonel Grey Tynemouth and Colonel Scriven Shrewsbury. Lord Glencairn was already in arms in Scotland, and towns were to be seized in Ireland. As Cromwell had already sent 10,000 men to Scotland England was seriously denuded of troops.

At first it was hoped to launch the rising before the meeting of the first Protectorate parliament in September 1654, but then it was postponed until October, then till November, then December, and finally until March. For the problems proved insuperable, and the royalists rapidly divided into a party of action and one of caution. It was true that Cromwell's Protectorate was a minority government, with the majority of people in the country hostile or indifferent. But the more responsible royalists believed that a rising could not succeed unless there was active dissension in the army, or unless the Levellers and Anabaptists were ready to start a rising, or both. But Thurloe had a highly efficient intelligence service. As well as being Secretary to the Council, he had control of posts. Letters were systematically opened, and many royalist letters fell into his hands. He also had paid spies both in Paris and about Charles himself, and he was well aware of what was going on. The leaders of disaffection at home were systematically picked off. Major-General Harrison was arrested in September 1654, then invited to dine with Cromwell, and warned 'not to persist in those deceitful ways whose end is destruction'. When he persisted in plotting with the Levellers, he was again arrested and sent to Carisbrooke Castle, where he remained for the rest of the Protectorate. In November the three colonels, Saunders, Alured and Okey were arrested, and dismissed from their commands. In Scotland Colonel Overton was arrested for conspiring against Monck, and sent to England and imprisoned. During January and February 1655 other officers were arrested and either cashiered or imprisoned, and thus the resistance in the army was effectively neutralised, with no prospect of advantage to the royalists. Moreover, those officers were not royalists, but republicans opposed to Cromwell's 'tyranny'. The Fifth Monarchist preachers, Rogers, Feake and Simpson were also imprisoned.

Throughout 1654 Thurloe was well informed of the activities of conspirators. As early as February he was uncovering a conspiracy centring in the Feathers Tavern in Cheapside, and the enquiries went on for months. The plot seems to have included a plan for seizing Whitehall and assassinating Cromwell. A number of obscure persons made confessions, and one named Gerard admitted having kissed the king's hand in Paris. He and another royalist named Vowel, a schoolmaster of Islington, were executed.[34] How well Thurloe was informed was illustrated by the case of Henry Seymour, who had left England with the Protector's passport, nominally on private business, but in fact to carry messages from the marquis of Hertford and the earl of Southampton to the king.[35] When he returned in June he was arrested, and interrogated by Cromwell. When he denied having seen the king, Cromwell described the room in which they had met, and some of the things said, and he proceeded to ask about the conversation of Sir Edward Hyde, and his friendship with Lord Hatton. It was clear that Cromwell knew a great deal about the activities of the Stuart Court. Seymour was sent to the Tower.[36]

During 1654 Charles was faced with difficult decisions. He was naturally anxious for a royalist rising, and realised how important it was that he should show enthusiasm and readiness to further any attempt to unseat Cromwell. He maintained a full correspondence with the Sealed Knot and other royalists in England. But whether he was in Paris, Aix or Cologne, he was far from the scene of events; communications were difficult, and he was never in possession of sufficient facts to be able to give a clear order, whether to launch a rising, or to postpone it. Yet it was just such a clear order that the royalists wanted. Some were ready for immediate action, some thought that a rising could not succeed without a mutiny in the army, or a foreign invasion. All expected the early appearance of the king. All that Charles felt able to do was to leave the final decision to the royalists on the spot, and this was a recipe for failure. The Sealed Knot were increasingly against a rising, but this earned only the exasperated contempt of the more sanguine royalists. Hyde's part in all this was to urge caution and restraint. He had a realistic opinion of Cromwell's military strength, and little confidence in the hotheads who would rush into premature action. He wrote to Nicholas in June 1654, 'Many light foolish people propose wild things to the King, which he civilly discountenances, but of which they brag; and hence it probably is that that has fallen out at London, by which many honest men are in prison. There are some honest men who will stir when it is fit.'[37] But the king had to contend with letters such as that from the earl of Atholl from Scotland, saying that the king's forces were 'very considerable, and increase daily, many noblemen and gentlemen having heartily joined; nothing could be so advantageous to the service as the king's hastening to come to them'. Yet by the time this letter reached Charles in August, the Scottish rising was virtually over. Hyde had always tended to discount royalist stories in Scotland, in view of past experience, and was not surprised at Middleton's failure in 1654.[38]

After the battle of Worcester Hyde had a wholesome respect for Cromwell's ability and his military strength. He was also inclined to discount his difficulties. In June 1653 he wrote:

I do believe that Cromwell will be much more modest than the Conventicle [i.e.

the Rump] he dissolved, and I cannot imagine that there are any of those divisions in the army which other men fancy.

And later he wrote of the

general discourses we have of differences between Cromwell and Harrison and his officers, but I give little credit to it; he is too wise a man, and knows too well the number of his friends out of the army, to proceed as he does if he suspected his own credit and strength and power in the army.[39]

He did however think that the opposition of the army officers would be strong enough to prevent Cromwell from taking the crown, but this in part was wishful thinking.[40] He always believed that the Republic would one day break up by internal divisions, because he believed that the forces of tradition would ultimately reassert themselves, but he did not think the time had yet come, and he never had great faith in royalist conspiracies. He wrote to Nicholas:

I have really more hope from (internal divisions) than from all the armies and fleets you and your enterprising friends will be able to draw together.

However he equally realised the dangers which would follow a royalist disillusionment at the king's lack of enthusiasm.

Repeated postponements of the rising did indeed cause widespread uncertainty and disillusionment. In January 1655 Ormond wrote to Hyde that 'the King's business seems so broken that they must wait for an opportunity to begin anew'. One calling himself 'J Brerley' wrote to the king lamenting the absence of a commander-in-chief (probably he favoured Ormond). Early in February a member of the Sealed Knot calling himself 'Upton' wrote to the king that their opinion was 'that since no rising in the army is now to be hoped for, and the fleet is gone, any rising of the king's party would only be to their own destruction'.[41] Ormond was particularly concerned at the growing divisions among the royalists. He wrote on 12 February:

The Sealed Knot dissuade all from a rising now as being precipitate and unseasonable; the others charge the Knot with coldness, and say that they are forced to rise at once by the discovery they believe Cromwell to have made of the plot. The Knot will appear if commanded by the King, although desirous to remain quiet; he must therefore either forbid the enterprise or direct them to help it, as otherwise all will certainly be lost.[42]

But this was just what the king did not do. Instead he sent Wilmot, earl of Rochester to England with full authority to act as he thought best. Charles's letter to Lord Willoughby stated that he could not direct him what to do, 'not being informed by his own friends of the grounds of their proceeding'. He urged however that if there was a rising at all, all would join in it.[43] Others sent on separate missions to England were Daniel O'Neill, Sir Joseph Wagstaffe, Nicholas Armorer and Trelawny, the latter sent by Hyde to the west country.

Rochester's task was to co-ordinate activities, and O'Neill's to persuade the Sealed Knot to take part. They found that a February rising had already been postponed, and O'Neill reported that he found everything in such confusion that he almost despaired. Rochester seems to have aroused some new energy, and it was hoped that, although Kent could not rise because of the presence of troops, yet the west country, Cheshire, Shrewsbury, Yorkshire and the north were ready. The second week of March was appointed as the time for action.

There had been so many postponements that many had lost heart, and there was probably confusion over the appointed date. On 8 March about 100 cavaliers gathered in Yorkshire, instead of the expected 4000, and those who did appear, rapidly dispersed. Similarly at Rufford in Nottinghamshire, the home of Sir George Savile, some 300 royalists gathered, but dispersed when they found they were so few. Sir George was prudently in London. There were similar gatherings and rapid dispersals at Morpeth, Shrewsbury and Chester. Some leaders, as at Morpeth (Colonel Edward Gray) and Chester (Sir Thomas Harris) were already under arrest.

The only action therefore was in the west country. Trelawny had contacted the agents there; they had met Rochester in London, and asked for the assistance of Sir Joseph Wagstaffe, a stout old royalist soldier. He and Edward Penruddock were to initiate the action. On Monday 12 March some 200 cavaliers rode into Salisbury at the time of the Assizes, and seized the judges and the sheriff. Wagstaffe wanted to hang them at once, but Penruddock refused. The king was proclaimed, and the gaols thrown open, and then, since a contingent from Hampshire had not arrived, they decided to ride into Dorset in the hope of gathering recruits. But a number of local leaders, including Sir Humphrey Bennett and Sir John Grenville, were already under arrest, and only a handful of recruits joined them. The marquis of Hertford and most of the country gentry remained silent. Desertions began as the frightened rebels pushed on towards Cornwall. Cromwell despatched his brother-in-law, Major-General Desborough in pursuit, but before he could catch up with them, a Captain Unton Cooke and a troop from Exeter dispersed the remaining royalists, a mere 200 men, at South Molton, and some fifty were taken prisoner. Penruddock's rising was over. In the ensuing trials three were executed at Salisbury, fourteen at Exeter (including Colonels Penruddock and Grove), and several at Chard. All over the country there were numerous arrests, and several hundred prisoners were sent to the plantations. It was significant however that the king's envoys, Rochester, Wagstaffe, O'Neill, Nicholas Armorer, all got away to the continent, for in spite of the ignominious failure of the rising, the royalists had many friends among local justices and gentry, and in London.

Why, then, was the failure so complete? First, it is clear that the repeated postponements had resulted in confusion and disillusionment, and many men were loathe to move in such doubtful circumstances. Second, the cavaliers lacked a central command which had general respect. The Sealed Knot were shrouded in mystery, and the king refused to appoint a single commander, saying that he alone would be the General. Yet he was too far away, too ill-informed to make decisions, and forced to rely upon the Sealed Knot, who were opposed to a rising at this time, and were conspicuous by their absence in March. As Clarendon wrote, royalists failed to trust, and were loathe to communicate with each other, since any man might be a spy, and Cromwell's prisons were full of suspected conspirators. There is no doubt that there were many royalists in most parts of the country, but few of them were prepared to risk their lives in so doubtful an enterprise. In the *History* Clarendon portrayed Charles as always suspecting that the enterprise would fail, and that the leaders 'were not equal to so great work'.[44] But this was Hyde's view rather than the king's, and Charles was more inclined to encourage action than to urge caution. Hyde himself came in for severe criticism as 'the chief manager' of the enterprise, and the Louvre party were loud in their condemnation. Captain Peter Mews wrote to Nicholas:

You would hardly credit how severely the miscarriage of the business reflects upon Sir Edward Hyde, for being by most supposed to be, if not the sole, yet the chief manager of this design, the whole weight lies upon him, and though something in general may fall upon his Majesty, yet the hottest charge is upon him; and it is not here [in Paris] talked in corners that if Sir Edward Herbert and Lord Jermyn had been interested in the design, the miscarriage would have been laid at their door.[45]

Mews had his own reasons for disliking Hyde, and Nicholas had already had a brush with him on the subject in the previous January, when he reported to the Secretary,

many things to the prejudice and disparagement of Sir Edward Hyde, as that he makes himself here sole minister of state, takes on him alone the sole management of all business, and made me here but a cypher; adding withal that I brought him first to Court and had been a principal means of his preferment there.

This was an obvious attempt to sow discord between Nicholas and Hyde, and was typical of the venom which the Louvre party encouraged. But Nicholas stoutly defended Hyde:

I am sure you cannot but know the great friendship and kindness that hath been long, and is still, between Sir Edward Hyde and me. And though I have known him long, yet I assure you his own abilities and loyalty got him the great esteem and favour he had with the late King before I had the happiness to be intimately acquainted with him. So far have I been from being instrumental to his preferment in Court, where he wanted not many great friends that, if it had been needful, would and could have therein served him far better than ever I could. As he is faithful and industrious in the King's business, so he is certainly best versed in all his Majesty's present affairs, having been constantly employed therein these many years, and by his sedulity and dexterity is without doubt most able at present to manage the same. And yet, for all that, I do not find that he doth meddle in other men's offices further than to contribute his assistance for the better despatch of his Majesty's affairs. I can therein say for myself that, as soon as I came to Court, he did in a very friendly and generous manner deliver to me all things that belonged to my place; which in my absence he executed in a very friendly manner and with much respect and kindness for me. And I may tell you truly, that I am glad of and find ease in his assistance in the business that related to my employment; wherein his experience and knowledge of the present state of business is a great advantage to me in performance of my duty in such things as are incumbent upon me, so as, though others may think me therein a cypher, because my friend assists me in it, yet I assure you I take it for a great, and it is a singular, contentment to me.[46]

It was a remarkable testimonial to Sir Edward Hyde from his closest colleague, but the back-biting went on against him, and so long as royalists were so bitterly divided among themselves, their cause was gravely weakened.

No doubt Hyde was partly at fault. His sharp tongue and natural exuberance offended. For instance, the earl of Norwich made it plain to Nicholas in May 1655 that, although a member of the Council, he was reluctant to join the king because of his dislike of Hyde. He wrote that Hyde's 'overvaluing himself and undervaluing others, together with his grasping at too much, hath and will, if it be permitted, bring irrecoverable inconveniences, if not ruin, to affairs'. He added however that

I think him, as Secretary Nicholas doth, a very honest, right principled man in the main, and shall ever do him and his the best service I can, though not rely upon or submit unto his rules, as perhaps he may expect.[47]

What divided so many men from Hyde, apart from conflicts of personality, was their conviction that if the royalists were to succeed, they must seek allies, whether among Presbyterians, Independents or Levellers. This was why Hyde referred to the Louvre party as 'the Presbyterian gang'. But Hyde always fought shy of such connections, believing, in the light of the experience of events after 1642, that such bargaining could only be detrimental to the fundamentals of Anglicanism and Monarchy. He believed that one day the nation would again turn to the Monarch because he was necessary for constitutional stability, and that half-baked alliances would do more harm than good. The earl of Norwich thought otherwise, and wrote to Nicholas in June 1655 that Hyde was

certainly a most unfortunate man, though I can never believe him a dishonest, for you will never find that any party, be it Presbyter, Independent or Cavalier, will be contented to come under *his* government; and remember I tell you so, who truly am so far from wishing him the least ill, as that I would serve him and his with all my heart.[48]

The bitterness and hostility of the Louvre party, not only towards Hyde, but even the king himself, increased when Charles left Paris. Lord Hatton, who remained in Paris, but was a friend of Secretary Nicholas, and kept him informed of events there, wrote that there were among them 'base persons that, to do a displeasure to Sir Edward Hyde and honest men, would destroy the king and his affairs'.[49] Relations between Charles and his mother came to a crisis in the autumn of 1654 over her plans for the duke of Gloucester, now aged fourteen. In October the duke's tutor, Lovell, wrote to the king the startling news that he had been dismissed by the queen, and that she intended to effect the boy's conversion to Catholicism.[50] This was confirmed by Lord Hatton on the 20th:

I do assure you the Papists are already busy with their old prophecy that Henry IX must repair what Henry VIII ruined. My hand trembles . . . Believe it, Sir, no minute must be lost for prevention, and no middle way will do it. Certain it is the Queen did lately tell the Duke of Gloucester that the return to England was laid out of her thoughts and all wise men's, and that there was no way left him to rise but his book and the Church.[51] [Her objective was clearly a cardinalate for her son.]

The boy was then to be sent to receive instruction from the Jesuits. At the news Hyde wrote that 'never in his life did he see the King in so great trouble and perplexity'. On 10 November Charles wrote to his mother that if the story was true, 'he cannot expect she either believes or wishes his return to England', since the news of the duke's conversion would have disastrous consequences among his Protestant subjects, who must suppose that he had consented to the instruction.[52] He wrote also an impassioned letter to Lord Jermyn that if he did not use all possible means to prevent it, he need not think ever to hear from the king again. He despatched Ormond with these letters, and with instructions to bring his brother away from France. The queen was unrepentant, declaring that she had a higher duty even than that to the king, but she met with unexpected resistance, not only from Gloucester, who remained loyal to 'the last words of his dead father', but also from Jermyn and the Louvre party, who had been shaken by the threat contained in the king's letter. She made a final attempt to persuade the duke to go to the Jesuits, but when he refused, she gave up, and Ormond left Paris in December, escorting the prince to Antwerp. The whole incident had further soured relations between the king and the Louvre party, and henceforth he rarely corresponded with them. Lord Hatton had warned Nicholas of the dangers of the king's letters to the queen, since she usually read them aloud to the company, and any information contained in them would speedily be transmitted to London. Henceforth the queen's party were largely in ignorance of the king's plans.

That their attitude verged now upon disloyalty was shown by an incident recounted by Sir George Ratcliffe, who had been merely the bearer of a letter from the king to the queen. For this he was soundly berated by Lord Jermyn. Radcliffe replied that he had been merely the bearer of a letter, but

his Lordship told me that it was in my power to have the king's command or not to have it; I might have chosen whether I would have it or no . . . My lord said I might have excused myself from obeying it . . . that allegiance does not extend to all things.[53]

From such incidents it was clear that the queen was becoming as big a millstone around the neck of her son as she had been around the neck of her husband.

How much of the queen's hatred was focused upon Hyde was revealed a few months later when her daughter, the Princess of Orange offended her. The princess had been kind to Lady Hyde in finding her a house at Breda; and, taking a liking to Hyde's daughter Anne, invited her to become one of her ladies-in-waiting. Hyde was reluctant to agree, but gave way to persuasion. The news however enraged the queen, and in July 1655 Lord Hatton wrote that she would not rest until the girl had been dismissed.[54] Hyde wrote to Lady Stanhope, the princess's principal lady, that his fears had been justified, and that 'my poor girl' would be a serious cause of conflict between the queen and the princess.[55] However the princess would not give way, and once again the queen had to accept defeat. Lady Hyde then gave up her house in Breda and moved to Cologne with her husband, and the following year their fifth child was born.[56]

Cromwell made peace with the Dutch in April 1654. His prestige in Europe was high, and he was in the happy position of finding his alliance sought by both Spain and France, each against the other. With a fleet of 160 ships and a large army, he could either continue an active foreign policy, or concentrate upon a peaceful settlement at home and the disbandment of a part of his forces. Lambert was for the latter policy, but at a council in July 1654 Cromwell came down in favour of the Western Design, namely an attack on the Spanish West Indies, with the prospect of captured treasure, together with the comfortable belief that the will of God was being done in aiming a blow at the leading Catholic power. This policy would entail a restoration of good relations with France, and the expulsion of the Stuarts from French territory. In August Admiral Penn and Colonel Venables received instructions to attack the Spaniards by land and sea, and they were sent off to attack Hispaniola, and ultimately to effect the conquest of Jamaica. In November 1655 the Treaty of Westminster completed the alliance with France. The Spanish, still at war with France, did all they could to avoid war with England, and for months refused to regard the English attack on the West Indies as an act of war. Thurloe wrote that they sat helplessly waiting to hear where the blow would fall, their only defence being the belief that God would not let them be defeated. Not until March 1656 did they actually declare war on England.

This seemed to provide the royalists with a new opportunity. As early as August 1655 Hyde had written to Don Luis de Haro, the Spanish minister suggesting aid for the king, 'A small countenance from a powerful friend will give such life to those who are only waiting for such a conjuncture that too much cannot be expected from it'.[57] The Spanish government still hoped to avoid war and made no reply but Hyde persisted. He wrote to Sir Henry de Vic, Charles's envoy in Brussels, suggesting that the king should come to Brussels, even without a formal invitation, and he boosted the possibilities of 'kindling a fire in Ireland and Scotland, as well as England, and so make work for Cromwell at home'.[58] The Spaniards procrastinated until March, when Charles was permitted to come to Bruges, accompanied by the marquis of Ormond. In April they completed a secret treaty, whereby the Spaniards promised 6000 troops and sufficient transport for an invasion of England, when the king should be in possession of a suitable port in England. Charles in return agreed that when he regained his throne he would help Spain against the Portuguese, would return all West Indian conquests, and would suspend the penal laws against the Catholics.[59] Charles certainly regarded the treaty as a great achievement, and wrote to Hyde that it would make him 'caper in spite of his gout'. Hyde replied that it was the most cheerful news he had received for seven years.[60] Not the least achievement was that Philip IV agreed to pay Charles an allowance of 6000 guilders a month, with 3000 guilders for the support of the duke of Gloucester. Charles was also permitted to raise four regiments on Spanish soil, which, pending the invasion of England, would be available to aid the Spaniards. The commands were given to Ormond, Wentworth, Rochester and Newburgh, and as Ormond's name was sufficient to induce some eight hundred Irish to leave French service and join the king, this greatly increased his prestige, and was a bonus for the Spaniards. It also entailed Charles severing his remaining connections with France. He now refused his French pension, and the duke of York was required to leave French service and join the king in Bruges. With him came the earl of Bristol, who rapidly earned high praise from the Spaniards for his military prowess. It was Bristol who suggested to Charles that Henry Bennett should be sent as envoy to Spain, an event which had important consequences for Hyde later.

Meanwhile a spy had been discovered at Charles's Court. Henry Manning was a handsome young Catholic, the son of a royalist colonel who had been killed at Alresford, where the son himself was also wounded. He came to the king at Cologne about January 1655, with, as Clarendon wrote, 'a store of good clothes and plenty of money'. He said that he had disposed of his father's estate, and wished only to avenge his father's death in the service of the king. Hyde's suspicions were at once aroused, because he said he brought with him offers of help from the earl of Pembroke, which Hyde (who knew Pembroke well) disbelieved. Hyde warned the king, but Manning's charm prevailed, and he was always seeking to know royalist plans so that he himself could be in the thick of the conflict. When the king went to Zeeland secretly at the time of the projected royalist risings, Cromwell at once learnt of it, and suspicion fell on Manning. Letters were intercepted at Antwerp, and Manning's letters to

Thurloe were discovered. Arrested on 5 December 1655, and faced with the letters, Manning confessed that he had written to them for money. Some of the information contained in the letters was a fabrication, describing Council meetings which never took place, with the purpose of inflating Manning's importance, but he also gave the names of royalist agents who were subsequently arrested in England. Manning was closely interrogated by Ormond, Culpepper and Nicholas, found guilty of treachery, and sentenced to death. Manning's pathetic letters to Nicholas begging for mercy did him no good, and about 15 December he was taken to a wood outside Cologne by Sir James Hamilton and Major Armorer, and shot. The Cologne authorities, if they knew of it, were complacent, and the main fear was that Cromwell might take reprisals upon royalist agents, but this did not happen. Manning was by no means the only spy Thurloe had about the king, but he was the only one to be exposed and to pay the full penalty.[61]

In May 1655 Manning's letter of intelligence to Thurloe announced that royalist hopes were now pinned on an alliance with the Levellers, and that there was a plot afoot to assassinate Cromwell.[62] There was a germ of truth in this. Colonel Edward Sexby had served in Cromwell's army, and had been one of the leading 'agitators' in 1647. He served the Commonwealth in various capacities, in Scotland and abroad, but broke with Cromwell at the establishment of the Protectorate, and thereafter became his inveterate enemy. He took a leading part in the rising in the west country in 1655, and narrowly escaped arrest. The approaching Anglo-Spanish conflict gave him a new opportunity. His hostility to Cromwell was such that he was ready to contemplate alliance with any who would further the Protector's downfall. The royalist Sir Robert Phelipps met him in Antwerp in May 1655, and wrote to Nicholas: 'I am fallen into an acquaintance with a most eminent Leveller . . . He told me that, if things were handsomely managed, the King and Kingdom both might receive great benefit thereby. . . . I will assure you he is the principal man of that faction now out of Cromwell's power'.[63] Nicholas, who had earlier had contacts with John Lilburne, and well understood the Leveller attitude, pointed out that he might equally well be one of Cromwell's spies. Phelipps had further talks with Sexby in June, and was much impressed with his attitude. Sexby claimed to have 'so great an interest both in the army, city and country that indubitably they should be able to pull down that false perjured rogue Cromwell'. He admitted honestly that 'he could not say what advantage the king would reap thereby, for that they do but abuse the king who persuade him that their intent is to establish him'. He admitted that a restoration of the monarchy would be difficult, but he said that he had no objection to it so long as the supremacy of parliament was established, and so long as those who had bought crown, episcopal or delinquents' lands were secure in their possession. Phelipps wrote that the alternative to a royalist-Leveller alliance might be a Presbyterian-Leveller alliance, which would exclude the royalists for ever.[64] This was his chief concern, but it was obvious that Sexby's conditions, honestly stated as they were, were hardly inviting to the royalists. It was also clear that Sexby was a good deal more interested in obtaining Spanish help than the modest help the royalists could offer. From Spain he asked £150,000 to effect the overthrow of Cromwell. Fuensaldagna, the Spanish Secretary in Brussels, was interested, and sent the plan to Madrid. The Pope's Nuncio was also interested in view of the Levellers' endorsement of religious toleration, and Father Peter Talbot, titular Archbishop of Dublin, an egregious busybody, repeatedly pressed the royalist-Leveller alliance upon both the king and Hyde.

Sir Marmaduke Langdale, who had great credit with the royalists in England, took over the discussions with Sexby in June 1655. In September however he warned the king of the dangers of an alliance with any party 'which had been in blood against your Majesty', and urged: 'for God's sake beware of letting your own friends any more appear in arms, unless they have either a foreign army to countenance them, or some considerable party of the army to join them'.[65] This was the lesson drawn from the failure of the Penruddock rising. However, negotiations continued, not only with Sexby, but also with Richard Overton, who expressed his pleasure in the king's 'affections to the public'.[66] For a time Sexby disappeared on a secret mission to Madrid, and when he returned there was evident disagreement between him and Overton. The latter found him 'very peevish', and Sexby told him that 'if they should but offer to join with any of the king's party, it would ruin the design'. His attempts to win Spanish aid made little progress, and by December 1655 Nicholas was writing that he found Sexby 'no better than an agent of Cromwell, or at least no friend to the King's interest'. Henceforth Sexby concentrated upon plans to assassinate Cromwell, which Secretary Nicholas refused to endorse in any way. Like Hyde, he had no objection to the assassination of the Protector, and indeed wrote that those who effected it would certainly be well rewarded,[67] but he refused to be a party to it, or in any way to involve the king's name. Sexby, himself a master of disguises, was in England in June 1656, to discuss the seizure of Portsmouth with Wildman and Sir Robert Shirley, but as Wildman was in Thurloe's pay, the plan was not likely to succeed. Thurloe had a further success in the summer of 1656 when he enlisted in his service no less a person than Sir Richard Willis, a member of the Sealed Knot. Willis had come to the conclusion that the royalist cause was hopeless, and being always heavily in debt, he was ready to sell royalist information. In general he would not write letters, but met Thurloe or his agents in London taverns. He would not divulge information which would actually endanger the lives of royalists, but henceforth any general royalist rising could not take place without Thurloe being forewarned.

Meanwhile Sexby enlisted Miles Sindercombe and two associates to kill Cromwell at the opening of parliament in September 1656. At the last moment their nerve failed them, but they produced another plan to kill him in Hyde Park. This also failed, so in January 1657 they produced a Guy Fawkes plan to blow up the Protector and set fire to Whitehall. The plot was discovered and Sindercombe and Cecil were arrested. Cecil revealed the whole plot, and it became clear that Cromwell's life had been in danger for months.

From the first Hyde regarded the discussions with the Levellers with considerable reserve, believing that no good could come of them, and fearing that his colleagues would commit the king to making dangerous concessions. In December 1656 Sexby submitted a plan to the king, saying that he did not mind whether the royalists or the Levellers began a rising against Cromwell, but that if it were to be the Levellers, there must be no mention of the restoration of the king until after Cromwell was destroyed. This confirmed Hyde's worst fears, and he drew up instructions to govern future relations with the Levellers:

If any such proposition be made in order to the obliging Sexby's party, as implies great alterations in the Church or State, as lessening the power of the Crown, and devolving an absurd power to the people, or if overtures be made for the pardoning any of those who had immediate hands in the murder of his Majesty's Father, it will be easily made to appear that it is impossible for his Majesty to promise any alteration of the fundamental Government of the Kingdom.

The king, he wrote, would not make extravagant promises 'as the Monarchical interest cannot be preserved by giving any satisfaction to the Republican, nor the Episcopal or Catholic interest with complying with the Presbyterian'. He was convinced that neither the Republican nor the Presbyterian interest could succeed on their own, and that the royalists remained ultimately the only alternative to the Protectorate, and it was essential therefore that they should not compromise their position.[68] Captain Titus at Amsterdam was Hyde's main informant on Sexby's exploits, and he sent him details of the failure of the Sindercombe plot which fully confirmed the wisdom of Hyde's stand. Sexby showed Titus the optimistic letters he received from England, and till the end continued his plots to kill Cromwell. The two men probably combined to write a pamphlet entitled *Killing no Murder*, which Hyde read in May 1657 with considerable pleasure because of its witty presentation. He had no idea who wrote it, but was amused at its dedication to Cromwell.[69]

Sexby dared to return to England in June, but as he was embarking for Holland in 1657 he was betrayed and arrested. He made a full confession of his activities, and died in prison without trial in January 1658. There were no more serious plots against Cromwell's life.

# The End of the Commonwealth

Superficially Cromwell's government appeared strengthened and confirmed by the failure of the Penruddock rising. In January he dissolved his troublesome parliament. From the summer he enforced a much stricter control of the press, so that *Mercurius Politicus* and *Publick Intelligencer* were the only permitted newspapers. In October he issued a misnamed *Declaration against the Royal Family of the Stuarts*, forbidding delinquents to possess arms or to keep Anglican chaplains or schoolmasters. When Archbishop Ussher went to him to seek an indulgence from the harsh penalties of the law, Cromwell received him kindly, but 'told him that he had been advised by his council not to grant any indulgence to men who were restless and implacable enemies to his person and government'.[1] Above all, from August onwards he issued commissions to the Major-Generals to suppress 'all Tumults, Insurrections, Rebellion, or other unlawful Assemblies', and to prohibit 'horse-races, cock-fightings, bear-baitings, state-plays, or any unlawful Assemblies . . . forasmuch as Treason and Rebellion is usually hatched and contrived against the State upon such occasions'; they should also be concerned for the poor, suppress drunkenness and blasphemy, and keep a strict watch on persons coming from abroad. England was thus subjected to a form of military government such as it had never known before, and to a central authority far more potent than that of the Stuarts. In one sense it was an abnegation of parliamentary government, and in another it was an admission of the strength of the threat of the enemies which opposed it. Cromwell might boost his prestige by posing as the European defender of Protestantism, and declaring war on Spain (October 1655), but if he could not obtain general acceptance at home, his regime would always be in danger.

Since he had dissolved parliament in January 1655, he was under no obligation to call another one until 1658, but he summoned one for September 1656, mainly to deal with the desperate financial situation, but also to make further progress towards constitutional stability. Again unwanted members were excluded from taking their seats; some hundred were forcibly excluded, and some fifty or sixty more voluntarily abstained. No king ever dared to act in this way, and once again the nation was reminded that the regime rested upon force. To parliament Cromwell identified the enemies. Spain was 'a natural enemy', but at home they included the Levellers, Commonwealthsmen and Fifth Monarchists, while Charles Stuart, with the aid of Spain, was preparing an army for invasion. Such threats would justify the existence of the Major-Generals and the continued rule of the army, but they also made the financial problem more urgent.

For a time the House turned aside to deal with the unfortunate James Naylor. They were hostile to the growth of the sectaries, and in particular the Quakers. Naylor was a follower of George Fox, and was an eloquent preacher with an extraordinary power over women. At Bristol he re-enacted Christ's entry into Jerusalem, riding on an ass to the acclamation of his hysterical admirers. Parliament considered the case, was appalled at the story, and ordered Naylor to be pilloried, whipped, branded, to have his tongue bored with a hot iron, and to suffer perpetual imprisonment. Apart from humanitarian considerations, Cromwell was concerned to know by what constitutional authority they had acted, but the sentence was carried out all the same. Some members however did show contrition. Colonel Sydenham, member for Dorset declared,

We live as Parliament but for a time, but we live as Englishmen always. I would not have us be so tender of the privileges of Parliament as to forget the liberties of Englishmen . . . We have not a power here to do as we please.[2]

In January 1657 the House was alarmed at the discovery of the Sindercombe plot, and again the issue of security was raised. Downing, the member for Carlisle argued that

Governments are best which are upon proof and long experience of our ancestors, such whereby the people may understand their liberty, and the Lord Protector his privileges . . . I cannot propound a better expedient for the preservation, both of his Highness and the people, than by establishing the government upon the old and tried foundation.

This was carried further on 23 February when Sir Christopher Pack, a rich Merchant Adventurer and member for the City, introduced a Remonstrance calling on Cromwell to settle the succession and assume the title and dignity of king. Some furious debating followed, the opposition being led by Lambert. Cromwell spoke on 7 March, declaring that 'for his part he loved the title of king, a feather in a hat, as little as they did'; but he urged that the constitution needed 'a check or balancing power' to offset the power of the Commons, and this required a Supreme Magistrate and a second chamber, as witness the case of James Naylor. On the 25th the House persisted with a resolution that the Protector be pleased to assume the title of King of England, and two days later they presented Cromwell with the Humble Petition and Advice, the Speaker urging him to accept the crown. The Protector asked for time to consult God and his own heart.[3] It was widely assumed that he would accept, but Colonel Desborough told him bluntly that if he accepted, neither he,

Lambert nor Fleetwood would any longer support him. Finally in a speech to the House in the Banqueting Hall on 8 May, Cromwell refused the title of king, but agreed to the remaining provisions of the Humble Petition and Advice. His title would be 'Lord Protector of the Commonwealth'; a second chamber would be created; all royalists were disfranchised, and the revenue was fixed at £1,300,000, £1,000,000 for the armed forces and £300,000 for government, 'no part thereof to be raised by a land tax'. This settled, parliament went into recess.

The arrest of Sexby in July removed the most dangerous of Cromwell's enemies, but a conspirator named Gardiner was taken in Whitehall in August, with two pistols intended for his assassination. The Fifth Monarchists had been neutralised by the arrest of their leaders, Harrison, Courtney, Carew, Rogers and Feake. These were however released from prison in 1656, and conspiracies at once began again, centred in All Hallows in Swan Alley, and Coleman Street, where Feake preached that Cromwell's government was no different from that of Charles I. But Fifth Monarchists were losing ground as the reign of King Jesus seemed indefinitely deferred. However a few fanatics remained, and Thomas Venner, a wine-cooper, and his Coleman Street congregation, planned a rising for April 1657. But many Fifth Monarchists prudently refused to take part without a clear sign from God. No such sign appeared; Thurloe's spies kept him fully informed of the plans, and when the saints attempted to assemble at Mile End Green, they were arrested, and Venner was sent to the Tower, where he remained until 1659. He was to lead a more dangerous rising in January 1661, before the Fifth Monarchist movement finally died away.

The royalists were greatly confused over the prospect of Cromwell's assumption of the crown. Hyde feared it above all things because he saw it as a step towards a return to tradition and normality which would make a Stuart Restoration more difficult. Other royalists however thought that it would be the signal for an army revolt against Cromwell, which would give royalists and Levellers their chance. But this hope was rapidly dispelled, and Sir Allan Broderick wrote to Hyde in June 1657, that there was 'at present a general tranquillity in this nation', those who opposed the assumption of the crown being pleased that they had defeated it, and those who supported it convinced that they would achieve their aim next session.[4] Much of Hyde's time was spent in the fruitless task of trying to extract greater aid from the Spaniards. Although the Sealed Knot were as opposed as ever to further risings, there were many royalists in England who thought otherwise. The king wrote to the earl of Bristol in July 1657:

Every week brings me letters from my friends in England, to know against what time I will expect them to be ready, and what they may depend upon from me; and if this winter pass without any attempt on my part, I shall take very little pleasure in living till the next.[5]

Hope had somehow to be kept alive, but, so long as Cromwell lived, action seemed more unlikely than ever. In September Hyde wrote to Nicholas that money was so lacking that at dinner the king was being asked 'to content himself with one dish.' To Rumbold, one of the most useful of his contacts in England, he wrote complaining that 'our friends want so much confidence in each other that they rarely confer together or send us advice, and simply awaited 'some extraordinary act of providence', rather than taking action. He continued that if the king were to land without a general rising, 'he would be overpowered as he was at Worcester, whilst all men sat still and looked for the effect of the first battle'. Hyde indeed had to speak with two voices. He must encourage the royalists in England to all the activity of which they were capable, while secretly realising that there was little which could be done. Secretary Nicholas, who still favoured the assassination of Cromwell as the best hope for the royalists, received Hyde's gentle reproof when he wrote:

You and I shall never differ in opinion in what should be done with or against Cromwell, yet there will or may be very honest and very wise men who dissent from us in the particular you mention [i.e. assassination], and give very solid reasons for doing so, which will not deserve to be thought fond fancies. [13 September 1657][6]

Hyde's attitude during these years must have been very difficult for his contemporaries to understand, and this had much to do with the hostility he incurred from so many royalists. For to them he appeared always to be opposing other men's points of view, opposed to those who favoured an alliance with the Presbyterians, or the expeditions to Scotland, or understandings with the Levellers, or assassination plots, or the political manoeuvres of the queen and the Louvre party. It seemed a natural inference that he wished to keep the reins of power entirely in his own hands. There was truth in this, for the king was often beset by hare-brained schemes of courtiers which could only do harm. But beyond this there was in Hyde's mind a conviction which few men understood, that the restoration of the monarchy was ultimately inevitable, because it lay in the logic of history, or, in different terminology, because it was the will of providence. Men might help or hinder the process, but they could not direct it, because they could never be certain of the consequences of anything they did. Thus he wrote to Nicholas in October 1657:

For his Majesty's journey into Scotland, you were against it, and if I had been with you I should as much have dissuaded it, yet I think neither you nor I do now wish that he had not gone, and if he had not, he would have been thought to have overslipped an opportunity to have recovered his three kingdoms. You were for the King's journey hither [to Brussels] and I against it, yet I know no reason that you should repent your advice since you thought it the most probable to produce good effects; and I am sure I have reason to be glad he came. If he had not, would not all the world have said, if he had followed his own business all would have been well?

When we have faithfully advised what to our understanding is best, let us not be out of love with it because it hath not success.[7]

As the king's minister, Hyde must encourage royalist activity wherever feasible, but his inclination was to await the guidance of Providence. The cold douch which he had to administer to many half-baked ideas made enemies of men like the earl of Norwich, who wrote, 'Whilst Sir E.H. thus absolutely stands at the helm, you will hardly see many that will pull at a rope or manage a sail, for 'tis not now a time to compliment when all lies at stake.'[8] Like many royalists, Norwich was hungry for office and responsibility at a time when the king had little to give, and he vented his spleen on Hyde.

In 1657–8 Hyde and Nicholas needed all the philosophy they could command, for the king's situation appeared dark indeed. In spite of the treaty with the Spanish, no money had been received by August 1657 and the king was treated with scant respect, and with an obvious unwillingness to help him in launching an attack on England, even if such a project had been feasible. Nicholas placed part of the blame on the king who often seemed more intent upon the delights of Spanish society than on the business in hand. He wrote that 'till the King shall himself take more majesty on him, he will always . . . find every day more and more neglect and disesteem . . . We are not sensible enough of our afflictions, but endeavour to spend our days in pleasure, while the hand of God is on us, which prolongs our punishment.'[9] Ormond also complained of the king's 'immoderate delight in empty, effeminate and vulgar conversations [which] is become an irresistible part of his nature'.[10] Nicholas, like Hyde, always believed that royalist misfortunes had been God's judgment upon them. In fairness to Charles it must be said that there was little for him to do. A treaty between Cromwell and the French for a joint expedition against Spanish Flanders had been followed by a successful campaign in which Mardyke was captured in October. The royalists fought on the Spanish side, and Charles, in his longing for action, accompanied Don Juan during the defence of Mardyke; and the marquis of Ormond, who was with him, had his horse shot under him. Not only Hyde, but the Spaniards, protested at the unnecessary risk to the royal person, and Charles returned ruefully to Brussels.[11]

Spanish resources were stretched to the limits, and there was little enough they could spare Charles, but the attack on Mardyke did spur them to offer him 150,000 crowns if he could acquire a suitable port for a landing in England.[12] But the chance of this appeared small, for there was a vicious circle: the Spaniards were unwilling to offer money until a rising in England was certain, and Charles could not begin an attempt on England without money and transport, and until the Sealed Knot were willing to rise. The Spanish would value the king in proportion to the difficulties he could make for Cromwell, and these appeared to be slight. There were troops and seamen ready to join the king, if only he had the money to pay them, but in November

Charles was writing to the Princess of Orange to beg for a jewel he might pawn for £1500, so desperate was he for money.[13]

However, the king, Ormond, Hyde and Nicholas all agreed that a rising must be attempted during 1658 if they were to retain credibility with the Spanish, and in December 1657 Hyde was busy drafting a Proclamation to be issued when the king set out for England, promising government according to law, a general pardon for all except regicides, the summoning of parliament, and a Church settlement with the advice of the clergy and parliament.[14] Information from England was so confused that Ormond offered to go to assess the situation: if a rising seemed possible, he would encourage it, if not 'he would compose them to be quiet'. Hyde characteristically opposed the journey as being far too dangerous, but Ormond brushed this aside, and the king agreed to the mission. The great need was secrecy, and it was given out that Ormond was going to Cologne to recruit troops. Instead he slipped away to Holland, and hiring a bark, he landed on the Essex coast. He played his part superbly, using disguises, and fitting in naturally with whatever society he found himself in. In London he was concealed by Sir Philip Honywood, and met a group of royalists at an apothecary's shop, but he soon found that they had no plans for a rising. He met some members of the Sealed Knot, including Colonel Russell and Sir Richard Willis, but they were chiefly concerned with emphasising the difficulties in the way of action. He discussed the possibility of seizing Hull, or Bristol, or Shrewsbury, but found the royalists in such confusion, with some refusing to speak to others. Hyde had set great store on a rising in the west country, but it was clear that there were no plans in progress. He heard that Lord Saye and Colonel Richard Norton were ready to support the monarchy on conditions, but Ormond did not consider bargaining a part of his task. In Sussex a young royalist, John Stapley was eager to organise a rising, and John Mordaunt was attempting the same in Surrey, but Ormond did not trouble to see them for without much more effective organisation a general rising was impossible. Ormond found plenty of hostility towards the Protectorate, but the royalists were too divided and suspicious of each other for effective action. He did however come to the conclusion that the earlier policy of seeking an agreement with Sexby and the Levellers had been a mistake, and that the royalists might now seek an alliance with the Presbyterians. But he was in great personal danger, for Sir Richard Willis, a member of the Sealed Knot, had probably informed Cromwell of his presence in England, although he would not reveal where he might be found. Ormond decided there was no more to be done, and after a month's stay in England he made his way through Sussex, guided by the king's physician, Dr Quartermaine, and made his escape to France, reporting to the king on 18 February that no rising in England was yet possible.[15]

Daniel O'Neill, who had accompanied Ormond to England, stayed on to make further contacts and to explore the possibility of a Presbyterian alliance,

..nd on 24 March he sent Hyde a graphic description of his findings. He wrote that he had met several members of the Sealed Knot; that they were either very reserved towards him, or were very ill-informed of the king's situation; that they trusted few, and were themselves mistrusted by the more ardent royalists; that their only idea of a rising seemed to be to get on their horses to join the king once he should have landed. With great difficulty he persuaded a number of royalists from Bristol, Gloucester, Windsor and Shrewsbury to meet him. The first half-hour was spent in 'venting their discontents' against Hyde for encouraging preparations for a rising, when he knew that the king could not come; and also against Ormond, for coming, since his visit had so alarmed Cromwell that both royalists and Presbyterians had suffered for it. It was clear that 'those that have their estates and liberty, negotiate by halves', and that there would be no rising without specific orders from the king.[16]

Since the failure of the attempts to reach an understanding with Sexby and the Levellers, some royalists had come to the belief that they should seek an alliance with the Presbyterians, since in their opposition to Independency, Levellers and Fifth Monarchists, some Presbyterians were coming round to the idea of a restored monarchy. John Mordaunt strongly supported the idea, believing that a rising in England was impossible without the support of such influential Presbyterians as the earl of Manchester, Lord Denbigh, Lord Saye, Lord Robartes and Sir William Waller. Ormond had instructed Lord Belasyse to contact the earl of Manchester, but it was Manchester himself who first raised the question. A long conference followed, and O'Neal reported that it revealed a division of opinion among the Presbyterians. The moderates, like Manchester, Denbigh and Waller were content with the promise of their lives and estates, but others, led by Lord Saye and Lord Robartes wanted to insist upon the terms of the Newport Treaty offered to Charles I. He also noted a hostility towards Hyde:

There has been industry used to lessen your credit with the Presbyterians. I am told all comes from Palais Royal and their friends.

Hyde could afford to ignore the snub, for it was clear that no rising was possible for the time being in England, and that even if the king had an equipped invasion force, he would be unable to get it out of Ostend harbour past the waiting English fleet.[17] In England the news of Ormond's presence had been followed by a general round-up of royalist suspects. Thurloe uncovered a plot for a rising in London, the leaders of which were mostly merchants like Robert Manley and John Sumner. Some forty or fifty people were arrested, six were condemned to death, and three actually executed. Sir Henry Slingsby, found guilty of trying to suborn the garrison of Hull to betray the city, and Dr John Hewitt, the incumbent of St Gregory's in St Paul's Churchyard, an active royalist agent, who had so recently been begging Hyde for the future reward of a deanery, were both executed in June 1658. The luckiest of the accused was John Mordaunt, younger son of the earl of Peterborough, who was acquitted by the casting vote of the president of the court, after his wife had seen to it that the key witness against him was missing. He was a fervent royalist, and when he was released from prison he remained in London to work for the cause, and especially for an alliance with the Presbyterians. His arguments had considerable influence upon the king and Hyde, and he did much to undermine confidence in the continued usefulness of the Sealed Knot. His chief defect was an over-enthusiasm which meant that his despatches had usually to be discounted.

However inadequate royalist plots appeared to be, and in spite of Thurloe's police system, it was evident that the Protectorate was breaking down under internal strains. When the Commons met on 20 January 1658 the excluded members were allowed to take their seats, and the opposition led by Sir Arthur Hesilrige renewed their attacks. Cromwell warned the House of the dangers of a royalist invasion, but the Commons preferred to concentrate upon Cromwell's Other House. According to the Venetian envoy, some members declared that if they had wanted a king it would have been better to have recalled Charles Stuart, and there was talk of taking the armed forces out of the hands of the Protector. The Commonwealthsmen wanted a return to parliamentary sovereignty. It was becoming clear that there was a revulsion against a dictatorship of the Protectorate, and Cromwell was coming to realise that he could rule neither with nor without a parliament. With changing issues many earlier revolutionaries had now become men of moderation. This is well illustrated in the case of Lord Saye and Sele, once a fierce critic of Charles I. When invited by Cromwell to sit in the Other House he refused, writing to his friend Lord Wharton:

The Government of this Kingdom according to the right constitution thereof and execution agreeable thereunto, I think to be the best in the world; being a mixture of three lawful governments in that manner that it hath the quintessence of them all, and thereby also the one is a boundary unto the other, whereby they are kept from falling into the extremes which either are apt to slip into, Monarchy into Tyranny and Aristocracy into Oligarchy, Democracy into Anarchy; now the chiefest remedy and prop to uphold this frame and building and keep it standing and steady is . . . the Peers of England, and their power and privileges in the House of Lords, they have been as the beam keeping both scales, King and people, in an even posture, without encroachments one upon another to the hurt and damage of both. Long experience hath made it manifest that they have preserved the just rights and liberties of the people against the tyrannical usurpation of Kings, and have also as steps and stairs upheld the Crown from falling and being cast down upon the floor by the insolency of the multitude from the throne of government.[18]

But the authority of the peers had been destroyed, and was being replaced by a House nominated by one man. Might was now right: 'it is dominion if it succeed, but rebellion if it miscarry, a good argument for pirates upon the sea, and for thieves upon the highway, fitter for Hobbes and atheists than good men and Christians'. Hyde would have endorsed every word of this, for it was an argument for the return to the traditional constitution.

Attacked by supporters of 'the Good Old Cause' on the one side, and deserted by men of moderation on the other, broken in health and weary in spirit, Cromwell addressed the Commons on 4 February 1658. He declared that he had never sought the office of Protector:

> I would have been glad to have lived under my woodside, to have kept a flock of sheep rather than undertake such a place of government as this is; but undertaking it by the advice and petition of you, I did look that you that did offer it unto me should have made it good . . . I would not have accepted of the government unless I knew there would be a just reciprocation between the governor and the governed.[19]

He accused them of playing the game of 'the King of Scots', and with this reproof he dissolved them. In the following months the chief domestic concern was the succession of plots, both monarchist and Fifth Monarchist, and in May he set up a new High Court of Justice to try the suspects. The trial and execution of Dr Hewitt affected Cromwell's own family, for Cromwell's daughter Elizabeth Claypole was his friend, and the news of his execution was said to have hastened her own death a few weeks later. Cromwell's third daughter Mary, who had married Viscount Fauconberg, was similarly involved in an attempt to save the life of Sir Henry Slingsby. Abroad Cromwell's prestige remained high, for on 4 June his troops won a brilliant victory over the Spaniards at the Battle of the Dunes, and ten days later Dunkirk surrendered. But this did little to raise the gloom of Cromwell's last months. He had been ill for over a year, and he died on 3 September 1658, having nominated his son Richard as his successor.

Clarendon, who viewed Cromwell's career with the intense interest of a historian, as well as of an opponent, made no attempt to conceal his admiration for his achievements. He was, he wrote

> one of those men whom his very enemies could not condemn without commending him at the same time, for he could never have done half that mischief without great parts of courage and industry and judgment. And he must have had a wonderful understanding in the natures and humours of men, and as great a dexterity in applying them . . . Wickedness as great as his could never have accomplished those trophies, without the assistance of a great spirit, an admirable circumspection and sagacity, and a most magnanimous resolution.[20]

What fascinated Clarendon was the way in which Cromwell imposed taxation, punished dissidents, bullied judges and imprisoned counsel for the defence, far more effectively than Charles I had ever been able to do.[21] It seemed to him poetic justice that Cromwell should have tasted some of the intransigence of opposition such as he himself had displayed against the monarchy. It was a prodigious achievement to have reduced all three kingdoms to his obedience,

But his greatness at home was but a shadow of the glory he had abroad. It was hard to discover which feared him most, France, Spain or the Low Countries, where his friendship was current at the value he put upon it . . . There is nothing he could have demanded that either of them would have denied him.

Clarendon was grateful to Cromwell for his merciful treatment of the royalists:

He was not a man of blood, and totally declined Machiavel's method, which prescribes upon any alteration of a government, as a thing absolutely necessary, to cut off all the heads of those, and to extirpate their families, who are friends to the old one.

Clarendon thought that Cromwell's last months were clouded because in some sense he had lost his way:

Cromwell never had the same serenity of mind he had been used to after he had refused the crown, but was out of countenance and chagrin, as if he were conscious of not having been true to himself.[22]

These were Clarendon's thoughts recollected in tranquillity, but in September 1658 he had to be concerned with more immediate matters. There were great disillusionment and mutual recrimination among royalists at the failure to effect risings during the year, and his first fear was that royalists might rush into rash acts. It was true that, as one of his correspondents wrote, 'Dick Cromwell . . . sits like an ape on horseback', but the danger was that he might be unseated by Lambert, who would be a greater danger, or, worse still, that the Commonwealth might be restored. Thus he wrote to Rumbold, 'We know very well that this good change must be attended with other alterations, before any eminent fruit will appear to the King; and his Majesty doth not expect that his friends should do any rash thing for him.'[23] Secretary Nicholas hurriedly drafted a Declaration of Charles II offering a free pardon to all except regicides who should support the king's restoration, but it was never published.[24] Hyde had to restrain the enthusiasm of men such as the earl of Bristol, who were for immediate action before any new regime could take root,[25] for he knew how feeble were the king's resources in the Low Countries. Instead, his advice to all his agents in England was to continue preparations for action, to concentrate upon winning allies, but also to see that, when a parliament should be called, the royalists should win seats. One other line of action was open to them. The king, Hyde, Ormond, Nicholas and Culpepper all agreed that the key to the future might well lie with General Monck in Scotland, and one of Hyde's correspondents reminded him that Sir John Grenville, a stout royalist in Devonshire, had Monck's brother as parson of his parish of Kilhampton in Cornwall, and enquired whether good use might not be made of the fact. Hyde at once drafted a letter from the king to Sir John Grenville:

I am confident that George Monck can have no malice in his heart against me, nor hath he done anything against me which I cannot very easily pardon.[26]

It was however some months before Grenville agreed to act.

The accession of Protector Richard was at once endorsed by the army, and Thurloe wrote with relief 'there is not a dog that wags his tongue, so great a calm are we in'; though he added that there were murmurings in the army 'as if his highness were not general of the army as his father was'.[27] Richard Cromwell was a gentle and harmless country gentleman, but Clarendon thought this a possible disadvantage to the royalists, since 'The dead is interred in the sepulchre of the kings . . . ; and his son inherits all his greatness and all his glory, without that public hate that visibly attended the other.'[28] One might despise Richard, but one could not hate him. The new Protectorate had certain advantages. Oliver Cromwell had quelled the leaders of the Levellers and Fifth Monarchists. 'Freeborn' John Lilburne was dead, Thomas Harrison and Robert Overton had been imprisoned, and other officers cashiered and silenced. The old religious fanaticism was losing its fire, and a new spirit of reasonableness (or materialism) was abroad. Hugh Peters, whose sermons had done so much to stoke up the fires of hatred in his Fast Sermons, admitted the change in his sermon to parliament in January 1658, 'He said religion was left by our ancestors (as, for instance, Smithfield and later times) hot, fiery hot; but it was now fallen into lukewarm hands. We do not boil up our religion to the height'.[29] When in the parliament of January 1658 it was suggested that a new convocation of divines might be summoned, it was opposed by a member named Highland:

I am glad to see such care of religion; but there is not that necessity at this time for an assembly. This is but calling them from feeding their flocks. Moral things are as necessary as religious. To feed and clothe the naked and oppressed. It is religion to pay your debts. Superstition is banished.[30]

Thus the new voice of the age of reason could already be heard in the land.

The ecclesiastical situation continued to be confused, but there was a steady swing away from the revolutionary tendencies of the 1640s. The initial attack on the Laudian bishops had been aimed against only a small number of prelates. It had led on to the abolition of episcopacy, the sequestration of church lands and the proscription of the Book of Common Prayer. But the efforts of the Westminster Assembly to substitute a Directory of Worship, combined with the Solemn League and Covenant, were a dismal failure. Scottish Presbyterianism was never acceptable to more than a small minority of English people, and the rise of Independency after 1647 defeated attempts at uniformity. County committees ruthlessly expelled about one-quarter of the 9000 incumbents in the country, but three-quarters of the clergy were undisturbed during the Interregnum. Many of them were low church Anglicans unaffected equally by Laudianism or extreme Puritanism. Many were able to insert parts of the Prayer Book into their services without causing comment. In 1654 Cromwell appointed a commission of Triers to test the qualifications of ministers for their godliness and zeal, but this was a test many moderate clergymen could survive. Many Anglican and royalist clergy did not scruple to take the 'Engagement' promising to be true and faithful to the Commonwealth, since they had no intention of joining in a rebellion. The bishops had been demoralised by the execution of Laud, and most were content to retire into rural obscurity, where Cromwell was prepared to leave them. But they also kept in touch with their clergy and quietly awaited better days. Anglican services were regularly available in London during the Protectorate, although with risks attached. When John Evelyn went to celebrate Christmas day 1657 at the service of Peter Gunning, one of the most popular preachers in London, at the chapel of Exeter House, the congregation found the chapel surrounded by troops, and they were questioned whether they were praying for Charles Stuart.[31] But this did not deter Gunning from continuing to hold his popular services. Brian Duppa of Salisbury continued an unobtrusive episcopate. Henry Hammond was the leading high church Anglican, whose death in 1660 prevented him from exercising his influence on the Restoration settlement, but there were many others, George Bull, Robert Sanderson, Jeremy Taylor, Ralph Brownrigg and Gilbert Sheldon, who quietly awaited a royal and Anglican restoration. When bishop Wren of Ely was released from prison he published his pamphlet *Monarchy Asserted* in answer to Harrington (1659).

In the search for church unity, Archbishop James Ussher in 1641 had proposed a modified form of episcopacy, with increased powers for presbyters, suggested by the early Christian Church of Ephesus.[32] In 1656 a group of moderate Anglicans, including Ussher, John Gauden and bishop Brownrigg met Secretary Thurloe with a view to bringing about an agreement between moderate Anglicans, Presbyterians and Independents. The Independents were obdurate, since they would not agree to any central control, but an agreement between moderate Presbyterians like Richard Baxter and Edward Reynolds on the one hand, and Archbishop Ussher and John Gauden on the other seemed possible. However nothing came of the meetings, but they mark a growing sense of need for a moderate compromise, for on the one hand Edward Reynolds denounced the 'boundless and universal liberty' practised by the sectaries, and on the other many moderate Anglicans like Gauden, Stillingfleet or Whichcote, felt that, although episcopacy was desirable, yet it was not essential to salvation, and that the necessary discipline might be attained another way. There was then under the Protectorate some drawing together of royalist-Anglicans and Presbyterians (although not yet agreement between them), both on ecclesiastical and political grounds, and the greater divide was between them and the Independents, who not only rejected ecclesiastical discipline, but also stood for the 'Good Old Cause' against both Protector and Monarch.

The Presbyterians had always accounted themselves monarchists in the 1640s, and the army judged Pride's Purge to be a necessary preliminary to the trial and execution of the king. With the fall of the monarchy, many Presbyterians accepted the situation, but some remained monarchists, and some went into exile. Their political leader, Denzil Holles, went into exile, but successfully resisted all royalist attempts to win him to the service of Charles II in the 1650–51 period, and in 1654 he accepted Cromwell's pass, and returned to live quietly in England. But a number of Presbyterians were involved in the royalist conspiracy of 1650; three prominent Presbyterian ministers of London, Christopher Love, William Jenkins and Thomas Case were arrested, and Love was executed.[33] During the 1650s Charles II could count on Lord Willoughby of Parham, Edward Massey, Richard Graves, Alderman James Bunce and Silas Titus as firm supporters among the Presbyterians. Yet it would be quite wrong to suggest that there was a royalist-Presbyterian alliance, for the distance between them was still great, and it was less theological than political. However much the royalists needed allies, if the Protectorate was to be overthrown, there was a great legacy of mistrust to be overcome before Hyde and his friends would accept a Presbyterian alliance except on their own terms. For it was the Presbyterians who had tried to impose the Covenant on Charles I and had shared in bringing about his downfall; while the Scottish Presbyterians had humiliated Charles II, showing that they intended that if he reigned, he should not rule. Moreover, when Ormond visited England early in 1658, he found the Presbyterians unprepared to act, and divided between those ready to accept the king, and those who wished to impose the old terms upon him. Moreover, many Presbyterians like John Glyn and John Maynard had apparently accepted the Protectorate. Presbyterians like Sir Richard Onslow, Lord Broghill and William Pierrepoint were among those who pressed Cromwell to accept the crown,[34] and the earl of Manchester and Lord Wharton, although favourable to Charles, consented to sit in Cromwell's Other House. The Presbyterians therefore, although veering in the direction of a conservative solution to constitutional and ecclesiastical problems, certainly did not in 1658–9 speak with one voice, or show any positive intention of restoring the monarchy. But the arguments in favour of a return to traditionalism were heard in the debates of January 1658 on Cromwell's Other House. Sir Arthur Hesilrige strongly opposed the creation of a second chamber:

The Commons of England will quake to hear that they are returning to Egypt, to the garlick and onions of a kingdom ... We are yet a Commonwealth.[35]

But Major Beake, member for Peterborough, thought differently:

The rule to bring us to stability is to have recourse to the ancient constitution . . . They that say 'Set not up a King, a House of Lords, for God has poured contempt upon them', let me retort upon them: God has also poured contempt upon a Commonwealth.

To which Sir Anthony Ashley Cooper made the enigmatic comment: 'Admit Lords, and admit all'. If the Protectorate foundered, this view would become the most likely alternative.

Financial pressures required Protector Richard to summon an early parliament. The new franchise introduced by the Instrument of Government was abandoned, and the parliament which met on 27 January 1659 was elected on the old franchise. The debates which ensued in the following weeks are some of the most interesting in the history of parliament. Sir Arthur Hesilrige led the campaign for a return to the Commonwealth. He glorified the achievements of the Long Parliament:

We were a glorious Parliament for pulling down. I hope this will be glorious for setting up.

Cromwell had been a usurper, and now was the time for a return to the sovereignty of the people. Henry Neville, member for Reading, on the other hand regarded the Long Parliament as 'an oligarchy, detested by all men that love a Commonwealth'.

We that are for a Commonwealth are for a single person, senate and popular assembly. I mean not King, Lords and Commons. I hope that will never be admitted here.

John Bulkeley, member for Christchurch, who had suffered exclusion by Pride's Purge, and had no fond memories of the Long Parliament, declared that 'he would not set the crown upon the head of the people', and concluded,

To acquiesce in that which they see is against the sense of the nation were madness.

Sir Arthur Hesilrige declared that there had been greater maladministration since 1654 than in five hundred years before; that when Charles I asked for £720,000 it was thought to be unreasonable, but that the current debt might be as high as £3,000,000. He then admitted that

the people care not what Government they live under, so as they may plough and go to market.

Colonel Briscoe agreed with him: 'All forms of Government are in themselves indifferent . . . [but] this Government of a single person is fitter for us.'[36]

The republicans had some effective speakers, but when it came to the vote Sir Arthur Hesilrige's motion was defeated by 217 : 86. The House was clearly in favour of government by one man, a House of Lords, and a House of Commons. But a traditional House of Lords was one thing; one nominated by the Protector, and filled with military men was another. There were lively fears expressed at the continued domination of the army. The army according to Ludlow was divided into three factions.[37] A considerable number of officers wanted a return to the Commonwealth; a second group, known as the Wallingford House party, headed by Fleetwood and Desborough, had at first endorsed Protector Richard, but had become disillusioned with him, and were seeking to replace him and a third group were prepared to accept him. On 6 April the Wallingford House party drew up a Remonstrance to the Protector, complaining of arrears of pay and the threat to the Good Old Cause, and demanding a remedy.[38]

The Remonstrance was at once attacked in parliament. Lord Falkland declared:

You have been a long time talking of three estates. There is a fourth which, if not well looked to, will turn us all out of doors. They have not only made resolutions, but have had the impudence to print them. I am against their meetings, and would have them suppressed.[39]

The House feared that another Pride's Purge was imminent. But they had no power to control the army, nor had they taken steps to reduce the deficit of over two million pounds, which might have met the army's grievances over arrears of pay.[40] Strengthened by the resolution of the House, Richard tried to dissolve the Council of officers. They refused to obey him, and Colonel Desborough went to the Protector 'and told him that if he would dissolve his Parliament, the officers would take care of him; but that, if he refused so to do they would do it without him, and leave him to shift for himself'.[41] Richard gave way, and dissolved parliament (22 April 1659). Whitelocke commented that the army remonstrance 'was the beginning of Richard's fall, and was set on foot by his relations', for Desborough was Richard's uncle by marriage, and Fleetwood was his brother-in-law.[42] And if the army was busy dismantling the Protectorate, the parliament had shown itself ineffectual in preserving it. Interesting though their consitutional discussions had been, they had not succeeded in passing a single act. Certain conclusions had however emerged, first that there was an overwhelming majority in favour of a mixed constitution; second that there had been an almost complete absence of religious issues discussed in the debates; and third, that there was a growing indifference to the particular form of government, so long as it worked, and so long as people could plough and go to market in peace.

Richard was now the helpless tool of the army. The Wallingford House party wished to continue a nominal Protectorate, governing without the aid of a parliament, but in the end they bowed to the wishes of the Commonwealths-men and recalled forty-two members of the old Rump which had last met in

April 1653. Thus Speaker Lenthall, Bulstrode Whitelocke, Alderman Pennington, Sir James Harrington, Edmund Ludlow, Sir Henry Vane and Sir Arthur Hesilrige again took their seats, but when the secluded members from Pride's Purge attempted to join them they found themselves still excluded. In May Protector Richard retired quietly into private life, the Commonwealth was restored and a Council of State of thirty-one members was set up, of whom only one, Sir Horatio Townshend, was a royalist.

During these weeks of rapid change there was little the royalists could do but wait upon events. Many had suffered severely from sequestration and decimation tax, and were demoralised by the failure of the Penruddock rising. However much they wished to see the return of the monarchy, they were not prepared to risk lives and estates in futile risings which could not hope to succeed against a powerful army. They were reluctant to join in conspiracies when anyone might be a spy, and they were often bitterly divided over personalities and tactics. The Sealed Knot were opposed to premature action, and resentful of younger hotheads. Hitherto Charles II's ministers had been inclined to seek an understanding with the Commonwealthsmen like Lilburne and Sexby, but now John Mordaunt, who had so recently escaped execution in England, and henceforth was one of Hyde's most active agents, pressed instead for an understanding with the Presbyterians, whom he regarded as men of moderation.[43] But the Presbyterians themselves were too divided to be regarded as a coherent party. Mordaunt had a poor opinion of the Sealed Knot, and wrote to Hyde:

I am sure we want a good pilot, and that want may be our ruin; our dissensions continue still amongst ourselves . . . Most persons named are upon the reserve, and so little consideration of duty to the King, that unless an angel should appear to them, I begin to fear their overwise cautiousness will not be satisfied.[44]

To these divisions between the more cautious and the more active royalists must be added further divisions stirred up by the queen's party, who bitterly resented the fact that the king had almost ceased to correspond with them, and who placed the blame squarely upon Hyde. In their hostility, some of them even discussed the possibility of replacing Charles by his brother James as the candidate for the throne, with French and Catholic help. One of Hyde's correspondents wrote in April 1659:

Your lordship cannot imagine the malice of the Lady Herbert against the good King, it is so great that it makes her unnatural . . . This woman hath belched out such devilish and damnable slanders, and makes it her daily practice so to do, that I shall but beget a trouble in you to send them. The Lady Newport is another of these jewels. These are two great trumpeters of the Duke of York, and I think they cannot do it emphatically enough but by railing at his Majesty . . . I hope to see the day when such cattle as these shall be whipped at the cart's tail.

George Morley, the future bishop of Worcester, had occasion to warn the duke that his many Roman Catholic friends could only do harm to the king's chance of restoration. All Hyde's efforts to win the aid of Catholics either in Rome or England had had scant success. He wrote to Mordaunt:

I know not how it comes to pass, but the Presbyterians gain much more credit with the Catholics than we do.[45]

The reason was however that they thought their chances of toleration greater from the moderate Presbyterians.

Hyde had a most difficult part to play in face of so much confusion. On the one hand he must be ready for any eventuality, which meant encouraging the activists in England, and for this he had four main agents and correspondents in Mordaunt, Rumbold, Titus, and Broderick. He must also be ready to seek alliances where they could be found, whether they were republican, Catholic or Presbyterian, but always with the proviso that the price of an alliance must not be to the detriment of the monarchy or the Anglican Church. But with so many divisions among the royalists he was never sanguine of their chances of making a successful rebellion in England, and he believed that the best hope lay in a free parliament which would peacefully restore the monarchy. He was encouraged by Sir William Waller's prediction that a free parliament would do just that. But behind all his thinking was the conviction that ultimately the restoration of the king was inevitable because it lay in the logic of history. It seemed so obvious to him that he wondered that Richard Cromwell, St John and Thurloe did not see it also, and combine to restore Charles at once.[46]

In March 1659 the king, mistrusting the zeal of the Sealed Knot, issued a secret commission to a committee of six, known as 'The Trust', to co-ordinate operations, consisting of Mordaunt, Lord Belasyse, Lord Loughborough, Colonel John Russell, Sir William Compton and Sir Richard Willis. Hyde assured Mordaunt that the arrangement was known only to the king, Ormond, Nicholas and himself. By May Mordaunt was able to report a wide network of royalist activity. Lynn was favoured as the port most likely to receive Charles, since Lord Willoughby and Sir Horatio Townshend were influential in Norfolk and Lincolnshire. Major-General Massey (who had once defended Gloucester against Charles I) and Captain Titus, after a mission to the west country, reported contacts with William Clayton of Bristol and Colonel Alexander Popham. Lord Newport was expected to seize Shrewsbury, and Sir George Booth to raise Cheshire. Sir Thomas Middleton was active in north Wales, Sir John Grenville in Cornwall, Sir Thomas Peyton and Sir William Waller in the south-east, and Lord Falkland, Mr Howe, John Talbot, Ralph Delaval and Lord Belasyse in areas between Oxfordshire and the north.[47] Mordaunt thought some of the royalists were very ready to leave the fighting to others, and he mistrusted also the Presbyterians, especially Major-General Brown.[48] Heedless of danger himself he could never understand the power which still remained with the Army, and the royalists' instinct for self-preservation.

Hyde trusted Sir Richard Willis, and could not understand why he so steadily opposed action. It was therefore a great shock to him to receive from Samuel Morland, one of Thurloe's subordinates, indisputable proof that Willis was a traitor. Morland sent letters which Willis had written to Thurloe under the surname of Thomas Barret, and it was clear that he had sold himself to Thurloe since 1656. Willis, a royalist from the beginning of the Civil War, rose to be a Major-General and Governor of Newark in 1645, but had then been replaced by Lord Belasyse. A bitter quarrel between the two men ensued, and it was unfortunate that ten years later they found themselves both members of the Sealed Knot. This rivalry was sufficient to cripple the organisation. Willis was always desperately short of money. The best that could be said for him was that he seems not to have endangered the lives of particular royalists. In June 1659 a royalist named Paul posted a placard in London charging Willis with being a traitor.[49] The news came at a most unfortunate time, and had a depressing effect on many royalists who now felt their lives in danger.

Mordaunt however pressed on with his plans for a general rising, and claimed to have an impressive list of promises from royalists in most counties. The problem was that most promises were contingent upon the king's early arrival in England, but the king's resources were so modest, and he was so lacking in transport, that he could not safely set out, at least until he had a secure port, either in Kent or at Lynn. Hyde warned Mordaunt that the chances of aid from France or Spain were slight, yet at the same time Mordaunt was writing:

Sir J. Grenville gave us last night an account of Cornwall and Devonshire. They are in a good posture, but not willing to engage unless some descent from abroad, or in order to second any attempt begun by others.

The same was true of most parts of the country. Another factor which Hyde had always to bear in mind was the exuberant optimism of Mordaunt, which always required considerable discount. Hyde gave Mordaunt every encouragement, but at the same time wrote to his close friend Ned Villiers:

I have had too much experience of the temper of our friends in England to be over-confident that they will begin any action, and I am sure any rash undertaking which could be suddenly suppressed would be a great blow to the King, and give the enemy all imaginable advantage.[50]

Mordaunt visited the king in July, and the date of the rising was fixed for August. Charles agreed to go at once to Calais or Boulogne to be ready to cross to England. But Mordaunt was now much less happy at the prospects, for the Sealed Knot were refusing to co-operate, and Broderick reported that the Presbyterians feared that if the king was restored by the royalists alone, 'he would be more absolute than his father was in the height of his prerogative', and they urged that the royalists should wait for a co-operative effort, so as to restore the king 'upon the true basis, liberty and property'. On 28 July Charles wrote to Mordaunt that unless there was a general rising there should be none at all.[51]

On the 31st however Sir George Booth, a wealthy Presbyterian who had been a Parliamentarian, raised a rebellion at Warrington, and with the help of the earl of Derby and about five hundred men occupied Chester, except the castle, which held out. The rebels declared, not for the king, but for a free parliament, and the laws, liberty and property of the nation. Lambert marched towards them with about 3500 men, but it took thirteen days for him to approach and meanwhile no other part of the country rose to join the rebellion. The result was therefore a foregone conclusion. Lambert met the rebels near Nantwich and dispersed them. Some thirty rebels were killed, and three hundred captured. Booth escaped, was later captured in woman's clothes, but he was never brought to trial. Willis had not known of the Booth rising beforehand, and the Council was taken unawares. Elsewhere, in Kent and the south-west there were numerous arrests of suspected royalists. Kent, where an invasion was expected, suffered particularly. Broderick was arrested, Hyde suspected through Willis' information to Thurloe.[52] The king, who had gone to St Malo ready to embark for Cheshire, or any other English port, instead took the urgent advice of Sir Henry Bennett, and went to Fuentarabia to try to extract some benefit from the Franco-Spanish peace negotiations.

Mordaunt and his friends were understandably bitter at the failure of the rising, and placed the blame chiefly on the inaction of the Sealed Knot, among whom, they claimed, 'more knaves will be found than Sir Richard Willis.'[53] Hyde was inclined to agree with them.

However mismanaged the Booth rising had been, and however disorganised the royalists were, it was clear that the number of rebels involved did not reflect the extent of royalism in the country. Hyde placed his hopes upon the virtual certainty that in England the Rump and the army must come into conflict. The army, although divided between Commonwealthsmen and 'Grandees', yet combined in hostility to the Rump, while the Rump lived in fear of another forcible expulsion by the army. In these circumstances the importance of General Monck was crucial. Sir John Grenville agreed to send Nicholas Monck to his brother. He was too cautious to carry letters from the king, but he memorised them, and they presumably contained the king's offer of wealth and rank in return for his support. He reached Scotland in August 1659, and was received by the General in a sphinx-like silence. According to his biographer Gumble, Monck and his wife were tempted, but he was far too cautious a man, and far too aware of the difficulties, to make any decision, especially as the Booth rising had just collapsed. When Nicholas Monck left Scotland in October, he still had no idea of his brother's intentions, and Sir John Grenville reported this to the king on 2 December.[54]

Meanwhile in September 1659, a group of army officers, flushed with their victory over the rebels, met at Derby, and drew up a petition to parliament, demanding the appointment of Fleetwood as permanent commander-in-chief, with Lambert as his deputy, the settlement of arrears of army pay, and other demands regarded as insulting by parliament. When the petition was submitted to Monck he ostentatiously refused to sign. Encouraged by this, the Rump demanded the suppression of the petition.[55] It was a challenge Lambert could not refuse. Mordaunt correctly assessed the situation when he wrote:

Lambert is so put to it by Sir Arthur Hesilrige and Thomas Scot that he is either lost or must loose them. And the House will either be dissolved or purged unless by a common consent new writs be issued out.[56]

The army replied with another petition, and parliament countered by revoking the officers' commissions, and putting Fleetwood's command into a commission of seven. Lambert's reply was swift: he surrounded the House with his troops and prevented them from sitting. He was now master of the situation, and royalists were divided between the fears that he would set himself up as the successor to Protector Oliver, and the hope that he might opt for the king. Lord Hatton wrote to Hyde a hysterical letter that the best solution would be for Charles to marry Lambert's daughter:

The race is a very good gentleman's family, and Kings have condescended to gentlewomen and subjects. The Lady is pretty, of an extraordinary sweetness of disposition, and very virtuously and ingenuously disposed . . .[57]

But the real question was what attitude General Monck would adopt. He made it plain that he supported parliament: in letters to the Speaker, Fleetwood and Lambert, he protested at the arbitrary action of the army.[58] He gave no sign that he was for the monarchy, but wisely kept his options open: he merely stood for the authority of the civil power against the domination of the army. This was an astute policy which would gather to his support all those, of whatever opinion, who feared continued military rule. Thus although Lambert marched his army from London to Newcastle in November, and blocked Monck's road to England, Monck knew that his letters to the City of London proposing the recall of parliament[59] were having the desired effect. Sir John Grenville, for instance, read them with great satisfaction, deducing that, 'it is now most apparent to all men living, there can never be any happy settlement without his Majesty's establishment'.[60]

Since the failure of the Booth rising, royalist correspondence had made depressing reading. Much time was spent raking over the causes of failure, and trying to apportion blame. Since Hyde was certain that Sir Richard Willis had been a traitor, but a number of the Sealed Knot refused to believe it, the dispute continued. The most active royalist was still Lord Mordaunt, but his letters steadily pressed for a royalist invasion, to take advantage of the political confusion, advice which was simply not practical, and which the king and Hyde were too shrewd to encourage. Charles and Ormond spent futile weeks at Fuentarabia seeking French and Spanish help. Hyde maintained a silence on such efforts which he suspected would achieve little, or resorted to irony:

[Secretary Nicholas] and I do not pretend to be so sharp-sighted as other men, into the affections and inclinations of the cardinal and court of France, yet we presume to think that the little experience we have had may enable us to guess which is the way to do our business in England, as well as any men.

To Mordaunt he wrote that it was necessary that the king should let the Sealed Knot know that 'he is master of his own affairs, and that he will be obeyed'.[61] The attitude of the Louvre party continued to be sour: when Ormond was received by the queen, she declared that if she had been trusted, the king would have been in England by now. Hyde was delighted with Ormond's ungallant reply, that 'if she had never been trusted, he had never been out of England'![62] If Charles had had to rely on the royalists alone for his restoration, his chance of achieving it would have seemed slight.

However the tide was flowing irresistibly in their favour without much effort on their part. The Rump reassembled on 26 December. Unfortunately we cannot follow its debates as in the Protectorate parliaments, for there is no Burton's Diary for the period, but it is clear that the Rump failed to find a solution to any of the outstanding problems of the time. There was still a little of the mystique of legality about this shrunken body, but by now the demand was for a free parliament. The Rump failed to agree on whether government should be by one man, whether there should be a second chamber, whether there should be complete religious toleration, or even what the word 'Commonwealth' really meant. Sir Henry Vane and Sir Arthur Hesilrige were its outstanding members. Both were fiercely opposed to both the monarchy and the Protectorate. Vane's views were often confused and mystical, and it is hardly possible to make out of them a coherent theory. He believed that 'the original of all just power' was the people, but that the people had failed to establish a perfect commonwealth because of the obtrusion of selfish interests; they needed therefore to be led by good men. He won the support of the sectaries, and seems to have looked to Lambert to achieve religious toleration. Hesilrige stood forth as the champion of liberty and an advocate of a free parliament, in spite of the fact that it would surely restore the monarchy. The two men began by co-operating, and ended by quarrelling, and between them prevented perceptible progress in the Rump.[63]

In these circumstances, having securely garrisoned Scotland, Monck crossed the Tweed on 1 January 1660, with four cavalry and six infantry regiments, and began a leisurely progress southwards. At his approach

Lambert's forces melted away, and Monck found York in the friendly hands of Fairfax. Monck's purpose was an enigma. He was naturally cautious, and perhaps had decided to be guided by events. Hyde found it alarming that he had not given the royalists any indication of his intentions. But his march southwards took on the aspect of a triumphal procession, as he received petitions from all sides, asking for the return of the secluded members or for a free parliament. If there were few requests for a return of the monarchy, it might have been because many country gentlemen, like Lord Falkland in Oxfordshire, regarded it as the most likely outcome of a free parliament. Monck returned non-committal answers to all, saying that he was but a servant to the parliament; however to the gentlemen of Devon he gave a more informative opinion, that 'Monarchy cannot possibly be admitted for the future in these nations, because its support is taken away'. There is no reason to suppose that this was not his opinion at the time. It was clear however that the royalists were utterly dependent upon him, for the king admitted that without the help of France or Spain (which was not forthcoming) he could not transport even 3000 men across the channel.[64]

When Monck reached St Albans, he requested the Commons to withdraw other troops from London, and they agreed. Fleetwood, who declared to the Speaker that 'the Lord had spat in their faces', threw up his command, and the Commons required Sir Henry Vane to retire to Raby. In the counties there was a growing movement for the non-payment of taxes until a free parliament was called, and the press took up the cry. The redoubtable William Prynne had for a year been writing pamphlets attacking the Rump, and demanding a free parliament and the restoration of the House of Lords and monarchy, and in December he received a letter of thanks from the king.[65] As Monck approached London, the tension between the City and the Rump increased, and when on 2 February a regiment at Somerset House mutinied and were joined by apprentices in Leadenhall Street, the Speaker requested Monck to enter London to restore order. He did so next day, with considerable display, and to the ringing of church bells.

The Rump was now entirely dependent upon Monck's good will, but when he addressed them on 5 February, he still gave no clue as to his intentions, beyond expressing his preference for a free parliament. The householders of the City, supported by the Common Council, were refusing to pay taxes until there was a free parliament. Monck was ordered by the Council of State to march into the City, to arrest the ring-leaders on the Common Council, to take down the gates and portcullises and the posts and chains of the City. He obeyed, and on 9 February began the work; but when his officers refused to continue, he changed his mind. If the choice lay between obeying the discredited Rump and obliging the City, there was no doubt which Monck would choose. Instead of continuing with his mission, he wrote to the Speaker urging that they should issue writs for a free parliament, and should end their own sittings by 6 May. Pepys, who was present at the reading of the letter, recorded the satisfaction of some of the moderates, and one of them taunted the angry Hesilrige with, 'Thou man, will thy beast carry thee no longer? Thou must fall'. Pepys was also at the Guildhall, where Monck was received with 'such a shout I never heard in all my life, crying out "God bless your Excellency". . . . In Cheapside there were a great many bonfires, and Bow bells and all the bells in all the churches as we went home were a-ringing.'[66] The night of celebration was named the Burning of the Rump. Next day, a Sunday (12 February), Monck attended the service in St Paul's with the Lord Mayor.

Clarendon believed that if the Rump had accepted Monck's policy meekly they could still have retained his loyalty, but they sought to undermine his authority as commander-in-chief by putting the command into a commission of five, with Fleetwood restored as commander-in-chief. This was a fatal mistake. They also attempted to impose an Engagement on all members of loyalty to the Commonwealth 'without a King, single Person or House of Lords', a committment neither Monck nor the Presbyterians would make. On 21 February seventy-three of the secluded members were allowed to take their seats, and the Rumpers were swamped. When Monck addressed members on that day, he declared that the old foundations of monarchy were too broken ever to be restored; that the restoration of the king would mean the restoration of prelacy, whereas he preferred a moderate Presbyterian government combined with liberty of conscience. He proposed the dissolution of parliament and new elections.[67] In the light of subsequent events, it is easy to suppose that Monck was playing a deep and subtle game, designed to keep the factions in parliament, the City and the army in step, while working all the time for a restoration of the monarchy. But this is to endow Monck with a prescience he did not possess. It is preferable to accept his words to parliament as a fair reflection of his opinions. The difficulties in the way of a restoration of the monarchy seemed insuperable; he disliked prelacy, and wanted a Presbyterian government. He had so far given no word of encouragement to the royalists. What changed the whole situation was the result of the elections to the Convention. The Cavaliers fought the elections with vigour and success, and were returned with a majority. This was certainly Clarendon's opinion of Monck. He wrote:

without doubt he had not to this hour entertained any purpose of thought to serve him, but was really of the opinion he expressed in his paper, that it was a work impossible; and desired nothing, but that he might see a commonwealth established in such a model as Holland was, where he had been bred, and that himself might enjoy the authority and place which the prince of Orange possessed in that government. He had not, from his marching out of Scotland to this time, had any conversation with any one person who had served the King, or indeed had he acquaintance with any such.[68]

The election results were as much a surprise to Hyde as they were to Monck and the Presbyterians. The electors pronounced against both radicals and Cromwellians. There was a strong Presbyterian minority, but many of them like Edward Montagu, John Robinson and Sir Richard Brown, were also good royalists. Hitherto Hyde had feared that a restoration might be possible only on the basis of some treaty, such as had been offered to Charles I at Uxbridge, but the election results entirely changed the situation.[69] He could now hope to avoid a treaty, and he could afford to brush aside Monck's demand for a confirmation of all land sales.

In spite of unanswered questions, Sir Thomas Peyton wrote in February 1660 that the Presbyterians now desired the king's restoration. But the king had still had no word from Monck, and Hyde was alarmed to hear that he had been offered Hampton Court as a reward for his services (which in the event he saw fit to refuse). But he understood Monck's difficulties in having to satisfy all parties, and his wisdom in saying that all problems must be left to the next parliament.[70] That Monck had still not made up his mind is suggested by a conversation he had with his chaplain Dr Price. Monck declared that the restoration of bishops 'could never be done; for not only their lands are sold, but the temper of the nation is against them'. Price replied that the royalist party was much stronger in the country than he supposed, and that prudence required that he did not pronounce against bishops. Monck concluded: 'Well then so much I will promise you, that I will not be engaged against bishops'.[71] Monck and his wife (a very determined woman) were popular with the Presbyterians, attended Mr Calamy's church, and also heard Dr Reynolds preach before the Lord Mayor, calling on the General to consummate the structure of government 'with a head stone', which was taken to mean a call for the restoration of the monarchy. Many Presbyterians still hoped that it would be a restoration within the terms of the covenant. Monck still kept his own counsel.

It is not surprising if Monck found the situation paradoxical. For how was it that the royalists, divided and factious, found their situation so suddenly improved? Mordaunt and a few others had been tireless in their efforts to rally support, but the change was not due to them, but to a growing conviction that no other regime could offer stability and security of property without the threat of military government or popular upheaval. And the change was not sudden. For seven years there had been a steady movement away from government by a single chamber, towards one of three estates, of one man, a second chamber and a House of Commons. So long as Oliver Cromwell lived, his prestige ensured the papering over of the cracks, but his death had been followed by a return to the radicalism of Hesilrige, Vane and Scot, in conflict with the Grandees of Wallingford House, and it was this return to a revolutionary situation that convinced men of property that the monarchy alone could offer conditions of stability. Sir James Harrington had argued that to restore a senate was the half-way house to restoring the monarchy, and that 'if we in England can have any monarchy, we shall have no commonwealth', and in his last work in 1660 he admitted that 'if the senate and the popular assembly be both royalists, they both will and can restore monarchy'.[72] Harrington related political power to private property, and for all his tortuous writings he had come to recognise that by 1660 the propertied classes were turning to the restoration of the monarchy. For good measure he added the aphorism that if the king came in and called a parliament, it would be a parliament of proprietors, and would turn republican in seven years.[73] It was a perceptive, although not entirely accurate, prophecy.

# The Restoration Effected

In March 1660 Pepys wrote that 'everybody now drinks the King's health without any fear, whereas before it was very private that a man dare do it'.[1] On the day the Long Parliament was dissolved a man painted out the sign 'Exit tyrannus' where Charles I's statue had stood. Many royalists were quietly released from prison. Monck's services were crucial, not only in bringing about the peaceful end of the Long Parliament, but also in curbing the exuberance of the Commonwealthsmen in the army, and his master-card was to refer all controversial questions to the new parliament. The attitude of many army officers was expressed by Lord Broghill, writing from Ireland on 17 March:

I hope, whatever a free parliament shall enact, we shall all actively or passively obey. I am fully persuaded the army is of that persuasion; and indeed, where can we rest, if that be not our foundation? Whatever supreme authority we own, we ought to obey.[2]

It was not until late in March 1660 that Monck consented to reveal his hand, and then only in strict privacy. He had come to place great trust in the advice of William Morrice, a west country royalist and friend of Sir John Grenville. Morrice urged Monck to receive Grenville, and he agreed. Grenville presented the letter which the king had written the previous July, offering to be guided entirely by him if he would serve him. Monck replied:

I hope the King will forgive what is past, both in my words and actions . . . for my heart was ever faithful to him; but I was never in a condition to do him service till this present time. And you shall assure his Majesty that I am now not only ready to obey his commands, but to sacrifice my life and fortune in his service.[3]

Monck advised the king to issue a general pardon, to agree to accept the decision of parliament about crown and church lands, and to guarantee liberty of conscience. He also insisted that the king should leave Brussels and move to Breda, since it was certain that the Spanish would never help him, and the Catholic connection could do him only harm. All this Grenville must commit to memory, since Monck would write nothing. Grenville and Mordaunt hastened to Brussels with the vital information. On 27 March Charles wrote to

Monck indicating acknowledgement, and saying that he 'knew Monck's power to do him good or harm too well not to desire him for a friend'.[4]

The king and Hyde were naturally gratified that Monck had declared for the monarch, albeit in secrecy, but were alarmed at his conditions. They had no intention of surrendering crown and church lands, nor extending a pardon to regicides, and as to religious toleration 'the complying with all humours in religion, and the granting a general liberty of conscience, was a violation of all the laws in force, and could not be comprehended to consist with the peace of the kingdom'.[5] Hyde hastily drafted letters to Monck, to the Speaker of the Commons, to the House of Lords, to the Lord Mayor of London, and to Monck and Montagu jointly as commanders of the fleet. Hyde during the previous weeks made various drafts of a Declaration, which finally emerged as the Declaration of Breda. Charles had to make a hasty departure from Brussels, for Hyde had been told of Spanish intentions to prevent his going. He reached Breda on 4 April, the date on the Declaration and all the letters, and Grenville and Mordaunt were despatched with them to England. The letter to Monck praised the concern of the army 'for the preservation of the protestant religion, the honour and dignity of the king, the privileges of parliament, the liberty and property of the subject, and the fundamental laws of the land'. That to the Speaker of the Commons stressed the importance of both parliament and monarchy to the happiness of the people, and promised 'there is nothing that you can propose that may make the kingdom happy, which we will contend with you to compass'. The letter to the House of Lords congratulated them on their return to their traditional authority. That to the Lord Mayor and Aldermen of London contrasted traditional English liberties with 'the most arbitrary and tyrannical power' of 'a few ill men'. That to the fleet was a simple call for its return to allegiance to the monarchy.

The Declaration of Breda was most carefully worded. It granted pardon 'to all our subjects . . . who within forty days shall lay hold upon our grace and favour . . . excepting only such persons as shall hereafter be excepted by Parliament'. It promised 'liberty to tender consciences, and that no man shall be disquieted or called in question for differences of opinion in matter of religion which do not disturb the peace of the kingdom'. The question of land grants was referred to the decision of parliament, and finally the army was promised all arrears of pay.[6] Hyde, who was the author of the letters and the Declaration, had thus decided to stake a great deal on the return of a royalist parliament, for all the most difficult questions were referred to their decision.

This was not something of which he could be certain; indeed he was confused about the situation in England; he complained that 'the face of things varies so much and so often, and what falls out at night so wholly crosses what was depended on in the morning', that he could not be sure of anything.[7] In March he received alarming news from Lady Bristol that the Presbyterian Junto were meeting daily to discuss policy, and express great bitterness against the King's party, and say they cannot be secure if they permit so much as a kitchen-boy to be about the King of his old party, and that he must be so fettered as he should not write a letter but that they must know the contents of it . . . They have already shared the bear's skin amongst them; Lord Manchester is to be Lord Treasurer, etc.[8]

She was warning Hyde delicately that he himself was threatened, and there was a core of truth in what she wrote. Manchester, Northumberland, Saye and Sele, Bedford, Crewe, Ashley Cooper, Denzil Holles, Pierrepoint, Annesley, Swinfin, Major-General Browne, were among the leading Presbyterians, and there was talk of the need to impose conditions on the king's return on the lines of the Treaty of Newport offered to Charles I: the confirmation of the sale of church and crown lands, and the exclusion of royalists, especially Hyde. In view of the recommendations Monck had sent the king, it is clear that at first he agreed with at least some of these terms.

On the other hand in the weeks before the meeting of the Convention, there was a steady flow of letters from gentlemen who wished to secure their estates by making their peace with the king. Sir Harbottle Grimston for instance had been accounted a good Presbyterian, and was one of the members secluded by Pride's Purge. In the Convention Parliament he was made Speaker by what appeared to be a Presbyterian manoeuvre, yet in fact he had already made his peace with the king, and promised to 'make it the business of his life to expiate his former crimes', and he made a good start by warning Charles of Presbyterian intentions to make him a Doge of Venice:

Presbytery is a very ill foundation to Monarchy, and therefore it must be laid with great care and circumspection. You know what your Father suffered by them and yourself also in Scotland. . . . The conditions questionless will be hard, and I believe much after the nature of those sent your Father at the Isle of Wight: the most dangerous one is that of the Militia, without which the King is scarce himself.[9]

In the Convention Grimston practised fulsome oratory in praise of monarchy, and was duly rewarded with the mastership of the rolls, for which it was said he paid £8000. This is merely one instance which helps to explain why the Presbyterian threat so rapidly fell away once the return of the king was a certainty.

In March Lady Willoughby wrote to Hyde that she thought that Sir Anthony Ashley Cooper could now be won over. Charles had written to him before, but Ashley Cooper was too cautious to reply. Now Hyde, relying partly on the fact that his uncle by marriage was the earl of Southampton, wrote personally to him, and gained his adherence to the king.[10] Lord Fairfax, Colonel John Birch, Edward and John Harley, made overtures to the king and were well received. Lauderdale, who had recently been released from Windsor Castle, also declared for monarchy without conditions. But those

Presbyterians who took the religious question seriously, still hoped for an understanding with moderate episcopalians such as Dr Morley on the basis of comprehension. On 4 May Morley reported that he thought the Presbyterian ministers would be prepared to accept episcopal government and liturgy, so long as they could 'use such arbitrary forms as they themselves shall think fit, without mixing anything prejudicial to the government of the Church and State as they shall be settled'. He thought they had no desire themselves to be bishops, but might be gratified by such gifts as the Mastership of the Savoy, or prebends at St Paul's or Westminster.[11]

There was a further difficulty to be overcome, namely the concerted effort, in which Mrs Monck joined, to prevent Hyde from returning to England. A rumour was circulated that Hyde had asked the king to grant him the estates of Sir Anthony Ashley Cooper. Morley warned Hyde of this, and the injury it would do him with Ashley Cooper. Colonel Robert Philips wrote that Hyde's enemies were trying to arouse Monck's jealousy of his influence with the king. The duke of Buckingham and the Louvre party were certainly engaged in the intrigue and Mordaunt wrote that Dr Clarges (Mrs Monck's brother) was a great enemy of Hyde's, and had been offered £1000 to keep him out of England. But Hyde also had powerful friends, and Henry Coventry wrote that he had won over Ashley Cooper, and convinced him there was no truth in the rumour, and when the time came, Hyde returned to England without hindrance.

The elections to the Convention changed the state of chronic uncertainty. Historians have found it difficult to quantify the groups in the Convention; it used to be thought that there was a Presbyterian majority, but this has long since been disproved. The difficulty arose from the fluid nature of the groups involved. Professor J R Jones estimated that there were 208 new members, 110 active royalists, and over 180 active parliamentarians. Trevallyn Jones identified 250 Anglican-royalists and about 90 active Presbyterians.[12] Without explanation these figures can be misleading, since a man accounted a parliamentarian in the light of his past record, might, like Sir Harbottle Grimston, become a firm supporter of monarchy in 1660. Similarly, those accounted Presbyterians at the outset split into two, the moderates abandoning their attempts to limit the crown, and accepting an unfettered monarchy. The king was therefore restored with much greater ease than had been expected.

The Convention Parliament met on 25 April 1660, and between then and the end of May when the king returned, the political Presbyterians made their final attempt to impose limitations on the monarchy. Sir Walter Earle proposed that all the great officers of state should be appointed by parliament. Some particularly wanted this to apply to the office of Lord Chancellor, in order to exclude Lord Hyde. Sir Matthew Hale wanted some such terms as were offered to Charles I at Newport, but Monck would have none of it. He said that there was now a peace in the nation which should not be disturbed, that there should be no delay in bringing over the king, and any terms to be offered the king might be deferred until he was in England. He moved that the king should be at once sent for. In the House of Lords, where ten peers at first took their seats and where the earl of Manchester and his friends dominated, it was proposed to exclude not only royalist peers, but also young peers who had taken their titles since 1648. Again Monck intervened and insisted on the admission of the young peers, which raised the number to thirty-six and destroyed the Presbyterian predominance. The return of royalist peers had to await the arrival of the king.*[13]

No question concerned Hyde more deeply than that of religion, and he was inclined to open his thoughts on the subject more freely to the faithful John Barwick than to anyone else. To him in a letter of 2 April Hyde wrote:

The Presbyterians, and their humours and appetites must be now so well known that I hope no arts or artifices are omitted to dispose them for their own sakes, as much as possible to repair the ruins they have made; and then the worst of them will be so contradicted and controlled by the best, that the schism will appear. There are some of them who have been eminent enough, when they were against us, who now either really are, or are willing to appear converted as well to a piety towards the Church as a loyalty towards the King.[14]

Hyde saw that the so called Presbyterian party was not, and never had been a united party, that it contained 'political' as well as religious Presbyterians. He hoped to be able to win over some who, like the earl of Manchester, would be satisfied with their estates and with high office, or with preferment within the church, leaving irreconcilables in a small minority. Thus he instructed Barwick to work with Morley and other Anglicans, to

enter into conversation, and have frequent conferences with those of the Presbyterian Party; that if it be possible, you may reduce them to such a temper as is consistent with the good of the Church: And it may be it would be no ill expedient to promote that temper, to assure them of present good preferments in the Church. But in my opinion you should rather endeavour to win over those, who being recovered, will have both reputation and desire to merit from the Church, than be over-solicitous to comply with the pride and passion of those who propose extravagant things.[15]

However, it was not only the Presbyterians who showed 'pride and passion', for Hyde complained bitterly of 'the very unskilful passion and distemper of some of *our* divines in their late sermons, with which they say both the General and the Council of State are highly offended, as truly they have reason to be', and he urged Barwick, Morley and the bishops of Ely and Salisbury 'to conjure those men to make a better judgment of the season, and not to awaken

* Abernathy argued that Monck continued to work with the Presbyterians to impose terms on the king, but it seems more likely that once he was assured of the royalist majority in the Convention, he abandoned the Presbyterian position, and backed an unconditional return.

those jealousies and apprehensions which all men should endeavour to extinguish'.[16]

In the event the Presbyterians failed to impose any conditions on the monarchy. Morley and Barwick were prepared to discuss religious questions, but not to make promises, and Manchester and Northumberland, who wished to impose political terms were defeated by the royalist majority in the Commons, and by the skill of General Monck, who argued that all such questions should await the king's return. Charles II was proclaimed on 8 May, and on the 11th representatives of both Houses were despatched to Breda. Edward Montagu commanded the fleet which arrived at The Hague on 14 May. Pepys was present, and was one of those who kissed the king's hand, and found him 'a very sober man, and a very splendid Court he hath in the number of persons of quality about him, English, very rich in habit'. Montagu and Pepys also called on Lord Chancellor Hyde, who was, as so often, 'bed-rid of the gout', but who spoke 'very merrily' to Montagu's son and to Pepys.[17] The King received the representatives of both Houses, the City of London and a group of Presbyterian ministers, including Reynolds, Calamy, Case and Manton. The king received the latter kindly, but when they pressed him not to use the Book of Common Prayer in England, he reminded them that 'he had referred the settling all differences of that nature to the wisdom of the parliament', and that 'whilst he gave them liberty, he would not have his own taken from him'.

On the quarter-deck, during the voyage to England, Charles told at length the story of his escape after the battle of Worcester, and made Pepys 'ready to weep to hear the stories that he told of his difficulties'.[18] On landing at Dover Charles was met by General Monck, and received from the mayor a richly ornate Bible, a book, the king said, he valued above all things. Dr Gumble, the biographer of General Monck, who was close to the king, saw 'his majesty's countenance on his first landing, where he did see a mixture of other passions besides joy in his face', and thought 'he had the remembrance of the cruel persecution of both his father and himself'. It was an acute observation. Charles spent the weekend at Canterbury, where he had the first taste of difficulties to come, for Clarendon said that he was so besieged by importunate royalists with stories of their sufferings that he retired nauseated and exhausted. He was also taken aback by being presented with a list of some seventy men Monck recommended as suitable members of his Privy Council, 'only two of whom had ever served the king', namely the marquis of Hertford and the earl of Southampton. But Monck made it clear to Hyde that they were merely recommendations, and not in any way intended to influence his decision. Charles admitted Monck and Ashley Cooper to the Privy Council, and Montagu, Hertford, Southampton and Monck to the Garter, and held his first Privy Council. Morrice was appointed Secretary of State. The king also attended service in Canterbury Cathedral, which Clarendon noted 'was very much dilapidated and out of repair', but where 'the people seemed glad to hear the Common Prayers again'.[19]

On Blackheath on 29 May, his birthday, the king reviewed perhaps 20,000 troops, and the whole journey to London was a triumphal procession. John Evelyn 'stood in the strand, and beheld it and blessed God: And all this without one drop of blood, and by that very army, which rebelled against him: but it was the Lord's doing, *et mirabile in oculis nostris*: for such a Restauration was never seen in the mention of any history, ancient or modern, since the return of the Babylonian Captivity'.[20] Evelyn said that there were such crowds anxious to kiss the king's hand that for some days he scarcely had time to eat. He was received by both Houses of Parliament, the earl of Manchester made a fulsome speech, and the Speaker of the Commons a long and tedious speech, to both of which the king replied that he was so weary with his journey that he could make no fitting reply.

Charles's first request to the Convention Parliament was that the royalist peers should be admitted to the Lords, and this was at once agreed to, thus effectively ending Presbyterian hopes of controlling the House. An attempt on the part of the political Presbyterians to pass a bill for the Confirmation of the privileges of parliament failed, and it died at the second reading. The second request of the king was that members should expedite the Act of Pardon and Oblivion. Some of Charles I's judges were already in custody, and some others surrendered under the forty-days clause of the Declaration of Breda. On 8 June the Commons decided that the number of those to be excepted beyond the judges be limited to twenty, but a further list of forty-two was drawn up of those to be subject to penalties not extending to life. Several members, including John Hutchinson, Francis Lassells and Robert Wallop were expelled the House. Others, like Bulstrode Whitelocke, were proposed for exception, but acquitted. It was no part of the king's wishes to drag out the retribution, and on 18 June Secretary Morrice delivered a message urging the House to expedite the Act. Members returned thanks, but proceeded to add a further nine to the exceptions, including the notorious trouble-maker Hugh Peters. It was a task royalist members found very congenial.

A more fundamental problem was that of the land. Lord Mordaunt, in his attempts before 1660 to win over Presbyterians and others to accept a restoration, found this the most urgent question after that of personal safety. It involved the fate of crown and church lands, which had been sold off, and also the lands of delinquents, who had been dispossessed or sequestrated. Many people, including Monck, had thought that a restoration would be impossible if dispossession of purchasers was likely to be the consequence. Many officers, for instance, had done well out of the purchase of lands at knock-down prices. Mordaunt's questions on the subject had presented the king and Hyde with great difficulties in the uncertain times of exile. Their intention was clearly that crown and church lands must be restored entirely.

Hyde therefore drafted an equivocal answer for the king. In July 1659 he wrote:

I know not what to say more to these who are possessed of my lands or the Church lands, or my friends, than that if any will frankly engage in my service and shall perform any thing of merit in it, I will make him an equal recompense for what he shall lose by returning to his duty, and this I think will satisfy any man who doth in his heart wish me well. But if I should make any general offers to that purpose, it would discredit me with many good men, and make little impression to my advantage with those who are most concerned, men naturally giving little credit to promises which are hardly possible to be performed.[21]

This could be taken to mean that while men of exceptional service to the crown could be compensated for the loss of crown or church lands, no general promise would be made, since this would alienate far more people than it would satisfy. However the Presbyterians pressed the point that without a general confirmation of purchases, a restoration would be impossible. In January 1660 Alan Broderick, one of the keenest of the royalists, wrote to Hyde that some sober Presbyterians, and other good men had proposed a general confirmation of purchases in return for a fixed revenue of £2,100,000 per annum from customs and excise, and a fixed stipend of £2000 per annum for each of the twenty-six bishops, with £8000 for their officials, to be raised out of impropriations. Such proposals had no attraction for Hyde, who was determined on the recovery of all crown and church lands. In April 1660 he wrote to Dr Cosin:

I hope at least, if the unreasonable warmth and indiscretion of our own friends do not do mischief, that the Church will be preserved in a tolerable condition, and *by degrees recover what it cannot be had at once.*[22]

He was complaining of 'the indiscretion of our friends upon some late sermons which have been preached, with such unseasonable menaces, and contempt of the Presbyterians, as if the High Commission were up again, and the Church possessed of her entire jurisdiction'. He had every intention that the church should regain both lands and jurisdiction, but by easy stages and conciliation, not by hostility and provocation.

The Presbyterians had a chance to get their way before the return of the king. In agreement with Monck, they produced a bill for the confirmation of all sales; it passed its second reading on 4 May, but was then lost in committee. A second bill was defeated on 22 June by a handsome majority.[23] On 13 May Broderick sent Hyde the details of Presbyterian intentions,[24] but by then it was becoming clear to Hyde that he could rely on the royalist and Anglican majority in the Commons to defeat the measure.

The question of crown and church lands was much more clear-cut than that of royalist lands. Some royalist lands had been confiscated or sequestrated, but others had been sold voluntarily, perhaps to pay fines or to finance the war effort. Dr Thirsk has shown that in 1660 the lands of fifty royalists in south east England were distributed among 257 people.[25] Sometimes estates had changed hands several times. The king and Hyde had skilfully left the problem to the decision of parliament, but it was one on which the Convention were not anxious to act. In September they urged the king to set up a commission to look into the question of crown and church lands, with a view to bringing about private agreements between owners and purchasers. If, for instance, a man had acquired crown or church lands at advantageous terms, perhaps ten years' purchase, he had already had value for money, and if he now became the lessee of the same lands, no injustice would be done. The commission was set up by proclamation on 7 October, and worked well in bringing about private arrangements. The king wrote to the archbishop to urge him to extend considerate treatment to purchasers of church lands. The work of the commission continued after the dissolution of parliament, and by the time of the Cavalier Parliament its work was all but complete. The fate of royalists' lands was much more uncertain. Great peers like the earl of Inchiquin (in Ireland), the earl of Bristol, the earl of Winchelsea, the marquis of Newcastle, Lord Gerrard, Lord Brandon and Lord Culpepper recovered their estates by private Act of Parliament. The duke of Ormond recovered his estates by royal declaration, later confirmed by Act of Parliament. But no general provision was made, and the question was left until the next parliament.

Finance was another problem urgently facing the Convention Parliament. The heavy burden of debt had been one of the main reasons for the fall of the Protectorate. The disbandment of the armed forces was urgently needed, but could not be effected until arrears of pay could be cleared. The cost of bringing back the monarchy was not negligible, since the royal apartments had to be refurnished, and the Cloth and Chair of State cost £1721, the royal robes and regalia £900, and so on. £50,000 had been sent to Holland for the king's use, and it was soon necessary to borrow money from the City, which however, was readily subscribed. In May a monthly assessment of £70,000 for three months was agreed upon, and the Court of Wards and Liveries, and all feudal tenures, were abolished in return for a settled revenue of £100,000 a year to the crown. The House also were informed that the outstanding debts on the excise amounted to £210,000 because in the confusion of changes of government merchants had ceased to pay.[26] During June the House found the Indemnity Bill a more congenial subject than finance, and on the 18th Secretary Morrice had to urge them to give the subject their attention. Lord Falkland and Pierrepoint pointed out that the army and navy were costing £6000 a day, and that the trained bands would be adequate for defence. Colonel Birch argued that an army was inconsistent with a free parliament, and that £260,000 would secure the disbandment of ten regiments of foot.[27] £4800 was voted for the maintenance of the garrison of Dunkirk. In July the Tonnage and Poundage Bill was passed and sent to the Lords, and a new

Book of Rates approved. On 28 July the king gave assent to both bills, and the Speaker declared with some pride

That it never was the custom of parliaments to charge the people with payments until their liberties and grievances were first confirmed and redressed; yet, out of the greatest truth and confidence that ever subjects had in a prince, the house of commons did now go out of their way, and had now supplied his Majesty's necessities with the greatest gift that ever prince of this kingdom had ever given him by his people.[28]

This had not been approved without opposition in the Commons, from Sir John Northcot and Sir Henry Hungerford, but it had been strongly supported by Sir George Downing and Denzil Holles. Charles gave an enigmatic reply: 'For the confidence they had in him, he only desired this, that they would retain it, until he deceived them'.[29]

In July the Commons turned to the question of settling the royal revenues, and a committee was appointed to consider them, including Sir George Downing, Ashley Cooper and Sir George Booth. At this time it was the Lords who seemed to be dragging their feet, for they were still bogged down in the Bill of Indemnity, and on 1 August the Commons had to remind them of the urgency of the financial situation. Denzil Holles for instance pointed out that twenty-four ships lay in harbour for want of £94,000 to pay their crews, and that there was a charge of £16,000 a month. But instead of dealing with finances the two Houses spent much of August in conflict over the terms of the Indemnity Bill, the Lords wanting a harsher bill than the Commons. Some of the late king's judges had surrendered themselves in the belief that the offer of forty days in which to give themselves up implied a pardon. The Lords rejected that. No fewer than three conferences between the two Houses during August failed to secure agreement. At the third conference on the 22nd Lord Chancellor Hyde (his appointment dated from 1658) attempted to give guidance. He pleased the Commons when he said that Charles II had told him that the execution of his father was not the work of the parliament, 'but of a very wretched and very little company of miscreants'. But the murder of a king was a terrible deed, and the offenders should not escape justice, nor should Sir Henry Vane, Sir Arthur Hesilrige, John Lambert and Daniel Axtell, who were still actively dangerous men. After the conference the Commons were as fiercely divided as before, but it was finally decided that those who had surrendered should not be executed but by Act of Parliament, and the bill was then passed.*

Thus on 29 August Charles gave the royal assent to a number of bills, one confirming judicial proceedings since 1642, another making 29 May a day of

---

* Clarendon's proposal was that if a person had surrendered himself by 6 June, and should be legally attainted of treason and murder, then execution should be suspended 'until his Majesty, by the Advice and Assent of the Lords and Commons in Parliament shall order the Execution'. Sir Arthur Hesilrige was not considered important enough to stand trial.

perpetual Thanksgiving, the Bill of Pardon and Indemnity, a Poll Bill for the disbandment of the forces, and a bill against excessive usury. In his speech the king promised

that I will not use great severity except in such cases where the malice is notorious, and the public peace exceedingly concerned.

He thanked them for the Poll Bill, but pointed out that this did nothing for his own finances:

I have not so much money in my purse as when I came to you. The truth is, I have lived principally ever since upon what I brought with me, which was indeed your money, for you sent it to me. The weekly expense of the Navy eats up all you have given me by the Bill of Tonnage and Poundage. Nor have I been able to give my brothers one shilling since I came into England, nor to keep any table in my house but what I eat myself: And that which troubles me most is to see many of you come to me at Whitehall, and to think that you must go elsewhere to seek your dinner.[30]

This human touch had the desired effect, for the Commons proceeded to vote £10,000 for the duke of York and £7000 for the duke of Gloucester, and to refer the whole subject of the royal revenues to its committee.

On 4 September Sir Heneage Finch reported from the committee that the present revenue of the crown appeared to be £819,398, and that the need was for a revenue of £1,200,000. The monthly assessment of £70,000 was extended for a further two years. When the House adjourned on 13 September Chancellor Hyde made an extraordinary speech full of patriotic fervour. He declared that the king did not take it unkindly that some members had doubted whether the king would in fact disband the army, since no other Prince in Europe would be willing to do so. It was 'an Army to which victory is entailed, and which could hardly fail of conquest wheresoever he should lead it . . . an Army whose order and discipline, whose sobriety and manners, whose courage and success, hath made it famous and terrible over the world'. He described how often the royal brothers in exile had witnessed and admired the army's achievements, and speculated what they could do with such a force! But a standing army was contrary to English traditions, and would be disbanded. The rest of the speech was an impassioned plea for reconciliation:

My Lords and Gentlemen. The King is a suitor to you . . . that you will join with him in restoring the whole nation to its primitive temper and integrity, to its old good old manners, its old good humour, and its old good nature. Good Nature! a virtue so peculiar to you . . . that it can be translated into no other language, hardly practised by any other people: and that you will by your example . . . teach your neighbours and your friends . . . how to learn this excellent art of forgetfulness.

He asked that 'the old reproaches of Cavalier and Roundhead and Malignant be committed to the grave':

Let not piety and godliness grow into terms of reproach, and distinguish between the Court and the City and the Country; and let not piety and godliness be measured by a morosity in manners, an affectation of gesture, a new mode and tone of speaking . . . Very merry men have been very godly men; and if a good conscience be a continual feast, there is no reason but men may be very merry at it.

On the subject of religion:

Religion is a sad argument indeed. It is a consideration that must make every religious heart bleed, to see Religion, which should be the strongest obligation and cement of affection . . . made now by the perverse wranglings of passionate and froward men, the ground of all animosity, hatred, malice and revenge: And this unruly and unmanly passion sometimes, and I fear too frequently, transports those who are in the right, as well as those who are in the wrong, and leaves the latter more excusable than the former.

He declared that the king would shortly be issuing a Declaration on the subject:

And I hope God will so bless the candour of his Majesty in the condescensions he makes, that the Church, as well as the State, will return to that unity and unanimity which will make both King and People as happy as they can hope to be in this world.

The speech has been quoted at length because it was perhaps the finest speech that the Chancellor ever made, and because it revealed so eloquently the magnanimity he wished to display. It was a plea for conciliation, and it was intended as a preliminary to a religious settlement which was his dearest wish. It is to this subject that we must now turn.

# Religion: Uniformity and Indulgence

The most difficult question of all remained to be solved, that of finding a church settlement. The alliance between the Laudian bishops and the crown had been so close that the fall of one seemed inevitably to entail the fall of the other. The aphorism 'No bishop, No king' had finally been shown to be true. Anglicans had then found themselves challenged by Rome on one side, and by Presbyterians and sectaries on the other, and in order to meet the challenge it was necessary to reexamine the theological and political bases of Anglicanism, which had sometimes seemed uncertain. In doing so, Anglicans were led on to reassess the historical nature of their church, to see it as approximating to the conditions of the primitive church, and the Reformation as a return to traditional ways and a rejection of the objectionable innovations of the Papacy. While Anglicans still asserted the divine right of kingship, this did not entail an endorsement of absolutism, but of the rule of law and traditional constitutional practice. It did however regard the king as the apex of that constitution and a guarantee of constitutional stability, and it did see the church as the guardian of that stability against the anarchy of the sects or the tyranny of the Presbyter, who was but 'the old priest writ large'. To understand the nature of the religious settlement of 1662, we should explore this thought-world a little further.

In one sense the work had already been prepared by Richard Hooker's *Laws of Ecclesiastical Polity*, a work directed mainly against the Presbyterians, but seeking to explore the whole theological basis for the church. The root of his thinking lay in the idea of law, not as an act of will, but as an expression of reason. God Himself was bound by his own law of reason, and man was bound by the law of nature. Law was the principle enabling all things to fulfil their purpose. But men had a second bridge to God, namely the Scriptures, and both were the source of wisdom:

As her [i.e. wisdom's] ways are of sundry kinds, so her manner of teaching is not merely one and the same. Some things she openeth by the sacred books of Scriptures; some things by the glorious works of Nature: with some things she inspireth them from above by spiritual influence; in some things she leadeth and traineth them only by worldly experience and practice.[1]

Scripture did not contain all wisdom; both Scripture and reason were necessary to man's happiness. But in Hooker's view of law there lay a paradox, for whereas he spoke of law as the reflection of reason, he spoke of it also as reflecting the will of the community:

Laws they are not which public approbation hath not made so.[2]

Political power may have originated in conquest, but in the course of time it had come to be the expression of the will of the community. The Scriptures laid down an unalterable moral law, but there were many things which were left to the will of the community, and in England

The parliament together with the convocation annexed thereunto, is that whereupon the very essence of all government within this kingdom doth depend; it is even the body of the whole realm; it consisteth of the king, and of all that within the land are subject unto him.[3]

He was not here claiming the supremacy of parliament, but thinking of the historical growth of the rule of law. Tradition was itself a guarantee of reason, and of God's approbation,

In which respect, I cannot but commend highly their wisdom, by whom the foundations of this Commonwealth have been laid; wherein though no manner, person, or cause, be unsubject to the King's power, yet so is the power of the King over all and in all limited, that unto all his proceedings the law itself is a rule. The axioms of our regal government are these: *Lex facit regem*; the King's grant of any favour made contrary to the law is void, *Rex nihil potest nisi quod jure potest*.[4]

Hooker regarded the church and the commonwealth as a single society, governed by reason and the Scriptures. He regarded episcopacy as instituted by Christ and the Apostles; but there were many things in church government which might be regarded as 'things indifferent', and each society might settle these things for themselves. The Scriptures did not, for instance, say that there should always be bishops, and if they once became proud and tyrannical the community might decide to abolish them:

Wherefore lest bishops forget themselves, as if none on earth had authority to touch their states, let them continually bear in mind, that it is rather the force of custom, whereby the Church having so long found it good to continue under the regiment of her virtuous bishops, doth still uphold, maintain and honour them in that respect, than that any such true and heavenly law can be shewed . . . that the Lord himself hath appointed presbyters for ever to be under the regiment of bishops, in what sort soever they behave themselves.[5]

It was a warning the Laudian bishops would have done well to ponder. Hooker warned also against the anarchy of Puritanism, and the 'restless levity' of the Anabaptists, which would lead to a world turned upside down, and he called upon them to, 'Think ye are men, deem it not impossible for you to err'.[6]

Some of the clergy took Hooker's advice, and reexamined their position. One of the most effective of these was Joseph Hall (1574–1656), bishop first of

Exeter, then of Norwich. A favourite of James I, who appointed him dean of
Worcester, he was sent by the king as his representative to the Synod of Dort
in 1618, where he said he learnt the value of bishops by seeing the divisions
among the Dutch who lacked them.[7] He watched with impatience the
arguments of Remonstrants against Counter-Remonstrants, Calvinists
against Arminians, and he preached a notable sermon before the Synod on the
text: 'Be not righteous over much, neither make thyself overwise'.[8] He argued
that there was too much dispute about abstract theology, in the course of
which men forgot they were Christians and brothers. He warned James I of
the coming catastrophe:

May it please Your Majesty: There needs no prophetical spirit to discern, by a
small cloud, that there is a storm coming towards our church: such a one as shall
not only drench our plumes, but shake our peace. Already do we see the sky
thicken, and hear the winds whistle hollow afar off, and feel all the presages of a
tempest.[9]

But if James sensed an approaching storm, he thought himself well able to deal
with it, and he forbade Hall to publish his *Via Media: The Way of Peace*, in
which he sought a reconciliation between Calvinist and Arminian theology.

One of the great controversies with the Puritans was the question whether
the Church of England at the Reformation had become a completely new
church or whether it was a continuous church which merely rejected the
errors and innovations of Rome. Following the lead of Richard Hooker and
John Overall, Hall argued the antiquity of the Anglican Church, and he
angered the Puritans by recognising the Roman Church as a 'visible',
although imperfect, church. In 1640 Hall, then bishop of Exeter, was
commissioned by Archbishop Laud to write *Episcopacy by Divine Right*, in
which he argued for the continuity of bishops since apostolic times. What,
then, was the objection? Was it merely to the word episcopacy? Was it to the
fact that bishops sat in parliament? If they did not, what would become of the
third estate? It was the first of a number of pamphlets published between 1640
and 1642 in defence of the bishops. One of the best was *An Humble
Remonstrance to the High Courts of Parliament* (1641), in which he argued that
episcopal government had existed for fifteen hundred years, that it was
instituted by the Apostles, and therefore deserved to continue. But, if bishops
were found to be claiming a jurisdiction which did not belong to them they
could be restrained. The claim to *jure divino* for episcopacy was attacked from
two sides, from those Erastians who saw bishops as having tenure from the
crown, and from those who defended the position of the Reformed Churches.
To the first he replied that bishops held at once from God and the king. To the
Puritans he answered that bishops should not be a cause of conflict, since
notable Calvinists like Jacobus Lectius had admired episcopacy, and since 'we
love and honour those Sister-Churches, as the dear spouse of Christ ...

While Geneva itself praiseth our Government . . . let it not be suffered, that any ignorant or spiteful sectaries should openly curse it'.

There followed an interminable controversy, in which Hall was attacked by five Puritan divines calling themselves Smectymnuus. Hall fought, not for victory but for peace and reconciliation. He declared:

Methinks controversy is not right in my way to heaven, however the importunity of an adversary may force me to fetch it in.[10]

He would have agreed with Matthew Arnold, who wrote of Puritanism:

This fatal self-righteousness, grounded on a false conceit of knowledge, makes comprehension impossible; because it takes for granted the possession of truth, and the power of deciding how others violate it; and this is a possession of superiority, and suits conquest rather than comprehension.[11]

Hall was prepared to regard episcopacy, less as a divine, than as a historical institution which had lasted fifteen hundred years, had worked well, and had produced great scholars and men of piety. But his moderation was of no avail. Charles I translated him to Norwich in 1641, a centre of Puritanism, where Matthew Wren had raised so many enemies. He was one of the twelve bishops impeached in July 1641. In 1643 he was evicted from his see, and witnessed the desecration of his cathedral:

What work was here! What clattering of glasses, what beating down of walls! What tearing up of monuments! . . . What a hideous triumph on the market-day before all the country, when, in a kind of sacrileous and profane procession, all the organ-pipes, vestments, both copes and surplices . . . and the service-books and singing-books that could be had, were carried to the fire in the public market-place.[12]

Hall continued to write and preach until his death in 1656.

Anglican clergy found themselves fighting an action on two fronts, against Roman Catholicism and Presbyterianism, and this had led them to rely heavily on their alliance with the crown. The Civil War did nothing to shake their belief in the divine right of kings, but brought a certain shift of emphasis. It is seen in the writings of John Bramhall, bishop of Londonderry, and in 1660 archbishop of Armagh. In his *The Serpent-Salve* (1643) he derived the right of the crown 'from the law of God, the law of nature, and the law of nations'. The king's original power rested on conquest, but absolute power did not long continue, but was modified by laws and charters. Laws and constitutions were the products of time:

All great and sudden changes are dangerous to the body natural, but much more to the body politic. Time and custom beget reverence and admiration in the minds of all men: frequent alterations produce nothing but contempt . . . Those states are most durable which are most constant to their own rules. The glory of Venice is perpetuated . . . by that sanction or constitution, that it is not lawful for any man to make mention of a new law to the Grand Council, before it have been first discussed and allowed by a select company of their most intelligent, most experienced citizens.

He spoke highly of the 'lawful rights and just privileges of Parliament'. What he opposed was Henry Parker's assertion of the supremacy of the people, which had superseded the law of the land, and imposed a High Commission in every parish more burdensome than the High Commission itself.

So farewell Magna Carta and the laws of England for ever, if this man may have his will: and welcome the judicial law of Moses.[13]

He was prepared to recognise the need to reform ship money, Star Chamber, the High Commission, even the vote of bishops in the Lords. He endorsed Charles I's words 'that Parliaments are so essential a part of the constitution of this kingdom, that we can attain no happiness without them'. But he could not admit parliament's supremacy over the king. The king was an essential part of the constitution. Thus Bramhall rejected absolute power of any kind: the only safe power was one bound by the law and constitution.

With the abolition of episcopacy, the sequestration of church lands, and the execution of the king, the Anglican Church suffered shipwreck, and seemed in real danger of extinction. Its full restoration could come only with the restored monarchy, but meanwhile Anglicanism was kept alive by men like Henry Hammond, Sanderson, Duppa, Brownrigg, Sheldon, Morley and Ussher. Henry Hammond was regarded as in some ways their leader. Appointed rector of Penshurst in 1633, archdeacon of Chichester in 1643, and canon of Christ Church Oxford in 1645, he had attended the king whenever allowed to do so. When he was expelled from Oxford in 1648, he took refuge with Sir Philip Warwick at Clapham, Bedfordshire, and continued to use the Book of Common Prayer in the local church. In 1650 he moved to the household of Sir John Pakington in Worcestershire, where he remained in study until his death in 1660. He personally attended the king in Worcester in 1651. Three stout volumes of his writings testify to his zeal in keeping alive the Anglican position in face of the attacks of both Presbyterians and Romanists. His *View of the New Directorie and Vindication of the Ancient Liturgie of the Church of England* emphasised, not only the ancient origins of the Anglican liturgy, but also that the New Directory rejected the work of the sixteenth century reformers which had been 'written in blood, and delivered down to us by the martyrdom of most of the compilers of it'. His *Of the Power of the Keyes of Binding and Loosing* (1651) traced with great erudition the claim that the power of bishops derived directly from the Apostles, and showed that the power of presbyters was quite distinct and subordinate, and did not extend to ordination or confirmation. His *Discourse on Papal Infallibility* (1650) was in part a reply to Romanist attacks on Lord Falkland's *Discourse on Infallibility*.

The mere assertion of infallibility on the part of the Church of Rome, he declared, was no proof:

If you could but be brought to think it possible you might be deceived, we could then find place in you for *Scripture* and *reason* to make impression: but till then you have that terrible prejudice against them, whensoever they are produced against you; and when they are urged for you, they are to little purpose, only to confirm you in the belief of that which you are already infallibly persuaded to be infallible.

Hammond was convinced that if the Anglican Church was to be saved there was a need to restate its theological foundations. Hence such works as his *The Doctrine of the Church of England concerning Church Festivals* (1657). The extent to which scepticism had become a part of seventeenth century thought is shown by his *Of the Reasonableness of the Christian Religion* (1650). Hammond rejected the tendency of liberal thinkers to make reason the test of religion:

Right reason is able to judge of all merely moral objects, whether any thing be good or bad morally; of natural objects in matter of fact . . . But of supernatural truths, such things as it never discerned in nature . . . in these it is no way judge of these . . .

From the amount Hammond managed to publish, and the fact that he was left comparatively undisturbed, for long periods using the Book of Common Prayer in public services (as did many other Anglican ministers), it is clear that Anglicanism found means of survival. Sanderson and Duppa were left undisturbed; bishop Skinner of Oxford and bishop King of Chichester secretly ordained a new succession of clergy. There were dangers, and it was necessary to be discreet, but there was also some connivance on the part of the authorities. Evelyn attended Anglican services in London. At Oxford the dean of Christ Church and Vice-Chancellor John Owen, permitted three hundred Anglicans to hold Sunday services in the house of the scientist Dr Willis, without attempting to hinder them. Baxter in 1653, when he attempted to reach agreement with the episcopalians, found them to be of two sorts:

the old common moderate sort, who were commonly in doctrine Calvinists and took Episcopacy to be necessary *ad bene esse Ministerii et Ecclesiae* but not *ad esse*, and took Reformed Churches as true churches . . . The other sort followed Dr. Henry Hammond and (for ought we knew) were very new and very few.

This somewhat oversimplified the truth. It is true that some Anglicans, like Ralph Brownrigg, bishop of Exeter, and Gauden, later bishop of Exeter, were ready to accept a modified episcopacy, whereas Hammond thought it necessary to retain the essential structure of the Laudian church, but he interpreted Laudianism in clear and intelligible terms, relying on rational persuasion rather than coercion. The central issue for him was the need to save episcopacy, and there is some evidence that he feared that a Restoration might be too harsh. When, a little before his death in April 1660, he declared that he was ready to say his *Nunc dimittis*, he added 'Indeed I do dread Prosperity. I do really dread it', he may have feared excessive Anglican reaction, or simply have disliked the thought of episcopal responsibility falling upon him.[14]

We have seen that Lord Falkland, Hyde and their friends at Great Tew, had developed a liberal theology which combined a veneration for the early church, a sense of historical continuity, with a rejection of dogmatism either of Geneva or of Rome, and a defence of the rights of conscience. They did not defend the Laudian bishops in their ceremonial excesses or their jurisdictional claims. But the simultaneous fall of the monarchy and the Anglican church convinced Hyde that one could not be restored without the other. He never regarded bishops as *jure divino*, but as ancient historical institutions. He once said that the Huguenots had rejected bishops only because the latter would not ordain their ministers,[15] and he came to regard episcopal ordination as the corner-stone of the church, and bishops an essential part of the constitutional structure. During the Civil War perhaps three-quarters of the clergy of England managed to remain undisturbed in their parishes; the Puritan alternatives were minority movements. If the moderates could be brought within the church, extremism would die away.

There was then, during the Interregnum, a real attempt to re-think the Anglican position. One of the men at the heart of the discussion was John Cosin, who was particularly obnoxious to the Puritans. A protégé of Laud and Neile, he had helped Montague to write his *Appello Caesarem*, which so infuriated the Commons. As prebendary of Durham, he fell foul of his fellow Prebendary, the Puritan Peter Smart. As Master of Peterhouse, Cambridge, he introduced elaborate adornments and ceremonies, to the scandal of William Prynne. When he went into exile, the king appointed him chaplain to the queen's household in Paris. He saw it as his chief task to defend the Anglican position against the argument of the Roman Catholics on the one hand, and the Calvinists on the other. At Hyde's request, he wrote his *Regni Angliae Religio Catholica*[16] to give foreigners a true understanding of the Anglican position. He was shabbily treated by the queen, who cared little for the Anglican Church, and left him almost without means of support,[17] and dependent upon the charity of such men as Sir Ralph Verney and John Evelyn. In his effort to emphasise the Protestant character of Anglicanism, he entered into close relations with the Huguenots of Charenton, near Paris. He also had long discussions with Cyril, archbishop of Trebezond, and found the Anglican position closer to that of the Greek Orthodox than of the Roman Church. He was deeply distressed by the queen's attempt to secure the conversion of the duke of Gloucester to Catholicism, and succeeded in keeping the boy faithful to his father's church.

In 1655 he raised the question of the survival of episcopacy in England.

Bishop Goodman of Gloucester had just died; most of the remaining bishops were old, and if they died without replacements, what would become of apostolic succession in the Anglican church? The difficulty was that there were no deans and chapters to complete the election of new bishops, and Cosin suggested that new bishops might be collated by royal warrant, and receive the laying on of hands by one or more of the remaining bishops. The king and Hyde approved the proposal, but it met with a stubborn resistance from the bishops in England. Wren of Ely, Brian Duppa of Salisbury, Brownrigg of Exeter and Skinner of Oxford professed to dislike the departure from tradition, although the more likely reason was their fear of taking any step which might embroil them with the Protector. Moreover Brownrigg and Skinner were the only bishops who were still permitted to preach, and they were not anxious to lose the privilege. They also disapproved of the proposal that the king might appoint to Irish bishoprics (where bishops were by royal appointment) men who might then be transferred to English sees. In 1659 the subject was again raised by John Barwick, one of the most reliable of Hyde's correspondents. Barwick and Richard Allestrey had been employed as agents and messengers by Charles I, and were then used as messengers by the bishops to pass messages between them, since they feared to meet. Barwick's great fear was for the extinction of the Anglican Church, and he pressed Hyde to beseech the king to grant a commission to the bishops in England 'to meet together after the custom of the Primitive Church to elect other bishops by their unanimous suffrage'. The king agreed, but again the bishops failed to move, paralysed apparently by fears of falling foul of the Commonwealth. Charles nominated Henry Hammond, the most eminent of living Anglicans to the see of Worcester, but Duppa objected on the grounds that it was too rapid a promotion for one not yet a bishop.[18]

Hyde was extremely irritated by the negative attitude of the bishops. It was true that Wren of Ely was still in prison, that Juxon of London was too old and ill to act, but he had relied on Wren and Duppa to muster the other bishops, and he was disappointed in them. In a letter to Barwick on 8 July 1659 he revealed the main cause of his worry. He sensed that the restoration of the monarchy might have to depend on some agreement with the Presbyterians, and that for that purpose it would be necessary to have a strong episcopal bench to conduct the negotiations. If the restoration was long delayed there might be no bishops left capable of conducting the business of the church. On Hyde's instructions, Barwick went on another round of visits to the bishops, but found them no more willing to act than before. The bishop of Ely 'desired to be excused as to the recommending of any person either to Carlisle or any other dignity'. Barwick wrote that those who were old, or who had dependant wife and children, had the strongest temptation to do nothing.[19] Hyde replied with some exasperation (29 September 1659):

The King hath done all that is in his power to do, and if my Lords the Bishops will not do the rest, what can become of the Church? The conspiracies to destroy it are very evident, and if there can be no combination to preserve it, it must expire. I do assure you, the names of all the Bishops who are alive, and their several ages, are as well known at Rome as in England; and both the Papist and the Presbyterian value themselves very much upon computing in how few years the Church of England must expire.[20]

He could only urge Barwick again to press Duppa into action. In a letter in November he wrote that it would be a miracle if half the bishops survived the winter, and when in January 1660 he heard of the death of Brownrigg of Exeter, he wondered how he could have explained his lack of zeal for the Church.[21]

In the event, nine Anglican bishops were still alive at the Restoration, and the many vacancies enabled the rapid promotion of the aged William Juxon to Canterbury, Gilbert Sheldon to London, John Cosin to Durham, Brian Duppa to Winchester, Humphrey Henchman to Salisbury, George Morley to Worcester (Henry Hammond having died), Robert Sanderson to Lincoln, John Gauden to Exeter, as well as George Griffith, William Lucey, Benjamin Laney, Hugh Lloyd, Richard Stern, Brian Walton, and Gilbert Ironside to lesser sees. It was a powerful bench, and Gilbert Sheldon (once a member of the Great Tew Circle) was in the key position of London, ready to succeed the aged Juxon at Canterbury. When he came to write his *History*, Clarendon omitted any account of the bishops' reticence during the years before 1660, presumably because it was no part of his purpose to show the bishops in a bad light, but at the time their attitude caused him considerable irritation. It was sufficient to recognise that the church returned chastened and with renewed vigour.

On the other hand the sectaries had lost much of their millenarian fervour, and many Presbyterians had become reconciled to the return of the monarchy, and even to episcopacy. Richard Baxter fully approved the restoration:

I make no doubt but God permitted all this for good; and that as it was their treason to set up Oliver and destroy the king, so it was their duty to have set up the present king instead of Richard.[22]

The great need of the time, Baxter wrote was, for 'prudent charity', and a recognition of the need for 'unity in things necessary, and liberty in things unnecessary, and charity in all'. George Morley conducted talks with the Presbyterian leaders, especially Calamy, Reynolds, Baxter and Manton, and on 4 May (three weeks before the king's return) reported to Hyde that they had agreed to episcopal government and the Anglican liturgy, 'so they may be permitted before and after their sermons and upon occasional emergencies, to use such liturgy forms as they themselves shall think fit, without mixing of anything prejudicial to the government of the Church and State as they shall be settled'.[23] He thought that they themselves showed not interest in being bishops, but would welcome some preferments such as the Mastership of the Savoy, the Provostship of Eton, or a prebend at St Paul's or Westminster. He thought that the Presbyterians would not be strong enough to prevent, but might hinder, a settlement if agreement was not reached. The main stumbling block seemed to him to be non-episcopal ordination, but he suggested that reordination might be a solution. Morley seems to have given no specific promises, but persuaded the Presbyterians to trust the king. When Reynolds, Calamy and the others waited on Charles in Holland they seem to have pressed for at least a modification of the Prayer Book. They received no such promise from the king, but left elated with the warmth of Charles's reception, and convinced that they could achieve comprehension within the Church. Reynolds, Spurstowe, Woodbridge, Manton, Bates, Calamy and Baxter were all appointed royal chaplains. When the king returned to England the Presbyterians frequented the Court, and the king met them at the earl of Manchester's residence.

Clarendon makes it clear that the first concern of the king was to secure the disbandment of the army and the receipt of a secure revenue for the crown, and these two subjects, together with the Bill of Indemnity, occupied much of the first months of the Convention Parliament. The business of the Court was very efficiently managed by Heneage Finch, Sir Edward Turner, Job Charlton and Roger Palmer, and they were ably supported by Sir George Downing and Sir Alan Broderick. The strength of Anglicanism was shown in the debates on religion on 9 and 16 July, when Sir Trevor Williams, Serjeant Hales, Alan Broderick and Lord Falkland all spoke in favour of a return to the Thirty-Nine Articles and the Church of Charles I. Sir Heneage Finch said they were but returning to the traditions of the past hundred and forty years. On the other side Sir John Northcot 'spoke very highly against Deans and Chapters, saying that they did nothing but eat and drink and rise up and play', although he did not oppose the bishops. William Prynne said he could not be for the bishops 'unless they would derive their power from the king, and not vaunt themselves to be *Jure Divino*'. Some spoke highly of bishops, some were for a moderate episcopacy, and some were for leaving the whole matter for the king's decision. Sir Anthony Ashley Cooper urged enigmatically that 'our religion was too much mixed with interest; neither was it ripe enough now to handle that subject', and he moved that the whole subject be laid aside for three months. Sir John Northcot reminded the House that many Presbyterians had been active in bringing in the king. In the end it was agreed to leave the matter to the king, who would be desired to consult with the leading divines.[24]

The Presbyterians did have one success. In July they introduced another bill for the settling of ministers in their existing livings. The managers succeeded in delaying the bill until September, but it then passed, and received the royal assent on 13 September. This success was a signal for the king to call for an adjournment.

The moderation shown by the Presbyterian leaders greatly disappointed the Scottish Presbyterians. James Sharp reported to Edinburgh from London in June:

Some leading Presbyterians tell me they must resolve to close in with what they call moderate Episcopacy, or else open profanity will upon the one hand overwhelm them, or Erastianism (which may be the design of some statesmen) on the other. I am often thinking of coming away; for my stay here is to little purpose.[25]

James Sharp regretted that Calamy, Manton, Reynolds and Baxter had consented to be royal chaplains, on condition that they would confine themselves to preaching until they were prepared to use the Prayer Book. He concluded that there were 'no considerable number, and no party in England that will join with you [the Scots] for settling Presbyterian government and pursuing the ends of the Covenant':

Discerning men see that the gale is like to blow for the Prelatic Party, and those who are sober will yield to a liturgy and moderate Episcopacy which they phrase to be effectual Presbytery. I know this purpose is not pleasing to you, neither to me.

He declared that 'the generality of the people are doting after Prelacy and the Service Book', and that Dr Crofts had preached before the king saying that he had been justly punished for accepting the Covenant in Scotland, and that God would punish him further if he did not break with the Presbyterians of his Privy Council. Hyde was very concerned at the possibility of a militant Presbyterianism raising its head in Scotland.

Even before the debates in the Convention, the king had instituted talks with the leading Presbyterians, through the earl of Manchester, the Lord Chamberlain, and Lord Broghill. The ministers Calamy, Reynolds, Ash, Baxter, Wallis, Manton and Spurstow met the king at Hyde's house, Worcester House, and Baxter wrote that they 'exercised more boldness at first than afterwards would have been borne'. Baxter asked the king not to turn out godly ministers because they had been appointed during the usurpation, 'The King returned a gracious answer, and said "that it must not be by bringing one party over to the other, but by abating somewhat on both sides and meeting in the midway" . . . Old Mr. Ash burst out into tears of joy.'[26] Charles asked them to draw up proposals for an agreement, and the Presbyterians withdrew to Syon College to consult their colleagues (24 June 1660).

According to Baxter, the Presbyterians reached agreement in the next two or three weeks upon a paper based on Archbishop Ussher's plan for a modified episcopacy:

About discipline we designedly adhered to bishop Ussher's model without a word of alteration, that so they might have less to say against our offers as being our own.[27]

Discussions followed at Worcester House. In the Privy Council Ormond, Southampton and Nicholas were opposed to concessions to the Presbyterians, while Monck, Manchester, Annesley and Holles favoured them. Ashley Cooper and Northumberland seem to have favoured toleration. The great question was the attitude the king and Hyde would adopt. Charles, after his experiences in Scotland, had no reason to show partiality to the Presbyterians, but he was not secure enough on his throne to modify the policy of conciliation he had so far pursued. Hyde too had indelible memories of the treatment of Charles I at the hands of the Presbyterians.* On the other hand he had no sympathy with high flying prelacy. He was an Erastian and a realist, who believed that monarchy and Anglicanism were inseparable, but that it was still possible to bring moderate Presbyterians within the Anglican fold. Charles showed no obvious preference for the Anglican bishops, and avoided their service in Westminster Abbey on the day of his return to London. High Anglicans like Brian Duppa and John Cosin played no part in negotiations leading up to the Declaration of Worcester, although Hyde had George Morley and Dr Gunning as advisers. On 22 October the king and Hyde submitted the Declaration to the Presbyterians, and Hyde at once raised the embarrassing question of toleration for the Independents and Anabaptists. This was a trap, for if the Presbyterians approved of toleration they would be extending toleration to both Roman Catholics and sectaries, but if they refused, they would be claiming special privileges for themselves, and, as Baxter wrote, 'all sects and parties would be set against us'.[29] They asked therefore for the exclusion of Socinians and Papists, to which Charles replied that 'there were laws enough against the Papists'.

This is a reminder that the Catholics presented another problem, for it was necessary to achieve a peaceful Ireland. During the royal exile there were frequent rumours that Charles had become a Catholic. It was not true, and we have seen to what lengths he went to save his brother Gloucester from his mother's attempts at conversion. But he was well disposed towards Catholics, and had gratitude for the help they had given him in his escape after Worcester. The Catholic cause was now encouraged by the queen and Louvre party, and especially by Walter Montague (abbot of St Martin's near Pontoise, and brother to the earl of Manchester) who exercised considerable influence in Ireland. His correspondent at Court was Richard Bellings, Latin Secretary

---

* Baxter commented on the use of the term Presbyterian: 'And here you may note by the way the fashion of these times and the state of the Presbyterians. Any man that was for a spiritual, serious way of worship (though he were for moderate Episcopacy and liturgy) and that lived according to his profession, was called commonly a Presbyterian, as formerly he was called a Puritan, unless he joined himself to Independents, Anabaptists, or some other sect which might afford him a more odious name'.[28]

to the king, who had been with him during his exile, and was no friend to Hyde. His attitude can best be assessed by his remark to Montague, 'If you can propose any expedient that, embroiling Episcopacy, will not advance Presbytery, it will be most welcome.'[30]

From all these conflicting currents the Worcester House Declaration emerged on 25 October 1660. The king declared that the peace of the State and the church were bound together, and his experiences of the Reformed Churches on the Continent during his exile qualified him to compose differences, for there were still 'unquiet and restless spirits' ready to 'continue their bitterness against the Church'. He believed that episcopacy was 'the best means to contain the mind of men within the rules of government', and that there was a wide measure of agreement upon the liturgy and endowment of the church. He required bishops to be men of learning, virtue and piety; he would appoint suffragan bishops, and require that episcopal jurisdiction should not be exercised without the assistance of presbyters. Confirmation would be only with the consent of the minister:

And though we do esteem the liturgy of the Church of England . . . to be the best we have seen . . . yet, since we find some exceptions made against several things therein, we will appoint an equal number of learned divines of both persuasions to review the same and to make such alterations as shall be thought necessary.

Meanwhile such questions as kneeling at communion, the use of the cross in baptism, and the surplice, were to be regarded as 'things indifferent', and left to the decision of the synod; nor would it be necessary to subscribe to more than the doctrinal clauses of the XXXIX Articles.*

The question must be asked: who was the author of the Declaration? Hyde had certainly written the first draft submitted to the bishops and Presbyterians on 22 October, and that draft was harsher than the final version. His first concern was for the integrity of the Anglican church, but he was also a realist hoping to win over the moderate Presbyterians. The king was less committed to the bishops, and more anxious for a toleration which would extend also to Roman Catholics, which would be anathema to the Presbyterians. After the meeting on the 22nd Baxter was convinced that he had lost, but Charles appointed two Presbyterian laymen, Denzil Holles and Annesley, who had rejected the views of Baxter, to arbitrate further with the bishops and Presbyterians. They produced a more moderate draft, which was then probably passed to Hyde, who may have then written the final version. Baxter was pleasantly surprised at the final result, and he certainly regarded Hyde as its chief author, for after its publication he went to him: 'I was so much . . . pleased with it that . . . I gave him hearty thanks'. Hyde then asked him if he would accept a bishopric. He asked for time to consider. In discussing the matter

* Pepys, who had no love for the bishops, declared on 30 October 1660: 'We did read over the King's Declaration . . . Very well penned, I think; to the satisfaction of most people'.

with Reynolds and Calamy, all three thought they might accept. Baxter wrote on 1 November again thanking Hyde for the Declaration, declining a bishopric for himself, but saying that he thought his friends would accept, and asking that Presbyterian ministers should not be dispossessed. Perhaps this was the deciding issue, for in the end only Reynolds accepted a bishopric (Norwich). Manton refused the deanery of Rochester, William Bates refused the deanery of Lichfield, and Edward Bowles refused the deanery of York.

For some time the see of Lichfield was left vacant in the hope that Baxter would accept it. His refusal is a little difficult to understand, since he was gratified by the Declaration, and indeed defended it before a meeting of London Presbyterian ministers, on the grounds that it was not a restoration of the old bishops, 'that there is the same name, but not the same thing'; and to John Gaudin he declared that there was nothing in the Anglican liturgy which he could not accept. Presumably the reason lay in the fact that many Presbyterian ministers were inevitably being dispossessed by those who had been sequestrated during the Interregnum.

Two further points should be made about the Declaration. When Hyde read it to the assembled clergy and ministers on 14 October he added: 'that others also be permitted to meet for religious worship, so be it they do it not to the disturbance of the peace; and that no Justice of the Peace or officer should disturb them'. This was a concession to the Independents which neither the bishops nor the Presbyterians liked, and was finally omitted.[31] The Declaration therefore amounted to a private agreement with the Presbyterians alone.

The second question is to ask whether the king and Hyde were sincere in making the Declaration, or whether they were merely fighting for time in which to achieve an Anglican triumph. Charles had not the deep attachment to the Anglican Church which his father had had, and there is some truth in Richard Belling's remark that he was more interested in gaining a revenue and a wife than in establishing episcopacy.[32] Hyde was deeply attached to the Anglican Church as an essential concomitant of monarchy, although he had a poor opinion of some of the bishops. But the main purpose of both men in 1660 was to achieve a stable restoration. Neither could be sure that the conflict was at an end. To win over the Presbyterians and to offer the Independents the right to peaceful worship (which had been Hyde's intention) would be a major step towards achieving their end. The weakness of the agreement however lay in the different assumptions which each side made. Hyde hoped that with minor variations the Presbyterians would conform to the liturgy of the Prayer Book; the Presbyterians that in return for the agreement they would be able to continue to use the Directory of Worship, and would retain their livings. Thus Clarendon complained that no sooner had the Declaration been issued than the London ministers petitioned 'that the wearing the surplice, and the using the cross in baptism, might be absolutely abolished out of the church'.

Clarendon regarded this as a breach of the agreement, and concluded 'that nothing but a severe execution of the law can ever prevail upon that classis of men to conform to government'.[33]

When parliament reassembled, the Presbyterians tried to convert the Declaration into an Act, and it was clear that they regarded it as a charter for toleration. So did those who opposed the bill. Sir Thomas Meres said that it would 'make all papists and other heretics rejoice, since it would wholly remove all conformity in the church'. Secretary Morrice and Sir Heneage Finch thought so too. The bill was supported by Henry Hungerford, Walter Young, William Prynne and others, but was finally defeated by 157 to 183 on 28 November 1660.[34] It was a margin too narrow for comfort, and the king looked forward to an early dissolution. There remained however the problem of finance. The revenues, estimated at £819,000, were still far short of the £1,200,000 required. No provision had been made for the £100,000 voted in lieu of the Court of Wards, and it was disputed whether the money should be raised by a land tax or by excise. Some argued that justice required a land tax, others that either tax would be more burdensome than the original Court of Wards, but in the end the landed interest won, and it was decided to raise the money by an excise on beer and ales. The arrears of the army and navy were to be met by a further monthly assessment of £70,000 for six months.

This matter settled, the Convention Parliament was dissolved on 29 December, with euphoric speeches from the Speaker, who called it 'a healing parliament, a reconciling, peace-making parliament, a blessed parliament', and from the king, who said that its actions had increased his 'extraordinary affection and esteem for parliaments'. Chancellor Hyde's speech was in a more sombre vein. He regretted that the House had not seen fit to introduce a Militia Bill, for a number of dangerous persons had been arrested, and had revealed the existence of a plot, 'they have confessed that there is a party of the late disbanded officers and soldiers and others, full of discontent and seditious purposes, and a resolution to attempt the change of the present government and to erect a republic'. This was a reference to the plot of Major-General Overton, a Fifth Monarchist, allegedly to burn Whitehall and kill the king and Albemarle. Some forty people had been arrested, and the danger had passed, but the rumour was that Ludlow was expected to arrive to conduct a general rising in the country. Hyde therefore emphasised the need for continued vigilance. He also had a warning to Presbyterians and Independents which forms the clearest statement we have of his attitude to the church in 1660:

We may tell those who still contrive to ruin the Church, the best and best-reformed church in the Christian world ... that God would not so miraculously have snatched this church as a brand out of the fire . ... to expose it again to the same rapine, reproach and impiety. That Church, which delights itself in being called catholic, was never so near expiration, never had such a resurrection ... God Almighty would not have been at the expense and charge of such a deliverance but in the behalf of a church very acceptable to him.[35]

Hyde's words form a valid commentary on his intentions in the Worcester House Declaration. It was a period of great confusion; the monarchy could not yet be said to be safely enthroned. It was not merely that it was so difficult to distinguish moderate dissenters from sectaries and fanatics, Anabaptists, Quakers and Fifth Monarchists. It was difficult also to dissociate dissenters of any kind from the events which had brought down the monarchy. It was a period of violence and retribution, during which Major-General Harrison, John Carew, Thomas Scot, Hugh Peters, Axtel, Hacker and the other regicides were tried and executed. Pepys was present when Harrison was hanged, drawn and quartered at Charing Cross on 13 October:

Thus it was my chance to see the King beheaded at Whitehall and to see the first blood shed in revenge for the blood of the King at Charing-cross.

It was the period in which bishops for the first time took charge of their dioceses, and tried to establish order. In the Winchester diocese, where the bishop confirmed as many as 600 people in one day, twelve ministers refused to subscribe or to 'yield to reason'.[36] The Act for the Confirming and Restoring of Ministers, passed by the Convention in September 1660, was essentially a moderate measure: where clergy had been sequestrated they should regain their benefices; where they were irreconcilables they should be dispossessed, but the remainder were to be confirmed in their parishes. There were some 700 or 800 sequestered clergy still living; the number of irreconcilables was not high. Ministers who applied for royal confirmation in their benefices, and who were not challenged by better claimants, readily achieved the king's confirmation. Hyde, Sheldon, Earle and Morley acted as a committee advising the king on royal patronage. Many of those who applied might have been accounted Puritans, but it would have been physically impossible to find staunch Anglicans to fill hundreds of benefices, and the upheaval would have been damaging to the prospects of a peaceful settlement. The king and Hyde had won the praises of Baxter and his friends for their friendliness towards men whose loyalty was not in doubt, and thus the changeover was achieved with the minimum of disturbance.[37] Moreover, Hyde and his committee had their hands full with royal appointments to bishoprics, deaneries, prebends and archdeaconries. Nearly 250 such appointments were made by September 1660. With so many at the king's disposal, it was easy to beg such plums as the church had to offer. Often Charles's liberality went beyond what might have been thought prudent, as when Presbyterians were offered the deaneries of Lichfield, Rochester and York; but there is no evidence that Hyde protested, and in any case the Presbyterians refused.

Of the bishops, nine were survivals of the past. Of the new appointments Sheldon and Morley had been members of the Great Tew Circle, and were closest to Hyde's views. Some owed their appointment to the king's favour: Humphrey Henchman had aided Charles in 1651, Nicholas Monck (Hereford) was brother to the General and an ardent royalist, and John Gauden won the king's favour, perhaps because of his claim to be the author of *Eikon Basilike*. Some bishops were shadowy figures who made little mark. There was thus no evidence of a plan about their appointments. Gauden and Reynolds were distinctly Low Church, but this did not prevent the former from regarding the Worcester House Declaration with some cynicism. He wrote that its purpose

was only in order to compose at present the minds of all his good subjects to some calm and Christian temper until such further expedients might be applied by his Majesty's wisdom and charity, as should not only allay former civil differences, but wholly remove the uncomfortable dissensions of his loyal subjects of the Church of England.[38]

It would be easy to underestimate the uncertainties and confusion which existed in England during the winter of 1660–1. To the royalists the sectaries, Anabaptists, Millenarians, Fifth Monarchists and Quakers represented dangerous and subversive forces working in secret to overthrow the monarchy. The Overton Plot of November was followed by that of the fanatical Fifth Monarchist Thomas Venner, a cooper by trade, in January 1661. Leading a group from their meeting house in Coleman Street, he issued forth into the streets with the cry of 'King Jesus and the heads upon the gates', and although numbering only thirty or forty, they were armed, and terrorised the city for four days before they were rounded up. Some thirty were arrested, Venner died of his wounds, and thirteen were executed. On the 10th a royal Proclamation forbade the meetings of Anabaptists, Quakers and Fifth Monarchists except in church, and empowered justices to tender the oath of allegiance to suspected persons. The refusal of Quakers to take any oath increased the suspicions against them. It was said that within a few weeks some 4000 people were in prison, 500 of them in London, although most were released when they were found not to be subversive.[39]

Hyde had therefore to tread warily between extending an indulgence according to the Worcester House Declaration and restraining subversives. By the end of the year some 695 ministers had been ejected, 290 of them to make way for sequestered Anglicans, the others for such reasons as refusal to use the Book of Common Prayer. When such cases were referred to Hyde he usually tried to mitigate the circumstances without offending the bishops or the Anglican squires. For there was a widespread feeling that the Declaration had given away too much, and while Hyde tried to maintain good relations with the moderate Presbyterians, there were many intransigents like the pamphleteers Crofton and Firmin, who attacked the bishops and exalted the

Covenant. Although, as would soon be apparent, the mood of the country was strongly royalist and Anglican, that of London was much more doubtful. When in October 1660 Pepys watched the bishops in their vestments in Westminster Abbey at the translation of Dr Frewen to the Archbishopric of York, his comment was: 'But Lord, at their going out, how people did most of them look upon them as strange creatures, and few with any kind of love or respect' (4 October 1660). In November he heard his minister 'begin to nibble at the Common Prayer', although the people did not know the responses, and for the first time in his life he heard the organ played in Westminster Abbey. In March 1661 the government was highly alarmed to learn that the City had elected two Presbyterians (Alderman Sir William Thompson and Alderman William Love) and two Independents (Alderman John Foulke and John Jones) as members of Parliament. The king and Hyde, who had constantly before them the fear that there would be a re-enactment of the Long Parliament, were alarmed, and guards were strengthened in the City. Pepys commented (20 March 1661),

they [the elected members] are thought to be Anabaptists, and chosen with a great deal of zeal, in spite of the other party that thought themselves very strong – crying out in the hall, 'no bishops, no Lord Bishops'. It doth make the people to fear it may come to worse, by being an example to the countries to do the same. And indeed, the bishops are so high, that very few do love them.

Zachary Crofton, the leading Presbyterian subversive, who preached so violently against the bishops, was imprisoned. But when Baxter applied to the bishop of London for licence to preach, it was granted.

The king's commission for the Savoy Conference was issued on 25 March, and the Conference met on 8 April: twelve bishops and nine assistants on one side, one bishop, eleven divines and nine assistants on the other. Although Archbishop Frewen presided, the Anglican case was conducted by Gilbert Sheldon. He began by proposing that as it was the Presbyterians who had desired the conference, they should submit their proposals in writing. Richard Baxter at once fell into the trap by agreeing, whereas the wiser Presbyterians regarded this as hardly fulfilling the agreement to 'meet together and consult'. At the end of a fortnight Baxter produced, not a few modest changes, but what amounted to an entirely new liturgy. Some of the moderate Presbyterians saw the futility of this procedure, and ceased to attend the conference, and Reynolds went over to the bishops. Proceedings continued until July, but the result was a foregone conclusion. Sheldon did not often attend, but left the debate to Morley, Henchman and Cosin. Morley accused Baxter of having 'a furious eagerness to engage in disputation'. Only Gauden had a friendly word for the Presbyterians. In the end Cosin clinched the argument by asking whether there was anything in the Book of Common Prayer contrary to the Word of God; if not, the Presbyterian proposals were 'mere expediency'.[40]

The conference broke up without a single concession from the bishops. This was the only possible conclusion, for if the bishops had accepted the four hundred proposals Baxter's industry had produced, they might as well have accepted the entire Directory of Worship.

Long before July the conference had been overshadowed by more spectacular events. On 20 April the king created Lord Hyde earl of Clarendon, Lord Capel earl of Essex, and sixty-eight Knights of the Bath; on the 23rd he was crowned with great magnificence and full Anglican rites. Pepys was delighted with the spectacle, and said that he was 'sure never to see the like again in this world'. The parliamentary elections had gone well for the king, and the example of the City of London was not followed in the counties. Parliament met on 8 May, and in his speech the king asked parliament to confirm all the legislation of the Convention (which was not a true parliament), and especially the Act of Indemnity. Clarendon makes it clear that this was particularly necessary, because many royalists who had suffered at the hands of the parliament-men, resented seeing them go scot-free now that the king had returned.[41]

The Lord Chancellor followed with a powerful speech which pointed out first that the revenues deemed necessary by the Convention had not been provided, and that there were still serious arrears of pay in the army and navy. Then, turning to religion, he declared that there must be limits to the rights of private conscience. If there were genuine objections to the present oaths, then let them be changed,

But still let there be a yoke: let there be an Oath, let there be some law, that may be the rule to that indulgence, that, under pretence of liberty of conscience, men may not be absolved from all the obligations of law and conscience . . . Nor is it reasonable to imagine that the distemper of twenty years can be rectified and subdued in twelve months.

He described the dangers which had been revealed in the Venner Plot. His great fear was that 1640 might come again, and he asked for the 'utmost severity' against seditious preachers who were trying to re-enact those days:

What good Christian can think without horror of these Ministers of the Gospel, who by their functions should be the messengers of peace, and are in their practice the only trumpets of war, and incendiaries towards rebellion! . . . If you do not provide for the thorough quenching these firebrands, king, lords and commons shall be their meanest subjects, and the whole kingdom kindled into one general flame.

If the old laws were not sufficient, then new laws must be devised to secure the peace of the kingdom. He contrasted the days of the Commonwealth, when

abject men who could neither write nor read, would make laws for the government of the most heroic and the most learned nation in the world . . . No man undervalues the common people of England, who are in truth the best and honestest, aye and the wisest common people in the world ... [But] it is the privilege, if you please, the prerogative of the common people of England to be represented by the greatest, the learnedest, and wealthiest and wisest persons that can be chose out of the nation.[42]

Finally he referred to the trade advantages which might follow from the Portuguese marriage, and was at pains to underline that it had the unanimous approval of the Privy Council.

The speech fully revealed Clarendon's distinction between genuine rights of private conscience and the unacceptable dangers of turbulent dissent. It also revealed his aristocratic view of society as a guarantee of stability, and the importance he attached to the Privy Council as the central instrument of executive government, by which that stability was guaranteed.

In some respects the Commons responded promptly to Clarendon's words, for a bill was at once introduced 'for Safety and Preservation of His Majesty's Person and Government', making it an offence punishable by praemunire to say that the Long Parliament was not dissolved, or to endeavour to change the government of either church or state. The two Houses agreed to the burning of the Solemn League and Covenant by the common hangman. They also agreed to consider providing 'a full, constant and standing revenue, such as might befit the support of so great and good a Prince'. The need was great, for there was an outstanding debt from the past of well over £3,000,000, but here the mountain first brought forth a mouse, for the House resorted to a bill for a 'free and voluntary present to his Majesty' from those willing and able to aid him, with a limit of £400 on the gifts of peers. This was followed in July by a bill increasing the excise to £400,000, and by the end of the year by a bill granting the king £1,200,000 a year to be raised by an assessment of £70,000 a month for eighteen months. In June there was a bill against tumults and disorders which forbade petitions signed by more than twenty persons, on pain of fines and imprisonment. The use of such petitions by subversive elements in the early days of the Long Parliament had not been forgotten. After further prompting from the king, the Act of Indemnity was confirmed. The Act of the Long Parliament disabling bishops from sitting in the Lords was repealed, and a further Act in 1662 recalled them to the Lords.

A more complicated measure was the Corporation Act, entitled 'An Act for the Well Governing and Regulating of Corporations'. At the Restoration the charters of many towns were Cromwellian, and the royalists could not be expected to accept them. Some towns, like Norwich, voted the king a free gift of money, and then petitioned for a renewal of their charters. This was often readily granted, for the king and Chancellor had not the time or staff necessary to check local conditions. Complaints were often made therefore that 'seditious persons' still held office in some towns. If the Chancellor listened to these complaints, he could investigate the corporation by Quo Warranto proceedings, and these might result in surrendered charters and new ones being issued. But this was a slow and piecemeal system, and a more general method was thought necessary. By the Corporation Bill all mayors, aldermen and other officials and magistrates were required by 1663 to take the oaths of supremacy and allegiance, and to forswear the Solemn League and Covenant. All officials unjustly dispossessed in the past should be restored to office, and no official should be appointed in future who had not taken Anglican Communion. Commissioners for the enforcement of the Act (appointed by the Crown) were to hold office until 1663.[43]

There was considerable opposition to the bill in the Commons: 136 voted against its second reading. The Lords, inspired by the duke of York, wanted an even harsher measure, by which all charters would have to be renewed by 1662, and the Crown would have the right to appoint all town clerks, recorders and mayors; but when these amendments were returned to the Commons on 24 July, they were rejected, on the grounds that 'nothing enacted by their Lordships seems to us to provide for present safety'.[44] On the other hand when William Prynne published a pamphlet opposing the bill as being contrary to Magna Carta, it was voted to be 'illegal, false, scandalous and seditious', and Prynne was forced to make an abject submission to the House (15 July). Ever since 1660, ejected royalists in the towns had been petitioning for reinstatement, and had received a sympathetic hearing from the king and his ministers. Now the Crown could proceed either by commissioners, or by Quo Warranto, and the commissioners had almost unlimited powers to exclude or appoint whom they pleased in the corporations, although their powers expired in 1663. There was no such time limit on the use of Quo Warranto writs. They had been used since the reign of Edward I, and frequently by the early Stuarts in the case of Horsham, Dover, Canterbury, Bath, and other towns. After 1660 they were effective in bringing about the surrender of charters at Preston, Taunton, Bristol, and other towns.

In 1661, when the City of London returned four opposition members, it was decided that all new charters should require the nomination of aldermen, recorders and town clerks by the Crown,[45] but when a royalist majority was returned in the elections, this was not proceeded with. But Quo Warranto proceedings were instituted against Berkhamstead, Maidstone, Bridport and Minehead in the following years. However in general until the 1670s there was peace in most towns. The Corporation Act was often laxly enforced, and Occasional Conformity was early practised by those eager for office, while those who wished to avoid it, could always make use of the Act. Dr Evans finds the decade 1663–73 'uncommonly tranquil' in Norwich:

There are no signs of bitterly disputed elections, conflicts between the corporation and the citizens . . . Religious tension seems to have been minimal . . . Relations between the corporation and Whitehall remained good, and local enthusiasm for King Charles did not subside.[46]

The City of London, which in any case was almost bankrupt, experienced political peace until the late 1670s.[47] It was only after 1679 that Charles II and James II returned to a concerted campaign against the corporations.

Clarendon had no special connection with the initiation or passage of the Corporation Bill, and he does not even mention it in his *Continuation*. Yet one of the charges made against him at his impeachment in 1667 was 'that he hath caused Quo Warranto's to be issued out against most of the Corporations of England, immediately after their Charters were confirmed by Act of Parliament; to the intent he might receive great sums of money from them, for renewing their Charters; which, when they complied withal, he caused the said Quo Warranto to be discharged'.

As Lord Chancellor he was involved in the issue of Quo Warranto writs, but there is no proof at all that he ever cancelled them in return for bribes, and this charge was as unfounded as many others raked up against him in 1667. It is probable however that he approved of the Corporation Act as fully as did the king.

To return to the theme of the settlement of religion, in July 1661 a bill was passed for restoring the bishops to their seats in the Lords. Clarendon describes how it ran into opposition from the earl of Bristol who tried to persuade the king that the bishops in the Lords would be an obstacle to achieving toleration for Catholics. Clarendon remonstrated with the king and persuaded him to change his mind, and next day he had the bill engrossed and carried in the Lords when the earl was not present. Henceforth, Clarendon wrote, 'the earl of Bristol was a more avowed and declared enemy to him than he had before professed to be'. Clarendon wrote with understanding of Charles's attitude to Roman Catholics, that the king, having lived so long outside England, and in contact with French Catholics, was ignorant of the fierce penal laws which existed in England. He describes how, one day, during their exile, he had to inform the king of the background of those Laws in the history of the religious conflicts in the reigns of Elizabeth and James I; to which the king replied that whatever the history of the penal laws, it was evident that the Catholics were no longer a danger, and that he would be glad to see the laws removed.[48] Although Clarendon well knew the king's views, his anger against the earl of Bristol boiled over in the Lords in July when, in answer to a speech stressing the loyalty of the Catholics to the king, he reminded the House, 'that the whole Irish nation (some very few excepted) joined in rebellion against the King, and but for that rebellion, neither Presbyterian nor Independent, nor Anabaptist had been able to have done any harm in England. ... It was that which produced all the mischief that succeeded in England'.[49]

Convocation met in May 1661, and in June the clergy were invited to consider a church settlement. Thereafter the bishops were engaged in considering a revision of the Prayer Book. Clarendon wrote that there were two schools of thought, those who thought there should be no change in the Prayer Book, lest the Catholics should say that the church had again changed its position; and those who thought it wise to make concessions to the Presbyterians. In the light of later experience, Clarendon was in no doubt that the former was the wiser course, since 'It is an unhappy policy, and always unhappily applied, to imagine that that classis of men can be recovered and reconciled by partial concessions, or granting less than they demand. And if all were granted, they would have more to ask.'[50] Both the Convocation and parliament ignored the proceedings at the Savoy Conference. On 25 June a Bill of Uniformity was introduced into the Commons and received its third reading on 9 July. But the bill hung fire in the Lords and parliament was adjourned from 30 July to 20 November. Even then the Lords were reluctant to consider the bill, presumably because the king and Clarendon discouraged it. By November Charles's financial position was becoming desperate, and it was essential that the Commons should approve the fixed revenue of £1,200,000. This took precedence in the king's mind over all other considerations, and on the 20th, having urged the necessity for a constant revenue, Charles told the Commons that the difficulties in the way of a religious settlement 'I confess to you are too hard for me'. He proposed therefore to leave it to the decision of parliament. This was a challenge the Commons were very ready to accept. On 15 December Sir Thomas Meres introduced a bill purporting to confirm an act introduced by William Prynne in the last parliament confirming the settlement of ministers. In fact however the bill introduced so many innovations as to amount to a new bill, the chief being that ministers must have had episcopal ordination.[51] In its new form it passed the Commons on 8 January 1662. The Lords were equally divided between those who supported the bill and those who preferred Prynne's original bill. Clarendon was still committed to the policy of the Worcester House Declaration and the pacification of the Presbyterians, and he persuaded seven of the bishops to support the first bill. He had the support also of the duke of York and (for once) the earl of Bristol and the Catholic Lords, and the Lords sent amendments back to the Commons which amounted to the return to the first bill. These the Commons at once rejected (19 February).

On 28 January the Commons sent a message to the Lords to expedite the Uniformity Bill, but the Lords decided to delay decisions on the bill until the revised Prayer Book was available. It had been completed in December, but was not ready for submission to the Privy Council until 24 February. The Lords gave it their approval on 17 March, and then turned to the Uniformity Bill. At this point Clarendon announced that the king wished a proviso to be inserted in the bill enabling him to retain any minister in the possession of a living, even though he was non-episcopally ordained, and exempting him from wearing the surplice, so long as he employed another minister to perform Anglican baptisms. This would be in effect to achieve Prynne's bill by other

means. Clarendon regarded it as doing no more than fulfilling the Declaration
of Breda and the Worcester House Declaration, and as giving the king the
power to distinguish between moderate and subversive dissenters, and he
carried with him the support of the moderate bishops, Sheldon, Morley,
Gauden and Reynolds. The proposal was however bitterly attacked by the earl
of Bristol, who saw it as merely favouring the dissenters, whereas he wanted
the king to use the dispensing power in favour of Roman Catholics. After a
serious contest Clarendon carried his proviso by a small margin, but when he
proposed that the clause requiring ministers to renounce the Covenant be
omitted, he was defeated by 39 to 26, with Sheldon voting against him. When
the amendments were sent back to the Commons they were all rejected.

Clarendon's proposals had landed him in great difficulties. He had
alienated the Anglican majority in the Commons, who regarded him as too
favourable to the Presbyterians; he had split the bishops in the Lords, and he
had increased the hostility of the earl of Bristol and his friends. The question
must be asked why he had placed himself in this predicament. We cannot gain
guidance from his *Life*, for on this subject his account is particularly vague and
untrustworthy. There is no doubt at all of his own lifelong belief in the need
for Anglican supremacy. Why not then simply allow the Act of Uniformity to
run its course? Either he considered the king bound by his Declarations to do
his best to win over the moderate Presbyterians, after which the extremists
need not be feared, or he was being pressed by the king to pursue a course
against his better judgment. The monarchy was not yet free from danger: a
further plot had been uncovered in December and January for a rising which
would bring about the seizure of Shrewsbury, Coventry and Bristol.[52]
Clarendon was genuinely disappointed when Baxter refused a bishopric, and
still more when on 25 May he decided to surrender his pulpit and cease to
preach. His sympathies for dispossessed ministers were real: when Baxter
asked him whether former congregations could safely aid such ministers, he
replied 'Aye, God forbid but men should give their own according as their
charity leads them.'[53] But the real answer lies in Clarendon's relations with the
king. For reasons we shall explore more fully in the next chapter, relations
were strained between them by 1662. Clarendon's open hostility to Lady
Castlemaine and his championing of Queen Catherine had incurred
Charles's anger. Charles was determined to win religious toleration, at least
for Catholics, and he was under no obligation to take the advice of the Lord
Chancellor. As early as June 1662 he was listening to advice from Sir Henry
Bennet unknown to Clarendon, advice which Clarendon would have regarded
as very dangerous. For the moment there was no real danger, for Charles still
relied heavily upon Clarendon. But it behoved the latter to do all he could to
meet the king's wishes.

In a speech to the Commons in March 1662 Charles had made great play
with his Anglicanism:

Gentlemen, I hear you are very zealous for the Church . . . I thank you for it. . . .
But I must tell you, I have the worst luck in the world if, after all the reproaches of
being a Papist whilst I was abroad, I am suspected of being a Presbyterian now I am
come home. I know you will not take it unkindly if I tell you that I am as zealous for
the Church of England as any of you can be . . . that I am as much in love with the
Book of Common Prayer as you can wish, and have prejudice enough to those that
do not love it . . . and you may be confident, I do as much desire to see a Uniformity
settled as any amongst you: I pray you trust me in that affair.[54]

The Act of Uniformity having been passed, parliament was prorogued on 19
May, and in his closing speech the Lord Chancellor spoke with approval of the
Act, since 'the temporary suspension of the rigour of former laws hath not
produced that effect which was expected'; but he added significantly 'the
execution of these sharp laws depends upon the wisdom of the most
discerning, generous and merciful prince . . . [who] having had more
experience of the nature and humour of mankind . . . can best distinguish
between the tenderness of conscience and the pride of conscience'.[55] This was
clearly a reference to a plan he had already in mind for the use of the royal
powers of suspending or dispensing with the laws. In the *Life* Clarendon
claimed that the king had promised Albemarle and the Presbyterians that he
would suspend the Act for three months, before he consulted Clarendon, and
that the latter had replied that if he had made a promise he must endeavour to
carry it out.[56] This may well be true, but Charles must often have heard the
Chancellor's views on the royal prerogative, and Clarendon had done his best
to have the proviso inserted in the Uniformity Bill.

However this might be, once parliament was prorogued, Clarendon
proposed a discussion of the constitutional position between the judges and
the bishops, in the presence of some of the Privy Council. On 10 June there
assembled at Hampton Court the judges headed by Chief Justice Bridgeman
and the Attorney-General Geoffrey Palmer, Archbishop Juxon and the
bishops of London and Winchester, together with Clarendon, Albemarle,
Ormond, Morrice and Nicholas. The question before them was whether the
king could suspend the Act of Uniformity for three months. The bishops
refused to be a party to any such measure, and the lawyers regarded it as
illegal. Clarendon wrote that he alone spoke for it, and thus encountered the
ill-will of the bishops, 'yet he never declined in the least degree his zeal for the
government of the church, or the interest of [the bishops]'.[57] He must have
expected the bishops and lawyers to refuse, but he also knew the king's
determination, and perhaps that his enemies were gaining the king's ear. Also,
he was under some obligation to the Presbyterian leaders to help them where
possible. There remained the dispensing power by which the king could
dispense with the law in the case of particular ministers. At the king's
suggestion the Presbyterian leaders petitioned him on 20 August for
individual letters of dispensation. The lawyers were again consulted and gave

their approval. The Act of Uniformity was to come into force on St Bartholomew's Day, 24 August 1662 and the bishops were away in their sees, but Sheldon was specially summoned to a meeting of the Privy Council on the 28th, at which the king announced that 'he intended an Indulgence, if it were at all feasible'. The strongest opposition came from bishop Sheldon, who

> in a warm speech declared that it was now too late to think of suspending that law; for that he already in obedience to it, had ejected such of his clergy as would not comply with it the Sunday before. . . . Nor could the resolutions of the Council Board justify his contempt of a law which had passed with an unanimous consent and upon such mature deliberation of both Houses. Should the sacred authority of this law be now suspended, it would render the legislature ridiculous and contemptible. And if the importunity of such disaffected people were a sufficient reason to humour them, neither the Church nor the State would ever be free from distractions and convulsions.[58]

According to one account, there was a violent altercation between Sheldon and Clarendon,*[59] but in the end Sheldon's view carried the day.

It is clear then that Clarendon was in favour of the exercise of the royal prerogative in favour of indulgence. It was in accordance with the spirit of the Declarations of Breda and Worcester House, and with the promises made to the Presbyterian leaders. It would indeed have been very difficult for him to oppose outright a policy to which Charles was so committed, without forfeiting his good will at a time when his enemies would have welcomed his fall. But apart from this it must be remembered that in 1662 the political situation was very uncertain, with plots and rumours of plots among the disbanded soldiery and disaffected sectaries. The three regicides Okey, Corbet and Barkstead were executed in April, and Sir Henry Vane followed in June, still proclaiming that the Long Parliament had not been dissolved, and that no court was able to try him. Clarendon repeatedly referred to the importance of avoiding a repetition of 1640, and he was nervous about the consequences of a rigid enforcement of the Uniformity Act. He was certainly shaken by the firm stand Sheldon had made even against the king. Thus George Morley, who had just succeeded Brian Duppa as bishop of Winchester, wrote to him on 3 September, saying that he was sorry to hear that Clarendon was so apprehensive, that the officers of the City militia were entirely in favour of the Act of Uniformity being enforced, that he did not

---

* That it was certainly violent is reflected in bishop Sheldon's letter to Clarendon two days later:

And now, my Lord, not being able to wait upon you today as I intended, and having this occasion to send, give me leave to complain of your great unkindness upon Thursday, in offering to expose me to certain ruin by the parliament or the extreme hatred of that malicious party in whose jaws I must live, and never giving me the least notice of it. You cannot blame me if it be sadly resented . . .[60]

It is not easy to see how Clarendon could have 'exposed him to certain ruin by the Parliament', but it is clear that Sheldon had been surprised by the line Clarendon had taken.

think that the Presbyterians would join with the sectaries and disaffected 'and risk their wealth and lives by forfeiting the Act of Indemnity', and that they were in no position to begin a war. He encouraged Clarendon's failing spirit by saying that God who had restored the king and his church would not suffer his enemies to prevail.[61] Morley was right in assessing the immediate consequences of St Bartholomew's Day, for some 1800 ministers were ejected, about a thousand of them Presbyterians, without violence.

For the time being the question of indulgence was shelved, and the Act of Uniformity was allowed to run its course. In October 1662 the king required Secretary Nicholas (now approaching the age of seventy) to retire, and Sir Henry Bennet, formerly Keeper of the Privy Purse, was appointed to his place. The appointment made a considerable stir. Nicholas wrote to the duke of Ormond:

I am told, and have some reason to believe, that this my remove was designed at Somerset House, and principally by my lord of Bristol, the lord St. Albans and Sir Henry Bennet; and it is here thought by some, that the design is not on me alone, but that it aims higher.[62]

The threat to Clarendon was obvious, and Ormond must have thought so too, for he wrote to Clarendon asking for information. The latter replied on 25 October in considerable gloom that he was being blamed by both sides for not pleasing them, as if he were the sole determinant of policy ('But you know, what will be, will be, in spite of the Chancellor.'). He then continued in code (so that we may be sure that the words reflected his true feelings):

I cannot tell you that I find whatever other people discourse, my credit at all diminished with the king. He takes pains sometimes to persuade me the contrary; yet this late change makes a great noise, and gives occasion to others to raise a thousand rumours of other alterations and removals of which I do not think there is the least ground. That which breaks my heart is that the same affections continue still, the same laziness and unconcernedness in business, and a proportionable abatement of reputation; and this makes a greater impression upon my mind and spirits than heretofore, by my not having that faithful bosom I had to discharge myself into, nor that friend, nor any other who is ready to bear that part in speaking plainly and honestly in proper seasons.

No letter Clarendon wrote better revealed his difficulties. The king still treated him kindly, although he was not above letting him feel his displeasure on occasion. But Clarendon felt his isolation now that Nicholas had gone, with Ormond distant in Ireland, and Southampton increasingly unwilling for action of any kind, while Somerset House the Queen Mother's residence, continued as a centre of opposition to him, and beyond there were the disappointed royalists who blamed the Chancellor for not fulfilling all their ambitions. Pepys, who was usually not far from the mark in assessing the rumours he heard, commented that 'the young men get uppermost' at Court, and that 'none in Court hath more the King's ear now than Sir Charles Berkeley and Sir Henry Bennet and my lady Castlemaine . . . all which things do trouble me much' (17 October 1662). When Clarendon wrote to Ormond again on 1 November, the gloom had somewhat lifted, and he declared that 'there was not the least grounds for any of those jealousies which were whispered abroad upon the late alteration of the Secretary'.[63] Bennet treated the Chancellor with respect, and no doubt Charles had continued to consult Clarendon as usual. He was therefore disposed to make the best of the situation. It seems probable however that nervous tension may have brought on a severe attack of gout which incapacitated him from 13 December until March. He was so ill that he could hardly sign his name or leave his bed.

It is surely significant that three days after the onset of Clarendon's illness we have the first mention of the proposed Declaration of Indulgence, when Bennet wrote to Ormond saying that the discontents of the dissenters might be allayed before parliament met on 18 February 1663. The Declaration of Indulgence was submitted to the Privy Council on 26 December, was approved, and was published at once. It declared the king's intention of seeking the concurrence of parliament in a relaxation of the Act of Uniformity in the case of tender consciences by the use of 'that power of dispensing which we conceive to be inherent in us', and that it was not his intention to exclude the Roman Catholics from its benefits. Clarendon explained his own part in it in a letter to Ormond, and as the duke was his closest and most honoured friend, we may be sure that it was the exact truth. He described how

One day when I was in great pain, Sir H. B. came to me and told me that the King observed a great spirit of malice abroad, infusing jealousies into the people; and therefore his Majesty resolved, as an antidote against that poison, to publish a declaration which was prepared, and he was sent to read it to me. I was surprised, having never heard word before of such a purpose. When I had heard it, I made many objections against several parts of it, and some doubt of the reasonableness. Sir H.B. departed. Some time after, when I was in the same indisposition, he came again to me, told me he had made such alterations as he thought would answer all my objections, and that the King resolved that it was time to publish it, and then read it again to me. I told him, by that time he had writ as many declarations as I had done, he would find they are a very ticklish commodity; and that the first care is to be that it shall do no hurt. This is all I know of it.

This is confirmed by Sir Henry Bennet's letter to Ormond that he had read the Declaration 'period to period' to the Chancellor, and that 'it is falsely suggested that Clarendon was not privy to it'.[64]

It is true that the Chancellor had been the author of the earlier declarations in favour of some form of indulgence, and in September he had written to Ormond that he feared the 'severe execution of the Act of Uniformity may add more fuel to the matter that was before combustible enough'; but it is clear that the Declaration of Indulgence was not his doing. He disapproved of the

Catholic clause, but what alarmed him most was the knowledge that Charles was now taking advice from men who were no friends to the Anglican Church. Pepys as usual is a fairly accurate guide to the times; he heard in the City 'that Sir H. Bennet is a Catholic, and how all the Court almost is changed to the worse since his coming in, and they being afeared of him. And that the Queen-Mother's Court is now the greatest of all' (17 February 1663). What was common gossip in the City must have been well known to Clarendon, who could not but feel his whole position and policy threatened.

When parliament reassembled on 18 February 1663, the king did his best to defend his Declaration of Indulgence. He was, he said,

in my nature an enemy to all severity for religion and conscience, how mistaken soever it be, when it extends to capital and sanguinary punishments, which I am told were begun in Popish times.

He hoped that the Catholics would have some share in his indulgence, which did not however extend to holding office. His loyalty to the Anglican Church was complete,

and yet, if the Dissenters will demean themselves peaceably and modestly under the government, I could heartily wish I had such a power of indulgence to use upon occasions as might not needlessly force them out of the kingdom, or, staying here, give them cause to conspire against the peace of it.[65]

The reply of the Commons was swift and unequivocal: an Indulgence, it declared, could not be accepted; the Declaration of Breda was not a promise, but was limited by what parliament should advise, and no such advice had ever been given. Laws could not be dispensed with but by Act of Parliament, and an Indulgence 'would establish schism by law, and make the whole government of the Church precarious . . . It will in no way become the gravity or wisdom of a parliament to pass a law at one session for Uniformity, and at the next session to pass another law to frustrate or weaken the execution of it.'[66] The vote the previous day that the question should be put gave a majority of 161 to 119 for the Address. The king put a bold face on the defeat and made a characteristic reply: 'He gave us hearty thanks for our many thanks; that never any King was so happy in a House of Commons as he is in this . . . that we could never differ but in judgment; and that must be when he did not rightly express himself, or we did not rightly understand him; but our interest was so far linked together, that we would never disagree.' The Commons, thus satisfied, turned to consider a bill to hinder the growth of Popery, and then the subject nearest the king's heart, the needs of the royal revenues.

These events, it must be remembered, took place during Clarendon's long illness. The French ambassador indeed believed that the illness was diplomatic, and that the king had instructed him to absent himself from the House if he could not support his policy, and this may have been true. A bill to implement the royal policy of indulgence was introduced into the Lords, and had reached the committee stage on 13 March. But on 12 March Clarendon returned to the Lords, and no more was heard of the bill. By this time even the pro-Catholic Somerset House party around the Queen Mother wanted the abandonment of indulgence, for fear that it would merely induce a further round of persecution. Clarendon attempted to walk a tightrope, indicating that the king was abandoning the policy of indulgence, defending the king's general attitude of tolerance, yet making it clear that he himself disapproved of the Declaration of Indulgence, which was not the king's, but the work of others with perhaps other intentions. There is no doubt that this was his real opinion. When pressed by Lord Ashley on the subject, he replied that what worried him was the 'wildness and illimitedness' in the bill, and that 'it was Ship-Money in religion, that nobody could know the end of'.[67] He meant that just as ship money might have developed into a permanent tax outside parliamentary control, so Indulgence might permit Catholics to become bishops, or Presbyterians to swamp the church. The words may have slipped out in the heat of debate, and Charles was justifiably annoyed at them, but they were certainly Clarendon's true opinion. When he said that the king was 'more worthy to be trusted than any Man alive' in the exercise of a policy of indulgence, so doubtful a statement had to be interpreted as meaning that it was true so long as Clarendon guided policy, but would not be true in less responsible hands.[68]

There remains the document written in Clarendon's own hand, entitled *Touching Liberty of Conscience*. It is a clearly argued defence of the policy of indulgence as the best way of settling the problems of a divided kingdom; affirming that the king did not intend full toleration, but only indulgence towards those of 'true tenderness of conscience'; that being head of the church the king did have prerogative powers in such matters; that persecution would never stamp out dissent, and so on.[69] The document convinced Abernathy that Clarendon was wholeheartedly in favour of the Declaration of Indulgence. But Dr Green's interpretation is to be preferred,[70] that the document was more likely written at the request of the king in defence of his policy than a statement of Clarendon's own opinions. It is to be noticed that the style and argument of the Sloane Ms. are far superior to the Declaration of Indulgence, which was not Clarendon's work. It is not surprising if Clarendon was dissatisfied with the latter, even though he could defend the general idea of indulgence.

It is not surprising if historians have differed in interpreting Clarendon's religious policy in the first years of the Restoration, for it often seemed vacillating and tortuous. The reasons are not hard to seek. His devotion to the Anglican Church is beyond question. He detested Presbyterianism more even than Independency because, with the experience of Scotland and the 1640s behind him, he regarded Presbyterianism as the greater danger to monarchy.

But it was clear in 1660 that a Restoration could not take place without the good-will of the Presbyterians, hence the toleration implied in the Declarations of Breda and Worcester House. But thereafter the Anglican Church appeared much stronger, and Presbyterianism much weaker, than had been supposed, and Hyde's attempts to bring the moderates into the church had been only partially successful. By 1662 other influences were gaining the ear of the king, and the danger of Catholic toleration grew with the influence of Bennet, Bristol and Berkeley. But with the king's determination to pursue the policy, there was nothing for Clarendon to do but to allow it to run its course, relying on parliament to block it. When in March 1663 Charles himself had begun to doubt the policy, Clarendon could emerge again in the hope of regaining control of policy. On 19 March he had the first private audience of the king for some time. Charles seems to have admitted to doubts about his policy, and Clarendon seized the opportunity to lecture him on the dangers of taking advice from ignorant courtiers. This is not likely to have had much influence, beyond annoyance, on the king. Nor was Clarendon's standing in parliament much enhanced by recent events, for whereas the royalist-Anglican members were irritated by the general support he had given to a policy of toleration, supporters of the Declaration of Indulgence regarded him as an enemy to the royal policy. Worst of all, Bennet persuaded the king that Clarendon was behind the resistance to the king's policy: at least this was what Clarendon thought. On 11 April he wrote a letter in cypher to Ormond, expressing his deep depression that the king appeared to believe the accusations, whereas, he 'could as easily turn turk as act that part', and he declared that he had defended the king's policy 'as if I had been the contriver of the counsels'.[71] He felt embittered and lonely, and for the moment thought of resigning. By the time he came to write his *Life* he had come to the conclusion that the policy of indulgence was a mistake, since it raised dissenters' hopes without bringing about a single conversion. What so impressed him by 1662 was the strength of Anglican sentiment both in parliament and the country and as the opponents of Anglicanism tended to be Clarendon's opponents, his alliance with the church became confirmed.[72]

# The Restoration in Scotland and Ireland

Charles II had a much freer hand in Scotland than he had in England.

The whole frame of the ancient government of Scotland had been so entirely confounded by Cromwell, and new modelled by the laws and customs of England, that is, those laws and customs which the commonwealth had established; that he had hardly left footsteps by which the old might be traced out again.[1]

Thus Clarendon summarised the position in Scotland. Cromwell had broken the dominant power of the kirk, and imposed seven years of English rule, during which the Presbyterian factions of Resolutioners and Protesters struggled to control the church, and the Scottish nobility came increasingly to recognise that the only hope for their resurgence lay in the return of the monarchy. Robert Baillie, in spite of his staunch Presbyterianism, wrote despondently in November 1658:

The country lies very quiet; it is exceeding poor; trade is nought; the English have all the money. Our Noble families are almost gone: Lennox has little in Scotland unsold; Hamilton's estate, except Arran and the barony of Hamilton, is sold; Argyll . . . is no more drowned in debt than public hatred, almost of all, both Scottish and English; the Gordons are gone; the Douglases little better; Eglinton and Glencairn on the brink of breaking; many of our chief family estates are cracking; nor is there any appearance of any human relief for the time. What is become of the King and his family we do not know.

It was significant that in the situation his thoughts turned to the monarchy. By June 1660 he was writing to Lauderdale:

I was one of those who, in my heart, and all needful expressions, adhered to the king in all his distresses.[2]

As a barefaced lie, it was no worse than many others told at this time as the Scots strove to obliterate the past and make their peace with the king. If Charles was to find useful servants in Scotland, he would not have to look too closely into their records. Baillie's chief hope was that, as Charles had sworn to the Solemn League and Covenant, he would remain loyal to it.

The humiliation which Charles II and his father had received at the hands of the Presbyterians were not likely to endear them to him, but he had a tolerance which sprang from a fundamental indifference to Scottish affairs, so long as there was peace. At his restoration he naturally took the first advice on Scotland from General Monck, who had governed Scotland so successfully. Monck, and still more his wife, favoured the Resolutioners, and hoped that the Presbyterians would be pacified. For this purpose he summoned James Sharp to London to argue their case. Sharp, later archbishop of St Andrews, has had a bad press for his duplicity, but his position was more understandable than has sometimes been admitted. In London he found the conviction that Presbyterianism was inimical to monarchy, and that for this reason it was essential that episcopacy should be restored. He wrote:

If I were convinced that moderate Presbyterian Government could not be as consistent with the king's interests as Episcopal, I would disclaim it. I remember I said to the king while my lord Lauderdale was by, that now his majesty had an opportunity to secure his interest in the Church of Scotland, and if it were not done, I was not to be blamed; the king did then smile, saying to me, 'you will be counted a malignant when you come home'. I have since my return professed to the brethren . . . that I see no way for the Church of Scotland to redeem themselves and their doctrines and practices from the imputations which lie upon them . . . but to disown whatever hath been prejudicial to the king's interest, and make it appear that his authority may be as much owned in this Church as in any other of his dominions, for I saw evidently that for us ministers in Scotland there is no reserve but in the king's favour and countenancing of us.[3]

To Sharp then the fundamental issue was not episcopacy, but the need to recognise royal supremacy, as the only way to achieve peace in Scotland after twenty-two years of disruption and conflict.

Charles appointed the earl of Middleton as his Commissioner in Scotland, with the earl of Glencairn as Chancellor, the earl of Rothes President of the Council, and the earl of Lauderdale as Secretary of State. He was careful always to keep his Scottish administration distinct from his English ministers. Clarendon approved of Middleton's strong measures against the Presbyterians, but would have preferred Newburgh to Lauderdale as Secretary of State because of the latter's Presbyterian background. Lauderdale had been an Engager back in 1648, and was one of those sent to urge Charles II to come to Scotland in 1649, during when he made secret contacts with the queen's party. He made peace with the kirk in 1650, was captured after the battle of Worcester, and imprisoned until 1659, during which time he maintained his mask of piety. He readily adapted himself to the Court of Charles II, paid court to the royal mistress, and entered into the amusements of the Court in a way that Clarendon could never do. His letters, and those of Sir Robert Moray, often show Charles delaying business while he went riding, fox-hunting or racing, or to his laboratory, although to little real purpose. Burnet described Lauderdale:

He made a very ill appearance: he was very big: his hair red, hanging oddly about him: his tongue was too big for his mouth, which made him bedew all that he talked to. . . . He was the coldest friend and the violentest enemy I ever knew'.[4]

In spite of his uncouth appearance, he was a scholar, well read in Latin, Greek and Hebrew. He became an acceptable companion to Charles, and rapidly made himself master of Scotland.

Middleton believed that since the Scottish parliament would do all that the king asked, it would be a pity to engage in half-measures.[5] James Sharp agreed with him, and advised the Presbyterians to trust the king:

The truth is, we have been so many years out of the channel of subjection and obedience to the magistrate as we know not how to return to it.[6]

Sharp, like many of the nobility, was coming to the conclusion that a moderate episcopacy was the only way to ensure the subordination of the church to the Crown. Lauderdale on the other hand, at first was more cautious, believing that the Covenant was still strong in Scotland, and that a Presbyterian settlement would be wiser.[7] For a time Middleton's policy prevailed.

The Scottish parliament met in January 1661, and at once began dismantling the Presbyterian establishment. The Covenant was forbidden, and in March the Recissory Act annulled all legislation since 1633. Even Sharp was shocked at the draconian nature of the Act:

We were promised and expected moderation, but what shall be expected when such acts pass?[8]

But the king clearly intended to restore episcopacy, mainly for political reasons, and in this Sharp acquiesced. Clarendon's erastianism was indicated by his remark:

God preserve me from living in a country where the church is independent from the State and may subsist by their own acts: for there all churchmen may be kings.[9]

Lauderdale, if he at first had doubts about episcopacy, none the less saw to it that the Lords of the Articles were restored, with a negative voice over the business of parliament, and that the National Synod would similarly be entirely under the control of the crown. In September a proclamation abolished presbytery because of the 'unsuitableness thereof to his Majesty's monarchical estate',[10] and restored church government by bishops. It had the support of the nobility and upper classes, and even the moderate Presbyterians were prepared to acquiesce as the price to be paid for the restoration of royal authority. In November 1661 James Sharp was nominated archbishop of St Andrews, James Hamilton, formerly a Covenanter, became bishop of Galloway, Andrew Fairfoul became archbishop of Glasgow, and Robert Leighton bishop of Dunblane. They were episcopally ordained and consecrated by English bishops in Westminster Abbey, and then returned to Scotland to consecrate the other bishops (December 1661).

In the second session of parliament in May 1662 the Act of Episcopacy was ratified, and the Declaration of Allegiance was imposed on all office-holders. An Act of Indemnity was passed, but it was to take effect only after offenders had paid heavy fines. These fines were an integral part of Middleton's policy, and many of them found their way into his pocket.

Thus far the king, and certainly Clarendon, supported Middleton's policy against Lauderdale. But Middleton overplayed his hand. He tried to secure the dismissal of Lauderdale's chief Presbyterian supporter, the earl of Crawford-Lindsay, the Treasurer, but this the king, who had no doubts on Crawford's loyalty, refused. Second, the Indemnity Act provided for the exclusion of twelve men, who were to be declared incapable of holding office. Members of Parliament were each to prepare a list of twelve names on a billet, and Middleton saw to it that the names of Lauderdale and Crawford-Lindsay were included. Lauderdale however was able to reveal the plot to the king. Middleton hastened to London to defend himself, but when the Scottish Council met in February 1662, Middleton was dismissed as Commissioner and replaced by the earl of Rothes. However he remained as General of the forces and Commander of Edinburgh castle, and before Lauderdale could consider himself in control he must be dismissed from these, together with his friends, the earl of Newburgh, Captain of the Guard, and Lord Tarbat, a Privy Councillor. Clarendon disapproved of billeting, but he did not wish to see the complete removal of Middleton, upon whom he thought the episcopal policy in Scotland depended.[11]

Some two hundred ministers, mainly Protesters, refused to take the oath of allegiance, and were evicted by February 1663 from their parishes. According to Burnet, 'their spirits were eager, and their tempers sour', but they had a great hold on their congregations, and too often they were replaced by inadequate ministers, who

were the worst preachers I ever heard: they were ignorant to a reproach, and many of them openly vicious. They were a disgrace to their orders.[12]

They earned the contempt of the parishes, and people deserted the churches to attend conventicles in barns or fields. An act against conventicles in 1662 had little effect. Troops were sometimes sent to suppress the conventicles, and prayer meetings developed into armed conflicts. North of the Tay episcopacy was in the main accepted, but in the south conventicles remained strong, although most of the nobility supported government policy. Rothes and Lauderdale showed themselves as efficient in enforcing episcopacy as Middleton had been, and they won the approval of Sheldon and the English bishops. The duke of Argyll had been tried for treason and executed in May 1661. Johnston of Warriston had escaped to the continent, but was captured and returned for execution in 1663. When he was brought before parliament Lauderdale wrote

I must confess I never saw so miserable a spectacle. I have often heard of a man feared out of his wits, but never saw it before.[13]

In the third session of parliament, Lauderdale was able to carry all his measures almost without opposition.

When in 1663 the earl of Bristol brought his impeachment of Clarendon, the rumour spread that Lauderdale supported him, but he wrote repeatedly to Sir Robert Moray (his eyes and ears in London when he was in Scotland) to deny it:

These are damned insipid lies. If liars will needs lie, why do they not colour them better?

and again

it were not possible to make me depone against the meanest servant, much less against the king's Chancellor, without his Majesty's knowledge and his warrant.

At the time of the Derwentdale plot he wrote to the king that Scotland was so quiet, that if he should require aid anywhere in his kingdoms, Scotland would be able to provide it. But he could not rest so long as Middleton remained in any position of authority. Lauderdale attacked the great expense of the troops, pointed out that Middleton himself had received £30,000, and he proposed the disbandment of the forces except for a troop of horse and six companies of foot. He urged the dismissal of Middleton from his comands, the dissolution of parliament and the return to government by Privy Council:

For we have been so long overwearied with the government of pretended parliaments that the people will never think the King's government perfectly settled nor themselves secured from changes and afterclaps until this Parliament be at an end.

Should another parliament be called, the Privy Council could see to it that it would be as loyal as the last. All this was very agreeable to the king, and in January 1664 Middleton resigned his offices of Captain-General and Keeper of Edinburgh castle. The parliament of 1663 had established a national synod of archbishops, bishops and presbyters, but as it could consider only such matters as were submitted to it by the king, it had no dangerous implications for the king or episcopacy.[14]

The fall of Middleton did the Presbyterians no good, for affairs were now governed by Rothes, Commissioner to the Scottish Parliament, archbishop Sharp of St Andrews, Alexander Burnet archbishop of Glasgow, and Lauderdale. The latter was personally opposed to the harsh policies of the triumvirate, but dared not openly resist them, and the repression was effected, first through a court of High Commission, and then by Sir James Turner and his troops. The Dutch War stirred resistance, for Presbyterians had close relations with the Dutch, and the Pentland Rising of November 1666 was sparked off by Turner's harsh measures. The rising was easily suppressed, but the king was alarmed, and decided that a more moderate policy was needed. Rothes was persuaded to become Lord Chancellor instead of Treasurer (October 1667), and the Treasury was put into commission. A new moderate government rested upon Lord Tweeddale and Sir Robert Moray. Archbishop Sharp could always be relied upon to come into line with any policy which had the approval of the king. Archbishop Alexander Burnet remained hostile, and in correspondence with Archbishop Sheldon, but the new policy prevailed for the time being. Sir James Turner was dismissed from his command, and brought to trial.

Clarendon had been associated with Middleton and the establishment of episcopacy in Scotland. Once the latter was achieved, he was satisfied, and he had little direct concern with Scottish affairs. His relations with Lauderdale were never close, and at first he suspected the latter's Presbyterian leanings, but this proved unfounded. Scotland after 1660 received but scanty treatment in his *Life*. His interest in Ireland was much greater.

Ireland indeed presented a much more complex problem than Scotland to the government of Charles II. Clarendon wrote humorously that it was so intricate that 'nobody had a mind to meddle with it', and that he himself had begged the king 'that no part of it might ever be referred to him'.[15] He could write about it therefore with some detachment, but with a nonetheless caustic pen. When Henry Cromwell ceased to be Lieutenant of Ireland, Lord Broghill, president of Munster, and Sir Charles Coote, president of Connacht, remained to make advances to the king, and to welcome his return. A Convention Parliament restored the old constitution, and Charles II was proclaimed in Dublin on 14 May 1660. Monck was appointed Lord Lieutenant of Ireland, with Lord Robartes his deputy. A deputation was sent to the king with a present of £20,000, and with them came a host of men who hoped to make the most of their opportunities. Clarendon wrote ironically that

all who served the king were furnished with suits enough to make their fortunes, in which they presently engaged themselves with very troublesome importunity to the king himself, and to all others who they thought had credit or power to advance their desires. Nor was there any other art so much used by the commissioners in their secret conferences, as to deprave one another, and to discover the ill actions they had been guilty of, and how little they deserved to be trusted, or had interest to accomplish.[16]

There was every intention to make the Restoration in Ireland a Protestant triumph, in spite of the fact that 800,000 out of a population of 1,200,000 were Roman Catholics. The latter were branded with responsibility for the terrible Irish rising of November 1641. Clarendon commented:

The miserable Irish alone had no part in contributing to his majesty's happiness; nor had God suffered them to be the least instruments in bringing his good pleasure to pass, or to give any testimony of their repentence for the wickedness they had wrought, or of their resolution to be better subjects for the future: so that they seemed as a people left out by Providence, and exempted from any benefit from that blessed conjuncture in his majesty's restitution.[17]

The Anglican Church was at once restored. Eight Irish bishops had survived the Commonwealth, headed by John Bramhall, bishop of Derry. He was nominated Archbishop of Armagh in August 1660, and in January 1661 two archbishops and ten bishops (including Jeremy Taylor, bishop of Down and Connor) were consecrated in Dublin. Jeremy Taylor preached on the doctrine of Apostolic succession. Bramhall was a strong upholder of the royal supremacy, a tolerant man who thought that the church could embrace both Calvinists and Arminians and he left his mark on the Irish church.[18] By the King's Declaration of 30 November 1660, the church was to regain the lands it had in 1641, but this proved easier to declare than to effect.

The problem of the land was by far the most difficult one which faced the Restoration government in Ireland. Indeed, it was so complex that a just settlement was almost impossible to obtain. The principles of the Declaration of 30 November were that all implicated in the rebellion from October 1641 forfeited their land to the crown; and all lands possessed by the Adventurers (i.e. those who had invested in land as part of the war effort) on 7 May 1659, and all lands granted to officers and soldiers, were confirmed to them. The king had a moral obligation to the Adventurers, and to have decided otherwise for the soldiers would have been to court rebellion. Innocent Papists (i.e. those who had taken no part in the rebellion) who had lost their lands simply by virtue of being Catholics, or who had been moved to Connacht or elsewhere in the west, could recover their lands. Those royalists who had gone into exile could recover their lands, and if they had passed into the hands of adventurers or soldiers, the latter were to be accommodated elsewhere. Some peers like Ormond, Inchiquin, Albemarle, Orrery and Anglesey immediately recovered their estates, as did the Church. A commission of thirty-six was appointed to implement the Declaration, all Protestants, and all with their own interests in possessing land, although some were genuinely anxious to do justice to the Catholic population.

The greatest obstacle to a settlement was that there simply was not enough land to go round. The Irish parliament was elected in May 1661. It was entirely Protestant: only one Catholic was elected, and he could not take his seat because of the oath of supremacy. The Lords were strongly Anglican, but the Commons had a substantial Presbyterian minority. The Bill of Settlement was submitted to them in May 1662; they could reject it, but not amend it. Albemarle was persuaded to give up the Lord Lieutenancy in favour of the duke of Ormond, who, although a Protestant, was the chief hope of the

Catholic population, for he was universally respected as a just and honourable man. His presence in Ireland was badly needed, for the administration was in chaos, and the attempts to work out a land settlement almost at a standstill. Albemarle agreed to resign, and the king decided upon the appointment without the Chancellor's knowledge. Clarendon describes how the king asked him what he thought of such an appointment, and he replied 'that the king would do very ill in sending him, and that the duke would do much worse if he desired to go'; but the king replied that the appointment had already been made.[19] Clarendon of course was thinking how much weaker his own position would be in England without the presence of Ormond; to him Ireland was but a secondary matter.* The departure of Ormond and the appointment of Bennet as Secretary of State would be a double blow to him.

Ormond arrived in July 1662, in time to give the royal assent to the Act of Settlement. Seven able men were appointed commissioners to carry out its terms, and a Court of Claims opened in September, with the purpose of sifting the claims. The task was a daunting one, and the commissioners soon ran into trouble with the Irish parliament, in which the Adventurers were strong, being accused of being far too favourable to the Irish, and admitting spurious claims. The Adventurers resisted, and the commissioners found they lacked powers of compulsion. There were necessarily crowds of malcontents, whose claims could not all be met, disbanded soldiers, owed arrears of pay, adventurers who had lost land, and so forth. Many complaints were carried to the king, and the result was a further Bill of Explanation, which was supposed to be merely explanatory, but in fact went beyond to state new principles. Clarendon writes with sympathy of the Irish 'who without doubt for many years had undergone the most cruel oppressions of all kinds that can be imagined, many thousands of them having been forced, without being covered under any house, to perish in the open fields for hunger'.[20] Their claims were bound to conflict with those of the Adventurers, and both could quote the Act of Settlement on their behalf. Many claims were fraudulent, and the commissioners were too often gullible. Their task was made much harder by the promises made by the king, who, from good nature or indolence had given far more promises than could be easily fulfilled. Clarendon for instance thought his concern for the marquis of Antrim to be far above the latter's just deserts.[21]

Clarendon and Ormond opposed the new clauses inserted into the Bill of Explanation, partly because they gave legality to many of the king's promises but they were overruled. The time for the commissioners expired in August 1663; by then they had apportioned 800,000 acres, but only one-sixth of the claims had been heard. It was now clear that there was too little land to settle outstanding claims, and the Act required all claims to be reduced by one-third,[22] the resultant land to be distributed among the Irish. It met with

* In describing the appointment Clarendon gives one of his rare dates, and gets it wrong by two years (1664 instead of 1662).

opposition from the Adventurers in the Dublin parliament, but Ormond succeeded in carrying it in December 1665.

Clarendon makes it clear that he himself was concerned with Irish affairs only as a member of the Council, and that he firmly refused offers of land there. The king did however confer on him a grant under the Great Seal, which he could not refuse, and he used the money, about £6000 to purchase land in Wiltshire from the earl of Portland.[23] He also on occasion intervened in cases of hardship, as with Richard Bellings, an Irish Catholic who had served the king in exile, and to whom Clarendon persuaded the king to grant £400 p.a. pending the recovery of his Irish lands. Bellings was subsequently used by the king to solicit a cardinal's hat for Lord Aubigny, and to attempt an understanding with Pope Alexander VII, in both of which he failed. Clarendon was blamed in his impeachment for the attempt in which he may not have been directly involved.

The duke of Ormond administered Ireland with great skill, honesty, and with absolute loyalty to the crown. He earned the gratitude of the dispossessed Irish Catholics, and had little difficulty with the Irish parliament. A perennial problem was that Ireland cost England more than was raised in taxes, so that there was an annual deficit of over £30,000. The land problem was too intricate and complex for any entirely just solution to be possible, but Ormond had done his best to make it acceptable to all parties. Nonetheless, there must needs be many malcontents ready to intrigue against him. Worst of all from Ormond's point of view was the fact that he had earned the hostility of the duke of Buckingham, who, at least since 1663, had hankered after the Lord Lieutenancy of Ireland, and who envied the only duke who so far surpassed him in power. Ormond's fate was to be inseparably bound up with that of his friend Clarendon, and the fall of one was merely a prelude to the fall of the other.

# The Chancellor under Challenge

From the beginning the Restored monarchy of Charles II was beset with disunity and factions among the royalists. The six or eight members of the Sealed Knot who had directed the royalist cause in England during the Interregnum, and had been too cautious or too wise to join in premature risings, looked with contempt on the younger royalists such as Viscount Mordaunt with their enthusiasm for action. In any case they played little part in the politics of the Restoration. No one had served the king more selflessly in the years 1658–60 than Mordaunt, but he made himself so many enemies that at the Restoration, Clarendon wrote, he was 'totally neglected'. Royalists who remained in England tended to feel that they had borne the heat of persecution, while those in exile were living in Parisian luxury; while those who were in exile blamed them for submitting so readily to Cromwell's rule. Too many royalists, Clarendon wrote, gave themselves to drinking and debauchery, and had exalted opinions of the compensation now due to them for their past sufferings.[1] He lamented that too many of his old friends, the duke of Richmond, the earl of Dorset, Lord Capel and Lord Hopton, were dead. Only the marquis of Hertford, the earl of Southampton, the duke of Ormond and Secretary Nicholas remained. Many of the exiled royalists, especially the Louvre party headed by the Queen Mother, Jermyn (now earl of St Albans) and Sir Charles Berkeley, regarded Clarendon's influence with the king with unconcealed hostility, and when they exchanged the Louvre for Somerset House they became a powerful faction, always ready to undermine the Chancellor's position at every opportunity. Instead therefore of a strong and united royalist party, there were factions and jealousies which would make the work of any minister difficult without the steady support of the king.

Clarendon's constitutional theory was much closer to a Tudor prototype than to later constitutional practice. As early as the fifteenth century Fortescue had drawn a clear distinction between a prince who ruled politically (i.e. according the the laws of the land) and one who ruled regally (i.e. as a despot). Charles I's Answer to the Nineteen Propositions stated exactly Hyde's theory of mixed monarchy. He recognised the Commons as 'an excellent Conserver of liberty', but he rejected Pym's claim to parliamentary sovereignty. When Charles I rejected the Nineteen Propositions with the answer *Nolumus Leges*

*Angliae mutari*, he was making the same reply as the barons had made at Merton in 1236. Events after 1640 had confirmed Burghley's aphorism that 'he knew not what an act of parliament could not do in England', but the consequences had been so revolutionary that Clarendon fell back on the idea of a fundamental law which was close to that of Sir Edward Coke, who regarded it as equivalent to customary law, which bound the king as much as all his subjects. Like Burghley, Clarendon venerated the law, respected the power and privileges of parliament, but thought that the laws of England were 'grounded upon truth and reason'. Parliament had an essential legislative function, but the key institution of government was the Privy Council. Clarendon did however misunderstand the working of the Tudor Privy Council, which was not, as he imagined, a body shaping policy. In fact the great queen consulted her principal councillors individually, and never accepted a theory of collective responsibility of the Council. Hers was a personal monarchy the success of which rested upon her genius. Clarendon imagined that it was a system by which the great men of the land, and the great officers of state, without a 'first minister' or favourites, took governmental decisions under the eye of a vigilant monarch. It was certainly not like that under the early Stuarts, when the work of the Council was overshadowed by royal favourites and incompetent kings. Yet Clarendon's ideal of government rested on this idealised view of the Privy Council. He wrote in his *History*:

The truth is, the sinking and near desperate condition of monarchy in this kingdom can never be buoyed up but by a prudent and steady council attending upon the virtue and vivacity of the king; nor be preserved and improved when it is up, but by cherishing and preserving the wisdom, integrity, dignity and reputation of that council: the lustre whereof always reflects upon the king himself; who is not thought a great monarch when he follows the reins of his own reason and appetite; but when, for the informing of his reason, and guiding his actions, he uses the service industry and faculties of the wisest men. And though it hath been, and will be, always necessary to admit to those counsels some men of great power, who will not take the pains to have great parts; yet the number of the whole should not be too great; and the capacities and qualities of the most should be fit for business; that is, either for judgment and despatch, or for one of them at least, and integrity above all.[2]

Years later in exile, his views were the same: the Privy Council

is the most sacred, and hath the greatest authority in the government of the state, next the person of the king himself, to whom all other powers are equally subject: and no king of England can so well secure his own just prerogative, or preserve it from violation, as by a strict defending and supporting the dignity of his privy council.[3]

This was to give the theory of 'mixed monarchy' a new interpretation. Carried to extremes, it would be reminiscent of the mediaeval claim that

The magnates are the king's right hand (*membrum regis principale*), and without them the king cannot attempt or accomplish anything,[4]

except that Clarendon was not thinking of governance by the great magnates, who must however be included, but by faithful servants of the crown such as Southampton, Secretary Nicholas and himself. It was not an arrangement which would have suited Queen Elizabeth, and it would not suit Charles II. Clarendon complained of 'the ill principles the king had received in France, and the accustomed liberty of his bedchamber' which instead of respecting the views of the Privy Council as a body, led him to prefer cabals. But the Privy Council of Clarendon's ideal was impossible in practice, either under Charles or under any of his successors.

Charles's first Privy Council of about twenty-nine members, had to be a heterogeneous collection of former exiles, resident royalists, Presbyterians and ex-Cromwellians. By 1663 its number had increased to nearer forty, and it was always too large and too diverse for the efficient conduct of government. Business therefore was conducted largely by committees, the chief of which was the Secret Committee for Foreign Affairs, which emerged in June 1660. Anyone might be summoned to it at the king's will, but the chief members were the duke of York, Clarendon, Southampton, Ormond, Albemarle, Nicholas and Morrice. Ormond soon departed for Ireland, but Clarendon managed to conduct business via this committee during the first years of the Restoration. It prepared business which was later submitted to the whole Council. Charles was content to leave much of the drudgery of government to Clarendon, who willingly undertook it.

In the eyes of contemporaries Clarendon was virtually 'first minister', yet he himself was at pains to deny it. He wrote that his desire was to give his full attention to the work of the Lord Chancellor, and that he merely directed affairs during the first months of the Restoration because he had been closest to the king's business for many years, and because the king trusted him. He intended, he said, to act in a wider capacity only until the Privy Council was firmy established. He was content to share power with the other leaders of the Privy Council. Albemarle was in 1660 in a position to dictate his own terms, and in addition to being Captain-General of the forces and Lord Lieutenant of Ireland he chose the office of Master of the Horse. Clarendon said that he was 'an immoderate lover of money', and 'the vile good housewifery of his wife', made full use of the enormous patronage within his gift. The duke of Ormond, at first Lord Steward, soon succeeded Albermarle in Ireland, and his absence was sorely felt by the Chancellor. Clarendon praised the Lord Chamberlain, the earl of Manchester, for his 'gentleness and justice', and thought him 'the most worthy to be received into the trust and confidence of the king'. The earl of Southampton, who became Lord Treasurer, was, according to Clarendon, 'the most valued and esteemed of all the nobility', and the friendship between the two men was so close 'that neither of them concluded any matter of importance without consulting the other'.[5] Sir Edward Nicholas, Clarendon's oldest friend, and Albemarle's nominee, Sir William Morrice, a staunchly royalist Presbyterian, worked well together as Secretaries of State. These were the men who conducted affairs in the first years of the Restoration.

In addition to the Committee for Foreign Affairs, of which Clarendon was a principal member, a Committe for Plantations was set up in July 1660, and a Committee of Trade in August 1660.[6] Apart from the Navigation Act it can hardly be said that Charles II's government had a colonial policy, and the councils were open to pressure from the enterprising and the powerful. Clarendon was concerned with colonial affairs since petitions were often addressed to him, and the Great Seal was often necessary for official documents. Moreover he was always a member of the Committee of Trade, and he joined the Committee for Plantations in September 1662. He was a member of a committee to consider the settlement of New England in May 1661, and in September 1662 the Committee for Plantations 'seriously debated and discussed the settlement for the plantations in New England, and the Lord Chancellor then declared that his Majesty would speedily send Commissioners to settle the respective interests of the several colonies, the Duke of York to consider the choice of fit men.'[7]

English eyes were already on Peter Stuyvesant's colony of New Amsterdam, and even before it was captured, Charles II conferred on his brother the 'Duke of York's Grant' of the vast area between the Connecticut and Delaware rivers. In fact the New Englanders were already becoming troublesome, and reluctant to accept the Stuart regime, and Clarendon drew up his 'Considerations in order to the establishing his Majesty's interests in New England', some time in 1664. He urged

that as soon as they find a fit temper in that people, they then treat about the improvements of trade and the supply of timber, cordage, tar, etc. and endeavour to show the advantages of a better correspondence with England by their cheerful submission to the regulations of trade for his Majesty's dominions and plantations . . . The encouragements to all who submit to said regulations, but if any town or province do not submit, they will not be allowed to trade with England or any other colony. And whilst they [the Commissioners] shall be found not to intermeddle with their government or matters of religion, the stiff and factious party will want pretensions for stirring up the people to an eager opposition to the fair and reasonable proceedings of the Commissioners.

In March 1665 Clarendon addressed a further long letter to Samuel Mavericke, the Commissioner of New England, on the affairs of the colony. A letter of April 1666 showed that Clarendon already regarded the Massachusetts colony as the troublespot among the colonies.[8]

Another area of special interest was Carolina. During the Interregnum a considerable number of royalists had taken refuge in Barbados, and the island was suffering from over-population. Sir John Colleton, a prosperous planter, conceived the idea of settling Carolina, the region between Virginia and Spanish Florida, with the surplus population of Barbados. He captured the interest of Ashley Cooper, and in March 1663, Ashley Cooper, Clarendon and Albemarle, and others, were created Lord Proprietors of the new state of Carolina, in the hope of growing wine, oil, currants, raisins and silks, but *not* tobacco, ginger, cotton and indigo, which would compete with other colonies. The Proprietors reserved to themselves 20,000 acres, and offered a hundred acres to every settler, fifty acres to every man-servant and thirty acres to every woman-servant who were willing to take up the offer at a rental of ½d. an acre to the Proprietors. Each Proprietor invested a modest £75 in the enterprise; three counties were envisaged, named after Clarendon, Albemarle and Craven, and there was talk of establishing government by General Assembly. In January 1665, in agreement with Colleton, eighty-six adventurers were to be brought from Barbados, and the Lords agreed to arm and defend the fort at Port Royal (for which the king granted twelve guns to be sent from Ordnance), and each adventurer was to be granted 500 acres for every thousand pounds of sugar subscribed and paid within forty days. John Vassall was appointed Surveyor-General of the county of Clarendon. However the settlement was a failure, and in October 1667 Vassal reported 'the unhappy loss of their plantation on the Charles river', the county being declared unfit for Christian habitation, 'which hindered the coming of people and supply, so as the rude rabble of inhabitants were daily ready to mutiny against Vassall for keeping them there so long'.[9]

The Indians had killed their cattle, and it was not possible to persuade six men to remain. There was no better news from the settlement at Roanoke. It was not until after the fall of Clarendon that John Locke drew up his famous 'Fundamental Constitutions of Carolina', and another attempt was made to establish a settlement in 1670.

The third area of interest was Jamaica. In March 1662 the king gave permission to the duke of York to transport forty planters to Jamaica, twenty to be provided by Sir Charles Lyttelton, and twenty by the Lord Chancellor, together with five ministers and fifteen members of their families. When in September 1664 Sir Thomas Modyford was sent as Governor of Jamaica he took with him a further batch of settlers, and together they formed the parish of Clarendon, named in honour of the Chancellor. A flower still grows in Jamaica named after him.*

---

* The *cassis clarendonensis*. The index to plats in Jamaica shows that in 1666 Clarendon had a plat for 3000 acres in this parish, and this is confirmed by the 1670 census[10] The estate then passed to Thomas Lynch. I am grateful to Mr. Clinton V. Black, Jamaica Government Archivist for this information.

Clarendon's interests in the colonies were certainly limited, and he never made any money out of them, but as Chancellor, as member of the committees, and as a prospective investor, he was not without interests in their development, and the colonial issues illustrate the multifarious nature of the work of the Lord Chancellor in the first years of the reign of Charles II.

Whether he liked it or not (and he liked it more than he admitted in his *Life*), Clarendon had to act as first minister, for in 1660 problems were manifold, and governmental institutions primitive. He had to conduct Charles's foreign policy as well as domestic affairs, and he was used by the king to ward off the crowd of importunate royalists at a time when, as he wrote, 'the king had nothing to give'. It is not surprising therefore that he aroused a host of jealousy. Lord Salisbury expressed a typical royalist hostility when he declared that Albemarle had brought in the king 'for his own greatness', while leaving 'us' (i.e. the royalists) 'to be hanged'; and that the Lord Chancellor would 'never leave until he was another Cardinal Wolsey'.[12] Pepys learned at Westminster

that my Lord Chancellor is much envied, and that many great men, such as the Duke of Buckingham and my Lord of Bristol do endeavour to undermine him. [But that they were not likely to succeed,] 'for that the King (though he loves him not in the way of a companion, as he doth these young gallants that can answer him in his pleasure), yet cannot be without him for his policy and service'. (27 July, 1661)

In so tense a situation Clarendon was appalled when he heard that his daughter Anne had formed an attachment to the duke of York. The two had entered into some kind of marriage contract in November 1659 in Holland, and by the summer of 1660, when she was pregnant, the duke asked the king's permission to marry her. Charles consulted Southampton and Ormond, and they were sent to inform Clarendon. He received the news with consternation, convinced that it would be his ruin, and that he would be punished by banishment. He declared that he would rather his daughter were the duke's whore than his wife, and he urged the king to send Anne to the Tower. Charles displayed extraordinary kindness and tact, and once he knew that he was not being ruined, Clarendon grew calmer. The marriage had already taken place in secret on 3 September 1660 at Worcester House, the service being conducted by the duke's chaplain, with the earl of Ossory and Anne's maid as the only witnesses. There was nothing therefore to do but to accept it. The greatest indignation came from the Queen Mother and the Princess Royal, the latter declaring that she would never yield precedence to her former lady in waiting. So far the marriage was a secret, although Lord Ashley had his suspicions early in September when he told Southampton that he deduced it from the new respect Anne's mother was displaying towards her. As late as 7 October Lord Sandwich told Pepys that Anne Hyde was pregnant, and the king wished her to marry, but she would not: so little did well-informed people know at the time. The anger of the queen and the Princess Royal had some effect on the duke, who may have had second thoughts, but as Anne was approaching her time, the king required the judges and bishops to confirm the marriage.* A boy was born on 22 October, and was created duke of Cambridge. Charles throughout showed extraordinary sympathy with Anne, and great kindness towards Clarendon, including a gift of £20,000 in addition to lands at Cornbury and Wychwood Forest, a barony, and then an earldom.† Not so the duke of York's friends. The scurrilous Count Grammont recounted the story of how the earl of Arran, Lord Jermyn, Talbot and Thomas Killegrew concocted a rumour that they had had familiarity with Anne Hyde before her marriage, and Killegrew claimed to have lain with her. Later however Charles Berkeley admitted to James that he had fabricated the plot, and that he did it because he 'preferred the Duke of York's interest to Miss Hyde's reputation'.[14] Berkeley made a humble submission to Anne, which she readily accepted, but Clarendon, who knew how much the hostility of Somerset House was really aimed against him, never forgave Berkeley, and drew a black picture of him in his writings. The Queen Mother's hostility remained unabated, and Clarendon wrote that he refused to do anything to placate her, or even to come into her presence. But two men combined to make peace. Mazarin let the Queen Mother know that her return to France would not be welcome if there was friction in the royal family; and Charles asked Clarendon to meet his mother half-way in a reconciliation. The earl of St Albans visited him and asked him to wait upon the queen. She received him graciously, and on New Year's Day 1661 she was, with the marchioness of Ormond, godmother to her infant grandson. Anne was now fully accepted by the royal family (the Princess Royal having died of smallpox in December), and the crisis was past. Clarendon wrote however that he was so concerned at the number of enemies that he begged the king to allow him to retire, but Charles had replied that he was indispensable.[15]

The unpopularity of the marriage remained. Pepys who like everyone else was anxiously awaiting the news that Queen Catherine was pregnant, noted on 18 February 1661 that he was anxious that the duke of York should not come to the throne, 'he being a professed friend to the Catholics'. On 6 May he wrote heartlessly of the death of the duke of Cambridge, 'which I believe will please everybody'. This was before the duke of York had earned Pepys' respect as Lord High Admiral, but there was also resentment that Clarendon might be grandfather to a future king. Already there were rumours that Queen

---

* The duke of York's attestation that he had contracted with Anne Hyde at Houslardike on 9 August 1659 and lived with her secretly before coming to England, and married her on 3 September 1660 at Worcester House, was drafted by John Nicholas and dated 16 February 1661. Cal. V, p. 80.[13] The Privy Council declared any who questioned the legality of the marriage guilty of praemunire.

† He refused the offer of 10,000 acres in the Fen country.

Catherine was barren, and even that Clarendon had known of this before the marriage, and had planted his daughter in the royal bed: ludicrous accusations, but nonetheless repeated. In fact the king himself told bishop Burnet that the queen had been with child, and the physician Willis confirmed that she had once miscarried.[16]

As to the duchess of York, opinions differed with the degree of prejudice. Pepys found her 'a plain woman and like her mother' (20 April 1661). Count Grammont thought she was 'no perfect beauty, yet there were none at the court of Holland who eclipsed her', and bishop Burnet, who knew her best, found her 'a very extraordinary woman', with 'great knowledge, and a lively sense of things', who 'soon understood what belonged to a princess'. She bore the duke eight children, of whom only two survived.[17]

Meanwhile Clarendon was involved in the problem of the king's own marriage, all the more urgent now that his brother was married. The choice of a bride was closely bound up with relations with France and Spain. Charles had some reason for gratitude to Spain for hospitality in the Spanish Netherlands during the last years of his exile, but none at all to France, where he had been humiliated, and where Mazarin had consistently preferred an alliance with Cromwell to active support for the Stuarts. On the other hand, Charles's French connections were strong, and the power of France alluring. The Restoration took Mazarin by surprise, and he made the mistake of listening to the advice of the Queen Mother and Lord Jermyn, and sending Bordeaux to England, in company with Jermyn, with the object of making trouble for Hyde. On the latter's advice, Charles refused to accept Bordeaux, who returned home in disgrace. Although Bordeaux's career was ruined, Charles's prestige was enhanced, and the French had learnt the fallacy of relying on the Queen Mother's party. In fact Hyde had his own private channel of communication with Fouquet, the French Superintendent of Finances, through his agent Bastide de la Croix. Bastide began on the wrong foot by offering Hyde a bribe of £10,000 'a present only to supply the Chancellor's present occasions, and to furnish his house, in regard that his long banishment must have deprived him of those conveniences'.[18] Hyde was shocked, and at once refused, but continued to work closely with Bastide.

Among Charles's advisers opinion was divided between a pro-French and a pro-Spanish bias. The latter, it was argued, would ensure a share in the Spanish market, the former would enable further attacks on the Spanish Main. Since an alliance with Spain might entail the return of Dunkirk and Jamaica, Hyde saw the French-Portuguese connection as the better choice. For twenty years the House of Braganza had been fighting for independence from Spain, and sorely needed the prestige of an English alliance. It suited France, whose peace with Spain precluded direct help to the Portuguese, to persuade England to provide it instead. In his *Life* Clarendon was at pains to say that the first suggestion of a Portuguese marriage came from the earl of

Manchester, and from Charles himself. In any case, by October 1660 Hyde was drafting the terms of a marriage treaty, with two million crowns as the marriage portion, together with Tangier and Bombay and trading rights in the Portuguese empire.[19] The Chancellor was concerned however that this would involve military aid against Spain, hence the importance he attached to French aid. In April 1661 he asked Fouquet for a secret loan of £50,000 to relieve the king's difficulties, and this was at once granted. Bastide warned of strong opposition to the Portuguese marriage, not least from the earl of St Albans, who wanted a French marriage. The chief members of the pro-Spanish party were the earl of Bristol and Sir Henry Bennet, aided by the Spanish ambassador Batteville. They pressed for a marriage with a princess of Parma, until Bristol saw the two sisters, and found one 'very ugly' and the other 'monstrously big'.[20] Since no suitable Protestant could be found, the Portuguese marriage was decided upon. When the new French ambassador, d'Estrades arrived, he agreed to a French advance of two million livres to pay for 1000 horse and 2000 foot and ten ships to aid the Portuguese against Spain. Hyde continued his secret correspondence with Bastide, and sometimes used it to monitor St Albans's correspondence with Paris. It was then a shock to him to hear of the sudden fall of Fouquet in the summer of 1661. D'Estrades was now informed of the earlier secret correspondence, and although he made some difficulty about the payment of the two million livres, and said that it should be spread over three years, yet he endorsed the agreement.[21] It is thus clear that Clarendon was the minister responsible for initiating Charles's policy of looking to France for financial support.

The marriage contract was concluded in June 1661, and prudently stated that half the two million crowns marriage portion was to be on board before the princess embarked. Catherine of Braganza did not land in England until May 1662. The couple were married at Portsmouth on 21 May, a brief Catholic ceremony in secret preceding the Protestant marriage ceremony. Clarendon had scribbled a note to the king in April, 'You must have a Bishop with you, and he must marry you before you go to bed, and she is prepared to submit to it as a civil obligation for the legitimation of her children . . . You cannot be married by a Roman priest, therefore she must by a Bishop of yours.'[22] Charles wrote to Clarendon five days after the wedding that he was well satisfied with the attractions of his bride:

I cannot easily tell you how happy I think myself; and I must be the worst man living (which I hope I am not) if I be not a good husband. I am confident never two humours were better fitted together than ours.[23]

After a stay at Hampton Court, the queen arrived at Whitehall in May 1662, and there began a conflict of wills which was of great embarrassment to Clarendon. Barbara Villiers, daughter of Lord Grandison, and cousin to the duke of Buckingham, married to a Catholic royalist named Roger Palmer, was the king's mistress. She had borne him a daughter in February 1661, created countess of Sussex, and another in 1662, made countess of Lichfield. She was a woman of great beauty, who sent Pepys into erotic fantasies every time he saw her; and, with a mind of her own, she well knew how to handle Charles. When she was first presented to the queen, the latter received her graciously, not knowing who she was, but when she knew, 'her colour changed, and tears gushed out of her eyes, and her nose bled, and she fainted'.[24] Catherine had been brought up in strict retirement, hardly ever having left the royal palace, and she was quite unprepared for such a humiliation.[25] Charles too was humiliated at so public a scene before the whole Court, and he determined to have his own way. He now determined to raise Roger Palmer to an Irish earldom of Castlemaine, and to appoint Barbara Palmer a Lady of the Bedchamber to the queen, and until the latter agreed he would cease to visit her. Clarendon wrote that he would never have acted so harshly but for the importunities of his mistress, and the stories of the amours of his grandfather Henri IV whom he so much admired. Charles sent Clarendon to try to change his wife's mind. Clarendon hated the task:

It was too delicate a province for so plain-dealing a man as he was to undertake: and yet he knew not how to refuse it.[26]

His sympathies were entirely with the queen. He had been a close friend to Barbara's father, a royalist of the old school, but he detested the immoralities of the Court and the scandals which gave the king such notoriety. He would never make address to the lady, and never in his writings referred to her by name. The earl of Southampton similarly would never allow her name to appear in the Treasury accounts. But Charles was savagely determined to have his way. He wrote to Clarendon in an undated letter:

I think it very necessary to give you a little good council, lest you may think that, by making a further stir in the business, you may divert me from my resolution, which all the world shall never do; and I wish I may be unhappy in this world and the world to come, if I fail in the least degree what I have resolved; which is, of making my Lady Castlemaine of my wife's bedchamber: and whosoever I find use any endeavour to hinder this resolution of mine (except it be only to myself), I will be his enemy to the last moment of my life. You know how true a friend I have been to you. If you will oblige me eternally, make this business as easy as you can, of what opinion soever you are of; for I am resolved to go through with this measure, let what will come on it . . . Therefore, if you desire to have the continuance of my friendship, meddle no more with this business.[27]

The king's determination was worthy of a better cause, but Clarendon could only submit. Charles's parenthesis 'except it be only to myself', is significant: he would listen to Clarendon's lectures in private, but in public he would be obeyed. Clarendon did indeed lecture him on the cruelty inflicted on the queen, and the contempt people had for prostitutes, and he wrote that 'the king heard him with patience enough', and 'did not appear displeased with the liberty he had taken.'[28] Clarendon saw the queen twice, but was met with tears, and her determination to return to Portugal rather than submit. Charles replied by bundling her retinue back to Portugal, apart from the countess of Pensalva and a few servants. But then the queen learned prudence, and suddenly accepted the lady, 'was merry with her in public, talked kindly of her, and in private used nobody more friendly'. Clarendon was immensely relieved. He wrote to Ormond on 17 July 1662:

The King is perfectly recovered of his indisposition . . . I wish he were as free from all other. I have had, since I saw you, three or four long conferences, with much better temper than before. I have likewise twice spoken at large with the Queen. The Lady [Castlemaine] hath been at court, and kissed her hand, and returned that night. I cannot tell you there was no discomposure. I am not out of hope.[29]

Clarendon's contempt for Lady Castlemaine was repaid with active hostility. At first, he said, it took the form merely of witty mimicry which amused the king, but later she was an active centre of opposition to everything the Chancellor did.

The Portuguese marriage was a marked success for Clarendon in the sense that it was carried through in the teeth of considerable opposition from Spain, the pro-Spanish party headed by the earl of Bristol and Sir Henry Bennet, and from the Queen Mother and her party. The French had learnt the strength of Clarendon's position, and advised the Queen Mother to drop her hostility to him, and this had its effect when she withdrew her opposition to the duke of York's marriage, and when she attended the christening of his son, before returning defeated to France in January 1661. For Clarendon the prime purpose of the marriage treaty was that it would cement good relations with France, and this seemed fulfilled when Louis XIV wrote to him in December saying that he considered him the principal minister of his friendship with Charles II, and that the new French ambassador, the comte de Comminges had been instructed 'to address Clarendon with confidence on all affairs of his negotiations'.[30] What this referred to we shall see in a moment; but the Portuguese alliance brought the prospect of two million crowns to Charles's beleaguered treasury, together with Bombay and Tangier, while it was hoped that France would foot the bill for the military expedition sent to Portugal. Finally, Clarendon hoped that he had gained French support in England's continued maritime disputes with the Dutch. But few of these hopes were entirely fulfilled. The Portuguese defaulted on the payment of the marriage portion. Louis XIV sent 200,000 crowns in February 1662, which enabled Charles to send 3000 foot and 1000 horse to Portugal, under the command of the earl of Inchiquin; but thereafter Louis found an excuse to send no more money; Tangier proved an expensive luxury, and Louis XIV had no intention of aiding England against the Dutch; while Clarendon had invoked the bitter hostility of the Spanish government.

Louis's flattering letter referred to the negotiations for the French purchase of Dunkirk. As one of Cromwell's spectacular acquisitions, Dunkirk aroused a good deal of patriotic feeling in England but it presented the government with formidable problems. The cost of its upkeep was at least £100,000 a year.[31] Hyde told d'Estrades in August 1661 that the king had already spent £400,000 on its garrison and defences. Its harbour was thought to be of little use without the construction of an expensive mole; it would be difficult to defend in the event of renewed war between France and Spain, and might involve England in the war. Nor was it thought to be of much importance to the herring fisheries. On the other hand it was the prize of a Cromwellian victory, and its return to France would open the way to further French aggression in the Netherlands, and enable privateers to prey again on English shipping. Clarendon's account of the sale of Dunkirk cannot be regarded as entirely accurate. He wrote that in the Privy Council only the earl of St Albans opposed the sale, while Southampton, Sandwich and Clarendon were strongly for it. But d'Estrades's despatches make it clear that Albemarle and Morrice opposed the sale, and did all they could to delay it, while Sandwich and Southampton, although in favour of the sale, thought the price too low. D'Estrades was anxious to push through the negotiations as quickly as possible, fearing the growth of opposition in England. There seems little doubt that the negotiations were conducted by Clarendon, that Southampton, Sandwich, Albemarle were consulted, but that it was submitted to the full Privy Council only shortly before the treaty was signed. Hyde opened the negotiations with d'Estrades in August 1661, asking seven million livres, d'Estrades countered with an offer of two million livres, and after hard bargaining they agreed on five million. The agreement was signed in October 1662, two days after Sir Henry Bennet became Secretary of State and began to organise opposition to the Chancellor.

The sale of Dunkirk must therefore be regarded as primarily Clarendon's work, although he had the full support of the king and the duke of York. He saw the sale as a matter of financial necessity: the king simply could not afford an annual expenditure of £100,000 on a garrison of doubtful value. The wider consideration of the growing threat of France to the Spanish Netherlands did not concern him. What did concern him was the two-fold consideration that he was cementing good relations with France, and providing the monarchy with a nest-egg which he wrote should 'be preserved for some pressing accident, as an insurrection or the like'. However the good will of Louis XIV was more a comfort to an insecure monarchy than a real political asset, and the idea of a nest-egg proved illusory. The money arrived at the Tower of London in 293 chests of silver coins in November 1662. Within a few weeks more than two-thirds of the 4,654,000 livres (£327,000) actually paid (allowing 12%

discount for cash), was swallowed up to pay arrears in the army and navy and the expenses of the royal household. £100,000 was allocated to the mint for recoinage, but was almost at once transferred to the City bankers as security for loans. It was therefore impossible to set aside a substantial sum for 'some pressing accident'. Moreover those who thought that Louis XIV had gained a bargain were probably right, for he made the payment to England the excuse not to pay the 1,500,000 livres towards the cost of the Portuguese expedition, which in effect brought the price of Dunkirk down to a little more than three million livres.[32]

The sale of Dunkirk was unpopular among patriots, Cromwellians and City merchants, and at once there were rumours of bribery and corruption. Sir Thomas Carew, a disaffected MP forecast to Pepys in November 1661 that there would be trouble when parliament met since 'they see things carried so by my Lord Chancellor and others that get money themselves, that they will not endure it' (12 November 1661). The accusation that Clarendon built Clarendon House ('Dunkirk House') out of the bribes received in the sale was quite unjustified. When in March 1661 Bastide had offered him a bribe of £10,000 he had been horrified, and at once refused it. The money from the sale is all accounted for in the Treasury Books, and there was no bribery or corruption. But the money was so quickly dissipated that it was natural that suspicions should be aroused.

The sale of Dunkirk, and especially Clarendon's reference to 'some pressing accident, as an insurrection', underlines the extreme insecurity of the early days of the Restoration monarchy. There was, to begin with, a severe economic depression. The revenues fell far short of the £1,200,000 estimated as necessary by parliament. Over the reign Professor Chandaman estimates that it averaged only £945,000, and that although parliamentary grants totalled over the whole reign £4¾ millions, so as to produce an average total of £1,170,000, the average is greatly aided by the improved financial conditions of the later years of the reign.[33] In the early years of the Restoration the situation was much grimmer. In July 1660 Hyde estimated the revenues at only £784,100. Moreover when economic conditions began to pick up about 1664, there followed war, plague and fire to reverse the progress.[34]

With the perspective of time, there has been a tendency for historians to play down the dangers of insurrection after 1660, and certainly the attempts to raise rebellion seem ineffectual. But it did not seem so at the time. England had experienced twenty years of disruption. It was difficult to believe that the great numbers of disbanded soldiery and religious fanatics would disappear without trace. The grim days of the Civil War, and the formidable strength of the parliamentary enemy, left an indelible impression on Clarendon's mind. Renewed insurrection was a constant fear. The Venner plot in January 1661 was followed by the so called Presbyterian plot in Worcestershire in November. In December the king sent a message to parliament of a new plot, and Clarendon submitted evidence for a rising of Commonwealthsmen and disbanded soldiers, directed by a committee of seven including Sir James Harrington and Major Wildman. Wildman was supposed to have a plan to seize Shrewsbury, Coventry and Bristol and to overthrow the government. In 1662 Albemarle dismantled the defences of Coventry, Northampton, Gloucester and Taunton as possible centres of trouble. In November 1662 there was uncovered a plot of old army officers to seize the king and the duke of York and begin a revolution, and four of the ring leaders were tried and hanged. Indeed the Privy Council seems to have spent much of its time considering plots and rumours of plots. How real a threat these plots were it is difficult to say, but there is no doubt they were taken seriously by the Council at the time. Some argued that they re-enforced the need for a stern application of the Act of Uniformity, while on the other hand the king thought his Declaration of Indulgence a more satisfactory safety-valve. Clarendon vacillated between the two policies, but it is easy to see why he wanted a reserve fund for emergencies.

On the whole the Portuguese marriage treaty proved more a liability than an asset. Of the £350,000 marriage portion only about half was paid before 1668, and far more than this was expended on the Portuguese expedition, while Tangier brought an annual expenditure of £55,000, and constant friction with the Moors, with little strategic or commercial benefit to England.[36] Moreover the Portuguese alliance renewed the prospect of war with Spain, for the Spanish feared the English occupation of Tangier, with its possible threat to the Spanish treasure fleet, resented the English military successes in Portugal against the forces of Don Juan José, and suffered the continued raids of the buccaneers on the Spanish Main. The Spanish ambassador Batteville was therefore sent to England to oppose Clarendon in every way, to co-operate with the political opposition, and to encourage rebellion in England and Ireland. Unfortunately for him, he was involved in the famous struggle for precedence with the French ambassador which in September 1661 led to a clash in the Strand in which six Frenchmen were killed and thirty injured. Public opinion was on the side of the Spaniards: Pepys' comment was 'indeed, we do naturally all love the Spanish and hate the French' (30 September 1661). Clarendon's accusations of treasonable activities against Batteville led Philip IV to recall him, but his agents remained active both in England and Ireland. The marquis Caracena, with his headquarters in Brussels, was the leader of the Spanish war party, and did all he could to foment risings across the Channel, taking advantage of the discontents of the disbanded soldiery and religious dissenters, and the unpopularity of the new chimney tax. With the enforcement of the Act of Uniformity due on St Bartholomew's Day, the danger of insurrection seemed so great that Charles asked Sir Henry Bennet, keeper of the privy purse, to submit his views. Sometime in the summer of 1662, Bennet wrote to the king that 'the dissatisfaction towards the present

Government (though, God knows, very undeservedly) is become so universal that any small accident may put us into new troubles, though they should not as yet be thoroughly designed by those that wish for them'.[37] He argued that in the event of a renewal of civil war the most important lesson to be learnt from the past was the importance of the king maintaining his hold on London, and if the regular troops were concentrated there, as they must be, the rest of the country would be under-defended. A new Militia Act had been passed in 1662, which gave the king a free hand in military affairs,[38] and Bennet's advice was to make full use of it to hold the country firm for the next three months, and then, with the aid of parliament, to attempt to mitigate the discontent with a policy of Indulgence.

The king's military strength was small. Some 40,000 men had been disbanded in 1660, and returned to civilian life. After the sale of Dunkirk, its garrison too was disbanded. In November 1660 the 1st Foot Guards of 1200 men were raised under the command of Colonel John Russell, a former member of the Sealed Knot, and they were instrumental in suppressing the Venner rising of January 1661. In February the 2nd Foot Guards were raised from Albemarle's most trusted men, with himself as colonel. Charles's Life Guards became the Royal Horse Guards ('the Blues') in 1661, numbering 500, for the personal protection of the monarch. These formed the nucleus of a standing army, which, together with the garrisons, cost some £189,724 a year. It was far too small to be a danger to liberty, but after the experience of Cromwell there was a great fear of military power, and Charles's army was sufficient to earn Clarendon the charge in his impeachment that he had 'designed a standing army to be raised, and to govern the kingdom thereby'; a charge no more substantial than the others.

A crucial turning point in Clarendon's career was reached with the appointment of Sir Henry Bennet as Secretary of State in October 1662. He was the son of Sir John Bennet, a judge of the Prerogative Court of Canterbury, who had been fined and imprisoned for bribery in 1621. Henry proved himself a good classical scholar at Christ Church, Oxford, and, being a staunch royalist, entered the service of lord Digby in 1643. He saw some military action, and received a sabre-cut across the nose during a skirmish near Andover in 1644, which he advertised by a black patch for the rest of his life. He made numerous diplomatic journeys on the continent, and became a great favourite with the Queen Mother at Saint Germain. In 1648 he became secretary to the duke of York, and when Charles II came to Paris he was a member of a young set, including his cousin Will Crofts, Lord Wilmot, Daniel O'Neill and William Coventry, whose wit and humour pleased the king. The duke of York however disliked him, and in 1654 Bennet wrote to Charles, then at Cologne, begging to be allowed to join him. The king was delighted to receive him, to the annoyance of the duke of York. Charles wrote to his brother:

You must be very kind to Harry Bennet, and communicate freely with him; for as you are sure he is full of Duty and Integrity to you, so I must tell you that I shall trust him more than any other about you, and cause him to be instructed at large in those Businesses of mine.[39]

Bennet was genial and witty, and brought with him all the gossip of Paris, which pleased the king who developed an easy familiarity with him. At the same time Bennet was careful to show deference to Hyde, Ormond and Nicholas, and thus to win their approval. In 1656 Charles thought of making Bennet Secretary of State, but then sent him as ambassador to Spain, where he remained for the next four years. There he developed strong pro-Spanish sympathies, and was thus opposed to Hyde's policy of friendship with France and alliance with Portugal.

He returned to England in 1661 with a grand equipage which offended Hyde, and an exotic habit of dress, which caused much comment. But Hyde welcomed him, perhaps regarding him as a possible ally against the influence of Sir Charles Berkeley with the king.[40] On the other hand he protested against his being appointed Keeper of the Privy Purse, an office which had been promised to one of Hyde's relatives. Hyde found Bennet a seat at Callington in Cornwall in June 1661, but Bennet soon assessed the political situation, and preferred the company of the earl of Bristol and Lady Castlemaine. In January 1662 he begged the king to make him ambassador to France, but Louis XIV would not accept so pro-Spanish an envoy. He wanted the lucrative post of Postmaster-General, held by Colonel Henry Bishop, but Clarendon in Council upheld the latter's claims, to the annoyance of the king.[41] Bennet was clearly avid for power, and he submitted to the king in the early summer of 1662 a memorandum, which greatly impressed Charles. It referred to the 'universal dissatisfaction towards the present government', and the likelihood of renewed conflict over religion. He urged the necessity of holding London by military force, and using the new militia to hold down the rest of the country, pending a reassessment of religious policy. He aimed now at nothing less than the Secretaryship of State. Since Morrice, as Albemarle's nominee, could not be moved, it was decided that Nicholas, now over seventy, must be persuaded to retire. John Ashburnham was sent by the king to offer Nicholas £10,000 and a peerage if he did so. Nicholas was willing to go, refused a peerage, but asked for a higher fee, and in the end, Clarendon commented, 'it cost the king very little less than £20,000 to bring in a servant whom few cared for, in the place of an old servant whom everybody loved'.[42]

It was a severe blow to Clarendon, who had first opposed the change, and then refused to do anything to influence Nicholas. The latter, on the other hand, half suspected that Clarendon had been in the intrigue. More seriously, O'Neill wrote to Ormond:

I can assure you the king is very much unsatisfied with the Chancellor, first for the opposition, and then for the little assistance he gave him in the removing of Mr. Secretary Nicholas.[43]

The sale of Dunkirk, the open conflict with Lady Castlemaine, and the uncertainties following the enforcement of the Act of Uniformity, all made this a trying time for Clarendon, but he was determined to make the best of it. He wrote in cypher to Ormond on 25 October:

I cannot tell you that I find, whatever other people discourse, my credit at all diminished with the King. He takes pains sometimes to persuade me the contrary; yet this late change makes a great noise, and gives occasion to others to raise a 1000 rumours of other alterations and removals, of which I do not think there is the least ground.[44]

His chief concern, he added, was the idleness and fecklessness of the king. But this was to put a bold face upon the situation, and Ormond knew better. As early as 15 October he had requested the king:

that my correspondence in what may relate to your service may be with Sir Henry Bennet, and that you will be pleased to declare it, as that I may be freed from the distraction of receiving your pleasure as to public transactions from more than one hand.[45]

To Clarendon however he asked that they continue to correspond in code, believing that Bennet's appointment was the work of 'the junto at Somerset House', and that it presaged 'further and greater alterations' in offices of state.[46] He urged that they should continue in close communication.

The appointment was bound to have serious consequences for Clarendon. A Secretary of State could be a powerful minister, dealing with foreign and domestic affairs. He would be in direct correspondence with all ambassadors, and would be able to influence all policies. Previously Clarendon and Nicholas had worked in complete harmony, and the Chancellor was the directing force. The change would be masked for some time because Bennet continued a tactful deference towards the Chancellor, but never again would the latter be in so unchallenged a position. Bennet had no doubt sensed the vacillations in Clarendon's policies; he disapproved of his foreign policy, and favoured a more tolerant religious policy. Although as always his instinct was to keep a foot in both camps, yet he acknowledged the influence of Lady Castlemaine in bringing him into office, and the Lady, the earl of Bristol, the duke of Buckingham and Sir Charles Berkeley formed a powerful anti-Clarendonian clique, able to entertain the king with ribaldry at the Chancellor's expense, and to offer him policies of which Clarendon disapproved.

For the moment however, Clarendon's difficulties seemed to relate more to the earl of Bristol. From the meeting of the Long Parliament the two young men had been close friends, together with Culpepper and Falkland. George

Digby had opposed ship money, supported the Triennial Bill, disliked prelatical bishops, and was brave enough to defend Strafford. Clarendon wrote that he had 'a most wonderful facility to arrive at a greater pitch of being beloved than any man I ever knew'. By June 1641 he was a member of the Court party, and was created Baron Digby. By the Spring of 1642 he had joined the king at York, and in 1643 he succeeded Falkland as Secretary of State. His advice to Charles I often savoured more of audacity than of wisdom, but his optimism and dash made him a live wire, and his friendship with Hyde seemed assured. When Hyde and Culpepper joined the Prince's Council in the West, Prince Rupert and Digby were the chief influences about the king. But Rupert lost the city of Bristol and Digby was defeated at Sherbourne in Yorkshire in 1645, and these disasters hastened the end for the king. In the king's council Rupert accused Digby of treason, which the king indignantly rejected, calling him 'my best subject'. Digby never saw the king again, but went to Ireland to join Ormond. He was still Secretary of State, and kept up a close and friendly correspondence with Hyde, full of admiration for the wisdom and integrity of Ormond, and full of optimism that the Irish Catholics might be persuaded to provide the king with an army in England. All that was needed, he convinced himself, was that the Prince of Wales should appear in Ireland to lead it.

Clarendon gives an amusing account of Digby's attempts to persuade the Prince to go to Ireland, first in Jersey, and then in Paris. With a fatuous optimism he spoke of an army of 12,000 men awaiting only a leader. He hoped that with Scots, Irish and French help, an attack could be made on England, but he entirely failed to persuade Hyde, or to convert the queen, or to win Mazarin's financial backing, and in July 1646 he returned to Ireland. His friendship with Hyde was unimpaired, and he left his son John in the latter's care in Jersey. When in the following year he returned to France, he entered French service, but joined Charles II at Bruges in 1656, and distinguished himself in military service with the Spaniards. It seems likely that by now he doubted whether the Stuarts would ever be restored, and in 1659 he was converted to Catholicism, perhaps with a view to entering Spanish service permanently. The news however was a great shock to Hyde, who said that he did not see how Bristol (he had succeeded his father in 1653) could ever again hold office: 'The noise and scandal of this defection and apostasy in a sworn counsellor of the king, and one of his secretaries of state, made it necessary for the king to remove him from both those trusts, which he had made himself incapable to execute by the laws of England.'[48] His dismissal was certainly a shock to the earl. At the Restoration he remained in Paris for a time, although he was in the House of Lords by July 1660. He thus ostentatiously avoided the scramble for rewards, but may have relied on the good offices of his old friends Clarendon and Ormond, for he must have argued that his services to the monarchy was little short of theirs. The king did give him £10,000, but there was no offer of office. As the Sherborne estates had been settled on his eldest son, he was a poor man. With his £10,000 he purchased Wimbledon House, and the king granted him also Ashdown Forest and lands in Sussex. But it was power he wanted, and he blamed Clarendon entirely for his exclusion from it. Clarendon had indeed put their old friendship behind him, and become cold and distant. The fact that he was a Catholic did exclude him from office, but perhaps his lack of political judgment was also partly responsible. Clarendon might however have shown greater tact in view of their long friendship. As it was, Bristol quickly emerged as the leader of the pro-Spanish party. He did everything possible to hinder the Portuguese marriage, even making a journey to Parma to inspect the princesses Spain suggested as possible brides. As a Catholic he strongly supported the Declaration of Indulgence, and he found a useful ally in Lady Castlemaine.

Burnet describes how at the time of the Declaration of Indulgence, Bristol summoned the leading Catholics to his London house, and after an oath of secrecy 'told them now was the time for them to make some steps towards the bringing in of their religion, that they should endorse the cause of the dissenters'.[49] Lord Aubigny supported him, saying that now it was in the interest of England to prevent trading men from leaving the kingdom for religious reasons. Lord Stafford told Burnet that he was present, but soon left, 'apprehending the earl of Bristol's heat'. Burnet said that the earl of Bristol and the duke of Buckingham regarded the Declaration as a victory over Clarendon. Sir Henry Bennet was not at the meeting, but he knew all about it, and now that he was Secretary of State, it was clear that there was a change in the political climate. Pepys wrote on 17 October 1662:

To Westminster Hall . . . Here I am told how things go at Court; that the young men get uppermost, and the old serious lords are out of favour. That Sir H. Bennet being brought into Sir Edward Nicholas' place, Sir Ch. Berkeley is made Privy-purse – a most vicious person, and one whom Mr. Pierce the surgeon today did tell me that he offered his wife £300 per annum to be his whore. He also told me that none in the Court hath more the King's ear now than Sir Ch. Berkeley and Sir H. Bennet and my Lady Castlemaine, whose interest is now as great as ever . . . all which things do trouble me much.

One of those who attached themselves to the earl of Bristol was Sir Richard Temple of Stowe, the member for Buckingham, who Godfrey Davies desscribed as 'a typical politician in a corrupt and selfish age'.[50] In 1660 he found himself with an estate worth £3500 a year and debts amounting to £12,000. He sought the usual remedy of employment at Court, and for this purpose attached himself to the Secretary Sir William Morrice, but without result. In 1663 therefore he moved on to the earl of Bristol. He told him that with royal authority he and his friends could carry the Declaration of Indulgence in the Commons. Bristol informed the king, who was interested. But Temple failed, and he then told Bristol that he could not co-operate with those who now managed the House, but that if the king would trust him and his friends, he would guarantee him a greater revenue than he could otherwise expect. This was noised abroad at Court, and on 13 June 1663 Coventry raised the matter in the House. The Commons requested the king to reveal the name of the Lord who had conveyed Temple's message to him. He named the earl of Bristol. At Bristol's request he appeared at the bar of the House to explain. In a masterly speech, he denied that there had ever been a message; he denied that he had ever received any reward for his services, or that he had ever asked for any, and then enlarged for half an hour on the inadequacies of the king's present ministers. All he had said was that if the king's affairs were better handled, he himself would undertake for the loyalty of the Commons.[51] The Commons were satisfied, but the king sent for Bristol to hear what he had said. When Bristol repeated it, the king said it was more 'vain, mutinous, seditious and false' than he had supposed. Bristol then fell on his knees, telling the king that he knew that all the enmity against him sprang from the Chancellor, and asking permission to charge him with high treason. He threatened that unless he withdrew his support from Clarendon, he would make damning revelations.[52] Charles said afterwards that he was so taken aback that he forgot to send him to the Tower. He replied that if Bristol had wished to impeach Clarendon he should have done so without informing him. O'Neill said that only Lord Aubigny was present; that Bristol had asked Bennet to be there, but he refused, saying that he had no wish to be a witness to his madness. Charles forbade Bristol to appear at Court.*

Bristol's acts were entirely motivated by a fanatical hostility towards Clarendon. O'Neill thought his precipitate actions were very embarrassing to Bennet and Ashley who would in different circumstances have been his allies. A few days later he carried his enmity further when in the Lords he exhibited Articles of high treason against the earl of Clarendon. The charges were a farrago of venom and nonsense: that he had abused the king's trust, that he had said that the king was inclined to Popery, and had a design to alter the established religion, that he had said that Bennet was a secret Papist, that he had sought a cardinal's hat for Lord Aubigny, the queen's almoner, that he had employed Papists on missions of trust, that he had said that the king intended to legitimise the duke of Monmouth, that he had abused the Commons, saying it was better to sell Dunkirk than be at the mercy of the Commons, that he had enriched himself by the sale of offices, and so on.[54]

David Hume's comment is the best:

The articles resemble more the incoherent altercations of a passionate enemy than a serious accusation fit to be dismissed by a court of judicature.

---

* Sir Richard Temple, having failed with the earl of Bristol, attached himself first to Arlington, and then to Buckingham. He was, as Clayton Roberts writes, one of the 'neglected men of talent who sought preferment at Court by making themselves considerable in Parliament'.[53] He and others like Seymour, Littleton, Howard and Galloway, were to lead the attack on Clarendon in 1667.

On 13 June the judges gave their unanimous opinion that one peer could not exhibit articles of high treason against another, and that even if all the charges were true they would not amount to treason. The king sent a message delivered by the Lord Chamberlain that several of the charges were to his certain knowledge untrue, and that they 'contained many scandalous reflections upon himself and his relations which he looked upon as a libel against his person and government'. Clarendon defended himself point by point, saying that if any one of the charges could be proved he would acknowledge himself guilty of the whole.[55]

Bristol had clearly overshot the mark, and with the displeasure of both the king and the Lords upon him, he went into hiding. For the time being Clarendon appeared vindicated, but there is no doubt that the previous ten months had been traumatic. The appointment of Sir Henry Bennet as Secretary of State, his long period of illness, his ambiguous part in the Declaration of Indulgence, the friction with the king over his relations with the queen and Lady Castlemaine, together seem to have neutralised Clarendon's political influence in 1663. At first he tried to put a bold face upon it, as when he wrote to Ormond in October 1662 that his credit was not at all diminished with the king; yet in the same letter he wrote fatalistically: 'you know, what will be, will be, in spite of the Chancellor'. In April 1663 he told Ormond that

since your departure I have had so unpleasant a life as that, for my own ease and content, I rather wish myself at Breda, and have hardly been able to restrain myself from making that suit . . . Sir Henry Bennet and his friends have more credit, which I do not envy them, except for our poor Master's sake, for he doth every day so weak and unskilful things as he will never have the reputation of a good minister, nor is in any degree able for that promise.[56]

Clarendon's correspondence becomes so thin for most of 1663 as to suggest that he had almost ceased to function as an active Minister; and it is significant that when Charles prorogued parliament in July, the Lord Chancellor was not present to make his customary address.

This is borne out by the *Diary* of Samuel Pepys, who had an excellent eye and ear for affairs at Court. In January 1663 he wrote: 'I find there is nothing almost but bawdy at Court from top to bottom.' In February he heard 'that Sir H. Bennet is a Catholic, and how all the Court almost is changed to the worse since his coming in, they being afeared of him'. In April the earl of Sandwich told him, 'great differences there are at Court, and Sir H. Bennet and my lord Bristol and their faction are likely to carry all things before them (which my Lord's judgment is, will not be for the best) and particularly against the Chancellor, who, he tells me, is irrecoverably lost'. In conversation with Sir Thomas Carew Pepys learnt of

the unhappy posture of things at this time; that the King doth mind nothing but pleasures and hates the very sight or thoughts of business. That my Lady

Castlemaine rules him . . . If any of the sober councillors give him good advice and move him in anything that is to his good and honour, the other part, which are his councillors of pleasure, take him when he is with my Lady Castlemaine and in a humour of delight, and then persuade him that he ought not to hear or listen to the advice of those old dotards or councillors that were heretofore his enemies, when God knows it is they that nowadays do most to study his honour. It seems the present favourites are now my Lord Bristol, the Duke of Buckingham, Sir H. Bennet, my Lord Ashley and Sir Ch. Berkeley, who among them have cast my Lord Chancellor on his back, past ever getting up again; there being now little for him to do, and waits at Court attending to speak to the King as others do . . . It is feared it will be the same with my Lord Treasurer shortly.

There could hardly be a more graphic picture of the state of affairs, with the Chancellor waiting in the queue for an audience of the king, to discuss policy which had been decided among the 'councillors of pleasure' in Lady Castlemaine's apartments. Only the duke of Albemarle was safe in the king's favour, but he was not a member of what Pepys called 'the Cabinet', and even he 'is envied enough'.[57] In June Pepys was expecting Clarendon's imminent fall, and 'praying God a worse doth not come in his place'. From this the Chancellor was saved by Bristol's insanely precipitate action, and by July Pepys was recording that 'my Lord Chancellor grows great again'.[58] But if he was free from Bristol, he was more than ever dependent upon Sir Henry Bennet and his friends.

Bennet had already turned his attention to building up Court influence in the Commons. At some time which cannot be exactly determined, but may have been in January 1663, while Clarendon's illness continued, the Secretary of State put before the king a plan for the more efficient organisation of the Court party in the Commons.[59] He argued that many members were often uncertain what the royal policy was, and that there were members like Thomas Clifford who could be used to organise a more coherent party.

Clarendon in his *Life* describes the system he had so far adopted with respect to the Commons. He wrote that he and the earl of Southampton had daily conferences with a few acknowledged royalists to consult on the business of the House,

all without any noise, or bringing many together to design, which ever was and ever will be ingrateful to parliaments, and, however it may succeed for a little time, will in the end be attended with prejudice.[60]

He had grim memories of the power of cabals in the Long Parliament, and wished to avoid building up a Court party, which would offend the independence of the House. He thought it sufficient to concert procedure with confirmed royalists, who would give direction to debates. He did not name them, but presumably they included men like the Solicitor-General Heneage Finch, Sir Thomas Meres, Henry Coventry, Sir Robert Paston, Sir

Hugh Pollard, Sir John Denham and Sir John Berkenhead. Until 1663 the system had certainly worked well, for the royalist-Anglican majority held, and there was little to divide members from the Court, except the rumours of Court extravagance and immorality,* and in particular the Declaration of Indulgence, in which the Commons gained their way. Sir John Berkenhead organised publicity by editing the Court newsbook *The Kingdomes Intelligencer* and *Mercurius Publicus*, until he was replaced in 1663 by Sir Henry Bennet's nominee, L'Estrange. Clarendon told Charles that his royalist friends had conducted affairs in the Commons without ever earning 'the odious name of undertakers, which in all parliaments hath been a brand'. He well remembered the sorry figures Charles I's ministers had cut in the early days of the Long Parliament, unless like St John they threw themselves in with the opposition. But his argument failed to convince Charles, who ordered him to use Thomas Clifford and Winston Churchill in the future organisation of the Commons. Churchill seems never to have played a significant part, but Clifford soon became Bennet's man in the Commons, and thus, Clarendon wrote, 'many other alterations followed by degrees, though not at once'.[61] Henceforth the Commons were confused by being offered two Court parties, one looking to Clarendon, and strongly Anglican, the other looking to Clifford and Bennet; and if to this is added the political influence of the duke of Buckingham, the confusion is increased.

When parliament met again in March 1664, the king announced that the Derwentdale Plot was at an end, and a number of ring leaders had been hanged, that the old spirit of enmity was still abroad, and that 'we are not yet at the bottom of that business'. A plot for a rising had first been uncovered by John Cosin, bishop of Durham, involving ex-soldiers and Anabaptist fanatics. A network of conspiracy stretched from Durham, Westmorland and Cumberland, to Yorkshire (where John Atkinson, known as The Stockinger of Askrigg, was the organiser), and to London, where there was a council of six, all old soldiers of Cromwell's day, Blood, Locker, Wise, Jones ('Mene Tekel'), Crew and Lee. Atkinson confessed that the plan was to seize the Tower and Whitehall and to kill the king, the dukes of York and Albemarle, and the Lord Chancellor. Atkinson and a number of others were executed, and investigations went on into 1665, but the last of the major conspiracies of the Restoration years was over. Since some of the conspirators had called for the recall of the Long Parliament, and others had said that under the Triennial Act of 1641 the parliament of 1661 was already dissolved, parliament hastened to pass a new Triennial Act (1664) which declared that the Act of 1641 was 'in derogation of His Majesty's just rights and prerogative inherent in the

---

* This is a constant theme among Pepys's friends, who showed a good deal of incomprehension about the costs of government. Thus Roger Pepys, member for Cambridge, and Samuel's cousin, exclaimed with wonder to him in June 1663 that since coming to the throne the king had received no less than £4,000,000! So modest a sum left little room for great extravagance.

Imperial Crown of this realm for the calling and assembling of parliaments'. The king was asked to ensure that the interval between parliaments should not be above three years. This done, parliament was again prorogued from May to November 1664. By that time the issue which overshadowed all others was the dispute with the Dutch, and Clarendon faced his most serious crisis since 1660.

# 'An Immoderate Desire to Engage the Nation in War'

Anglo-Dutch relations in the seventeenth century form a complicated pattern of friendship and rivalry. Queen Elizabeth had supported the Dutch against Spain, and Protestantism formed a bond between the two countries facing a common Catholic enemy. The marriage of William of Orange to Charles I's daughter was intended to cement that alliance, as was that of William of Orange and James II's daughter later. But religious ties and dynastic links proved less effective than the growing fact of economic rivalry. For while the English were engaged in civil wars, the Dutch were gaining mastery of the cloth trade, the herring fisheries, and the Baltic trade in grain and timber, and compared with Dutch expertise, at first the English were merely amateur traders. During the civil wars the sympathies of the House of Orange were with the Stuarts, but with the death of William of Orange in 1650 the Republicans gained the upper hand. They were not interested in an alliance with the Commonwealth or Protectorate against Spain, where they had important markets, and Cromwell's idea of a Protestant alliance came to nothing. The Dutch sought only economic advantage wherever it could be found. The first check to Dutch domination of the carrying trade came with the English Navigation Act of 1651. Thereafter relations deteriorated rapidly as the Dutch complained of cargo seizures, and the English complained of Dutch brutalities in the East Indies and elsewhere. In the first Anglo-Dutch War of 1652–4 the Dutch suffered heavy losses but the peace treaty of Westminster of April 1654 was entirely inconclusive. The real lesson to be drawn from it was probably the futility of fighting such a commercial and maritime war, but this lesson was not learnt, and the problem of Dutch rivalry was inherited by the Restoration government.

Charles II refused to recognise legislation passed by the Commonwealth or Protectorate, so the Navigation Act had to be re-enacted, and that of 1660 was very much more efficient than that of 1651. Together with the Staple Act of 1663, it formed the basis of the mercantilist system which prevailed for the next century and a half, and was one of the sources of England's commercial prosperity. Its principal author was Sir George Downing. Downing's parents emigrated to New England when he was fifteen, and he was one of the first graduates of Harvard College. Returning to England, he served Cromwell in various capacities, and in 1657 was sent as Resident at The Hague, where he rapidly decided that the Dutch were the greatest rivals to English prosperity. In 1660 he found it easy to make his peace with the Restored monarchy, explaining his earlier errors by the biased education he had received in New England. His appointment at The Hague was confirmed, and he proved himself as efficient in the pursuit of regicides as formerly he had been in pursuing royalists.[1] He was also a leading advocate of a tough policy towards the Dutch.

Charles II and Clarendon did not so much formulate a policy towards the Dutch as have one thrust upon them. Charles had some reason for gratitude for the splendid send-off the States had given him on his return to England, and Clarendon, always aware of the political uncertainties and the financial weakness of the Crown, was always anxious for peace. As early as November 1660 a Dutch embassy arrived to discuss the possibility of an alliance, but they found a host of obstacles. The greatest was the Navigation Act, which obviated the Dutch claim to free trade. There was Selden's theory of 'Mare clausum', in conflict with the Dutch theory of 'Mare liberum'; there was the Dutch invasion of the herring fisheries from the Shetlands to Yarmouth. There was the clear intention of the Dutch to monopolise East Indian trade, and in particular their refusal to evacuate Pularoon, in the Spice Islands, which the English had claimed since 1623. There were long-standing claims to compensation by the East India Company for seizure of ships and cargoes, and the English attached quite special importance to the two ships the *Bona Aventura* and the *Bona Esperanza*, which had been seized by the Dutch in 1643. The East India Company alone made claims against the Dutch amounting to £300,000. There were other issues. The marriage treaty with Portugal annoyed the Dutch, for they were still at war with Portugal, and resented the cession of Bombay and Tangier, which could be used as bases against Dutch shipping. Also the Stuarts attached great importance to the restitution of the House of Orange. In December 1660 the Princess of Orange died in England, leaving her eleven-year-old son William to the protection of her brother Charles II, and this was deeply resented by De Witt and his party. Downing was convinced that the restoration of the Prince of Orange was an essential condition for peace with the Dutch, and he sought an alliance with the Orange party in their opposition to De Witt.[2]

Charles II's problem was that he could not afford to pursue a policy towards the Dutch which appeared weaker than Cromwell's had been. As early as July 1661 Clarendon was writing to Bastide that 'the whole nation, but not the king desires a fair war with the Dutch'.[3] Clarendon, who was not greatly interested in the commercial aspects of the conflict, but much more in the stability of the monarchy, placed his hopes in the understanding with France. If Louis XIV supported Charles, surely the Dutch would not dare to risk a war. But the fallacy here lay in the fact that Louis XIV had no intention of playing the English game, or of supporting the House of Orange, which he assumed would always be pro-English. For him the prime consideration was the isolation of Spain, and for this purpose an alliance with De Witt would be the best move. It was true that Colbert viewed Dutch economic power with as much hostility and envy as Downing did, but for the time being this fact was concealed. Louis's alliance with the Dutch republic, signed in March 1662, was a setback for Downing, but he continued to rely on the considerable opposition in the other states of the United Provinces to the domination of Holland's commercial interests, and his belief that the Franco-Dutch alliance could not hold once De Witt appreciated Louis's designs in the Spanish Netherlands. When Charles II protested to Louis about the alliance, he replied blandly that it was in England's interests, since without it the Dutch would ally with Spain, and he added that once the English and the Dutch had made peace Charles would be welcome to enter the alliance.[4]

The Franco-Dutch alliance in no way deterred Downing from pressing England's claims. He was convinced that they were just, and that England's commercial prosperity depended upon curbing Dutch dominance. But De Witt was equally adamant, and he looked to the French alliance, not only to support him against England, but to enable the Dutch to apply a restraint on French ambitions in the Spanish Netherlands. Both sides displayed a stubbornness which made compromise impossible.

Clarendon was always in danger of being swept along by Downing's uncontrollable determination. In August 1662 Downing revealed what concerned him most when he sent Clarendon a memorandum on the growth of the Dutch woollen industry, which was now providing France, Poland and even England with cloth, so that England had become merely 'the poor man's clothier'. If the Navigation Act were relaxed, he wrote, there would soon be few ships left in England. In such matters Clarendon was largely in Downing's hands. On another occasion Clarendon wrote that having discussed his despatches with the king, the duke of York and the Lord Treasurer, they agreed that a treaty with the Dutch, if 'dexterously managed, would secure to England the best trade of Christendom', and that Downing, 'with his knowledge of trade and the Dutch, was best qualified to conduct the affair' (18 March 1664). So Downing was given a free hand to carry on the negotiations very much as he wished. When the question of the *Bona Esperenza* and the *Bona Aventura* was raised, Clarendon had to ask Downing what the question was, since he had not heard of it. He was always ready to give way to the expert. When Clarendon wrote to him that he thought that the question of the Prince of Orange should be left out of the peace talks with the Dutch (a very sensible suggestion), Downing brushed it aside with the reply that that would be to play De Witt's game, and he continued to press the prince's claims.[5] Downing and De Witt between them made a peaceful settlement impossible.

Moreover, it must be remembered that Clarendon was no longer conducting foreign policy as he had done at first. The duke of York was actively interested in English sea-power. The Royal African Company was incorporated in 1663 with the duke as President, and the king and Sir Henry Bennet were among the shareholders. Bennet as Secretary of State, was in favour of a vigorous foreign policy, and was hot for a war which might yield rich profits. Neither the king nor Clarendon wanted war, but as the latter wrote, Charles could not 'seem less careful of his subjects than Cromwell was'. Neither believed that it would really come to war. Thus Clarendon asked whether the two ships *Bona Esperenza* and *Bona Aventura* were really worth a war, and Charles asked the Dutch ambassadors, 'And pray, what is Cape Verde? A stinking place – is this of such importance to make so much ado about?'[6] But the lure of gold and slaves was a potent force, and there was bitter rivalry on the Gold Coast. Robert Holmes was sent out by the Royal African Company to avenge Dutch attacks on Capo Corso, and in the Spring of 1664 he captured Cape Verde, Goree and most of the Gold Coast. It is true that Charles disavowed Holmes, and sent him to the Tower, but he did not offer to hand back the forts, which De Ruyter was duly sent to recapture. In August the English seized New Amsterdam. In December Sir Thomas Allin attacked the Smyrna fleet off Cadiz, and captured three ships. When parliament met in April 1664, feelings were running high when a parliamentary committee listed the injuries received from the Dutch, and a resolution called on the king to redress them. Still neither the king nor Downing expected war: Downing argued that a show of strength would force the Dutch to climb down. Charles wrote to his sister (2 June, 1664):

The States keep a great bragging and noise, but I believe, when it comes to it, they will look twice before they leap. I never saw so great an appetite to a war as is, in both this town and country, especially in the Parliament men, who, I am confident, would pawn their estates to maintain a war. But all this shall not govern me.[7]

When he wrote again a fortnight later he was convinced that the moderation shown by the Dutch ambassadors portended that they were afraid of war and would surely in the end give way. In September he wrote that there was no need for the Dutch to provoke England, 'for except myself I believe there is scarce an Englishman that does not desire passionately a war with them'. Much as Charles claimed to be uninfluenced by popular clamour, the prospect of 'parliament men pawning their estates to maintain a war', together with rich prizes to be won at sea, was alluring to him. In November the duke of York was ordered to put the fleet in a state of readiness for action, and a hundred-and-thirty Dutch ships were seized in English ports. When France offered mediation, Bennet replied that there must be victory first.

However, nothing could be done without money, and Clarendon describes how the king instructed him and the Lord Treasurer to summon a group of their supporters in the Commons to a meeting at Worcester House in January 1665, to be told that it was no longer a question of whether there should be war, but how that war should be carried on, and how the money should be raised. Sir Henry Bennet and Sir William Coventry were for asking for a modest sum sufficient to get the fleet to sea, but Clarendon and Southampton thought that a single vote for the war would be likely to gain acceptance, and would be more likely to alarm the Dutch, and that the required sum was £2½ million. But since so large a sum had never before been granted at one time, it was decided that it should not be proposed by a minister, but that the independent Norfolk landowner, Sir Robert Paston, should propose it. Next day the House was astounded to hear the size of the supply.[8] Witcombe has shown that the Commons did not accept it as easily as Clarendon's account implies, and that there were always about a hundred members ready to oppose such measures. But the majority held, and in February a money bill was carried, voting a total of £2,477,500, to be spread over three years.[9] Clarendon commented sardonically that

this brave vote gave the king the first liking of the war: it was above what he had expected or indeed wished to be proposed.[10]

Clarendon regarded it as a personal triumph over the war-monger Sir Henry Bennet. With his supply secured, the king declared war on 4 March 1665.

Both sides were concerned at the line the French would adopt. Charles wrote to his sister in August 1664 that he was anxious to know what he could expect from Louis, and in December he wrote optimistically that 'he believed his friendship to France is and will be more considerable than that of the Hollanders'.[11] But this was to deceive himself, for Louis regarded the conflict as a nuisance impeding his plans for the isolation of Spain, and although he had no intention of aiding the Dutch actively, he saw fit to warn Charles that he must honour his alliance with them. His attempts at mediation were genuinely intended. What he would have preferred to war would have been for the Dutch and the English to renew relations with France pending the death of Philip IV of Spain.

De Witt had the same problem of uncertainty over French intentions, but he did not hesitate. In June 1665 he sent out the largest Dutch fleet ever mustered, over a hundred ships. It was heavily defeated by the duke of York off Lowestoft. Admiral Obdam's flagship blew up; and that eighty ships managed to return to port was mainly due to the skill of Cornelius Tromp. For Charles the greatness of the victory was overshadowed by the fact that his close friend Sir Charles Berkeley, now earl of Falmouth, was killed in the battle. Clarendon, who thought that Berkeley had had a pernicious influence on the king, wrote that people were amazed to see the king's floods of tears at the news, and he added that considering the influence Falmouth might have acquired with time, it was perhaps no bad thing that he was removed from the scene.*[12]

Clarendon thought that if the French had pushed mediation at this point, peace might have been obtained.[14] Arlington did instruct Downing to offer peace terms on the basis of a war indemnity, satisfactory terms in the East and on the Guinea coast, and restitution of the Prince of Orange.[15] De Witt however rejected them. In September 1665 Philip IV of Spain died, and the French threat to the Spanish Netherlands became imminent. In these circumstances Charles himself suggested peace to the Dutch ambassador. De Witt well understood the danger of the French threat, but he remained adamant that the English quarrel must be settled first, in spite of the fact that many of his countrymen, including the Orange party, was calling for an alliance with England against the French threat.

Charles II, in his search for allies, in September 1664 sent Henry Coventry to Sweden and Gilbert Talbot to Denmark, with a view to building up a northern alliance against the Dutch. It was a somewhat unlikely enterprise, for Denmark was in the pay of France, and the Swedes were suspicious of Danish intentions. But the English victory off Lowestoft encouraged the Danish king, and his very poverty was an added inducement to listen to Talbot's proposal. A rich Dutch East Indian convoy had rounded Scotland and taken refuge in the Norwegian port of Bergen. The earl of Sandwich, who now commanded the English fleet, was cruising off the Dogger Bank hoping to intercept De Ruyter. In July 1665 it was proposed that he should detach a squadron of some fourteen ships to attack the Dutch convoy in Bergen harbour. The King of Denmark would make a show of protest, but in fact would sanction the attack, and would share the proceeds, which were estimated at six million pounds. The King of Denmark agreed, and on July 31 the detachment under Tiddeman arrived off Bergen. But the Danish governor had received no conclusive orders, and required them to wait. But Tiddeman could not afford to wait, and on 2 August he attacked, only to be met by a bombardment from the shore forts, which cost him the lives of 118 of his men before he broke off the engagement. Meanwhile De Ruyter had safely reached his home port. Sandwich redeemed the failure to some extent by capturing nine East Indiamen worth £200,000. Arlington sent Thomas Clifford to Copenhagen in a further attempt to win Danish aid, and in September a treaty was signed, which Denmark had no intention of honouring.

Arlington's whole northern policy rested on the hope that Denmark and Sweden would set aside their hostility towards each other, but this proved impossible, and the fear of France prevented any action against the Dutch.

---

* This was also Pepys' opinion: 'I do not meet with any man else that so much as wishes him alive again, the world conceiving him a man of too much pleasure to do the King any good.[13]

The attempt to win over the Great Elector was equally abortive. Arlington sent Sir Walter Vane to urge war on behalf of the House of Orange, with the offer that if it were restored, 'we would hearken to very moderate terms of accommodation'.[16] Clarendon disapproved of this policy of trying to force the House of Orange on the Netherlands as likely to prove counter-productive, even though the inland states like Overijsel and Gelderland were pro-Orange, and opposed to the preponderance of the commercial interests of Holland. In February 1666 Arlington tried again, drafting new terms to be sent through Sir Gabriel Sylvius, a faithful servant of the Orange family: if England could be sure of a Dutch alliance against France and the restoration of the Prince of Orange, the king would be willing to accept a lower indemnity, and allow the commercial conflict to settle itself.[17] Again the terms were rejected by De Witt, and Arlington wrote ruefully to Ormond:

I am afraid De Witt is so powerful and so engaged with France that we shall get nothing of them but what we get by fighting.[18]

The only ally England managed to procure in the war against the Dutch was the fighting bishop of Münster. Clarendon describes how the bishop sent to him a monk of the Benedictine abbey of Lammspring in Westphalia, offering to attack the Dutch from the land side in return for a substantial subsidy, and holding out hopes of further German support, and even the good will of France. Arlington sent Sir William Temple to negotiate, and by a treaty of 13 June 1665 the bishop undertook to provide 30,000 men in return for 500,000 rixdollars payable in three instalments. In October 1665 the bishop's troops entered Overijsel and Groningen. But by then he found himself threatened by the French. Sir Walter Vane failed to persuade the Great Elector to join in, concluding that 'they that are able to give most are likely to have this court'. In fact by February 1666 the Great Elector promised the Dutch to intervene with troops if the bishop did not make peace. Threatened with the displeasure of the Emperor, the fighting bishop had no alternative but to retire and disband his forces. Clarendon implies that too much had been expected of the alliance.*[19] in view of its flimsy nature. Dryden might fulminate against the bishop:

> Let Munster's Prelate ever be accurst,
> In whom we seek the German faith in vain,

but the true moral was in the next verse:

> Happy who never trust a Strangers will,
> Whose friendship's in his interest understood![21]

In October 1665 Clarendon frankly explained to Henry Coventry, English

---

* In April 1666 Sir William Temple reported the bishop's words that 'if he had but one friend on this side of the sea, he would never have been forced into such a peace'.[20]

envoy to Sweden, the predicament of English foreign policy. The threat of France to the Spanish Netherlands, and Louis's alliance with the Dutch, really required 'a good understanding with Spain'. But Spain would do no more than 'look on', and set a price on the purchase of their friendship by the return of Tangier and Jamaica, so that the king had given up all hope of Spain since the death of Philip IV. An alliance of England, Spain and Sweden 'would be the foundation of peace and security to the Empire', but England could not afford to purchase the Swedish alliance, and there was no hope from either Denmark or Moscow. Clarendon was already looking beyond the Dutch war to the threat which France posed to the peace of western Europe. Coventry made it clear to the Swedish government that England's policy was 'to keep the balance between France and the House of Austria', and hence the need for a Spanish-Swedish-English alliance, but Sweden emphasised that without substantial subsidies there could be no offer of assistance. French diplomacy was already active in Stockholm, and by January Coventry was writing that it was already too strong to be combatted.[22]

Thus by 1666 England's diplomatic efforts were everywhere a failure, and it was necessary to make a supreme effort to achieve a decisive victory at sea. Both fleets were at sea in June. The English made a fatal initial error by heeding a false rumour that a French fleet was coming up the Channel from the Mediterranean, and divided their fleet. They thus fought the Four-Days' Battle (1–4 June) at a grave disadvantage, and suffered heavy losses, with six ships captured, seventeen destroyed and 8000 men killed, wounded or prisoners. The Dutch had losses of about one-quarter these figures. By a supreme effort the English reversed the decision in the St James's Day Fight (25 June) off the mouth of the Thames, in which the Dutch lost about twenty ships and 7000 men. The English thus regained command of the sea, and Albemarle and Prince Rupert were able to go on to inflict damage on Dutch shipping in the Vlie, estimated at a million pounds. It might have been argued that in this desperate struggle in 1666 the honours were about even. But England was exhausted, the government at its wits' end for money, and the country was reeling under the disasters of the Great Plague of 1665 and the Fire of London of 1666, with the consequent impoverishment of the people, dislocation of trade, destruction of property and interruption of administration and tax-collecting. In October Charles expressed himself ready for peace on the basis of a return to the *status quo ante*.

The Dutch were equally exhausted, but De Witt conducted their affairs with superior statesmanship. Negotiations were long drawn-out. When Charles proposed peace talks at The Hague, where he knew there was a strong peace party, De Witt refused, and finally in February 1667 it was agreed to talk at Breda. Charles then made the fatal decision to lay up his fleet. The reason was clearly stated in a letter of the earl of Orrery to Clarendon in March. Parliament had granted the king by a Poll Bill and an Act of Assessment a total of £1,800,000. If he could save an appreciable part of this, he could avoid meeting an angry parliament in October.[23] But De Witt was well informed of it, and saw that it gave him the chance of a final victory. Louis XIV also concluded that England's weakness removed the last obstacle to sending his troops into the Spanish Netherlands. Charles's double policy was landing him in trouble. He regarded the French alliance as a basic need to protect him against his rebellious subjects. Arlington however was reacting to the French threat to the Spanish dominions, and was anxious for an early peace and a Dutch alliance. Clarendon, who had initiated the pro-French policy, was veering round to Arlington's position, but was inhibited from adopting it both by his loyalty to the king, and his dislike of Arlington. While Arlington was negotiating with the Dutch, Clarendon was employing the earl of St Albans in Paris to win the good offices of Louis XIV. His letters make it clear that he did so on the king's instructions, and without any abatement of his own mistrust.[24] With that engaging frankness he often used in his letters and conversations, he told St Albans that he thought the king and the duke of York 'to be over-inclined to France', but that the king wished Louis to know that he did not seek a Spanish alliance against France. St Albans replied that Louis genuinely wanted peace 'upon the principle of being at liberty for another business', and would 'do all fair offices to get Charles II satisfaction'. Charles, as a face-saver, was making the single demand for the surrender of Pularoon, in the East Indies. St Albans' advice was that if the king wanted a speedy peace, he should give up the claim to Pularoon and concentrate upon developing the American colonies, 'the best roots for enlarging the English Empire'. Clarendon replied that the good offices of France would prove Louis's friendship, and facilitate 'those noble designs which may contribute to the greatness of both crowns',[25] but he indicated that Pularoon would not be insisted upon at Breda.

The French genuinely sought to effect a peace, but De Witt knew what he was about, and by June the Dutch fleet were at sea with explicit instructions to attack up the Thames. On June 12 and 13 Sheerness and Chatham were attacked, wharves and shipping captured or destroyed, and Westminster itself was at the mercy of the Dutch if they had dared so much. There was no help for it now but to accede to all the Dutch demands. They retained Pularoon and the Gold Coast forts. England's only gain was New Amsterdam. The Treaty of Breda was signed by Lord Hollis and Henry Coventry on 21 July. A needless war, entered upon lightly by king and parliament, had landed Charles in a grave predicament, and was to prove a disaster for the earl of Clarendon. The only beneficiary was Louis XIV, who could use Charles's weakness to bind England more securely to French power, while French troops advanced unimpeded into the Spanish Netherlands.

# Parliament and Impeachment 1666–7

In the first years of his reign Charles II had good reason to be satisfied with his parliaments, which had restored the monarchy without conditions, had admitted the 'miseries and calamities' of the previous twenty years, and the mistakes of the Long Parliament in usurping sovereignty, and had often shown itself to be 'more royalist than the king'.[1] The only substantial point of conflict had been over the king's Declaration of Indulgence, over which the king had been compelled to give way gracefully in return for the vote of supply. Charles had accepted the establishment of Anglicanism without entirely abandoning his desire for some kind of toleration for Catholics and dissenters. Clarendon never swerved from his belief that Anglicanism must be established, but he used his influence where possible to mitigate the rigours of the law. When the Lancashire Presbyterian Adam Martindale, who had welcomed the Restoration, was imprisoned at Chester, Richard Baxter drew Clarendon's attention to it, and he intervened with the Lord Lieutenant, the earl of Derby to secure his release.[2] When William Kiffin was accused of subversion, Clarendon gave him friendly advice, and Kiffin wrote that although he was often denounced, he was never arrested, 'my Lord Chancellor being very much my friend'.[3] When in 1663 twelve dissenters were sentenced to death at Aylesbury, Kiffin saw Clarendon, who at once secured from the king a reprieve and royal pardon.[4] Many men did indeed suffer imprisonment under the so called 'Clarendon Code', but the laws were those of parliament, and the enforcement the work of zealous justices of the peace, who thought they were dealing with subversives. The difficulty was to distinguish between peaceful men of conscience and subversives, and as there were constant rumours of plots, and enough evidence that they really existed, the law leaned towards security rather than toleration. The great fears in the minds of the governing classes were fed with the memories of twenty years of religious fanaticism.

Clarendon's management of the business of the Commons by daily consultations with a few trusted royalists, without attempting to build up a royalist party, which, he felt, would offend the House, appears to have worked well up to 1666. This was mainly because the Commons had a strong Anglican majority which provided its own cohesion, and its efforts were mainly in accord with Clarendon's wishes. We have seen that there was a change when Bennet was appointed Secretary of State in 1662, and when, on the king's orders, he began building up a group of ambitious young men in the Commons, like Thomas Clifford, William Coventry and Sir Thomas Littleton. By May 1663 Pepys was complaining of the king's 'counsellors of pleasure', Lady Castlemaine, the duke of Buckingham, the earl of Bristol, Sir Henry Bennet, Lord Ashley and Sir Charles Berkeley, 'who among them have cast my lord Chancellor on his back, past ever getting up again'.[5] Yet the earl of Bristol's attempt at Clarendon's impeachment was a fiasco which caused hardly a ripple of interest in the Commons. In so far as there was a difference of principle between Clarendon and these 'counsellors of pleasure', it was opposition to a rigid Anglicanism, and the desire to gain toleration for Catholics, and also for dissenters who were beginning to contribute to the commercial life of the country, but this was secondary to the personal hostility and jealousy they felt towards the Chancellor, whose influence with the king seemed undiminished. There was indeed a growing desire among Presbyterian sympathisers and men of moderation for some modification of the penal laws. In spite of the Derwentdale Plot of 1663 there was a growing feeling that a distinction should be made between peaceful dissenters and trouble-makers, and the Conventicle Bill passed the Commons in 1663, but was held up, perhaps deliberately in the Lords, until parliament was prorogued. When the bill came up again in May 1664, the Lords again tried to amend it by including some relief for 'occasional conformists', but the Commons would have none of it. The final bill referred to 'the growing and dangerous practices of seditious sectaries and other disloyal persons', and forbade meetings in conventicles of more than five persons, on penalty of five shillings for the first offence and ten shillings for the second. The war supply of £2,477,500, although not without opposition, was carried by comfortable majorities in February 1665.

In the general enthusiasm for war, the war party was in control and Clarendon played a subordinate part. He wrote of the parliament which met at Oxford during October 1665, that it 'preserved an excellent harmony', 'insomuch as never parliament so entirely sympathised with his majesty'. This was confirmed by the Venetian Giustiniani who reported that in the Commons 'the authority of the Chancellor prevails'.[6] The plague had raged during the summer in London; many established ministers had fled, and dissenting ministers often openly took their places. In the midst of war there were fears of renewed subversion, and the Commons reacted angrily by producing the Five Mile Bill, requiring all dissenting ministers to take an oath that it was not lawful to take up arms against the king, and that they would not 'at any time endeavour any alteration of government either in Church or State', or else not to come within five miles of a town.[7] The bill was not carried without serious opposition, especially in the Lords, where the Lord Treasurer Southampton, the earl of Manchester, Lord Wharton and Lord Lucas all opposed it. The most interesting argument came from the Lord Treasurer, Clarendon's close friend, who argued that the bill would only be further provocation, and that 'he did not know that our laws are like the Medes and Persians which were not to be altered'. Lord Lucas argued that he himself could not take an oath which made it impossible to change the law. Archbishop Sheldon on the other hand argued that all the oath meant was that it was the intention of parliament to maintain the monarchy and the Anglican church. George Morley, bishop of Winchester, argued that one who would refuse the oath must be a dangerous person, and he painted a vivid picture of the work of subversive ministers in Guildford:

If there be no laws there can be no society, and if they will not come under these laws what shall we say? All must live under a rule or none must. We desire only security.[8]

Clarendon was absent from the House for eleven of the sixteen days of its meeting, laid low with gout, and if he had a strong opinion on the bill, he did not express it. There is no reason to suppose that he disagreed with George Morley.

The Commons readily extended the licensing act, and voted £1,500,000 for the war. Moreover, at the suggestion of Downing, an Appropriation clause was added to the finance bill. Treasury business was in the soporific care of the earl of Southampton, who was quite incapable of reforming a primitive and defective system. Sir George Downing, an unpleasant character, but a very able man, had studied the Dutch system of finance. As early as August 1661 he had submitted a paper arguing that unless the king could increase his revenues to at least £1,500,000, the Dutch were bound to win in any conflict. In September 1662 he submitted to Clarendon a paper explaining the new theory of credit:

No Prince can ever be so rich as to be able to carry on his affairs by the strength of his purse without credit, but if he is once able to get up to a punctual order in his Treasury and keeps to it, he will not want credit and consequently money. If a punctual order of payment on loans were made, the King could take up money on as easy terms as any merchant on the Exchange.[9]

Judging from the number of financial papers among the Clarendon manuscripts, the Chancellor must have been much concerned with money matters, partly because of Southampton's lethargy, and partly because of the Chancellor's theory of government by Privy Council or its committees. It is unlikely that Clarendon understood Downing's argument, which however did convince the king. His argument was that the supply bill for 1665 should contain an appropriation clause, 'to make all the money that was to be raised by this bill to be applied only to those ends to which it was given, which was the carrying on the war, and to no other purpose', which would be 'an encouragement to lend money, by making the payment with interest so certain and fixed, that there could be no security in the kingdom like it'.[10] A tax so appropriated would be paid direct to the Exchequer, and loans were to be repaid in strict rotation at the interest rate of six per cent. This was to become standard practice after 1667. Clarendon opposed the innovation as an infringement of the royal prerogative, but it was supported by Coventry, Arlington and the duke of York, and Clarendon says that opposition died away once it was known that the king wished it to be passed.

Clarendon describes how one day in 1665 the king sent for him to complain of the Lord Treasurer Southampton. He said that, in spite of his unquestionable integrity,

he was not fit for the office he held: that he did not understand the mystery of the place . . . That his bodily infirmities were such that many times he could not be spoken with for two or three days, so that there could be no despatch. . . . That all men knew that all the business was done by Sir Philip Warwick (his secretary)[11]

but that he loved him too much to disoblige him, and he asked Clarendon to persuade him to resign. Clarendon asked whom he would make Treasurer in his place. The king replied that he would put the Treasury into commission. This was anathema to Clarendon's whole system of government in which a Lord Treasurer played a key role in government by Privy Council, and he argued against the change, and moreover persuaded the duke of York to join him in his protest. Charles therefore dropped the subject. Clarendon never understood the new ideas which Downing was infusing into the administration, and it was a misfortune that Southampton continued in office until his death two years later.

Clarendon says that Lord Ashley was given a peerage at the Restoration, and was made Chancellor of the Exchequer, in spite of being a Cromwellian, mainly because he was Southampton's nephew by marriage. He shared his uncle's tolerant views towards dissenters, but in other respects came to recognise Southampton's deficiencies as Lord Treasurer. Perhaps also he was tired of having little to do as Chancellor of the Exchequer, while all financial business was transacted by Sir Philip Warwick at the Treasury. He therefore drifted over to Arlington's camp, where, according to Clarendon there was held out to him the prospect of succeeding his uncle as Treasurer.[12] When the appropriation clause of the supply bill came under discussion, its novelty was such that the king wished it to be discussed in his presence, and since Clarendon was prostrate with gout the council meeting was held in his bed-chamber. Clarendon said that he had never seen the clause, and Southampton had read it only an hour or two before. Ashley, Arlington, Coventry and Downing were present. The king recognised the dangers of creating too rigid a precedent, but in the end came down in favour.

Clarendon had some harsh words for Downing for setting on foot a project without due consultation, and told him 'that it was impossible for the king to be well served, whilst such fellows of his condition were admitted to speak as they had a mind to; and that in the best times such presumptions had been punished with imprisonment by the lords of the council, without the king's taking notice of it'.[13] Clarendon treated the incident as part of the conspiracy against him on the part of Arlington and his friends, and failed to understand the need for new administrative methods to meet the exigencies of war. His reference to 'the best times' was a reminder that he still held fast to that imaginary period of English history, when all government business was conducted by the great Lords of the Privy Council. But it is not surprising that he had made Downing one of his bitter enemies.

The third controversial issue raised in the Oxford Parliament of 1665 was the Irish Cattle Bill. Irish landowners found it profitable to export cattle to England for a final period of fattening before being sold on the English market. This trade was favoured by the crown because of the increased revenue it yielded, and because it increased the prosperity of Irish agriculture. It was favoured by English consumers, who thought the price of English beef too high, and also by manufacturers who exported goods to Ireland in return for cattle. It was favoured also by landowners in the west country and Norfolk who pastured the cattle; but it was opposed by most of the great land-owners as bringing down the price of English beef. In 1663 a measure was passed to exclude Irish and Scottish cattle for six months every year. The duke of Ormond, the greatest landowner in Ireland, led the protest, but the measure passed. However, ways were soon found to circumvent the law, and in the Oxford Parliament Sir Richard Temple introduced a bill totally prohibiting the importation of Irish cattle (18 October). Sir Heneage Finch led the opposition, arguing that it would ruin Irish agriculture and be a heavy blow to the king's revenue, but it passed by 80 : 68, and was sent to the Lords. The king was known to disapprove of the bill, but he could not risk his revenues by offending the Commons. In the Lords Clarendon and the duke of York opposed the bill, but it passed the second reading and went into committee. On the 31st however parliament was prorogued, and Irish landowners had a respite until the next session.[14]

The work of the Oxford Parliament has been reviewed in some detail because it is necessary to establish that until October 1665 both the king and Clarendon had good reason to be satisfied with the parliaments. If there was growing opposition to Clarendon, Southampton and Ormond among the younger politicians led by Arlington, they had not yet been able to make their mark in parliament. Nor can we be sure that they had a concerted plan to undermine Clarendon's position. When he came to write his *Life* he was in the mood to see conspiracy in every action, and it is often not possible to prove that he was wrong. He saw the attempts to get rid of Southampton as really aimed against himself, and Ashley's sudden defence of the appropriation clause as part of the plan to succeed his uncle as Treasurer. It may have been so, but it may equally have been genuine conviction that Southampton's fall was in the national interest.[15] The failures of the Dutch war would change the situation.

Pepys gives a vivid picture of the way in which the Dutch War was conducted. There were some who always doubted its wisdom: William Coventry told him in May 1664 that there was little justification for it, that the injuries inflicted by the Dutch were greatly exaggerated, and that the Dutch could not injure the growth of English trade if only English merchants were more enterprising. He claimed to have made his views known to Clarendon and Arlington, albeit late in the day, in April 1665.[17] Pepys himself doubted whether the war would succeed, and was shocked at the crudity of the preparations for it:

We to a committee of the Council to discourse concerning pressing of men; but Lord, how they meet; never sit down – one comes, now another goes, then comes another – one complaining that nothing is done, another swearing that he hath been there these two hours and nobody came. At last it came to this: my Lord Annesley, says he, 'I think we must be forced to get the King to come to every committee, for I do not see that we do anything at any time but when he is here'. And I believe he said the truth. And very constant he (the king) is at the council-table on council-days.[18]

When on 12 April Pepys went to discuss Naval finances with the Lord Treasurer, he left with an inimitable picture of Southampton wringing his hands and asking

'Why, what means all this, Mr. Pepys? . . . Why will not people lend their money? Why will they not trust the King as well as Oliver? . . .' And this was all we could get, and went away without another answer. Which is one of the saddest things that at such a time as this, with the greatest action on foot that ever was in England, nothing should be minded.

By January 1666 political factions were so marked that Pepys feared to be seen talking to Sir William Coventry (an anti-Clarendonian) for fear of offending his patron the earl of Sandwich and Sir George Carteret, Treasurer of the Navy (both Clarendonians), and he concluded that the only safe course for him to pursue was 'to keep out of harm's way'. By July he had concluded that the only real man of business in the conduct of the war was Sir William Coventry.[19]

Pepys' patron, the earl of Sandwich, came in for serious criticism after the failure of the Bergen expedition in 1665, and this was not lessened by the rich prizes which he subsequently captured at sea, for he and his men plundered part of them for their own benefit. Sandwich was ill-advised enough to sell spices and silks on the London market for £5000. The incident ruined his reputation, and caused a scandal. Both Clarendon and Arlington defended him, and he received a pardon under the Privy Seal, but at a time when the fleet was so hampered for lack of money, it created an ugly impression. Sandwich was superseded in the command of the fleet by Prince Rupert and Albemarle, and he was sent to the embassy in Madrid, where he did useful work.[20]

The debaucheries of the Court were increasingly the talk of the town, and were thrown into a still more lurid light by the miseries which attended the war and the plague of 1665. In December 1665 Lady Castlemaine gave birth to a fifth child (created first earl and then duke of Northumberland). Clarendon wrote that if the queen could have produced a child, Charles would have restrained his 'inordinate appetites and delights,[21] but at Oxford she had either a real or an imagined miscarriage, and Charles consoled himself elsewhere. Lady Castlemaine's influence was not diminished, but he was infatuated with the beauty and the chastity of young Frances Stewart, who nonetheless resisted his importunities. Then in April 1667 she suddenly eloped with the duke of Richmond. It was an event which redounded however unfairly, on Clarendon.*

The fanaticism of the millenarians and Fifth Monarchists had subsided a good deal, but there was still a widespread belief that 1666 was to be 'the Year of the Beast', in accordance with the prophecy in Revelation xiii, 18: 'Here is wisdom. Let him that hath understanding count the number of the beast: for it is the number of a man; and his number is Six hundred threescore and six'. Clarendon wrote that 1666 was 'a year long destined by all astrologers for the production of dismal changes and alterations throughout the world, and by some for the end of it'.[23] For years, careful records had been kept of blazing stars and other phenomena which portended evil. Thomas Ewins, Congregational minister in Bristol, interpreted these as foretelling God's judgment on France, England and the Dutch.[24] Vavasor Powell, the Welsh Fifth Monarchist, repeatedly foretold disaster for 1666. A prophecy of Thomas Becket was supposed to have been discovered in Somerset with the same foreboding. It was not only fanatics who believed such things. On 25 February the earl of Sandwich told Pepys that

he dreads the issue of this year, and fears there will be some very great revolutions before his coming back again [he was departing for Spain].

Aubrey noted that all his affairs 'ran kim kam' that year, and for him, as for many people, the Great Fire of London and the disasters at sea seemed a fulfilment of the prophecy of doom. It is true that these superstitions were rapidly being outmoded by the new spirit of enquiry reflected in the Royal Society. The prophecies were treated derisively by John Spencer, later dean of Ely, and John Dryden wrote his 'Annus Mirabilis' to give a different interpretation to the year as one of victory over the Dutch. Dryden portrayed

---

* Pepys was shocked also at the way the duke of York paraded his mistress, Lady Denham, in public. Evelyn called it 'bichering', since the duke followed her about like a dog.[22]

Charles II as the tender father of his people, without entirely ignoring his weaknesses:

> Or, if my heedless Youth has stept astray,
> Too soon forgetful of they gracious hand,
> On me alone thy just displeasure lay,
> But take thy judgments from this mourning land.

It was Dryden's purpose to regard the Dutch War as opening the way to a new prosperity, and that had been the popular view in 1664:

> Thus to the Eastern wealth through storms we go;
> But now, the Cape once doubled, fear no more:
> A constant Trade-wind will securely blow,
> And gently lay us on a spicy shore.[25]

Few people were ready to echo his optimism in 1666. The Great Fire of London profoundly shook the nation, dislocated the administration, seriously diminished the royal revenues, and greatly increased the sense of foreboding. In such an atmosphere factions were bound to grow, as men looked for scapegoats upon whom the blame for all the disasters could be pinned. As the September parliament approached, Pepys nervously looked to the navy accounts. He estimated the total revenues for the period September 1664–September 1666 at £5,590,000, and the whole charge of the navy at £3,200,000, and wondered what had become of the remaining £2,390,000.[26] He was right to be concerned, for parliament met on 21 September, when the ashes of London were still warm, to hear a grim report on national affairs from the king.

Charles in his opening speech referred to the 'dismal ruins' of the fire. He was now fighting two powerful enemies France and the Dutch; in spite of the great sums parliament had granted, all had been spent, and he had seriously to anticipate the revenues. Clarendon wrote that the situation was worse than even the king realised:

Monies could neither be collected nor borrowed where the plague had prevailed, which was all over the city and over a great part of the country; the collectors durst not go to require it or receive it . . . The two great branches of the revenue, the customs and excise, which was the great and almost inexhaustible security to borrow money upon, were now bankrupt, and would neither bring in money nor supply credit: all the measures by which computations had been made were so broken, that they could not be brought to meet again.[27]

If to this were added the 'deluge by fire', and the setbacks of the war, it was easy to see why the House had not 'a better countenance'. One of its first acts was to set up a committee 'to receive information of the insolence of Popish priests and Jesuits and the increase of Popery', thus identifying the favourite suspects for causing the fire of London. A month later the House petitioned the king for the banishment of all priests and Jesuits except those who served the queen. On 26 September Sir Philip Warwick submitted the public accounts, Sir George Carteret (Treasurer of the Navy) the navy accounts, and Colonel Legge, and Sir John Duncombe the Ordnance accounts, and a committee was appointed to examine them. When the House came to consider the raising of a supply of £1,800,000, they became bogged down in discussions of how the money should be raised, whether by excise, poll tax, land tax, a tax on sealed paper, or by monthly assessment. Andrew Marvell wrote that the delay was 'not from any want of ardor in the house to supply the public necessities, but out of our house's sense also of the burthen to be laid upon the subject, and a desire therefore to do it in the most prudent eligible and easy manner'.[28] On 11 October Sir Richard Temple proposed that £1,600,000 should be voted the king for war purposes. The Court party replied that this would not be enough, and after 'a long and hot debate', the House agreed to £1,800,000.[29] On the 16th it was debated whether it should be raised by a land tax, or by an excise, the Court party favouring the latter. Debates continued during November, and early in December William Garraway proposed tacking to the Poll Bill a provision to establish a commission of both Houses to examine the accounts of the expenditure of the previous grants totalling over four million pounds. There were doubts about its constitutional legality, but it was carried by 119 to 83.[30] This could hardly have occurred if some members, accounted supporters of the Court, had not voted for the measure, and the king reacted angrily. Pepys correctly assessed the situation:

how angry the Court is at the late provision brought in by the House. How still my Lord Chancellor is, not daring to do or say anything to displease the Parliament. That the Parliament is in a very ill humour, and grows every day more and more so. And that the unskilfulness of the Court and their difference among one another is the occasion of all, not agreeing in what they would have, and so give leisure and occasion to the other part to run away with what the Court would not have.[31]

Pepys correctly noted that the king would rather prorogue parliament and do without the money than accept the proviso. Next day the Commons withdrew the proviso and decided to put the measure into a separate bill. Pepys wrote that the reason for the king's attitude was that £400,000 had gone into the privy purse since the beginning of the war, and that the king had just settled the debts of Lady Castlemaine totalling £30,000, facts he would not like to see investigated.

Clarendon certainly advised the king to resist the implied invasion of his prerogative, and his views on the confusion in which the Court party found themselves can be deduced from the remarks of his secretary, Matthew Wren, whom Pepys met at dinner on 15 December:

By and by comes in Matt Wren from the Parliament-house, and tells us that he and all his party of the House, which is the Court party, are fools, and have been made so this day by the wise men of the other side – for after the Court party had carried it yesterday so powerfully for the Paper Bill, yet now it is laid aside wholly, and to be supplied by a land tax – which, it is true, will do well, and will be sooner finished, which was the great argument for the doing of it – but it shows them fools, that they would not permit this to have been done six weeks ago, which they might have had. And next, they have parted with the Paper Bill; which, when once begun, might have proved a very good flower in the Crown as any there. So doth really say that they are truly outwitted by the other side.[32]

When the bill for an accounts commission reached the Lords in December, Clarendon persuaded them to set it aside in favour of a petition to the king to nominate his own commission. The Court party was clearly in disarray, and Clarendon placed the blame principally upon the duke of Buckingham, who gathered round him a number of members of the Commons, including Sir Richard Temple, Sir Edward Seymour, William Garraway and Sir Robert Howard. He

invited them to his table, pretended to have a great esteem for their parts, asked counsel of them, lamented the king's neglecting his business, and committing it to other people who were not fit for it; and then reported all the license and debauchery of the court in the most lively colours, being himself a frequent eye and earwitness of it.[33]

Buckingham was as much an evil genius to Charles II as his father had been to Charles I. Enormously rich, a gambler and playboy, he was entirely unprincipled, and without any capacity for administration, but with an itch for power. He was the kind of man a wise monarch would have banished for ever from Court, but Charles found him amusing and tolerated his antics, and most politicians found it advisable not to alienate the duke. Even Arlington described himself as 'ever an humble servant of the Duke of Buckingham'.

The financial question was complicated enough, but there were other problems which bedevilled the smooth working of this session. Buckingham chose to make the Irish Cattle Bill a major issue. It was suspected that he did so chiefly as a means of striking a blow at the only duke who could rival him in influence, the duke of Ormond; and a blow at Ormond was a blow also at Clarendon.[34] The bill did indeed genuinely divide political opinion, for whereas landowners like Sir Charles Harbord, Sir William Doyley and Sir John Holland, benefitted from the trade and opposed the bill, a majority supported it in spite of the king's known dislike of it. It was feared that even if the bill was passed, the king would circumvent it by issuing trade licences under the prerogative, and in order to prevent this it was proposed to insert in the bill a declaration that the trade was a 'nuisance'. The king could hardly use the prerogative to permit a trade which had been declared *malum in se*. However the Solicitor-General Heneage Finch protested that such a declaration would be an infringement of the prerogative.[35] The House concurred, and by 106 to 102 sent the bill back to committee. So narrow a vote suggests that a concerted effort on the part of the Court could have secured the bill's rejection. But the Privy Council was divided, with Buckingham and Ashley supporting the bill, and Clarendon opposing it. Clarendon makes it clear that it was not simply a matter of faction, but that many honest men favoured the bill, and in these circumstances the king listened to the advice of Sir William Coventry, who argued that resistance to the bill might endanger the voting of supply. Accordingly Charles let it be known that he was content for members to follow their own judgments and consciences.[36] With this assurance, the bill passed the Commons on 15 October by 165 to 104, and was sent to the Lords. In his final speech Heneage Finch warned the Commons that if they continued to subordinate Irish interests to those of England, they would be laying up for themselves great problems for the future.

The battle was now transferred to the Lords, where the earl of Anglesey led the opposition to the bill, and where debates were heated as Buckingham and Ashley made the bill their own. Buckingham threw off his natural indolence to attend every debate, and he and Ashley showed how much this was a personal conflict which had little to do with the prosperity of agriculture. Ashley for instance declared that if Irish rents rose as English rents fell, the duke of Ormond would have a greater revenue than the duke of Northumberland, a thing, Clarendon added sardonically, 'not to be endured'.[37] Buckingham declared that anyone who opposed this bill 'had either no Irish interest or an Irish understanding', which Lord Ossory, eldest son of the duke of Ormond, took to be an insult to his father, and challenged him to a duel. The two agreed to meet in Chelsea Fields, but the fight did not take place, as Buckingham claimed that he went to the wrong place. The Lords considered both men equally guilty of offending the rules of their House, and Ossory was sent to the Tower, and Buckingham to the custody of Black Rod. Released after a few days, Buckingham was again in trouble when he fell to blows with the marquis of Dorset, and knocked off the latter's periwig, at a conference between the two Houses, and again the sentence of the Lords was that the two should be sent to the Tower for a few days.[38]

The arguments for and against the Irish Cattle Bill continued. It was pointed out that the trade was worth £25,000 a year; that the Irish spent £330,000 a year in England, and that counties like Norfolk, Suffolk and Kent actually profited from the trade. The Lords removed the word 'nuisance', and replaced it by 'mischief', and when the duke of Ormond offered 15,000 bullocks or 20,000 barrels of beef for the relief of the poor of London, the Lords included the offer in the bill. In this form it passed on 23 November. The Commons however feared the use of the prerogative to circumvent the bill, and restored the 'nuisance' clause, and rejected Ormond's offer as savouring too much of a propaganda move. A deadlock developed between the two Houses. At a conference between them on 9 January 1667 the Lords argued that the 'nuisance' clause was an infringement of the royal prerogative; the Commons argued that it had been used before, and that it was necessary to prevent the use of the dispensing power. Both sides stuck to their positions, and the Commons made it plain that the supply bill was threatened. The matter was discussed in Privy Council on 13 January, and Arlington argued that only surrender over the Irish Cattle Bill would ensure the Supply Bill. Clarendon argued that the interests of one kingdom ought not to be subordinated to those of another, nor the interests of Norfolk, Suffolk and Kent be subordinated to those of other counties; and finally that the royal prerogative must be defended at all costs. Clarendon wrote that he offended the Commons, not only by opposing the bill, but by urging the king and the Lords to preserve their respective rights against the encroachments of the Commons. He wrote that he was warned to be more cautious of what he said, in view of the enemies he was making, but 'in that, as in many things of that kind that related to the offending of some men, he was uncounsellable'. Moreover, he wrote that the things he said in Privy Council were freely repeated by his enemies to members of the Commons. Thus his enemies gathered strength.[39]

Charles preferred Arlington's advice to Clarendon's on the Irish Cattle Bill, and the duke of York was sent to urge some Lords to drop their opposition. Even so they were reluctant to comply, but in the end Archbishop Sheldon and most of the bishops, and the duke of York and his friends, abstained from voting, and the bill achieved a majority. However, eight peers entered a protest against the 'nuisance' clause and the challenge to the prerogative.[40]

Two other matters increased the tensions of this session. The first sprang from charges against Viscount Mordaunt. As we have seen, he had been one of the most ardent of the young royalists, who had done the king great service in the years 1658–60, but had managed to make so many enemies that he was virtually discarded at the Restoration, being fobbed off with the governorship of Windsor Castle in 1661. On 2 November 1666, one William Taylor brought a petition to the Commons against Mordaunt. His story was that, having been a faithful servant to Charles I, he had attempted to stand for election in the borough of Windsor, but that Mordaunt had secured his defeat, had ejected him from his quarters, and had arrested and imprisoned him, refusing to accept his bail of £2000; that he had been ejected a second time in 1664, and again been illegally imprisoned. The petition was referred to the Committee of Privileges, and on 21 December William Prynne was responsible for drawing up articles of impeachment against Mordaunt for acts 'contrary to the great Charter, and other laws and Statutes of this Realm and Liberties of all the Commons and Freemen of England'. Prynne was in his element searching for precedents for impeachment, and it was obvious to many that this was intended as a dress rehearsal for a much greater occasion. In January 1667 there was a clash between the two Houses, when the Lords proposed that

Mordaunt should sit during his trial and be granted counsel for the defence, whereas the Commons wished him to stand at the bar of the House, and be denied counsel. When on the 25th the bill for the Monthly Assessment was ready for the Lords, the Commons decided to hold it up, lest the king prorogued parliament before the Mordaunt case was heard. On the 31st the Lords informed the Commons that they had 'the right of judging in what manner the Lord Mordaunt should be tried', and the Commons resolved that 'they should not depart from their privilege, nor agree that the Lord Mordaunt should sit within the Bar at his trial'. It was deadlock.[41]

The second matter to engage the attention of the Commons was the Canary patent. The wine of the Canary Islands was popular in England, and the English were virtually its sole purchasers; but its price was so high that some merchants petitioned in March 1664 for a charter of incorporation which would enable them to bargain more effectively with the Spanish producers. The subject was fully discussed in Privy Council in the king's presence; the farmers of the customs were consulted, and Clarendon wrote that the decision was unanimously in favour of incorporating the trade. The Solicitor-General was directed to prepare the letters patent under the Great Seal for the incorporation of the Canary merchants. Clarendon says that months passed without protest being made, but when the charter was ready for the Great Seal, the Lord Mayor and Aldermen of London entered a caveat on the grounds that the merchants concerned were not freemen of London. The Chancellor accordingly persuaded the merchants to accept a clause requiring them to become freemen within a given time. There were also protests from merchants of the west country that they would be excluded from the trade, and Clarendon was told that the matter would be raised in parliament. He therefore again deferred affixing the seal, but when parliament was prorogued in March 1665 without the question being raised, he issued the charter on 17 March. The 'Governor and Company of Merchants trading to the Canary Islands' were to have a monopoly of the trade.

The very word 'monopoly' tended to infuriate seventeenth-century parliaments. Professor Kenyon refers to 'the insensate fury with which parliament fell upon the monopolists' in 1621, and John Pym made monopolies one of his main grievances in April 1640.[42] On 9 October 1666 the Commons set up a committee to inspect the patent and charter of the Canary Company, and all other similar charters. On the 29th the committee reported that the Canary Company 'was a monopoly and destructive to trade, and therefore illegal'.[43] They expected the charter to be cancelled forthwith, but no action was taken before parliament was prorogued on 8 February 1667. On the 17th however Pepys' informant told him

that unless the King doth do something against my Lord Mordaunt and the patent for the Canary Company before the Parliament next meets, he doth believe there will be a civil war before there will be any more money given, unless it may be at their perfect disposal.

Apparently the king thought so too, for Mordaunt resigned his post and went into exile, and the Canary patent was cancelled on 18 September 1667. Clarendon's account of the Canary patent seems entirely accurate, and he refuted the accusation that he had received a bribe, although he admitted that some months after the charter had been issued, he received a present from the governor of the company, as did many other people, according to the custom of the time. But rumours spread, and Pepys heard that Clarendon's secretary, Matthew Wren had received a £5000 bribe from the company.[44]

At the very end of the session, parliament passed the Monthly Assessment and Poll Bills, giving the king £1,800,000. On 8 February Charles prorogued them until October, with a promise that he would appoint his own commissioners to investigate expenditure and to root out 'fraud and cozenage'.[45] Thus ended the most turbulent session the king had yet encountered. At the root of the problem was the dissatisfaction at the cost of the war compared with its limited achievements. He had to remind them in his closing speech that if people grumbled at heavy taxes they must remember that wars could not be fought without them. Discontent was not directed at the king himself, nor the war leaders, who might still achieve victory, but vented itself on side issues, against Catholic priests and Jesuits, the Irish cattle trade, Lord Mordaunt and the Canary patent. It would need only military failure to turn this irritability into a more ruthless search for scapegoats. At the same time it must be recognised that if the Court party had stood firm, there would have been much less effective opposition. But instead of a single Court party there were now the proliferation of factions, with Clarendon, Buckingham, Arlington and Ashley each having his adherents in the Commons. Clarendon described how Buckinghim built up his following there by patronage and flattery,* and how he attended the debates in the Commons to influence their course.[46] Ashley showed that his hostility to Ormond was as great as Buckingham's. Arlington was more subtle, keeping a foot in both camps, and continuing to write friendly letters to Ormond about the strength of feeling against Irish cattle, without doing anything to stem it.[47] Clarendon's ideal of government by an active and united Privy Council was thus proving a pipe dream, and if it failed, his usefulness to the king would be at an end. The ebullient royalism of 1661 was being replaced by a critical attitude to which Charles referred in a speech in January 1667:

You have manifested a greater distrust of me than I deserved. I do not pretend to be without infirmities: but I have never broken my word with you; the nation never had less cause to complain of grievances, or the least injustice or oppression, than

---

* The chief members were Sir Richard Temple, William Garraway, Sir Edward Seymour and Sir Robert Howard.

it hath in these seven years it hath pleased God to restore me to you. I would be used accordingly.[48]

It should now be clear why the king had no thoughts other than of peace. The Dutch, with French aid, were too strong for him to expect a victory, and parliament was becoming increasingly reluctant to continue to finance a war. When Pepys saw Clarendon in February,

he doth confess our straits here and everywhere else arises from our out-spending our revenue; I mean, that the King doth do so.[49]

In the *Life* he describes how Charles set up the commission to examine accounts, but carefully excluded from its jurisdiction the prize money for which Lord Ashley was responsible, which had gone directly into the royal purse. Meanwhile confusion among his advisers grew. Clarendon describes how, after Buckingham's turbulent conduct during the late session of parliament, one of his servants had reported to Arlington the duke's suspicious conduct suggestive of a conspiracy, and how he had visited an astrologer, Robert Heydon, to have the king's horoscope cast. As this came within the reach of the statute of treason, and as Arlington was very ready to investigate the activities of a political rival, Heydon was arrested, his papers seized, and he was sent to the Tower. Letters in Buckingham's handwriting were sufficient to persuade the Privy Council that his acts were treasonable, and the king sent the sergeant at arms with a warrant under the sign manual for his arrest. But Buckingham eluded the clutches of the sergeant, and went into hiding. Pepys reported the gossip on 3 March when he wrote that 'this silly Lord hath provoked by his ill-carriage, the Duke of York, my Lord Chancellor, and all the great persons, and therefore will most likely die'.

Buckingham remained in hiding until June, when he sent his secretary Thomas Clifford to Clarendon professing his innocence, and asking for advice. This is an interesting comment on the relations between the two men. Clarendon had always despised Buckingham's idiosyncracies and way of life, but he wrote that Buckingham had always treated him with apparent respect, and now had enough confidence in his integrity to put himself into his hands. Clarendon replied that so far as he knew, Buckingham had done nothing which put his life in danger, and that he need fear no conspiracy against him. He advised him to surrender himself to the Tower. Clarendon said that he took his stand on strict legality, knowing that Arlington was telling the king that the Chancellor favoured Buckingham, while he told Buckingham's friends that Clarendon was determined to destroy him. Buckingham took Clarendon's advice and surrendered himself to the Tower. He was examined by a select commission, but the evidence against him was thin, and the king was tired of the whole affair. The duke was therefore released, and a fortnight later was again at Court, ready to join his cousin Lady Castlemaine in hostility to the Chancellor.[50]

While the king was deciding to lay up the fleet in anticipation of an early peace, confusion grew in the administration. In April Pepys reported that Sir George Carteret and Sir William Coventry were at each other's throats over Navy finances, and on the 26th he walked for two hours with Evelyn

talking of the badness of the Government, where nothing but wickedness, and wicked men and women command the King. That it is not in his nature to gainsay anything that relates to his pleasures. That much of it arises from the sickliness of our Ministers of State, who cannot be about him as the idle companions are, and therefore give way to the young rogues.[51]

He was referring to Albemarle and Southampton (who were both ill), and to Clarendon who for once was free from gout. The rumour then was that Arlington would soon succeed Southampton as Lord Treasurer, and Pepys thought that it would be a disastrous move if he and 'his gang' came to power.

He [Evelyn] tells me that of all the great men of England, there is none that endeavours more to raise those that he takes into favour than my Lord Arlington; and that on that score, he is much more to be made one's patron than my Lord Chancellor, who never did nor will do anything but for money.

Arlington had successfully built up a parliamentary party for himself, and Clifford was his 'bribe-master-general'. The slur that Clarendon sold offices was often repeated, but was largely unwarranted. Indeed many men who were now against him had sought his patronage unsuccessfully, and Clifford himself was one of them.

Clarendon's chief concern during the Spring of 1667 was to secure French aid in making the Dutch peace, for which purpose he used the earl of St Albans in Paris. His personal affairs were in great confusion. During the Great Fire, while he was at Whitehall, his wife, fearful that Worcester House in the Strand would soon be engulfed, bundled the family possessions into carts and lighters and sent them to Twickenham. As his lease of the house expired at Michaelmas, he did not return there, but took refuge with the earl of Burlington, whose daughter had married Clarendon's second son Lawrence Hyde, later earl of Rochester. For his own great house, Clarendon House, was still unfinished. It was being built on land given by the king on the north side of Piccadilly, opposite the north end of St James's Street. Begun in 1664, Burnet said that Clarendon planned simply 'a good ordinary house', but that, not understanding such things, he was run into a vast charge of about £50,000, three times as much as he had intended.[52] During the plague year he kept some three hundred men working on the house, which he thought would be acceptable during a trade depression, but in fact it aroused only resentment at so much ostentation. It was nicknamed Dunkirk House, or Holland House, implying that it was built out of either French or Dutch bribes, since he was known to be opposed to the war. Pepys and Evelyn visited the house several times in the course of its construction, and Pepys wrote that it was 'the finest pile I ever did see in my life, and will be a glorious house'. The view from the roof he described as 'the noblest prospect that ever I saw in my life, Greenwich being nothing to it'. By May 1667 Clarendon was at last installed in his new house, and Pepys, who attended a meeting of the Tangier committee there, wrote, 'Mightily pleased with the nobleness of this house and brave furniture and pictures, which indeed is very noble.'[53]

It was however a great mistake, confirming as it did popular views of the Chancellor's corruption, and increasing the envy of his enemies. When later he went into exile, he urged his son to tell his friends that 'if they would excuse the vanity and folly of the great house, he would undertake to answer for all the rest of his actions himself'.[54]

In May there occurred what Clarendon called 'a fatal breach in his fortune' with the death of his closest colleague, the earl of Southampton. Pepys, who knew more of the working of the administration than anyone, commented:

There is a good man gone; . . . though, for certain, the slowness (though he was of great integrity) of this man, and remissness, have gone as far as to undo the nation as anything else that hath happened; and yet, if I knew all the difficulties that he hath lain under, and his instrument Sir Philip Warwick, I might be brought to another mind.[55]

W A Shaw paid tribute to the honesty of his administration at the Treasury, but his methods were old-fashioned, and most of the work was left to his secretary Sir Philip Warwick. Clarendon describes how, when Downing and Coventry wished to introduce a more efficient way of raising loans by the use of the appropriation clause, they had to do it without the knowledge of the Chancellor or the Treasurer, by direct intervention of the king. The change would enable them to raise loans at six per cent instead of higher rates, but the two traditionalists saw it as offending the bankers who were accustomed to advance loans. W A Shaw wrote:

The truth was that Charles II returned to a bankrupt inheritance. The country had been exhausted by the financial demands made upon it by Cromwell's strong policy . . . The taxable capacity of the country had been exceeded.[56]

Southampton continued to use traditional methods, and was impervious to new ideas, and Clarendon saw the suggestions of Downing and Coventry as acts of disloyalty undermining a system sanctified by the past. The Dutch War imposed an intolerable strain which neither Southampton nor Clarendon knew how to relieve. Even when Southampton was dying, Clarendon begged the king not to dismiss him; but once he was gone Charles insisted, against Clarendon's advice, on putting the Treasury into commission as a first step towards reform.

The active members of the commission were Lord Ashley, Sir William Coventry, Sir Thomas Clifford and Sir John Duncombe. Clarendon feared that their main purpose would be to denigrate Southampton's memory, but Pepys, who knew better, declared:

I am of another mind, and my heart is very glad of it, for I do expect they will do much good, and that it is the happiest thing that hath appeared to me for good of the nation since the King came in.[57]

He was delighted to hear that Sir George Downing was appointed its secretary, and that it began at once to institute economies with a new air of efficiency. When the Dutch launched their devastating attack in the Medway early in June, Sir William Coventry was the most active member of the commission on the scene.

In the ensuing panic in London, Pepys hurried his gold out of London, and thought of hiding his silver in the latrine. The City talked loudly of treason, not only among the Catholics, but within the government, and in Westminster Hall Clarendon was insulted with shouts of 'Dunkirk House'. The capture of the *Royal Charles* and the burning of the *Royal James* and other ships was a final indignity. In the Privy Council, Pepys reported, 'they were ready to fall together by the ears, arraigning one another of being guilty of the counsel that brought us into this misery, by laying up all the great ships.'[58]

An angry mob broke down the trees before Clarendon's house, smashed his windows, and set up a gibbet with the words: 'Three sights to be seen; Dunkirk, Tangier and a barren Queen', three things blamed upon the Chancellor. The blame for the laying up of the ships was placed, not on Clarendon, but on Coventry. Clarendon wrote that at the Court itself (apart from the king and duke of York) there was 'such wild despair and even ridiculous apprehensions, that I am willing to forget'.[59] In the City the cry was for a parliament, and this was supported in Council by the Treasury Commission on the grounds that without further money, the king could do nothing. Clarendon however stoutly opposed, on the legal point that a prorogued parliament could not be recalled before the appointed date in October. He foresaw that there would be little likelihood of more money, and every likelihood of a grim post mortem. His advice was for a dissolution of parliament and new elections.[60] It was a dangerous proposal, for the king could not count upon the return of a more loyal parliament, and Charles rejected it. Clarendon then advised that they set their minds to making a speedy peace and to repair the damage done before October. But the king opted for the recall of parliament for 25 July.

When parliament met, the king delayed proceedings for four days, while he awaited news of the signing of the peace. The Commons, in ill-humour, used the time to debate a motion by Sir Thomas Tomkins, seconded by William Garraway, urging the king to disband his army of 12,000, which he had raised to meet a possible invasion, as soon as peace was signed, and it was passed without dissent. The wildest rumour was spread around the city, that the king would dispense with parliament, and hold down the country with his army while he imposed a general excise. The duke of York was suspected of being the strong man behind the plan, and Clarendon, his father-in-law, was reported as saying that Queen Elizabeth had dealt with the Armada in 1588 without the aid of a parliament. The presence of the troops undoubtedly aroused much alarm, and Pepys asked how it was that a king who had been restored with so much loyalty in 1660, 'could devise to lose so much in so little time'. By 29 July it was known that the peace was signed, and Charles was able to prorogue parliament until 10 October, but not without an angry protest that they could 'persuade any sober person that he did intend to govern by a standing army'.[61] The day of reckoning was thus put off for a few weeks.

The Court was plunged into the utmost confusion. Sir George Carteret told Pepys that 'they are at Court all in factions, some for and others against my Lord Chancellor, and another for and against another man; and the King adheres to no man, but this day delivers himself up to this and the next to that, to the ruin of himself and business', while 'the gaming, swearing, whoring and drinking' continued, so that Carteret had dared to tell the king of 'the necessity of having at least a show of religion in the government, and sobriety; and that it was that that did set up and keep up Oliver, though he was the greatest rogue in the world'.[62]

It was Charles's misfortune to be constantly compared with Cromwell, to his disadvantage. Members of parliament dispersed in ill-humour at having been brought to Westminster to no purpose, and there were repeated rumours that it would never be called again. If it did meet again, any member of the administration might be called to account. All connected with the war felt themselves threatened. Sir George Carteret hastily exchanged his office of Treasurer of the Navy for the safer haven of the Treasurership of Ireland. Coventry told Pepys that he and Arlington were as much under threat as Clarendon, and Pepys himself, in the greatest alarm, had his treasure hidden in his father's garden. There was therefore a powerful incentive in many minds to fasten attention upon the Chancellor.

Clarendon, for his part, knew his many enemies, and wrote that he 'was guilty of that which he had used to accuse the archbishop Laud of, that he was too proud of a good conscience'.[63] Feeling that he had done no wrong, he placed all his confidence in the continuance of the king's support. He wrote that 'he was in truth weary of the condition he was in', and had asked the king 'that he might retire from all other business, than that of the judicatory'.[64] This might have been the most equitable solution. Clarendon was not a great lawyer, and as Chancellor rarely took important decisions without the aid of two judges; but he was conscientious, with a great sense of the dignity of his office, and he would have continued to perform his duties as well as another. But Charles was under heavy pressure to dismiss him, and had come to the conclusion that he was now a liability. Sir William Coventry certainly believed that he should go, since he had become an obstacle to administrative reform. Arlington saw the advantage in diverting popular wrath against the Chancellor. By the middle of July the duke of Buckingham was released from the Tower, to find himself more popular than ever. Pepys, who thought his release entirely to the king's discredit, was amused to hear people 'speak kindly of the duke as one that will enquire into faults'.[65] Buckingham would certainly make the most of the next session of parliament, and was hot for Clarendon's impeachment. Finally, Lady Castlemaine was an old enemy, and it was said that the decision to dismiss him was taken in her apartments.

On 9 August Clarendon received a great blow with the death of his wife, with whom he had been happily married for over thirty-five years, and who had borne him nine children. A fortnight later the king sent the duke of York to tell him that he had received information that the next parliament would certainly impeach the Chancellor, and that in order to save him, Charles wished him to surrender the seals of office. Clarendon wrote that he received the news as if it had been a warrant for his execution.[66] What shook him most was the knowledge that the king had withdrawn his support. It was reasonable for Charles to require his resignation; it was hardly honest to threaten a parliamentary impeachment. If an impeachment was being planned, it must be the work of the leaders of the parliamentary factions, and they would not have gone so far had they not been certain of the approval of the king. When Charles received Clarendon on 26 August he told him that resignation would be the best way to preserve him from impeachment, and that his innocence would not save him if it came to a trial, any more than it had saved Strafford. Clarendon replied stoutly that he would not wish it to be known that he had retired voluntarily, that he had never broken the law, and that his dismissal would be a blow to the crown, since 'men would not know how securely to serve [the king], when they should see it was in the power of three or four persons who had never done him any notable service . . . to dispose him to so ungracious an act'.[67] While the king talked of 'the great power of the parliament', Clarendon replied that he could not know how parliament would act, and that he believed that his own following in the Commons would be stronger than that of the two who were his enemies (he meant Coventry and Arlington). He even asked the king to remember the fate of Richard II, and made some uncomplimentary remarks about Lady Castlemaine which he afterwards regretted.[68] As he left the royal presence and crossed the garden, Lady Castlemaine ran to the window in her dressing gown, and stood with Arlington and Bab May (Privy Purse) mocking as he passed. According to Nathaniel Crew, the old man looked up and said, 'O Madam, is it you? Pray remember that if you live, you will grow old'.[69]

All was not necessarily lost, for there was a widespread belief that his fall was the result of a Court intrigue. Anglesey wrote to Ormond on the 27th 'that many, out of zeal to justice and the King's service, interposed with His

Majesty in his behalf, that at least he might be left to a fair trial, and not borne down by the cry of the people'.[70] Sir George Carteret told Pepys that he believed that Clarendon would recover from the attack, as he had from Bristol's attack four years before; and Pepys thought that the prestige of the Court was so low that it might restore Clarendon's popularity. The duke of York stoutly defended him, but this was not necessarily an advantage, for the duke's intentions were widely suspect. Pepys heard that there had been high words in the Privy Council between the duke and Sir William Coventry, his secretary, and that the latter had declared 'that what he did was in obedience to the King's commands; and that he did not think any man fit to serve a prince that did not know how to retire and live a country life'.[71] Clarendon's son, Cornbury, told Ossory that indeed his father had been willing to retire, until he heard of the design to dismiss him, when he suddenly changed his mind. The die was cast on 30 August, when at seven in the evening the king sent Secretary Morrice to Clarendon for the seals of office, and Bab May fell on his knees before the king telling him 'that he was now king, which he had never been before'. Sir Alan Broderick's comment to Ormond however was that he 'beseeched Almighty God to grant that the King may find as good a man to keep the seals'.[72]

Coventry was perhaps the only man acting against Clarendon from mainly disinterested motives, and Pepys asked him 'what was the great matter that grounded his desire of the Chancellor's removal'. He wrote darkly:

He told me many things not fit to be spoken, and yet not anything of his being unfaithful to the King; but, he told me that while he was so great at the Council-board and in the administration of matters, there was no room for anybody to propose any remedy to what was amiss or to compass anything, though never so good for the Kingdom, unless approved of by the Chancellor, he managing all things with that greatness which now will be removed, that the King may have the benefit of others' advice.[73]

Clarendon and his friends at first welcomed the meeting of a parliament, believing in his innocence. But the most ominous fact, which Pepys at once discerned, was that the king had deserted the Chancellor, and had let it be known that he would not oppose an impeachment. This was to throw Clarendon to his enemies, and to make his defence impossible without throwing much unsavoury light on the Court. Many people could not fail to ask what was the point of this sudden attack on the Chancellor, who could not in any way be held personally responsible for the failure of the Dutch war. The suspicion was that it was an indirect attack upon the duke of York, for now that the queen's barrenness was certain, there were many who did not relish James as Charles's successor. Pepys recorded that the birth of another son to the duke on September 14 'settled men's minds mightily', but in fact it alarmed his enemies more, and the rumour spread that Charles and his brother were on bad terms, and that the king intended to legitimise the duke of Monmouth, or to seek a divorce and remarry, and that he intended to give Monmouth the command of the army. More immediately disturbing was the fact that, to the amazement of all, the duke of Buckingham on 23 September was restored to the Council and his place in the Bedchamber, and soon appeared to have re-established his influence over the king. Pepys was amazed to see him sitting again in Council, with all his old panache:

It is wonderful to see how this man is come again to his places, all of them, after the reproach and disgrace done him, so that things are done in a most foolish manner quite through.[74]

When parliament met on 10 October 1667 Lord Keeper Bridgeman announced that the king was ready to lay his accounts before the House:

he doth assure you, he will leave everyone concerned to stand or fall according to his own innocence or guilt.

The two Houses returned their thanks to the king, especially for disbanding his forces, for cancelling the Canary patent, and for the dismissal of Clarendon, and the king replied:

as for the earl of Clarendon, I assure you I will never employ him again in any public affairs whatsoever.[75]

On 15 October the Commons appointed a committee to examine the accounts, and next day a committee to enquire into the miscarriage of the late war, and a further committee to enquire into the reasons for the sale of Dunkirk, 'and whether any money were paid into the hands of any private person'. The first committee met on 19 October, and at once plunged into an enquiry into the responsibility for the division of the fleet in June 1666. The duke of York came under attack for his failure to pursue the Dutch on the night of 3–4 June, and the blame was placed on one of his officers, Henry Brouncker, who had given orders to slacken sail while the duke was asleep, in order to protect him from the dangers of battle. Prince Rupert and the duke of Albemarle submitted a full narrative of the reasons for the division of the fleet. They ascribed it to faulty intelligence, which led Albemarle to believe that the Dutch would not be at sea before Prince Rupert had dealt with a French fleet from Brest. They went on to castigate 'the intolerable neglect in supplying of provisions during the whole Summer's expedition, notwithstanding the extraordinary and frequent importunities of our letters . . . directed to Sir William Coventry'. Further blame was laid on the 'horrible neglects of his Majesty's officers and the workmen of his yards', and the culpable decision not to keep the fleet in being during the Spring of 1667. Albemarle specified the faulty intelligence he had received from Arlington, and the incompetence of Commissioner Pett in the defence of Chatham during the Dutch attack in June.

In the course of the enquiry Sir William Coventry, who himself had been under attack, was ill-advised enough to produce a letter which reflected severely upon the judgment of the duke of Albemarle, who just before the Dutch attack on the Thames ports had written to the king that Chatham was well defended, and that the positioning of a chain across the harbour made the harbour safe from attack, whereas the Dutch had dealt with it in a half-hour. Albemarle was furious, but the committee ignored the implication. Indeed the conduct of the enquiry was chaotic, and earned Pepys's contempt:

Lord, what a tumultuous thing this committee is, for all the reputation they have of a great council, is a strange consideration; there being as impertinent questions, and as disorderly proposed, as any man could make.[76]

Pepys, with his expert knowledge, discerned no less than fourteen miscarriages in naval affairs, but they escaped the eye of the committee. Amidst so many technical details, it was easy for the latter to ignore the responsibility of the big fish. No blame was attached to Albemarle, and indeed the House carried a vote of thanks to him and to Prince Rupert for their conduct of the war, to the amazement of Pepys, who commented

I know not how, that blockhead Albemarle hath strange luck to be beloved, though he be, and every man must know, the heaviest man in the world,

although he admitted that he was 'stout and honest to his country'.[71] Commissioner Pett on the other hand was small fry, and the House fastened upon his 'great and high crimes', and had him arrested and brought to the Bar of the House.

In one sense the whole enquiry into the miscarriage of the war was overshadowed by political considerations, especially the coming impeachment of Clarendon. No word of criticism was permitted against the king, but the duke of York received none of the thanks of the House accorded to Prince Rupert and Albemarle. Those who might be useful against Clarendon were left unscathed by the enquiry. Sir William Coventry, who had been especially consulted by the king in August, had been one of the most insistent that Clarendon must go. No doubt he hoped to replace Morrice as Secretary of State, but instead he had alienated the duke of York, and offended Albemarle without gaining recognition from the king. An honest administrator, he was finding the political game too deep for him, and by October he was beginning to regret his part in the attacks on Clarendon, for he now saw that the fall of the Chancellor might be followed by the fall of Arlington, and the supremacy of Buckingham and the idle crowd which surrounded him. He told Pepys 'that he never was an intriguer in his life, nor will be, nor of any combination of persons to set up this or fling down that, nor hath in his own business this Parliament spoke to three members to say anything for him, but will stand upon his own defence, and will stay by it'.[78] But this was no way to succeed in the politics of Charles II's reign, and within a year Coventry was facing political extinction.

However there was another aspect to the crisis. The Commons could not by themselves secure a conviction, and the Lords had no intention of repeating the mistakes of the 1640s. The attack upon Clarendon in the Lords was led by the duke of Buckingham and the earl of Bristol, but this itself was counter-productive, for few wanted to see Clarendon replaced by Buckingham, and it was known that the attack on Clarendon was aimed indirectly at the duke of York. He at the time was in isolation suffering from smallpox, and in his absence Buckingham spent long hours closeted with the king. Moderate men shrank from the conflict which would ensue once the king's brother returned to health. Most of the bishops foresaw a threat to the Anglican church, and all but three of the bishops voted against the impeachment. Pepys, who followed all this with perception, was horrified at the thought of a government dominated by Buckingham and Bristol. He repeated a remark of Buckingham's that he was allowing the king to suffer indignities at the hands of parliament, 'that I may hereafter the better command him'.[79] This was what moderate men feared.

Thus the Lords refused to commit Clarendon by 102 votes to 28. It might indeed have been better if they had allowed the case to come to immediate trial, for there was every chance that the Lords would have acquitted him. Pepys reported that the duke of York, who had recovered from his illness, now regarded the king as 'a slave to the duke of Buckingham', and that his friends were disgusted 'that the King doth in this do the most ungrateful part of a master to a servant that ever was done, in this carriage of his to my Lord Chancellor'.[80] How seriously the approaching triumph of Buckingham was regarded was reflected in Evelyn's remark 'that he did believe we should soon see ourselves fall into a Commonwealth again'.[81] If these views spread, there was every likelihood that the Lords would acquit Clarendon. Charles must have realised this, and sent several messages indirectly to Clarendon hinting that his best course was to escape, all of which he stoutly rejected. Finally Clarendon described how the king sent the duke of York to tell him that it was absolutely necessary that he be gone. Clarendon took this as a command, and on 30 November he rode away on horseback, with his two sons and a few friends, as far as Erith, where he found a boat ready. Contrary winds kept him at sea for three days and nights, before he reached Calais in safety. Clarendon did not say what argument the duke of York had used, or what promises, if any, were made to make him change his mind. Hitherto he had been determined to stand trial, confident of being acquitted by the Lords. He might simply have been obeying the king's command, or York might have warned him of Buckingham's plan to try him by a specially nominated committee which might have sat after parliament had been prorogued, and which would have been packed with Buckingham's nominees, and would certainly have condemned him. But this would have been such an unprecedented course as to be very unlikely.

It was soon apparent that the House of Commons was less concerned with finding the truth about the miscarriage of the war than with fighting a battle for the life of Clarendon. Sir Hugh Cholmly told Pepys that the ex-Chancellor's enemies were out for his head. The subject of impeachment was raised in the Commons on 26 October by Sir Edward Seymour, and discussion ensued whether there should be immediate impeachment, or whether charges should be formulated and evidence taken. The anti-Clarendonians were modelling their campaign on the impeachment of Strafford, and indeed on one occasion sent up Strafford's impeachment to the Lords in mistake for Clarendon's. They knew the difficulty of proving specific charges, and wanted impeachment by common fame, without evidence. The use of the Strafford precedent was dangerous, for parliament had already reversed his impeachment, and Sir Heneage Finch reminded the House that it was their taking declaratory powers

which I fear hath brought us into a reckoning of blood, which we have not yet paid for . . . Though I know not what the legislative power of a parliament cannot do, yet it is not in the power of the parliament, king, lords nor Commons, to declare anything to be treason which is not in the common law felony before . . . Your own act this parliament shews that all done by Strafford was not treason.

Serjeant Maynard agreed, arguing that 'where life is concerned you ought to have a moral certainty', and that common fame was not sufficient ground on which to accuse a man of treason.

It was agreed therefore to reduce the charge to Articles, and these were presented to the House on 6 November by Sir Thomas Littleton. The first charge, in imitation of that against Strafford, was that Clarendon had 'designed a standing army to be raised, and to govern the kingdom thereby, had advised the king to dissolve this present parliament, to lay aside all thoughts of parliaments for the future, to govern by a military power, and to maintain the same by free quarter and contribution'. Others were that he had said that the king was a Papist at heart, that he had received bribes for the Canary patent, that he had sold offices, that he had 'gained for himself a greater estate than can be imagined to be lawfully gained in so short a time', that he had advised and effected the sale of Dunkirk, that he had issued *quo warranto* proceedings against corporations, that he had betrayed secrets to the enemy during the last war, and finally that he was the principal author of the fatal counsel of dividing the fleet in June 1666. There were seventeen charges in all, and the last indicated the desperate lengths to which the accusers were driven to make a case, and there were others equally fatuous.[82]

The leaders of the attack were mostly followers of Arlington or Buckingham, politicians so far disappointed of advancement, and ready to make the wildest charges. Such were Sir Edward Seymour, Sir Thomas Littleton, Sir Robert Howard, Sir William Lowther, Sir Richard Temple, Sir Charles Wheeler and Sir Thomas Osborne. Many of them had been accounted good royalists in 1660, but lacking preferment since, had come to regard Clarendon as the obstacle to their advancement. Often their accusations savoured more of envy than of common sense. Sir Edward Seymour declared that the accused 'makes the earth groan by his building, the monument of his greatness'. Sir Thomas Littleton accused him of manufacturing plots in order to excuse the raising of an army. Sir Thomas Osborne complained that 'no man ever held more employments. No vessel to swim without his hand to the rudder. No money issued out of the Treasury without his approbation', and he quoted against him his remark that 'four hundred country gentlemen were only fit to give money, and did not know how an invasion was to be resisted'. Sir Charles Wheeler repeated the old story that Clarendon had been in Cromwell's pay, and he accused him of 'oppressing the duke of York till his alliance with his daughter'.

It was clear that even if all they said was true, it would have little to do with treason. The Clarendonians took their stand less on a defence of Clarendon than on exposing the weakness of the position of the accusers. Sir Heneage Finch, as we have seen, made notable speeches, and so did Serjeant Maynard. The anti-Clarendonians wanted merely a charge resting on common fame, since they knew how difficult it would be to prove any of them. Seymour argued that precedents and rules of evidence might bind the lower courts, but could not bind the high court of parliament; that it should be sufficient for the Commons to accuse, for the Lords to accept. Littleton argued that it was sufficient for the Commons to impeach a man of high treason, without giving reasons:

It [parliament] cannot be malicious to a part of itself, nor affect more power, than already it hath; which is absolute over itself, and parts, and may therefore do, for the preservation of itself, whatsoever is not repugnant to natural justice.

To which Heneage Finch replied that the Lords were not there to register the will of the Commons, but to act as judges according to the law.

The accusers were on more solid ground when they discussed the sale of Dunkirk. Sir Robert Howard argued that if the king could sell Dunkirk, he could sell Tangier, and if Tangier, why not London? Sir John Vaughan pointed out the difference: Tangier was a marriage portion, and therefore could be sold, but Dunkirk was acquired by arms, and therefore could not be sold, since it was an integral part of the kingdom. On the charge of Clarendon's correspondence with the enemy it was agreed that this could not be proved without bringing in foreign witnesses, which the House decided not to do, but the charge was allowed to stand. The final vote against Clarendon of 161 to 89, was on 11 November and next day the impeachment was sent to the

Lords, with the request that Clarendon be sequestered from parliament and committed to safe custody.

This the Lords refused to do. On 15 November[83] they replied that the Commons had submitted no specific evidence of treason. For a fortnight there was deadlock. A conference between the two Houses on 28 November turned mainly on an interpretation of Strafford's trial. The Lords argued that it could not be used as a precedent, since the present parliament had reversed its decision:

They could not allow all for good that was done in parliament . . . nor would the Commons, if they reviewed the transactions of the Long Parliament. They absolutely denied the newest precedent to be the best. Antiquity was always venerable; laws and old precedents, with a constant course to them were most to be esteemed . . . The last drops of a river make not a stream or course, but a constant current. It seemed contrary to natural justice and reason that a person accused should be punished before he knew his crimes.

The Lords denied that the Commons had the power to imprison without trial, which the Petition of Right had denied to the king and his Council. They had too-recent memories of the use of power by the Long Parliament to wish again to submit to the domination of the Commons. After a long debate the Lords stuck to their position, and on 29 November refused to commit Clarendon. The commons voted that the Lords' refusal was 'an obstruction to the public justice of the kingdom, and a precedent of evil and dangerous consequence'.

Clarendon was much less concerned with the charges made against him than with the shattering realisation that the king had withdrawn all support from him. He wrote to the king on 16 November begging to know the reason for his displeasure. Lord Berkeley had told him that it arose from the king's belief that he had encouraged the elopement of Frances Stuart with the duke of Richmond, and he assured the king of his complete innocence in the matter.[84] Charles was indeed angered by the elopement, and wrote to his sister that

I cannot so soon forget an injury which went so near my heart.[85]

But the reason for his displeasure towards Clarendon went much deeper. He excused his dismissal of the Chancellor in a letter to Clarendon's great friend Ormond:

The truth is, his behaviour and humour was grown so insupportable to myself, and to all the world also, that I could not longer endure it, and it was impossible for me to live with it and do those things with the Parliament that must be done or the government will be lost.

He added that

This revolution already seems to be well liked in the world and to have given a real and visible amendment to my affairs.

To his sister he was even more frank:

There can be nothing advanced in the Parliament for my advantage till this matter of my Lord Clarendon be over, but after that I shall be able to take my measures so with them, as you will see the good effects of it. I am sure I will not part with any of my power, nor do I believe that they will desire any unreasonable thing.

Charles saw the fall of Clarendon as the simplest way of escaping from the predicament into which the Dutch War had left him. Once the wrath of parliament was quieted, he could renew his control of events. He saw it as a tactical move which would head off a revolt, free him from the last vestiges of control by the Council, and leave him free to choose his ministers and his own policy.

The king's dismissal of his Chancellor in 1667 was not unreasonable, for Clarendon had become an obstacle to administrative reform, and Charles had developed a personal dislike for the man who had guided him from his youth, and so often lectured him on his shortcomings. As Clayton Roberts wrote: 'Clarendon's austere morality, censorious counsels and ungovernable temper had become quite insupportable to Charles'. The king's friends who gathered in Lady Castlemaine's apartments mimicked and ridiculed the old man, and looked forward to the day when his restraining hand would be removed. Charles might have been wiser to have left Clarendon as Lord Chancellor on the understanding that he confined himself to his legal duties. But he not only dismissed him, but actively encouraged the impeachment, which would not have begun but for the knowledge that the king approved. His reasons he made clear in his letter to his sister: he would gratify parliament, divert it from probing into the mistakes of the Dutch war, escape from the remaining controls of the Privy Council, and be freer than ever to pursue his own policy. It is even possible that Buckingham promised him that he could secure a larger parliamentary grant. The short-term advantage to the king seemed assured. What he failed to realise were the long-term consequences. The fact that the king's chief minister had been brought down by the hostility of the Commons was masked for the moment by the appearance that the king and Commons were acting in concert, but it was a fact all the same. The fate of Clarendon in 1667 foreshadowed that of the Cabal in 1673, and the earl of Danby in 1678-9. In one sense historians (J R Tanner and Keith Feiling for example) were right to see Clarendon's fall as a step towards achieving ministerial responsibility to parliament, but Charles saw it as a step towards achieving a more personal form of government, which in the long run led to the revolution of 1688. It marked the end of Clarendon's attempt at conciliar government, which had already shown signs of cracking by 1663, but yet had given stable government at least until 1666. Charles had little to complain of in his parliament until he experienced the consequences of a war which was none of Clarendon's making.

And what of the Commons? Why were they so hostile to Clarendon? Clarendon had indeed made enemies. There were old royalists embittered at their lack of reward at the Restoration, and those who were jealous of Clarendon's influence with the king. There were those who resented the Act of Indemnity. There were the Presbyterians and dissenters, who saw him as the pillar of Anglicanism. Yet these were not the men who advocated impeachment. It has been the purpose of the foregoing account to emphasise the smooth relations between government and parliament until 1666. Impeachment was the brain-child of the factions led by Arlington and Buckingham, who saw Clarendon as the great obstacle to their personal advancement. The leaders of the attack in the Commons, Sir Edward Seymour, Sir Robert Howard, Sir Thomas Osborne, Sir Richard Temple, Thomas Clifford, and the others, were ambitious young men hungry for office. And they had their reward. Sir Thomas Osborne and Sir Thomas Littleton became joint Treasurers of the Navy, John Trevor became Secretary of State; Buckingham appropriately became Master of the Horse, and even Sir Richard Temple and Sir Edward Seymour eventually obtained minor offices. When the Commons first met in October 1667, their first thought was to investigate the reasons for the failures of the war. The first vote in the impeachment proceedings was a defeat for the anti-Clarendonians by 172 to 103. But as the latter redoubled their efforts, and piled up the fatuous charges, the independent country members were won over to believing the charges. After all, Clarendon House *was* a major blunder; if Clarendon *had* disclosed the king's secrets to the French (there was no proof), he was certainly guilty of treason. The sale of Dunkirk *looked* like a national humiliation . . . and thus a majority was built up. Those men who like Sir William Coventry and his brother Henry, who sought only the truth, were soon overwhelmed and disgusted by the course of events, and Sir William, the ablest man of them all, found his political career all but over. The earl of Strafford had been brought down, without justice, but because he was seen as an instrument of despotism. Clarendon was brought down because he was an obstacle to the ambitions of his rivals, and the intentions of the king.

Charles wanted to be rid of Clarendon without the possible embarrassments of an impeachment. Accordingly, he sent the bishop of Hereford with the message that 'if the chancellor would withdraw himself into any parts beyond the seas', he would not be prevented. Clarendon replied that he would go only if the king expressly commanded it. That command came on 29 November, when the duke of York sent Clarendon's close friend, Morley, bishop of Winchester, with the message that 'it was absolutely necessary for him speedily to be gone, and that he had the king's word' that he would not be prevented. Clarendon waited no longer, but at once took coach, with his two sons and two servants, to Erith, where a boat awaited him. Taking leave of his sons, he went aboard, was delayed by contrary winds, but reached Calais three days later.

On 3 December Lord Cornbury delivered to the Lords his father's vindication of himself. He denied that he had acquired a fortune by corrupt methods. Except what he had received by the king's bounty, 'I have never received or taken one penny but what was generally understood to be the just and lawful perquisites of my office'. He declared that he was in debt by over £23,000, and that once his debt was paid his income would be about £2000. The king had given him a total of £26,000, and the profits of his office amounted to £2000 a year. To the second charge that he had acted as chief minister, he denied that it was so. Before the king's return his affairs had been conducted jointly by Ormond, Culpepper, Nicholas and himself, and thereafter by the Privy Council. 'For more than two years I never knew any difference in the councils, or that there were any complaints in the kingdom.' But after Arlington became Secretary, 'my credit since that time hath been diminished'; those since appointed to the Council have mostly not been his friends.

I have been so far from being the sole manager of affairs, that I have not in the whole last year been above twice with his majesty in any room alone, and very seldom in the two or three years preceding. And since the parliament at Oxford, it hath been very visible that my credit hath been very little.

As for the Dutch war, he declared that he had always opposed it, that it had failed through lack of allies, and that he had always refrained from attempting to give advice as to how it should be managed. But he continued to be a member of the Council; 'nor was there ever any thing done but upon the joint advice of at least the major part of those who were consulted with'.

Pepys thought that this attempt to defend himself was a mistake in that it only enfuriated the Commons. He commented that he had learnt that 'it is seldom any wrong to a man to say nothing, but for the most part it is to say anything', and that 'nothing but this unhappy paper hath undone him'.[86] It was however not in Clarendon's nature not to seek a full vindication, and it is not clear that Pepys was right. On 13 December the Lords sent down a bill for Clarendon's banishment; the Commons demanded instead a proclamation for his return to stand trial. This the Lords refused, and the bill for banishment was carried. Already the steam was going out of the attack, for the vote on 18 December was only 65 to 42, and the attempt to obtain an Act of Attainder, which would have deprived him of his estate, failed. Some members were having second thoughts. John Swinfen, member for Tamworth, was bold enough to declare that to act merely upon reason of state was contrary to honour and justice:

The power of parliaments is indeed great; it hath no bounds but the integrity and justice of parliaments. If reason of state be a motive of parliament to banish one man, so it may be for many.

He concluded that to banish Clarendon without any charge being proved against him, was to the dishonour of parliament. In the Lords a strong minority opposed to Clarendon drew up a protest which was signed by twenty-seven peers, headed by Buckingham, Albemarle, Bristol, Arlington and Pembroke, and including the bishops of Durham and Hereford. Arlington who had played a far more subtle game than Buckingham in the affair, now showed his true colours.

Buckingham was the principal author of the impeachment of Clarendon, and appeared to be the main influence in Charles's government. That influence rested upon his promise to the king of better management of the Commons, and increased vote of supplies. But he found this more difficult than he imagined. When parliament met in February 1668 after an adjournment, the king announced an alliance with the United Provinces and Sweden, and requested financial support for the fleet. When Buckingham's friends moved to return thanks to the king for his speech, the House laid it aside without a question. When the issue of supply was pressed, the House preferred to continue probing the miscarriages of the war (no evidence produced in any way reflecting on Clarendon). When Buckingham's friends pressed for some toleration for dissenters, the House replied with a petition to the king for a proclamation against Conventicles, and by May the Commons had plunged into a conflict with the Lords over Skinner's Case. Buckingham's credit was thus severely shaken at Court.[87]

For Buckingham however the fall of Clarendon was only a preliminary to the overthrow of the duke of Ormond, for he longed for Ormond's offices of Steward of the Household and Lord Lieutenant of Ireland, and there were plenty of malcontents in Ireland willing to help him achieve his ends. The government of Ireland must be made as difficult as possible, and evidence must be sought of corruption and mismanagement. It should now be clear why the duke of Buckingham had headed the campaign for the Irish Cattle Bill, and why attempts were made to prevent the export of wool to Ireland. Buckingham's minions in the Commons, Sir Robert Howard, Sir Thomas Littleton, Sir Charles Wheeler, Sir Edward Seymour and William Garraway, looked in vain for evidence of illicit trade licences or alienation of crown lands, which could be advanced against Ormond. On 7 March Sir Charles Wheeler accused Ormond of having received £200,000, 'concluding that (except Lord Clarendon) nobody had been so burdensome, and gotten so vastly as the Duke of Ormond'.[88] The charge was so ill-founded that no-one could be found to second him, but it was a warning of what was to come.

The news of Clarendon's fall was a great shock to Ormond. He wrote kindly to the fallen Chancellor on 6 September 1667, and Clarendon replied:

The truth is, I know not what to say, the world is so much altered since I writ last. The great affliction I lay under in the unexpected loss of my wife, which I did not apprehend full two days, had (I thought) pretty well prepared me to quit this world; yet I cannot tell you that the other, which followed within a few days, did not exceedingly surprise me, and even astonish me. Nor in truth am I yet recovered out of that trance, nor can I imagine how from being thought a pretty wise fellow, I became suddenly to have no understanding, and to be of no use.[89]

The only fault he could accuse himself of, was having been too outspoken, of 'insolence and sauciness in debate'. At this time he had no thought of an impending impeachment. His concern was that his estate was so encumbered with debt that he was not sure how he could live without office. He intended to stay at Clarendon House during the winter, and 'at the spring shall retire into some corner of the country, where I may be able to get bread'.

However he reckoned without Buckingham. John Nicholas wrote:

The Duke of Bucks. is the great man who carries all before him, and hath, as it's said, undertaken to his Majesty by his interest in the House of Commons to make them do whatsoever he shall desire.[90]

The bargain was struck with Charles in October: it involved the impeachment of Clarendon and a promise that Arlington and Sir William Coventry would be unscathed, and a promise of extra supplies for the king.

After Clarendon's flight, his eldest son, Lord Cornbury, wrote to Ormond to explain his actions. His father, he wrote,

never stirred, so long as he saw any probability of being brought to his trial in Parliament; though all his friends from the first opening of this session persuaded him to leave the Kingdom, fearing his innocence (though never so great) would not be able to protect him against the fury and malice of his adversaries. He hath had all other baits imaginable to be gone; the King himself having often intimated as if he would be glad my father were out of the way; and some of his very enemies did not stick to undertake . . . that if he were once gone, there should be no further proceeding against him. But all this moved him not, till it was too evident that the House of Commons aimed at nothing so much as to break with the Lords, upon their refusal to commit him without special matter alleged . . . To this dilemma things were brought; so that 'twas impossible to avoid a rupture between the two Houses: which my Father might not be the cause of . . . and being informed from very credible hands that there was *a design to prorogue the Parliament on purpose to try him by a Jury of Peers* (by which means he might fall into the hands of the Protesting Lords), he resolved to withdraw, and accordingly found an opportunity of transporting himself to Calais, where he arrived on Wednesday last . . . Thus your Grace sees the inevitable ruin and destruction of a person who hath spent near thirty years in the service of the Crown; . . . If this storm proceeded only from the power and malice of a particular faction, it were to be struggled with; but being from the anger and displeasure of the King (the ground whereof he could never yet by any means discover) makes his misfortunes insupportable.[91]

By then Ormond knew that his own affairs were being investigated, and he wrote to his son that what he really wanted to know was what attitude the king was adopting.[92] In January 1668 he knew that Sir William Coventry was delving into his accounts, but he still trusted that Arlington was his friend. In February he wrote that

Either the Duke of Bucks and his undertakers will succeed, or fail; if the first I am well pleased to have no part in the honour; if the last, his and their credit with the King and the world will soon vanish. I am sure it ought to do.[93]

His chief concern was that he had incurred a heavy debt in the service of the crown, and had not yet received the money due to him under the Act of Settlement. If he once left office he knew that he would never be paid. He decided therefore in May to go to London to defend himself against the spurious charges against him. He knew that Buckingham was his mortal enemy, but thought he could succeed if Arlington supported him. But Arlington as usual played the subtle game of trying to stand well with both sides. He had no desire to see a triumphant Buckingham, but at the same time feared Ormond's powerful support for the anti-Clarendonian party. For a time it seemed that Buckingham had failed in his attack on Ormond, and in February 1669 the latter was writing that he believed that he would not be removed. However, in May the king informed him that he intended to change the government of Ireland, and Ormond's administration was at an end. He had fallen before the same political intrigue which had brought down Clarendon.

The 'Undertakers' entirely failed to fulfil their bargain with the king, and by 1670 Buckingham's following in the Commons had perhaps shrunk to seventy. There was poetic justice in the fact that in January 1674 he in turn came under the attack of the Commons as part of the campaign to overturn the Cabal and reverse the French alliance, which was associated in the mind of the Commons with arbitrary government and the spread of Popery. On 7 January he was accused in the Lords of a scandalous liaison with the countess of Shrewsbury, whose husband had died after a duel with the duke. On 13 January he was accused in the Commons of promoting Popery and the French alliance, of speaking treasonable words against the king, of misusing his powers as Lord Lieutenant of the West Riding, of imprisoning the king's subjects, of raising money illegally, of killing the earl of Shrewsbury and of adultery with his wife, of sodomy and other crimes.[94] He had taught the Commons to use the weapon of impeachment, and they were apt pupils. Buckingham made a poor defence, and the king deprived him of most of his offices. He never held a public position again.[95] Charles was left to bear the consequences of the Treaty of Dover and a disastrous third Dutch war. By 1673 his government faced bankruptcy, and a triumphant House of Commons forced upon him the humiliation of the Test Act. It was the nadir of the reign.

# Conclusion: Clarendon, History and Politics

The anguish of Clarendon's exile was relieved only by the thought that it had been the result of a conspiracy by a very few men, and that the king would soon pardon him, although he realised that the Act for his banishment made this much more difficult. Meanwhile banishment began with humiliation and discomfort. Louis XIV had no wish to offend the English parliament, and made it clear that he was not welcome in France. When Clarendon wrote to his old enemy, the earl of St Albans in Paris, he received no comfort. Stress brought on another attack of the gout, and in travelling to Rouen, his coach overturned, and he was injured. Since the French king made it plain that he wanted him out of France, his first thought was to go to Avignon, but on receipt of a message from the duke of York that he should return and defend himself, he left Rouen for Calais. Here his gout was so bad that he was bed-ridden, 'nor for many nights closed his eyes'. He was angered by further messages from the French foreign minister that he must be gone, and replied sturdily, 'that though the king was a very great and powerful prince, he was not yet so omnipotent as to make a dying man strong enough to undertake a journey'. At this point however the French attitude changed, for the news arrived of England's Triple Alliance with Sweden and the Dutch, and it was no longer necessary to placate parliament. For six weeks Clarendon lay prostrate. Then as the prospect of returning to England receded, he returned to Rouen, where he stayed until April, before resuming his journey to Avignon.[1]

At Evreux he was attacked by some English mercenaries, who pillaged his belongings and dealt him a blow on the head, before he was rescued by the authorities. He spent some time recovering at Bourbon, and reached Avignon in June, where he was received as a celebrity. He then heard that his old friend the Viscountess Mordaunt was at Montpellier, and found the town delightful. He therefore decided to move there, and remained nearly three years. The authorities were friendly, and the presence of Lady Mordaunt was a great consolation. Here he found peace,

And it pleased God in a short time, after some recollection, and upon his entire confidence in him, to restore him to that serenity of mind, and resignation of himself to the disposal and good pleasure of God, that they who conversed most with him could not discover the least murmur or impatience in him, or any unevenness in his conversations.[2]

It was natural that in these circumstances his thoughts should again turn to his writings, but now his purpose was different. He had begun his *History* in 1646 in an attempt to understand the nature of the Great Rebellion. His purpose now was 'to vindicate himself from those aspersions and reproaches which the malice of his enemies had cast upon him in the parliament'.[3]

Clarendon's first task was to write a vindication of his actions from the charges of impeachment, and this he sent to his son in July 1668, and it was printed in an abbreviated form in the *Continuation*.[4] He then turned to write the *Life*, which he began in July 1668. His *History*, written between 1646 and 1648 had been completed as far as Book vii, when it was laid aside. There was necessarily some overlap, but the *Life* could take on a more personal note, and could be freer in its criticisms. Characters merely mentioned in the *History* could be fully drawn in the *Life*. By November 1669 he had completed the first three parts of the *Life*. Parts iv, v and vi, written between November 1669 and May 1670, were later largely incorporated into the later Books of the *History*. He was seriously handicapped by being cut off from his papers. In the early years of his exile, his children were not allowed to visit him, but in 1671 the prohibition was relaxed, and his second son, Laurence Hyde, was granted a pass to visit him. In 1672 the visit was repeated, and Laurence brought many of the papers his father needed. In June 1671 Clarendon moved to Moulins in order to ease communications with England; during the next year Books viii to xvi of the *History* were completed, and in June 1672 the *Continuation* of the *Life* was begun. Written under these extreme difficulties, the wonder is not that his writings contained inaccuracies, but that so much was remembered, and that so many judgments have stood the test of time. His chronology was faulty; there are few dates, and those given were often wildly innacurate. His books then do not make easy reading, and require a fair knowledge of the period from other sources before their value emerges. In general the earlier writings of 1646–8 are more trustworthy than Books ix–xvi, because they were written nearer to the events. He was not a soldier, and his military assessments are often doubtful. Yet with all the imperfections, which historians delight to discover, his books remain an indispensable source for the period, and no-one could write a history of the period without close attention to his judgments.[5]

In a sense this whole book has been in the nature of a commentary upon Clarendon's *History*, but it is fitting that we should attempt a brief assessment of it as a whole. Professor Knights, in a perceptive essay upon the work, wrote:

It is more than *political* wisdom . . . This is *moral* wisdom. It is this that constitutes Clarendon's greatness as a historian: that there is a constant reference beyond politics – beyond, that is, the conflict of forces – to the human ground. We touch here on Clarendon's representative significance. The wisdom. . . . grows not simply out of 'politics' but out of 'culture': it is not merely a result of reading, though Clarendon had read widely in the classics; it is the product of a civilised tradition and of habits of civilised intercourse . . . He was the product of a society within which there was a highly developed sense of the person, a society for which personal and moral issues mattered, and which possessed a language in which these issues could be intelligently discussed.[6]

The tolerant humanism of the Great Tew circle shaped the standards by which he judged men and events. Horace Walpole called him 'the Chancellor of human nature', and wrote that as a historian

his majesty and eloquence, his power of painting characters, his knowledge of his subject, rank him in the first-class of writers.[7]

Indeed it is Clarendon's character-studies which perhaps first seize the attention of the reader. His assessments often show intense interest in human nature, as when he writes of the first duke of Buckingham:

If he had an immoderate ambition . . . it does not appear that it was in his nature, or that he brought it with him to the court, but rather found it there, and was a garment necessary for that air.

and of Archbishop Laud who

thought he could manage and discharge the place and office of the greatest minister in the court . . . without any other friendship or support than what the splendour of a pious life, and his unpolished integrity, would reconcile him to; which was an unskilful measure in a licentious age.[8]

'Unpolished integrity' is a splendid phrase when applied to Laud. We have quoted already his assessments of the characters of the principal members of the Great Tew circle, which must always remain one of the most important sources for our understanding of them. More remarkable perhaps is the cool detachment with which he writes of men who might have been regarded as his opponents, in particular John Pym and Oliver Cromwell. He had great respect for them both, and more than a little admiration for Cromwell. His interest as a historian and student of human nature transcends any partisanship he might have felt.

Sir Charles Firth[9] was concerned that there was an apparent contradiction between the undue importance which Clarendon attached to individual actions and his later belief that God's will would be fulfilled despite the intentions of individuals. But there was no real conflict between the two views. Clarendon adhered to the Arminian doctrine of Free Will; men could choose their course of action, but there would always be a price to pay for breaking the moral code, and the wicked would not in the end frustrate the will of God, and might even be unknowing instruments of his purpose.[10] Thus the Restoration of 1660 was brought about less by the actions of the royalists than by the disintegration of the Protectorate, and General Monck, 'was instrumental in bringing these mighty things to pass, which he had neither wisdom to foresee, nor courage to attempt, nor understanding to contrive'.[11] Similarly he wrote to the countess of Morton in March 1650,

I have long thought our nation will be either utterly extinguished under this great judgment, or be restored and preserved by such an extraordinary way, as we shall not be able to assume any part of it to our own wits and dexterity; for methinks, God Almighty exceedingly discountenances all the designs which our natural reason is apt to flatter us with.[12]

It is significant that nowhere in his *History* did Clarendon attempt to assess his own part in bringing about the Restoration.

Belief in a moral order lay at the base of all Clarendon's thinking. In December 1646 he wrote to Secretary Nicholas:

When I come to be hanged, Mr. Secretary, I will have a better defence than saying I meant well, and thought in prudence this was the best way to serve the king; when, by the better and known sense of the law, I have done that which I ought not to have done. I like prudence well; and where the law allows a latitude, am as like to be deceived by my own reason as another man; but if ever I quit the foundation of my innocence upon confidence of King or Parliament, and go out of that known tract, in hope that my own wit find a better way, I will in the next place renounce all known Divinity, and trust my own spirit for a new religion.[13]

He argued that not even to save the king's life should there be any acceptance of dishonourable terms, and this was why he was so pessimistic about achieving a settlement after Charles I's military defeat. There could be no peace without restoring the king to his just position,

and how ridiculous soever this seems, it will appear more necessary, the nearer men draw near to the conclusion. And even they who are most peremptory against it now, will every day meet with somewhat in their journey, that will reform them. And all this makes me believe . . . that there will be yet no peace . . . it not being for God to wrap up the horrid impiety of the people in a sudden calm.[14]

Moreover to Clarendon the moral law and constitutional law were so closely bound together as to be almost synonymous. Thus, when discussing negotiations between Charles I and Parliament, he wrote in October 1647:

In God's name, distribute as many personal obligations as can be expected, but take heed of removing landmarks and destroying foundations; whilst you insist upon those, you have a place to fix your foot upon, but recede from one of those, and they will be too hard for you . . . Abandon your principles, and there is no judge of reason left but plurality of voices and strength of hands. . . . Believe it, though a war may be carried on by a new model, a firm peace can never be established but by the old.[15]

Another important aspect of Clarendon's *History* is the quality of his historical judgments. To choose examples almost at random, when he blamed Buckingham for two speedy dissolutions of parliament, and wrote that he was 'utterly ignorant of the ebbs and floods of popular councils'[16] or when he wrote that in the 1630's 'England enjoyed the greatest measure of felicity that it had ever known'; or when he criticised the feebleness of the king's ministers in 1640, when 'everyone thought it enough to preserve his own innocence'; or when he estimated the fourth earl of Bedford as 'a wise man, and of too great and plentiful a fortune to wish a subversion of government', Clarendon was making historical judgments which were perceptive and accurate. His remarks were often trenchant and caustic. Professor Trevor-Roper has said of Clarendon that 'of all historians, he is probably the greatest master of disdain', and he quotes his opinion of the earl of Arundel, a general 'who had nothing martial about him but his presence and his looks'; and Archbishop Abbott who 'had been head or master of one of the poorest colleges in Oxford, and had learning sufficient for that province'.[17] Such judgments add attic salt to the quality of his history.

The credibility of Clarendon's *History* has indeed recently been attacked by Ronald Hutton.[18] He rests his case on the examination of three specific examples. The first is the assumption that while the upper classes tended to be royalist, the middle and lower classes favoured parliament. Modern research has indeed revealed a very complex pattern of social relationships, if indeed any pattern at all, with families sometimes split down the middle, so that father might fight against son, and brother against brother. Also, Clarendon perhaps did not recognise the widespread neutralism which pervaded the country. Yet Cromwell too doubted whether the journeymen of his army could ever be expected to beat the royalist gentlemen. When Clarendon wrote of the resentment felt when journeymen rode the countryside on horseback, lording it over royalist gentlemen, he was accurately reflecting the opinion of the time, as was Denzil Holles, when he wrote that it was a great evil 'that servants should ride on horses, and the princes walk as servants on the earth';[19] and he is confirmed by Professor Underdown, who wrote of 'the old leadership being pushed aside by energetic new men lower down the social scale'.[20]

The second example is when Clarendon says that the force which Lord Herbert met at Coleford in 1643 was 'a rabble of country folk', whereas it was in fact a regiment of parliamentary troops. It is more than possible that the rank-and-file of both armies in 1643 could have been described as a rabble, but the point is quite irrelevant to Clarendon's narrative, which was concerned with the fact that Colonel Lawley and his officers were shot.[21] 'Country people' was no doubt used in a pejorative sense, but without great damage to the accuracy of his history. More serious has been the criticism of Clarendon's treatment of the Western campaign, and perhaps the injustice done to Lord Goring and Sir Richard Grenville. It is true that Clarendon's account cannot be accepted in all its details, and that the whole story requires the researches of Mary Coate and A C Miller to put the record straight. It was a frustrating campaign in which personal feelings ran high, and Clarendon was writing to defend the Prince's Council from the attacks of Goring and Grenville. If there were inaccuracies in his treatment of the Western campaign, he had even greater difficulties in gaining the details of campaigns in the Midlands and the North. Yet when he had authentic sources, such as Hopton's narrative, his account was accurate, and he made great efforts to collect the relevant information from his contemporaries. Within the limits of three examples, much of what Hutton says can be accepted, but not the accusation that Clarendon's work was 'a brilliant network of statements designed to deceive', and that it was 'a fallacious portrait of events'.

Clarendon has often been accused of inaccuracy or bias on occasions when further research has shown that he was substantially correct. Thus his account of the situation in the City of London 1642–3, which Gardiner thought to be inaccurate, was based on *A Letter from Mercurius Civicus to Mercurius Rusticus 5 August 1643*, the accuracy of which has since been vindicated by the researches of Professor Pearl. Wormald has shown that Clarendon's account of Waller's Plot in 1643 is a good deal more accurate than that of Gardiner. Professor Trevor-Roper has shown that Clarendon's view of the part played by the fast-day preachers in stirring up the crowd, was both perceptive and accurate, and that he was right when he wrote: 'No good Christian can without horror think of those ministers of the Church who, by their function being messengers of peace, were the only trumpets of war and incendiaries towards rebellion.'[22] The military events of 1644, of which Charles I was particularly proud, were taken by Clarendon from Sir Edmund Walker's *The Happy Progress and Success of the Arms of King Charles I, 1644*, the Ms. of which was copied out by Hyde, and the accuracy of which has not been impugned. Clarendon was intensely interested in human character, and his work is studded with priceless assessments of the political figures of his day.

As the earlier chapters of this book have attempted to show, it is not always easy to deduce from the *History* Clarendon's own part in events. It was not his purpose in 1646–8 to advertise himself in his writings, and when he came to write the *Life* he was more concerned to trace his relations with the king than his early opposition to him. His political position appeared fluid as he changed from reformer to royalist, whereas the truth was that his constitutional conservatism was formulated in reaction to the unprecedented parliamentary challenge to the monarchy. Neither Hallam nor Gardiner understood the subtlety of his position. Both rather despised him because they were so sure that parliament was in the right that they gave little time to studying the other side.* They failed to see Hyde as the principle author of a new version of 'mixed monarchy', by which the king would return to the known basis of the

---

* Gardiner called him 'an essentially mediocre statesman', whose ideas were 'based on negations'.[23]

constitution, exercising his legitimate authority, but respecting the rights of parliament. No one can say whether Charles I would have adhered to Hyde's ideal if he had won the Civil War; much no doubt would have depended upon the conditions of victory; but it was the principle upon which Hyde effected the restoration of the monarchy in 1660. Wormald corrected the misjudgments of Hallam and Gardiner by showing that Clarendon wanted neither the complete victory of the king, nor the complete victory of parliament, but a return to the traditional constitution:

From the passing of the Grand Remonstrance to the end of March 1642 Hyde spent his time trying to persuade the King to adopt the policy which was precisely the one which Gardiner himself judged that the King ought to have pursued.[24]

Hyde was appalled by the prospect of civil war. He understood, much better than the king, the weakness of the latter's position, and the strength of parliament, and between 1642 and 1646 found himself in that most difficult of all political positions, of seeking a peace settlement while war was being waged.

Once those negotiations had failed, there was little more that he could do for Charles I. The latter expected him to write his *History* as a vindication of the monarchy, and sent him documents for this purpose. But this was not the book Hyde intended to write, and it is significant that he laid aside his writing in 1648, when the fall of the monarchy appeared imminent. His great fear was that, in order to save his life, Charles might barter away the fundamentals of monarchy in church and state. But Charles stood firm, and Hyde venerated him for it. The speed of events had forced Hyde to review the situation in the light of history, and his transcendant purpose now was to preserve the 'foundations' of the constitution; he repeatedly wrote that the 'landmarks' must be preserved. He had never concealed the mistakes that the king had made before 1640, but he believed that the errors of parliament after 1642 were much greater. His sense of history, fully in the tradition of Richard Hooker, asserted itself as he was convinced that traditional development in church and state must sooner or later be resumed. Thus he always opposed the idea that the monarchy could be restored by foreign intervention, and was always doubtful about royalist risings in England. The Restoration would come about by the disintegration of the revolutionary forces, when the historical development would be resumed. It was the traditional monarchy he wished to see restored, divorced from the despotic tendencies of the 1630s.

It was also the church of Richard Hooker which he wished to be restored. The Great Tew circle had gone back to the study of the Early Fathers, as an antidote to the revolutionary ideas of the Reformation. They rejected the idea of Papal supremacy, but looked for a historically based religion. Their ideas accorded neither with the Counter-Reformation, High Anglicanism nor Calvinism. Many of their conclusions were fully in the tradition of Erasmus,

Hooker and Grotius. They concluded that there were many questions of theological nicety which could not be answered, and which were unnecessary to true belief, that conflict over them sprang from pride and passion rather than from a desire to find truth, and that ecclesiastical government must distinguish clearly between essentials and inessentials in matters of belief.

Hyde spent much time during his long exiles in the study of history and theology. As Lord Acton wrote, 'he had reflected more deeply than any man then living on the problem of Church and State; and he did not believe in the sacred fixity of divisions founded on schemes of Church government only'. During his final exile he wrote about the subject at great length. In an essay *Of the Reverence due to Antiquity*[25] he expressed impatience at too great a concern for the Early Fathers:

There is not, it may be, a greater obstruction in the investigation of truth, or the improvement of knowledge, than the too frequent appeal, and the too supine resignation of our understanding to antiquity . . . Nor doth it seem a natural thing that religion should arrive at its perfection in its infancy; nor doth it appear that the church could be in its full vigour in our Saviour's time, or in the time of the apostles.

St Augustine and Saint Jerome were learned and pious men, but they lacked 'all that learning which hath flourished in Europe since that time'. The Christian Church had grown through sixteen hundred years, and its problems were not the same as those of the fourth century. Clarendon wrote as a man of the Renaissance, aware of the intellectual strides which had been made since the Middle Ages, and this was his answer to those who had spent so long discussing the meaning of 'presbyter' in the early church. Some who had studied the Early Fathers had been led back to Rome, as Chillingworth had been for a time, but Clarendon was in no such danger. He wrote of the 'professed licence and incorrigible practice of wickedness' in the mediaeval Roman Church, and of its 'impure and unclean air'.

He was equally critical of the Reformation, when

novelties were introduced, which are always odious in religion; and the horrible outrages which in many places were committed, when all kinds of profaneness were applied to the removing some kind of superstitions; and the foul pretence of conscience made use of to pull down churches and interrupt all exercise of religion, to withdraw all duty and obedience from kings and princes, and to contemn all laws and government.[26]

Standing between Rome and the Reformation

it is not in our power to doubt but that the church of England is legitimately constituted, and founded upon all principles of Christianity, which our Saviour himself declared to be the foundation of his church. . . . We pronounce no anathema against those who are of another profession, but are well content that those tares shall grow till the harvest.

Clarendon was making a plea for the rights of private conscience, but he was also adamant that religion must not be allowed to be politically divisive:

A kingdom divided against itself cannot stand. Not that such a union is necessary to the peace thereof that all men must think the same thing, or concur in the same action; such a unity is not necessary nor requisite in private families, and would obstruct all growth of knowledge and improvement of virtue in all public kingdoms and states: but the division is most prodigious when all the kingdom will not obey one sovereign; when one part of it will submit to a sovereignty which their sovereign forbids, and which pretends to a power to depose the other.

When he wrote he was thinking, not of the Protestant Dissenters, but of the Roman Catholics whose allegiance was to the Pope rather than the king. At the same time he asked the Church of England 'not to make the plaster too wide and too broad for the sore it is to cover'; in short, not to make the controversy more than was necessary for national safety.

We find that conferences, disputations and books are so far from extinguishing the fire, that they do not allay the heat of it; on the contrary, they raise the spirit to a ruder blaze, and that people to an insolence, the enduring whereof is dishonourable to church and state.[27]

Theological controversy would settle nothing, and would only fan the flames:

There is no hope of any concord between us from any determination of the fathers; and they who most cry up their authority, and pretend to be entirely governed by them, do in truth most contradict their opinions and undervalue their persons.

These ideas were reflected in Clarendon's attitude to the Restoration of the church after 1660. There was no question but that the Anglican Church must be restored, because this was a prime condition for national unity. With the experience of the previous decades, when Puritans had destroyed episcopacy and ultimately executed the king, and when Irish Catholics had revolted and looked to Rinuccini and the Pope rather than to the monarchy, suspicions against them were bound to continue. Charles I had died for the episcopal church, and thus the alliance between church and state had to be renewed. But Clarendon was anxious 'not to make the plaster too wide and too broad'. He hoped that the Presbyterians would find a place within the church, and many of them did. In 1660 he could not be sure of the strength of the royalist and Anglican cause, and the uncertainties in his actions have caused historians some difficulty in interpretations. Moreover it must be remembered that he was not the sole director of policy. The king, the bishops and parliament, as well as the Chancellor, shaped the legislation of the time, and all the evidence suggests that Clarendon, while standing firm on the 'foundations', was anxious to extend accommodation to all whose loyalty was not in doubt.

Clarendon's attitude to church and state is most clearly set out in his

*Animadversions . . . . By a Person of Honour* (1673). At Oxford Hyde had been friends with one Hugh Cressy, who became a member of the Tew Circle and canon of Windsor thanks to the patronage of Lord Falkland. In January 1647 Hyde was shocked to hear that Cressy had not only been converted to Rome, but intended to become a priest.[28] In 1662 the young Anglican rector of Sutton, Edward Stillingfleet, published his *Irenicum*. He wrote, he said, 'not to increase the controversies of the times, nor to foment the differences that are among us', but to still them. He wrote very much in the spirit of the Great Tew Circle. It was incredible that there should be conflict among Christians:

He that came to take away the insupportable yoke of Jewish ceremonies, certainly did never intend to gall the necks of his disciples with another instead of it.

Christ's only commission to the Apostles was to teach what he had commanded them:

Not the least intimation of any power given them to impose or require any thing beyond what himself had spoken to them, or they were directed to by the immediate guidance of the Spirit of God . . . The Apostles valued not *indifferencies* at all, and those things it is evident they accounted such, which whether men did them or not, was not of concernment to Salvation.

Churches differed in their rites and customs according to tradition, but had no basis for claiming a monopoly of the truth in them, and he accused the Catholic Church of fanaticism in such matters.

Cressy sprang to the defence of his church in a pamphlet *Fanaticism fanatically imputed to the Catholic Church*, and in turn accused Falkland, Chillingworth and the Great Tew Circle of Socinianism and the exaltation of private opinion. The work naturally attracted Clarendon's attention, and in 1673 he replied with his *Animadversions*, published anonymously 'By a Person of Honour'.

The work shows to what an extent his ideas had been formed in his early years. He quotes in detail a sermon by a Mr Lushington he had heard at Oxford over forty years before. He claimed that Anglicans had as great respect for the Early Fathers as any church, but he denied that all problems could be solved by reference to them, because the Fathers did not answer all questions, and did not always say the same thing. The ultimate test of belief must be, not authority, but reason. The essential requisites of the Christian faith were simple, and they need not be complicated by the subtleties of theologians. Beyond the essentials of the Christian faith all was merely a matter of opinion. Religious forms differed according to tradition and climate:

It would be very incongruous where genuflexion is neither the posture of reverence or devotion, to introduce a command for kneeling; and there are many particulars worthy of the same consideration.

One of the greatest causes of civil conflict had been the distinction between the ecclesiastical and the temporal power:

That unreasonable, inconvenient and mischievous distinction of Ecclesiastical and Temporal, as it exempts things and persons from the civil justice and sovereign authority, and as it erects another tribunal and sets up another distinct sovereign jurisdiction superior and independent upon the other, hath cost the Christian world very dear in treasure and in blood, and hath almost heaved that government . . . off the hinges.

The metaphor of the hinges he had used once before when drafting one of Charles I's replies to parliament, and it is clear that he was thinking here of the causes of the Civil War.

No work of Clarendon's shows to better advantage his deeply religious nature than his *Contemplations and Reflexions upon the Psalms of David: applying those Devotions to the Troubles of this Time*. Begun at Jersey in December 1647, continued in Spain, and completed at Montpellier in February 1670, and dedicated 'To my children', it was a work of devotion which brought consolation in times of trouble and despair. In a work of nearly four hundred pages, Clarendon wrote commentaries on each of the psalms, and added to each a prayer. The theme throughout is that however much virtue and innocence may seem to be defeated, yet God will in the end not allow wickedness to triumph; but this will be in God's own time, and not as man dictates. The great difference between a merely moral man and a good Christian is that the first depends solely upon the dictates of natural reason, while the second knows that God's will be done. 'The true Christian can never want true comfort, whatsoever condition befalls him.' But religion is not a recipe for resignation, but for action:

Though it is not easy to know all that we may believe, it is not at all hard to know what we are to do, and what we are not to do. The religion of the brain may admit a thousand disputations, when that of the heart is contracted into one proposition, in which all men agree, Love God and keep his Commandments.[29]

If the people were being punished, it was for their own sins:

It would be too great a Prerogative for the King himself to be able to make a land fruitful that affects to be barren . . . . to make a proud, faithless and perverse nation happy and flourishing, which will not understand nor walk in those ways which lead unto their peace.

The conclusion was:

Let us therefore make the right use of our afflictions, improve ourselves, and grow the better by them; learn and study, and practise that Christian virtue of patience, which we are sure is not only necessary for the condition but as necessary for that condition our own wishes would carry us to, will not only mitigate, and even take away the pain of our sufferings, and so disappoint our enemies of their greatest triumph.

On the theme of politics, one of the most interesting of his essays was on Liberty.[30] Liberty [he wrote] is the charm which mutinous and seditious persons use to pervert and corrupt the affections of weak and wilful persons, and to lead them into rebellion against their princes and lawful superiors. Men would undergo restraint and compulsion in the name of liberty, when they would never submit to them under an ordered government. Men could pursue selfish ambitions and inflict tyranny in the name of liberty, which would never be accepted if their true motives were understood. But true liberty must be defined and regulated by law:

The law is the standard and the guardian of our liberty; it circumscribes and defends it; but to imagine liberty without a law is to imagine every man with his sword in his hand, to destroy him who is weaker than himself; and that would be no pleasant prospect to those who cry out most for liberty.

He would have nothing to do with a contract theory of government whereby men could withdraw their obedience from the institutions of their ancestors:

From this resentment and murmur, war and rebellion have arisen which commonly leave men under much worse conditions than their forefathers had subjected them to.

There was much in his attitude to liberty which was reminiscent of Hobbes, but their conclusions were very different. Clarendon regarded Hobbes as a dangerous and subversive thinker. In July 1659 he wrote to his friend Barwick:

Mr. Hobbes is my old friend, yet I cannot absolve him from the mischief he hath done to the King, the Church, the Laws and the Nation: And surely there should be enough to be said to the politics of that man, who having resolved all Religion, Wisdom and Honesty into an implicit obedience to the Laws established, writes a Book of Policy which I may be bold to say, must be by the established laws of any Kingdom or province in Europe condemned for impious and seditious; and therefore it will be very hard if the fundamentals of it be not to be overthrown.[31]

Hobbes had been appointed tutor in mathematics to the Prince of Wales in 1645, but when the *Leviathan* was published in 1651, fears that his atheism might infect the prince led to his banishment from Court in 1652. After the Restoration Charles II received him kindly, and gave him a pension of £100 a year. Clarendon however had hoped that someone within the church would refute Hobbes: John Bramhall had had a controversy with him in Paris about free will:

The question at that Time was, and still is,
Whether at God's, or our own Choice we Will.[32]

But there had been no adequate attempt to refute *Leviathan*, and Clarendon in exile, having finished his *History*, undertook the task in *A Brief View and Survey of the Dangerous and Pernicious Errors to Church and State in Mr. Hobbes's Book entitled Leviathan* (1673). It was a major work of 322 pages, and we need not follow Clarendon through all his objections to Hobbes, but the work is important to us in that it provides a useful statement of Clarendon's political thought.

Clarendon wrote that Hobbes had

taken upon him to imitate God, and created Man after his own likeness, given him all the passions and affections which he finds in himself . . . (and thus) comes at last to institute such a Commonwealth as never was in nature, or ever heard of from the beginning of the world till this structure of his'.[33]

The book 'shakes the principles of the Christian religion'; the author 'hath no religion, or he is no good Christian'. Clarendon rejects Hobbes' picture of man in a state of nature:

Nor can anything be said more contrary to the Honour and Dignity of God Almighty than that he should leave his master-workmanship, Man, in a condition of war of every man against every man, in such a condition of confusion 'That every man hath a right to everything, even to one another's body' . . . He deprives man of the greatest happiness and glory that can be attributed to him, who divests him of that gentleness and benevolence towards other men by which he delights in the good fortune and tranquillity that they enjoy . . .

Hobbes says that 'War is founded in Nature'; Clarendon on the other hand declares

We say that Peace is founded in nature; and that when the God of nature gave his creature, Man, the dominion over the rest of his creation, he gave him likewise natural strength and power to govern the World with peace and order.

In Hobbes' *Leviathan* a subject had no liberty or rights of property in face of the Sovereign, for they are determined for him; and all this 'upon the extravagant supposition of a consent (a contract) that never was given'.[34] There never was such a social contract whereby men surrendered their rights, and thus

it is to no purpose to examine the Prerogatives he grants to his sovereign because he founds them all upon a supposition of a contract and covenant that never was in nature, nor can ever reasonably be supposed to be'.

He asks where the laws of nature propounded by Hobbes were to be found, and he condemns Hobbes' 'magisterial assertions against the dignity and probity of mankind, and the honour and providence of God Almighty'.

Clarendon rejects Hobbes' view of the law as essentially the command of the sovereign. His own view of the law is much closer to that of Hooker:

All Government so much depends upon the consent of the People that without their consent and submission it must be dissolved, since where nobody will obey, there can be no command, nor can one man compel a million to do what they have no mind to do.[35]

He argued that Hobbes claimed for his sovereign a power claimed by no ruler in history. It was a threat to the liberty and right to property of the subject if, as Hobbes declared, the sovereign had absolute rights over the lives and property of his subjects. It reminded Clarendon of the Divine Right claims of Mainwaring and Sibthorpe, to which he had been so opposed in his youth. Liberty and the rights of property, he declared, were not mere words, but 'the fundamentals of Government'. Even Hobbes had admitted that 'no law can be conceived to be good, though it be for the benefit of the Sovereign, if it be not necessary for the People', and Clarendon asks how this could be reconciled with his assertion 'that all laws which establish any Propriety to and in the People are invalid and void'? No sovereign in Europe made such claims. Nor could law be regarded as being merely the will of the sovereign: could he, in fact, change the inheritance laws of a people without creating confusion?

All governments subsist and are established by firmness and constancy, by every man's knowing what is his right to enjoy, and what is his duty to do . . . If power of interpretation of Law be vested in the Person of the Sovereign, he may in a moment overthrow all law.

Clarendon equally rejected Hobbes' materialist Erastianism, by which all matters of faith were governed by the will of the ruler. We need not pursue this in detail, but one remark of his is particularly significant. The Christian religion, he wrote,

depends solely upon the universal veneration of the Scripture; upon which, if secular and politic interests did not fan a small fire (that would easily be extinguished) into a flame, there are not in sixteen hundred years many such differences grown in the interpretation thereof, as must exclude any pious believer from Heaven, if in his life he carefully observes those precepts in the understanding whereof every man of all parties agrees.[36]

Here he spoke with the same voice as that of the Great Tew circle by which the fierce religious conflicts of the previous century-and-a-half melted away in comparison with the great truths of Christianity upon which all Christians could agree.

The great difference between Clarendon and Hobbes was that while the latter was portraying a Utopia similar to Plato's, Clarendon based his ideas firmly upon history. Indeed, he accused Hobbes of having read too little history, in spite of the fact that he had translated Thucydides.

Clarendon wrote with deep conviction; he wrote also to while away the long hours of exile; but he wrote also in the hope that he would catch the eye of the king, who might relent and allow him to return to England. When he finished his *History* he wrote to Charles:

I have performed a work, under this mortification [i.e. exile], which I began with the approbation and encouragement of your blessed Father, and when I had the honour to be near your Majesty, and which, if I do not overmuch flatter myself, may be for the honour of both your Majesties. But if your Majesty's compassion towards an old man, who hath served the Crown above thirty years, in some trust, and with some acceptation, will permit me to end my days, which cannot be many, in my own country, and in the company of my own children, I shall acknowledge it as a great mercy, and do so entirely resign myself to your Majesty's pleasure, that I do assure your Majesty if the bill of banishment were by your Majesty's grace repealed, I would sooner go into the Indies than into England, without your particular direction or licence.[37]

This appeal went unheeded, but his son Laurence was permitted to visit him, and thus encouraged, he wrote again to Charles in June 1672:

Since by your Majesty's permission I have enjoyed the comfort of my son's company, I hope your Majesty will likewise give me leave to cast myself at your feet for that your gracious condescension, and to protest that I have never committed a fault against you willingly in my life, but have always, and do, love your Majesty with all the passion, and served you with all the faculties of my soul . . .[38]

This meeting with no better response, he tried again with his dedication of his book against Hobbes. He was resolved, he wrote

by God's blessing, never to displease you whilst I live, or after I am dead; retaining still a hope . . . that your Majesty will at some time call to your remembrance my long and uncorrupted Fidelity to your Person and your Service.

But Charles was more likely to have approved of Hobbes' book than of Clarendon's insistence that a ruler must be bound by the law, and again the appeal failed. Further letters followed, one in March 1674, and finally three letters in August, one to the king, one to Queen Catherine and one to the duke of York. To the king he wrote with a final touch of pathos:

I do confess the opinion I had that I knew your Majesty very well, and the assurance I had, that you knew me better than any other man could do, was, under my dependence upon God's providence, all my security, which made me neglect all other arts, and possibly some necessary wariness, which might have preserved me, how unsuccessful soever that confidence hath proved, I will never depart from it, nor practise any other artifices or devices towards my restoration, but by all humble supplication to your self . . . The wound was inflicted only by your own hand, and no other can cure it: nor do I wish the cure to be sooner administered than your Majesty thinks fit to vouchsafe it. If the sufferings I have already undergone (greater it may be than your Majesty believes) be not sufficient ransome for all my presumption and sauciness, which are all the crimes I am conscious of, and which no doubt may be thought great crimes towards Princes, though they be the natural products of long service and much favour and bounty, I shall with all possible resignation wait upon your own time . . . And I must still make it my most humble suit to your Majesty . . . that you will believe, that I never received a penny whilst I had the honour to serve you from any man, that was not just and warrantable by all the rules and practice of the best men who were my predecessors. . . .[39]

Charles however maintained a stony silence until the end.

In view of the constant accusations of corruption against Clarendon, and his stout denials, some attempt should be made to assess his wealth at the time of his exile. Clarendon said that in 1660 the king gave him £20,000. He purchased Clarendon Park in Wiltshire, from which he took his title, from the duke of Albemarle, for £18,000, and as there was a mortgage on it dating from Charles I's time, Charles II cancelled it for £20,000 in 1663. It was the wanton cutting of timber at Clarendon Park for the use of the navy, which brought Pepys into the displeasure of the Chancellor in 1664.[40] However for some reason Clarendon seems never to have obtained the full ownership of Clarendon Park, for in 1667 it reverted to the duke of Albemarle. In 1662 Clarendon received a grant of a half-year's rent due from the soldiers and Adventurers in the counties of Meath, Wexford and Kilkenny, which should have amounted to £20,000, but Clarendon said that he never received more than £6000. He was also possessed of various estates, either by royal gift, or by purchase, namely 29½ acres in Westminster, a house and ten acres in south Lambeth, the manors of Langley, Leafield and Ramsden, together with woodlands and house and grounds in Wychwood forest; the rangership of the royal manors of Woodstock, for which he paid £134 rent; the property of 'Long Acre', worth £8000 and Wychcott, Witney and Twickenham, with rents equalling £600 p.a. He received also from the king land in Westminster from Coventry Street to Hyde Park Corner. Lister thinks that he may have received royal gifts to the total value of £60,000, and that his salary as Chancellor may have amounted to £5000 p.a. It was not an excessive reward in return for his services to the monarchy. He was certainly unwise to have embarked upon the building of Clarendon House at the cost of £50,000, and at the time of his exile he left debts of over £40,000, a fact which does not encourage belief that there had been corruption.[41]

He left his sons considerable problems. Henry Hyde, born in June 1638, was acting as his father's secretary, copyist and decipherer by 1655. In 1660 he married the daughter of Lord Capel, and in 1667, as Lord Cornbury, he became Lord Chamberlain to Queen Catherine. The queen had always regarded Clarendon as her friend, and Cornbury became a favourite with her, which enabled him to ride out the storm of his father's fall. He was so incensed by the treatment of his father that he joined the anti-Court party, was an enemy of Arlington's, and attached himself to the duke of York, his brother-in-law. Laurence Hyde, Clarendon's second son, was an able man, member for Oxford University and Master of the Robes to the king in 1661. He skilfully defended his father in 1667, but remained in favour at Court, and went on to be ambassador to Poland, one of the Lords of the Treasury, First Lord, earl of Rochester, Lord President of the Council, Lord Lieutenant of Ireland and Lord Treasurer under James II. After Clarendon's exile the two brothers had considerable problems in administering the family estates, and in

June 1671 Clarendon wrote to Cornbury showing that £10,000 were owing to Laurence, and that Long Acre was mortgaged for £6000. He advised the immediate sale of Clarendon House, together with other lands, after which there should remain sufficient income to permit the development of Cornbury Park, and the completion of the building there:

I would be very glad that you would in all places plant as much as you can, and even repair those walnut trees in the ground which are decayed, for . . . I do hope to live, as old as I am, to see that ground enclosed with a good brick wall.[42]

Cornbury completed the magnificent east wing of Cornbury Park in 1677, using Hugh May as the architect.

Nothing perhaps throws more light on Clarendon's interests than pictures which he collected at Clarendon House, for which Evelyn is our chief informant. In December 1668 he dined with Lord Cornbury, and in a long letter next year to Pepys he enumerated the pictures he had seen there. Clarendon's purpose, he wrote, was 'to furnish all the rooms of state and other apartments with the pictures of the most illustrious of our nation, especially of his Lordship's time and acquaintance, and of divers before it'. There were portraits of the first duke of Buckingham, Horace and Francis de Vere, Sir Walter Raleigh, Sir Philip Sidney, the earl of Leicester, Burghley, Cecil, Walsingham, Bacon, Ellesmere, Treasurer Weston, Cottington, Duke Hamilton, Bristol, Northumberland, Falkland, Digby, Charles II, Albemarle, Sir Edward Coke, Geoffrey Palmer, Selden, Sir Robert Cotton, Dugdale, Camden, John Hales, Archbishop Laud, Juxon, Sheldon, Morley and Duppa, Sanderson, Brownrigg, Donne and Chillingworth, Sir Thomas More, Fisher, Fox, Chaucer, Shakespeare, Beaumont and Fletcher, Spenser, Waller, Cowley and Butler (Hudibras), the last being hung in a special place of honour. Evelyn said that he himself had sent him many portraits, including Wolsey, Gardiner, Cranmer, Ridley, Latimer, Ussher, Hooker, Sir Francis Drake and Sir Richard Hawkins. Some no doubt had been sold by indigent royalists, others were presents from suitors, and many were of small value. We may entirely discount Lord Dartmouth's accusations in his edition of Burnet's *History* that they were acquired by plunder and corruption. Some are known to have been by Cornelius Jansen and Van Dyck, but many were merely copies of portraits of his close friends. Many royalists had had to sell pictures during the Interregnum, there was a depressed market, and prices were low. Evelyn makes clear that many were gifts:

When Clarendon's design was once made known, anybody who either had them of their own, or could purchase them at any price, strove to make their court by these presents, by which means he got many excellent pieces of Van Dyck, and the originals of Lely, and the best of our modern masters' hands.

But Evelyn makes it clear also that there was no trafficking in favours:

Whatever my Lord Clarendon's skill, whether in law or politics, the offices of state and justice were filled with men of old English honour and probity . . . There were indeed, heinous matters laid to his charge which I could never see proved.

When he disposed of Clarendon House, the second earl transferred the pictures to Cornbury Park. He soon found himself in financial difficulties, and sold Cornbury to his brother in order to satisfy his creditors. The earl of Rochester died intestate in 1711. The third earl of Clarendon, son of the second earl, was a degenerate who died in 1723, and the title passed to his cousin Henry, who united the titles of Rochester and Clarendon. In 1751 he was forced to sell Cornbury to the duke of Marlborough. Henry's daughters married respectively the earl of Essex and the duke of Queensberry, and on Henry's death the pictures were divided between the countess of Essex' two daughters and the duchess of Queensberry. Horace Walpole saw the duchess of Queensberry's pictures at Amesbury, in Wiltshire, and later they passed to Lord Douglas at Bothwell Castle. The elder daughter of the countess of Essex married the Hon Thomas Villiers, and when he was created earl of Clarendon in 1776, the younger daughter, who had married the earl of Granard, returned her share of the pictures to the new earl, and in the early nineteenth century they were gathered at the Grove, the seat of Lord Clarendon in Hertfordshire.[43]

Clarendon's great library was sold off by auction in 1756. The catalogue is preserved in the Bodleian Library, and well illustrates the breadth of his interests, including as it did 37 volumes of the General Councils, 20 volumes of the *Annales Ecclesiastici* of Baronius, 6 volumes of St Bernard, 6 volumes of P. Gassendi, Dugdale's Monasticon, the complete works of Aristotle, Plato, Cicero, Tacitus, Seneca, Livy, Thucydides, Demosthenes, Bede, Hooker, Grotius, a large number of works on the Papacy, the sermons of Donne, the works of Hammond, Chillingworth, Hales, Pascal and a numer of French, Italian and Spanish writers. A sale of Clarendon Mss. in 1764 included his letters, Mss. and writings on theology, law, speeches and parliamentary journals. Clarendon's papers were bequeathed in 1751 to the trustees for the University of Oxford by his great-grandson, Henry Viscount Hyde. The Clarendon Building, designed by Nicholas Hawksmoor in 1713, is traditionally supposed to have been financed out of the profits of the *History*, and when further profits accumulated, the trustees spent £12,000 on the building of the Clarendon Laboratory in 1868.[44]

This was an entirely appropriate memorial to Clarendon, for, as Professor Trevor-Roper declared in 1974, 'Few men have loved Oxford as Edward Hyde did'.[45] He was proud to become Chancellor of the University in October 1660, and one of his first acts in exile was to resign the office. It cannot be said that he left a great mark on the University, but he loved to ride down from Cornbury in state, to be received by civic dignitaries and University authorities, and to preside over its affairs. His first visit was in September 1661, when the Masters of colleges gathered at St Mary's, and a watch was kept on the steeple for his coming over Shotover hill. As the Chancellor approached in a coach drawn by six Flanders mares, accompanied by Lord Falkland, Lord Lieutenant of the county, and most of the county gentry, the Masters and doctors of the University processed to receive him at Magdalen, where he spent the night. Anthony Wood noted that Clarendon's wife and another gentlewoman dined at high table, 'a thing rarely seen', and against all custom. As was perhaps inevitable after a Restoration, the Chancellor conferred a prodigious number of honorary degrees, including 28 D.D.s. He seems to have had a particular enmity against the Puritan Principal of his old college, Magdalen Hall, Dr Henry Wilkinson, telling him sharply that 'his house did not confrom to the Common Prayer:

I hear your hall entertaineth not only factions but debauched scholars, for, as he understood from the proctors, there were more of that house taken in the night time at inns, ale-houses and whorehouses than any house in Oxon hath.[46]

Later when Wilkinson presented him with a Bible, the Chancellor reminded him jokingly that he was still as much attached to the Prayer Book. When Wilkinson invited Clarendon to dine at Magdalen Hall, presumably to see the state of the college for himself, Clarendon refused, saying that 'he entertained a company of factious people in his house'. Wood says that Wilkinson went away fuming, not least because he had spent £26 on sweetmeats. Clarendon was entertained at St John's and All Souls, where he specially viewed John Selden's books.

Henry Wilkinson was finally excluded as Head of Hall under the Act of Uniformity of 1662, and at the same time Conant ceased to be Rector of Exeter, and a number of Fellows retired from Exeter, Lincoln and Pembroke. Neither in 1660 nor in 1662 was there any great upheaval in the University. The continuity which was such a notable feature of the period of the Interregnum, was equally a feature of the Restoration. Clarendon came again to Oxford from Cornbury in September 1663, to prepare for a royal visit. On the 23rd Charles II, his queen, and the duke and duchess of York dined at Cornbury, and then rode on horseback to be officially received at Christ Church. While Clarendon listened to sermons and read in the libraries, the king and the duke went fox-hunting. The final visit was in September 1665, when the king came from Salisbury to preside over the Oxford Parliament, during the Plague.

The Hyde family seems to have had a singularly happy and close relationship. Edward Hyde venerated the memory of his father, and was always grateful for the assistance given him in his career by his uncle the Lord Chief Justice. A letter of Laurence Hyde to his elder brother Edward in 1634, in a mood of youthful banter, catches the relationship between them:

Ned,

I could have sent you this message by a footman, without a letter, but that I would give you the advantage of having as witty a letter of mine as I have of yours, and then we may read them both together in all companies, and I chose your way of conveying letters, a Porter, that I may be as like you as I can, only that he is paid to his journey's end, and you use to pay your messengers but half-way; all copies come something short of the originals, and that makes me come short of you in so many things . . .[47]

On Edward's second marriage to Frances, daughter of Sir Thomas Aylesbury, in 1634, the latter wrote to Henry Hyde of his son:

Long before I heard from you I was thoroughly confirmed in my opinion of his worth which will make him welcome to any man that has reason and good sense . . . What they have is with God's blessing and ours . . . They are now both content, and God bless them. My wife says Amen.[48]

Frances plays small part in Clarendon's story or his correspondence, but the marriage seems to have been entirely happy. During their exile they had long periods of separation, but she was singularly uncomplaining. A few of her letters have survived, and one of them, written in her beautiful copy-book hand, says much for her patience and devotion, and is worth quoting: it is dated 29 September 1658 from Breda:

My Dear Hart,

I was glad to receive yours of the 26 for from the hour you left till this morning I could not so much as hear of you, which was some trouble to me, but God be thanked you are well . . . I hope before this time the old lady hath left the house, and then you will give me leave to come to you. The thing I proposed to myself, was to have been at Antwerp this next Saturday and so to have come to you on Monday night with John Leane. This I am ready to do tomorrow, but if you will give me leave to come then, you will give me great satisfaction, you know my desire of being with you, and when you consider that and how fast the winter approaches, I hope you will name Saturday for the longest [i.e. latest] day . . . My dear Hart, I pray God keep you well and bring me quickly to you. Ever your own . . .

They had nine children, but three died in infancy. To bring up a large family in exile presented great problems, and Lady Hyde could not have managed without the help of the Aylesbury family. William Aylesbury, her brother, the part-translator of the historian Davila, brought his mother and father and two sisters (one of them Lady Hyde, together with her children) to Antwerp from England in 1649. He offered to support them for a year if Edward Hyde would support them thereafter, to which Hyde agreed. Lady Aylesbury and her daughter 'Aunt Aylesbury' became devoted to the children, and played a large part in their upbringing. Frances Hyde's first son Henry was born in 1638. Her last child was born in March 1660, while the three previous children were left to the care of Lady Aylesbury and her daughter. Lady Aylesbury was an inveterate letter-writer, her favourite correspondent being Henry the eldest grandson, to whom she sent constant messages for her daughter about her young children. Charles was sickly, and she had to report in March 1660 that 'truly none hath hopes of him but myself', and he was indeed soon to die. Frank was old enough to be sent to his mother in 1660, but with Aunt Aylesbury's strict instructions to 'see that all his linen be aired both for his bed and body'. However even Aunt Aylesbury was tiring of being a foster-mother, for Lady Aylesbury wrote in March 1660 to 'my dear Harry' to tell his mother that 'she will look after no more when Frank is out of her hands'. Mercifully nature limited the number of offspring to nine.

Anne Hyde, for whom her father showed special affection, early developed an independent character. Her letter to her brother Lorie in October 1654 reveals a mixture of affection and sisterly solicitude:

Dear Brother,
    This is to show you that I will not always be so lazy as not to answer your letters, and indeed I will never be so without a just cause, for I am never better pleased than when I am talking with you as methinks I am when I am writing to you. I am sorry to hear you do not go to Cologne with my Father, for I wish you might see as much as is possible now you are abroad, but our present condition will not permit us what we most desire, but I doubt not of a happy change, and then you will have all that is fit for you, which I most earnestly wish you, and truly it is one of the things I beg daily of almighty God to see you a very good and happy man . . . I am ever yours most affectionately, A.H.

As we have seen, Sir Edward Hyde was reluctant to agree to her becoming a Maid of Honour to the Princess of Orange. He was later concerned to hear that she had taken part in a play, but was mollified to know that it was with the full approval of the princess. Anne replied, in a fine, strong hand:

I received yours of the 19 but yesterday, and am very glad you were not displeased with me. I am sure I shall never willingly give you cause to be so, and it would be the greatest trouble to me in the world if ever you are it. For the business of the play, I assure you I shall never do any such thing without her Highness' command, and when that is I am confident your Lordship will not be displeased with me for it, and in that and all things else never have nor never will give anybody any just cause to say anything of me; Mrs. Culpeper is this day gone to her brother's wedding. When she returns I hope your Lordship will give me leave to see you somewhere. In the meantime I humbly beg your and my Mother's blessing upon
    My Lord, your Lordship's most dutiful and obedient daughter
                                                        Anne Hyde.

In spite of her protestations, there were two occasions when she gave her father grave displeasure. We have already seen the shock, bordering on panic, which gripped the Chancellor when he heard of his daughter's pregnancy and marriage to the duke of York, and the consequences of it dogged him for the rest of his political life. But once her marriage was accepted, Clarendon combined paternal affection with a new respect for her exalted rank. In a letter of August 1663 she wrote to him that she was going to Bath with the king and queen, and would do her best to visit Cornbury, and adds, 'I long very much to hear from you how my Mother does, for I heard she was not well'. Among the family papers is a mock-solemn document purporting to be an adjudication by Hugh May, Clarendon's architect, in a wager between Clarendon and the duchess of York for £20: he gives the award to the duchess.[49]

The second occasion for displeasure was in 1671, when Clarendon was at Montpellier, and learnt of his daughter's conversion to Roman Catholicism. He wrote to her that

no distance of place that is between us. . . . in respect of the high condition you are in, can make me less your father, or absolve me from performing those obligations which that relation requires from me.[50]

He thought she had been swayed by 'some fallacious argument of antiquity and universality . . . The common argument that there is no salvation out of the Church, and that the Church of Rome is that only Church, is both irrational and untrue. There are many Churches in which salvation may be attained . . . There is indeed but one faith in which we can be saved . . . If the Apostles preached true doctrine, the reception and retention of many errors does not destroy the essence of a Church; if it did, the Church of Rome would be in as ill, if not in a worse condition than most other Christian Churches, because its errors are of a greater magnitude, and more destructive to religion.' Thus to the end Clarendon retained the views of the Tew Circle. He begged her to consult him further, and wrote with concern to the duke of York, not knowing that he was already a Catholic. Anne retained her new faith, but died shortly afterwards (March 1671), aged 33, worn out with child-bearing. She had produced four sons and four daughters, but only two daughters survived her, both destined to be Queens of England.

Clarendon took a keen interest in the welfare of his three eldest children, but seems to have been content to leave the others to the care of the Aylesbury grandmother and aunt. Henry was with his father, and by the age of sixteen was already acting as his father's secretary, copyist and decipherer. Laurence tried his hand at writing to Henry in French in 1654; he longed to be in Cologne with his brother, and wrote wistfully:

I do not doubt but that you have always enough employment, but when you do write I should be very glad if you would send some news to me, and I cannot think but that being in a place so near the King, you should hear some kind of news every day.[51]

Even at this stage Aunt Aylesbury kept an eye on Henry's welfare, for Laurence added the enigmatic P.S.: 'My Aunt Aylesbury desires you to wash your hands in warm water before it is too late'. Henry later, as Lord Cornbury, became Lord Chamberlain to Queen Catherine, with whom he was always a favourite. He was strongly incensed at the treatment his father received at the time of his impeachment, and joined the anti-Court party, with special enmity towards Arlington. He was strongly attached to his brother-in-law the duke of York, and later served as his Lord Privy Seal. Laurence proved the abler man. He became Master of the Robes to Charles II, and was skilful enough to remain in favour at Court when his father fell from power. He was ambassador to Poland, one of the Lords of the Treasury, First Lord, and, as earl of Rochester, was Lord President of the Council and Lord Lieutenant of Ireland. It was Laurence who attended his father in exile when it was possible, and the two brothers had the final task of publishing their father's great work.

A historian has recently asked why it was that Clarendon, who left such inimitable portraits of his contemporaries, left no full portrait of Charles II.[52] One reason no doubt was that he still hoped for a recall to England, but as he had no intention that his manuscript should be published either in his lifetime or that of the king, that could not be the main reason. It must lie in his veneration for monarchy, whatever the short-comings of the monarch. Perhaps then the absence of a full-length portrait amounts to an accusation, and it is true that those who knew Charles II best were those who left the most critical assessments of him. (Not until Halifax wrote of him after 1688 did a more tolerant picture begin to emerge.) But if Clarendon did not write a final assessment of Charles II, he left plenty of information to serve as guidelines. He had great respect for his intelligence, and admired the personal bravery he displayed during the Worcester campaign. Having been closely associated with him since Charles was a boy of fifteen, he had genuine affection for him, although he never lost the habit of lecturing him and reminding him of his duties as king. There was never any doubt with Clarendon that Charles was king, and that the ultimate decision must be his: his main regret was that Charles so often put off decisions.

In the first two years of the Restoration, relations between the king and Clarendon were close and friendly, for both were uncertain of the strength the monarchy could assume, and Charles relied heavily on his Chancellor's advice and his capacity for hard work. The relationship is well revealed in the notes which passed between the two during meetings of the Privy Council. For example, July 1660:

King: What do you think of my Lord Berkeley's being Deputy of Ireland, if we can find no better?
Chancellor: Do you think you shall be rid of him by it, for that is all the good of it.
(In the end the appointment went to Lord Robartes)

August 1660:

Chan.: I pray be pleased to give an audience to my lord Broghill . . . If you will give him leave to attend you tomorrow morning at 8 of the clock, I will give him notice of it.

King: You give appointments in a morning to others sooner than you take them yourself; but if my Ld. Broghill will come at 9 he shall be welcome.

(Next month Broghill was created earl of Orrery)

5 October 1660:

King: I am going to take my usual physic at tennis. I send you here the letters which my Ld. Aubigny desires me to write. Look them over, and if there be no exceptions to them, return them by twelve a clock for I would willingly despatch them this afternoon.

November 1660:

Chan.: My Lord Treasurer and I will be at my chamber at Whitehall by 3 of the clock, that if your Majesty please, we may attend you an hour before the Council sit. God keep you.

December(?) 1660

King: I would willingly make a visit to my sister at Tunbridge for a night or two at farthest. When do you think I can spare that time?

Chan.: I know no reason why you may not for such a time (2 nights) go the next week, about Wednesday or Thursday, and return time enough for the adjournment . . . I suppose you will go with a light train.

King: I intend to take nothing but my night bag.

Chan.: Yes, you will not go without 40 or 50 horse!

King: I count that part of my night bag.

In September 1661 Clarendon asked leave to visit Cornbury. The king replied:

He must be a harder hearted man than I that can refuse you a few days in a place you are so well pleased with as I perceive you are with Cornbury . . . Have a care of the game about Cornbury that I may have good sport next year when I come thither.

December 1661:

Chan.: You know the Committee is to meet on Monday at my chamber here. If you do not call some of us before you, that we may be of one mind, we shall be little the better for meeting with the other Committee.

King: I will be with you at Worcester House on Sunday in the afternoon. Do you warn those Lords you think fit to meet me there.[53]

There are many such informal notes, and they reflect a close and harmonious relationship between the king and his Chancellor. But they become much less frequent after 1662, and, in his last years, as we have seen, Clarendon declared that he was hardly ever alone with the king. Charles had grown self-confident, was a master of deception and at keeping his own counsel, and much influenced by his younger ministers and friends. We may judge of Clarendon's later relationship with Charles by an incident he gives without date. He describes how on one occasion Arlington and he were discussing disapprovingly the immoralities of court life which Charles encouraged, when the king entered and asked what they were talking about. Instead of prevaricating, Clarendon told him bluntly that his mode of life was the talk of the town, and that it could do the monarchy nothing but harm. Charles listened patiently to the moral discourse which the Chancellor hoped Arlington would endorse, instead of which the Secretary turned the subject into raillery, and the king and he teased Clarendon that 'now he grew old, and considered not the infirmities of younger men'. Clarendon became angry, and said that he used 'too plain expressions which it may be were not warily enough used, and which the good lord forgot not to put the king in mind of, and to descant upon the presumption, in a season that was more ripe for such reflections'.[54] In earlier times Clarendon's moral lectures had been accepted by the king, but no longer, when Buckingham and his friends were doing all in their power to mock him. Yet Clarendon persisted:

He did beseech his majesty not to believe that he hath a prerogative to declare vice virtue, or to qualify any person who lives in a sin and avows it, against which God himself hath pronounced damnation, for the company and conversation of innocent and worthy persons. And that whatever low obedience, which was in truth gross flattery, some people might pay to what they believed would be grateful to his majesty, they had in their hearts a perfect detestation of the persons they made address to.

Clarendon wrote that Charles suffered from 'that unfixedness and irresolution of judgment that was natural to all his family of the male line, which often exposed them all to the importunities of bold, and to the snares of crafty men'.[55] The confusion into which Charles's affairs fell by 1673, when he was to find a strong minister in Danby, seemed to bear out Clarendon's strictures.

When Clarendon's *History* first appeared in print there were enthusiastic responses from Pepys and Evelyn. Pepys wrote in August 1702 to the second earl of Clarendon:

I am but this morning come from the third reading of your noble Father my Lord Chancellor Clarendon's *History* with the same appetite I assure you to a fourth that ever I had to the first; it being most plain that that great story neither had nor could ever have been told as it ought but by that hand and spirit that has now done it . . . [It is] such a lecture of Government for an English Prince as I won't distrust but you may yet live to be thanked and to thank God for.[56]

Evelyn was even more enthusiastic. He wrote to Pepys in January 1703:

I cannot but let you know the incredible satisfaction I have taken in reading my late Lord Chancellor's *History of the Rebellion*, so well, so unexpectedly well, written; the preliminaries so like that of the noble Polybius, leading us by the courts, avenues and porches into the fabric; the style masculine, the characters so just and tempered, without the least ingredient of passion or tincture of revenge, yet with such natural and lively touches as shews his Lordship knew not only the persons outside, but their very interiors; whilst he treats the most obnoxious . . . with a becoming generosity and freedom.

Like Professor Knights, Evelyn sensed that it was essentially a moral work; it would provide, he wrote, a model for great ones as to how they should act, and how 'to make their treading sure by the virtue of justice, moderation and public spirit':

I acknowledge myself so transported with all the parts of this excellent History that, knowing (as I did) most of the persons then acting the tragedy and those against it, that I have no more to say but much, very much to admire . . . It required no little skill, prudence and dexterity to adventure so near the heels of truth without danger or just resentment of those who deserved so ill as no reflections could have been severe enough.[57]

On Clarendon's fall, Archbishop Sheldon stood forth as the leader of the Clarendon party, and Clarendon's sons were later the leaders of the Tory party committed to the defence of the Anglican Church. When Clarendon's son published the *History* in 1702–4, he certainly regarded it as a triumph for the Tory party. In its preface he declared that two of Clarendon's greatest achievements had been 'the act of oblivion and indemnity, and the act of uniformity, by which the people of England were quieted in their minds, and settled in their possessions, and the church of England redeemed from the oppressions it had lain under'. Queen Anne was advised that

From this History your majesty may come to know more of the nature and temper of your own people than hath yet been observed by any other hand. . . . And though your majesty will see here, how a great king lost his kingdoms, and at last his life, in the defence of this church, you will discern too, that it was by men who were no better friends to monarchy than to true religion that his calamities were brought upon him . . . And a truth it is which cannot be controverted, that the monarchy of England is not now capable of being supported but upon the principles of the church of England.

The intention clearly was that the *History* should become an instrument of Tory propaganda, and accordingly it was attacked by the Whigs. Oldmixon, for instance, in a ridiculous work, attempted to show that Clarendon's Mss. had been tampered with by the Tories, not least by Dean Aldrich of Christ Church, and further attacks came from the Whig Edmund Smith in 1710. All this was completely disproved by John Burton in his *The Genuineness of Lord Clarendon's History Vindicated* (1744). He argued that Oldmixon dared not impeach the integrity of Clarendon himself, so had resorted to charges of forgery by the editors, for which there was not a shred of evidence. The purpose, he said, was 'to blast the credit of Lord Clarendon's History', which was strange since

It might be expected that since this history contains a strenuous defence of the Liberties and Rights of the Subject against the encroachments of the Crown in the former part of King Charles I's reign, it might have escaped the censure of those who affect to be thought zealous of the same cause.

Here Burton showed a clearer understanding of Clarendon's work than the latter's son showed in his Preface. It is true that Clarendon's loyalty to the Anglican Church remained until the end. In a letter to Lord Cornbury in June 1671 he wrote:

There is no doubt, every good man would depart from many little things, if the doing so would firmly unite the Presbyterians to the Church – which, I confess, I think impossible; for the truth is, they are a pack of knaves; and they who appear less violent will immediately lose the party, who will make no other use of the concessions which they shall be granted, than to ask anew and more unreasonable things: and any kind of yielding that proves not fully effectual, will be attended with great scandal to the Church, which shall never be thought to be settled upon any sound . . . [illegible] . . . but still to hearken to new expedients. If the Presbyterians once believed that nothing would be yielded to them, and all their hopes were desperate, it would be the best measure to reduce them. They are as much afraid of the Papists and Independents too as any sober man can be, and will join against them as soon as their own hopes are at an end.[58]

But the purpose and scope of his *History* far transcended the narrow confines of his sons' Toryism. He was writing a work which he intended to stand alongside the historians he had studied so carefully, Tacitus, Livy, Plutarch, Cicero and Machiavelli. At first his intention was to show what had gone wrong, what errors had been committed even by the king himself. Later it was to complete the story of his times and vindicate his own part in it. The result was, in Trevor-Roper's words, 'a majestic, olympian work, untouched by the bitterness of exile'. He knew the Puritan leaders, Pym, Hampden, St John, the younger Vane, Essex, Warwick and Manchester, and was able to leave incomparable portraits of them. He knew they were not revolutionaries in the modern sense of the word, seeking to destroy church and state, but in fact sought a constitutional balance which was not so very different from his own, yet were led on step by step until an impasse was reached. When Tom May published his *History of the Parliament* in 1647, Hyde must have read it, and it must have reinforced his intention to give another version of the events of the Long Parliament, and one which would inevitably reflect the philosophy of the moderates of the Great Tew Circle.

And what was that philosophy? It was essentially conservative and empirical. The form of government, indeed the structure of society, had evolved over a great period of time, and was reflected in the law of the land and the customs of the people. Society was a growing organism, but violent change was inimical to culture and tradition. Society could not be confined into some mediaeval framework, any more than the church could be limited to the forms which existed in the time of the Early Fathers. The human mind had made great strides since the days of Erasmus and Luther. Many of the dogmatic certainties of the past had been successfully challenged, and human reason must be allowed to operate in a spirit of mutual tolerance. But just as Burke defended the principle of liberty at the time of the American Revolution, but turned to the defence of tradition in his *Reflections*, so Falkland and Hyde opposed the misuse of executive power in 1640, yet came to defend tradition in the end. Falkland was no advocate of the bishops, but he refused to believe that their errors justified their extinction. Clarendon in his *Animadversions* declared that 'no reformation is worth the charge of a civil war'. War drove men to extremes, whether of Puritanism, or of royalism, and, contemptuous as he was of Presbyterian intransigence, he was equally irritated by intransigent bishops. The only safe path was for men of moderation to defend the fundamentals, what he called the 'foundations', while permitting discussion in a spirit of tolerance of those things which were inessential or 'indifferent'. Clarendon therefore was fully in the tradition of Erasmus, Hooker, Bacon, Grotius, Selden, Chillingworth and the Cambridge Platonists, who laid the basis for the men of the Enlightenment. His true successors are Hume, Gibbon and Burke.

Clarendon continued writing until the end. According to Aubrey,

as he was writing the pen fell out of his hand. He took it up again to write: it fell out again. So then he perceived he was attacked by death, sc. the dead palsey.

He died at Rouen on 9 December 1674, in the presence of his second son; his body was brought back quietly to England and was buried in Henry VII's chapel, Westminster Abbey. The grave is unmarked. By his will, proved at London 14 December 1675, he left his property, his papers and writings to his two eldest sons, Henry Lord Cornbury and Laurence Hyde. He commended his daughter Frances to the kindness of her brothers, since he could leave her nothing.[59] He made no mention of his two younger sons, one of whom was drowned in the frigate *Gloucester* in 1682. The original manuscripts of his *History*, mostly written on large sheets in his own tiny, crabbed hand, may be seen in the Clarendon Mss. 112, 114-20 in the Bodleian Library, and the modern editions of his work are based on a careful collation of these originals. They remain the outstanding monument to Clarendon's genius as a statesman and historian.

# Abbreviations

Abbott: Abbott W C, *The Writings and Speeches of Oliver Cromwell*, Harvard University Press, Cambridge, Massachusetts, 1937.

Abernathy: Abernathy G R, 'Clarendon and the Declaration of Indulgence'. Transactions of the American Philosophical Society, 1965.

Baxter: Baxter, Richard, *Reliquiae Baxterianae*: or Mr Richard Baxter's narrative of the most memorable passages of his life and times. Published from his own original manuscript by Matthew Sylvester, T Parkhurst, London. 1696, 3 parts.

BIHR: *Bulletin of the Institute of Historical Research.*

Bod.: Bodleian Library.

Browning: Browning A (ed.), *English Historical Documents*, vol. 8. Eyre & Spottiswoode, London, 1953.

Burnet: Burnet G (Bishop of Salisbury), *History of my own time*, Thomas Ward. London 1724, vol. 1, edited by G Burnet, vol. 2 edited by Sir Thomas Burnet.

Burton: Burton T, *Diary of Thomas Burton*, first published from the original autograph ms. in 1828, Henry Colburn, London.

Cal. Cl. Sp.: *Calendar of the Clarendon State Papers* preserved in the Bodleian Library. Ed. by Rev O Ogle and W H Bliss under direction of Rev H O Coxe, (vols. 2, 3 ed. by Rev W Dunn Macray, vol. 4 ed. by F J Routledge under direction of Sir Charles Firth), Clarendon Press, Oxford, 1872.

Carte Mss.: Mss. in the Bodleian Library.

Carte: Carte T, *An History of the Life of James, Duke of Ormonde*, J J & P Knapton, London, 1936.

Cl. Mss.: Clarendon Mss. 1–154, Bodleian Library.

Cl. SP.: *State Papers collected by Edward earl of Clarendon*, commencing from the year 1621, containing the materials from which his *History* and *Great Rebellion* was composed, and the authorities on which the truth of his relation is founded. Vols. 1 and 2 ed. by R Scrope, vol. 3 ed. by T Monkhouse, Oxford, 1767–86.

Coate: Coate Mary, *Cornwall in the Great Civil War and Interregnum 1642–1660*, Clarendon Press, Oxford, 1933.

Cobbett: *Cobbett's Parliamentary History of England from the Norman Conquest in 1066 to 1803*. From which last-mentioned epoch it is continued downwards in the work entitled The Parliamentary Debates. 36 volumes in all, vols. 1–7 published by R Bagshaw, vols. 8–12 by Longman & Co. London 1806–12, vols. 13–36. Longman & Co. London. 1812–20.

Cont.: Clarendon. A Continuation of his *History*. See *Life*.

CSPD: *Calendar of State Papers Domestic Series*, of the reign of Charles I 1625–6 1648–9 etc) preserved in . . . Her Majesty's Public Record Office, 1625–38 ed. by J Bruce, 1638, 1639 ed. by J Bruce and W D Hamilton, 23 vols'., Longman & Co., London 1858–97.

*Calendar of State Papers Domestic Series* of reign of Charles II 1660–1 (1661–2 etc) preserved in the State Paper Department of Her Majesty's Public Record Office. Ed. by M A E Green, 1671 (etc) ed. by F H Blackburne Daniell, Longman & Co., London 1860 etc.

CSPVen: *Calendar of State Papers and Manuscripts* relating to English Affairs existing in the archives and collections of Venice and other cities of North Italy. Ed. by Rawden Brown vols. 1–6, G C Bentinck vols. 8–12, Allen B Hinds vols. 13 etc. Stationery Office, London 1864.

D'Ewes: D'Ewes, Sir Simon, *The Journal of Sir Simon D'Ewes* ed. by W H Coates, 1942 (Yale Historical Publications).

DNB: *Dictionary of National Biography*, Oxford University Press, 1920 etc. 22 vols.

Ec.HR: *Economic History Review*.

EHR: *English Historical Review.*

E.: British Library, *Thomasson Tracts* being *A complete collection of Books and Pamphlets* begun in the year 1640 by special command of King Charles I, London (?), 1685 (?). Now in the British Museum as *Catalogue of the Pamphlets*, Books, Newspapers and Manuscripts relating to the Civil War, the Commonwealth and Restoration, collected by G Thomasson 1640–61.

Evelyn: Evelyn John, *Memoirs illustrative of the Life and Writings* of John Evelyn comprising his Diary from 1641 to 1705–6, and a selection of his familiar letters, whole first published from original ms. ed. by W Bray, 2 vols. H Colburn, London, 1818.

Everitt: Everitt Alan, *The Community of Kent and the Great Rebellion, 1640–1660*, Leicester 1966.

Gardiner: Gardiner S R, *Selected and Edited Documents of the Puritan Revolution*, Clarendon Press, Oxford, 1979 edit.

Grey: Grey, Anchitell, Parliamentary Debates, 1667–94. T Becket and P A De Hondt, London, 1769, 10 vols.

H: Clarendon, *The History of the Rebellion and Civil Wars in England* begun in 1641 with the precedent passages and actions that contributed thereto, and the happy end and conclusion thereof by the king's blessed restoration, Oxford, 1704.

Hexter: Hexter J, *The Reign of King Pym*, Harvard University Press, Cambridge, Mass., 1941.

HJ: *Historical Journal.*

HMC: Historical Mss. Commission.

Huntingdon LQ: *Huntingdon Library Quarterly*.

JC: *Commons Journals* vols. 1–81. 8 November 1547 to 31 May 1826. London 1724, etc.

JMC: *Journal of Modern History.*

Keeler: Keeler M F, *The Long Parliament 1640–1641*, Philadelphia, 1954.

Kenyon: Kenyon J P, *The Stuart Constitution 1603–1688: Documents.* Cambridge University Press, 1966.

Knyvett: *The Knyvett Letters 1620–1644*, ed. by B Schofield, Norfolk Record Society, 1949.

Life: Clarendon, *The Life of Edward earl of Clarendon* . . . containing i. an account of the Chancellor's life from his birth to the Restoration in 1660, ii. A continuation of the same and of his history of the Grand Rebellion from the Restoration to his banishment in 1667. Printed from his original ms. Oxford, 1759.

Lister: Lister T H, *Life and Administration of Edward first earl of Clarendon*, 3 vols., London, 1838.

LJ: *Lords' Journals.*

Nalson: *An Impartial Collection of the great affairs of State*, 2 vols., London, 1682.

Pepys: *The Diary of Samuel Pepys*, ed. by R C Latham and W Matthews, 11 vols., George Bell & Sons, London, 1970–83.

Rushworth: Rushworth John, *Historical Collections of Private Passages of State*, Newcomb for G Thomasson, London, 1659.

Tanner Mss.: Bodleian Library 59–63.

Thurloe: Thurloe John, *State Papers*, 7 vols., London, 1742.

TRHS: *Transactions of the Royal Historical Society*.

Verney: *Memoirs of the Verney Family during the Civil War*, 4 vols. Longman, London, 1872.

Warwick: Warwick Sir Philip, *Memoirs of the reign of King Charles I*, London 1701.

Weston & Greenberg: *Subjects and Sovereigns: The Grand Controversy over Legal Sovereignty in Stuart England*, Cambridge, 1981.

Whitelocke: Whitelocke Bulstrode, *Memorials of the English Affairs*, 4 vols., London, 1682.

# Notes

## CHAPTER I
### EARLY LIFE AND INTELLECTUAL INFLUENCES

1 – Neale, J. E., *Elizabeth I and her Parliaments*, Cape, London. 1953, 2 vols. p. 377; Notestein, Wallace. *The House of Commons 1604–1610*, Yale, 1971.

2 – *Life*, 1, 7.

3 – Prest, W. R., *The Inns of Court under Elizabeth and the Early Stuarts 1590–1640*, Longman. London 1972. p. 6; Clarendon. *A Collection of several tracts of Edward Earl of Clarendon, published from his original ms.* London. 1727.

4 – *Life*, 1, 13–14.

5 – Lister, vol. 3. p. 4.

6 – Burnet, vol. 1, p. 159.

7 – 'An Eclogue on the Death of Ben Jonson in *Jonsonus Virbius*, ed. by Viscount Falkland, 1638, p. 6.

8 – Quoted in Dunlap, R. (ed.), *Poems of Thomas Carew. Poems with his Masque. 'Coelum Britannicum'*. Oxford, 1949, p. 6.

9 – *Life*, 1, 26.

10 – *Ibid.*, 1, 27.

11 – *Ibid.*, 1, 34.

12 – Chrimes, S. B. (ed.), *Sir John Fortescue, De Laudibus Legum Anglie*, Cambridge Studies in English Legal History, Cambridge University Press, 1942, p. 79.

13 – Kenyon, J. P., *The Stuart Constitution 1603–1688*, Cambridge University Press, 1966, pp. 4, 34, 33.

14 – Laud – *The Works of the Most Reverend Father in God William Laud*, Oxford (London printed), 1847–60, 7 vols., vol. 3, p. 390.

15 – Selden, John, *Table Talk*, being the Discourses of John Selden Esq (edited by R. Milward). London, 1689.

16 – *Life*, 1, 37.

17 – *Life*, 1, 48.

18 – Viscount Falkland, (Lucius Cary), *Discourse of Infallibility* edited by Thomas Triplet, John Hardesly, London, 1651, preface.

19 – Mathew, David, *Age of Charles I*, Eyre and Spottiswoode. London, 1951, p. 224.

20 – *Life*, 1, 41.

21 – Hartley. T. E., *Proceedings in the Parliaments of Elizabeth I*. Leicester University Press, 1981, 2 vols., vol. 1, p. 34.

22 – O'Day, Rosemary, *English Clergy: Emergence and Consolidation of a Profession, 1558–1642*, Leicester University Press, 1979.

23 – Neale, J. E., *op. cit.* p. 418.

24 – Knight, W. S. M., *Life and Works of Hugo Grotius*, Sweet and Maxwell, London, 1925, pp. 144–46.

25 – Brandt G., *Historie der Reformatie*, Amsterdam, 1677, 4 vols., vol. 2, p. 348.

26 – Bacon, Francis, *A Wise and Moderate Discourse concerning Church Affairs*. To be found in the Library of Christ Church, Oxford, 1641.

27 – Hales, John, *Tract concerning Schism and Schismatics*, 1638, Bodleian Library.

28 – Above *Tract* republished in Hales's *Golden Remains of the ever memorable Mr John Hales* edited by P. Gunningham with a preface by J. Pearson, London, 1659.

29 – *Life*, I, 55.

30 – Morley, John, *Works of Lord Morley*, Macmillan, London, 1921, 15 vols., vol. 3, p. 480.

31 – *Life*, I, 57; Orr, R. R., *The Thought of William Chillingworth*, Oxford University Press, Oxford, 1967, p. 30.

32 – Chillingworth, William, *The Works of William Chillingworth*, J. Walthoe, London, 1719(?), 4 parts, letter to Sheldon, p. 4.

33 – Chillingworth, William, *Nine Sermons included in the third edition of The Religion of Protestants a safe way to Salvation*, Oxford, 1638, p. 57.

34 – Chillingworth, William, *Works op. cit.* vol. 6. p. 56.

35 – Morton, T., *Good Counsels for the Peace of Reformed Churches by some reverend and learned bishops and other divines*. Translated out of the Latin, Oxford, 1641.

## CHAPTER 2
### THE SEEDS OF CONFLICT

1 – *Cl. SP.*, vol. 2, pp. 228–9.

2 – *H.*, I, 1–4.

3 – cf. Elton, G. R., *The High Road to Civil War* and Russell, Conrad, (ed.) *The Origins of the English Civil War*, Macmillan, London, 1973.

4 – *H.*, I, 12.

5 – Prestwich, M., *Cranfield: Politics and Profit under the early Stuarts; the career of Lionel Cranfield, Earl of Middlesex*, Clarendon Press, Oxford, 1966.

6 – *H.*, I, 49.

7 – Lister, vol. I, p. II.

8 – *H.*, I, 50.

9 – *Ibid.*, I, 64.

10 – *Ibid.*, I, 67–71.

11 – *Ibid.*, I, 94.

12 – *Ibid.*, I, 128.

13 – See Sharpe, Kevin (ed.), *Faction and Parliament, Essays on Early Stuart History*, 'The Earl of Arundel, his Circle'. Oxford University Press, Oxford, 1978.

14 – Alexander, M. V. C., *Charles I's Lord Treasurer: Sir Richard Weston*, Macmillan, London, conclusion.

15 – *Life*, I, 63–4.

16 – Heylyn, Peter, *Cyprianus Anglicus: or the history of the life and death of William Laud*, London, 1668, p. 56.

17 – *Life*, I, 18.

18 – *H.*, I, 145.

19 – *Life*, I, 22–3.

20 – *Ibid.*, I, 25.

21 – The whole story is told at length in Whitelock. vol. I. pp. 53–62. See also Spalding, Ruth, *The Improbable Puritan: A Life of Bulstrode Whitelock*, Faber, London, 1975.

22 – Whitelocke, vol. I, p. 76.

23 – Spalding, Ruth, *op. cit.*, pp. 51–64.
24 – Whitelocke, vol. 1, p. 76.
25 – Historical Manuscripts Commission, 6th Report, App. p. 28.
26 – *H.*, 1, 150.
27 – *Ibid.*, 1, 151.
28 – Kenyon, J. P., p. 34.
29 – *H.*, 1, 73.
30 – *Ibid.*, 1, 166–84.
31 – *Ibid.*, 1, 195.
32 – *Ibid.*, 1, 206.
33 – *Ibid.*, 2, 9.
34 – Burnet, G., *The Memoires of the Lives and Actions of James and William, Dukes of Hamilton and Castleherald etc.* R. Royston, London, 1667, in 7 bks.
35 – *H.*, 2, 34.
36 – *Life*, 1, 75.
37 – *H.*, 1, 164.
38 – *Life*, 1, 72.

CHAPTER 3
EDWARD HYDE THE REFORMER

1 – *The Earl of Strafford's letters and despatches with an essay towards his life by Sir G. Radcliffe.* W. Knowler, London, 1739, 2 vols., vol. 2, p. 190.
2 – Rowe, V. A., 'The Influence of the Earls of Pembroke on Parliamentary Elections', *EHR*, 1935; Gruenfelder, J. K., 'The Election to the Short Parliament 1640' in *Early Stuart Studies* edited by Reinmuth, University of Minnesota Press, 1971.
3 – Cope and Coates, 'Proceedings of the Short Parliament', Camden Society, London, 1977, p. 137.
4 – *Cl. Mss.*, no. 18; Cope and Coates, *op. cit.*, p. 248.
5 – Cope and Coates, *op. cit.*, p. 140.
6 – *Ibid.*, p. 70.
7 – *Ibid.*, p. 86.
8 – *Ibid.*, p. 182.
9 – *Ibid.*, pp. 187–92.
10 – *Ibid.*, p. 195.
11 – *H.*, 2, 73: Cope and Coates, *op. cit.*, pp. 192–95.
12 – *JC.*, 13 April–5 May, 1640.
13 – *H.*, 2, 81.
14 – *Life*, 2, 77–8.
15 – *Cl. SP.*, vol. 2, p. 83.
16 – Strafford, *op. cit.*, vol. 2, p. 408.
17 – *Cl. SP.*, vol. 2, p. 89.
18 – *Ibid.*, vol. 2, p. 95.
19 – *Ibid.*, vol. 2, p. 97.
20 – *Ibid.*, vol. 2, p. 112.
21 – *H.*, 3, 70.
22 – Wedgwood, C. V., *Thomas Wentworth, first Earl of Strafford: A Revaluation.* Jonathan Cape, London, 1961, pp. 305–8.
23 – *H.*, 2, 130.
24 – Willcox, W. B., *Gloucestershire: A Study in Local Government, 1590–1640*, New Haven, 1940 (Yale Historical Publications). Quoted in Keeler, M. F., *op. cit.*, p. 36n.

25 – Keeler, M. F.
26 – *Cal. Cl. SP.*, vol. 1, nos. 209, 211.
27 – Keeler, M. F.
28 – Russell, Conrad, 'The Parliamentary Career of John Pym 1621–29' in *The English Commonwealth* edited by Peter Clark, A. G. R. Smith and Nicholas Tyacke, Leicester University Press, Leicester, 1979.
29 – *H.*, 3, 3.
30 – *Ibid.*
31 – *Ibid.*, 3, 8.
32 – *JC*, November 23, 28, 30, December 7.
33 – Rushworth, vol. 5, p. 21.
34 – *Ibid.*, vol. 5, p. 24.
35 – *Ibid.*, vol. 5, p. 33.
36 – *Ibid.*, vol. 5, p. 55.
37 – *Ibid.*, vol. 5, p. 113; *JC*, 16 December.
38 – *JC*, 7 December.
39 – Rushworth, vol. 5, p. 86.
40 – *H.*, 3, 15.
41 – Rushworth, Vol. 5, p. 128; Whitelocke, vol. 1, p. 114.
42 – *Life*, 1, 87.
43 – *Ibid.*, 1, 89.
44 – Rushworth, vol. 5, p. 154.
45 – *Ibid.*, vol. 5, p. 39.
46 – *Ibid.*, vol. 5, p. 145.
47 – *Ibid.*, vol. 5, p. 170.
48 – *Ibid.*, vol 5, p. 184.
49 – *Ibid.*, vol 5, p. 188.
50 – *Ibid.*, vol 5, p. 196.
51 – *H.*, 3, 108; Whitelocke, vol. 1, p. 123.
52 – Whitelocke, vol. 2, p. 125.
53 – *H.*, 3, 135.
54 – Wedgwood, C. V., *op. cit.*, p. 367.
55 – *H.*, 3, 140.
56 – Rushworth, vol. 5, p. 238.
57 – *H.*, 3, 47.
58 – 22 April, 1641. *H.*, vol. 3, p. 158; Rushworth, vol 5, p. 230.
59 – *H.*, 3, 25.
60 – *Ibid.*
61 – Roberts, Clayton, 'The Earl of Bedford and the Coming of the English Revolution'. *JMH*, 1977.
62 – DeLisle Mss. Historical Manuscripts Commission, 6. London, 1966: 346.
63 – H., 2, 89.
64 – H., 3, 159, 161.
65 – *Ibid.*, 3, 165.
66 – Rushworth, vol. 5, p. 239.
67 – *Ibid.*, vol 5, p. 250; Gardiner, S. R. *op. cit.*
68 – *Cal. Cl. SP.*, vol 2, no. 295.
69 – *H.*, 3, 54.
70 – *H.*, 3, 87.

## CHAPTER 4
### THE ASSAULT ON THE MONARCHY

1 – Rushworth, vol. 5, p. 21.

2 – Dering, Sir Edward, *Collection of Speeches, 1642*, Edward Griffin for F. Eglesfield and Jo Stafford, London, 164–2.

3 – Gardiner, S. R. *op. cit.*, 135.

4 – H., 3, 67; Clarendon's view is not entirely sustained by Anthony Fletcher (*The Outbreak of the Civil War*, E. Arnold, London, 1981, ch. 3), but he shows that popular opposition was whipped up by the Puritan preachers Stephen Marshal and Cornelius Burges. Fletcher suggests that popular hostility to the bishops was wider than Clarendon admitted.

5 – Rushworth, vol. 5. pp. 30, 33.

6 – *Ibid.*, vol. 5, p. 154.

7 – Nalson, *op. cit.*, vol. 1, p. 768.

8 – Rushworth, vol. 5, p. 206.

9 – Dering, Sir Edward, *op. cit.*, p. 62.

10 – *H.*, 3, 150.

11 – *JC*, under those dates.

12 – *H.*, 4, 240–2.

13 – Nalson, *op. cit.*, vol. 2, p. 277.

14 – *Life*, 1, 89.

15 – *Ibid.*, 1, 91.

16 – *JC.*, 17 June.

17 – Rushworth, vol. 5, pp. 333–44; *H.*, 3, 158.

18 – Nalson, vol. 1, p. 663.

19 – Rushworth, vol. 5, p. 307.

20 – *H.*, 4, 237.

21 – Nalson, vol. 2, p. 310.

22 – *H.*, 3, 248.

23 – *Ibid.*, 3, 255.

24 – September, 1641, Rushworth, vol. 5, p. 386.

25 – *H.*, 4, 8.

26 – Rushworth, vol. 5, p. 392.

27 – Pennington, D. H., and Thomas, Keith (ed.), *Puritans and Revolutionaries: Essays in 17th Century History, Presented to Christopher Hill*, Oxford University Press, Oxford, 1978.

28 – Nalson, vol. 2, p. 496.

29 – D'Ewes, p. 6.

30 – Nalson, vol. 2, p. 496.

31 – Manning, Brian, *The English People and the English Revolution*, Heinemann Educational, London, 1976.

32 – D'Ewes, p. 15.

33 – Rushworth, vol. 5, p. 394.

34 – *Ibid.*, vol. 5, p. 394.

35 – D'Ewes, pp. 26–8.

36 – *Ibid.*, p. 30.

37 – Nalson, vol. 2, p. 601.

38 – *H.*, 4, 31.

39 – R.E. Bax., p. 28.

40 – D'Ewes, p. 44.

41 – *Ibid.*, pp. 51–2.
42 – *Ibid.*, p. 105; Kenyon.
43 – D'Ewes, pp. 149–51.
44 – *Ibid.*, p. 183; Sir John Holland's *Diary*, quoted in Coate, p. 184; *H.*, 4, 50.
45 – Warwick, p. 201.
46 – D'Ewes, p. 126.
47 – Verney, p. 121.
48 – *H.*, 4, 67.
49 – *Ibid.*, 4, 74.
50 – *Ibid.*, 4, 76.
51 – D'Ewes, pp. 213–15; Manning, Brian, *op. cit.*, pp. 54–64; *H.*, 4, 108.
52 – D'Ewes, p. 223.
53 – *H.*, 4, 82–5; D'Ewes, p. 219; *JC*, 2 December.
54 – D'Ewes, pp. 225, 230; *JC*, 3 December.
55 – *JC*, 3 December, 1641.
56 – D'Ewes, p. 245; *H.*, 4, 97.
57 – D'Ewes, p. 305; *JC*, 16–17 December.
58 – Manning, Brian, *op. cit.*, p. 66.
59 – D'Ewes, p. 337.
60 – Speech of 24 December, 1641, D'Ewes, p. 346.
61 – *H.*, 4, 114; D'Ewes, p. 346.
62 – *H.*, 4, 115.
63 – D'Ewes, p. 365.
64 – Rushworth, vol. 5, p. 471.
65 – *Life*, 1, 93.
66 – *Ibid.*, 94.
67 – Gardiner, p. 233.
68 – *Life*, 2, 41.
69 – *JC*, 5 February, 1642.
70 – Manning, Brian, *op. cit.*, pp. 85–95.
71 – *JC*, 3 January.
72 – *H.*, 4, 154.
73 – Somers, Baron John, *A collection of scarce and valuable tracts*, F. Cogan London, 1748, 4 vols., vol. 4, p. 344.
74 – *H.*, 4, 155.
75 – *Ibid.*, 4, 197.
76 – *Ibid.*, 4, 203
77 – Rushworth, vol. 5, p. 508.
78 – Somers *Tracts* vol. 4, p. 357.
79 – *H.*, 4, 206.
80 – *JC.*, 13 January.
81 – *Life*, 2, 6.
82 – Verney, p. 157.
83 – *Life*, 2, 14.
84 – Rushworth, vol. 5, p. 525.
85 – Verney, pp. 157–60.
86 – Gardiner, p. 245.
87 – *Ibid.*, pp. 241–2.
88 – Verney, p. 163; *JC*, 15 March
89 – Rushworth, vol. 5, p. 559.
90 – Verney, p. 171.

91 – *H.*, 4, 255.
92 – *Ibid.*, 4, 338.
93 – *H.*, vol. 4, p. 217.
94 – *JC*, 22 February.
95 – *Life*, 2, 27.
96 – *JC*, 28 February.
97 – *JC*, 2 March.

CHAPTER 5
THE SEARCH FOR PEACE

1 – *Life*, 2, 30, 34.
2 – *JC*, 12 March, Rushworth, vol. 5, 528–31.
3 – *Cl. SP.*, vol. 2, p. 13.
4 – Rushworth, vol. 5, p. 538.
5 – *Life*, 2, 39.
6 – *Cl. SP*, vol. 2, p. 1, 41.
7 – *JC*, 29 March.
8 – *H.*, 5, 31.
9 – Cliffe, J. T., 'The Yorkshire Gentry' *op. cit.*, University of London Historical Studies 90/Athlone Press 1976, pp. 321, 336.
10 – Dering, Sir Edward, op. cit.
11 – Twysden, Sir Roger, Journal. Archaeologia Cantiana, London, 1858, vol. 1.
12 – Everitt, pp. 94–104; Woods, T. P. S., *Prelude to the Civil War: Mr Justice Malet and the Kentish Petitions*.
13 – Gardiner, vol. 10, p. 182.
14 – Gardiner, Dorothy (ed.), *The Oxinden Letters*, Constable & Co, London, 1933, p. 313.
15 – Rushworth, vol. 5, p. 566; *H.*, 5, 89–91.
16 – *H.*, 5, 152.
17 – *Life*, 2, 41.
18 – *Ibid.*, 2, 54.
19 – *Ibid.*, 2, 58.
20 – Gardiner, p. 249; *H.*, 5, 320.
21 – *Life*, 2, 61.
22 – Weston and Greenberg, p. 303 n. 11.
23 – Knyvett, pp. 101, 105, 107, 13 July, 1643, p. 118.
24 – Quoted in Spalding, Ruth, *The Improbable Puritan, op. cit.*
25 – Rushworth, vol. 5, pp. 754–5.
26 – *Ibid.*, vol. 5, p. 753.
27 – *Ibid.*, vol. 5, p. 755.
28 – *Cl. SP.*, vol. 2, p. 144.
29 – *Ibid.*, vol. 2, pp. 144–9.
30 – *H.*, 5, 340.
31 – *Ibid.*, 5, 346.
32 – *Ibid.*, 5, 357–61.
33 – Rushworth, vol. 5, p. 779.
34 – *H.*, 5, 372.
35 – *Ibid.*, 5, 374.
36 – Warwick, p. 196.
37 – *H.*, 5, 415.

38 – Somers *Tracts*, vol. 4, p. 372.

39 – *H.*, 5, 430.

40 – *H.*, 6, 5.

41 – *Life*, 2, 67.

42 – Coate, pp. 35–8; Edgar, F. T. R. *Sir Ralph Hopton: the King's man in the West: a study in character and command*. Clarendon Press, Oxford, 1968.

43 – Hobbes, Thomas, *Leviathan or The Matter, Forme and Power of a Commonwealth, ecclesiasticall and civill*, Andrew Crooke, London, 1651, p. 315.

44 – Godolphin, Sidney, 'Hymn' in *The Poems of Sidney Godolphin* edited by Dighton, William, The Clarendon Press, Oxford 1931 (Tudor and Stuart Library).

45 – *H.*, 6, 86.

46 – *Ibid.*, 6, 99.

47 – Rushworth, vol. 6, pp. 3, 18, 20.

48 – *Ibid.*, vol. 6, pp. 29–33.

49 – *H.*, 6, 151.

50 – *Ibid.*, 6, 196–206.

51 – Fletcher, Anthony, *The Outbreak of the English Civil War* (*op. cit.*) has recently provided a much needed corrective to this omission.

52 – Rushworth, vol. 6, pp. 62–3.

53 – *Ibid.*, vol. 6, p. 111.

54 – *Life*, 3, 2.

55 – Hexter, p. 50.

56 – Gardiner, p. 62.

57 – Rushworth, vol. 6, p. 261.

58 – *Life*, 3, 5.

59 – *Ibid.*, 3, 10.

60 – *Ibid.*, 3, 15.

61 – Rushworth, vol. 6, p. 202.

62 – *H.*, 6, 14.

63 – *Ibid.*, 6, 326.

64 – *Ibid.*, 6, 383–397.

CHAPTER 6
### TWO SOVEREIGN CONTENDING POWERS

1 – *H.*, 7, 21–3.

2 – *H.*, 7, 26, 45, 50; Rushworth, vol. 6, p. 322.

3 – Gardiner, S. R., *History of the Great Civil War 1642–49.* Longman & Co., London. 1886, 1891, 3 vols., vol. 1, p. 72.

4 – *H.*, 7, 69.

5 – *Ibid.*, 7, 72.

6 – *Ibid.*, 7, 87–91; Coate *op. cit.*, p. 68.

7 – Coate, p. 72.

8 – *H.*, 8, 31.

9 – Coate, p. 75.

10 – The Original Letter, found at Padstow, is reproduced in Coate, Mary, p. 77; *Cl. SP.*, vol. 2, p. 155.

11 – Coate, p. 89.

12 – *H.*, 7, 132–3; Coate, p. 99.

13 – *Life*, vol. 3, p. 34.

14 – Whitelocke, p. 74.

15 – D. N. B.

16 – *H.*, 7, 180.

17 – *Ibid.*, 7, 248.

18 – Trevor-Roper, H. 'Scotland and the Puritan Revolution' in *Religion, Reformation and Social Change*, Macmillan, London, 1963.

19 – *H.*, 3, 34.

20 – Rushworth, vol. 6, p. 472.

21 – Wedgwood, C. V., *The King's War*, Collins, London, 1958, p. 278.

22 – Rushworth, vol. 6, p. 376.

23 – *H.*, 7, 413.

24 – *Life*, 3, 41.

25 – *H.*, 7, 326.

26 – *Ibid.*, 7, 327.

27 – *Ibid.*, 7, 371.

28 – *Ibid.*, 7, 372–5.

29 – *Ibid.*, 7, 383.

30 – *Ibid.*, 7, 387.

31 – *Ibid.*, 7, 403.

32 – *Cl. SP.*, vol. 2, p. 175.

33 – *H.*, 7, 405.

34 – *Ibid.*, 7, 416.

35 – *Ibid.*, 8, 2.

36 – *Ibid.*, 8, 98.

37 – *Ibid.*, 8, 101.

38 – *H.*, 8, 116; Coate, p. 148 is more kind to Goring.

39 – *JC.* vol. 2, p. 625. Quoted in Crawford, Patricia, 'Denzil Holles', *RHS*, 1979, p. 74.

40 – Crawford, *op. cit.*, pp. 86–7, Speech of 21 February.

41 – Pearl, Valerie, 'Oliver St John and the "Middle Group" in the Long Parliament', *EHR*, 1966; 'The "Royal Independence" in the English Civil War', *TRHS*, 1968.

42 – MacCormack, Professor John, *Revolutionary Politics in the Long Parliament*, Harvard University Press, Cambridge, 1974.

43 – Neale, J. E., *History of the Puritans*, vol. 3, p. 346.

44 – Baillie, Robert, *Letters* first published from ms. of author for William Creech and William Gray, Edinburgh, 1775, 2 vols., vol. 2, p. 117.

45 – *Ibid.*, vol. 2, p. 145.

46 – Gardiner, p. 271.

47 – Baillie, Robert, *op. cit.*, vol. 2, p. 164.

48 – *Ibid.*, vol. 2, p. 169.

49 – *Ibid.*, vol. 2, p. 205.

50 – *Ibid.*, vol. 2, p. 212.

51 – *Ibid.*, vol. 2, p. 225.

52 – *H.*, 8, 167.

53 – Baillie, *op. cit.*, vol. 2, p. 216.

54 – *Manchester's Quarrel*, Camden Society, London, p. 92.

55 – *H.*, 8, 184.

56 – Baillie, *op. cit.*, vol. 2, p. 246.

57 – *Ibid.*, vol. 2, p. 205.

58 – Whitelocke, vol. 1, p. 111.

59 – *H.*, 8, 187.

60 – Trevor-Roper, H., 'The Fast Days of the Long Parliament' in *Essays in British History*, Macmillan, London, 1964.

61 – *H.*, 4, 172.
62 – Higgins, P., 'The Reactions of Women' in Manning, Brian (ed.), *Politics, Religion and the English Civil War*, E. Arnold, London, 1973.
63 – *H.*, 8, 189.
64 – Whitelocke, vol. 1, p. 112.
65 – *Cl. SP.*, vol. 2, p. 179; The terms were drafted by Hyde.
66 – *H.*, 8, 227–32.
67 – *Ibid.*, 8, 233.
68 – *Ibid.*, 8, 241.
69 – *Ibid.*, 8, 243.
70 – *Ibid.*, 8, 246, 248, 252.
71 – Rushworth, vol. 6, p. 718.
72 – *Ibid.*, vol. 6, pp. 941, 943, 945.
73 – *Life*, 3, 51.
74 – Napier (17th century text), vol. 2, p. 177, Quoted in Wedgwood, C. V., *The King's War. op. cit.*
75 – *H.*, 8, 253.
76 – *Life*, 3, 56.

CHAPTER 7
FROM UXBRIDGE TO THE ENGAGEMENT

1 – Laud, *Works, op. cit.*, vol. 3, p. 247.
2 – Lister, vol. 3, p. 8.
3 – *H.*, 9, 26; Miller, A. C., *Sir Richard Grenville of the Civil War*, Phillimore, Chichester, 1979; Coate, p. 172.
4 – *H.*, 9, 33, 38.
5 – *Ibid.*, 9, 42, 47, 54, 65.
6 – *CSPD*, 1645–7, 46.
7 – Coate, pp. 181–7.
8 – *H.*, 9, 70.
9 – *Ibid.*, 9, 74.
10 – *Ibid.*, 9, 79.
11 – For a full account of the siege see McGrath, Patrick, 'Bristol and the Civil War', Historical Association, 1981; Sprigge, Joshua, *Anglia Rediviva*, R. W. for J. Partridge, London, 1647, p. 121.
12 – *H.*, 9, 90.
13 – *Cl. SP.*, vol. 2, p. 195.
14 – *Ibid.*, vol. 2, p. 188.
15 – Abbott, vol. 1, p. 200.
16 – *H.*, 9, 96.
17 – Coate, p. 192 ff; Miller, A. C. *op. cit.*, p. 124.
18 – *H.*, 9, 101.
19 – *Cl. SP.*, vol. 2, p. 196.
20 – *Ibid.*, pp. 189, 192.
21 – *Ibid.*, vol. 2, p. 209–12.
22 – Rushworth, vol. 7, pp. 215–220.
23 – Charles 1st in 1646: *Letters to Henrietta Maria*, Camden Society, London, 1856, no. 6.
24 – *Ibid.*, 14.
25 – *Cl. SP.*, vol. 2, p. 207, February 1646.
26 – Charles 1st in 1646, *op. cit.*, p. 18.

27 – *H.*, 9, 117.
28 – *Ibid.*, 9, 134.
29 – *Cl. SP.*, vol. 2, 206.
30 – Chevalier, Jean, *Journal* edited by J. A. Messervy, 1914; vol. 1, p. 287; Hoskins, Elliott, S., *Charles II in the Channel Islands: A contribution to his biography and to the history of his age*, London, 1854, 2 vols.
31 – *H.*, 10, 6.
32 – Chevalier, Jean, *op. cit.*, vol. 1, p. 290; *Cl. SP.*, vol. 2, p. 287.
33 – *Cl. SP.*, vol 2, pp. 230, 235.
34 – Rushworth, vol. 7, p. 249.
35 – *Cl. SP.*, vol 2, p. 226.
36 – Charles 1st in 1646, *op. cit.*, pp. 20, 29.
37 – *H.*, 10, 26–31.
38 – Charles 1st in 1646, pp. 32, 41, 45.
39 – *Cl. SP.*, vol. 2, p. 236.
40 – *Ibid.*, vol. 2, p. 238.
41 – *H.*, 10, 38–44; Clarendon wrote a 'Memorandum concerning the Prince's remove from Jersay, 25 June, 1646', which is printed in Hoskins, Elliott, S., *op. cit.*, vol. 1, pp. 429–39. It gives a vivid account of the discussions.
42 – *Cl. SP.*, vol. 2, p. 307.
43 – *H.*, 10, 54; *Cl. SP.*, vol. 2, pp. 244, 247, 243, 248, 254.
44 – *H.*, 10, 65; Rushworth, vol. 6, pp. 309, 319.
45 – *Cl. SP.*, vol. 2, pp. 264, 266, 267, 268, 270, 275, 330.
46 – *H.*, 10, 68.
47 – *Cl. SP.*, vol. 2, p. 308.
48 – Ludlow, Edmund, *Memoirs*, Vivay, 1698, 1699, 3 vols., vol. 1, p. 144.
49 – Kishlansky, M. A., *Rise of the New Model Army*, Cambridge University Press, 1980, p. 114.
50 – *H.*, 10, 82.
51 – H., 10, 104.
52 – *The Clarke Papers: Selections from the papers of William Clarke, Secretary to Council of the Army 1647–49 and to General Monck and the Commanders of the Army in Scotland 1651–60*, edited by C. H. Firth, Camden Society, London, 1891–1901. 4 vols., vol. 1, p. 477.
53 – Gardiner, p. 311.
54 – Abbott, *op. cit.*, vol. 1, p. 435.
55 – *H.*, 10, 88.
56 – Dr William Young's testimony at Hugh Peter's trial 1661, Abbott, vol. 1, p. 454.
57 – *H.*, 10, 93.
58 – *Cl. SP.*, vol. 2, App. 37.
59 – *H.*, 10, 115–19.
60 – Crawford, Patricia, 'Denzil Holles' *op. cit.*, p. 150 ff.
61 – Kishlansky, M. A. *op. cit.*, p. 244.
62 – *Ibid.*, pp. 255, 259.
63 – Gardiner, p. 316.
64 – *Cal. Cl SP.*, vol. 2, no. 295.
65 – *H.*, 10, 122.
66 – *Ibid.*, 10, 125.
67 – Ashton, Robert, *The English Civil War*, Weidenfeld, London, 1978. p. 294.
68 – Aylmer, Gerald, (ed.), *The Levellers in the English Revolution*, Thames & Hudson, London, 1975.
69 – *H.*, 10, 126.

70 – Aylmer, Gerald, *op. cit.*, p. 24.
71 – Rushworth, vol. 7, p. 628.
72 – Pearl, Valerie, 'London's Counter Revolution' in Aylmer, '*The Interregnum: The Quest for Settlement 1646–1660*; Macmillan, London 1974; and Ashton, Robert, *op. cit.*, p. 303.
73 – *H.*, 10, 129.
74 – *Ibid.*, 10, 134–6.
75 – Rushworth, vol. 8, pp. 871, 880.
76 – Abbott, p. 563.
77 – Rushworth, vol. 8, p. 948; Everitt *op. cit.*
78 – Rushworth, vol 8, p. 952; Gardiner, p. 347.
79 – *H.*, 10, 147.
80 – Rushworth, vol. 8, p. 953.
81 – *H.*, 10, 151.
82 – *Cl. SP.*, vol. 2, p. 403.
83 – *H.*, 10, 158, 165, 170.

CHAPTER 8
### THE BEGINNING OF THE *HISTORY* AND THE FALL OF THE MONARCHY

1 – *Cl. SP.*, vol. 2, p. 241.
2 – *Life*, 5, 1.
3 – *Cl. SP.*, vol. 2, p. 246.
4 – *Ibid.*, vol. 2, p. 288.
5 – *Ibid.*, vol. 2, p. 333; he meant that parliament had learnt some of their tactics from D'Avila.
6 – *Ibid.*, vol. 2, p. 334.
7 – *Ibid.*, vol 2, p. 289.
8 – *Ibid.*, vol. 2, p. 350.
9 – *Ibid.*, vol 2, p. 328.
10 – *Ibid.*, vol. 2, p. 318
11 – *Ibid.*, vol. 2, p. 335.
12 – *Ibid.*, vol. 2. p. 291.
13 – *Ibid.*, vol. 2, pp. 306–10.
14 – *Ibid.*
15 – *Ibid.*, vol. 2, p. 316.
16 – *Ibid.*, vol. 2, p. 403.
17 – To Culpepper, 8 January 1647 *Cl. SP.*, vol. 2, p. 326.
18 – *Cl. SP.*, vol. 2, pp. 328, 338, 346.
19 – *Ibid.*, vol. 2, pp. 384, 391.
20 – *Ibid.*, vol. 2, pp. 408–9.
21 – *H.*, 11, 23.
22 – *Life*, 5, 21–2.
23 – *Cl. SP.*, vol. 2, p. 276.
24 – *H.*, 11, 77, 99.
25 – *Ibid.*, 11, 44.
26 – *Cl. SP.*, vol. 2, p. 411.
27 – Everitt, pp. 238–41.
28 – Ketton-Cremer, R. W., *Norfolk in the Civil War*, Faber, London, 1969, p. 335 ff.
29 – *H.*, 11, 85.

30 – *Cl SP.*, vol. 2, p. 417.

31 – *Ibid.*, vol. 2, pp. 422–3.

32 – *Cal. Cl. SP.*, vol. 1, no. 2897.

33 – *Cl. SP.*, vol. 2, pp. 455, 459.

34 – Somers *Tracts op. cit.*, vol. 6, p. 301.

35 – Underdown, D., 'The Parliamentary Diary of John Boys', *BIHR*, 1966.

36 – *H.*, 8, 241.

37 – Lister, vol. 3, p. 51.

38 – Rushworth, vol. 8, pp. 1101, 1133.

39 – *Cl. SP.*, vol. 2, pp. 425–44.

40 – *Ibid.*, vol. 2, p. 448.

41 – Colonel Cook's narrative in Rushworth vol. 6, p. 1346.

42 – Lilburne, *The Legal Fundamental Liberties of the People of England revised, asserted and indicated, London*, 1649. App. B., p. 254, Clarke Papers, vol. 2.

43 – Clarke Papers, vol. 2, pp. 73–120, 140, 147.

44 – Underdown, D., *Pride's Purge* p. 139.

45 – Ashton, *The English Civil War, op. cit.*, pp. 341 ff.

46 – Abbott, vol 1, p. 718; Wedgwood, C. V. *The Trial of Charles 1st*, p. 169.

47 – *LJ*, vol. 10, p. 641.

48 – Rushworth, vol. 8, p. 1382.

49 – Wedgwood C. V., *The Trial of Charles 1st, op. cit.*, p. 100.

50 – *Ibid.*, pp. 155 ff.

51 – *H.*, 11, 157.

52 – Rushworth, vol. 8, pp. 1403–25.

53 – Ludlow, *Memoirs, op. cit.*, vol. 1, p. 217.

54 – *H.*, 11, 243.

55 – *Ibid.*

56 – See Wedgwood C. V., 'European Reaction to the Death of Charles 1st', in Carter, *From the Renaissance to the Counter Reformation*, Random House, New York, 1965.

CHAPTER 9
### IRELAND, SCOTLAND AND SPAIN

1 – *Cl. SP.*, vol. 3, p. 1, To Hatton, 4 February 1648.

2 – *Ibid.*

3 – *Cl. SP.*, vol. 2, p. 470.

4 – *Ibid.*, vol. 2, pp. 168–9.

5 – *Ibid.*, vol. 2, p. 201.

6 – Somers *Tracts, op. cit.*, vol. 8, p. 508.

7 – *Cl. SP.*, 2, p. 473.

8 – *H.*, 12, 17.

9 – To Lord Hatton, 12 April 1649, *Cl. SP.*, vol. 2, p. 479.

10 – Nicholas, Sir Edward, Correspondence of Sir Edward Nicholas, Secretary of State, edited by G. F. Warner, London, Camden Society, 1886, 4 vols., vol. 1, p. 115.

11 – To Berkeley, 12 April 1649, *Cl. SP.*, vol. 2, p. 478.

12 – Nicholas Papers, *op. cit.*, vol. 1, p. 123.

13 – *Life*, 5, 29; *H.*, 12, 40.

14 – *Cl. SP.*, vol. 2, p. 481.

15 – Nicholas Papers, vol. 1, pp. 138–47, 'specious' meant pleasant or acceptable, without cynical overtones.

16 – *H.*, 12, 50.

17 – *Ibid.*, 12, 64.
18 – Carte, *Life of Ormonde.*
19 – C. V. Wedgwood's phrase, see *Montrose*, Collins, London, 1961, p. 133.
20 – *Cl. SP.*, vol. 2, App. pp. 51–4.
21 – *Ibid.*, vol. 3, p. 544.
22 – *Ibid.*, vol. 3, p. 526.
23 – *Ibid.*, vol. 2, p. 537; 18 March to Jermyn, vol. 2, p. 528.
24 – To the Countess of Morton, vol. 2, p. 529.
25 – *Ibid.*, vol. 2, p. 517.
26 – *Ibid.*, vol. 2, p. 522, 18 March 1650.
27 – *Ibid.*, vol. 2, p. 530.
28 – *Ibid.*, vol. 2, p. 540.
29 – *Ibid.*, vol. 2, p. 524.
30 – *H.*, 13, 5.
31 – *Ibid.*
32 – Clarke Papers, vol. 2, p. 205.
33 – Carlyle, T, *Oliver Cromwell's Letters and Speeches*, London, 1845, p. 136.
34 – Thomas Weston to Nicholas, *Cl. SP.*, vol. 2, p. 65.
35 – Somers *Tracts*, vol. 6, p. 119.
36 – Nicholas Papers, vol. 1, p. 221.
37 – *Cl. SP.*, vol. 2, p. 546.
38 – *Ibid.*, vol. 2, p. 562.
39 – A detailed account of his escapes is in *Cl. SP.*, vol. 2, pp. 563–71, by William Ellesdon.
40 – *CSP Ven.*, pp. 28, 129.
41 – *H.*, 12, 83.
42 – *H.*, 12, 90; *Life*, 5, 43, 106.
43 – *Cl. SP.*, vol. 2, pp. 504, 507.
44 – *H.*, 13, 16.
45 – *Cal. Cl. SP.*, vol. 2, no. 421.
46 – *Ibid.*, vol. 2, p. 499.
47 – Nicholas Papers, vol. 1, p. 182.
48 – Lord Hatton to Nicholas, 13 September 1650, Nicholas Papers, vol. 1, p. 195.
49 – *Ibid.*, vol. 1, p. 173.
50 – *Ibid.*, vol. 1, p. 195.
51 – *Ibid.*, vol. 1, p. 218.
52 – *Ibid.*, vol. 1, pp. 233, 241.
53 – Nicholas to Hyde, 21 October 1651, Nicholas Papers vol. 1, p. 278.
54 – *Ibid.*, vol. 1, p. 276.
55 – *Cal. Cl. SP.*, vol. 2, nos. 492, 507, 521, 578, 583, 590.
56 – Nicholas Papers, vol. 1, pp. 279–83; *Cal. Cl. SP.*, vol. 2, nos. 599, 601, 609.
57 – *Life*, 6, 25.
58 – *Ibid.*, 6, 16.
59 – Cosin, John, *Works*, edited by J. Sansom, John Henry Parker, Oxford, 1843–55, 5 vols., vol. 4, p. 241.
60 – 3 December 1649, *Cl. SP.*, vol. 2, p. 499.
61 – Nicholas Papers, vol. 1, pp. 157, 174.
62 – Osmond, P. H., *Life of John Cosin, Bishop of Durham 1660–1672*, A: R. Mowbray, London, 1913.
63 – *Life*, 6, 29.

CHAPTER 10
ROYALISTS AND THE COMMONWEALTH

1 – Gardiner, pp. 384–8.

2 – *Cal. Cl. SP.*, vol. 2, no. 575.

3 – Gardiner, S. R., *History of the Commonwealth and Protectorate 1649–1660*, Longman & Co., London, 1894–1903, 3 vols., vol. 1, pp. 399–410.

4 – Holles, Denzil, *Memoirs of Denzil Lord Holles from 1641 to 1648*, for T. Goodwin, London, 1699, pp. 1, 207.

5 – Crawford, Patricia, 'Denzil Holles', *RHS*, 1979.

6 – Nicholas Papers, vol. 1, p. 106.

7 – Hyde to Sir Toby Mathew, 23 May, 1650, Lister, vol. 3, p. 54.

8 – *H.*, 8, 165.

9 – Worden, Blair, *The Rump Parliament 1648–1653*, Cambridge University Press, Cambridge, 1974, p. 76.

10 – Roots, Ivan, *The Great Rebellion*, 1642–60. Batsford, London, 1966, p. 138.

11 – See for example, Underdown, D., *Pride's Purge, Politics in the Puritan Revolution*, Oxford University Press, Oxford, 1971; and Worden, Blair, *The Rump Parliament, op. cit.*

12 – *H.*, 14, 1.

13 – Worden, Blair, *op. cit.*, p. 23.

14 – *Ibid.*, p. 69.

15 – Whitelocke, vol. 3, pp. 148, 170.

16 – Gardiner, S. R., *Commonwealth and Protectorate, op cit.*, vol. 1, p. 248.

17 – *H.*, 14, 1–4.

18 – Webb, John, (ed.) *Military Memoir of Colonel John Birch*, Camden Society, London, 1873, p. 217.

19 – Morrill, J. S., *Cheshire 1630–60: County Government and Society during the English Revolution*. Oxford University Press, Oxford, 1974, p. 78.

20 – Everitt, pp. 159–62.

21 – *H.*, 12, 150.

22 – Among the extensive literature on the subject, special attention should be paid to Tatham, G. B., 'The Sale of Episcopal Lands', *EHR*, 1908; Thirsk, Joan, 'The Sale of Royalist Land', *EcHR*, 1952; Habakkuk, H. J., 'Public Finance and the sale of Confiscated Property'. *EcHR*, 1965; Holiday, P. G., 'Land Sales and Repurchases in Yorkshire', *Northern History*, 1970.

23 – Verney, vol. 3, p. 9.

24 – Abbott, vol. 3, p. 453.

25 – Ludlow, *Memoirs, op. cit.*, vol. 1, p. 379.

26 – Gentles, Ian, 'The Sales of Bishops' lands in the English Revolution'. *EHR*, 1960.

27 – Walker, John, *Sufferings of the Clergy*. London. 1714; Matthews, A. G., *Walker Revised, being a revision of John Walker's Sufferings of the Clergy during the Grand Rebellion*, Clarendon Press, Oxford, 1948.

28 – Green, I. M., 'The Persecution of "scandalous" and "malignant" parish clergy'. *EHR*, 1979.

29 – Everitt, p. 225.

30 – Morrill, J. S., *op. cit.*, p. 181.

31 – Underdown, D., *op. cit.*, p. 34.

32 – Morrill, J. S., *op. cit.*, p. 245.

33 – Howell, R., *Newcastle-upon-Tyne and the Puritan Revolution*, Oxford University Press, Oxford, 1967, p. 165.

34 – *Ibid.*, pp. 197, 196, 193, 346, 208.

35 – Evans, J. T., *Seventeenth Century Norwich: Politics, Religion and Government 1620–90*, Oxford University Press, Oxford, 1980.

36 – *Ibid.*, pp. 108, 125, 176–82.

37 – Pearl, *London and the Outbreak of the Puritan Revolution*, Oxford University Press, Oxford 1961. Brenner, R., 'Civil War Politics of London's Merchant Community', *Past and Present*, February, 1973.

38 – *Lettres du Cardinal Mazarin*, Amsterdam, 1690, 2 vols., vol. 2, p. 335; see Knachel, P. A., *England and the Fronde: The Impact of the English Civil War and Revolution on France*, Cornell University Press, New York, 1967.

39 – Jean de Montereul, Diplomatic Correspondence, vol. 1, p. 71.

40 – *Cal. Cl. SP.*, vol. 2, no. 160; *Cl. SP.*, vol. 3, p. 129.

41 – *H.*, 13, 124.

42 – *Cl. SP.*, vol. 3, p. 124.

43 – *H.*, 13, 146.

44 – Nicholas Papers, vol. 1, p. 310.

45 – *H.*, 13, 151–2.

46 – *Cl. SP.*, vol. 3, p. 71.

47 – *Ibid.*

48 – *Ibid.*, vol. 3, p. 48.

49 – *Ibid.*, vol. 3, p. 47.

50 – Lister, vol. 3, p. 63.

51 – *Ibid.*, vol. 3, pp. 73–83.

52 – *Cl. SP.*, vol. 3, p. 154.

53 – *Ibid.*, vol. 3, p. 211.

54 – *Ibid.*, vol. 3, p. 86.

55 – *Ibid.*, vol. 3, p. 170, 6 June 1653.

56 – *Ibid.*, vol. 3, pp. 171, 173–4.

57 – *Cl. SP.*, vol. 3, pp. 178, 187; *Cal. Cl. SP.*, vol. 2, no. 595.

## CHAPTER II
### ROYALISTS AND THE PROTECTORATE

1 – cf. the Army petition, June 1652, Whitelocke, vol. 3, p. 433 and the legal reforms drafted but never carried. Somers Tracts, vol. 6, pp. 177–245.

2 – Whitelocke, vol. 4, p. 6.

3 – Ludlow, Edmund, *Memoirs, op. cit.*, vol. 1, p. 357.

4 – Thurloe, vol. 1, p. 249.

5 – Abbott, vol. 3, p. 19.

6 – Whitelocke, vol. 3, p. 468.

7 – *Cal. Cl. SP.*, vol. 2, nos. 1136, 1519.

8 – *H.*, 14, 12–13.

9 – *Ibid.*, 14, 15; this view has been disputed by Austin Woolrych, *Commonwealth and Protectorate*, Oxford University Press, Oxford, 1982, ch. 6.

10 – *Cal. Cl. SP.*, vol. 2, no. 1153.

11 – *H.*, 14, 26.

12 – *Ibid.*, 14, 43.

13 – Abbott, vol. 3, p. 447.

14 – Thurloe, vol. 1, p. 366.

15 – *Cal. Cl. SP.*, vol. 2, no. 1232.

16 – *Cl. SP.*, vol. 3, p. 181.

17 – *Cal. Cl. SP.*, vol. 2, no. 170.

18 – Somers *Tracts*, vol. 6, p. 299.

19 – Abbott, vol. 3, p. 524.

20 – *Cal. Cl. SP.*, vol. 2, no. 1226.

21 – *Ibid.*, vol. 2, 1214, 'the King is so much given to pleasure that if he stay in Paris, he will be undone'.

22 – *Ibid.*, vol. 2, no. 1232.

23 – *Ibid.*, vol. 2, no. 970.

24 – *Ibid.*, vol. 2, no. 1515.

25 – *Ibid.*, vol. 2, nos. 1473, 1425.

26 – *H.*, 13, 138.

27 – *Ibid.*, 13, 140.

28 – Nicholas Papers, vol. 2, p. 15.

29 – *H.*, 14, 59–61.

30 – *Cal. Cl. SP.*, vol. 2, no. 1714.

31 – *Ibid.*, vol. 2, no. 1657.

32 – *Ibid.*, vol. 2, no. 1736.

33 – *H.*, 13, 115.

34 – *H.*, 14, 36; Thurloe, vol. 2, passim.

35 – *H.*, 14, 82.

36 – Nicholas Papers, vol. 2, p. 100.

37 – *Cal. Cl. SP.*, vol. 2, no. 1937.

38 – *Ibid.*, vol. 2, nos. 1949, 1957.

39 – *Cl. SP.*, vol. 3, pp. 170, 198.

40 – *Ibid.*, vol. 3, p. 208.

41 – *Cal. Cl. SP.*, vol. 2, nos. 33–5, 39.

42 – *Ibid.*, vol. 3, no. 47.

43 – *Ibid.*, vol. 3, no. 67.

44 – *H.*, 14, 123.

45 – Nicholas Papers, vol. 2, p. 267, April, 1655.

46 – *Ibid.*, vol. 2, p. 175.

47 – *Ibid.*, vol. 2, p. 279.

48 – *Ibid.*, vol. 2, p. 317.

49 – *Ibid.*, vol. 2, p. 123.

50 – *Cal. Cl. SP.*, vol. 2, no. 2033.

51 – Nicholas Papers, vol. 2, p. 109.

52 – *Cal. Cl. SP.*, vol. 2, no. 2062.

53 – Nicholas Papers, vol. 2, p. 162.

54 – *Ibid.*, vol. 3, p. 4.

55 – *Cl. SP.*, vol. 3, no. 274.

56 – *Life*, 6, 38–46.

57 – *Cl. SP.*, vol. 3, p. 275.

58 – *Cal. Cl. SP.*, vol. 3, nos. 188, 196.

59 – *Ibid.*, vol. 3, no. 301.

60 – *Ibid.*, vol. 3, nos. 309, 313.

61 – *H.*, 14, 138–44; Nicholas Papers, vol. 3, pp. 149–211.

62 – Thurloe, vol. 3, p. 428.

63 – Nicholas Papers, vol. 2, p. 298.

64 – *Ibid.*, vol. 2, p. 340.

65 – *Cl. SP.*, vol. 3, p. 277.

66 – Nicholas Papers, vol. 3, p. 43.

67 – *Ibid.*, vol. 3, pp. 118, 145, 264.
68 – *Cl. SP.*, vol. 3, p. 315.
69 – *Ibid.*, vol. 3, pp. 325, 335, 343.

CHAPTER 12
THE END OF THE COMMONWEALTH

1 – Ussher, James, *The Whole Works of James Ussher*, C. R. Elrington (ed. vols. 1–14), J. H. Todd (ed. vols. 15–17), Dublin, 1847–64. 17 vols., vol. 1, p. 273.
2 – Burton, vol. 1, p. 274, 30 December, 1656.
3 – *Ibid.*, vol. 1, pp. 363, 378, 396–400.
4 – *Cl. SP.*, vol. 3, p. 349.
5 – *Ibid.*, vol. 3, p. 351.
6 – *Ibid.*, vol. 3, pp. 362–4.
7 – *Ibid.*, vol. 3, p. 372.
8 – Nicholas Papers, vol. 3, p. 15.
9 – *Ibid.*, vol. 3, pp. 8, 10, 13, 15.
10 – *Cl. SP.*, vol. 3, p. 387.
11 – *Ibid.*, vol. 3, p. 374.
12 – *Ibid.*, vol 3, p. 367, earl of Bristol to Ormond, September, 1657.
13 – *Cal. Cl. SP.*, vol. 3, no. 1190.
14 – *Ibid.*, vol. 3, nos. 1251, 1253.
15 – *H.*, 15, 87–91: Carte, vol. 2, p. 176; Clarke Papers, *op. cit.*, vol. 3, p. 147.
16 – *Cl. SP.*, vol. 3, p. 391.
17 – *Ibid.*, vol. 3, pp. 394, 396.
18 – Firth, C. H., *EHR*, 1895.
19 – Clarke Papers, vol. 3, p. 136.
20 – *H.*, 15, 147.
21 – *Ibid.*, 15, 150.
22 – *Ibid.*, 15, 152, 156, 143.
23 – *Cl. SP.*, vol. 3, pp. 407, 409–10.
24 – Nicholas Papers, vol. 4, p. 72.
25 – *Cal. Cl. SP.*, vol. 4, no. 85.
26 – *Cl. SP.*, vol. 3, pp. 417, 420.
27 – Thurloe, vol. 7, p. 372.
28 – *H.*, 16, 2.
29 – Burton, vol. 2, p. 346.
30 – *Ibid.*, vol. 2, p. 333.
31 – Evelyn, vol. 1, p. 308.
32 – Ussher, *op. cit.*, vol. p. 531.
33 – Worden, Blair, *The Rump Parliament*, *op. cit.*, p. 243.
34 – Whitelocke, vol. 4, p. 289.
35 – Burton, vol. 2, p. 402.
36 – *Ibid.*, vol. 2, pp. 414, 27, 134, 107, 256, 260.
37 – Ludlow, Edmond, *Memoirs*, *op. cit.*, vol. 2, p. 61.
38 – Whitelocke, vol. 4, p. 342.
39 – Burton, vol. 4, p. 449.
40 – *Ibid.*, vol. 4, p. 441.
41 – Ludlow, *op. cit.*, vol. 2, p. 69.
42 – Whitelocke, vol. 4, p. 342.

43 – *Cl. SP.*, vol. 3, pp. 432, 444.

44 – *Ibid.*, vol. 3, p. 451.

45 – *Ibid.*, vol. 3, pp. 457, 482.

46 – *Ibid.*, vol. 3, pp. 444, 454, 448.

47 – *H.*, 16, pp. 24–6; *Cl. SP.*, vol. 3, pp. 460–61; Nicholas Papers, vol. 4, p. 74.

48 – Nicholas Papers, vol. 4, pp. 97, 114.

49 – Nicholas Papers, vol. 4, p. 169; Clarke Papers, vol. 4, p. 304.

50 – Clarke Papers, vol. 4, pp. 484, 500.

51 – *Ibid.*, vol. 4, pp. 526, 536.

52 – *Cal. Cl. SP.*, vol. 4, no. 326.

53 – *Ibid.*, vol. 4. nos. 347, 363.

54 – *Ibid.*, vol 4, no. 618.

55 – Clarke Papers, vol. 4, pp. 57–60.

56 – *Letter Book of John Viscount Mordaunt, 1658–1660*, edited by Mary Coate, Camden. Third Series, vol. 69, 1945, p. 54, 7 October 1659.

57 – *Cl. SP.*, vol. 3. p. 591; cf., Mordaunt, *op. cit.*, p. 59.

58 – Clarke Papers, vol. 4, p. 66.

59 – Old Parliamentary History, vol. 22, p. 46.

60 – Mordaunt, *op. cit.*, p. 116.

61 – *Ibid.*, p. 143.

62 – *Cl. SP.*, vol. 3, p. 342.

63 – On Vane see Rowe, V. A., *Sir Henry Vane the Younger. A Study in Political and Administrative history*. Athlone Press. London, 1970, and Judson, M. A., *The Political Thought of Sir Henry Vane the Younger.* (Haney Foundation Series). University of Pennsylvania Press, Pennsylvania, 1969.

64 – Mordaunt, *op. cit.*, 162.

65 – *Ibid.*

66 – Pepys, 9–11 February 1660.

67 – Somers *Tracts*, vol. 6, p. 550.

68 – *H.*, 16, 133.

69 – Abernathy, p. 47.

70 – *Cal. Cl. SP.*, vol. 4, nos. 568, 585.

71 – Kennet, White, *Register and Chronicle, Ecclesiastical and Civil*, London, 1728.

72 – Harrington, James, *Pour Enclouer le Canon*, H. Fletcher, London, 1659; *Ways and Means*, printed for J. S., London, 1660; Pocock, J. G. A., (ed), *The Political Works of James Harrington*, Cambridge, 1977.

73 – Aubrey, J., *Brief Lives, edited from author's mss. by Andrew Clark*, Clarendon Press, Oxford, 1898, p. 125.

## CHAPTER 13
### THE RESTORATION EFFECTED

1 – Pepys, 6 March 1660.

2 – Thurloe, vol. 7, p. 859.

3 – Price, John, *The Mystery and Method of His Majesty's Happy Restoration*, London, 1680, p. 784.

4 – *Cal. Cl. SP.*, vol. 4, no. 620; Skinner, Thomas, *Life of General Monck*, London, 1676 (Latin ed.), English edition edited by William Webster, W. Bowyer, London, 1723, p. 274: *H.*, 16, 162–8.

5 – *H.*, 16, 171.

6 – *Ibid.*, 16, 181–204.
7 – *Cl. SP.*, vol. 3, p. 685.
8 – *Ibid.*, vol. 3, p. 705.
9 – *Ibid.*, vol. 3, p. 712.
10 – *Ibid.*, vol. 3, p. 600.
11 – *Ibid.*, vol. 3, p. 738.
12 – Jones, J. R., *Cambridge HJ*, 1963; Jones, Trevallyn *EHR*, 1964.
13 – Firth, C J., *The House of Lords during the Civil War*, Longman & Co., London, 1910, p. 283; *LJ*, vol. 11, p. 13.
14 – *The Life of the Reverend Dr John Barwick, translated into English by the editor of the Latin Life (Hilkiah Bedford)*. J. Bettenham, London, 1724, p. 514.
15 – *Ibid.*, p. 523.
16 – *Ibid.*, pp. 515–21.
17 – Pepys, 17 May 1660.
18 – *Ibid.*, 23 May 1660.
19 – *H.*, 16, 243–5; *Cont.*, 11–13.
20 – Evelyn, vol. 3, p. 246.
21 – *Cl. SP.*, vol 3, p. 512.
22 – *Ibid.*, vol. 3, pp. 644, 732.
23 – Habakkuk, H. J., 'The Land Settlement and the Restoration', *TRHS*, 1978.
24 – *Cl. SP.*, vol. 3, p. 747.
25 – Thirsk, Joan, 'The Restoration Land Settlement', *JMH*, 1954.
26 – *JC*, 31 May 1660.
27 – Cobbett, *Parliamentary History*, vol. 1, p. 75.
28 – *Ibid.*, vol. 1, p. 94.
29 – *JC*, p. 104.
30 – Cobbett, *Parliamentary History*, 29 August 1660.
31 – *Ibid.*, vol. iv, p. 122.

## CHAPTER 14
### RELIGION: UNIFORMITY AND INDULGENCE

1 – Hooker, Richard, *Laws of Ecclesiastical Polity*, printed by John Windet, London. Part 1 contains books 1–4, part 2 book 5. Books 6 and 8 first published 1648 and book 7 in 1661. 8 books, bk. 2, chap. 1, para. 4.
2 – *Ibid.*, bk. 1, ch. 10, para. 8.
3 – *Ibid.*, bk. 8, ch. 6, para. 11.
4 – *Ibid.*, bk. 8, ch. 2, para. 13.
5 – *Ibid.*, bk. 7, ch. 5, para. 8.
6 – Preface, bk. 11, p. 1.
7 – Hall, Joseph, *Episcopacy by Divine Right*, printed by R. B. for N. Butter, London, 1640; *Works*, T. Pavier, M. Flesher and J. Haviland, London, 1625, vol. 10, p. 151.
8 – Works, vol 11, p. 477.
9 – *Ibid.*, vol. 10, p. 489.
10 – *Ibid.*, vol. 1, p. 400.
11 – Arnold, Matthew, *Puritanism and the Church of England*, Smith, Elder & Co., London, 1870.
12 – Hall, Joseph, *The Shaking of the Olive Tree*, London, 1660.
13 – Bramhall, John, *Works, edited by John Vesey, Archbishop of Tuam*, Printed at His Majesties Printing House, Dublin, 1676, 4 vols., vol. 3, p. 297.

14 – Fell, J., *Life of Henry Hammond*, London, 1661, p. 206; Packer, J. W., *The Transformation of Anglicanism 1643–60 with special reference to Henry Hammond*, Manchester University Press, Manchester, 1969.

15 – *Cl. SP.*, vol. 2, p. 738.

16 – Cosin, John, *(Works), Regni, Angliae Religio Catholica*, vol. 4, p. 339.

17 – Nicholas Papers, vol. 1, p. 159.

18 – Barwick, P., *Life of John Barwick*, p. 241.

19 – *Ibid.*, pp. 423–8, 435–49.

20 – *Ibid.*, p. 449.

21 – *Ibid.*, pp. 461–8, 488.

22 – Baxter, Richard, *The Autobiography of Richard Baxter: being the Reliquiae Baxterianae abridged*. Introduction and notes by J. M. Lloyd Thomas. J. M. Dent & Sons, 1931.

23 – *Cl. SP.*, vol. 3, p. 738. London and Toronto, E. P. Dutton & Co., New York, 1925, p. 90.

24 – Cobbett, nos. 79, 82.

25 – Kennet, White, *Register and Chronicle, op. cit.*, 10 June, 1660.

26 – Baxter, *Reliquiae Baxterianae*, I, ii. 30.

27 – *Ibid.*

28 – Baxter, *Autobiography*, p. 154.

29 – *Ibid.*, Autobiography, p. 153.

30 – *Cal. Cl. SP.*, vol. 5, no. 28.

31 – Kennet, White, *op. cit.*, p. 280.

32 – *Cal. Cl. SP.*, vol. 5, no. 49.

33 – *Cont.*, 144; Petition of the London Ministers 16 November, 1660.

34 – Cobbett, Parliamentary History, p. 160.

35 – *Ibid.*, p. 168 ff.

36 – *Cal. Cl. SP.*, vol. 5, no. 53.

37 – Green, I. M., *The Re-establishment of the Church of England, 1660–1663*, Oxford University Press, Oxford, 1978, pp. 39–60, 64.

38 – Gauden, John, *Considerations touching the Liturgy*, London, 1661, p. 33.

39 – Kennet, White, *op. cit.*, p. 355.

40 – *Ibid.*, pp. 433, 499.

41 – *Cont.*, 185.

42 – Kennet, White, *op. cit.*, p. 182.

43 – Sacret, 'Restoration Government and Municipal Corporations', *EHR*, 1930.

44 – *JC*, 24 July.

45 – CSPD, 1661–2, no. 539.

46 – Evans, J. T., *Seventeenth Century Norwich, op. cit.*, p. 47.

47 – Levin, Jennifer, *The Charter Controversy in the City of London, 1660–1680, and its consequences*, Athlone Press, London, 1969, chs. 1–2.

48 – *Cont.*, 295.

49 – Kennet, White, *op. cit.*, p. 498.

50 – *Cont.*, 311.

51 – Kennet, White, *op. cit.*, 15 December, 1661.

52 – *Ibid.*, 10 January 1662.

53 – Powicke, F. J., *A Life of the Reverend Richard Baxter 1615–91*, Jonathan Cape, London, 1924.

54 – *JC*, 3 March, 1662.

55 – Cobbett, P. H., pp. 247–58.

56 – *Cont.*, 338.

57 – *Ibid.*, 341–2.

58 – Kennet, *op. cit.*, 28 August, 1662.

59 – *Mercurius Publicus* Printed by order of The Council of State (by H. Muddiman). London, 1660–63, nos. 35, 579.

60 – Cl. Mss., no. 72, quoted in *EHR*, 1929.

61 – *Cal. Cl. SP.*, vol. 5, no. 266.

62 – Lister, vol. 3, pp. 223–5.

63 – *Ibid.*, vol. 3, p. 228.

64 – *Ibid.*, vol. 3, pp. 233, 231.

65 – Cobbett, P. H., 18 February, 1663.

66 – *JC*, no. 440.

67 – Green, I. M., *op. cit.*, p. 223.

68 – CSP Ven., vol. 33, p. 238.

69 – British Museum, Sloane Mss. no. 4107. f. 260–4; Abernathy, p. 90.

70 – Green, I. M. *op. cit.*, p. 220.

71 – Carte Mss. no. 47; Green, I. M. *op. cit.*, p. 224.

72 – Cont., 1, 310, 333.

CHAPTER 15
### THE RESTORATION IN SCOTLAND AND IRELAND

1 – *Cont.*, 1, 35.

2 – Baillie, Robert, *Letters and Journals*, Edinburgh, 1775, 3 vols., vol 3, p. 387.

3 – Lauderdale Papers edited by O. Airy, Camden Society, London, 1884–5, 3 vols., vol. 1, p. 47.

4 – Burnet, vol. 1, p. 101.

5 – *Cont.*, 106.

6 – Lauderdale Papers, vol. 1. p. 56.

7 – *Cont.*, 100 ff.

8 – Lauderdale Papers, vol. 1, pp. 71, 81.

9 – MacKenzie, Sir G., Memoirs of the Affairs of Scotland from the Restoration of King Charles II, Privately Printed, Edinburgh, 1821, p. 55.

10 – Register of the Privy Council of Scotland, vol. 1, pp. 28, 30.

11 – Burnet, vol. 1, p. 152.

12 – *Ibid.*, pp. 157–8.

13 – Lauderdale Papers, vol. 1, pp. 142, 158, 161.

14 – Burnet, vol. 1, p. 204.

15 – *Cont.*, 107.

16 – *Ibid.*, 108.

17 – *Ibid.*, 226.

18 – Bramhall, John, *Works, edited by John Vesey, op. cit.*, vol. 1, p. 18.

19 – *Cont.*, 235.

20 – *Ibid.*, 242, 244.

21 – *Ibid.*, 247–52, cf. the case of the earl of Tyrconnell; pp. 262–9.

22 – Clarendon wrongly says one-fourth, *Cont.*, 276.

23 – *Ibid.*, 276, 281–2.

## CHAPTER 16
### THE CHANCELLOR UNDER CHALLENGE

1 – *Cont.*, 1, 35.
2 – *H.*, 3, 53.
3 – *Cont.*, 2, 913.
4 – *Vita Edwardi Secundi*, Medieval text, author unknown, p. 28.
5 – *Cont.*, 44, 46.
6 – *Acts of the Privy Council of England and Colonial Series*, edited through the direction of the Lord President of the Council by W. L. Grant and James Munro under the general supervision of Almeric W. Fitzroy. Hereford, 1908–12, 6 vols. 1613–18.
7 – *Ibid.*, 25 September 1662.
8 – *Calendar of State Papers. Colonial Series*, edited by W. N. Sainsbury, Longman & Co., London, 1860 etc. 1661–8 nos. 706, 963, 1184.
9 – *Ibid.*, nos. 547, 536, 904, 1601.
10 – *Ibid.*, vol. 8.
11 – *Cont.*, 47.
12 – *Cal. Cl. SP.*, vol. 5, no. 175.
13 – *Ibid.*, vol. 5, p. 80.
14 – Grammont, *Memoirs du Mareschal De Grammont* compiled by his son the 2nd Duke of Grammont, Paris, 1716.
15 – *Cont.*, 68–73.
16 – Burnet, vol. 1, p. 174.
17 – *Ibid.*, vol. 1, p. 170.
18 – *Cl. SP.*, vol. 3, suppl. 1.
19 – *Cal. Cl. SP.*, vol. 5, no. 56.
20 – *Cl. SP.*, vol 3, 4, 9, suppl. 8.
21 – *Cal. Cl. SP.*, vol. 5, no. 144.
22 – Macray, W. D., (ed.) *Notes which passed at meetings of the Privy Council between Charles II and the earl of Clarendon 1660–1667*, London, 1896, p. 67.
23 – Lister, vol. 3, p. 197.
24 – *Cont.*, 362.
25 – Lister, vol. 3, p. 156.
26 – *Cont.*, 365, 367.
27 – Lister, vol. 3, p. 209.
28 – *Cont.*, 369, 392.
29 – Lister, vol. 3, p. 209.
30 – *Cal. Cl. SP.*, vol. 5, no. 285.
31 – Clarendon said it was £120,000. *Cont.*, 458.
32 – Grose, C. L., 'The Dunkirk Money', *JMH*, 1933.
33 – Chandaman, C. D., *The English Public Revenue. 1660–1688*. Clarendon Press, Oxford, 1975, pp. 263–4.
34 – *Cal. Cl. SP.*, vol. 5, no. 45.
35 – *CSPD*, 1661–2, nos. 253, 347, 422–511.
36 – Chandaman, *op. cit.*, p. 130.
37 – Lister, vol. 3, p. 198.
38 – Childs, J., *The Army of Charles II*, Routledge, London, 1976, p. 220.
39 – *Miscellanea Aulica*, p. 108, Bod., 55b, 140.
40 – Macpherson, James, Original Papers, London, 1775, vol. 1, p. 23.
41 – Carte Mss., no. 32, 13 September, 1662.
42 – *Cont.*, 438.
43 – Carte Mss., no. 34.

44 – Lister, vol. 3, p. 227.

45 – Carte Mss., no. 34.

46 – *Ibid.*, no. 34, 19 October.

47 – *H.*, 9, 127–31.

48 – *Cont.*, 160.

49 – Burnet, vol. 1, p. 193.

50 – Huntingdon L. Q., 1940–1.

51 – Cobbett, P. H., 1 July, 1663, Daniel O'Neill to Ormond: Carte Mss. nos. 328, 296, 20 June, 1663.

52 – *Cont.*, 474.

53 – Roberts, Clayton, 'Sir Richard Temple: "The Pickthank Undertaker" ' in *HLQ*, 1977–8.

54 – Cobbett, P. H. 10 July, 1663.

55 – P. H., 13 July, 1663; Lister, vol. 3, p. 247.

56 – Lister, vol. 3, pp. 225, 244.

57 – Pepys, 15 May, 1663.

58 – *Ibid.*, 3 July, 1663.

59 – Lister, vol. 3, p. 231.

60 – *Cont.*, 395.

61 – *Ibid.*, 413.

## CHAPTER 17
### 'AN IMMODERATE DESIRE TO ENGAGE THE NATION IN WAR'

1 – *Cont.*, 518.

2 – *Cal. Cl. SP.*, vol. 5. 16 August, 1661.

3 – *Ibid.*, 15 July 1661.

4 – *Ibid.*, vol. 5, no. 194.

5 – *Ibid.*, vol. 5, no. 196, August 1661.

6 – Quoted in Feiling, Keith, *British Foreign Policy, 1660–1672*, Macmillan & Co., London, 1930, p. 125.

7 – Bryant, Arthur, (ed.) *The Letters, Speeches and Declarations of King Charles II*, Cassell & Co., London, 1935.

8 – 'The silence of the house was not broken; they sat as in amazement'. Cont., p. 542.

9 – Cobbett, P. H., 9 February 1665: Witcombe. D. T., *Charles II and the Cavalier House of Commons 1663–74*, Manchester University Press, Manchester, Barnes & Noble, New York, 1966.

10 – *Cont.*, 543.

11 – Bryant, *op. cit.*, pp. 163, 172.

12 – *Cont.*, 650.

13 – Pepys, 9 June, 1665.

14 – *Cont.*, 658.

15 – Geyl, P., *Orange and Stuart*, Weidenfeld, London, 1969, p. 204.

16 – Geyl, *op. cit.*, p. 218.

17 – *Ibid.*, p. 228.

18 – Carte Mss. no. 46, quoted in Geyl *op. cit.*, p. 234, February 1666.

19 – *Cont.*, 553; See C. H. Firth's article in *EHR*, 1906.

20 – *Cal. Cl. SP.*, vol. 5, no. 541.

21 – Dryden, John, *Annus Mirabilis, the year of Wonders 1666*. Printed for H. Herringman. London, 1667.

22 – *Cal. Cl. SP.*, vol. 5, nos. 509, 510, 524.
23 – *Ibid.*, vol. 5, 22 March 1667.
24 – *Ibid.*, vol. 5, 2 March 1667.
25 – *Ibid.*, vol. 5, 13 March, 15 April, 1667.


CHAPTER 18
PARLIAMENT AND IMPEACHMENT 1666–7

1 – See preamble to the Act for the preservation of the king, 1661. Browning, p. 63.
2 – *The Life of Adam Martindale written by himself*, edited by R. Parkinson, Chetham Society, Manchester, 1845.
3 – *Remarkable Passages in the Life of William Kiffin written by himself* edited from the original ms. by W. Orme, London, Perth (printed). 1823. p. 46.
4 – Whiting, C. E., *Studies in English Puritanism from the Restoration to the Revolution, 1660–1688*, SPCK, London, 1931, p. 112.
5 – Pepys, 15 May, 1663.
6 – *Cont.*, 776; CSPD Ven., 1664–5, no. 312.
7 – Browning, p. 383.
8 – Robbins, C., 'The Oxford Session of the Long Parliament of Charles II'. *BIHR*, 1948.
9 – *Cal. Cl. SP.*, vol. 5, nos. 125, 271.
10 – *Cont.*, 787, 788.
11 – *Ibid.*, 811.
12 – *Ibid.*, 777.
13 – *Ibid.*, 794–804.
14 – Edie, Carolyn, 'The Irish Cattle Bills'. Transactions of the American Philosophical Society, 1970.
15 – Haley, Kenneth, H. D., *The First Earl of Shaftesbury*, Clarendon Press, Oxford, 1968, p. 183.
16 – Pepys, 29 May, 1664.
17 – HMC Rep 5/315.
18 – Pepys, 9 January, 27 February, 1665.
19 – *Ibid.*, 28 January, 6 July, 1666.
20 – Harris, F. R., *Life of Edward Mountague KG first earl of Sandwich 1625–72*, John Murray, London, 1912.
21 – *Cont.*, 856.
22 – Pepys, 26 September, 1666.
23 – *Cont.*, 827.
24 – Hayden, R, Bristol Record Society, vol. 27, 1974.
25 – Dryden, John, *Annus Mirabilis. op. cit.*, vol. 5, p. 304.
26 – Pepys, 10 October 1666.
27 – *Cont.*, 941.
28 – *The Poems and Letters of Andrew Marvell*, edited by H. M. Margoliouth, Clarendon Press, Oxford, 1927, 2 vols., vol. 2, p. 42.
29 – *Diary of John Milward Member of Parliament for Derbyshire, September 1666 to May 1668*, edited by Caroline Robbins, Cambridge University Press, Cambridge, 1938. pp. 20–21, 25.
30 – *Ibid.*, 56; *The Poems and Letters of Andrew Marvell. op. cit.*, vol. 2, p. 46.
31 – Pepys, 10 December 1666.
32 – *Ibid.*, 15 December 1666.

33 – *Cont.*, 951.
34 – *Ibid.*, p. 954.
35 – Milward, *op. cit.*, p. 15, 5 October.
36 – *Cont.*, 962.
37 – *Ibid.*, 967.
38 – *Ibid.*, 976–8.
39 – *Ibid.*, 990, 997.
40 – *LJ*, vol. 12, p. 74.
41 – Milward, *op. cit.*, p. 76.
42 – Kenyon, *Docs.* pp. 57, 201.
43 – Milward, *op. cit.*, pp. 18, 33.
44 – Pepys, 17 February, 1667; 25 October 1666; *Cont.*, 630.
45 – Cobbett, P. H., 8 February, 1667.
46 – *Cont.*, 951–3.
47 – Carte Mss. no. 46, f. 440.
48 – Cobbett, P. H., 18 January, 1667.
49 – Pepys, 20 February, 1667.
50 – *Cont.*, 1121 ff.
51 – Pepys, 26 April, 1667.
52 – Burnet, vol. 1, p. 249.
53 – Pepys, 14 February, 9 May, 1667.
54 – *Cont.*, 1068.
55 – Pepys, 16 May, 1667.
56 – Shaw, W. A., 'The Beginnings of the National Debt' in *Historical Essays*, edited by T. F. Tout and J. Tait. Publications of the University of Manchester History Series no. 6, 1907., p. 392.
57 – Pepys, 22 May, 1667.
58 – *Ibid.*, 14 June, 1667.
59 – *Cont.*, 1096.
60 – *Ibid.*, 1101.
61 – Cobbett, P. H., 29 July 1667.
62 – Pepys, 27 July, 1667.
63 – *Cont.*, 1117.
64 – *Ibid.*
65 – Pepys, 17, 22 July, 1667.
66 – *Cont.*, 1134–5.
67 – *Ibid.*, 1140.
68 – *Ibid.*, 1142.
69 – *Ibid.*, 1143; Pepys, 27 August, 1667; Crew, Nathaniel, *Memoirs of Nathaniel, Lord Crew*, Camden Society, London, 1893.
70 – Carte Mss. no. 46.
71 – Pepys, 30 August, 1667.
72 – *Cont.*, 1147; Carte Mss. no. 46.
73 – Pepys, 2 September, 1667.
74 – *Ibid.*, 12, 14, 25 September, 1667.
75 – Cobbett, P. H., 10 October 1667; *JC*, 16 October 1667.
76 – Pepys, 22 October, 1667.
77 – *Ibid.*, 23 October, 1667.
78 – *Ibid.*, 28 October, 1667.
79 – *Ibid.*, 16, 17 November, 1667.
80 – *Ibid.*, 27 November, 1667.

81 – *Ibid.*, 30 November, 1667.
82 – Browning, no. 193.
83 – All references in this paragraph refer to Cobbett, P. H., on the dates given.
84 – *Cont.*, 1181.
85 – Bryant, Letters of Charles II, *op. cit.*, pp. 204, 205.
86 – Pepys, 6 December 1667.
87 – Carte, *Life of Ormonde*, vol. 2, p. 363.
88 – *Ibid.*, vol. 2, p. 364.
89 – *Ibid.*, vol 2, app. p. 38.
90 – Egerton, F. H., *The Life of Thomas Egerton, Lord Chancellor of England*, now constitutes the Egerton Mss. in the British Museum, Paris, 1828 (?).
91 – Carte Mss. no. 53, 8 December, 1667.
92 – *Ibid.*, no. 63.
93 – *Ibid.*, no. 71.
94 – Grey, *Debates*, vol. 2, p. 244.
95 – See Pritchard in Huntingdon L. Q., 1981.

## CHAPTER 19
## CONCLUSION: CLARENDON, HISTORY AND POLITICS

1 – All the references in this paragraph to be found in *Cont.*, 1207, 1215, 1218.
2 – *Ibid.*, p. 1242.
3 – *Ibid.*, p. 1243.
4 – *Ibid.*, p. 1246 ff.
5 – See Firth, C. H., 'Clarendon's *History of the Rebellion*, in *EHR*, 1904.
6 – Professor Knight's article in *Scrutiny*, 1947.
7 – Walpole, Horace, *A Catalogue of the Royal and Noble authors of England, with lists of their works*, Strawberry Hill, 1758, 2 vols.
8 – *H.*, 1, 72, 145.
9 – Firth, Charles, *EHR*, vol. 19.
10 – All this is made clear in Clarendon's *Contemplation on the Psalms of David*, in the Bodleian Library.
11 – *H.*, 16, 115; Wormald, Brian, H. G., *Clarendon: Politics, History and Religion, 1640–1660*, Cambridge University Press, Cambridge, 1951.
12 – *Cl. SP.*, vol 2, p. 529.
13 – *Ibid.*, vol. 2, p. 306.
14 – *Ibid.*, vol. 2, p. 333 to Sir John Berkeley, January 1646.
15 – *Ibid.*, vol. 2, p. 379.
16 – *H.*, 1, 12.
17 – Trevor-Roper, H., 'Clarendon and the Practice of History', in Fogle (French, R.). *Milton and Clarendon etc.*, pp. 21–50, 1965.
18 – Hutton, Ronald, 'Clarendon's History of the Rebellion', *EHR*, 1982.
19 – Holles, Denzil, *Memoirs of Denzil Lord Holles from 1641 to 1648*. For T. Goodwin, London, 1699. p. 1.
20 – Underdown, *Pride's Purge, op. cit.*, p. 34.
21 – *H.*, 6, 291.
22 – Pearl, Valerie, *London and the Outbreak of the Puritan Revolution, op. cit.* Wormald, Brian, *Clarendon, op. cit.*; Trevor-Roper, Hugh, 'The Fast Days of the Long Parliament', in *Essays in British History, op. cit.*
23 – Gardiner, vol. 10, p. 169.

24 – Wormald, Brian, *op. cit.*, p. 116.

25 – Clarendon, Montpellier 1670, in *Essays Moral and Entertaining*, edited by J. S. Clarke, London, 1815, 2 vols.

26 – Clarendon, *Against the Multiplying Controversies*, Moulins, 1672.

27 – *Ibid.*

28 – *Cl. SP.*, vol. 2, p. 322.

29 – Psalms, 19, 72, 37.

30 – Clarendon in *Essays Moral and Entertaining. op. cit.*

31 – *Life of John Barwick, op. cit.*, p. 429.

32 – Hobbes, Thomas, *The Moral and political works of Thomas Hobbes of Malmesbury. To which is prefixed the Author's Life, extracted from that said to be written by himself*, London, 1750.

33 – Clarendon. *A Brief View and Survey of the Dangerous and Pernicious Errors to Church and State in Mr Hobbe's Book entitled Leviathan.* (1673), pp. 29, 9, 28, 59.

34 – *Ibid.*, pp. 83, 52.

35 – *Ibid.*, pp. 45, 124–6.

36 – *Ibid.*, p. 207.

37 – Cl. Mss. no. 87.

38 – *Cl. SP.*, vol. 3, supp. 40.

39 – Cl. Mss. no. 87.

40 – Pepys, 14 July, 1664.

41 – Lister, vol. 2, passim.

42 – Lister, vol. 3, p. 478 ff.

43 – Ellis, George, James, Welbore, Agar, *Historical Inquiries, respecting the character of Edward Hyde, Earl of Clarendon*, John Murray, London, 1827; Lewis, Lady Maria Theresa, *Lives of the Friends and Contemporaries of Lord Chancellor Clarendon*, London, 1852, 3 vols.

44 – Firth, C. H., 'Edward Hyde, Earl of Clarendon, as statesman, historian and Chancellor of the University', Lecture delivered on 18 February, 1909, Clarendon Press, Oxford, 1909.

45 – Trevor-Roper, Hugh, 'Edward Hyde, Earl of Clarendon', Tercentenary Lecture, Clarendon Press, Oxford, 1975.

46 – Wood, Anthony, *The Life and Times of Anthony Wood, antiquary at Oxford 1632–95 described by himself.* Collected from his diaries and other papers by Andrew Clark, Oxford, 1891–95 (Oxford Historical Society Publications, vols., 19, 21, 26, 30, 40). 5 vols.

47 – Cl, Mss. no. 129.

48 – *Ibid.*

49 – The above letters are all in Cl. Mss. no. 150.

50 – Lister, vol. 3, p. 481.

51 – *Ibid.*

52 – Roebuck, W. G., 'Charles II: The Missing Portrait'. Huntingdon L. Q., 1974–5.

53 – Macray (ed.), *Notes which passed at Meetings of the Privy Council between Charles II and the Earl of Clarendon 1660–1667*, London, 1896.

54 – *Cont.*, 920–1.

55 – *Ibid.*, 927, 928.

56 – Tanner, J. R., (ed.) *Private Correspondence and Miscellaneous Papers of Samuel Pepys 1679–1703*. G. Bell & Sons. London, 1926, 2 vols., vol. 2, p. 266.

57 – *Ibid.*, vol. 2, p. 301.

58 – Lister, vol. 3, p. 481.

59 – Cl. Mss. no. 154.

# Index